Marketing Tourism, Hospitality and Leisure in Europe

Series in Tourism and Hospitality Management

Series Editors:

Professor Roy C. Wood
The Scottish Hotel School, University of Strathclyde, UK

Stephen J. Page
Massey University, New Zealand

Series Consultant:

Professor C. L. Jenkins
The Scottish Hotel School, University of Strathclyde, UK

Key textbooks in this series:

Books in this series are available on free inspection for lecturers considering the texts for course adoption. Details of these and any other International Thomson Business Press titles are available by writing to the publishers (Berkshire House, 168-173 High Holborn, London WC1V 7AA) or by telephoning the Promotions Department on 0171 497 1422.

Marketing Tourism, Hospitality and Leisure in Europe

Susan Horner
and John Swarbrooke

Sheffield Hallam University, UK

INTERNATIONAL THOMSON BUSINESS PRESS
I ⓣ P An International Thomson Publishing Company

London • Bonn • Boston • Johannesburg • Madrid • Melbourne • Mexico City • New York • Paris
Singapore • Tokyo • Toronto • Albany, NY • Belmont, CA • Cincinnati, OH • Detroit, MI

Marketing Tourism, Hospitality and Leisure in Europe

Copyright © 1996 S. Horner and J. Swarbrooke

First published by International Thomson Business Press

I(T)P   A division of International Thomson Publishing Inc
The ITP logo is a trademark under licence

British Library Cataloguing-in-Publication Data
A catalogue record for this book is available from the British Library

First edition 1996

Typeset by Photoprint Typesetters, Devon
Printed in the UK by the Alden Press, Oxford

ISBN 0 412 62170 3

International Thomson Business Press   International Thomson Business Press
Berkshire House   20 Park Plaza
168–173 High Holborn   13th Floor
London WC1V 7AA   Boston MA 02116
UK   USA

http://www/thomson.com/itbp.html

Contents

PART 3   THE MARKETING MIX AND TOURISM, LEISURE
AND HOSPITALITY

Series Editors' Foreword

The International Thompson Business Press Series in Tourism and Hospitality Management is dedicated to the publication of high quality textbooks and other volumes that will be of benefit to those engaged in tourism, hotel and hospitality education, especially at degree and postgraduate level. The series has two principal strands: core textbooks on key areas of the curriculum; and the *Topics in Tourism Hospitality* series which includes highly focused and shorter texts on particular themes and issues. All the authors in the series are experts in their own fields, actively engaged in teaching, research and consultancy in tourism and hospitality. Each book comprises an authoritative blend of subject-relevant theoretical considerations and practical applications. Furthermore, a unique quality of the series is that it is student oriented, offering accessible texts that take account of the realities of administration, management and operations in tourism and hospitality contexts, being constructively critical without losing sight of the overall goal of providing clear accounts of essential concepts, issues and techniques.

The series is committed to quality, accessibility, relevance and originality in its approach. Quality is ensured as a result of a vigorous refereeing process, unusual in the publication of textbooks. Accessibility is achieved through the use of innovative textual design techniques, and the use of discussion points, case studies and exercises within books, all geared to encouraging a comprehensive understanding of the material contained therein. Relevance and originality together result from the experience of authors as key authorities in their fields.

The tourism and hospitality industries are diverse and dynamic industries and it is the intention of the editors to reflect this diversity and dynamism by publishing quality texts that enhance topical subjects without losing sight of enduring themes. The Series Editors and Advisor are grateful to Steven Reed of International Thompson Business Press for his commitment, expertise and support of this philosophy.

Stephen J. Page
Massey University – Albany
Auckland
New Zealand

Roy C. Wood
The Scottish Hotel School
University of Strathclyde

Preface

This book is designed to offer a truly European perspective on marketing in the related fields of tourism, leisure, and hospitality. It is not simply meant to be a description of the situation in individual European countries. It is also an attempt to take a supra-national, pan-European view of the subject. The authors will endeavour to tackle questions such as is there now such a person as 'the European tourist'? However, before we plunge into the debates with which the book is concerned, perhaps we should begin by explaining why we believe there is a need for a book on European tourism, leisure and hospitality marketing in the first place.

Firstly, why European? Europe is increasingly becoming a true entity in political, economic and socio-cultural terms. It is where many elements of modern tourism, leisure and hospitality were born and grew to maturity. It is the most popular continent with international tourists and the home of some of the leading transnational corporations in tourism, leisure and hospitality. Finally, Europe is currently undergoing a period of fascinating change through which it is becoming, perhaps, more and more homogeneous, in spite of enduring national and regional differences.

Secondly, why tourism, leisure and hospitality? Why any of them and why all three together? These three industries, if industries they are, have all grown dramatically across Europe in recent decades. They have been in the vanguard of the development of modern consumer societies. The rationale for linking them together is that they are clearly interrelated, but, more than that, it is the authors' contention that the traditional demarcation lines that have existed between them are becoming increasingly blurred and meaningless. However, it is also true that, as the book will show, there are still some major differences between them.

Finally, why marketing? Because marketing is the 'buzz word' of modern management theory and practice in both the public and private sectors across Europe. The concept of marketing has been broadened to the point where it now appears to encompass most aspects of corporate life. It is particularly appropriate to take a marketing approach when one is looking at three service industries like tourism, leisure, and hospitality, for it is in such largely modern industries where staff and customers interact on a face-to-face basis that many modern innovations in marketing have been born.

The book has been designed to be both valuable, and, hopefully, stimulating for a variety of audiences, including :

- undergraduate and postgraduate students on tourism, leisure and hospitality courses;
- students on business courses who have an interest in service industries;
- students following vocational courses, for example GNVQ courses in the UK;
- lecturers who teach on tourism, leisure and hospitality courses;
- managers working for European tourism, leisure and hospitality organizations.

As the book is truly European, it should be relevant to these audiences in all European countries, not just the UK.

The text is split into a number of sections, as follows:

- Part 1 provides the context for the book and includes a discussion of the meaning of the terms, tourism, leisure and hospitality.
- Part 2 sets out the European dimension in terms of the supply and demand sides of tourism, leisure and hospitality, and the business environment of European tourism, leisure and hospitality organizations.
- Part 3 applies the marketing mix to the field of tourism, leisure and hospitality in Europe.
- Part 4 looks at the marketing planning process in relation to European tourism, leisure and hospitality organizations.
- Part 5 looks at how marketing practices and techniques vary between different sectors within tourism, leisure and hospitality across Europe, from airlines to theatres, destinations to fast-food outlets.
- Part 6 looks at topical issues in tourism, leisure and hospitality marketing including quality, ethics and green issues.

The authors attempt in addition to draw together some conclusions and make some predictions about the future development of tourism, leisure and hospitality marketing in Europe. They also offer a substantial bibliography for those who wish to undertake further reading on topics covered in the book. A glossary of terms for those readers who are unfamiliar with some of the terms used is also included.

Throughout the book, the points made are illustrated by a wide range of examples. For ease of reference a wide variety of case studies drawn from all over Europe have been included in a separate section. Those of particular relevance to individual chapters are referenced at the ends of the chapters concerned, while a comprehensive chart detailing the areas of coverage of each case study has also been provided.

A number of features have been incorporated in the book to make it easier for the reader to use and to make it a truly interactive text. These incude the following:

- Key concept boxes at the beginning of each chapter inform readers about the main issues they may expect to find covered in the test.
- Potential discussion points and/or essay questions are identified at the end of each chapter and case study.
- At the conclusion of each chapter an exercise is provided to help students, individually or in groups, to increase their understanding of the key topics covered in the text, and to explore how the concepts can be applied in practice.

We have endeavoured to write the book in a style that is easy to read and follow, particularly for European readers whose first language is not English. Only such readers can tell us to what extent we have succeeded in this aim.

Throughout the period we have spent writing this book, we have been careful to ensure that it did not become insular in two main ways. Firstly, we did not want to suggest that somehow Europe is a self-contained entity. Therefore, throughout the book, and in a specific chapter towards the end, we have looked at the relationship between Europe and the rest of the world. Secondly we recognize that tourism, leisure and hospitality do not exist in isolation from the rest of modern consumer society. A chapter at the end of the book explains this theme further.

Inspite of all our efforts we are, nevertheless, aware of the limitations of this book. There are not enough pages to fully explain this fascinating and hugely complex subject, and while we have tried to write the book from a European point of view, the fact remains that we are British.

Susan Horner
John Swarbrooke

Acknowledgements

While all the weaknesses of the book are solely our responsibility, many of its strengths reflect the help and support of many people and organizations. We can only thank a few of them here but the others know who they are, and, hopefully, they know how much we appreciate their help.

We would firstly like to thank Judith Mitchell who has typed every word of the book, quickly and accurately. Her patience and good humour were a constant source of strength to both of us during the months of hard work involved in writing this book.

We must also express our thanks to our many colleagues all over Europe who helped with the production of the book in a number of ways. These include:

- Monsieur M. Aline, Thalassa, Les Sables-D'Olonne, France;
- Professor Marin Bachvarov, Kliment Ohridski University, Sofia, Bulgaria;
- John Brown, Bord Fáilte, Ireland;
- Señor Josep M. Brugués, Port Aventura, Spain;
- Madame Jacqueline Clais, ESTHUA, Angers, France;
- Dr Franck Debos, Université de Nice, France;
- Señor Dendero – Futbol Club Barcelona, Spain;
- Monsieur Georges Dubœuf, France;
- Professor Giovanni Montemagno, University of Catania, Italy;
- Penny Manning, First Choice Holidays, UK;
- Robyn Griffith-Jones, The Victoria and Albert Museum, UK;
- Robert Hollier, European Travel Commission, Belgium;
- R.G. Marcall, Airtours plc, UK;
- Dr Thomas Mavrodontis, TEI Thessaloniki, Greece;
- Peter M. Moore MBE, Managing Director, Center Parcs, UK;
- Sue Moore and Abby McGowan, British Airways, UK;
- Señor Puyalto, Port Aventura, Spain;
- Dr Greg Richards, ATLAS Co-ordinator, Tilburg University, Netherlands;
- Dr Marco Robledo, Universitat des Iles Balears, Palma de Mallorca, Spain;
- Primrose Stubbs, Executive Director sales and marketing, Abercrombie & Kent, UK;
- Françoise Toussaint, Director of Corporate Communications, Accor, France.

It is important for us to place on record in addition our gratitude to our respective parents for all their help and support throughout our lives. We know that without the sacrifices they have made for us we would never have been in a position to write this book.

Finally, there is the enormous debt which we owe to our son John, who has brought us great joy. He made us laugh at times when writing this book was hard work and he made us see that life is about more than work. This book is dedicated to him.

It only remains now for us to wish you 'happy reading'. If you find this book useful and interesting, then all our efforts will have been worthwhile.

Best wishes

Veuillez accepter l'expression de nos sentiments distingués.

Mit den besten Wünschen

Cordiali saluti

Saludos

Поже Лания

Med venlig hilsen de bedote ønsker

En iyi dileklerimle

Introduction

This first section of the books sets the scene by answering three questions which are central to the whole book, namely:

- **Chapter 1: What is marketing?**
- **Chapter 2: What is Europe?**
- **Chapter 3: What are tourism, leisure and hospitality?**

First we will look at the marketing concept and examine some current trends and key issues in the theory and practice of marketing.

After that, there will be a discussion of what is meant by the term 'Europe'. This will involve looking at the idea of Europe in terms of a number of factors, including: history, economic systems, politics, demography and culture. At the same time we will consider whether or not Europe is becoming more, or less, homogenous.

Finally, in this section of the book, the authors will seek to offer definitions of tourism, leisure and hospitality. They will examine the interrelationships between these three sectors, and suggest that the distinctions between them are becoming increasingly blurred.

Europe

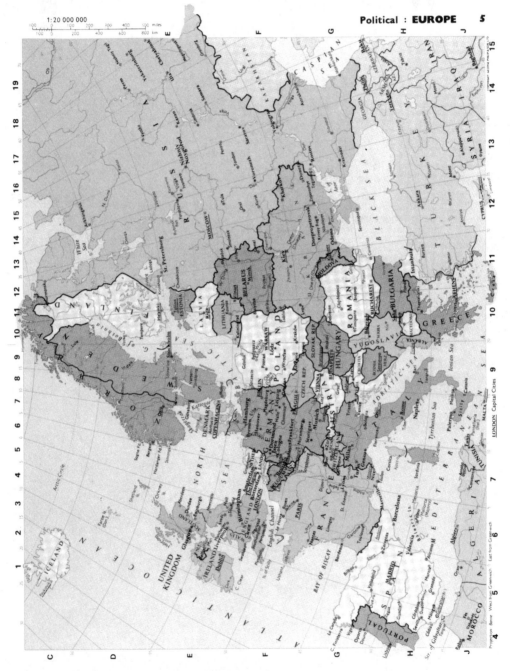

1:20 000 000

What is marketing? | 1

Key concepts

The main concepts covered in this chapter are:

- the scope and nature of marketing;
- definitions of the marketing concept;
- the application of marketing principles to profit-making and non-profit-making organizations;
- the differences between strategic and tactical marketing;
- service product marketing in comparison to the marketing of manufactured products.

INTRODUCTION

This chapter introduces the marketing concept. It looks at the historical development of marketing and discusses the application of marketing to different kinds of organization. The chapter also looks at the marketing function within the context of other management functions. Differences between product marketing and service marketing will be discussed. The chapter will review the reasons why marketing has become a highly fashionable influential subject in all aspects of the economy and society, and review some of the current contemporary marketing issues.

The main points covered in the chapter are as follows:

- introduction to the marketing concept;
- definitions of marketing;
- the historical development of the marketing concept;
- the application of the marketing concept to different kinds of organization;
- different approaches to the running of business organizations;
- the consequences of an organization adopting a marketing approach;
- the differences between strategic and tactical marketing;
- marketing and other business functions;

- a review of the differences between product marketing and service marketing;
- contemporary marketing issues.

INTRODUCTION TO THE MARKETING CONCEPT

What does marketing mean? For most people marketing constitutes selling and promotion. Marketing does indeed involve selling and promotion. If the products, however, have been designed to suit customer wants, selling and promotion will just be the icing on the cake.

The marketing concept is something of an enigma. It is a well recognized business function in many organizations, but the underlying concept of the marketing philosophy is rarely discussed. The introduction of a marketing department to many organizations involves the appointment of one or a number of personnel who organize promotional materials and nothing more. This, it must be stressed, does not constitute marketing.

Marketing is concerned with the relationship between buyer and seller, and the transactions involved in bringing this to a satisfactory conclusion. It could be argued that, unlike economics which concentrates on the relationship between supply and demand, marketing relies on the idea that the customer forms the central focus for all people working in the organization. The application of the marketing concept to an organization involves putting the customer at the centre of all decision-making processes in the business.

The marketing concept suggests that the overriding inclination of the organization will be to serve the final customer's needs and wants as the main priority. The organization will seek constantly to find out what the customer wants both today and in the future and work tirelessly to produce the products and services that are requested. This may mean that the organization has to make major shifts in its product and service ranges, and may even involve the organization moving into new markets and changing fixed asset bases.

There are fundamental problems with the organization adopting a consumer-led approach. It is often difficult for many people in organizations to see the final customer as being central to their individual roles. Many people in organizations are divorced from the final customers and it is difficult for them to see the logic of introducing the marketing approach.

Some organizations even have difficulty in recognizing who the customers are, particularly if the product or service is offered free of charge, or if the organization supplying it is the sole supplier. This can be particularly prevalent if the organization has been faced with a buoyant market position where demand outstrips supply. The logic here is that there have always been more customers demanding the products and services on offer, so why bother with any expensive marketing effort? Organizations in this type of market position tend to

```
< --------------------------------------------------------------------------------- >

Customer sovereignty          Customer manipulation

Customer is central focus of  Customer is manipulated to buy or use
business                      by whatever means legal or otherwise
```

Figure 1.1 The marketing continuum model.

look to marketing when market conditions become more difficult and customer demand starts to reduce.

The second reason for organizations having difficulty with putting the customer at the centre of the business is the fact that the implication of changing consumer demand on the organization may be too difficult to cope with. This is particularly apparent if the organization has long-term investments in fixed assets. The hotel chain with major investments in a group of prestigious hotels, or a theme park owner, faced with changing consumer demands would find it very difficult in the short term to change. The idea of total customer sovereignty, in a business which relies on substantial fixed capital assets, is impossible to implement in the short term.

Organizations often consider their customers' wants and needs, but also rely on persuading their customers to buy their existing products and services. The idea of persuasion rather than meeting customer needs and wants represents a totally different approach to the marketing concept. It is this idea of **customer persuasion** or at the most extreme **customer manipulation** which large numbers of the population interpret marketing to be. Marketing is often viewed by the man or woman in the street as aggressive hard selling by unscrupulous persons eager to make themselves vast profits.

The idea that organizations use **customer sovereignty** or **customer manipulation** in the extreme is wrong. It is more likely that the marketing approach can be expressed in terms of a continuum model as in Figure 1.1.

Organizations will tend to fall somewhere in the middle of the continuum, using some market research to find out about customer wants, but using some manipulation techniques to increase sales.

Vance Packard (1957) in his book *The Hidden Persuaders* portrayed a frightening manipulative view of the marketing function. The idea that consumers, including children, could be manipulated by marketing activity to buy products and services was seen by many as a horrifying vision of the marketing profession.

DEFINITIONS OF MARKETING

The definitions of marketing demonstrate the different approaches which academics have taken to the marketing philosophy. Marketing has been defined in many different ways, emphasizing different points. This is perhaps a reflection of the immature stage of development of the marketing discipline.

Philip Kotler (1994) the American marketing academic has defined marketing as follows:

> A social and managerial process by which individuals and groups obtain what they need and want through creating and exchanging products and values with others.

Levitt (1986) discusses the role of marketing as follows:

> a truly marketing minded firm tries to create value satisfying goods and services that consumers will want to buy.

This definition is useful because it identifies the importance of customer needs and wants as being central to the marketing function. Once the needs and wants have been identified, they must be met by producing goods and services which satisfy them and produce a successful deal for both producer and consumer.

Other academics suggest that the marketing concept can only work if it is embedded in the whole culture of the organization. The management guru Peter Drucker (1969), for example, considers this view in his definition:

> Marketing is not only much broader than selling, it is not a specialized activity at all. It encompasses the entire business. It is the whole business seen from the point of view of its final result, that is from the customer's point of view. Concerns and responsibilities for marketing must therefore permeate all areas of the enterprise.

This definition suggests that everybody in an organization involved in the marketing function should ultimately consider the final customer as being central to their activities at work. This suggests that marketing involves an encompassing philosophy which often means that an organization has to change its internal business culture to accommodate this new form of approach.

Tom Peters and Robert H. Waterman (1982) have been at the forefront of suggesting styles of management for organizations to adopt if they want to become 'excellent', and manage effectively during periods of chaotic change. Rosabeth Moss Kanter (1984) has suggested that organizations have to empower individuals to stimulate entrepreneurial spirit and become market leaders. The underlying culture of the organization needs to facilitate the exchange of goods and services for money or benefits by satisfying the target customers.

The Chartered Institute of Marketing, which is the professional body for practising marketers in the UK, defines marketing as:

> Identifying, anticipating and satisfying customer requirements profitably.

This definition explains how the marketing philosophy is to put the customer as the central focus for business decision-making. The definition has been criticised because of the word 'profitably'. It has been argued that many non-profit-making organizations can use the marketing philosophy to become more effective rather than simply more profitable. The definition is useful in that it identifies the role of marketing as being to identify the needs and wants of customers both now and in the future, and then meet them.

Academics from other European countries also define marketing as the methods which an organization can employ to result in successful transactions with customers. Lendrevic and Lindon (1990), for example, define marketing as:

> The assembly of methods and means at the disposal of an organization, in order to give favourable impressions to the public, to achieve the right objectives.

Table 1.1 summarises the main points which have come out of the definitions so far.

The marketing philosophy can therefore be seen to encompass a number of steps which can be summarized as in Figure 1.2.

Table 1.1 The main emphasis of each definition of marketing

Emphasis	Example
• Marketing is about putting the customer at the centre of the business	Kotler Chartered Institute of Marketing
• Marketing is about methods which can be used to gain favourable impressions	Lendrevic and Lindon
• Marketing is about the way in which the business develops its markets	Levitt
• Marketing is about organizing the culture of the business to become market and customer focused	Peters and Waterman Kanter Drucker

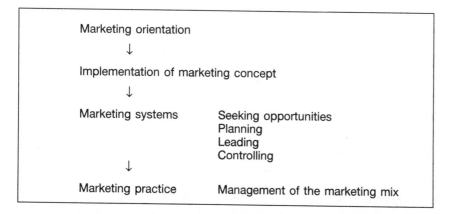

Figure 1.2 The marketing philosophy.

The practical application of marketing in business organizations involves an understanding of a number of theoretical disciplines.

- **Business and management disciplines.** An effective marketer must have an understanding of how organizations function and how they become successful. Marketing must be clearly defined within the whole business.
- **Social and behavioural disciplines.** The development and interpretation of a body of knowledge about customers and their behaviour, both now and in the future, is crucial in marketing.
- **Methodological disciplines.** The collection, analysis and interpretation of marketing data to help in determining marketing programmes is vital.

THE HISTORICAL DEVELOPMENT OF THE MARKETING CONCEPT

The marketing concept has been encouraged by the adoption in most parts of the world of capitalist ideas and free market principles. In the UK, for example, the 1980s and 1990s have been the era of the entrepreneur and free enterprise has been encouraged. This has been accompanied by the development of marketing as a business discipline.

Marketing is not a new phenomenon. It can be argued that marketing is as old as civilization itself. Early traders were very skilled at marketing in their daily exchanges. Entrepreneurs travelled the world to trade commodities which people wanted to buy.

The rise of industrialization ushered in a new era of mass produced products being marketed to mass audiences, including clothes and cars. Many of the brand names which are now universally recognized symbols of mass marketing, such as Coca Cola and Heinz, are already decades old.

The early 1950s saw a huge expansion in the supply of goods and services which often outstripped the demand. Most markets became buyers' markets and companies were faced with growing competition.

There have also been changes occurring in the business world more recently, which have encouraged the development of more sophisticated marketing techniques. The rapid growth in technological innovation over the last century has made the business environment much more challenging and has opened up many new marketing opportunities. This been accompanied by a general slowing down in population growth in many countries of the developed world. The population in the developed countries has become better educated and therefore more discerning in their purchases.

Competition in national markets has become much more intense and complicated. Coupled with this, there has been the growth of international players in many markets which have often challenged the national players in the markets which they historically considered very safe. These new European or international players have often used sophisticated marketing techniques to take a large section of the market share from the nationally based players. Whole national industries have been removed in very short periods of time by this new competitive situation.

This new competitive business situation has meant that it is difficult enough to survive, never mind become successful on a long-term basis. This has meant that a completely new philosophy of business has had to develop in which effective and efficient manufacturing processes is not sufficient. The answer to this new situation, it has been suggested, is to be the application of the marketing concept.

Theodore Levitt (1960) was one of the first management theorists to stress the importance of a marketing approach for business organizations and raise the profile of marketing as an academic discipline. In the influential article 'Marketing myopia' published in the *Harvard Business Review* in the summer of 1960, he argued that an industry should be a 'customer satisfier' rather than a 'goods producer'. He argued that there was a fundamental difference between marketing and selling. Selling focused on the needs of the seller, whereas marketing focused on the needs of the buyer. Marketing, he argued, was concerned with the idea of satisfying the needs of the customer by means of the product and the whole cluster of things associated with creating, delivering and consuming it.

Marketing, however, had been developing in businesses before this. The original idea of marketing had been developed by the fast moving consumer goods industries, typically in the United States of America from the 1930s onwards. Procter & Gamble, the American detergent and personal products company, was one of the first companies to develop the use of marketing techniques in a practical business organization.

Consumer durable manufacturers such as car makers were quick to adopt the marketing approach from the 1950s onwards. Service sector organizations became very interested in the application of marketing techniques during the 1970s and 1980s. Airlines and banks, for example, have been attracted to the marketing concept. The conversion of British Airways from a production-oriented company to a customer-led business by Lord King and Sir Colin Marshall which has led to huge financial success is one example of this.

Marketing for professional groups is also becoming popular. Accountants, solicitors and lawyers are beginning to use marketing techniques.

Non-profit-making organizations such as educational institutions, charities and local authorities have been showing great interest in the use of the marketing concept for their types of organization during the 1980s and 1990s. The use of marketing has enhanced consumer awareness. The use of marketing has not only improved profits for business organizations, but has also been used to promote governmental initiatives and enhance the profile and increase the income of voluntary organizations.

Marketing is increasingly being adopted on an international scale in all sectors of the economy. International marketing is increasingly studied as a separate discipline. This book will suggest that organizations operating on a European or international basis should treat the multinational perspective as an inherent part of their marketing effort.

THE APPLICATION OF THE MARKETING CONCEPT TO DIFFERENT KINDS OF ORGANIZATION

The development of the application of marketing occurred in the fast moving consumer goods industry. The previous section discussed this in more detail. Many other types of organization are now trying to adopt the marketing concept within their own business context. It is important to remember, however, that the different types of organizations will have fundamentally different sets of objectives. The marketing objectives of different types of organization are explored in Table 1.2.

The marketing programmes will be subtly different in these different types of organization so that the overall objectives of the organization can be met.The underlying philosophy of putting the final customer at the centre of business is applicable to all organizations.

Public sector organizations can be defined as agencies operated and organized by central and local government. This sector of industry has often been reluctant to incorporate the marketing philosophy into their business for a variety of reasons.

Marketing has often been considered by the officers of public bodies as being inappropriate because it has associations with competition and profits which do not fit in well with the aspects of social responsibility which these organizations are supposed to incorporate. There may even be issues regarding the ethics of collecting information during market research from the clients of public sector organizations, and issues around whether the data collected may be used for political

Table 1.2 The marketing objectives of different types of organization

Type of organization	Marketing objectives
● Profit-making	To make profits at specified return
● Non-profit-making and public sector	To maximize income and use it effectively and efficiently
	To meet objectives laid down by government or funding bodies within specified budgets
● Voluntary	To do most good for users of the services provided within the budget

reasons rather than in the client's interest in providing better services.

Kotler and Andraeson (1987) describe how their research carried out in the United States of America has indicated that many people within the non-profit-making sector have the view (often subconsciously) that marketing is basically bad due to aspects of wasting public money, and the perceived qualities of 'hard sell' promotion. Many of these ideas are currently being challenged. Scholes (1991), for example, outlines the changes which have occurred in the UK public sector due to the creation of compulsory competitive tendering and the creation of internal markets.

A change in management philosophy to a more market oriented approach has been forced upon public sector bodies faced with these legislative and administrative changes.

Kotler and Andraeson (1987) outlined a series of reasons for public sector and non-profit-making organizations which it is suggested should encourage the use of marketing techniques. These included:

- the organization is often surrounded by a series of key publics or stakeholders with whom it is important to maintain good working relations;
- adverse publicity in the media may have far reaching effects on the future operation of the organization;
- marketing will allow the organization to offer very innovative products and services;
- wider publicity regarding the public sector organization may open up opportunities to market segments which previously did not benefit from the product or service due to ignorance. Marketing in this way may even help the organization build on factors associated with social responsibility.

DIFFERENT APPROACHES TO THE RUNNING OF BUSINESS ORGANIZATIONS

Studies of organizations suggest that they fit roughly into three categories: the production oriented organization, the sales oriented organization, and the marketing oriented organization. The historical development of many organizations often takes the organization through these three stages sequentially, but this is not always the case.

The **production oriented** organization will concentrate all its efforts on producing the goods which the company knows it is good at producing and then trying to sell these goods. The organization should concentrate on producing products that are of the best quality and performance that customers will clamour to buy. Many old traditional industries have used this approach over long periods. This approach means that the managers put all their efforts into making the production processes better and more efficient. Little effort is spent considering the consumer. After all, they have always bought the products so why should things change now?

The **selling oriented** organization will produce products and then attempt to sell these products by the use of a variety of sales and promotion techniques. Profits will be obtained by sales volume. A good example of this type of approach is where a company is experiencing reducing sales levels and brings in a 'marketing officer' to try and address this problem. They spend time and money producing leaflets to promote the products without ever looking at the customer. Or a sales person is brought in to sell the product to potential customers, using 'hard sell' methods.

The **marketing oriented** organization considers the customer needs and wants before making any decisions about what to produce. Once production is started the customer is constantly monitored for changing patterns of buyer behaviour and the products and services constantly altered to meet these changing demands. Profits are achieved through customer satisfaction. The British Airways motto 'To fly, to serve' demonstrates the marketing approach.

THE CONSEQUENCES OF AN ORGANIZATION ADOPTING A MARKETING APPROACH

Interest in the application of marketing is intensifying in many organizations, including organization from the non-profit-making and public sectors. This is happening because it has been recognized that marketing can contribute to an improved performance in the marketplace.

Nigel Piercy (1992) suggests that there are stages which contribute to the development of market-led strategic change in organizations. These are summarized in Figure 1.3.

Piercy (1992) suggests that adoption of the market-led approach is essential for two reasons:

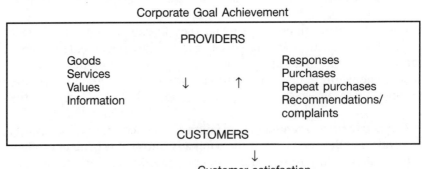

Figure 1.3 The development of effective marketing strategies in organizations. Source: Piercy (1992).

- that ultimately all organizations are forced to follow the dictates of the market (i.e. the paying customer) or go out of business;
- the organization can pursue organizational effectiveness by being 'market led' and focusing on the customer's needs, wants and demands.

The simplicity of the ideas of marketing as an underlying business philosophy seems obvious. The question which arises is why do organizations find it difficult to become market led and actually fail in the implementation stage? Piercy (1992) suggests that there are three main reasons for organizations finding it difficult to adopt marketing. These can be summarized as follows:

- there are considerable barriers to the introduction of marketing such as ignorance of customer characteristics, lack of information, inflexible technology and competitive threats which all come from the way in which an organization is run;
- being 'market led' may require substantial and painful upheaval in the way the organization is structured, the way decisions are made, the key values which are communicated to employees and managers, and how everybody in the organization does their job;
- the introduction involves a programme of deep-seated fundamental strategic change in organizations, not just hiring a marketing executive or doing more advertising or any other short-term tactical ploy.

The introduction of a marketing philosophy into an organization involves deep structural and cultural change which is often very hard to achieve in the short term.

THE DIFFERENCES BETWEEN STRATEGIC AND TACTICAL MARKETING

It is important that the differences between strategic and tactical marketing are understood. The real significance of a **strategic marketing plan** as opposed to a **tactical operational marketing plan** must be clearly defined if organizations are to operate marketing effectively.

McDonald (1989) differentiates between the strategic marketing planning process and the tactical plan by defining the strategic marketing plan as:

> having a greater emphasis on scanning the external environment, the early identification of forces emanating from it, and developing appropriate strategic responses involving all levels of managers in the process.

He suggests that a strategic plan should cover a three to five year time period. The operational plan or tactical plan is a much more detailed programme of work, often on a smaller area of the business and covering a shorter timescale. The tactical marketing plan will include details of how the organization is going to achieve its overall strategy.

Table 1.3 The marketing mix

P – Product	The good or service to be marketed
P – Price	The amount of money a customer has to pay to obtain the good or service
P – Promotion	All the methods of communicating the features of the good or service to the customer
P – Place	All the activities that enable the customer to obtain the product or service

The tactical marketing plan will include details of the appropriate annual **marketing mix** plans for each area of the business. The marketing mix is the term used to summarise the techniques which can be used by the organization to influence demand. E.J. McCarthy (1960) developed this framework as the **4Ps**. This is shown in more detail in Table 1.3.

MARKETING AND OTHER BUSINESS FUNCTIONS

It is vital that the marketing function fits into the whole business organization in an effective manner. It could be argued that if everybody is considered to be a marketer in an organization then a separate marketing function within an organization is not necessary. It is essential that everybody knows how they fit into the marketing activity which the organization undertakes.

Organizations which have incorporated marketing into existing business disciplines have tended to have a separate marketing department. This can be seen at Marriot Hotels who run their company in five main divisions:

- People;
- Finance;
- Product and Service;
- Sales and Marketing;
- Development.

There is often confusion about the role of marketing within the other functions of the company. Kotler (1994) discusses the importance of marketing in relation to other business functions. In some firms marketing is seen as just another function. In other firms it is given prime importance. The more enlightened firms put marketing at the centre of the business. The most enlightened, however, put the customer as the central focus of the business. Figure 1.4 shows this diagrammatically.

This chapter has tried to show the importance of marketing in bringing about success in organizations. Many strategic management academics are now beginning to recognize the importance of marketing as a central business function. Kenichi Ohmae (1982), for example, has expressed such views:

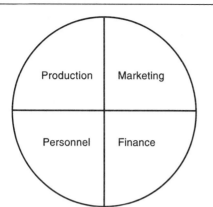

(a) Marketing as an equal function

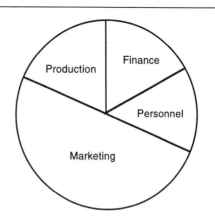

(b) Marketing as a more important function

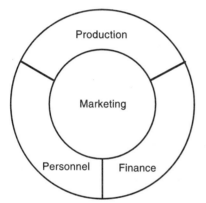

(c) Marketing as the major function

(d) The customer as the controlling function

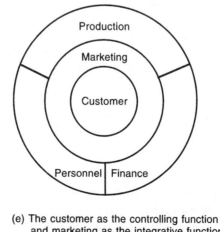

(e) The customer as the controlling function
and marketing as the integrative function

Figure 1.4 Alternative views of marketing in a firm.
Source: Kotler (1994).

In a free competitive economic world, there will be no stability in a corporation's performance if it allows its attention to be diverted from the basic mission of serving its customers. If it consistently succeeds in serving customers more effectively than its competitors, profit will follow.

Despite the obvious logic for using the marketing approach, there are still relatively few companies that practise it. Drucker (1985) has expressed concern about this situation:

Why after forty years of preaching marketing, teaching marketing, professing marketing, so few suppliers are willing to follow, I cannot explain. The fact remains that so far, anyone who is willing to use marketing as the basis for strategy is likely to acquire leadership in an industry or a market fast and almost without risk.

Most organizations it seems, still have far to go to become customer satisfiers.

IS THE MARKETING OF SERVICES ANY DIFFERENT TO THE MARKETING OF PRODUCTS?

It is widely accepted that the principles and practice of marketing techniques were developed by goods manufacturing industries. Literature which was published confined their examples to goods. There have been signs more recently of literature devoted entirely to the marketing of services. Books by Cowell (1984) and Bateson (1995) are examples of texts which have explored the application of marketing for service organizations. The techniques of marketing have been embraced more recently by service organizations which for a variety of reasons now try to make the marketing philosophy the central focus of the business. This has been particularly apparent when an organization has moved from the public to the private sector of the economy, forcing the organization to adopt a profit-orientated approach in the face of growing competition.

The developed countries of Europe have seen a gradual shift of emphasis in economic output from the product sector to the service sector. The development of services ranging from hotels to educational establishments and from airlines to leisure parks has been both rapid and complex. The importance of services to the economy of the United Kingdom can be shown with reference to employment and balance of payments statistics. This pattern is repeated in all the developed countries of Europe. There has been an increase in the numbers employed in services as opposed to manufacturing industries. Balance of payments statistics show the growing importance of services to the economies of Europe.

Many service organizations such as the banks and airlines have embraced the marketing philosophy. There are many service organizations, however, which have only just started to adopt the marketing philosophy. The marketing of higher education establishments, for example, has recently added a new perspective to service marketing.

THE ROLE OF MARKETING IN SERVICE INDUSTRIES AND THE MANAGEMENT OF INTANGIBLES

There has been considerable growth in the service sector in Europe as higher living standards and technological developments stimulated the growth of many service industries. The use of new technologies has revolutionized and expanded customer service. The trend towards a growing European service economy is predicted to increase by economists. The population of Europe is predicted to become richer and spend an increasing amount of their income on services.

Marketing theorists have attempted to define services in relation to their intangibility and the fact that a service never results in the ownership of anything, merely bringing the customer 'benefits' or 'satisfactions'.

Kotler (1994) defines a service as:

Any activity or benefit that one party can offer to another that is essentially intangible and does not result in the ownership of anything. Its production may or may not be tied to a physical product.

Rushton and Carson (1985) state that the fundamental differences between goods and service-marketing is that goods are produced whereas services are performed.

Theorists have attempted to clarify the definitions by stating that services have characteristics which distinguish them from products. The most commonly stated characteristics of services are as follows.

- **Intangibility**. Services have the characteristic of being intangible in that they cannot be seen, felt, heard, tasted or smelled before purchase.

  Bateson (1977) has refined intangibility further in that a service has a 'palpable' intangibility in that it cannot be touched by the consumer but also a 'mental' intangibility in that it can often be difficult for the consumer to grasp the idea of the service mentally.
- **Inseparability**. Services have the characteristic of an overlap between the production and performance of the service and the consumption of it. A service, in its purest form, has the provider and customer face to face. This should theoretically mean that the implementation of the marketing philosophy to the service industries should be an easier task, particularly in terms of being customer centred. Service organizations have the benefit of having face-to-face contact with the final customer.
- **Heterogeneity**. It is difficult for services to be provided to the same standard at every consumption occasion. This can be explained by reference to the example of a restaurant meal. Every time the same

customer visits the same restaurant for the same meal, the experience will be different according to occasion, moods, staff performance, etc.

- **Perishability**. Services have the characteristic of being perishable in that if the service is not sold, then the business can never be recovered. The empty hotel room or the seat on the train cannot be put into storage for later consumption. Empty rooms or seats mean lost business and therefore lost profitability.

  Services marketing is also often faced with widely fluctuating demands at different times or periods in the year.

- **Lack of ownership**. The customer only has access to the activity or facility when he or she buys a service. The customer never owns anything at the end of the transaction. Services often lead to feelings of satisfaction rather than a tangible item which can be shown to other people.

Academic theorists have looked at the differences between product and service marketing. Judd (1968), for example, has identified features which differentiate services from manufactured goods. These include the fact that services cannot be stocked and that channels of distribution, if they exist at all, are often short.

SERVICE MARKETING

It has been suggested that the marketing theories which were developed for the fast moving consumer goods industries can be adapted for organizations which market services. Grönroos (1980), for example, conducted research on service organizations in Sweden and Finland and suggested that traditional marketing literature could offer little to service organizations. Other academics have argued that service marketing requires a different approach and different concepts compared to product marketing (see Shostack (1977), for example).

One of the problems associated with the concept of 'service marketing' is the fact that many organizations never market true products or true services. Shostack has suggested that there is a goods-service continuum dependent on the level of tangibility in the product or service offered for sale (Figure 1.5).

Marketing theorists have also tried to develop new marketing theories to apply to service marketing examples. Booms and Bitner (1981), for example, have suggested an expanded marketing mix for services to try and recognize that people who perform or deliver the services are crucial and that setting, atmosphere and layout may be importance influences. The elements which need to be emphasised during the creation of marketing programmes for services are shown in Figure 1.6.

This expanded marketing mix stresses the importance of certain elements of the traditional marketing mix and suggests new categories for special attention – participants, physical evidence and process.

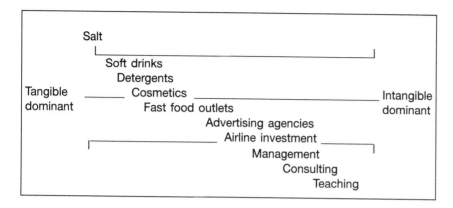

Figure 1.5 A goods–service continuum. Source: Shostack (1977).

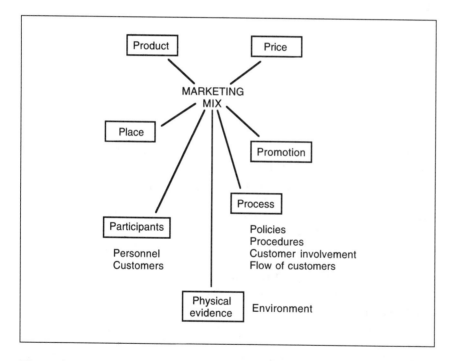

Figure 1.6 Elements to be emphasized during the creation of marketing programmes for services. Source: adapted from Booms and Bitner (1981).

ARE PRODUCTS AND SERVICES FUNDAMENTALLY DIFFERENT?

The philosophical question which must be asked is whether the marketing of services is substantially different from marketing products and whether the differences mean that fundamentally modified approaches are necessary when developing marketing programmes for services.

Levitt (1972) has questioned the view that service marketing is any different to product marketing. Levitt argues that all companies sell intangibles in a market rather than simple products. Industries which are generally associated with marketing services such as travel, repair, consulting, education and banking are not able to let the prospective customer try out or experience the product or service before purchase. Levitt argues, however, that the most basic of fast moving consumer goods, such as shampoo and pizzas, have a strong element of intangibility, just like the services, because the consumer can rarely experience these products in advance. Branding of products, for example, adds intangible elements to a very tangible item. It denotes quality and can make the item desirable.

The conclusion which could be drawn from this analysis is that although services do have some special characteristics which require different approaches to marketing, they have many characteristics which they share with products.

CONTEMPORARY MARKETING ISSUES

There are a number of contemporary issues which have been growing in importance in the marketing field during the last part of the twentieth century. The first of these is the growing interest being shown by **non-profit-making organizations** in the philosophy and practice of marketing. Charities and local authorities, for example, have already begun to operate strong public relations campaigns and have seen the advantage of segmenting markets and using branding techniques. The use of marketing has been recognized by the Countryside Commission, for example, in England, in an area of activity where marketing would once have been criticized for being ideologically unsound.

The second contemporary issue for marketing is the link of marketing to **quality** and **total quality management**. Total quality management (TQM) has become a management discipline in its own right. There is, of course, a great deal of similarity between the philosophy of total quality management and the philosophy of marketing. Total quality management requires that the products and services produced by an organization are right first time and that employees are working for the good of the organization and its customers. This is very close to an organization introducing a marketing-led philosophy. Both approaches usually involve a shift in the culture of the organization.

The third contemporary issue for marketing is the growth of interest in **ethical issues and social responsibility**. It can be argued that a clever public relations campaign can allow an organization to appear to be acting ethically and showing social responsibility without the underlying philosophy being present. It is clear that the addition of a 'green' product to a range of products which are questionable in terms of their formulation and positioning may not be enough in the future to satisfy the ever growing number of critics.

It may become unacceptable to advertise to children and to other groups in the population. It may not be sufficient for large companies to donate small amounts of money to charities and other good causes in order to improve the reputation of the organization in the eyes of the population, the customers and the shareholders. Acting ethically, and with social responsibility, in marketing is predicted to become a very important issue for all companies in the future.

CONCLUSIONS

This chapter has defined the marketing concept and considered various definitions of marketing. We have reviewed the history of marketing and the fact that marketing concepts were developed initially for production-oriented organizations. The chapter reviews the appliction of marketing to the service sector, public sector, voluntary sector and charitable organizations. Contemporary issues in marketing are also reviewed at the end of the chapter.

DISCUSSION POINTS AND ESSAY QUESTIONS

1. Discuss the extent to which the idea of consumer-led or customer-orientated marketing is feasible for tourism organizations.
2. Examine the ways in which the marketing of services differs from the marketing of manufactured goods.
3. Evaluate the ways in which marketing objectives and approaches differ between organizations in the public, private and voluntary sectors.

EXERCISE

Students should interview those responsible for marketing within several different types of tourism, leisure and hospitality organizations with the object of finding out their definitions of marketing and their views on the marketing concept.

The views of these managers should then be compared and contrasted with the definitions and ideas discussed in Chapter 1.

Finally, students should attempt to explain any differences which they identify between the views of practitioners and those of academics.

2 | What is Europe?

Key concepts

The main concepts covered in this chapter are:

- Europe in history;
- Europe as a geographical entity;
- Europe's political systems;
- economics and the idea of Europe;
- the demographics of Europe;
- European cultures and lifestyles.

INTRODUCTION

The purpose of this chapter is to look at what we mean when we talk about 'Europe'. The word 'Europe' is commonly used but rarely defined. This may be because there is a belief that a consensus exists as to what the term Europe means. Alternatively, the dearth of definitions may result from the fact that everyone has their own view of what constitutes Europe.

For marketing people, Europe is seen in terms of markets, fundamentally. Marketers increasingly talk about the European market, again without usually defining what they mean. Nevertheless this emphasis on Europe as a market is understandable given the creation of the so-called 'Single Market' in Europe in the early 1990s.

The growing influence of the European Commission has led many people in politics, the business world and the media to see Europe as synonymous with the European Union. As such the idea of Europe as an entity is often considered to be a relatively recent invention.

However, such a view ignores two crucial aspects of the concept of Europe, namely its history and geography. For while the Single Market and the European Union emphasize the unity of Europe, a study of its history and geography shows a more complex and fragmented picture, where conflict rather than agreement has often been the dominant agent of change.

To the student of history and geography, Europe is a patchwork quilt of different cultures shaped by historical events and geographical factors. Indeed it is this cultural diversity which poses the greatest challenge for those marketers who seek to practise European marketing with the development of 'Euro-brands' for 'Euro-consumers'.

Furthermore, the Europe of the European Union does not currently encompass a number of countries that have traditionally been thought of as an integral part of Europe. For example, it excludes Poland, the country whose invasion proved to be the catalyst for the last great war fought in Europe. It also does not include Switzerland, which has for decades fulfilled the roles of being Europe's neutral state during times of war and its trusted banker.

In view of these complexities, this chapter will attempt to answer the question: What is Europe? It will endeavour to do this by looking at the concept of Europe from a number of different points of view, including:

- its historical development;
- the geography of the continent;
- political systems and institutions;
- economic theories and systems;
- demographic factors;
- cultures and lifestyles.

In all of these cases, it is possible – although difficult – to gather evidence and reach some conclusions, as all of these aspects are to some degree visible and measurable.

However, it is important to recognize that Europe is not just something that can be looked at in such academic terms. It is also an idea, a concept which has stimulated the emotions and exalted the imagination of people for centuries. Likewise, the idea of a Europe united by choice has been a dream for those this century who have seen it as a way of achieving peace.

Yet as this idea of unification appears to be becoming more and more of a reality, voices are being heard which say this process could be more of a threat than an opportunity, a nightmare rather than a dream. They fear a loss of national sovereignty and identity and the dilution of the rich cultural differences which are themselves at the heart of Europe's appeal to non-European tourists.

This debate is taking place in a Europe which in the current century has seen its dominance of world affairs dramatically diminish. In military terms it lives in the shadow of the USA while in the industrial sphere the pace is now being set by the countries of the Pacific Rim. The future of Europe will undoubtedly be bound up with the process of globalization which is underway. It could be argued that an emphasis on a united Europe fails to recognize the reality that it is the global scale which now matters, not individual continents.

However, rather than trying to foresee the future, let us start by looking at Europe from a historical perspective.

HISTORY AND THE CONCEPT OF EUROPE

Europe does not have a single history, in spite of the numerous text-books which purport to be histories of Europe. Any history of Europe is usually a series of histories of different parts of Europe and what happened to them individually at particular times. They also discuss the relationship between these various parts in terms of war, trade, royal marriages and treaties, for example. But only rarely are they able to talk about Europe as a single entity.

Nevertheless, European countries have been prominent in the development of world civilization and history through the ages. In pre-history there were the cave painters of Spain and France and the society of the ancient Greeks. These were followed by the Roman Empire and the birth of Christianity in Europe. After that came the Vikings who went on to conquer large parts of Europe and discover distant lands. Then there came the great European cathedral builders of the medieval period, and the rise of great kingdoms which patronized the arts, such as that ruled over by the Dukes of Burgundy.

Later, the artists of the Renaissance enriched the world, while explorers began to discover the rest of the world and open it up to trade with Europe. This led to the development of European colonies in every continent which carried European influences to the four corners of the world. However, at the same time, the emigration of millions of Europeans to these colonies, particularly the USA, sowed the seeds of the eventual usurping of Europe's position in the world by the USA.

Europe was the cradle of the Industrial Revolution and the place where railways first began to transform the world. It is also the continent where the two World Wars of the twentieth century began and where Napoleon and Hitler tried to unite Europe by force and killed millions of people in the attempt.

Finally, in terms of the subject of this book, Europe is the birthplace of the modern tourism industry and is still the most popular destination for international tourists, of all the continents of the world.

Nevertheless, we still cannot talk about a history of Europe. However, in the future, we may increasingly be able to write a history of Europe as a single entity with the rise of the European Union and its enlargement to include the countries of Scandinavia and Eastern Europe.

GEOGRAPHY AND EUROPE

There has always been a debate as to whether Europe is a single geographical entity. Physically, it is thought to extend east to the Urals, south to the Mediterranean, north to the northernmost tip of Scandinavia and west to the western coasts of Ireland and Portugal. However, geographers have often split Europe into blocks such as Eastern, Western and Southern, which they felt represented distinct geographical entities in their own right.

Geographical features serve to both divide and unite Europe. The English Channel has kept the British isolated from developments in European consciousness and mountain ranges divide countries like Spain and France, and France and Switzerland. However, some rivers link European countries together, such as the Rhine.

Europe is covered by several climatic zones from the Mediterranean climates of the south, to the Arctic climates of northern Scandinavia. There are also substantial differences within Europe in terms of agricultural systems, vegetation and landscape, for example. There are different patterns of settlement. In all these cases, there are differences within individual countries, as well as within Europe as a whole.

However, one could also say that some of these differences between countries and within Europe are declining. Some commentators argue that many big cities are starting to look more alike while agricultural technology and policies are reducing differences in agricultural systems.

At the same time, Europe is being unified as a geographical entity by developments in transport and the media. Air services are bringing cities closer together, while countries are being linked by coordinated developments in fast rail services that cross national boundaries. Meanwhile, satellite television is exposing people to programmes produced in other European countries.

Yet, there is also a simultaneous growth in regional consciousness taking place in Europe, from the Basque Country to Macedonia. Regions are also developing which link two or more countries together, such as the so-called 'Euro-Regions' of Midi Pyrennées (France) and Catalonia (Spain) and Kent (UK) and Nord Pas-de-Calais (France).

POLITICAL SYSTEMS AND INSTITUTIONS IN EUROPE

Europe has been the birthplace of many major political philosophies such as liberalism, socialism and communism. With the fall of communism in Eastern Europe, Europe is increasingly being united through the adoption of liberal democratic systems by these Eastern European countries so that such systems are now dominant throughout the continent.

However, there are still fundamental differences between European countries in terms of their political systems and institutions. Examples of this include:

- countries with powerful elected assemblies and those where their power is more limited;
- the existence of republics and monarchies;
- countries where the participation of the people in the political system is high and others where it is much lower.

However, there are clearly now supranational institutions which are creating Euro-level political systems and institutions. Most notably there is the European Union with its elected European Parliament. European legislation is increasingly affecting people across Europe in areas such as labour rights, consumer protection, and health and safety.

Cooperation between European countries has also been facilitated for many years by the Council of Europe.

ECONOMIC THEORIES AND SYSTEMS IN EUROPE

Europe is the birthplace of many economic theories and is still the home of a range of economic systems including largely market economies and mixed economies where state intervention is substantial. However, since the end of communism in Eastern Europe there are no purely state-controlled economies in Europe. Furthermore, Europe possesses supra-governmental economic cooperation areas and free trade zones such as the Single Market.

However, the level of economic development is not uniform across Europe, as can be seen from Table 2.1 which compares the Gross Domestic Product (GDP) of a range of European countries in terms of US dollars per capita. Thus Europe's richest and most economically developed country, Switzerland, has a Gross Domestic Product which is nearly fifty times more than that of Bulgaria.

There are considerable variations between European countries in terms of other economic indictors. For example, inflation in 1993 stood at 1.3% in Denmark and 1.4% in Ireland, compared to 14.4% in

Table 2.1 Gross Domestic Product (GDP) of selected European countries, 1993 (US dollars per capita)

Country	Gross Domestic Product 1993 (US dollars per capita)
Switzerland	33 813
Denmark	25 453
Iceland	23 511
UK	16 183
Ireland	14 290
Spain	12 462
Greece	7 156
Hungary	3 698
Turkey	2 580
Romania	1 438
Bulgaria	727

Source: Euromonitor (1995).

Table 2.2 Percentage of the working population employed in different sectors in selected European countries 1993

| Country | Percentage of working population employed in: | | |
	Agriculture	**Manufacturing**	**Community, social and personal services**
Austria	7.1	26.0	23.9
Finland	8.6	19.6	32.1
France	5.2	20.4	32.1
Greece	22.2	19.2	19.8
Ireland	13.8	19.9	24.5
Netherlands	4.0	17.8	34.7
Norway	5.5	14.6	38.7
Sweden	3.4	18.3	40.4
Turkey	43.9	15.2	14.4
UK	1.2	20.1	33.4

Source: *European Marketing Pocket Book* (1995).

Greece, 66.1% in Turkey and 255.2% in Romania (Euromonitor, 1995).

Unemployment rates also vary drastically within Europe, from a rate of 4.5% in Switzerland in 1993 to 22.7% in Spain (Euromonitor, 1995).

There are also significant differences between European countries in terms of the sectors within which people are employed, as can be seen from Table 2.2.

Furthermore, wealth is not distributed in a uniform way within different European countries because of differences in taxation systems and social security policies, for example. However, again these are being affected by the growth of European Commission influence in these fields.

Industrial structure also varies from country to country in Europe, but we have witnessed the rise of European transnational corporations that hail from Europe and are mainly concentrated in Europe. These include names such as Renault, Philips, Center Parcs, Accor, Club Méditerranée, Nestlé, Netto, Aldi, LTU and Lego. Again the Single Market is helping the growth of such organizations as they increasingly seek to extend their influence to other continents.

DEMOGRAPHY AND EUROPE

In terms of population size, the countries of Europe are dramatically different. For example, Luxembourg, in 1994, had an estimated population of 400 000 while Malta was even lower at 367 000 and Liechtenstein had just 30 000 inhabitants. At the other extreme, Germany had 81 682 000, and Turkey some 58 848 000 (Euromonitor, 1995).

There are also significant differences in rates of population growth. For example, it is estimated that between 1990 and the year 2020 the total population of Italy will fall by 2.4% and that of Bulgaria by 2.1%.

By contrast during the same period it is expected that the population of Iceland will grow by 34.9%, and Turkey by 65.8% (Euromonitor, 1995). However, it is worth noting that, in general, rates of population growth are lower in Europe than in many other parts of the world.

European countries tend to have a relatively high population density in relation to other continents, reflecting the early urbanization and industrialization that took place in Europe. Nevertheless, there are still extreme variations within Europe. In 1994, the population density per square kilometre in Iceland was 2.6 and that in Norway 13.3. Conversely, the corresponding figures for Belgium and the Netherlands were 331.2 and 372.8 respectively (Euromonitor, 1995). European countries also vary in terms of the age structure of their populations, as can be seen from Table 2.3.

Increasingly, European countries are becoming multi-cultural societies, due to in-migration. Many of these in-migrants are from non-European countries, but they are often linked by past colonial ties to those countries in which they make their new home.

At the same time, there is a growing flow of people migrating between European countries. These people may be moving primarily to find employment, or they may be people from Northern Europe moving to Southern European countries like Spain when they retire.

While religious observance is perhaps declining across Europe overall, it is still an important factor in countries like Ireland, for example, and amongst some immigrant communities.

The European population, in general, is highly literate and a relatively high percentage of people continue with higher education in comparison to other continents. Nevertheless, there are still substantial national differences. Adult literacy rates vary from 70% in Turkey and 78% in Albania to 99% in many countries and 100% in Luxembourg (Euromonitor, 1995). In 1991, the latest year for which comparable

Table 2.3 The age structure of the population of selected European countries, 1993

Country	Percentage of population in the following age groups, 1993			
	0–14	15–34	35–54	55 and above
Austria	17.6	30.8	26.6	25.0
Bulgaria	18.5	27.6	26.9	26.9
Czech Republic	20.6	28.5	28.1	22.8
France	19.9	29.4	26.0	24.7
Germany	16.4	29.5	27.4	26.8
Greece	17.6	29.6	25.3	27.4
Ireland	25.7	31.1	23.9	19.4
Italy	15.5	31.1	26.2	27.2
Netherlands	18.3	31.5	27.9	22.3
Norway	19.2	29.8	26.3	24.8
Poland	24.6	29.2	26.0	20.2
Romania	22.8	29.7	25.3	22.4

Source: *European Marketing Pocket Book* (1995).

data is available, the percentage of people with a degree or professional qualification ranged from 13% in Ireland to 55% in France and 58% in Sweden (Euromonitor, 1995).

While the nature of the family is changing in Europe, marriage is still very popular. However, there has also been a growth in divorce in many European countries, although not in some countries where divorce is either not socially acceptable or may be virtually illegal. Thus in 1993, the rate of divorce was 0.5 per 1000 population in Italy but 3.0 in the UK (Euromonitor, 1995).

In addition, the nature of households is also changing in terms of household size, for instance. Thus in 1993, the average number of people in households within Europe ranged from 2.27 in Denmark to 4.33 in Turkey (Euromonitor, 1995).

In general, European countries share many similar characteristics in terms of demographics when compared to other continents. However, within Europe, there are, as we have seen, still large differences between individual countries.

There are, though, many common trends being felt across Europe, even if the starting points are very different. These include couples having fewer children and more people entering higher education. Perhaps, therefore, in demographic terms Europe is starting to become more homogeneous.

Clearly, the demographic indicators we have discussed here have massive implications for those organizations which wish to sell their products in European markets.

CULTURE AND EUROPE

Cultural diversity is the hallmark of Europe and is cited as perhaps the greatest challenge facing moves towards the unification of Europe.

Firstly, there is the issue of language. Although several languages such as English, French and German are quite widely spoken, there is no universally understood language in Europe. There are over twenty national languages and many regional languages such as Breton and Basque which are an intrinsic element of European culture.

There are many other differences in the culture of European countries of which just a few examples will suffice to illustrate the point. These include:

- different attitudes towards the environment and green issues from the countries of Eastern Europe where economic growth is the dominant theme and green issues are a lesser priority, to Scandinavia and the Netherlands where green issues and environmental concerns are an important aspect of daily life. For example, in 1990, 55% of glass and 58% of paper used in the Netherlands were recycled. The equivalent figures for Ireland were 8% and 15% respectively;

Table 2.4 National differences in consumer expenditure in different types of goods and services, 1993

Country	Percentage of consumer expenditure on:			
	Food	**Clothing**	**Health**	**Leisure**
Denmark	14.3	4.5	2.2	10.4
France	14.7	4.9	10.3	7.5
Greece	29.2	7.4	4.1	5.9
Hungary	16.4	3.4	4.5	10.9
Iceland	17.2	7.6	2.3	11.5
Ireland	18.8	5.6	4.2	12.5
Netherlands	11.2	5.7	13.2	10.1
Portugal	29.4	8.4	2.6	5.3
UK	11.4	4.5	1.5	10.2

Source: Euromonitor (1995).

- varying patterns of leisure activity, for example substantial differences between countries in the proportion of the population that is involved in sport as participants;
- the role played in society by women varies significantly between European countries such as Greece and Norway;
- eating habits, both in terms of eating out and what people eat in their own homes.

There are also considerable national differences, within Europe, in terms of consumer culture. Firstly, there are variations in consumer expenditure on different types of goods and services, as can be seen from Table 2.4.

However, it could be argued that in the field of consumer culture, Europe is becoming more homogenous, albeit at a slow pace. We are seeing the rise of transnational corporations in Europe, selling 'Euro-brands' while satellite and cable television is leading towards the growth of 'Euro-media'. Companies which are keen to expand into new national markets and the creation of the Single Market in Europe are both encouraging the Europeanization of consumption.

It may also be that this slow move towards homogeneity is more pronounced amongst younger consumers rather than older ones. Their education and language skills perhaps make them more amenable to the idea of 'Euro-branding'.

If this is the case, then Europeanization may come about, not through political action, but rather through consumerism, which may then need to be reflected in political change.

EUROPE AND THE REST OF THE WORLD

So far we have talked of Europe as if somehow it was a closed system, but clearly this is not the case. It is being constantly affected by countries outside the continent, and is in its turn influencing other parts of the world.

The effects of non-European countries on Europe

Non-European countries have influenced Europe dramatically in recent years and are continuing to do so. These influences include:

- the growth of American and Japanese companies setting up operations in Europe and seeking to sell their products in the European market;
- the increasing role played by American culture in the daily lives of many Europeans in terms of television programmes, music, the cinema, and food and drink, for example;
- the impact of Japanese management theory on the way in which management practice is viewed by academics and practitioners in Europe;
- the military, economic and political influence which the USA is able to exercise in Europe;
- migration from non-European countries to Europe.

The influence of Europe in the rest of the world

Europe as a whole, and individual countries within Europe, continue to exercise considerable influence in the rest of the world. European companies are becoming increasingly important players in the global market through names such as Accor and Marks & Spencer, for example. The European Union is now a major political entity in the world context and its influence will grow as new countries join. Individual countries are continuing to influence the wider world through aid programmes and the efforts of organizations like the British Council, spreading the cultural influence of individual European countries to other parts of the world.

CONCLUSIONS

Overall, it appears that while Europe is still heterogeneous, it is becoming a little more homogeneous all the time, particularly in terms of consumer cultures. The process is not uniform across Europe; it is happening perhaps more in certain countries and amongst particular age groups. It could be argued that homogeneity is a function of the actions of the European Commission, industry and education systems.

This process of homogenization could ultimately, if carried to its conclusion, pose a threat to tourism, as cultural diversity is one of the main motivations for tourists to travel between European countries, and to Europe from other continents.

However, our concern with Europeanization may blind us to a trend which is perhaps of even greater long-term significance, namely globalization. It may be that the globalization of industries, markets and cultures will occur before Europeanization, and will prove to be far more significant. In this process Europe may find its place in the geopolitics of the world becoming less important as economic power passes to the countries of the Pacific Rim.

DISCUSSION POINTS AND ESSAY QUESTIONS

1. Critically evaluate the statement that 'Europe does not exist!'
2. Discuss the factors that appear to be slowly making Europe a more homogeneous continent.
3. Examine the influences which events and trends in non-European countries are having on culture in Europe.

EXERCISE The group should split into six teams and each team should choose one of the following pairs of countries:

- Belgium and Bulgaria;
- Germany and Greece;
- Iceland and Malta;
- Poland and Portugal;
- France and Hungary;
- Sweden and Spain.

For each of your countries, you should prepare a profile which covers their history, geography, economy, population structure and culture. Each profile should be presented in written form in a report of no more than 3000 words and should be well supported by facts and figures.

You should then identify the key differences and similarities between your countries in relation to these five headings, and put them on OHP (overhead projector) acetates.

Each team should then present their OHP to the rest of the group.

At the end of the exercise, an attempt should be made to see if any general conclusions can be drawn from these 12 countries about the differences between Northern Europe, Southern Europe and Eastern Europe.

What are tourism, leisure and hospitality? | 3

Key concepts

The main concepts covered in this chapter are:

- definitions of tourism, leisure and hospitality;
- the relationship between tourism, leisure and hospitality;
- differences within Europe in terms of how tourism, leisure and hospitality are perceived;
- the ways in which the distinctions between tourism, leisure and hospitality are becoming increasingly blurred.

INTRODUCTION

This chapter covers three main issues. It:

- examines the ways in which tourism, leisure and hospitality are defined and perceived, across Europe;
- explores the relationships between tourism, leisure and hospitality, in the European context;
- argues that some of the traditional demarcation lines between tourism, leisure and hospitality are becoming increasingly blurred, and that symbiotic relationships between them are growing.

There has traditionally been a considerable degree of overlap and disagreement over the relationship between tourism leisure, and hospitality. Everyone agrees they are interlinked but we can never agree about the precise nature of the link.

Before we go on to look at this vexed question, let us begin by outlining some generally accepted definitions of tourism, leisure and hospitality to see if this helps to clarify the relationship between the three areas.

Tourism

Definitions of tourism tend to have several components. In general tourism is defined as a short-term movement of people to places some distance from their normal place of resident to indulge in pleasurable activities. While this sounds simple, it is not. For example, it does not encompass the lucrative field of business tourism where the main purpose of the trip is for work rather than play. We also have difficulty in deciding how far you have to travel to be a tourist or how many nights you have to stay away from home to be classified as a tourist. There is clearly a strong link between the ideas of tourism and travel.

Many people would find it difficult to identify a tourism industry. Instead most commentators might say that tourism is an activity serviced by a number of other industries such as hospitality and transport. If there is a tourism industry specifically, it is probably made up of the tour operation and retail travel sectors, which did not exist on any scale until the rise of modern mass package tourism.

Leisure

According to Collin, writing in 1994, leisure as a noun means 'free time to do what you want'. The same author defines the leisure industry as 'companies which provide goods and services used during people's leisure time (holidays, cinemas, theatre, amusement parks, etc.)'.

These definitions are so broad that they encompass a myriad of different activities and organizations that might, on the face of it, appear to have little in common. For example, one could argue that leisure encompasses rock climbing and playing bridge, gambling and church-going.

Hospitality

Collin defines the noun 'hospitality' as 'looking after guests well'. This term is an 'Americanism' but it is becoming increasingly used in Europe, in place of traditional phrases such as hotel and catering or *hôtellerie*. This is perhaps because it has a qualitative dimension, in other words looking after guests **well**, which makes it attractive in an era when quality management is a fashionable conception. The same author describes the hospitality industry as 'all companies involved in providing services for guests (hotels, inns, restaurants, and other recreational activities)'. This means hospitality is mainly concerned with the provision of places to sleep and food and drink. Not all hospitality consumers are tourists, therefore, as some will simply be people going to their local bar for a drink.

THE RELATIONSHIP BETWEEN TOURISM, LEISURE AND HOSPITALITY

It could be said that the three are different, although they are related, for tourism is an activity, leisure is a concept of time and hospitality is concerned with the supply side, in other words the provision of services.

In terms of the relationship between tourism, leisure and hospitality, there are a number of models which have been suggested but they all have weaknesses.

For some commentators, tourism and hospitality are merely subsets of leisure. However, this does not take account of the tourist activity and hospitality services which are related to business travel. Others argue that all three are separate yet there are clearly great areas of overlap between them. Ultimately it does not matter if we cannot easily see how they interrelate as long as we recognize that they do.

However, it would be wrong for us to end this brief discussion without highlighting the problems which this ongoing debate causes for marketing in all three fields. These include:

- a lack of clarity and problems of duplication and gaps in marketing research data;
- the absence in most European countries of a single strong professional body or lobby, speaking with one voice for all three areas, which reduces the potential influence of the views of tourism, leisure and hospitality interests on decision-makers;
- ongoing debates in tourism, leisure and hospitality education institutions and professional bodies that perhaps deflect some energy that might otherwise be spent on further improving the quality of education and training for marketing practitioners in all three areas.

For the purposes of this book, there are two main issues in relation to the nature of tourism, leisure and hospitality that are relevant, namely:

- how these three areas are perceived across Europe and whether they are viewed differently in various European countries;
- whether or not the three areas are becoming more closely linked over time, as activities, industries or in terms of the products they offer.

DIFFERENT PERCEPTIONS OF TOURISM, LEISURE AND HOSPITALITY ACROSS EUROPE

On the first issue, there has traditionally been a clear distinction between Northern Europe and Southern Europe. In the countries of Northern Europe, which tend to be the most industrialized and economically developed on the continent, leisure is a highly developed concept with a long history. Furthermore, in most of them, tourism is seen as an outbound activity where affluent people travel south in search of sun, or to other countries in search of new experiences. To these countries and their people, in spite of their domestic tourism industries, tourism is seen in terms of tour operators and travel agents facilitating their travel abroad while hospitality means the services they receive as consumers in other countries.

Conversely, the countries of Southern Europe are less industrialized and urbanized, with their population overall having lower disposable incomes than their Northern European counterparts. This has a number of implications for their perception of tourism, leisure and hospitality. Leisure is only beginning to be recognized as a concept. Furthermore, given that since the 1960s these countries have traditionally been receivers rather than generators of tourists, tourism and hospitality are generally seen in terms of the supply of services to meet the needs of these tourists. In some countries tourism is often seen as simply part of the hospitality sector, in other words, to quote Collin, 'looking after guests well', rather than as a separate subject. After all, as receivers rather than generators of tourists, specific tourism industry sectors such as outbound tour operators are not required. However, tourism industries do exist in Southern Europe usually in the form of destination-based 'travel agencies' which tend to perform functions such as organizing excursions and hiring cars to visitors.

We must recognize, though, that this picture is too simplistic and it does not take account of how things are changing over time. For example, while the countries of Southern Europe have not generated large numbers of outbound tourists in the past, they have large domestic tourism markets. Therefore, their industries have, simultaneously, to meet the needs of foreign visitors and their own population.

Secondly, some Northern European countries such as the UK, have significant inbound and domestic tourism markets, for whom they have had to develop destination-based services.

Finally, and most importantly, the situation is changing. As Southern European countries such as Italy and Spain become ever more economically developed and their populations have greater disposable income, they are becoming major generators, rather that just receivers, of international tourist trips. For many European countries, currently, their biggest increases in incoming tourists are from Southern European countries such as Spain and Italy. This is being accompanied by a development of the concept of leisure time, activity and expenditure in these countries.

Thus, the distinctions between Northern and Southern European countries are diminishing in relation to the ways in which tourism, leisure and hospitality are viewed.

However, recent political change in Eastern Europe is also leading to developments in the concepts of tourism, leisure and hospitality in the countries of this region of Europe. To countries desperately in need of foreign currency and economic growth, tourism is seen as a quick way of achieving both. Inbound tourism is being encouraged across Eastern Europe from Poland to Albania. At the same time, for the residents of these countries, the ability of increasing numbers of them to be able to travel abroad on holiday is a test of the political and economic results of the changes their countries have undergone.

These developments, however, are also making these countries realize that they must rethink their approach to tourism and hospitality in particular. State monopolies are being replaced by a market economy and private businesses are in competition with each other. In this situation, the poor service and lack of hospitality that characterized many Eastern European countries in the past have been identified as major obstacles to the development of a successful tourism industry. Much effort is therefore being put into customer care training, for example.

It would be wrong, though, to look at the issue of how tourism, leisure and hospitality are perceived just within the European context. As more and more Europeans travel to other continents for business and pleasure and viceversa, Europe is also being influenced by the attitudes of non-European cultures to tourism, leisure and hospitality. Several examples will serve to illustrate this point, including:

- the 'have a nice day' standardized service of American fast-food operators where the emphasis is on the speed of service;
- the high standards of personal service offered by the countries of the Pacific Rim;
- the specific needs and desires of non-European tourists such as the Japanese.

THE BLURRING OF THE DISTINCTION BETWEEN TOURISM, LEISURE AND HOSPITALITY

It is now time to turn our attention to the second question, namely to what extent the overlap between tourism, leisure and hospitality is growing, and the distinctions between them becoming more blurred.

Some have said this is a result of postmodernism, but whatever the reason it does appear to be a real phenomenon. Furthermore, it is a phenomenon which appears to be affecting both the demand side and the supply side in tourism, leisure and hospitality.

A number of examples can be used to illustrate this point:

- The resort complexes such as Club Méditerranée and Center Parcs offer both hospitality services and leisure facilities on the same site, under the ownership of one organization. Furthermore, they offer this mixture to a market which largely consists of tourists, in other words, people who have travelled away from home and are spending at least one night away from their normal place of residence.
- Theme parks are increasingly offering on-site accommodation units to encourage visitors to spend more time, and thus more money, on site. A good example of this is the Futuroscope theme park in Western France which now has several hotels, of different grades, within the boundaries of the park.
- The trend amongst hotels in most European countries is to build in-house leisure facilities for their guests such as gymnasia and swimming pools. This is seen as necessary to attract two very different groups of clients, namely leisure visitors at weekends, and business customers on weekdays.

- Leisure shopping is being developed as a tourist activity. Shopping is now used as a way of motivating trips to destinations as diverse as Liverpool in the UK, with its Albert Dock complex, the craft centres of rural Norway and the gold shops of Dubai.
- Sophisticated catering operations are being developed at visitor attractions to boost income. These can range from fast-food outlets to themed restaurants. Interestingly many of these current developments in Europe are mirroring earlier ones in North America.

At the same time, we are also perhaps seeing a reduction in the gap that has traditionally been seen between the leisure and pleasure and the business sectors of tourism, leisure and hospitality. For example, theme parks like Chessington World of Adventures are increasingly offering their facilities for corporate hospitality. Likewise the existence of leisure facilities such as golf courses are being used more and more by destinations to attract conference business, for instance.

We are also seeing some changes within the industrial structure of tourism, leisure and hospitality that are blurring the distinctions between the three sectors. For example, some tour operators are buying shares in, or taking full control of, hotels and hotel groups. A good example of this is the partial ownership of the leading Greek hotel chain Grecotel by the German tour operator TUI. Likewise, there are the hotel chains like Stakis in the UK which own and operate casinos, and tour operators and hotel chains offering holidays based on leisure pursuits such as white-water rafting, bicycling, painting and gastronomy.

However, it would be wrong to suggest that these examples of inter-relationships between tourism, leisure and hospitality are a recent phenomenon. For instance, in the early days of tourism, railway companies and airlines were major owners of hotels.

Nevertheless, the scale of the link between the three sectors is perhaps unprecedented and the sophistication of the links has not been seen before. This reflects the fact that tourism, leisure and hospitality are all relatively recent developments as 'major industries' and that they are still growing and developing at a very rapid rate.

The blurring of the distinction between the three sectors is a truly pan-European phenomenon, although there are national differences in its precise nature.

Perhaps, the clearest and most highly developed form of integration between the three is, ironically, an American import, the resort complex concept.

CONCLUSIONS

We have seen that there is not a consensus on what precisely the differences are between tourism, leisure and hospitality. Furthermore, we have also identified that these three words are viewed somewhat differently in different regions of Europe. However, the last section of the chapter is perhaps the most significant for if the distinctions between the three are becoming increasingly blurred, then such debates will become meaningless.

DISCUSSION POINTS AND ESSAY QUESTIONS

1. Discuss the differences and similarities between tourism, leisure and hospitality.
2. Outline the ways in which the concepts of tourism, leisure and hospitality differ between different regions within Europe.
3. Evaluate the extent to which the distinctions between tourism, leisure and hospitality are becoming increasingly blurred within Europe.

You should produce your own definitions of the following terms: **EXERCISE**

- tourism;
- leisure;
- hospitality.

Using your definition, select one tourism organization, one leisure organization, and one hospitality organization. You should then consider the following questions in relation to your chosen organizations:

(a) Why did you choose the particular organizations you selected?
(b) Does each organization fit completely in its respective category, with no links to either of the other two areas?
(c) If not, what are the links?
(d) Are there links between your organization and other industries, e.g. retailing or the media, for example.

You should conclude by evaluating your original definitions in the light of the findings from your study of these three organizations.

Conclusions to Part 1

The first three chapters have introduced the key concepts which underpine the philosophy of the book as a whole. These include:

- defining marketing;
- defining Europe;
- defining tourism, leisure and hospitality.

The European dimension

This part of the book looks at the European dimension to the subject of tourism, leisure and hospitality marketing, given that it is this European perspective which is, perhaps, the unique selling proposition – or USP – of this book.

Four chapters provide the European context for the rest of the book. They address the following topics:

- **Chapter 4: European consumers or consumers in Europe?** This chapter looks at the individual consumer and critically considers the concept of the 'European Consumer' in tourism, leisure and hospitality.
- **Chapter 5: The European market.** This chapter looks at tourism, leisure and hospitality markets within Europe. Again, it will try to identify national differences and pan-European similarities in the nature of markets in tourism, leisure and hospitality.
- **Chapter 6: The European tourism, leisure and hospitality industries.** This chapter looks at the supply side on a European scale. It looks at the types of organizations found in these three sectors and trends in the structure of the industry together with the rise of transnational corporations.
- **Chapter 7: The European business environment.** This chapter looks at both the macro- and the micro-environment of tourism, leisure and hospitality organizations. This means looking at political, economic, social and technological factors in relation to the macro-environment, and the organization itself, its suppliers, marketing intermediaries and existing customers together with its competitors in terms of the micro-environment. We will then attempt to judge to what extent the business environment across Europe is homogeneous or heterogeneous.

European consumers or consumers in Europe? | 4

Key concepts

The main concepts covered in this chapter are:

- trends in consumer behaviour, tourist typologies and purchase decision-making;
- factors facilitating the potential growth of the 'European consumer' including 'global efficiency' and 'consumer convergence';
- market segmentation and the European consumer;
- European models of consumer behaviour and lifestyle types.

INTRODUCTION

This chapter has three main sections, namely:

- a brief discussion of key consumer behaviour concepts in tourism, leisure and hospitality;
- an evaluation of the idea of the 'European consumer' in tourism, leisure and hospitality;
- an outline of some major current issues in consumer behaviour.

CONSUMER BEHAVIOUR IN TOURISM, LEISURE AND HOSPITALITY

In this section, we will briefly discuss three consumer behaviour concepts that are highly relevant to marketing in tourism, leisure and hospitality. These are as follows:

- motivators and determinants;
- typologies of tourists and tourist behaviour;
- the purchase decision-making process.

Given the limitations of space, we will mainly focus on tourism, although many of the points are also true of leisure and hospitality. We will also make some comment about leisure and hospitality where appropriate.

Motivators and determinants

Marketers must understand this crucial concept which underpins all consumer behaviour in tourism, leisure and hospitality.

Motivators are those factors that make people want to take holidays or undertake particular leisure activities. Determinants are of two types. There are those factors which determine whether or not a consumer will be able to take a holiday or not, for example. Then there are those factors that determine, if a consumer can take a holiday, which kind of trip they will be able to take. In other words, where they will go, when they will travel and what they will do when they are in their holiday destination.

Motivators can be divided into a number of categories, as follows:

- **physical** – relaxation, climate, health, sporting activity, sex;
- **emotional** – nostalgia, aesthetics, romance, escapism, fantasy;
- **cultural** – gastronomy, sightseeing, learning about an area's history;
- **status** – exclusivity, fashionability;
- **personal** – visiting friends and relations;
- **personal development** – learning a language or new skill.

When designing promotional campaigns, marketers need to reflect these different motivators in the promotional messages they send out about their products.

It is also important to recognize that different consumers can have different motivators for purchasing the same product. For instance, a weekend break to Paris could be a second honeymoon for some customers, a sightseeing trip for others and a chance for others to practise their French.

This example also shows that an individual consumer can be motivated by more than one factor at a time. While our honeymoon couple enjoy their romantic experience, they may also choose Paris because of its ability to satisfy their desire for good food, culture and improving their French.

The **determinants** which dictate whether or not consumers will be able to take any trip at all include: disposable income, work and family commitments, state of heath and the availability, or otherwise, of leisure time.

The factors which determine the type of holiday a consumer will be able to take include these same determinants, as well as the following:

- the availability of appropriate products;
- the information which is accessible to the consumer through brochures, guide books and the media;
- one's past experiences and those of the customer's family and relatives;
- consumer's perceptions of different types of holiday and particular destinations;

- preferences for different modes of transport;
- prices of different types of holidays, and the prices charged;
- at different times of the year, together with in-resort prices;
- fluctuations in currency rates;
- the views of other members of the group with whom the consumer will be travelling;
- the existence of special events that might lead a consumer to visit a place they might not otherwise visit because the event is located there.

Marketers need to recognize and take action on those determinants which they can influence.

Typologies of tourists and tourist behaviour and the marketing applications of these typologies

For many years, academics have sought to produce typologies of tourists and tourist behaviour. In many cases, however, these typologies have been based on little or no empirical data. It would, therefore, be rather unwise if marketers were to follow these typologies too closely when planning their marketing activities. Nevertheless, they do represent a good basis for practitioners to start to think about their consumers, particularly in relation to the ways which might help them segment their markets.

These typologies have a number of potential marketing applications in that they can:

- suggest the types of new products that might appeal to particular sorts of tourists;
- hint at which groups of tourists may be willing to pay a higher price in return for benefits like exclusivity and service, for example;
- indicate particular distribution channels that might be most effective for a certain type of tourist;
- help marketers decide which messages to target at specific types of tourist.

We must recognize that, while most typologies are based on commentators placing tourists into certain categories, it is equally important to understand the perceptions which tourists have of themselves. Marketing is as much about playing to perceptions which tourists hold about themselves as it is about the reality of their purchasing decisions.

This is well illustrated in tourism through the well-known debate about whether one is a **tourist** or a **traveller**. There is the idea that a tourist is someone who buys a package from a tour operator while the traveller is the person who makes their own independent arrangements for their vacation. The idea has grown up that somehow the latter type of behaviour is somehow superior or better than the former. Therefore, many people who buy tourist packages want to still see themselves as travellers. Therefore, marketers, particularly in small-scale tour operations, sell the image that their product is 'loose', is not a 'package' and is for the independently-minded traveller. In other words, they sell to their customer's desired perception of their own behaviour, not the reality of what they are actually buying.

We will now examine some of the tourist typologies that have been put forward to see what value they may have for tourism marketers.

Cohen (1979)

The sociologist, Cohen, split tourists into four types, as follows:

- **The organized mass tourist** is the tourist who buys a package holiday to a popular destination, largely goes around with a group of fellow tourists and may spend most of their time in their hotel or in its immediate environs.
- **The individual mass tourists** are the people who buy a looser package that allows them more freedom, such as a fly-drive holiday. They tend to stick to the beaten track but may occasionally do something more adventurous.
- **The explorer** makes his or her own travel arrangements and deliberately sets out to avoid contact with other tourists, while trying to meet local people. Nevertheless, they do want to have a certain level of comfort and security.
- **The drifter** tries to become part of a local community, albeit temporarily. This tourist has no planned itinerary and tries to totally distance themselves from tourism in every form.

Cohen categorizes the first type as institutionalized travellers while the latter two he terms non-institutionalized travellers.

Clearly, for tour operators it is the institutionalized travellers who represent their target market. On the other hand, destinations wishing to develop sustainable tourism would possibly prefer to target the non-institutionalized travellers.

Cohen (1979) also categorized tourists on the basis of the type of experience they were seeking, in other words:

- the **recreational** tourist where the emphasis is on physical recreation rather than culture or social content;
- the **diversionary** tourist who seeks a way of forgetting their everyday life;
- the **experiential** tourist who seeks authentic experiences;
- the **experimental** tourist who seeks close contact with the local culture;
- the **existential** tourists who seek to totally immerse themselves in foreign cultures and lifestyles.

Again, different messages about the product would need to be given to these different types of tourist.

Smith (1995)

Smith identified seven types of tourists, as follows:

- **Explorers** are a small group who almost travel as anthropologists, but are constrained by the fact that there are fewer and fewer new places to explore.
- **Elite** tourists are regular experienced travellers, travelling on expensive, perhaps tailor-made tours.
- **Off-beat** tourists aim to get away from other tourists.
- **Unusual** tourists make side trips from organized tours to experience some local culture.
- **Incipient mass tourists** are those who travel to well established resorts where tourism is not yet totally dominant. Nevertheless, they tend to seek out the familiar rather than looking for local culture.
- **Mass tourists** are part of a mass flow which expects the same standard of amenities as they receive at home.
- **Charter tourists** have little or no interest in the destination providing that they enjoy their holiday, which should feature food and standards of accommodation which are familiar to them.

Tourism organizations seeking to sell to these different types of tourists will need to present different messages to each group. For the 'off-beat' tourist they would promote the fact that the destination is quiet while the 'unusual' tourist would need to be told all about the optional excursion programmes on offer.

'Charter' and 'mass' tourists, on the other hand, would need to be reassured about the types and standard of food and accommodation in the resort.

Plog (1977)

Plog linked personality traits to tourist behaviour and contrasted the **psychocentrics** and the **allocentrics**. The former are less adventurous, inward-looking people who prefer popular resorts and prefer to be surrounded by other tourists. Allocentrics are more adventurous and outward-looking and like to take risks. They prefer unusual, exotic destinations and prefer to be more individual travellers. It is very difficult for tourism organizations to operationalize such a typology, as it would require sophisticated data on tourist personalities which is difficult to collect.

The post-tourist

Feifer (1985) and Urry (1990) have identified the development of the **post-tourist**, a product of the postmodern age. This tourist lives in an age of mass communication and information technology that allows the post-tourist to make informed choices about their holidays. This tourist recognizes that there is no such thing as an authentic tourist product and accepts pseudo-events for what they are. To them, tourism is a game and the post-tourist feels free to move between different categories. Today they may choose to be an independent traveller trekking in South America while next year they may choose a mass package holiday in Benidorm. It can be argued that this tourist renders traditional tourist typologies meaningless. This group also poses a great challenge for the tourism industry, with its sophisticated understanding of tourism packages and its unwillingness to fit into a neat type or segment.

The 'good' tourist

This highly moralistic and judgmental approach to classifying tourists has arisen in recent years, partly through the work of Wood and House (1991). The tourist is exhorted to behave in a way which is sustainable and responsible. They are also encouraged to feel good about behaving in this way. It is argued that most tourists can aspire to join this group if they modify their behaviour in particular ways. For tourism organizations this group may represent a potentially lucrative niche market which must be sold products it can feel good about buying.

Typologies and segmentation

Even from this brief list of some of the most well known typologies, it is clear that there are strong links between these typologies and the methods of segmenting markets. This point can be illustrated through several brief examples, as follows:

- Assumptions are often made that there are links between demographic segmentation and typologies, in that it is often believed that it is more likely that Cohen and Smith's 'off-beat' tourists will be younger, well educated people while Smith's 'elite' tourists will usually be older, more affluent people. Likewise, it is assumed that those with families will be less adventurous in their holiday behaviour than those without families.
- Several of the typologies, most notably that of Plog, are based firmly on the principles of psychographic segmentation in that they focus on the personality of the tourist.
- Concepts such as the 'post-tourist' are closely linked to another element of psychographic segmentation, namely lifestyles. For the post-tourist, tourism is just another aspect of their postmodern lifestyle.

Factors which limit the use of tourist typologies

There are a number of factors which restrict the potential use of tourist typologies in tourism marketing. These include:

- Making use of these typologies would require sophisticated research data on consumers and their attitudes, which is currently lacking in tourism. It is expensive to collect such data and it is problematic to undertake as tourists find it difficult to tell researchers how they behave and why they behave in that way. Alternatively, if one relies on observation as a basis for developing typologies, there is a danger of bias and prejudice on the part of the observers affecting the results.

- Those 'broad-brush' typologies are too simplistic and stereotypical to encompass the many different types of tourist behaviour that we observe in the real world.
- Most of the typologies do not allow for the fact that individual consumers can move between types in response to the input of different determinants in their behaviour. These determinants might include changes in levels of disposable income or amount of free time, new family circumstances, illness, and the need to compromise with the views of the other members of the group with which they will be taking a holiday.
- The majority of typologies are at least five years old and therefore cannot reflect changes in consumer behaviour which have taken place in recent years. Therefore many, for example, pre-date the introduction of newer types of products, such as long-haul holidays to exotic destinations designed for mass-market tourists.

Another weakness of these models for European tourism organizations is that they tend to be either based on American experience or are 'international' in that it is assumed that there are no national or cultural differences. Yet we know that there are significant national differences in patterns of tourist behaviour.

The purchase decision-making process

Clearly, if we are to optimize the effectiveness of our marketing activities, we need to understand how consumers make their decision to purchase tourism, leisure and hospitality products. Then we know where and when we need to intervene in this process to obtain the result we want. The problem is that while many models have been advanced, relatively little empirical research has been conducted in order to test these models against actual behaviour. Nevertheless, it is still worth looking at several of these models.

Gilbert (1991) has given us a model for the framework within which consumer decisions are made. This is illustrated in Figure 4.1. Meanwhile, Wahab, Crampton and Rothfield (1976) put forward a linear model of the decision-making process, as shown in Figure 4.2.

Schmoll (1977) developed a model which hypothesized that the decision was the outcome of a process with four elements, as follows:

- travel stimuli, including guide books, reports from other travellers and advertising and promotions;
- personal and social determinants of travel behaviour including motivations, desires and expectations;

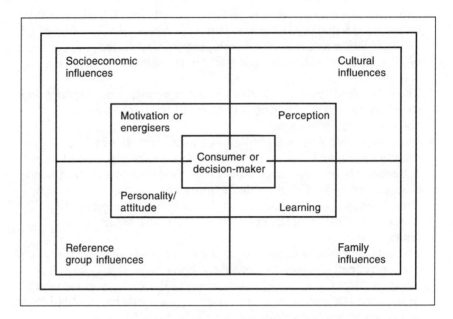

Figure 4.1 Consumer decision-making framework. Source: Gilbert (1991).

Initial framework → Conceptual alternatives → Fact gathering → Definition of assumptions → Design of stimulus → Forecast of consequences → Cost benefits of alternatives → Decision → Outcome

Figure 4.2 The Wahab, Crampton and Rothfield model of consumer behaviour. Source: Wahab, Crampton and Rothfield (1976).

- external variables including destination image, confidence in travel trade intermediaries and constraints such as cost and time;
- characteristics and feelings of the service destination such as the perceived link between cost and value, and the range of attractions and amenities offered.

Meanwhile, in 1982 Mathieson and Wall developed a linear five-stage model of the decision process that can be seen in Figure 4.3.

From a marketing prediction point of view, all of these models have two fundamental flaws, namely:

- they are stereotypical and generalized whereas it is clear that the process actually varies significantly between different groups of consumers;

Felt need/ Travel desire	→ Information collection and evaluation image	→ Travel decision (choice between alternatives)	→ Travel preparation and travel experiences	→ Travel satisfaction outcome and evaluation

Figure 4.3 Travel-buying behaviour. Source: Mathieson and Wall (1982).

- they do not have a time dimension so they do not tell the practitioner when they will need to intervene in the process in order to influence the final decision.

Given the European emphasis of this book, it is interesting to note that much of the literature in these fields of study is based on research carried out in the USA, Canada and Australasia, for example, rather than Europe. This should be borne in mind when one is evaluating the potential applications of the ideas contained in the literature to tourism, leisure and hospitality marketing in Europe.

Readers with a particular interest in consumer behaviour in the fields with which this book is concerned should consult the growing number of texts that deal with various aspects of the subject. These include the works of Plog (1977), Ross (1994), Sharpley (1994), Ryan (1995) and Urry (1990 and 1995).

THE EUROPEAN CONSUMER

The removal of trade barriers throughout Europe on 1 January 1993 opened up the possibility of operating a pan-European marketing strategy, at least as far as the member states of the European Union were concerned. This would mean that organizations could target on a pan-European basis rather than at a national level. The issue of whether pan-European consumers existed became a major issue of debate in the academic literature.

It was argued by Vandermerwe and L'Huillier (1989), for example, that large companies from America, Japan and Europe could start to target the unified market and use their huge marketing budgets to capitalize on the opportunities that existed. It was also argued that Europe would emerge as the most important market in the world, and that it would be more stable and lucrative than the United States and Japan.

The question now arises as to whether European customers do exist and whether these customers can be targeted by leisure, hospitality and tourism organizations. The alternative view is that there are consumers in Europe who show very different national and even regional buying behaviour. The second scenario would mean that organizations would have to target many groups of consumers across Europe with individually tailored products and services.

The emergence of the European consumer

The emergence of the European consumer, if in fact such a consumer does exist, can be explored from the supply side and the demand side. Two factors that were suggested by Halliburton and Hünerberg (1993) were the supply side factor that they termed **global efficiency** and the demand side factor they termed **customer convergence**.

Global efficiency

Global efficiency suggests that organizations will try to exploit common characteristics to gain efficiencies in production and marketing to produce products and services that cross national boundaries. Put in simple terms, it is cheaper for an organization to produce the same product that is sold in many different countries than it is to individually tailor a product to individual national characteristics. This is particularly relevant for large multinational organizations.

There have been conflicting ideas expressed by academics on the idea of globalization of products and services. The best example of a difference in opinion was shown by Theodore Levitt (1983) and Philip Kotler (1984).

Levitt argued that competition between companies would drive them to globalize products and services. Kotler on the other hand argued that globalization of products and services was restricted to a few special cases of products that could be rapidly rolled out into the market, or which were based on high technological development. He quoted the examples of Coca Cola and McDonald's as being very specialist cases, which could not be readily repeated. Most markets, he believed, would remain national. Companies would have to change products and services to meet national customer requirements.

Since 1984, there have been a number of articles that have supported the globalization approach (see Ohmae (1982) and Guido (1991)).

Similarly, there have been a number of articles that have argued against the principles of globalization (see Douglas and Wind (1987) and Kashani (1989)).

Homma (1991) has argued that there is a continued relevance of cultural diversity and that markets are moving from mass products to products designed to meet highly differentiated consumer needs in a variety of cultural settings. He argues that it is easy to generalize about European commonalities conceptually and intellectually, but the activity to date has proved to be less than useful at an operational level.

There are companies in the leisure, tourism and hospitality industries which have been actively trying to gain global or European efficiency by global or European marketing effort. McDonald's, for example, has been trying to roll out the same service and product concept, not just in Europe, but around the world. Disneyland Paris has been trying to globalize the concept of the theme park based on the Disney parent company, and target the European and international tourist. Experience to date seems to suggest that it is the large multinational corporations which can benefit from global efficiency and launch European or global products.

Customer convergence

The demand side factor which has been identified is customer convergence. This explores the idea that consumers from different countries are becoming increasingly similar in their habits and purchasing patterns. If consumers are converging in their habits and buying patterns, a European or global customer could exist.

The first question that should be addressed when questioning the emergence or not of a European consumer is the degree of customer convergence that is happening across the European Union. Customer buying behaviour is influenced by a series of factors including demographic characteristics, economic characteristics, psychographic characteristics and attitude and social position. It is also possible to compare and contrast spending patterns of individuals on specific products and services in different countries of the European Union.

Demographic data indicates that there are some differences in the age profiles of individual countries in the European Union. This is shown in Table 4.1.

In the countries that have highly developed economies, it can be seen that there are some striking similarities in the age profiles. Population forecasts up to the year 2020 also show that most of the countries of the European Union will have populations that will remain fairly static (Figure 4.4).

One consequence of this static population growth is that there is a general trend for the population in most of the countries of the Eco-

Table 4.1 European demographics – age distribution 1993

Country	% less than 20 years	% 20–39 years	% 40–59 years	% 60 + years
Belgium	24.3	31.3	24.2	21.1
Denmark	23.7	30.9	26.2	20.0
France	26.7	29.9	23.6	19.6
Germany, East *	25.5	32.2	30.2	18.3
Germany, West *	21.5	33.2	26.5	20.3
Greece	24.5	30.1	25.1	20.8
Ireland	34.9	27.7	21.0	15.2
Italy	22.6	31.4	25.2	21.3
Luxembourg	23.3	34.1	25.1	19.1
Netherlands	24.6	33.4	24.9	17.5
Portugal	27.4	28.7	23.7	19.5
Spain	25.8	30.6	22.3	21.2
United Kingdom	25.5	30.7	23.6	20.8

* Note that these figures were based on the borders of East and West Germany before the two countries were unified.

Source: Euromonitor (1995).

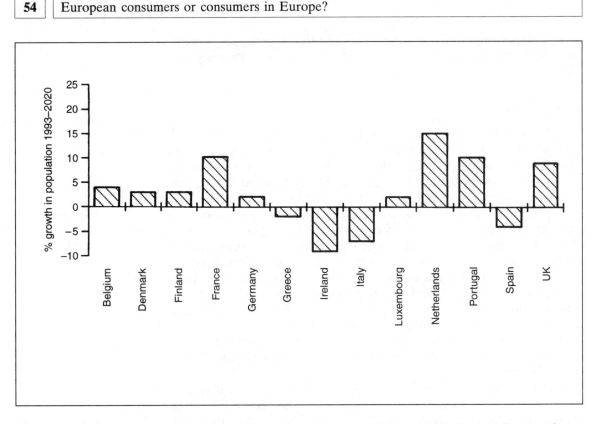

Figure 4.4 Europe's changing population: forecast growth rates to the year 2020. Source: Euromonitor (1995).

nomic Union to be ageing. Most countries will also see a decline in the numbers of individuals in the 15–44 age group band (Figure 4.5).

One of the major differences in demographic data between the countries of the European Union is the population density (Figure 4.6). Scandinavian countries such as Norway, Sweden and Finland have very low population densities in comparison to the densely populated countries of Germany, the Netherlands and the United Kingdom.

Data also reveals that there are similarities and differences between countries in the European Union and average household composition. The number of households containing single persons, for example, is much larger in some countries than others. Denmark and Germany, for example, have a very high percentage of one person households. The Southern European countries of Greece, Portugal and Spain have a much smaller percentage of one person households. This is explained in Table 4.2.

One of the strongest determinants of consumer buying behaviour is the level of wealth in the population. This is particularly important in the leisure, hospitality and tourism markets, because purchase of these products and services is often viewed as highly discretionary and non-essential.

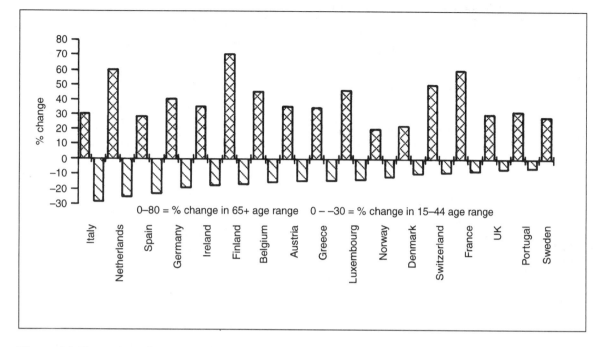

Figure 4.5 Europe's ageing population: forecast growth rates to the year 2020. Source: *European Marketing Pocket Book* (1995).

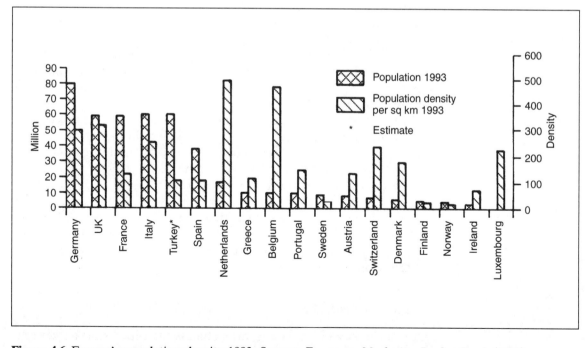

Figure 4.6 Europe's population density 1993. Source: *European Marketing Pocket Book* (1995)

Table 4.2 Europe's household characteristics (units: % of total households – latest year)

	Year	1 person	2 persons	3 persons	4 persons	5 + persons	Unspecified
Belgium	1981	23.2	29.7	20.0	15.7	11.4	
Denmark	1993	34.8	33.0	14.7	12.7	4.8	
France	1992	17.9	32.4	18.3	19.5	12.0	
Germany, East	1991	30.3	32.2	19.4	14.1	4.0	
Germany, West[1]	1991	33.6	30.8	17.1	13.4	5.0	
Greece[2]	1989	18.5	26.0	19.5	22.5	13.5	
Ireland	1986	18.2	20.3	14.8	16.1	30.6	
Italy	1990	20.7	24.5	23.5	23.5	7.8	
Luxembourg	1988	21.8	29.0	21.0	16.5	11.7	
Netherlands	1990	29.3	28.9	15.6	18.5	6.0	1.7
Portugal	1988	15.0	23.0	27.0	20.0	15.0	
Spain	1986	12.0	24.0	27.0	18.5	18.5	
United Kingdom	1987	25.0	32.0	17.1	13.1	6.0	6.8

1. Unified Germany.
2. Estimate based on current trends.
Source: Euromonitor (1995).

Gross Domestic Product (GDP) can be viewed as a measure which can compare the wealth of national populations. It is interesting to look at European GDP statistics to compare and contrast different countries (Figure 4.7). This will enable the marketer to assess whether the Euro-consumer does exist in relation to relative wealth.

Figure 4.7 shows that there are big differences across the European Union in relation to GDP. The Scandinavian countries have high GDP per capita, whereas the Southern European countries have relatively low GDP per capita.

The differences between regions of the European Union are also apparent. The major conurbations of Northern Europe are amongst the richest regions while many of the Southern European conurbations are the poorest.

From the data it can be seen that certain countries of Europe have similar patterns beginning to emerge. It should, in theory, be possible to identify groups of customers from this series of countries who share similar characteristics. The Euro-consumer could exist.

The data seems to suggest that countries in Europe are becoming more alike in their profile. The charts which have been studied in this chapter have also shown that there are also distinct differences between different European countries. This is particularly marked when comparisons are drawn between northern and southern European regions.

Market segmentation

One of the key techniques in marketing is the process of market segmentation, which has been used by practitioners to effectively target

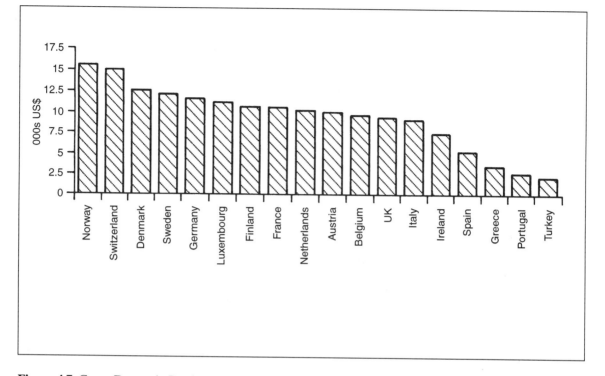

Figure 4.7 Gross Domestic Product per capita, 1993. Source: *European Marketing Pocket Book* (1995).

selected groups of the population with specially designed products and services.

Market segmentation is defined by Dibb, Simkin, Pride and Ferrell (1994) as:

> The process of dividing a total market into groups of people with relatively similar product needs, for the purpose of designing a marketing mix (or mixes) that precisely match the needs of individuals in a selected segment (or segments).

Successful use of market segmentation techniques allow the marketer to identify target groups of customers who have similar needs, and then design the marketing mix to meet their collective needs. A variety of techniques are used for market segmentation. It is not intended to give a full review of these techniques in this book, but to give a short summary of the various approaches used in tourism, leisure and hospitality marketing. For those readers who require a further discussion of the market segmentation process, you should refer to *Marketing Concepts and Strategies* by Dibb, Simkin, Pride and Ferrell (1994) or *Marketing in Travel and Tourism* by V.T.C. Middleton (1994).

There are five main techniques which are used for market segmentation: demographic, socioeconomic, geographical, psychographic and behaviouristic. These are explained below.

Table 4.3 Wells and Gubar lifecycle stages

Bachelor stage (young single people not living with parents)
Newly married couples without children
Full nest I (youngest child under 6)
Full nest II (youngest child 6 or over)
Full nest III (older married couple with dependent children)
Empty nest I (no children living at home, family head in work)
Empty nest II (family head retired)
Solitary survivor (in work)
Solitary survivor (retired)

Source: Worcester and Downham (1986).

Demographic segmentation

Demographic data is widely available and this has meant that marketers have used it extensively to segment markets. One example of a company which has used age as a way of segmenting a market is Saga Holidays. They identified a trend in the UK of an increasing market segment of the over 55s and decided to target them with holidays. The family lifecycle concept, which is an adaptation of demographic data, is also used widely in package holiday marketing. Table 4.3 shows the Wells and Gubar (1986) family lifecycle stages.

The family lifecycle has been used extensively in the marketing of tourism products. A package holiday company will market holidays to young single people, young families, empty nesters, and single retired people. Holiday brochures are deliberately targeted at these different lifecycle segments.

Socioeconomic segmentation

This group of variables, which could also be grouped with demographic or psychographic, includes income, occupation, education and class. Different techniques have been developed in different countries to enable the marketer to use socioeconomic variables as a basis for segmentation. The underlying principle here is that occupation, education and social class will determine which products the consumer buys.

The most commonly used socioeconomic method of segmentation in the UK is the JICNARS classification which assigns people into six categories (Table 4.4).

Geographical segmentation

The needs of a consumer are affected by their geographical location. Some products and services are targeted at national market segments and others can be targeted at international market segments.

Table 4.4 JICNARS classification

Social grade	Social status	Head of household's occupation	Approximate percentage of families
A	Upper middle class	Higher managerial, administrative or professional	3
B	Middle class	Intermediate managerial, administrative or professional	10
C1	Lower middle class	Supervisory or clerical and junior managerial, administrative or professional	24
C2	Skilled working class	Skilled manual workers	30
D	Working class	Semi and unskilled manual workers	25
E	Those at lowest levels of subsistence	State pensioners or widows (no other earner), casual or lowest grade workers	8

A – Upper middle class: The head of the household is a successful business or professional person, senior civil servant, or has considerabe private means. A young person in some of these occupations who has not fully established himself/herself may still be found in Grade B, though he/she should eventually reach grade A. In country or suburban areas, A-grade householders usually live in large detached houses or in expensive flats. In towns, they may live in expensive flats or town houses in the better parts of town.

B – Middle class: In general, the heads of B-grade households will be quite senior people but not at the very top of their profession or business. They are quite well off, but their style of life is generally respectable rather than rich or luxurious. . .non-earners will be living on private pensions or on fairly modest private means.

C1 – Lower middle class: In general it is made up of the families of small tradespeople and non-manual workers who carry out less important administrative, supervisory and clerical jobs, i.e. what are sometimes called 'white-collar' workers.

C2 – Skilled working class: Consists in the main of skilled manual workers and their families: the serving of an apprenticeship may be a guide to membership of this class.

D – Semi-skilled and unskilled working class: Consists entirely of manual workers, generally semi-skilled or unskilled.

E – Those at lowest level of subsistence: Consists of old age pensioners, widows and their families, casual workers and those who, through sickness or unemployment, are dependent on social security schemes, or have very small private means.

Source: Chisnall (1985).

ACORN (A Classification of Residential Neighbourhoods) is a system of geographical segmentation which incorporates demographic and socioeconomic variables. It works on the principle that customers who live in different residential neighbourhoods have different profiles in respect of the other variables. It divides the housing stock into 17 groups and 54 neighbourhood types, all of which it is suggested have different requirements. Table 4.5 shows this consumer targeting classification.

ACORN data is used extensively by the major brewers in the UK to identify the ideal location to site particular types of hospitality outlet.

Table 4.5 The ACORN consumer targeting classification

Categories	% population	Groups
A Thriving	19.8	1 Wealthy Achievers, Suburban Areas 2 Affluent Greys, Rural Communities 3 Prosperous Pensioners, Retirement Areas
B Expanding	11.6	4 Affluent Executives, Family Areas 5 Well-off Workers, Family Areas
C Rising	7.5	6 Affluent Urbanites, Town and City Areas 7 Prosperous Professionals, Metropolitan Areas 8 Better-Off Executives, Inner City Areas
D Settling	24.1	9 Comfortable Middle Agers, Mature Home Owning Areas 10 Skilled Workers, Home Owning Areas
E Aspiring	13.7	11 New Home Owners, Mature Communities 12 White Collar Workers, Better-Off Multi-Ethnic Areas
F Striving	22.8	13 Older People, Less Prosperous Areas 14 Council Estate Residents, Better-Off Homes 15 Council Estate Residents, High Unemployment 16 Council Estate Residents, Greatest Hardship 17 People in Multi-Ethnic, Low-Income Areas
Unclassified	0.5	

Source: CACI Limited, 1993 (source: OPCS and GROCS). Crown copyright 1991.
ACORN is a registered service mark of CACI Limited.

Psychographic segmentation

This method of segmentation is based on the idea that the attitudes and opinions of individuals dictate their behaviour as consumers. It tries to group people on the basis of shared attitudes and opinions. Socioeconomic groups which have already been discussed could be classed as a method of psychographic segmentation. The most quoted type of psychographic segmentation refers to **lifestyle**. In lifestyle segmentation, individuals are grouped according to their lifestyle. Lifestyle results from a combination of many factors including education, income, occupation, social contacts and individual preferences. Some of the lifestyle types are particularly relevant for tourism, leisure and hospitality organizations. The 'environmentally aware' group will probably be looking to purchase sustainable tourism products, for example. The 'health conscious' group will probably be looking to purchase healthier foods in a hotel and make use of leisure facilities, for example.

The materialistic lifestyles of the 1980s are supposed to have been overtaken by a more caring lifestyle in the 1990s. If this is the case, these changing lifestyles will have a fundamental effect on purchasing behaviour.

Individuals can also be grouped according to their **personality**. An extrovert individual, for example, will probably be looking to purchase a holiday which involves extensive opportunities to meet people. The introvert on the other hand will probably be looking to purchase a holiday which involves less social contact.

Behaviouristic segmentation

The final method of segmentation is referred to as behaviouristic. This category contains a number of variations which are listed below:

- **Purchase occasions**. Is the product purchased on a regular basis or as a one-off purchase?
- **Benefits sought**. What are customers hoping to gain from the product? This could be anything from an 'educational experience' at a museum to a 'romantic interlude' at a restaurant.
- **Attitude to the product**. This is where people are grouped according to whether they are enthusiastic or indifferent to the product. It includes whether the group are loyal to the product and whether they will purchase or use it again without question, or whether they will consider competitive products.
- **User status**. This means that people are non-users, ex-users, potential users, regular users or first time users.

Multi-variable segmentation

In reality, no one method of segmentation is satisfactory when the complexities of the tourism, leisure and hospitality markets are considered. It is only when more than one method are used together in an appropriate way that an accurate view of the customer group and the market can be compiled.

Organizations therefore often use more than one characteristic to segment markets. This is referred to as **multi-variable segmentation**. The use of additional variables can often lead to better positioning and targeting of the marketing mix.

Segmentation and the European consumer

To return to the question of whether there is such a thing as a European consumer, organizations must query whether it is possible to find market segments across national boundaries in Europe which have similar characteristics.

Work has been carried out by companies and academics to try and devise systems which will allow clusters of Euro-consumers to be targeted, based on customer convergence. These clusters of consumers will not necessarily be living in the same country, but will show remarkably similar demographic and economic characteristics which will cut across cultural and national boundaries. Some of the work on trying to identify Euro-clusters has concentrated on geographical segmentation techniques and some of the work has been based on lifestyle segmentation techniques.

Geographical segmentation techniques

Early work suggested that grouping of consumers could be done by applying the **golden circle** concept (D'Arcy et al., 1989). This suggested that if you considered Europe in terms of domestic wealth, then an area could be identified which included 50 million of the wealthiest people in Europe by drawing a circle with a 250 mile radius from Cologne.

This was expanded by Paitra in 1993 when he described the Euro-consumer as a manager of a large company, aged between 25 and 40, travelling a lot, working more than spending time on hobbies and often purchasing away from home. This person, he suggested, had similar behaviour in all the capitals of Western Europe, but represented only a tiny segment characterized by people who were hungry for services and technological products. The large multinational hotel groups and international airlines have tried to target this European manager with specially designed products and services.

Vandermerwe and L'Huillier (1989) have also suggested that Europe can be divided into six clusters based on cultural, geographic, demographic and economic variables.

Lifestyle segmentation

Research has also concentrated on the development of similar lifestyles trends in Europe.

A group of organizations involved in the Research Institute for Social Change (RISC) has been looking at the ways in which consumer values and attitudes have been changing across Europe. The major aspects of these changes are reported in Moorcroft (1987). The most important changes were also summarized by Gratton (1993) as being:

- a break with the traditions of economic security and status;
- a pursuit of individuality and rejection of stereotypes;
- greater informality and spontaneity;
- enjoyment of and belief in using all the senses for personal well-being and fulfilment;

- sensitivity and openness to contact with others;
- the integration of technology;
- adaptation to complexity and risk;
- disorientation and aimlessness.

These trends, according to Gratton, are leading to an ever increasing internationalization of tastes amongst European consumers, a process which has also led to a convergence of consumers' values and attitudes across the European Union.

Work by Homma (1991) indicated that despite there being cultural diversity, there were certain trends such as environmental issues which were becoming increasingly important.

Frontiers was a study carried out by the Henley Centre in cooperation with Research International to look at the strength of customer convergence in Europe. They found that certain characteristics were common across Europe. Young people in Europe, for example, were keen to obtain new brands but tired of them quickly.

ESOMAR (the European Society for Opinion and Marketing Research) have in recent years been trying to harmonize social grade classifications for a number of European countries. This is shown in Figure 4.8.

The EU countries covered are: Belgium, Denmark, France, Germany, Greece, Ireland, Italy, Luxembourg, the Netherlands, Portugal, Spain and the U.K. Research has been carried out by INRA (International Research Associates) for the European Commission.

Due to the diversity of wealth, lifestyle and educational levels in the different countries covered, it is often difficult to categorize individual populations using an 'average' scale or one that is already in use in another country.

Instead, the ESOMAR social grades (A, B, C, D, E1, E2, E3) are based on the terminal education age (TEA) and occupation of the main income earner (MIE). Also contributing to the social grade classification is the level of household ownership of 10 different durables.

Although the base of the classification remains constant, application of the 'rules' varies. In Denmark, for example, the average TEA was measured at 22 years while in Portugal it was just over 14 years. Since the distribution of TEA varies, the five age bands that represent TEA in the various countries are different. Similar variations apply to the range of occupations in the different countries.

The extremes of the scale are consistent in all countries. Thus grade A in any country will always refer to those in senior managerial or professional posts with a high TEA and a high level of wealth as indicated by their ownership of several items in the list of durables. Conversely, grade E3 refers to those in very low paid employment or who are unemployed with a low TEA and basic ownership of the durables. The definitions of the intermediate grades, however, vary.

As an example, grade E1 may be represented by skilled manual workers with a TEA or 17–18 in a more advanced country, but by unskilled manual workers with a TEA or 15–16 in a less developed country.

Figure 4.8 The ESOMAR social grade classification for Europe. Source: ESOMAR, quoted in the *European Marketing Pocketbook* (1995).

Because of the complexities described in Figure 4.8 it is not possible to provide a standard grid or to summarize the definitions for the different social grades in all of the countries.

Work carried out by the French company CCA in combination with the Europanel Network (an association of AGC-UK, GFK of Germany, Secodip of France and IHA of Switzerland) looked at the possibility of identification of the European customer. The measurement instrument covered five principal dimensions of human behaviour:

- objective personal criteria;
- behavioural attributes;
- attitudes;
- motivations and aspirations;
- sensitivities and emotions.

The work involved extensive sampling of individuals in 15 European countries. This research identified trends which were expressed on three axes.

The European lifestyles which emerged from the research were then regrouped into 'mentalities'. The were 16 'mentalities' were summarized by Mazanec and Zins (1994) and are shown below in Figure 4.9.

It was found in the research that the distribution of Euro-styles within the populations was different in different European countries. What is interesting about this research is that there is an underlying core of values and attitudes that transcend political and administrative boundaries. If the Euro-consumer is to be targeted by marketers, they must look to this type of segmentation.

The research carried out by Mazanec and Zins (1994) tried to relate tourist behaviour and the new European lifestyle typology. The Austrian National Guest Survey adopted the Eurostyles methodology in order to examine the lifestyle structure of travellers to Austria during the 1991–2 summer and winter season. The research found that the 16 original Euro-styles could not be considered to be ready-made segments for tourism marketing.

They suggested that the original lifestyle groups should be merged into groups of types which they termed **socio-targets**. This is shown in Figure 4.10.

What is very interesting about the research is that, once the grouping of styles had been found, it allowed segmentation to be developed on an international or European level. The possibility of defining segments across borders has thus demonstrated.

Sinus GmbH of Germany have also developed an international approach to consumer research, describing so-called social milieus in West Germany, France, the UK and Italy. The study made a sound milieu map for each country studied. By making a comparison of

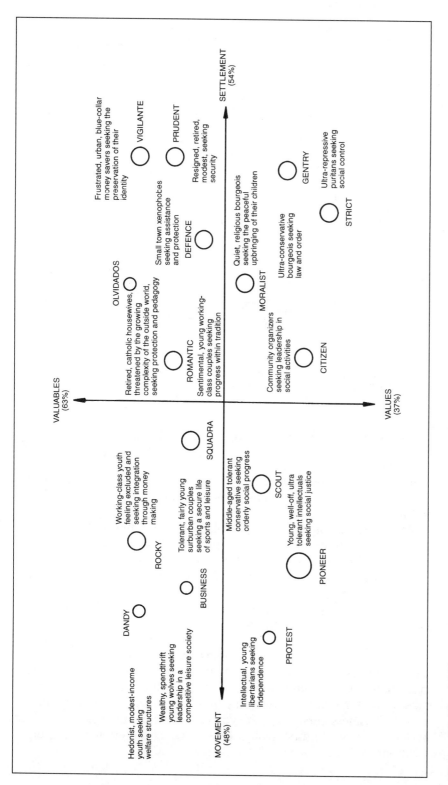

Figure 4.9 The 16 Euro-styles in Europe. Source: CCA/Europanel, quoted in Mazanec and Zins (1994).

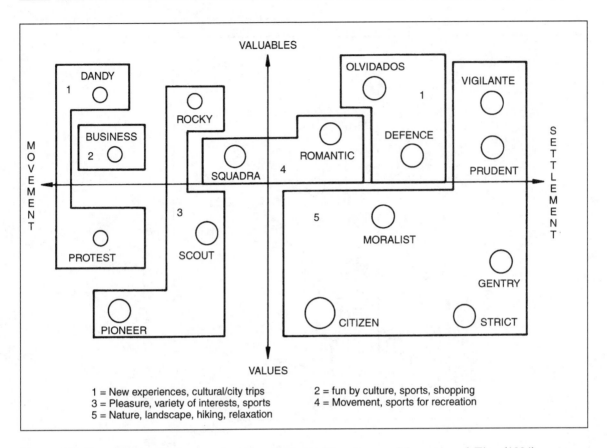

VALUABLES

DANDY
1

OLVIDADOS
1

VIGILANTE

ROCKY

BUSINESS
2

DEFENCE

ROMANTIC

SQUADRA
4

PRUDENT

M
O
V
E
M
E
N
T

S
E
T
T
L
E
M
E
N
T

3

5

MORALIST

PROTEST

SCOUT

GENTRY

PIONEER

CITIZEN

STRICT

VALUES

1 = New experiences, cultural/city trips
3 = Pleasure, variety of interests, sports
5 = Nature, landscape, hiking, relaxation

2 = fun by culture, sports, shopping
4 = Movement, sports for recreation

Figure 4.10 Target segments by travel motives and activities. Source: Mazanec and Zins (1994).

values, attitudes and beliefs in each social milieu across the four countries, a map of multinational target groups was drawn up. This is shown in Table 4.6.

The research showed that the upmarket segments, for example, shared a similar structure in the four countries . The trendsetter segment was also directly comparable in the four countries.

This sort of research seems to indicate that certain segments of the population can be selected and targeted by companies without reference to national characteristics. However, there is a need for more empirical research to be conducted in this area.

To conclude this section, it would appear that there is convergence of taste in Europe and clusters which can be drawn up with similar characteristics. At the same time, there is still a flourishing set of local customers. Large multinational companies will be amongst the first to take advantage of the new emerging consumers. The fast-moving wealthy business person and the young American influenced consumer perhaps will be the first groups to emerge as targets for these organizations.

Table 4.6 Multinational target groups: 35 social milieus in the four key European countries

UK	France	Italy	West Germany	Target group
• The upper class	• Les héritiers	• Neo-conservatori	• Konservatives-gehobenes Milieu	• Upper conservative mileus
• Traditional middle-class milieu	• Les conservateurs installés	• Piccola borghesia	• Kleinbürger-liches Milieu	• Traditional mainstream
• Traditional working-class milieu	• Les laborieux traditionnels	• Cultura operaia	• Traditionsloses Arbeitermilieu	• Traditional working class milieus
• Social climbers • Progressive working-class milieu	• Les nouveaux ambitieux	• Rampanti • Crisaldi	• Aufstiegs-orientiertes Milieu	• Modern mainstream
• Progressive middle-class milieu	• Les managers modernes	• Borghesia illuminata	• Technokratisch-liberales Milieu	• Trendsetter milieus
• Thatcher's children	• Les post-modernistes	• Edonisti	• Hedonistisches Milieu	• Avantgarde milieus
• Socially concerned	• Les néo-moralistes	• Critica sociale	• Alternatives Milieu	• Socio-critical milieus
• British poor	• Les oubliés • Les rebelles hédonistes	• Sottoproletariato urbano	• Traditionsloses Arbeitermilieu	• Underprivileged milieus

Note: The model takes into account all social milieus in those four countries except for the Italian *cultura rurale tradizionale* which has no comparable counterpart in the United Kingdom, France and West Germany.
Source: Sinus GmbH, Germany (1990).

There are certain common trends which can be targeted across national boundaries. Targeting of these market segments which cross national boundaries is vital for tourist authorities, multinational hotel chains and fast-food outlets alike.

MAJOR CURRENT ISSUES IN CONSUMER BEHAVIOUR IN TOURISM, LEISURE AND HOSPITALITY

There are a number of current issues in consumer behaviour which are of interest to tourism, leisure and hospitality organizations. We will now discuss some of these in the sections below.

Attitudes to the 'package holiday'

Many commentators are now claiming that consumers are beginning to reject the traditional package holiday in favour of more independent travel. If true, this represents a particular problem for tour operators in countries like the UK and Germany where the package holiday or FIT has come to dominate the outbound tourism market. However, it would be less of a threat to the industry in countries like France, where the package holiday has never become the dominant form of holiday-taking.

However, the idea that somehow the package holiday is in decline needs to be carefully considered. Millions of Europeans still buy packages every year.

What appears to be happening is not that consumers are rejecting package holidays, but rather that as they become more confident and experienced travellers, they are demanding new types of package. The tour operators are responding with more flexible packages to meet these demands, which are proving popular with consumers. These include fly-drive holidays and 'go-as-you-please' holidays that allow consumers to choose their own accommodation from a list provided by the tour operator.

The tour operation sector is also developing new types of packages to exploit new forms of consumer demand, including:

- special interest holidays, ranging from painting and wine appreciation to diving and golf;
- all-inclusive packages where everything is included in a single price, even drinks and entertainment;
- short duration holidays for those with limited spare time or those who want a short break in their routine. For example, a number of UK tour operators now offer day trips to a range of European cities;
- reasonably priced fly-cruises where people fly to the cruise embarkation port. This phenomenon has in recent years in the UK at least expanded the cruise market and encouraged many people to take their first ever cruise

Consumers who normally do not take package holidays seem happy to do so under certain circumstances, such as the following:

- where using a package allows them to travel to a destination they wish to visit much cheaper than they would be able to visit it on their own;
- to let them enjoy a destination that is difficult to visit as an independent traveller;
- if the consumer has children and packages offer big discounts for children and/or a programme of activities for children.

Travellers or tourists?

In many countries in Europe and beyond these two terms, which were once interchangeable, now have very different connotations. According to Sharpley (1994):

The former (traveller), in a touristic sense, is usually applied to someone who is travelling/touring for an extended period of time, probably back-packing on a limited budget. It denotes a spirit of freedom, adventure and individuality. The word tourist, on the other hand, is frequently used in a rather derogatory sense to describe those who participate in mass produced package tourism'.

Because of the negative connotations which are increasingly associated with being seen as a tourist, many people, when describing their holiday, stress those characteristics of it which appear to make them appear more like travellers. For example, they will emphasize that their holiday destination was 'unspoilt' or 'not commercialized' and they may also be at pains to tell people that during their holiday they had little or no contact with tourists of their own nationality.

Those responsible for tour operation marketing have recognized this phenomenon and are giving messages about their products which make them appear as if they are targeted at 'travellers' rather than tourists. They use phrases such as 'undiscovered' and 'off the beaten track'. Likewise they try to persuade potential customers that their packages are not packages at all but rather that they represent a tailor-made service for the independent-minded traveller. This is clearly linked to the developments in the concept of the package holiday which were discussed earlier in this chapter.

The 'green' consumer

In the late 1980s and early 1990s, 'green issues' became a major social and political concern in many European countries. This resulted in the growth of the so-called 'green consumer' whose behaviour as a consumer was influenced by their interest in a range of environmental issues.

This trend has also been felt to some extent in tourism, leisure and hospitality, albeit much more in some countries than others. In Germany, for example, consumers demand that hotels and destinations they visit take environmental issues seriously. Many of them are interested in whether hotels recycle material, for example, hence the fact that German tour operators such as TUI feel the need to produce environmental checklists and reports for the hotels they contract and the destinations they feature in their programmes. However, there appears not to be a similar level of concern amongst British or French tourists, for example.

If consumer concern is only relatively highly developed in a few European countries amongst leisure tourists, then it appears to be largely absent amongst business travellers. Very few such travellers seem concerned about the fuel used by aircraft, energy wastage in hotels, or the impact of golf courses developed on wildlife habitats.

It is not surprising therefore that in most European countries, outside Germany, the Netherlands and Scandinavia, most major organizations have taken little action beyond small, almost cosmetic gestures. Nevertheless, some organizations have sought to use these gestures to improve their image with consumers. Some have sponsored environmental awards while others have promised to donate an amount of money to an environmental cause for every booking they receive. This latter tactic is particularly clever, in marketing terms, because it makes customers feel good about buying a holiday that might otherwise be seen as environmentally irresponsible. In other words, a donation of £2 per holiday to a turtle conservation project can make consumers feel good about taking a trip to a resort where tourism is threatening the future of the same breed of turtles.

As we discuss later, in Chapter 30, perhaps in tourism, as in other spheres of consumer society, we need to stop talking about the 'green consumer' and talk instead of 'shades of green consumers'. In other words dark green consumers who will make sacrifices and pay more because of their benefits, and light green consumers who will not, but will only seek to buy greener products if they do not cost more.

Some tour operators are recognizing the dark green consumer as a separate segment and are attempting to target them with specific products which claim to be environmentally friendly holidays, or eco-holidays. These allow the tourists to feel they are enjoying themselves without harming the environment. Sales of such tourism products seem to be growing in popularity amongst European consumers.

Authenticity and tourism and leisure products

Authenticity is a major current debate in tourism and leisure and has been for a number of years, as can be seen in the writings of MacCannell and Urry, for example. The conventional wisdom has traditionally been that authentic is good and inauthentic is bad.

Yet, in recent years, it has been suggested that, according to Urry (1995):

> Some tourists might best be described as post-tourists, people who almost delight in inauthenticity. The post-tourist finds pleasure in the multitude of games that can be played and knows that there is no authentic tourist experience. They know that the apparently authentic fishing village could not exist without the income from tourism, or that the glossy brochure is a piece of popular culture.

Many tourism, leisure and hospitality organizations appear to be agreeing with this view as they develop a range of products which are explicitly inauthentic, which in turn appear to be very popular with consumers. These include virtual reality experiences, themed hotels and reconstructions of historical events.

Furthermore, in the visitor attraction sector, many consumers do not have the expertise to distinguish between the authentic and the inauthentic. For instance, most would not know if an authentic painting in a gallery were to be replaced by a modern copy. Likewise, some consumers appear to have difficulty distinguishing reality from fantasy, such as those people who treat soap opera characters as if they were real. In such a situation what is authenticity? However, there is a market segment for whom the search for authenticity is a major motivator. They want to visit the 'real' rural France, for example, and they will pay handsomely if they feel they are being given this opportunity. Such people represent an attractive target market for some organizations.

The desire for a total leisure experience

It appears that many of today's consumers are not content to simply visit a museum and look at artefacts for example. Instead they are looking for a total leisure experience. For a museum, this means they might expand it to provide the following facilities and services:

- a well stocked shop where visitors can purchase a souvenir of their visit;
- a range of catering facilities offering everything from a drink to a full meal;
- imaginative interpretation of the museum's contents including live interpretation using actors, computer simulations and 'walkman' tours.

This represents a challenge for many visitor attractions but it also offers them potential new lucrative sources of income.

The search for new experiences

Some consumers appear to be motivated by a need to enjoy new experiences. They may want to be seen to be trendy or perhaps they have simply become bored with the existing range of leisure and tourism products. The willingness of such consumers to pay a premium price for new experiences has led some unlikely organizations to offer some even more unlikely products to satisfy the demand. For example, in Russia, the military authorities sell tourists the chance to pilot a jet fighter or experience weightlessness by utilising the training facilities of the Russian space programme.

The desire to learn

Many people today are seeking to use their leisure time to learn something new, which is giving opportunities for organizations to develop new products. There are, thus, literally tens of thousands of people across Europe who are using their leisure time and their holidays to learn to:

- paint;
- cook;

- speak foreign languages;
- fly;
- scuba dive;

and a hundred and one other skills.

The quest for discounts

The pan-European recession of the early 1990s led organizations to use discounts to attract and retain customers. However, even as Europe begins to recover from this recession, many commentators are saying that consumers will still look for discounts, even if the European economies become buoyant. The argument goes that for consumers, discounts and the search for a bargain have now become part of their psyche. If true, this has potentially serious implications for tourism, leisure and hospitality organizations which would prefer not to discount because of the effect discounting can have on profit margins and product quality. This is particularly true in the business tourism field when companies have used discounts to reduce their travel bills. In a competitive world, where costs must be kept as low as possible, they are unlikely to be willing to go back to paying pre-recession prices.

It must be said that most of the trends in consumer behaviour which we have discussed in this section are based more on observation than on detailed empirical research, due to the lack of such research data in tourism, leisure and hospitality. For those who are interested, there is a discussion of the problems involved in researching consumer behaviour in tourism, leisure and hospitality in Chapter 32.

Nevertheless, what is clear is that some of the trends noted in this section are linked. There is no doubt that there is a relationship between attraction towards package holidays, the desire to be seen as a traveller and green issues. Likewise, the concepts of postmodernism and the post-tourist are relevant to both authenticity and the search for new leisure experiences.

CONCLUSIONS

In this lengthy chapter, we have looked at some of the key concepts in consumer behaviour in tourism, leisure and hospitality which are highly relevant from a marketing point of view. We have also seen that, in some ways, consumer behaviour is converging across Europe and becoming increasingly similar, which is laying the foundation for the development of pan-European markets in the future. At the same time, there are still some distinct national differences in consumer behaviour in tourism, leisure and hospitality. Finally, we have identified some current trends and issues in consumer behaviour that have important implications for tourism, leisure and hospitality marketing.

DISCUSSION POINTS AND ESSAY QUESTIONS

1. Examine the extent to which 'customer convergence' is occurring in Europe.
2. Discuss the application of the four classic methods of market segmentation to the market for any of the following types of product:
   (a) package holidays or FITs;
   (b) business class services of scheduled airlines;
   (c) fast food;
   (d) a golf course owned by a golf club;
   (e) conference facilities within a hotel.
3. Critically evaluate the various European lifestyle models – CCA/Europanel and SINUS GmbH for example – in terms of their accuracy and application in European tourism, leisure and hospitality marketing.
4. Evaluate the potential applications of the main typologies of tourists and tourist behaviour to the marketing of tourism products.
5. Discuss the main factors which might motivate tourists to take the following types of holiday:
   (a) a holiday in the Orlando region of Florida;
   (b) a skiing holiday in a fashionable Alpine resort;
   (c) a beach holiday in a lively Mediterranean resort.

Select a major tourism, leisure and hospitality organization which currently **EXERCISE** primarily offers its products to the residents of its own country.

Then imagine that you have been engaged as a consultant by the organization to advise it on how it might commence selling its products to residents of several other European countries. You should, therefore, undertake the following activities:

- identify the current market segments to which the product is currently targeted;
- advise the organization on whether or not their existing approach to segmentation might be appropriate for the new countries in which they may wish to begin operating;
- if it would not be appropriate, you should advise the organization on which approaches to segmentation may be more relevant for those countries.

Your results should be presented through a written report and a verbal presentation.

5 The European market

Key concepts

The main concepts covered in this chapter are:

- the identification of national differences and pan-European similarities in the European tourism, leisure and hospitality markets;
- domestic and international markets;
- markets for different tourism, leisure and hospitality products including tourist destinations, hotels and fast food.

The previous chapter looked at the concept of the 'European consumer' and suggested that there were some emerging groups which were present across Europe. These groups can be targeted with similar products and services.

This section will expand this idea further, by looking at the 'European market'. It will try to identify national differences and pan-European similarities in the nature of the markets in tourism, leisure and hospitality.

INTRODUCTION

The national markets of Europe are affected by three types of tourism. These are the 'inbound' market, the 'outbound' market and 'domestic' tourism. The tourism market in Europe does not involve a single 'industry' but a number of contributory organizations. These include:

- travel agents and tour operators;
- transport organizations including airlines, shipping companies and railways;
- commercial accommodation providers (that is, accommodation excluding staying with friends and relatives and second homes);
- catering establishments;
- visitor attractions;
- theme parks.

The tourism market of Europe is affected by the relative economic affluence of the populations in the individual countries.

Economic overview

The previous chapter showed that there are great differences in the Gross Domestic Product (GDP) per capita of selected countries in Europe. This ranges from the high GDPs of the developed countries – for example, Switzerland and Germany – to the low GDPs of the less developed countries of Spain, Greece and Portugal. If we include the Eastern European countries in the analysis, it can be seen that these countries have very low levels of GDP per capita (Figure 5.1).

The economies of Europe are generally characterized by relative affluence and ageing populations. The previous chapter showed, however, that this is an over-simplification of a much more complex picture. There is a great diversity between countries and even regions of Europe, coupled with local legal frameworks and cultural diversity. On the other hand, there is no doubt that the hospitality and tourism industries are global in nature.

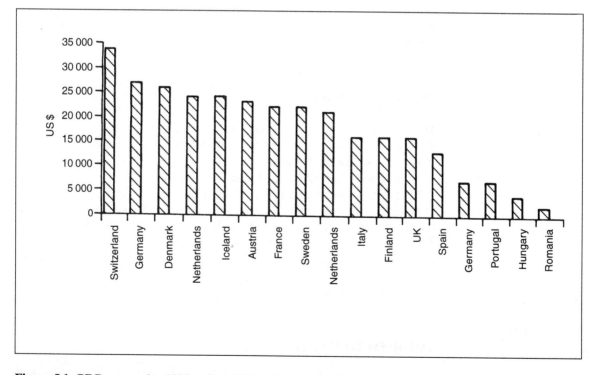

Figure 5.1 GDP per capita 1993: selected European countries.
Source: Euromonitor (1995).

It could be suggested that countries which have a higher level of wealth indicated by a high per capita GDP would show a pattern of high spending on leisure and tourism products, since these rely heavily on levels of disposable income. Data shows, however, that there is not a direct correlation between the two. There are motives for purchasing leisure products which are not necessarily linked to personal wealth.

Consumer spending

Figure 5.2 shows the spending by individuals in different countries of Europe on hotels and restaurants, expressed in dollars per capita. It can be seen that the Southern European countries, particularly Spain and Italy, spend larger amounts on hotels and restaurants than other more affluent countries such as Denmark and the Netherlands.

Spending on hotels and restaurants is therefore not totally dependant on the individual's wealth. This could be explained by levels of disposable income or differences in culture which show different purchasing patterns. The populations which are living in countries with high per capita GDPs could also be spending money on other areas of the leisure, tourism and hospitality industries.

It is clear from the data in Figure 5.2, however, that there are very different patterns of consumer spend for hotels and restaurants in different European countries.

Holiday preferences

Data which has been collected on consumer holiday preferences in European countries also indicates that there are massive differences between individuals from these countries. Table 5.1 shows the holiday preferences of individual European countries.

This data shows the distinct differences which exist between different countries. The Italians, Portuguese and Spanish like to stay at home for holidays. The French, rather surprisingly, also like to take domestic holidays. The populations from other countries such as Germany, the Netherlands and Belgium are much more adventurous in their destination preference and have a tendency to go outside their country for holidays.

TOURISM DEMAND

Tourism is accepted as being the largest economic activity in the European Union, and it has potential for future growth. The southern

European countries are particularly noted for attracting pleasure holidaymakers.

Holiday or leisure tourism

The developed countries of Europe show increasing patterns of consumption of holiday taking. Individuals in these countries are often taking more than one trip per year, either inside or outside their country of residence.

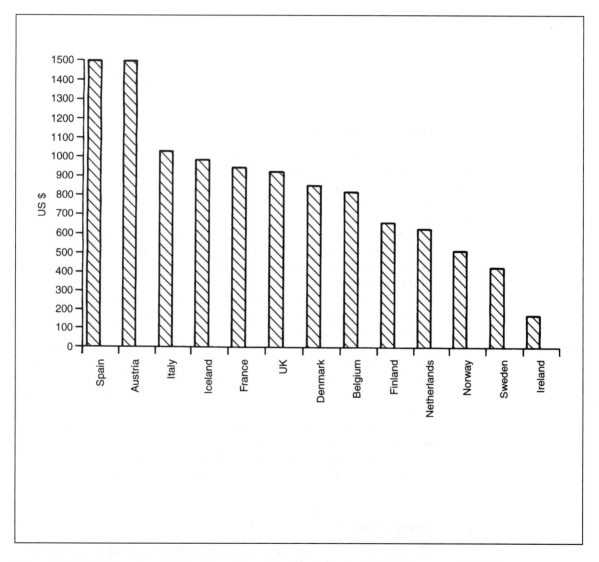

Figure 5.2 Consumer spend on hotels and restaurants (expressed in US$ per capita) 1993. Source: Estimates based on statistics in Euromonitor (1995).

Table 5.1 Holiday preferences: adults taking a holiday (6 days or over) by destination 1990 (units: % of adults)

EU	All holidays	Own country	Only in own country	Taking domestic holidays	Taking only domestic holidays
Belgium	47	17	11	36	23
Denmark	62	37	23	60	37
France	56	48	37	86	66
Germany, West	50	23	14	46	28
Greece	51	46	38	90	74
Ireland	40	21	19	52	47
Italy	46	39	34	85	74
Luxembourg	61	3	2	5	3
Netherlands	63	31	17	49	27
Portugal	41	38	35	93	85
Spain	39	35	33	90	85
United Kingdom	58	36	26	62	45

Source: Euromonitor (1995).

Domestic tourism in Western Europe

Domestic tourism in Europe varies considerably from country to country in relation to volume of demand from consumers, particularly in relation to foreign holidays (see Euromonitor, 1995). There are differences shown between the demand for holidays by different European countries.

Table 5.2 shows comparisons between countries of domestic holiday taking. The Swedes and French have the highest proportion of adults taking domestic holidays because there is a high ownership of second homes in these countries.

Countries do differ in terms of their holiday taking patterns. Table 5.3 shows that the Swiss take the most holidays with the Spanish taking the least holidays.

The patterns of demand for holidays by individual countries in Europe are therefore very different. The difference in geography of the European countries also means that the populations of different countries go to different geographical locations for their main domestic holidays. This can be seen in Table 5.4.

The seaside does, however, come out as the top geographic location for a domestic holiday in every European country. The most common length of the main holiday is 14 days. Multiple holiday taking of two or three holidays during the year is becoming common in Northern Europe.

Business tourism

The countries of Europe have seen the evolution of large national and multinational business organizations. This has generated the need for an increased level of business travel. The business person who reg-

Table 5.2 Western Europe – adults (18+) taking domestic holidays by country 1993

	% adults taking	Adults (million)	% share (Europe)
Sweden	50	3.3	3
France	48	19.3	21
Greece	46	3.0	3
Norway	40	1.3	1
Italy	39	17.4	18
Portugal	38	3.7	4
Switzerland	37	1.7	2
Denmark	37	1.6	2
UK	36	15.4	16
Spain	35	9.4	10
Austria	32	1.9	2
Finland	32	1.2	1
Netherlands	31	3.5	4
Germany	23	10.5	11
Ireland	21	0.5	1
Belgium	17	1.3	1
TOTAL	36	95.0	100

Source: Euromonitor (1995).

Table 5.3 Western Europe – overall holiday taking patterns 1993 (% adults 18+)

	Any holiday	Foreign	Domestic
Switzerland	70	51	37
Sweden	70	42	50
Netherlands	63	46	31
UK	58	32	36
France	56	19	48
Germany (West)	50	35	23
Italy	46	12	39
Spain	39	6	35
AVERAGE	52	25	36

Source: Euromonitor (1995).

ularly commutes across a variety of European countries is now a fairly common phenomenon. This has fuelled the growth of the international hotel chains aimed at this growing market segment.

Tourism may be generated from domestic or international markets for both sectors. The difference between holiday or leisure tourism and business tourism has been explained by Davidson (1994) as can be seen from Table 5.5. It can be seen that the distinction between the two types of tourism is often blurred. Business people who attend conferences, for example, are often accompanied by husbands or wives or

Table 5.4 European Union – domestic holidays by type of location 1993

	% main holidays*	Location favoured in
Seaside	52	Greece, Portugal, UK, Italy
Countryside	25	Netherlands, Denmark, Germany
Mountains	23	Germany, France
Cities or towns	19	Denmark, Ireland, Spain

* Multiple responses allowed for dual locations, hence > 100%
Source: Euromonitor (1995) from *Eurobarometer* and national sources.

Table 5.5 Leisure tourism and business tourism

	Leisure tourism	Business tourism	But ...
Who pays?	The tourist	The traveller's employer or association	Self-employed business travellers are paying for their own trips
Who decides on the destination?	The tourist	The organizer of the meeting/incentive trip/conference/exhibition	Organizers will often take into account delegates' wishes
When do trips take place?	During classic holiday periods and at weekends	All year round, Monday to Friday	July and August are avoided for major events
Lead time (period of time between booking and going on the trip)?	Holidays usually booked a few months in advance; short breaks, a few days	Some business trips must be made at very short notice	Major conferences are booked many years in advance
Who travels?	Anyone with the necessary spare time and money	Those whose work requires them to travel, or members of associations	Not all business trips involve managers on white-collar duties
What kinds of destinations are used?	All kinds: coastal, city, mountain and countryside locations	Largely centred on cities in industrialized countries	Incentive destinations are much the same as for upmarket holidays

Source: Davidson (1994).

children, and they often tag a short holiday onto the beginning or end of the conference.

Business tourism has the advantage of often bringing greater returns because it is often high cost. It can also have the advantage of generating business in off-peak times.

Business trips contribute substantially to the total tourism receipts in the world. In 1990 there were 425 million international trips made in the world and 63 million of these were on business (Davidson, 1994).

Table 5.6 International tourism in Western Europe 1995

Country	International arrivals (m) 1992	Tourism receipts ($ million) 1992
France	59.59	21 375
Spain	39.638	21 181
Italy	26.113	21 577
Austria	19.098	14 832
United Kingdom	18.535	13 683
West Germany	15.147	10 982
Greece	9.331	3 268
Portugal	8.884	3 721
Netherlands	6.049	5 004
Ireland	3.666	1 620
Norway	2.375	1 975

Source: Euromonitor (1995).

International tourism in Western Europe

International tourism receipts are a major source of revenue for most European countries. Table 5.6 shows a comparison between European countries in the levels of tourism arrivals and tourism receipts.

It can be seen that there are large differences between the European countries. France has been highly successful, for example, in developing a large number of international arrivals which bring large tourism receipts to the country.

The Eastern European countries are also showing promising development of tourism receipts which are growing rapidly. Table 5.7 shows the levels and development of tourism receipts for the period 1977–92. Poland has been particularly successful in the development of tourism receipts during this period.

The European countries also show differences in demand from international and domestic sources. This can be looked at by investigating the stay in accommodation split between international users and domestic users. Table 5.8 shows that some of the European countries rely on a large proportion of international tourists to fill their accommodation (see Ireland, United Kingdom, Luxembourg, Greece), whereas other countries rely more heavily on domestic tourists to fill

Table 5.7 The levels and development of tourism receipts in Eastern European countries

Eastern Europe	Tourism receipts ($ million) 1992	% growth 1977–92
Bulgaria	49	–79.1
Czech/Slovak Republics	1280	595.7
Hungary	1251	290.9
Poland	4100	2311.8
Romania	262	122.0

Source: Euromonitor (1995).

Table 5.8 Stay in accommodation – % split between international and domestic usage of accommodation 1992

Country	International	Domestic
Belgium[1]	47	53
Denmark[1]	45	55
France	37	63
Germany, West	13	87
Greece[2]	75	25
Ireland[3]	100	–
Italy	32	68
Luxembourg	88	12
Netherlands	31	69
Portugal	59	41
Spain	55	45
United Kingdom	82	18

1. Data refer to 1983.
2. Data refer to 1986.
3. Data refer to 1987.
Source: Adapted from Euromonitor (1995).

their accommodation space (see West Germany, Netherlands, Italy, France).

Different European countries also show distinct differences between the countries which their tourists come from. Details of these differences are shown in Table 5.9. The data shows some very interesting comparisons. Certain countries of Europe rely heavily on tourists coming chiefly from other European countries (see Belgium, Denmark, France, Greece, Italy, Portugal, Spain). Other countries rely heavily on tourists coming from outside Europe, particularly the USA (see West

Table 5.9 Principal countries of origin of foreign tourists 1992

	No. 1	%	No. 2	%	No. 3	%	No. 4	%
Belgium[1]	Netherlands	37.1	W. Germany	16.2	France	10.0	UK	9.8
Denmark[2]	W. Germany	35.2	Sweden	20.7	Norway	12.3	Netherlands	6.4
France[3]	W. Germany	21.1	UK	13.8	Italy	12.0	Belgium	11.9
Germany, East[1]	Czechoslovakia	3.9	USSR	3.8	Poland	1.1	Bulgaria	0.7
Germany, West	USA	12.7	Netherlands	1.4	UK	9.6	Sweden	6.6
Greece	UK	23.1	W. Germany	20.8	Italy	6.7	Netherlands	5.9
Ireland	UK	56.3	USA	11.7	W. Germany	7.1	France	6.9
Italy[4]	Switzerland	20.1	France	17.6	W. Germany	17.5	Austria	10.6
Luxembourg[2]	Belgium	27.2	W. Germany	14.6	Netherlands	13.7	France	9.8
Netherlands	W. Germany	20.7	UK	19.0	USA	10.4	Italy	6.2
Portugal	Spain	47.6	UK	14.4	W. Germany	9.1	France	7.3
Spain[4]	France	21.3	Portugal	20.9	W. Germany	14.0	UK	11.8
United Kingdom[4]	USA	14.8	France	13.6	W. Germany	12.4	Ireland	7.1

1. Data refer to 1988.
2. Data refer to 1988.
3. Data refer to 1987.
4. All visitor arrivals.
Source: Euromonitor (1995)

Germany, Ireland, Netherlands, United Kingdom). The order of the principal countries of origin is also very different for different European countries.

This data does show, however, the importance of European travel as a generator of revenue.

Seasonality of demand for tourism is also another key factor which can be compared for different European countries. Figure 5.3 shows the comparative seasonality data for a sample of European countries. It can be seen that for the UK, Italy and Spain, there is a peak in visitor arrivals in the summer months. Spain has a particularly high number of visitor arrivals in August.

National comparisons

The differences between the tourism markets in different European countries has already been investigated. It is interesting to bring together this data for country-to-country comparisons. Table 5.10 shows a comparison between the United Kingdom and France. The two countries which are situated in close proximity show very different trends in their tourism markets.

France has a much more developed tourism industry with regard to total arrivals and receipts. Both countries have very different profiles in terms of sources of visitors and accommodation patterns.

This analysis would seem to suggest that the individual countries of Europe have very different markets. Whether this is due to natural market conditions or because of differences in national tourism policy is not altogether clear.

Specific tourism markets

The evidence to date seems to suggest that there are large differences between the tourism markets of individual European countries. It is necessary to look at specific tourism markets to investigate this further. Let us look at the market for cities, for example.

Cities

Cities within Europe are marketed in their own right. They may be marketed for business tourism, for leisure tourism and for tourists on educational trips.

There is very little data available regarding the arrivals of tourists in individual cities. One piece of research which looked at this was carried out by Gotti and van der Borg on behalf of CISET. This research elaborated on data which was collected on individual cities in Europe, the results of which are shown in Table 5.11.

It can be seen that the origins of tourists to the cities studied in major European countries are very different. Oxford, for example,

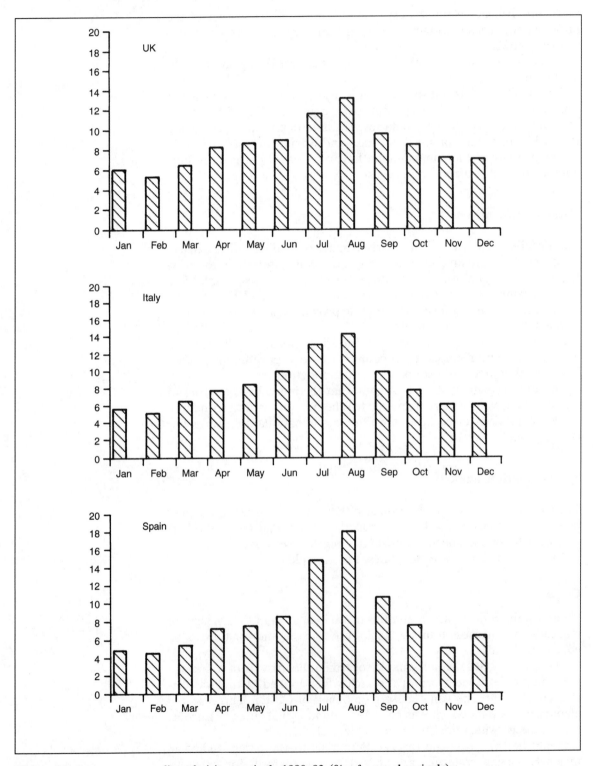

Figure 5.3 Average seasonality of visitor arrivals 1990–93 (% of annual arrivals).
Source: Economist Intelligence Unit (1995).

Table 5.10 Comparison of tourism in France and the United Kingdom

Factor	France	United Kingdom
Holiday consumers	High proportion of domestic consumers	Lower proportion of domestic consumers
Number of International arrivals (m 1992)	59.59	18.54
Tourism receipts 1992 ($ million)	21 375	13 683
Accommodation stay	Large % from domestic market	Large % from international market
Origin of tourist arrivals	1. W. Germany 2. UK 3. Italy 4. Belgium	1. USA 2. France 3. W. Germany 4. Ireland
Seasonality	Summer month bias	Summer month bias

Source: Adapted from various statistics.

Table 5.11 Arrivals of tourists by area of origin

	Domestic	Rest of Europe	USA	Japan
Aix-en-Provence	42.4	44.1	7.7	1.0
Amsterdam	7.3	n.a.	11.8	n .a.
Bruges	10.8	68.3	11.5	3.0
Florence	37.4	33.2	11.8	17.6
Oxford	60.0	17.0	13.0	2.0
Salzburg	16.7	42.9	10.7	4.5
Venice	26.3	36.0	17.8	11.1

Source: CISET (1995).

relies heavily on domestic visitors, whereas Bruges relies heavily on visitors from other European countries.

This data suggests that based on a small sample, different cities attract very different markets. This data could hide the fact that the same person, whether it be a business traveller or a leisure holiday-maker, is visiting many European cities over the course of a few years.

CONCLUSIONS

This chapter has looked at the concept of the 'European market' for tourism, leisure and hospitality services. It has been seen that there are some long-term pan-European trends which are beginning to emerge. In the affluent countries of Europe, the proportion of earnings after tax which the average European family spends on leisure goods, services and holidays will increase as standards of living rise. Examples of this shift to leisure include the obviously increasing number of families who are able to take multiple holidays per year. These families also often take many short breaks in a year and spend increasing amounts on entertainment, cars and leisure goods.

Leisure and tourism are therefore big and growing businesses. The economies of scale are, however, taking some time to develop and it is anticipated by analysts that the concept of pan-European multiple retailing and leisure branding in this sector will not develop fully until well into the next century.

The other important issue is the emerging status of the less affluent European countries which will continue to develop their industrial infrastructures.

There are pan-European similarities in the nature of markets in tourism, leisure and hospitality. These will be exploited to a greater degree by organizations in the future. The first example of pan-European marketing has been those companies which are beginning to target the international business traveller or the young consumer using an 'American' approach.

There are, however, subtleties in the markets which the national statistics and company financial data can disguise. Consider, for example, hotelier in any of the major European holiday destinations who is selling bedrooms in a medium sized hotel. Such a hotelier will be targeting a number of European countries, selling bedspaces by negotiation with a selection of the major tour operators such as TUI (Germany), Thomson (UK), LTU (Germany) and First Choice (UK).

For this hotelier, whether an individual or part of a larger group, this marketing is truly European in nature. You only have to sit down with the guests at mealtimes to discover this fact!

DISCUSSION POINTS AND ESSAY QUESTIONS

1. Discuss the main national differences found within Europe in terms of domestic tourism markets.
2. Identify the most important characteristics of the international tourism market within Europe.
3. Examine the main differences between the leisure tourism and business tourism markets.

Choose **two** of the following markets:

- theme park;
- fast food;
- budget hotel accommodation;
- package holidays (FITs).

For your chosen markets you should collect data on the size and nature of each market in your country and then on a European scale.

You should then highlight differences and similarities in each of the markets between different individual European countries.

Finally, you should outline any problems you experience in the collection and interpretation of the data for this project.

CASE STUDY

You can use Case study 22 on 'the European youth travel market' to illustrate some of the issues raised in this chapter of the book.

<table>
<tr><td>

6

</td><td>

The European tourism, leisure and hospitality industries

</td></tr>
</table>

Key concepts

The main concepts covered in this chapter are:

- the types of organization that exist within the supply side of tourism, leisure and hospitality;
- the role of transnational corporations in tourism, leisure and hospitality.

The previous chapter identified that there are some pan-European similarities in the nature of the markets in tourism, leisure and hospitality. This chapter will look at the supply side of the industry. It looks at the types of organizations found in these three sectors, trends in the structure of the industry and the rise of the transnational corporations.

INTRODUCTION

It is important to reiterate that the tourism market is not served by one industry but by a combination of different types of organization supplying very different products and services including:

- transport organizations;
- tour operators and travel agents;
- visitor attractions;
- the hospitality industry including commercial accommodation suppliers and restaurants.

These industrial sectors of tourism, leisure and hospitality are shown in Figure 6.1. Destination markets include countries, regions and individual cities and towns. This type of marketing involves a complex of interactive products and services which the visitor 'buys' (Figure 6.2).

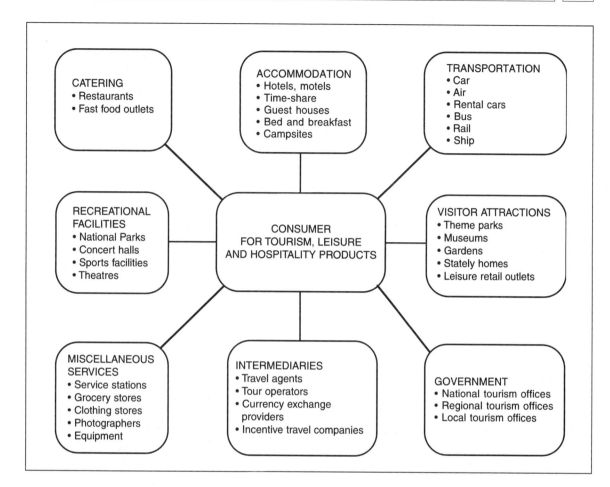

Figure 6.1 The industrial sectors of tourism, leisure and hospitality.

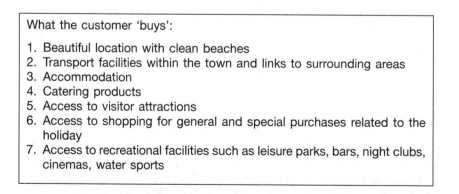

Figure 6.2 Destination market: large European seaside resort.

MARKET STRUCTURE

The European market for tourism, leisure and hospitality products has been developed by organizations of different sizes. These range from global organizations which have developed their business in Europe as part of their global strategy, to small local entrepreneurial organizations which rely on a very limited market catchment area.

The European leisure market is very fragmented in nature. Most of the major sections of the industry have a large multinational presence in the market. These multinationals, however, often only represent a small part of the total market size.

Most of the large operators have levels of business which only represent a small part of the total amount which is spent on tourism as a whole. Larger companies are, however, beginning to recognize that they can target consumers who have things in common across national boundaries. This can be considered, for example, with reference to a quote from the chairman of the leisure service provider, the Tussauds Group:

> Europe is a very fragmented market when it comes to leisure. There are already many existing facilities built into the cultural framework, such as museums, castles, parks and so on. But our feeling is that European leisure consumers have a lot more in common with each other than differences, which means that our expertise can be translated across countries fairly easily.
>
> (Chairman of Tussauds Group, interviewed in *Business Life* magazine, April 1994)

Leisure-related companies

The major players in the European leisure-related market are only small in comparison with the largest companies in Europe. This was identified in the Financial Times annual survey of Europe's largest companies by market capitalization (Table 6.1).

It can be seen from Table 6.1 that the industry has few very large operators. Private ownership or government control (either central or local) is still the norm in the leisure industry in countries as diverse as Germany, Italy, Spain and Sweden (Euromonitor, 1994). Tourist attractions, hotels and restaurants are almost invariably owned and operated as single units. The 'leisure conglomerates' which do appear in the list are largely UK-based and include the Rank Organization, Granada Group, Tussauds Group and Scottish & Newcastle. Further consolidation of the industry occurred in 1996 when Forte hotels was taken over by the Granada Group.

Table 6.1 Western Europe – largest European companies with leisure-related operations by market capitalization 1993

Company (rank in 500)	Country	Main	Capital (US$ billion)	Sales (US$ billion)	Staff (000s)
Top European					
1. Royal Dutch/Shell	UK/NL	Petroleum	88.8	83.9	127
2. BT	UK	Telecoms	40.9	20.2	170
3. Roche Holdings	SZ	Chemicals	35.7	9.1	56
Leisure related					
28. Grand Metropolitan	UK	Catering, misc.	13.2	12.1	102
76. Allied-Domecq*	UK	Drinks,catering	7.7	8.0	26
93. Bass	UK	Beer, leisure	6.0	6.6	84
130. Pearson	UK	Media, misc.	4.5	2.5	28
134. Eurotunnel	UK/FR	Transport	4.2	–	–
140. Rank Organization	UK	Leisure	4.1	3.2	42
151. Whitbread	UK	Beer, catering	3.8	3.6	65
153. Agence Havas	FR	Travel agency	3.8	5.0	12
175. Ladbroke Group	UK	Gaming, misc.	3.2	6.3	53
177. Granada Group	UK	Media, leisure	3.2	2.0	18
191. Scottish & Newcastle	UK	Beer, holidays	3.0	2.3	28
194. Forte	UK	Hotels	2.9	4.1	81
211. Accor	FR	Hotels	2.7	5.2	144
433. Greenalls Group	UK	Catering	1.2	0.8	8

* Formerly Allied-Lyons; acquired Domecq group in 1994.
NB. Three leisure companies dropped out of the Financial Times top 500 from the previous year. These were, with 1992 rankings, as follows:

- First Leisure Corporation (461), operating a mixture of entertainment venues and seaside resort attractions;
- Club Méditerranée (464);
- the French catering group Sodexho (481).

Source: *Financial Times*, quoted in Euromonitor (1994).

SECTORS OF THE EUROPEAN TOURISM, LEISURE AND HOSPITALITY INDUSTRIES

Airlines

The demand for airline travel in the business sector via scheduled airlines is international in nature. This is due to sophisticated distribution and computer reservation systems, and the fact that this product is largely based on international travel.

Other forms of air travel are demanded on a national basis. The development of charter airlines, for example, has occurred to supply the needs of domestic tour operators.

The airline industry is becoming global in that the major airlines are growing by acquisition, merger and franchising agreements. The growth of global route networks has been fuelled by the increasing trend to deregulation and privatization. It is predicted that there will be many changes which will occur in the European market in the next decade.

Airlines have also been subject to a high degree of national protection which has been encouraged by state ownership and government control of landing rights. This position resulted in the growth of a large number of individual airlines across Europe each having a fairly modest network of flights.

The need for sophisticated computer systems to service airlines coupled with the need for integrated airline services has stimulated the growth of mergers and alliances in Europe. This trend was summarized by Hamill in 1993 and is shown in Figure 6.3.

Airlines have been led into a period of extensive change with rapidly expanding computer systems. There has also been a growth in the marketing techniques used such as sophisticated market segmentation methods and branding policies.

The airline industry has therefore taken an international approach to strategic development and large European and international airlines are emerging as a result. It is predicted that the establishment of large airline companies and alliances will mean that Europe will be dominated in the near future by a small number of major players.

This is evident when the data on the ten largest international airlines is considered (Table 6.2). It can be seen that many of the major airlines are American. There are, however, three European airline companies which appear in the top ten – namely Air France Group (France), Lufthansa (Germany) and British Airways (UK).

The major European airlines are also establishing strategic alliances with both American and Far Eastern operators. British Airways, for example, has already established links with the US Air Group.

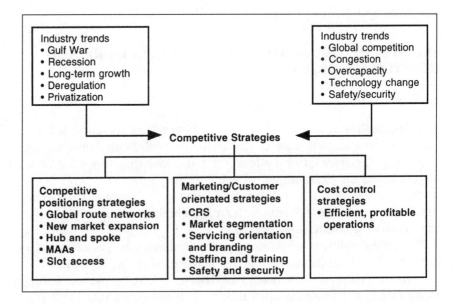

Figure 6.3 Competitive challenges and strategies in the world airline industry. Source: Hamill (1993).

Table 6.2 The ten largest international airlines by revenue: 1991

Carrier	Country	Revenue ($m)	Profits	Passenger miles in millions	Rank by revenue	Rank by passenger miles
American (AMR)	US	12 993	(240)	82.3	1	1
Air France Group	France	11 823	(122)	33.3	2	8
United Airlines	US	11 748	(332)	82.3	3	1
Japan Airlines	Japan	10 627	(100)	32.6	4	9
Lufthansa	Germany	9 713	(251)	32.6	5	10
Delta	US	9 170	(324)	62.1	6	3
British Airways	UK	9 064	685	40.9	7	6
Northwest	US	7 534	(3)	53.2	8	4
All Nippon Airways	Japan	6 634	55	23.0	9	12
US Air Group	US	6 544	(305)	34.1	10	7
Singapore	Singapore	3 044	521	21.7	20	13

() = loss.
Source: IATA, quoted in Hamill (1993).

The growth of the international carriers and the rapid development of the major European airports such as Schiphol (Amsterdam), Heathrow (London) and Charles de Gaulle (Paris) has meant that the market for airline tickets is rapidly becoming a European, if not global, market. This will continue to develop at a rapid pace particularly due to the sophisticated computer reservation systems.

Despite the differences shown in the way that airlines sell their products to their individual national markets, the large airlines which sell their airline tickets to the European or international traveller are perhaps the best examples of the development of a 'European market' in tourism, leisure and hospitality.

Tour operators

The demand for holidays, and particularly package holidays, has grown in Europe dramatically in recent years. This has resulted in the growth of a large number of tour operators across Europe.

While the vast majority of European tour operators are small-scale, a survey by the German travel trade publication *FVW International* showed that in 1991 there were 101 tour operators in Europe which were carrying more than 30 000 passengers. Of these 26 were German, 14 Swiss, eight Dutch, eight French and seven British, while three were based in Eastern Europe. However, it must be noted that the FVW survey usually underrepresents operators from Southern Europe. Nevertheless, it is estimated that in 1992–93 the companies featured in the FVW survey took 51.3 million people on holiday (Gratton and Richards, 1995).

In 1993, the eight largest European tour operators – five German and three British – accounted for 38% of all holidaymakers carried by the operators covered by the FVW survey. Furthermore, the trend in Europe has been towards larger carriers. In the case of the top 50 tour operators, the average number of holidaymakers carried through operators grew from 400 000 to 600 000 between 1988 and 1993 (Gratton and Richards, 1995).

Table 6.3 shows the turnover in millons of ECUs of Europe's 20 largest tour operators in 1991–92.

However, the European tour operator market is growing at a slower pace than previously, overall. In Northern Europe the market appears to have reached maturity, with little opportunity for rapid growth in the short term. On the other hand the market is growing significantly amongst the residents of Eastern European countries. Nevertheless, in general, the European package holiday market is becoming more competitive.

Therefore, it is not suprising that tour operators have been seeking to improve their sales volume and market share by expanding into the holiday market of other countries. A few examples will serve to illustrate this point, including:

- the taking over of the Scandinavian Leisure Group (SLG) by the UK tour operator Airtours;
- Club Med marketing its products to UK customers;
- the German operator ITS having an 80% stake in Holland International, the market leader in the Netherlands.

In 1993, German tour operators earned substantial proportions of their turnover from the activities of their foreign subsidiaries. They contributed 39% of the total turnover of ITS, 18% for NUR and 13% for TUI (Gratton and Richards, 1995).

If expanding into other national markets is one means by which tour operators can seek to improve their market position, then operators in some countries would appear to have one distinct advantage. In other words, they charge lower prices than those in other countries so that they should be able to attract customers from countries where prices are higher. An Economic Intelligence Unit (EIU) report of 1992, quoted by Gratton and Richards, show how prices differ across Europe.

The EIU survey established the average price in Europe for a 14-night holiday and then showed that the price of such a holiday in the UK and Spain was only 85% and 91% of the European average respectively. At the other extreme prices in Italy, Norway and Switzerland were all significantly above the European average (Gratton and Richards, 1995).

As well as price differentials, there are other reasons why we may see the growth of more and more transnational tour operators in Europe, including:

- the fact that the 'Single Market' will become more and more of a reality in Europe with each year that that passes;
- the growth of new outbound markets in Eastern Europe and Southern Europe;

Table 6.3 Europe's top 20 package travel companies 1991/1992[1]

Rank/company[2]	Turnover ECU (m³)	Turnover local currency	Sales growth on previous year (%)[4]	Own brand package travel as share of turnover (%)[5]
1. TUI (Germany)	2590 (Oct)	DM 5.30 bn	8.1	85.0
2. Thomson (UK)[7]	1623 (Dec)	£1.16 bn	10.1	64.0
3. NUR (Germany)[8]	1220 (Oct)	DM 2.50 bn[6]	25.0	90.0
4. LTU (Germany)	1206 (Dec)	DM 2.46 bn	8.6	75.0
5. Kuoni (Switzerland)	1190 (Dec)	Sfr 1.16 bn	−1.7	50.0
6. Club Méditerranée (France)[9]	1122 (Oct)	Fr 7.4 bn	−4.2	60.0
7. DER (Germany)	1056 (Dec)	DM 2.15 bn	4.9	40.0
8. NRT Nordisk (Sweden)	1019 (Dec)	Skr 7.59 bn	−1.5	40.0
9. ITS (Germany)	963 (Oct)	DM 1.97 bn	21.1	65.0
10. Owners Abroad* (UK)	916 (Oct)	£644 m	29.3	75.0
11. Nouvelles Frontières (France)	639 (Sep)	Fr 4.46 bn	14.1	80.0
12. Hotelplan (Switzerland)	606 (Oct)	Sfr 1.09 bn	49	89.0
13. SAS Leisure (Sweden)	556 (Dec)	Skr 4.14 bn	−0.6	60.0
14. Spies (Denmark)	540 (Apr)	Dkr 4.25 bn	−5.7	80.0
15. Grupo Viajes Iberia (Spain)	532 (Dec)	Pta 69.00 bn[10]	55.0	60.0
16. Airtours (UK)	412 (Sep)	£290 m	58.2	80.0
17. Arke Reizen (Netherlands)	347 (Oct)	G801 m	3.5	51.0
18. Center Parcs (Netherlands)[11]	347 (Dec)	G795 m[10]	10.0	100.0
19. CIT (Italy)	342 (Nov)	L525 bn	−1.2	40.0
20. Sun International (Belgium)	317 (Oct)	Bfr 13.4 bn	−19.1	70.0

* Owners Abroad has been renamed First Choice Holidays.
1. Criteria for inclusion: a minimum of 25% of turnover from own brand outbound package travel; 50% of turnover from sales of leisure-related travel; 25% of turnover from sales to destinations or in countries other than the country of head office.
2. Domicile of the company shown in the table. Where the parent company is in a different country, this is identified in the footnotes.
3. At rate prevailing on the last day of financial year. Some figures are rounded. Consolidated group turnover where available. The accounting principles underlying the figures vary considerably and are discussed in the EIU Special Report quoted as 'Source' below. Arke is an associate, not a subsidiary, of TUI, but it is included in the parent group's figures on the basis of a share of turnover rather than equity. Other companies in this table in which another group in the table is a minority shareholder are: TUI (DER); ITS (Sun International); and Grupo Viajes Iberia (NUR is a shareholder in two GVI subsidiaries).
4. Calculated on the basis of change in local currency.
5. Outbound and inbound package operations, including ground handling, seat only, seat booking and travel insurance where separate information is available. Incoming tour operating and ground services are regarded as an integral part of the company's package travel business, but it should be borne in mind that the extent to which there are synergies between the outbound and incoming operations varies considerably from group to group. Excludes airlines and travel retailing. Hotels and accommodation are also excluded where possible. Figures are generally authors' estimates.
6. Projection but no further result will be issued.
7. Thomson is a subsidiary of the Thomson Corporation of Canada.
8. Includes Sunsnacks which Neckermann bought from TEA during 1991 and an undisclosed allocation of turnover from its 49% stake in a joint venture with Kuoni in Austria, also acquired in 1991.
9. Includes Club Aquarius from April 1991.
10. EIU estimate.
11. Center Parcs is a wholly owned subsidiary of Scottish and Newcastle Breweries of the UK.

Source: Economist Intelligence Unit (1993).

- the development of ever more sophisticated computer reservation systems (CRS) which make transnational operation easier.

Finally, we need to remember that the majority of Eastern tour operators are not transnational; indeed most of them are small-scale. But many of these small and medium-sized operations are growing by successfully exploiting niche markets such as activity and special interest holidays. In the UK, for example, the Association of Independent Tour Operators (AITO) has over 200 member companies which offer such holidays.

Visitor attractions

Visitor attractions have been defined as:

> designated permanent resources that are controlled and managed for their own sake and for the enjoyment, amusement, entertainment, and education of the visiting public.
>
> (Middleton, 1994)

Middleton (1994) expands this definition by classifying visitor attractions into ten categories:

- ancient monuments;
- historic buildings;
- designated areas, parks and gardens;
- theme parks;
- wildlife attractions;
- museums;
- art galleries;
- industrial archaeology site;
- themed retail sites;
- amusement and leisure parks;

It is estimated by Europarks that there are 200 leisure parks in Europe which attracted more than 160 million visitors in 1993.

Visitor attractions have been categorized according to Swarbrooke (1995) into different groups according to their catchment areas. These include attractions which are very local in appeal. The second group includes attractions which have a regional catchment area, such as smaller theme parks. Relatively few attractions have primarily national catchment areas and are usually market leaders in their field. Alton Towers in the UK is one example of an attraction with a national catchment area.

Only a small number of attractions enjoy an international catchment area. These tend to be unique attractions which are world famous. Disney World is an example of such an international attraction.

Most attractions are marketed, therefore, on a local basis with small marketing budgets. It is the large international attractions which provide the opportunity for European or international marketing programmes.

These larger operations need substantial operating and marketing skills. The attractions must be funded by the right financial package, must have an appealing theme so that large numbers of customers are drawn each year, and must have access to a large catchment area to encourage the large numbers of customers which are required.

Disneyland Paris was the first European attraction which had a truly pan-European perspective. It has tried to develop the market for the attraction across a European catchment area. In response to the development of Disneyland Paris, other major theme parks have linked up to form a strategic alliance.

It was announced in Paris in June 1993, that five major European theme parks with a combined turnover of £130 million had joined together to push for higher standards and a wider understanding of the European market. The group also planned to increase their purchasing power, swap information about their markets, and develop new technology. The consortium also acts as a point of contact for pan-European activity such as promotions, sponsorship, travel trade packages and staff events. Details of the consortium are shown in Table 6.4.

This development is perhaps one of the first signs that as the Single Market in Europe becomes more a reality, there will be a growth in investment in new attractions coming from foreign companies. The decision of the Lego organization to develop a Legoland attraction in the UK on the site of the former Windsor Safari Park is an example of this type of development.

The European theme park industry is demonstrating confidence in the ability of large investments to promote attendances. Investments for 1994 include US$10 m at De Efteling (Netherlands), US$8 m at Bobbejaanland (Denmark), US$7 m at Parc Asterix (France), and US$7 m at Walabi Flevo (Netherlands). The largest single investment reported is the 'Galway' flight simulator at Phantasialand Germany, which is reported to have cost DM30 m (US$18 m) to develop. (Tourism Research and Marketing, 1994.)

France leads in terms of the total number of theme park attendances, though in 1993 there seems to be a steady growth in the number of attendances across Europe (Tables 6.5 and 6.6).

Table 6.4 The Great European Theme Parks Consortium

Established	–	June 1993
Total annual visitor numbers	–	9.8 million
Members	–	Alton Towers – (UK)
		Europa Park – (Germany)
		De Efteling – (Holland)
		Parc Asterix – (France)
		Liseberg – (Sweden)
Total staff	–	7000
Benefits	–	Sharing of information
		Promotional gain
		Technical development

Source: Leisure Opportunities (1993).

Table 6.5 European theme park attendance 1993

Region	Visitors (millions)
France	15.0
UK	11.5
Germany	11.0
Netherlands	7.0
Scandinavia	6.5
Belgium	4.2
Italy	3.0
Total	58.2

Source: *Tourism Research and Marketing* (1994).

Table 6.6 Attendance at some major European theme parks

Park	Attendance (000s)		
	1991	1992	1993
De Efteling (N)	2300	2500	2700
Duinrell (N)	1080	1180	1190
Futuroscope (F)	1000	1300	1900
Asterix (F)	1400	1000	1200
Tivoli (DK)	4000	4000	4100

Source: *Tourism Research and Marketing* (1994).

European parks have also started to attract more international visitors. It is estimated that Futuroscope, for example, the French theme park, attracted 40% of its visitors in 1993 from abroad. More detail on the Futuroscope market is presented in Figure 6.4.

European parks have been attracting more tourists from the UK because they are being increasingly featured in brochures from tour operators. Futuroscope, for example, had 25 000 UK visitors in 1993 compared to 12 000 in 1992, and has announced collaboration with 15 major UK tour operators. At the same time De Efteling welcomed 37 000 UK visitors in 1993 and the operators who delivered these visitors included North Sea Ferries, Holland Travel Service and Stena Sealink (now Stena Line). (Tourism Research and Marketing, 1994.)

These are the first signs that a 'European market' for large, well developed theme parks is beginning to develop.

Hotels

The hotel industry is increasingly making a global push to attract the world's top business and leisure travellers. Hotel chains now operate on every continent of the world, except Antarctica.

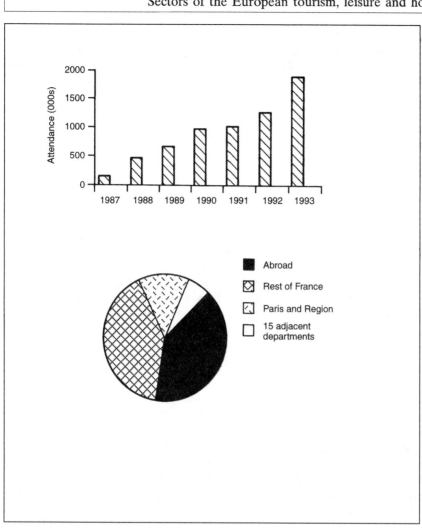

Figure 6.4 Futuroscope: attendance details 1987–93 and attendance profile 1993. Source: *Tourism Research and Marketing* (1994).

It has already been stated that the markets for hotel products in different European countries are very different. The split between international and national visitors and the total spend on hospitality products vary enormously between individual countries. Despite this, there is a push for the major hotel groups to become global in nature.

Europe is seen as a favourable location for hotel groups to develop, particularly as economies are beginning to grow following the recessionary period. It is estimated, however, that only approximately 10% of the total accommodation capacity in Europe is currently under a corporate flag.

It is expected that as the economies of Europe begin to recover from recession, then the performance of hotels will benefit. The entry of Austria, Finland and Sweden to the European Union in January 1995 may also fuel increased demand for hotel accommodation.

The global hospitality industry in terms of sales is dominated by the American corporations. If the leading hotel chains are ranked according to room numbers, a number of European based chains are present in the top 20 rankings. This is demonstrated in Table 6.7. It can be seen that companies such as Forte plc (UK), Accor (France), Sol Group (Spain) and Société du Louvre (France) are global players in terms of number of rooms. However, Accor and Forte (which was bought by the Granada Group in 1996) dominate the European hotel business.

International hotel chains have concentrated their activities on the major countries of region. Forte UK, for example, has developed an extensive portfolio of hotels located in continental Europe. This portfolio is shown in Table 6.8. It is estimated by Slattery, Feehely and Savage (1995) that this portfolio accounted for 13.1% of hotel profits in the year to end January 1994, and will represent 16.4% of hotel profits in the year to January 1997. Forte purchased Meridien from Air France in 1994 to help it develop its market in continental Europe.

The French based Accor group has also developed an increasing presence in all the countries of Europe, from a strong French foundation. Accor has developed their hotels from a strong portfolio of brands including Altea, Formule 1 and Novotel. The full range of brands is shown in Table 6.9 while Table 6.10 shows the numbers of hotels owned by Accor in selected countries of Europe. The company owns hotels in most Western European countries and is beginning to develop a portfolio of hotels in Eastern Europe.

Fast food chains

The unification in Europe and the growing openness in Eastern Europe has meant that there has been a tremendous opportunity for the rapid spread of the franchise fast food chains. The younger generation who have been influenced by American culture have been keen to visit these chains. The chains have also promoted the special occasion dining experience amongst youngsters across Europe – and indeed globally.

The acceptance by governments and consumers alike of this type of catering outlet has fuelled the tremendous growth of franchised fast-food restaurants in Europe, spearheaded by the chains McDonald's, Burger King and Pizza Hut. Research carried out as early as 1990 indicated that these chains had reached most of the major developed countries of Europe in large numbers, their restaurants tending

Table 6.7 Top 20 corporate hotel chains*

Rank 1993	Corporate chain headquarters	Rooms 1993
1	Hospitality Franchise Systems Parsippany, NJ USA	384 790
2	Holiday Inn Worldwide Atlanta, GA USA	340 881
3	Best Western International Phoenix, AZ USA	272 743
4	Accor Evry, France	250 319
5	Choice Hotels International Silver Spring, MD USA	229 784
6	Marriott International Washington, DC USA	173 048
7	ITT Sheraton Corp. Boston, MA USA	129 714
8	Hilton Hotels Corp. Beverly Hills, CA USA	94 952
9**	Forte plc London, England	78 691
10	Promus Cos. Memphis, TN USA	78 309
11	Hyatt Hotels/Hyatt International Chicago, IL USA	76 057
12	Carlson/Radisson/Colony Minneapolis, MN USA	75 986
13	Club Méditerranée SA Paris, France	65 128
14	New World/Renaissance Hotels Central, Hong Kong	55 591
15	Hilton International Watford, Herts,England	52 930
16	Inter-Continental Hotels London, England	48 510
17	Sol Group Palme de Mallorca, Spain	43 178
18	Westin Hotels and Resorts Seattle, WA USA	38 021
19	La Quinta Inns San Antonio, TX USA	27 960
20	Société du Louvre Paris, France	27 906

* This list contains chains which own all of their hotels, together with organizations which are franchisors and consortia.
** Forte was purchased by the Granada Group in 1996.
Source: *Hotels* (July 1994).

to be established in the cosmopolitan cities and major towns (Table 6.11).

Dominance by the American chains in the development of this sector of hospitality could lead to the inevitable question of whether the development of European markets in the future will be an 'Americanization' process rather than a 'Europeanization' process. What is clear is that the growth of the international restaurant franchise has been a

Table 6.8 Forte Hotels – continental European portfolio

Brand	Hotels	Rooms
Forte Agip	18	2 710
Forte Exclusive	9	1 559
Forte Grand	8	1 950
Forte Crest	5	1 121
Forte Meridien	8	3 493
County Hotels	2	115
Forte Travelodge	6	308
Forte other	4	639
Forte Relais	2	135
Unbranded overseas	5	840
Total	67	12 870

Source: Kleinwort Benson Securities (1995).
Note: Forte was taken over by the Granada Group in 1996.

Table 6.9 Accor 1995

	Number of hotels	Number of rooms
Altea	12	1 098
Arcade	6	351
Etap	28	1 907
Formule 1	310	20 356
Ibis	415	43 022
Mercure	242	28 705
Motel 6	748	84 498
Novotel	279	43 360
Partnership	7	329
Palm Azur	32	4 905
Pullman	17	2 156
Sofitel	117	22 123
Urbis	61	3 902
Total	2276	256 887

Source: Kleinwort Benson Securities (1995).

Table 6.10 Accor Hotels in Europe 1993

	Accor	Wagon-Lit (former)
France	668	153
Belgium	25	12
Germany	63	24
UK	24	–
Italy	5	–
Netherlands	17	13
Portugal	6	4

Source: Euromonitor (1994).

Table 6.11 Franchise restaurants in Europe

Restaurant	Country	Number of units
McDonald's	United Kingdom	320
	Germany	319
	France	115
	Spain	28
Burger King	United Kingdom	163
	Germany	70
	Spain	39
	France	18
Pizza Hut	United Kingdom	228
	Germany	41
	Spain	14
	France	3
Domino's	United Kingdom	42
	Germany	3
	Spain	3
	France	1
KFC	United Kingdom	271
	Spain	16
	Germany	10
TGI Friday's	United Kingdom	5
Taco Bell	United Kingdom	2
Sbarro	United Kingdom	1

Source: *Restaurants and Institutions* (1990).

major contribution to the globalization strategy of the hospitality industry.

The brewers

Many of the major companies which have key leisure interests in Europe have a foundation in the UK beer market. The brewers have diversified into the leisure market, from their more traditional brewing and retailing operations.

A summary of the major brewers in this market is shown in Table 6.12. It can be seen that the six major UK brewers have diversified into different sectors. They also control some of the major brands in the tourism, leisure and hospitality industries and have considerable interests in continental Europe.

CONCLUSIONS

This chapter has looked at the structure of tourism, leisure and hospitality in Europe. The conclusion to be drawn is that although there are signs that the larger organizations in all sectors are beginning to develop European markets, this development is limited at present. The two market segments which are being targeted are the international

Table 6.12 The major UK brewers and their presence in European leisure markets

Company	Trading brands	Operating sectors	UK turnover £m	Continental Europe turnover £m	Other details
Grand Metropolitan	Burger King IDV (Smirnoff, Cinzano, Baileys etc)	Food Drinks Retailing	1343	1550	Operates globally
Allied Domecq (previously Allied Lyons)	Hiram Walker Group (Canadian Club, Beefeater, Courvoisier, Tia Maria) Dunkin Donuts } US Baskin-Robbins	Spirits and wines Retailing Brewing Food manufacture Internal sales	2975	866	Owns pub chain in Hungary. Operates globally
Bass	Toby Holiday Inn Worldwide Gala Clubs Coral Hollywood Bowl	Brewing Pubs Hotels Soft drinks Leisure	3782	194	Joint venture with Prague brewers. Distributes Pepsi in the UK. Operates in US and other countries
Whitbread	Brewers Fayre Bowlingo Charlie Chalk Fun Factories TGI Fridays Lansbury Hotels	Beer and other drinks Pub partnerships Managed retail estates	2657 (UK – not divided)	N/A	Estimated that UK represents 95% of group's turnover
Scottish and Newcastle	Center Parcs Pontins Chef and Brewer	Beer Retail Leisure	1293	221	Leisure division Center Parcs and Holiday Club Pontin's had turnover of £335 million in 1993
Greenalls Group	Greenhall Devenish	Public houses Pub restaurants Motels Hotels Off-license Drinks and leisure	741 (UK – not divided)	N/A	2% of sales derived from hotels in US

Source: Based on company accounts (1994).

business traveller and the young person interested in American culture.

There are signs that some of the sectors which contribute to the European tourism, leisure and hospitality markets are recognizing this opportunity. It is predicted that there will be a growth in the size of organizations to help them exploit these opportunities.

It is important to recognize, however, that the market is still composed of many hundreds of thousands of small suppliers in both the public and private sectors of industry.

DISCUSSION POINTS AND ESSAY QUESTIONS

1. Discuss the patterns of ownership found in the airline, tour operation and hotel sectors
2. Choose a major European tourism, leisure and hospitality company. Describe how the organization has grown over time and explain why it has developed in this way.

Select **one** of the following sectors: **EXERCISE**

- visitor attractions;
- accommodation;
- arts and entertainment;
- catering;
- tour operations;

For your chosen sector you should:
(a) outline the balance between small businesses and large corporations within the sector;
(b) identify the respective roles of public, private and voluntary sector organizations
(c) discuss the involvement, if any, of major organizations in your sector, in other industries

---

CASE STUDY

You can use the Case study 19 on British Airways to illustrate some of the points made in this chapter.

7 The European business environment

Key concepts

The main concepts covered in this chapter are:

- the macro-environment including political, economic, social and technological factors;
- the micro-environment including the nature and structure of the organization itself, suppliers, marketing intermediaries, existing customers and competitors;
- the two-way link between the business environment in Europe and the business environment in non-European countries;
- factors that may potentially make the European business environment more homogeneous.

INTRODUCTION

This chapter looks at the European business environment in which tourism, leisure and hospitality organizations operate today. It examines the forces and factors that are in action within this environment currently, and assesses their likely impact on these sectors.

Where appropriate, the authors will highlight those areas where there are differences between these sectors and between different European countries in relation to the business environment. They will also indicate where the European business environment is being influenced by factors whose origins lie outside Europe.

For the purposes of this chapter, the business environment will be split into two parts, as follows:

- the **macro-environment** which is made up of societal forces that cannot be controlled by organizations. They can only try to anticipate them and respond to them as effectively as possible. We will consider these factors under four headings, namely political, economic, social and technological.
- the **micro-environment** consists of those factors that are within the immediate business environment of the organization. As such, they are capable of being either controlled or influenced by the organization. We

will consider these factors under five headings, in other words the organization itself, suppliers, marketing intermediaries, existing customers and competitors. The organization must seek to manage these factors in line with its objectives.

However, it is important to note that the two are interrelated. For example, the relationship between an organization and its suppliers and marketing intermediaries is partly influenced by a political factor, namely government legislation on contract law, to give just one instance.

THE MACRO-ENVIRONMENT

The macro-environment has an impact on the three elements of the marketing system, the product, the market, and the ways in which the product is marketed to the consumer.

Furthermore, in the context of this chapter, it is important to recognise that macro-environmental factors operate at three geographical levels at least, namely:

- The **national level** where the factor is purely significant for organizations operating within the domestic market of that one country. Nevertheless, this could also mean foreign companies who sell their product in that country. For example, a change in German tax law would have an impact on a French hotel chain that operates units within Germany.
- The **European level** where the factor is significant within Europe specifically. Given that Europe does not exist as a single political or economic entity at the moment, any such factors are likely to be confined to the member states of the European Union only. An example of this is the EC Package Travel Directive.
- Those issues which exist on a **global scale** and have an influence which is on a scale greater than Europe. An example of this is the computer reservation systems (CRS) which are becoming increasingly global in nature.

Clearly there are two sides to this set of factors. In other words, there are those which originate in Europe and go on to influence countries outside Europe, and there are those which, though non-European in origin, have an impact on the European business environment.

Many argue that, currently, tourism, leisure and hospitality organizations are living through a period when their business environment is particularly volatile. This perceived volatility has underpinned many recent developments in management thinking, such as the concept of 'Thriving on Chaos', championed by Tom Peters.

We will now begin to look at the current macro-environment in Europe to attempt to see how volatile it is in reality. Certainly, it is a truism that the macro-environment is always undergoing some change. It is therefore obvious that any discussion of it in this book can only ever be a snapshot taken at a specific time.

Political factors

Europe is clearly in a period of rapid political change, which is of great significance for the European tourism, leisure and hospitality sectors.

The national level

On the national level there are a number of political factors that influence the product, market, and marketing activity, within these sectors. A few examples will illustrate this point:

- **Government policies** on topics as diverse as the following:
  - governmental financial assistance for the tourism, leisure and hospitality sectors;
  - the funding levels enjoyed by local government;
  - individual and corporate taxation;
  - state ownership within the economy, including the privatization of state-controlled industries;
  - social security policies;
  - the quantity and dates of public holidays;
  - the curriculum in schools;
  - the conservation of historic buildings;
  - border controls and the freedom of movement granted to the citizens of a country;
  - relations with particular foreign countries.
- **Government legislation** on a range of issues including:
  - health and safety at work;
  - consumer protection;
  - advertising;
  - holiday entitlement;
  - transport operations.

These lists in relation to government policies and legislation are both short and selective but they do give an impression of the breadth of influence governments may have over these sectors.

Government policies and legislation are notoriously unpredictable as they usually reflect short-term domestic political factors such as election campaigns. However, **Political stability** is crucial, given that tourism, leisure and hospitality are all better in a country where the political situation is stable. Instability can take a number of forms, including:

- Politically motivated strikes and demonstrations which can disrupt sectors by closing down airports and rail networks, for example. Given the importance of tourism to many national economies, as well as the importance which citizens attach to their holidays, trade unions realize that disrupting tourism can give them a powerful weapon. French air traffic controllers, for example, have used this tactic successfully in recent years.

- Terrorism such that in some countries tourists are becoming deliberate targets. Terrorist groups who wish to undermine governments must seek to harm the national economy which may well mean attacking tourism, given that in many countries, tourism is a crucially important sector of the economy. In other cases, tourists may be attacked because of their perceived lack of moral values by terrorists whose motivation is both religious and political.

  It is often the perception of terrorism rather than the reality that has the greatest impact on our sectors. For example, although tourists have never been deliberately targeted during the years of conflict in Northern Ireland, the perception of the situation undoubtedly harmed the development of tourism in the region.

- Wars which make leisure activities impossible for the local population and make it unattractive or impossible for outsiders to take trips to the war zone. A sad example of this is the former state of Yugoslavia, where civil wars have seriously damaged the once booming tourism and hospitality sectors. Only when war ceases can such places begin to rebuild their tourism and hospitality sectors, which can be a long job.

- The extent to which governments are seen to be in control of the country, so that law and order can be maintained rather than day-to-day life being largely determined by groups who are not part of the state. This is clearly a problem in Russia with the rise of powerful organized crime syndicates.

A few examples will demonstrate that, while the impact of national political factors is predominantly domestic, they do have an influence on people and organizations beyond the national boundaries. These examples include:

- the civil war in the former Yugoslavia which forced foreign tourists and tour operators to seek alternative destinations, both within and outside Europe;
- the package of financial and non-financial assistance offered by the French government which helped persuade the Disney organization to site Disneyland Paris in France;
- the growing freedom of movement of citizens of the former Communist countries of Eastern Europe which is leading, slowly, to more of their population taking holidays in Western Europe.

The European level

If we turn our attention now to political factors which exist at a European level, the most important clearly relate to the European Union.

The European Commission affects tourism, leisure and hospitality within member states in a wide variety of ways, including:

- legislation such as the EC Package Travel Directive which was designed to improve consumer protection in the field of package holidays across all members states;
- the activities of its directorate DG XXIII which is charged with developing tourism within the European Union
- the funding of tourism projects through a range of schemes, including the European Regional Development Fund, for example. It is, probably, not an exaggeration to say that in some countries such as the UK more public funding for tourism has come from the European Commission than from national governments in recent years;
- European Union wide tourism marketing campaigns on themes such as cultural tourism involving organizations such as the European Travel Commission;
- policy and strategy at a European Union level, such as the Green Paper on Tourism Policy published in spring 1995;
- the implementation of the Single Market and the resulting moves towards the abolition of duty free the harmonization of sales taxes, the deregulation and liberalization of air fares, and the proposed single European currency.

The current wave of enlargement of the European Union means that these influences are affecting more and more countries. Nevertheless, it is important to recognize that the Union currently has just 15 member states, so that many of these factors are not directly experienced by many European countries. These include the countries of Eastern Europe, Switzerland, Norway, Iceland and Turkey, although some of these countries do enjoy some links with the European Union.

At a pan-European level, the Council of Europe continues to play a role in tourism, leisure and hospitality through its work in the field of conservation.

The global level

If we look at political factors on the global scale, we can see that they operate in two directions, as we noted earlier. Firstly, there are those factors which originate outside Europe, but which influence European consumers and organizations. These include:

- the peace process in the Middle East and political change in South Africa, which mean that both regions are now gaining in popularity as destinations with European consumers, tour operators and airlines. It is also making them more attractive places for potential investors from Europe;
- the policies and legislation of non-European governments. This includes the attitudes towards tourism of the governments of the main destination countries for European tourists such as the USA, Egypt, Israel, Kenya and Thailand, for example, together with that of other generating countries such as the USA and Japan.

Conversely, there are those European factors that influence consumers and organizations outside Europe, including the following:

- political change in Eastern Europe which is opening up opportunities for non-European tourists to visit Eastern Europe and for non-European companies to invest there and organize holidays in these countries. It is also creating a demand for Eastern Europeans to take tourist trips to destinations like the USA to visit friends and relatives;
- the European Commission's campaign to attract non-European tourists to visit Europe to arrest the decline seen in recent years in Europe's position in the global tourism market.

The only agency operating on a global scale in tourism and hospitality or leisure is the World Tourism Organization (WTO) based in Madrid. It brings together governments from around the world and is particularly active in the areas of global policy, data collection and training.

We have devoted a relatively large section of this chapter to political factors. This is because this is perhaps the aspect of the macro-environment in Europe, which is undergoing the most fundamental change today.

Economic factors

Many of the economic factors discussed below are clearly linked to politics. Economic policy is strongly linked to governmental political policies. In Europe, through the Single Market, we are seeing an ever closer link between political and economic policies on an increasingly European scale.

The national level

However, mirroring the structure of the last section we will begin by looking at economic factors at the national level. These include the following:

- interest rates which affect both market demand and investment in new physical products such as hotels, theme parks and leisure shopping complexes;
- inflation figures, given that the higher the level of inflation, the more difficult it is to engage in longer-term financial planning;
- levels of unemployment as these affect overall demand;
- social security benefits, which if they are low may mean that many people who are jobless, elderly or sick and may be unable to afford to purchase the products of the tourism, leisure and hospitality sectors;
- the distribution of wealth in society, in other words are a small group rich while the majority are relatively poor, or is wealth more evenly

distributed? This has an impact on the value and nature of demand and is largely influenced by taxation policies

- salary levels, which if high may encourage companies to try to find ways of reducing the labour needs of their operations;
- currency exchange rates which affect outbound tourists and those organizations which service their needs;
- countries with balance of payment deficits in general or specifically in relation to tourism may be motivated to bring in policies designed to boost tourism.

Clearly, these factors have implications beyond the national frontiers. For example, if a country has relatively high wage rates, hotel chains may seek to recruit staff from countries where pay rates are lower. Thus, German hotel companies recruit Turkish workers, while many London hotels recruit staff from the Philippines, for example. Likewise, low interest rates and a buoyant economy in a country may encourage investment from foreign companies.

The European level

At the European level, the key economic factors are increasingly those which are being influenced by the actions of the European Commission. As these are politically motivated, they were outlined in the section on political factors. They include:

- plans to abolish duty free sales between member states by the end of the decade;
- the idea of harmonizing sales taxes, both in terms of the rate and the goods and services on which they are levied;
- deregulation and liberalization of markets that have been largely regulated by individual national governments, such as air travel.

Perhaps, most significantly, there is the proposed single currency within the European Union. While fraught with difficulties, this project has enormous implications for tourism within the European Union including the tourist flows between members states, which have always been influenced by currency exchange rates. For example, the number of British visitors to France fell between 1992 and 1995 as the pound fell in value against the 'Franc fort' from around 9.5 in summer 1992 to 7.40 in spring 1996.

However, by removing the uncertainties in exchange rates, a single currency would make forward planning by the tourism industry a much more practical activity. But it could also take away the income that many travel agencies, and some hotels and airports, earn from currency exchange transactions.

For many types of tourism organization such as the ferry companies and some airlines, these economic factors are perceived to be a serious threat. For consumers, they seem to represent both a threat and an opportunity.

At the supranational but sub-European level, Eastern Europe again stands out as a distinctly different region. Its low level of economic development makes it attractively inexpensive for Western Europeans, hence the popularity of skiing holidays in Bulgaria and Romania. On the other hand, the lack of economic stability and high inflation rates put off potential foreign investors.

Within the pan-European context, differential levels of economic development and wealth between countries are still motivators of flows between certain countries. It is one of the reasons, along with others, why more Swedes visit Greece than vice versa!

The global level

On the global scale the only truly global economic factors are, perhaps, the trade treaties like the GATT agreement and the continuing moves that are increasing the power of transnational, vertically and horizontally integrated corporations. Europe is playing a leading role in this trend through airlines like British Airways, with its stake in US Air and Qantas, and hotel chains such as Accor with its ownership of the Motel 6 chain in the USA. However, Europe is also affected by this trend in reverse, hence the growing presence in Europe of McDonald's and Disney.

Finally, on the global scale, differences in levels of economic development are still a motivator for trips to certain regions. This is particularly true of tourist flows from Europe, where places such as Thailand, Goa Beach, the Dominican Republic and Cuba are becoming particularly popular for sun and sand holidays because they are inexpensive for most Europeans due to their relatively low level of economic development.

Social factors

These can, somewhat subjectively, be divided into several categories, namely:

- demographic factors, in other words, those concerned with population structure in terms of characteristics such as age, sex, religion, race, education and birth, death, and fertility rates;
- social concerns, like crime, health and environmental issues;
- the emergence of distinctive subcultures within societies, that share certain values and perhaps characteristics as consumers. It could be argued that these are at the core of the 'lifestyle marketing' which we have increasingly seen in the 1990s.

Demographic factors

At the **national level**, the most important demographic characteristics include:

- the age structure of the population which is important both in terms of the target markets for an organization's marketing and its recruitment policies;
- the role and influence of women in society and their participation in leisure activities, tourism for pleasure, and business travel. In some countries, including most of those in Western Europe, women are already important markets in tourism, leisure and hospitality;
- the existence of ethnic minority communities within individual countries, who may well differ from the majority of the population in terms of race, language and religion. These groups may provide well recognized valuable niche markets for airlines, who can sell tickets between the country where the person lives and the country where their families originally lived or still live. This is seen in relation to Turkish people living in Germany, for example.

The other side of this coin is where attempts are made to encourage people from ethnic minorities to take part in leisure activities in their country of residence. For example, great efforts have been made in the UK to encourage people from the Asian and Afro-Caribbean communities to experience countryside recreation.

If we look at these same three factors at the **European level**, we will see there are large differences between individual countries.

People in Western Europe have been told they are living through an explosion of the so-called 'demographic time bomb' where populations will become increasingly aged. This growth in older people reflects improved health care, for example, and is clearly being seen in countries like Germany and the UK. However, in other parts of Europe, the main characteristic of the population in terms of age is that of a youthful population. This is true not only in terms of numbers, but also spending power. Spain provides a good illustration of this point.

While the role of women in societies in Europe is, apparently, slowly becoming increasingly similar in different countries, there are still differences between some countries of Europe such as Norway and Greece, for example.

Finally, some European countries have large ethnic minority communities, largely as a result of immigration, while others have a relatively small such population. Generally, those countries with strong colonial traditions, such as Britain and France, and those where the demand for labour has outgrown indigeneous supply, such as Germany, tend to have the largest such communities. Conversely, smaller countries with no such colonial tradition such as Ireland tend to have small ethnic communities. However, in some countries, there are minority groups which are long established and are not a result of immigration, yet they remain culturally distinct from the rest of the population. This is true of the Walloons in Belgium, the Basques of Spain and the Corsicans in France.

In terms of the **global level** in relation to demographic factors, the main link between Europe and the rest of the world is principally a matter of demographic change in countries outside Europe where European transnational corporations sell their product.

Social concerns

Let us now turn our attention to social concerns, beginning with the **national level**. We will focus on the following concerns, which all have an influence on tourism, leisure and hospitality:

- crime;
- health issues;
- environmental issues.

Crime can discourage people from visiting places, particularly those which have developed a bad reputation in terms of crime generally, and against tourists specifically. On the other hand, if the appeal of the place is strong enough, it may simply result in tourists exercising more caution. Some Italian cities, and from time to time French autoroutes, have suffered in this respect.

Health issues can be both a threat and an opportunity for our sectors. A threat is posed if countries, or parts of them, are perceived to represent risks to visitors' health, in some way. For example, many beaches in the UK are perceived to be a health threat because of pollution. Other health threats present in some European countries include rabies, a water-borne virus in St Petersburg, and a relatively high risk of food poisoning in some of the hotter countries. In every country, skin cancer and AIDS are now widely recognized to be tourism-related diseases.

However, health concerns are also an opportunity for our sectors as we can see from the growth of leisure facilities within hotels, the resurgence of many spa resorts and the opening of numerous health farms. They have also provided new opportunities for caterers to develop new menus and themed restaurants.

Lastly are **environmental issues** which again represent both threats and opportunities for our sectors. The threats relate to concerns over what tourism can do to the physical environment in particular, such as high-rise development in coastal resorts and all the waste generated by hotels from water to packaging materials. These concerns might theoretically result in consumers rejecting organizations that they believe are involved in harming the environment. There is also a danger that governments will legislate if public concern reaches a serious level. Much of the industry is therefore currently engaged in attempting to regulate its own behaviour to prevent these threats becoming reality.

The opportunities lie in the fact that many consumers in some countries will pay a premium price for a more environmentally friendly product or will show brand loyalty to a company which it believes shows a responsible attitude towards the environment. A frequently quoted single example from the hospitality sector is the Hotel Ariston in Milan.

Again, if we consider these three issues on a **European level** we can see that there are substantial differences between individual European countries. **Crime**, for example, is not perceived to be on any significant scale in Scandinavia, even in the capital cities. Conversely, in Russia, for example, crime against tourists is almost an accepted part of life.

There are also situations in Europe where certain nationalities develop a reputation for criminal activities they perpetrate as tourists, rather than they themselves suffering from criminal activities. An example of this is the reputation which – rightly or wrongly – British 'lager louts' have in the coastal regions of Spain.

Across Europe there are also large variations in what is considered criminal activity that needs to be suppressed by the authorities. In cities like Amsterdam, for instance, organized prostitution is not only tolerated, but it has almost become an accepted part of the tourism product, just another aspect of the city's heritage. Meanwhile, in other European countries, prostitution is perceived as a serious problem to be actively discouraged.

When we move on to look at **health issues**, there are also large national variations. Again, Scandinavia is seen to be a place with few of the health risks outlined earlier, while countries like Russia are seen to be relatively much less healthy.

Finally, concern over **environmental issues** is far more highly developed in the countries of Northern and Central Europe, than those in Southern and Eastern Europe, generally. Maybe this reflects the fact that the former were industrialized and urbanized relatively early and so have had to face the resulting problems for longer. There are also variations between countries in terms of what are considered to be the most important environmental issues. In some it is industrial pollution while in others it is waste and recycling. Wildlife protection is a major political issue in some countries and of little significance in others.

Interestingly, in the three issues we have focused on here, there appears to be something of a division in Europe, between North and South, and East and West.

If we look at these issues on a **global scale**, what is instantly clear is that the differences within Europe appear minor compared to those between Europe and the rest of the world. As regards **crime**, for instance, there is no country in Europe where street crime and random killings reach the level found in many cities in the USA, while levels of assault and robbery in the street come nowhere near those found in many cities in Africa and South America. On the other hand, there are regions of the world where the level of casual street crime in Europe might appear high, such as much of the Middle East.

In terms of **health**, the differences are even more dramatic, with large areas of Africa and Asia subject to the risk of malaria, yellow fever, hepatitis, typhoid and cholera. However, again, there are also countries as healthy or even healthier than Europe as a whole, for example Canada.

In relation to **environmental issues**, there are also some variations. In some countries rampant development is the order of the day, with little concern for the environment. Examples of this include the Amazonian rain forest in South America and some of the newly industrialized countries of South East Asia. However, there are also many examples of countries with a strong environmental ethos outside Europe, like Canada.

Of these three factors, the one which has the most significance for the link between Europe and the rest of the world is perhaps health. Many people in Europe who can afford long-haul holidays are undoubtedly deterred from doing so because of the fear of ill-health or the need to have inoculations. However, as we have seen in the case of Florida, criminal attacks on tourists can result in short-term reductions in the number of Europeans willing to visit the place where these attacks took place.

Emergence of subcultures

Lastly, there are the subcultures. These are interesting because many of them appear to cross national boundaries. It is therefore largely irrelevant to seek to divide them into national and European level factors, as we have done elsewhere in this section. These subcultures include:

- 'Euro-students' who go to other countries to study;
- animal rights campaigners;
- teenage consumers;
- Internet users;
- participants in fashionable sports such as snow-boarding.

Three points can be made about these subcultures in relation to marketing, as follows:

- Each subculture is reflected in lifestyles, so that when targeting these market segments marketers need to adopt a lifestyle-based approach to their marketing.
- Most of these subcultures are dominated by younger people.
- They are all found in all or most countries of Europe to a greater or lesser extent. Perhaps these subcultures are the forerunners of the much-vaunted 'pan-European consumer'.

The first four groups listed earlier all have a relevance to marketing in our sectors. 'Euro-students' are major customers for packages such as the 'Inter-Rail' scheme, while animal rights campaigners are a threat to some types of visitor attraction, like zoos or bullfights. Teenage consumers are increasingly being offered the chance to take holidays separately from their parents, usually based on activities or special interests. Internet users may be the first to start using home-based new technology to access tourism products, thus bypassing the travel agent. The final group constitutes a niche market for the growing range of activities and special interest holidays.

However, it is also interesting to note that most of these subcultures probably originated outside Europe, particularly in the USA. Perhaps they are thus not a result of the development of a 'Euro-youth' subculture, but rather are evidence of the growing American global power in the media and consumerism.

Technological factors

The last of the four macro-environmental factors that influence the business environment of tourism, leisure and hospitality is also the one for which national boundaries are the least relevant. It could be argued that new technology is the key to the growth of the 'global village', which is making national boundaries appear less and less important for industries. This is clearly the case in tourism where technology is a catalyst for globalization. This is partly because the cost of developing these technologies is so great that cooperation between major national corporations in different countries is required, while the developments in communication technology are making communication on a global scale easier all the time.

We will, therefore, simply discuss each of the most significant technological developments and their implications for tourism, leisure and hospitality marketing. They can be divided into several categories, namely:

- operational technologies;
- communication technologies;
- transport technologies;
- product technologies.

Operational technologies

These include:

- **Computer reservation systems**. These are becoming ever more sophisticated. At one time most related just to the product of one company such as an airline or a hotel chain. Now there are, increasingly, global distribution systems (GDS) which are worldwide in coverage and link together the products of a large variety of suppliers. This makes it possible to put together ever more complex packages, but it also offers potential for travellers or travel agents to put together tailor-made individual itineraries.
- **Smart cards**. These can store a multitude of information and can be used for a range of purposes already, even at their current relatively low level of sophistication. They can function as keys to help guests gain access to hotels and individual bedrooms. In addition, airlines are experimenting with their use instead of tickets. For example, in May 1995, Lufthansa began such an experiment on their Frankfurt–

Berlin route. Both adaptations could reduce costs for organizations in terms of staff and ticket-writing.

- **Computer databases**. These can, increasingly, handle more and more data, so that marketing messages can be targeted more precisely to various target markets.
- **Computer-based management information systems**. These provide managers with up-to-date information on matters as diverse as stock levels, visitor numbers, financial performance and guests' tastes and preferences.
- **Food production and service technologies**. These are being utilized to reduce labour input and thus hold down costs.

Communication technologies

Tourism, in particular, is beginning to exploit these technologies. They include the following:

- **Multi-media systems**. Examples such as CD-ROM can give consumers direct access to three-dimensional images – and sounds – in relation to tourism products. In theory, therefore, a guest might call up an image of a resort that a tour operator is featuring, and then go on to study an image of the beach. They would then look at images of the hotel facilities such as the restaurant and swimming pool. Finally, they would look at the interior of the specific room they would be allocated, and the view from the window. In this way, the visitor would have realistic expectations and this should lead to less complaints from those consumers who believe that they have been misled by the traditional brochure.

  Some operators, such as Thomas Cook, are beginning to install multi-media kiosks in some branches, but multi-media systems are also, increasingly, being bought by people for installation in their own homes.
- **Interactive television**. In future this will allow people to not only receive information via their television, but will give them an opportunity to take action in response to this information. In other words, a consumer will be able to call up information on their television screen and then make a booking via the television.
- **The Internet**. This and other data services provided through computers can give consumers access to information on a worldwide scale.
- **Minitel**. The well-established Minitel system in France is an interactive system linked to the telephone. People in France who have this system in their home call up information on rail services and holidays, for example, and then make direct bookings via the small computer which is linked to their telephone. Such systems may become available in more and more European countries.

All four of these developments in communication technologies could have a dramatic effect on the distribution chain in tourism and hospitality. They give the consumer the potential ability to access information and book directly without the need for a marketing intermediary.

Amongst the areas where they could be used are the following:

- reserving theatre tickets;
- booking a hotel room;
- booking a package holiday.

The relevant intermediaries, including theatre booking agencies and travel agents, could thus be eliminated from the transactions. This has attractions for the theatres, hotels and tour operators who would no longer have to pay commission – usually around 10% – to these intermediaries. Thus they could either reduce their prices and/or increase their profit margins.

However, this scenario could fail to materialize for a number of reasons, including:

- intermediaries responding by emphasizing personal service and reducing commission rates;
- consumer resistance to using the new technologies;
- those who control the technologies deciding not to feature their competitors' information to prevent potential competition.

It is interesting to note that both the operational and communication technologies we have discussed could have another dramatic impact on the distribution of products in tourism specifically. Many of them, such as smart cards, will also increasingly be introduced by companies in other industries – food and clothes retailers and banks, for example. It is possible that these latter types of enterprise will increasingly use these technologies to begin to act as travel agents selling package holidays. Thus, in the future, the premises of such a business may offer the ultimate package holiday – the consumer may not only book the holiday there using a smart card and a multi-media system, for example, but may also purchase their clothes, sun tan creams and insurance as part of the package, using credit offered by the store or bank.

The last type of communication technology we will consider relates specifically to the business travel sector. It is argued that a number of ongoing technological innovations will reduce the need for business travel. These include:

- e-mail;
- video conferencing;
- computer conferencing.

However, while these will undoubtedly have an influence on business travel, they are unlikely to reduce it dramatically, given that business travel is thought important for two main reasons, namely:

- it is seen as a 'reward' by staff, or as a 'perk of the job'

- it is often essential for sales people to meet their customers face to face and socialize before the latter will agree to purchase.

Transport technologies

These have always been important, particularly to tourism, and at present the following seem to be the main relevant areas of innovation:

- **Fast trains, particularly the French TGV**. The introduction of a train capable of covering 500 kilometres in an hour will lead to increased competition on short-haul routes in Europe for airlines and could also stimulate the weekend break market, where speed is of the essence as time is limited. This fast train network will spread across Europe over time, until we have a pan-European fast rail service network.
- **The development of larger and faster aircraft**. These could reduce per capita costs and thus prices, while also making longer-haul destinations more accessible for short break holidays.
- **In-car navigation systems**. These will provide tourists travelling in a foreign land with a printout of a route to their chosen destination. They will also help motorists avoid traffic jams.
- **Faster ferries**, both conventional and those based on newer methods of propulsion and innovative design. These may speed up loading times which should make them more competitive.

Product technologies

In terms of product technologies the most important current development must be the field of **virtual reality**. Some people are claiming that virtual reality could destroy tourism and hospitality by taking away people's motivation to travel for pleasure. The argument is that virtual reality will offer people such incredible simulated experiences in their own homes, or in high street arcades and centres, that they will have no desire to travel to undergo the authentic experience.

Virtual reality uses sensations that are transmitted through gloves, helmets and complete suits to give the consumer a multi-media sensual experience that mimics reality. Thus, in the future, the consumer may be able to enjoy a range of virtual reality experiences, including:

- 'attending' a Pavarotti concert any night you want rather than having to wait until a concert is scheduled near your home town;
- feeling the sun on your face and hearing the waves lapping on the shore as you lounge on a beach on a deserted Pacific island
- enjoying a meal in a three-star Michelin restaurant in your own home.

The list of potential virtual reality experiences is almost endless.

But virtual reality is not only striving to be as good as reality, it aims to be even better than the real thing. For example, its interactive nature means you can do things you would never be allowed to do in real life, such as pilot a jet fighter or shoot someone in a gunfight in a Western saloon. It also allows you to be good at activities that in the real world are beyond your abilities, such as playing football for your national side or windsurfing when you cannot swim or are frightened of water.

Some have even suggested that virtual reality could be a valuable tool in the development of sustainable tourism. Even if people can be given a good simulated experience at home they may choose not to seek the equivalent authentic experience. In other words, a virtual reality trip around Venice may deter someone from making the trip to the real place. This could be a good way of reducing numbers of visitors to sites and cities that are already receiving too many.

However, this ignores the factors that motivate trips which would not be satisfied by virtual reality substitutes, namely:

- social contact with local people and other tourists;
- the status value attached to visiting the authentic place.

It is also true to say that virtual reality is currently only at a very early stage in its development, such that it is still dominated, perhaps, by products aimed at younger males. While visual images are often good, the other senses are not well catered for, particularly smell and touch. It is largely, too, more of an individual than a group activity. Nevertheless, virtual reality will be both a serious threat and a huge opportunity for the tourism and leisure sectors in the years to come.

In addition to virtual reality, there are other product technologies which are influencing tourism, leisure and hospitality, including:

- improved in-flight entertainment systems in aircraft;
- increases in our ability to create 'artificial environments' such as the domes at Center Parcs, which may one day lead to underwater holiday centrés, for example;
- new sports based on technological innovations.

Technology, as we said earlier, is truly transnational, and therefore will potentially influence the future for all European organizations. However, the pace and nature of technological change may vary significantly between European countries.

THE MACRO-ENVIRONMENT AND TOURISM, LEISURE AND HOSPITALITY ORGANIZATIONS

There is no doubt that the key factors in the macro-environment for different types of organizations within the European tourism, leisure and hospitality sectors are different. This is illustrated in Table 7.1, which outlines what the authors consider to be key issues in the field of macro-environmental threats and opportunities for six types of organizations. One threat and opportunity only are listed for each organization, although in reality there are clearly a number for each.

While this is a highly simplistic and generalized picture, a number of points do emerge, including the following:

- Some factors are highly relevant to more than one sector, for example virtual reality.
- A factor which is an opportunity for one type of organization (recession for a mass market, low price tour operator) can be a threat for others (such as international hotel chains). Likewise new communication technologies may allow tour operators to bypass travel agents so that they represent opportunities for the former but threats for the latter.
- Some factors can be both potential threats and opportunities for an organization. Virtual reality could thus be a threat for a theme park if it were introduced by competitors, but an opportunity if the theme park were first to introduce it. Whether a factor is an opportunity or a threat, therefore, is often a function of how the organization responds.

Clearly, Table 7.1 is highly subjective, but hopefully it does give an impression of the diversity of the business environment and the different ways in which the environment might affect different types of organization in tourism, leisure and hospitality.

We conclude the section with some general comments about the macro-environment in relation to tourism, leisure and hospitality organizations.

Firstly, it appears there may well be a difference between organizations in leisure and those in tourism or hospitality. Many leisure organizations are affected mainly by factors that are mostly domestic in nature, rather than is the case for most tourism and hospitality organizations where international factors are often very significant. For example, in terms of political factors, the most important for leisure organizations is probably domestic government policy on health and local government spending, for example. The most important factors for most tourism and hospitality organizations, on the other hand, will probably be international, for example the price of raw materials such as food and fuel which are sourced from abroad, global distribution systems and the impact of political change in other countries on market demand. Secondly, there are differences between the three sectors in terms of which factor is of most significance. For leisure organizations, social and economic factors such as health concerns and recession are very important, while for tourism and hospitality political factors and technological change are of crucial significance.

There are clearly also differences in the macro-environment based on other criteria, such as whether organizations are in the public, private or voluntary sector and their size. The macro-environment also clearly can vary dramatically between European countries, particularly in relation to the political, social and economic factors.

Table 7.1 Key issues in the macro-environment by different sectors

Type of organization	Political factors		Economic factors		Social factors		Technology factors	
	Opportunities	Threats	Opportunities	Threats	Opportunities	Threats	Opportunities	Threats
Local authority sports centre	Government policies to encourage people to exercise for the sake of their health	Government control on local authority expenditure	Economic recession	Growth of private sports centres and health farms	Growing concern over health	If medical opinion changes on the health benefits of exercise	New types of exercise equipment	Virtual reality
Private sector theme park	Reduction in corporate taxation	Stronger health and safety at work legislation	Growth in disposable income	Rise in interest rates	Increase in young people as a proportion of the population in some countries	Reduction in young people as a proportion of the population in some countries	Virtual reality	Virtual reality
International hotel chain	Political change in Eastern Europe, the Middle East and Southern Africa	Strong labour protection laws in the countries in which they hope to expand	Low interest rates	Recession	Environmental concerns about design, waste disposal, pollution, energy	Environmental concerns about design, waste disposal, pollution, energy	New food production service systems	New communication technologies such as e-mail, computer- and video-conferencing

Organization								
Major European airline	Deregulation and liberalization of the skies	Increased competition due to deregulation and liberalization of the skies	Reductions in fuel prices	Recession	Growing number of women business travellers	Environmental concerns over noise and pollution	New operational technologies, such as smart cards	New communication technologies, such as e-mail and computer- and video-conferencing Virtual reality
Major mass-volume, low-price tour operator	Single European currency	Further European Commission consumer protection legislation	Recession	Major fluctuations in currency exchange rates	Growth in the number of students and families who are likely to be major customers for their products	Fear of skin cancer and AIDS in mass-tourism destinations	Interactive television which will allow them to sell directly to consumers	
Small independent travel agency	Reductions in corporate taxation	Single European Currency which will reduce currency transactions on which commission is earned	Rise in disposable income	Recession	Growing number of older people who may want to buy high value holidays such as cruises	Any trend towards more independent travel	New global distribution systems installed in agencies	New global distribution systems accessible directly to consumers in their own home

It remains to be seen whether global trends and the actions of the European Commission will create a more homogeneous European macro-environment in the future.

Meanwhile, it is time to switch our attention to the micro-environment.

THE MICRO-ENVIRONMENT

We will consider the micro-environment under five headings as follows:

- the nature and structure of the organization;
- suppliers;
- marketing intermediaries;
- existing customers;
- competitors;

These elements are important controls or influences in the micro-environment of organizations in tourism, leisure and hospitality.

Each of the five elements will be considered in relation to the following questions:

- How do they vary between organizations in the tourism, leisure and hospitality sectors?
- How, if at all, do they differ between different European countries?

The nature and structure of the organization

There are a number of aspects of the nature and structure of the organization which have a direct bearing on its marketing function. These include:

- The range of products the organization offers, the market segments at what they are targeted, and the way in which the marketing function is organized to communicate with these markets.
- Whether the organization is in the public, private or voluntary sector. Stereotypically, public sector organizations have a complex set of objectives rather than simply commercial success. Local authorities, for example, often use tourism as a tool for urban regeneration or development, and as a way of improving infrastructure and amenities which are also of benefit to residents. They are controlled by politicians rather than by managers and boards of directors so that their decisions are often made for political reasons.

  Private sector companies tend to have a more straightforward set of objectives, namely profit maximization and increasing market share. Decisions are usually taken on the basis of financial considerations such as the reduction of costs and increasing income.

  For voluntary sector bodies, tourism is often a means to an end. In the case of the National Trust in the UK, for instance, the money generated from tourism is used to further the conservation work which is carried out by the National Trust. It is therefore often a matter of these bodies encouraging tourism, but not when it may conflict with the organization's main interest, which in this case is conservation.

The sector in which an organization exists is open to influence and control so it is appropriate to include it in a section on the micro-environment. For example, some local authorities in the UK, while in the public sector, have transferred their museums to voluntary sector trusts. A number have also placed the promotion of their area as a destination in the hands of private sector companies which they have set up with commercial partners. In both cases, the main reason for this has been to remove them from the bureaucratic restrictions that public ownership can entail.

- The structure of the organization, in other words whether it is monolithic or is subdivided into smaller units. If the latter, these units might be based on functional factors, as is the case with strategic business units (SBUs) for example, or geographical factors such as regions or countries. The choice of structure has implications for the nature of the product and the marketing function as well as the market.

  Also important in relation to this subject is the power of different departments within the organization, and whether or not it is a marketing centred organization or one where the finance department is all powerful and marketing is merely a small separate department.

- The decision-making structure of the organization is also highly significant from a marketing point of view. Sometimes decision-making is highly centralized, with all major decisions being taken by a head office that could be thousands of kilometres away from the place where the impact of the decision will be felt. Such geographical isolation of decision-making can lead to problems where centralized decisions do not make sufficient allowance for cultural differences between places. There is undoubtedly a trend towards decentralized decision-making so that decisions are taken locally by people who live in the area. While this can be very good from a local morale point of view, it can also lead to fragmentation.

- Corporate culture is an important factor and has been receiving increasing attention from management theorists in recent years. Cultures can vary in a range of ways, including between the following characteristics:
  - entrepreneurial or bureaucratic;
  - aggressive or defensive;
  - dynamic or inert;
  - risk-taking or cautious;
  - outward-focused or inward-focused;
  - backward-looking or forward-looking.

  Most corporate cultures, of course, fall somewhere between these extremes.

Table 7.2 The old manager and the new manager

The old manager	The new manager
• believes in ad hoc tactical marketing	• believes in strategic marketing planning
• practises crisis management	• practises forward planning
• makes decisions based on judgement, experience and intuition	• makes decisions based on marketing research and factual information
• does not delegate very much to subordinates	• constantly delegates appropriate work to colleagues wherever possible
• sees themself as leader, making all the key decisions and issuing orders	• sees themself as team manager, working with the rest of the team and managing through consensus
• believes in experience rather than eductational qualifications and training	• believes in experience and educational qualifications and training
• responds to financial problems by cutting costs	• responds to financial pressures by trying to boost income

- Linked to corporate culture is the issue of management styles which also vary. These are often characterized by the terms 'old' manager and 'new' manager. The main differences between both types of manager that are relevant to the marketing function are outlined in Table 7.2. This is clearly an over simplistic view and most managers fall between these two extreme positions. It is also possible for someone to be an 'old' manager on one issue and a 'new' manager on another.

The nature and structure of organizations does vary between tourism, leisure and hospitality, and between countries. However, great differences are also seen between organizations in one sector within a single individual country.

Nevertheless, there are a few generalizations we can make, which, although over-simplistic, do contain an element of truth. Firstly, the organizations in the private sector – e.g. hotels, tour operators and privately owned airlines – do tend to be more entrepreneurial and dynamic than those in the public sector, including municipal tourist offices, state airlines and sports centres. Secondly, management decision-making strategies and styles are, perhaps, more centralized and formal in Southern Europe than in Northern Europe, although this situation is slowly changing.

The suppliers

The relationship between a producer and its suppliers is crucial to the quality of the final product. This is true whether the suppliers provide goods or services to the organization. The supply function also influences the organization in terms of its costs, and thus its pricing policies and, ultimately, its profit margins.

In tourism, leisure and hospitality, links with suppliers are becoming ever closer due to two main factors, namely:

- The growing emphasis on quality, where the quality of the final product is largely dependent on the quality of goods and services provided by suppliers. For example, tour operators are reliant on the quality of rooms allocated to their clients by hotels while restaurant meal quality is partly dictated by the quality of the ingredients chefs receive from their suppliers.
- Product liability legislation which makes producers responsible for the product they sell, including any defect in it that may be the responsibility of the organization's suppliers. Under the EC Package Travel Directive, UK tour operators would be held legally responsible for the death of a client in a fire in a Spanish hotel if this were due to negligence on the part of a hotelier. Likewise, a restaurateur could be prosecuted in the UK under the Food Safety Act 1991 if guests suffered food poisoning due to a meal served in the restaurant, even if the fault were with the ingredients provided by the suppliers.

For these reasons, more and more organizations are seeking to develop closer and closer links with suppliers, to enhance product quality and reduce the risk of legal action.

At one end of the scale this can mean tight controls and occasional inspections by the staff of the organization. However, in extreme cases, it may mean organizations take over their suppliers through vertical integration, or simply set up operations so that they can supply themselves. Hence some hotel chains now have their food production facilities to produce ingredients and meals for their hotel restaurants.

In some cases, vertical integration can be a defensive tactic in a field where particular suppliers are essential. For example, tour operators often buy up or establish their own charter airlines so they are not dependent for flight seats on other carriers who may be owned by their competitors. For if a tour operator cannot obtain seats on flights, there will be no product for them to sell.

However, we must recognize that the supplier network in many tourism, leisure and hospitality organizations, is incredibly complex, as can be seen from Table 7.3. These networks can incorporate dozens or even hundreds of suppliers, large and small, at home and abroad.

There can be differences in supplier–producer relations between countries, based either on law or custom and practice. For example, in some countries bills are expected to be settled immediately while in other countries, payment is often made some time after the goods and services have been provided.

The supply chain in tourism, leisure and hospitality can be very complex and individual organizations can function both as producers and suppliers simultaneously. For example, a resort hotel is a producer in relation to some customers, while for a tour operator putting together a package, it is just another supplier.

Table 7.3 Suppliers – a private hotel and a local authority museum

A private hotel	A local authority museum
• Food and drink suppliers, both raw ingredients and pre-prepared meals and drinks	• Other departments of the local authority who supply financial, personnel and technical services to the museum
• Launderers	• Consultants who advise the museum on specialist matters
• Uniform suppliers	• Food and drink suppliers for the catering outlets
• Builders	• Souvenir products for sale in retail outlets
• Landscape contractors and gardeners	• Dealers from whom they buy artefacts
• Professional advisers such as accountants	• Members of the public who donate artefacts to the museum free of charge
• The schools, colleges and professional bodies that train their personnel	• The schools, colleges and professional bodies that train their personnel
• Equipment suppliers in relation to kitchens, for instance	• Contractors who make exhibition cases
• Furnishers, in terms of chairs and beds for example	• Equipment suppliers who provide tills for the catering or retail outlets, for example
• Interior decorators	• Furnishers, in relation to the museum displays and its offices
• Printers who produce their promotional literature	• Printers who provide their guides and catalogues and promotional literature
• Computer and telecommunications companies that install and maintain computers	• Stationers
• Stationers	

Given that all three sectors provide a service rather than a physical product, the difference between suppliers and product can be blurred. Services tend to give the user more freedom in terms of how they can use the service than would be the case with a manufactured product, which tends to have perhaps less potential ways in which it can be customized by the consumer. It is therefore possible to argue that, in relation to a consumer at least, a hotel is less of a producer of a final product and more of a supplier who provides the raw material from which the guests create their own individual product or experience.

Clearly the area of suppliers is a complex matter in the tourism, leisure and hospitality sectors.

Marketing intermediaries

The same complexity is true also for marketing intermediaries, namely those organizations which provide the interface between the producer and its customers.

Interest in marketing intermediaries has also been growing in recent years in tourism, leisure and hospitality, for the same reasons as was the case with supplier relationships, namely with regard to:

- quality, given that the messages given to potential customers by marketing intermediaries about the organization's products will affect the market image of the product;
- product liability legislation, by which producers may be held accountable in law for misleading representations of their product, through the EC Package Travel Directive, for example, in the case of tour operators.

Many tourism, leisure and hospitality organizations use an enormous range of marketing intermediaries, through both formal and informal relationships. Figure 7.1 illustrates the range of marketing intermediaries that may be used by a large chain-owned hotel.

As the diagram illustrates, most of the links with marketing intermediaries are two-way, or at least they should be, for they should also provide information on consumer feedback for the hotel. However, Figure 7.1 leaves out one vitally important set of marketing intermediaries, namely past customers. There is much research to show that in tourism, leisure and hospitality, many people make purchase decisions based on word-of-mouth recommendations from other people or on their own past experience.

Marketing intermediaries will vary depending on the type of customer being considered. Most business travellers are reached through their employers and specialist business travel agents, for example, while package tourists are communicated with through travel agents. Independent travellers, on the other hand, may rely heavily on tourist information centres and the media.

There are some differences between the intermediaries used by leisure organizations and by those in hospitality and tourism. The main difference appears to be that those used by leisure organizations tend to be much more local than those used by tourism and hospitality organizations. This may reflect the fact that leisure products often have a much more local market than their hospitality and tourism counterparts. Therefore, while leisure products such as local authority sports centres use local newspapers, their neighbourhood hotel may be using nationally distributed directories, and airlines will be making use of national newspapers in other countries.

There are also some national differences in relation to the use of certain types of marketing intermediaries. For example, in France travel agents are not as important as intermediaries for tourism products as they are in the UK. Likewise, while the travel media is an increasingly important intermediary in the UK, it is as yet of little significance in Greece. For example, although all four main television channels in the UK have a regular programme featuring holidays, there is apparently no such programme on any Greek channel.

As we noted at the beginning of this section, organizations can both be marketing intermediaries and use marketing intermediaries themselves at one and the same time. For example, a tour operator can be an intermediary for a hotel, but also needs intermediaries itself. This

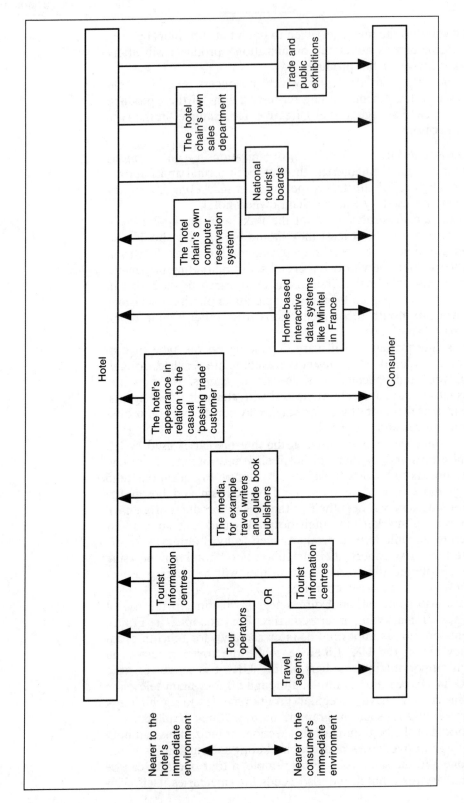

Figure 7.1 Marketing intermediaries used by hotels owned by major chains.

also illustrates that there can be more than one layer of intermediaries in other words, a hotel's message may well reach consumers via both tour operators and then the travel agents which are used by the operator.

Finally, the degree of control and influence an organization can exercise over its intermediaries does vary dramatically. For example, a hotel has far more influence over the way it is promoted by the company's own sales people than it does over guide books where everything is based on objective inspections.

Existing customers

Existing customers are an important element in the micro-environment of organizations in tourism, leisure and hospitality because the organization can influence them in ways which can enhance the effectiveness of its marketing activity. These ways include:

- impressing first-time visitors to a theme park, for example, by the quality of product and service offered so that they wish to visit again in the future;
- encouraging satisfied existing customers to persuade their friends and relatives to visit a particular hotel or resort, for instance;
- using incentive schemes to encourage increased use of the organization's products by existing customers. This is the rationale behind the 'Frequent Flyer Programmes' of airlines and the season tickets offered by some attractions;
- obtaining valuable data on the nature of the current market for the organization from existing customers, which can be used to improve either the product, or the way it is marketed, or both.

As these examples illustrate, the relationship between the organization and its customers is a two-way one where both influence each other.

Failure to successfully 'manage' existing customers can cause problems for organizations, particularly those which rely on repeat visits. There are times when the wishes of the existing customers can come into conflict with an organization's desire to attract new customers. For example, removing under-occupied first-class carriages on a train and replacing them with second-class ones because the existing second class accommodation is not adequate may upset the loyal first-class passengers who are regular users. This could lead to them changing their mode of travel to the airlines, with a loss of that premium price business for the railway.

The importance of keeping existing customers happy is summed up by the oft quoted account that while a satisfied customer might tell five people about a product, those who are not satisfied will probably tell 25 people about their dissatisfaction!

Competitors

There is a complex interrelationship between an organization and its competitors. They influence each other in a number of ways including:

- price levels;
- product development;
- distribution systems;
- promotional techniques;
- operational practices;
- corporate structure and culture.

Strategies in relation to competitors vary between organizations. Some aim for market leadership through innovation while others are content to follow where others lead and learn from their mistakes. Some decide to compete on price while others focus on product differentiation. While some organizations seem obsessed by their competitors, others seem unaware that they have any competition!

However, for competition to be relevant there has to be competition in the market and that is not true in some sectors of tourism, leisure and hospitality. Examples include:

- the European scheduled airline market where, in spite of the European Commission's 'liberalization' of the market, there is still not true and full competition. This is partly because many airlines are still in the ownership of the state and receive large public subsidies;
- local authority leisure provision which is limited by local government boundaries so that one authority will not offer a product in the area of a neighbouring authority. However, there can be limited competition from commercial sector operators;
- there can also be informal price-fixing in sectors such as hotels in some resorts and urban centres, for instance.

Finally, even if a market is competitive, it is not always easy to identify precisely who its competitors are. A theme park, let us say Parc Asterix in France, could be said to have a myriad of potential competitors, including:

- all other theme parks in the country (Disneyland Paris, and Futuroscope, for example) and even theme parks in adjacent countries such as De Efteling in the Netherlands;
- other attractions in the Ile-de-France which are aimed at a similar market, namely families. These might include special events like travelling fairs and circuses or permanent attractions such as La Villette;
- activities which appeal to families, although they are not formal attractions, and provide opportunities for them to spend their leisure time and disposable income. Such activities might include eating out, strolling in the park or even playing in the garden or on computer games at home.

Furthermore, an organization might have different competitors for different market segments. For instance, Alton Towers may compete against Blackpool Pleasure Beach for the custom of young single adults, while in the school trip market the main competitors may be museums and heritage centres.

THE MICRO-ENVIRONMENT AND NATIONAL DIFFERENCES

There are some striking national differences in relation to micro-environmental factors. Where they do exist, they are often seen in the following fields:

- management styles and decision-making with structures which are more formal in some countries, like Spain perhaps, than in Scandinavian countries like Sweden, for example. However, this difference is perhaps lessening as modern theories on management style gain broad acceptance across Europe;
- some elements of the supply chain where differences may reflect differences in contract law and business practice;
- in relation to some forms of distribution or marketing intermediaries, such as the home-based Minitel system in France which is not available in many countries;
- the issue of competition between countries with different levels of state intervention in the market. The UK, for example, has consistently over recent years reduced its role in the ownership and marketing of rail travel and air transport, while in other countries rail operators are still totally state controlled and the national airlines are still subsidized by the government.

In areas like competition, suppliers and marketing intermediaries, action by the European Commission is slowly homogenizing some of the features of the micro-environment, specifically within the member states of the European Union.

THE MICRO-ENVIRONMENT – A GLOBAL PERSPECTIVE

Interestingly, some aspects of the micro-environment are being influenced by forces outside Europe, including:

- the writings of American management theory researchers, such as Tom Peters, on corporate culture and structure
- Japanese theories on supply chain management;
- developments elsewhere in the world, such as the deregulation of the US airline industry in the 1980s which is providing some lessons for the liberalization of the European air travel market.

THE LINK BETWEEN THE MACRO- AND THE MICRO-ENVIRONMENT

There are clear links between the macro- and the micro-environment. A few examples will illustrate this point adequately, as follows:

- Corporate culture and ideas on management styles and organizational structures are often influenced by social and cultural changes such as the growing role of women in business and demographic changes.
- Technological developments are often a means by which some organizations can seek to gain an advantage over their competitors.
- Problems with the relationship between suppliers and producers and the need to protect existing customers can lead to political action in the form of legislation, hence the EC Package Travel Directive which was designed to protect consumers and make both suppliers and producers liable for the product they sell.
- Economic recession can change the basis of competition in a market when price becomes more important, and can also make organizations more concerned about building brand loyalty amongst their existing customers. It is often more cost-effective to do this than to try tempting people to become new customers in a very competitive market.

CONCLUSIONS

The European business environment is so complex and diverse that the drawing of all-encompassing conclusions is neither desirable or possible. The authors will therefore limit themselves to some observations.

- Any picture of the European business environment is, like the one presented in this chapter, by definition dated even on the day when the book is published. The macro-environment in particular is changing dramatically at present, particularly in relation to political change and technological innovation. We may simply be living through an era of rapid change and soon the pace may slacken; on the other hand perhaps, the business environment of today is the shape of things to come and rapid change is going to be the order of the day in the future.
- At the moment, business environments, particularly the macro-environment, also vary in many ways between different European countries. However, within the European Union, there are forces at work which are bringing them closer together. Nevertheless, as far as tourism, leisure and hospitality are concerned, it is probably still a case of the business environments of Europe rather than the European business environment.
- There are subtle differences between the business environment of tourism and hospitality organizations on the one hand, and leisure

organizations on the other. However, overall, there are probably more differences between organizations based on their size and type of ownership rather than based on to which of these three sectors they belong.

- There are many factors at play in the European business environment which have an impact outside Europe. The actions of European tourism, leisure and hospitality organizations are also affecting the business environment in non-European countries.
- Many of the factors in the European business environment of tourism, leisure and hospitality organizations are also influencing other sectors of the economy. They are particularly relevant to industries like food manufacturing and retailing, for example, or even education. In some of these other sectors the concept of a totally European business environment is perhaps nearer to realization than it is in our sectors.

These last two points are particularly important for we should never forget that tourism, leisure and hospitality are global activities, and are part of the broader consumer society as a whole.

Having set the scene and dressed the stage in this chapter, it is now time to look at the main tools of the marketer, the four Ps or the marketing mix. It is the way these tools, or props, are used by the marketers, or actors, that determines whether the marketing activity, or play, will be a success with the consumer, or audience.

DISCUSSION POINTS AND ESSAY QUESTIONS

1. Discuss the current impact of European Commission policies and directives on tourism, leisure and hospitality in Europe, and examine whether or not its influence is likely to grow in the future.
2. Evaluate the factors in the macro- and micro-environment which have encouraged some tourism, leisure and hospitality organizations to adopt strategies involving vertical integration.
3. Discuss what you consider will be the three most important factors in the macro-environment over the next five years for **one** of the following organizations:

   (a) Center Parcs UK;
   (b) TUI;
   (c) Accor;
   (d) Burger King;
   (e) Port Aventura;
   (f) Iberia.

EXERCISE Choose a specific organization within **one** of the following sectors:

- tour operation;
- airline;
- accommodation;
- arts;
- fast food.

For your chosen organization, produce a model of its current business environment, including both its macro- and micro-environment.

Bearing in mind its current policies together with trends in the sector and the world as a whole, produce another model of what you believe its business environment may be in ten years' time.

Finally, on one sheet of A4 paper, you should outline the assumptions and evidence on which you have produced this second model.

CASE STUDIES

You can use one or more of the following Case studies to illustrate some of the points made in this chapter:

1. Political change and hotel development in Eastern Europe;
18. Airtours plc, UK;
19. British Airways, UK;
21. The Victoria and Albert Museum, UK;
25. Accor, France;
28. Center Parcs, UK.

Conclusions to Part 2

Part 2 has explored some of the key issues which form an introduction to the book. It has looked at the issue of whether there is such a thing as a European consumer for tourism, leisure and hospitality organizations. The market and the industries have been explored and the business environment explored.

Some of the major points which have emerged from this part are:

- There are certain trends which are converging in Europe. This is leading to the growth of market segments which appear to cross national boundaries. There is still however, a flourishing set of local customers.
- There are signs that European markets are developing for tourism, leisure and hospitality products and that organizations are developing structures which can exploit these opportunities.
- Tourism, leisure and hospitality are all global phenomena which means that the business environment is extremely complex and difficult to handle.

The marketing mix and tourism, leisure and hospitality

PART

3

This part of the book examines the application of the marketing mix in tourism, leisure and hospitality, in other words the 4 Ps of product, price, place and promotion.

The four chapters will seek to identify similarities and differences in the 4 Ps between tourism, leisure and hospitality. Consideration will be given to how the concept of the marketing mix is changing within tourism, leisure and hospitality in response to a range of factors, including technological developments. Where appropriate, the chapters will also endeavour to highlight where there are differences in the application of the 4 Ps between different countries within Europe.

The four chapters in this part address the following topics:

- **Chapter 8: Product;**
- **Chapter 9: Price;**
- **Chapter 10: Place;**
- **Chapter 11: Promotion.**

Product 8

Key concepts

The main concepts covered in this chapter are:

- the concept of a product;
- core, actual and augmented products;
- the benefits customers seek from products;
- branding;
- product and market positioning;
- product lifecycle;
- new product development.

INTRODUCTION

Clearly, the product is at the heart of all marketing in tourism, leisure and hospitality. It is what gives consumers the benefits they are seeking and its production and delivery is the core activity of all tourism, leisure and hospitality organizations.

The aim of this chapter is to examine the nature and scope of the product in tourism, leisure and hospitality. It will therefore cover the following topics on the supply side:

- the types of products offered in terms of their designed characteristics, both tangible and intangible;
- the service element of the product;
- branding and package positioning.

We will also look at products from the demand point of view, for example in terms of the benefits consumers expect when they purchase a product.

The chapter will then go on to look at the concept of the product lifecycle in terms of its application to tourism, leisure and hospitality products. This will include a discussion of relaunches, together with a number of recent examples.

The process of new product development will then be examined, including the strategic question of whether pan-European products can be developed.

WHAT IS A PRODUCT?

The term 'product' is commonly used and often defined. Many definitions of the word exist, none of which are universally accepted. A large number of them are derived from manufacturing industries:

> A product is anything that can be offered to a market for attention, acquisition, use or consumption that might satisfy a want or need. It includes physical objects, services, persons, places, organizations and ideas.
>
> (Kotler, 1994)

In recent years, the growth of service industries has led to new concepts of product linked to the fact that in most services the product is a a mixture of tangible goods and intangible services. This concept has come to be known as the 'product/service mix' from which other definitions have flowed:

> The product/service mix is the combination of products and services aimed at satisfying the needs of the target market.
>
> (Renaghan, 1981)

Dibb, Simkin, Pride and Ferrell have defined a product as:

> Everything, both favourable and unfavourable, that is received in an exchange. It is a complexity of tangible and intangible attributes, including functional, social, and psychological utilities or benefits. A product can be of an idea, a service, a good or any combination of these three.
>
> (Dibb, Simkin, Pride and Ferrell, 1994)

These definitions again stress the tangible and intangible elements of the product/service mix.

Services are, of course, intangible and are the result of the application of human and mechanical efforts to people or objects. Services are often bought on the basis of promises of satisfaction. The holiday brochure, for example, offers you the promise of exotic locations and luxurious hotels. These promises are often strengthened with symbols. The UK tour operator, Thomson, for example, uses the symbol of a bird in flight to symbolize the idea that the consumer is going to fly away to new and exciting destinations.

There are a number of special characteristics that make services different from products. Most of them relate to the idea that 'services are consumed in the process of their production' (Sasser, Olsen and Wycoff, 1978). A number of factors make the problem of service marketing very different from that of product marketing. The concepts of intangibility, inseparability, perishability and heterogeneity have already been explored in Chapter 1.

These factors mean that the staff involved in producing and delivering the product are part of the product itself. The customer is also an inherent part of the production process.

It also means that service products cannot be standardized. This is very important when it comes to the development of quality management systems. The fact that a service is perishable and cannot be stored means that it is often difficult for the provider to manage the balance between supply and demand. Capacity planning and utilization are therefore vital management tasks.

The intangibility of the service means that the customer cannot inspect the item before purchase. Customers only have a 'feeling' left after consumption of the service. Coupled with this, the service will never be the same for the customer twice. The visitor experience of a restaurant, for example, may differ according to the conditions at different eating occasions.

Service providers do have the advantage of being face to face with the customer. This factor can alleviate some of the added complexities of services marketing if used correctly by the providers.

Work was carried out in the late 1970s and 1980s trying to develop a terminology for service products and there were different views put forward. (See Sasser, Olsen and Wyckoff, 1978; Grönroos, 1980; Eiglier and Langeard, 1981). The academics agreed that all services have different elements, which make up the total item which the customer purchases.

Sasser, Olsen and Wyckoff (1978) explained the concept further by reference to the example of an expensive restaurant. In this case there are goods and services on offer which they defined as:

- the physical items (e.g. food, drink);
- the sensual benefits or explicit services (e.g. taste, aroma, service);
- the psychological benefits or implicit services (e.g. comfort, status).

Tourism, leisure and hospitality products and services have a varying degree of tangible and intangible elements in their 'product-service mix'. Shostack (1977), for example, argues that a fast-food outlet has an equal mix of tangible and intangible elements, whereas an airline has a dominance of intangible elements.

THE THREE LEVELS OF PRODUCT

Kotler (1994) has expanded his original definition of products to include the service elements. He has termed this concept the three levels of the product, as shown in Figure 8.1. This emphasizes the fact that the product planner must think about the product at three levels.

This three level concept tries to explain the fact that the consumer does not just purchase a product, they purchase benefits such as brand names, service elements and after-sales service. The **core product** is what the customer is really buying. It consists of the main benefit or benefits the purchaser identifies as a personal need that will be met by the product. Marketers need to turn the core product into an **actual product**. The actual product will include features, brand name, quality, styling and packaging.

Finally, there is the **augmented product** which includes all the additional services and benefits the customer receives. The augmented product is the 'total product bundle that should solve all the customers' problems, and even some they haven't thought of yet' (Lewis and Chambers, 1989).

This model was developed with the manufacturing company in mind. However, it has been adopted, with modifications, to services, such as visitor attractions by Swarbrooke (1995), as illustrated in Figure 8.2.

Kotler envisages that all the elements of the augmented product are under the control of the producer. Swarbrooke (1995) points out that for service products such as attractions, some of the elements are outside the control of the service deliverer. The weather, for example, is outside the control of a visitor attraction provider, but may have potential positive or negative effects on sales.

The concept of the augmented product has also been developed for hospitality organizations. According to Buttle (1986), every hotel offers the same core product but this is modified and enhanced to make it more attractive to the target market. Competition, he says,

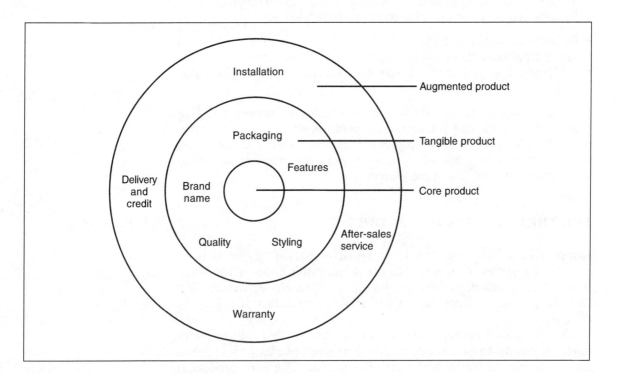

Figure 8.1 The three levels of product.
Source: after Kotler (1994).

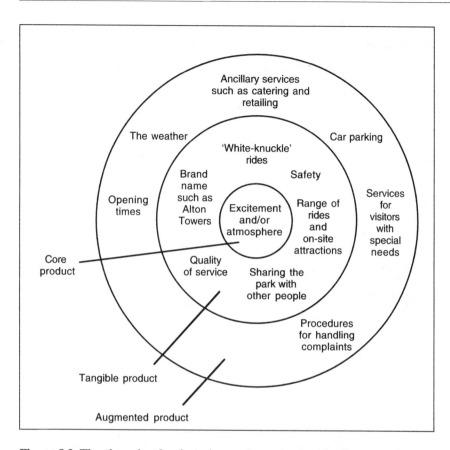

Figure 8.2 The three levels of product – the example of a theme park.
Source: Swarbrooke (1995), after Kotler (1994).

takes place largely at the augmented level. Buttle has also developed a list of ways in which accommodation and food service products are augmented, shown in Table 8.1.

Lewis and Chambers (1989) have also stressed the three levels of product for hospitality products. They talk about formal, core and augmented products, and define the formal product as the thing that the customer thinks they are buying – it is in fact what the customer can easily articulate. In truth, however, it may not be the real underlying reason why the customer is buying the product. They may be covering up their real needs which are much more deep-seated.

THE CONSUMER BENEFIT CONCEPT

Customers who are buying tourism, leisure and hospitality products are buying benefits not products. Bateson (1977) has argued that it is

Table 8.1 Hospitality augmentation

Accommodation	Food and beverage
Reservation system convenience	Speed of food service
Reservation system simplicity	Ordering convenience:
Acknowledgement of reservations	telephone
Lift attendants	advance orders
Room service	order-taking table staff
Standard of housekeeping	Complaints procedures
Courtesy	Advance reservations
Procedures for handling	Reliability of food/beverage
overbooking	quality
Information services	Customer advice on wines
Customer recognition	Provision of special foods
Credit provision	Cooking to order, e.g. steaks
Baggage handling	Acceptance of credit cards
Pet/child care	Variations in portions
Provision for disabled	Home deliveries
Group accommodation	Extent of non-available menu items
Discounts on club referrals, etc.	Fibre/calorie information
Cleaning/laundry	Provision of 'doggy bags'
Courtesy care	Function-catering facilities
Willingness to bill later	Quality of table appointments
	Entertainment
	Privacy/discretion

Source: Buttle (1986).

only through the idea of a consumer benefit that the service concept can be defined. As Bateson says:

> For any firm the 'consumer benefit concept' will be a bundle of functional, effectual and psychological attributes. It is important to separate this consumer benefit concept from the product itself.

The task of the marketer of tourism, leisure and hospitality products and services is to try and understand the benefits which customers seek. This is a complex issue, because different customer groups who purchase the same service may be seeking different benefits. As an example, some of the main benefits sought by groups of customers with different characteristics for a fast-food chain are shown in Table 8.2.

Clearly Table 8.2 is based on stereotyping. Nevertheless the idea of using customer characteristics to speculate on the types of benefits particular groups of customers will seek is a useful tool for the development of products and services.

However, customer characteristics are only half the story. The second factor which influences the benefits sought is the nature of the product itself. This was developed by Swarbrooke (1995) when he looked at certain types of attractions and the main benefits sought as shown below in Table 8.3.

The key to success in the development of tourism, leisure and hospitality products depends on the ability to match the product which is offered with the benefits sought by the customers. The matching of the two is a challenging process.

Table 8.2 Customers for a fast-food chain and the benefits sought

Customer characteristic	Main benefits sought
Young, adventurous personalities	• Excitement • New experience
Fashion-conscious	• Status • Being seen taking part in a fashionable activity
Families with young children	• Entertainment for children • Special events for children • Economy • Reliability
Health-conscious	• Healthy nutritional food • Clean environment
Elderly people	• Reliability • Safety • Economy

Source: Swarbrooke (1995).

Table 8.3 Types of attraction and benefits sought

Type of attraction	Main benefits sought
Theme park	Excitement Variety of on-site attractions Atmosphere The company of other users Value for money Light-hearted fun
Beach	Sun tan Sea bathing Economy Company of others *or* solitude
Cathedral	History Aesthetic pleasure derived from architecture Atmosphere – sense of peace and spirituality
Museum	Learning something new Nostalgia Purchasing souvenirs
Theatre	Entertainment Atmosphere Status
Leisure centre	Exercise Physical challenges and competing against others Status

Source: Swarbrooke (1995).

BRANDING AND PACKAGING

Branding and packaging are part of the product's tangible features that help customers decide which products to buy.

Branding

Kotler (1994) defines a brand as:

> a name, term, symbol or design or combination of them, intended to identify goods or services of one seller or group of sellers and to differentiate them from those of 'competitors'.

Brand names, logos or trade marks encourage people to buy particular products because they give the customers the benefits they are seeking. These benefits may range from familiarity and safety, to status and self-esteem. Branding offers particular advantages to organizations that are marketing services.

Given the intangible nature of services and the potential difficulty of differentiating one service from another, branding provides a significant method for achieving a degree of product differentiation.

Some tourism, leisure and hospitality organizations have developed a long-term branding strategy. Disney, for example, has developed a brand which offers customers a reliable product linking their film, video and leisure products.

There has also been a flurry of service organizations in the tourism, leisure and hospitality industries which have been implementing branding strategies in the last decade. Forte, for example, prior to its takeover by Granada, had developed a strong branding strategy. The company was transformed from the old Trust House Forte name into Forte on the back of a well-developed branding strategy. This allowed the company to develop internationally, which was a key objective of the branding strategy.

Organizations have also tried to use brands to give themselves a perceived improved image with customers. First Choice – the UK-based holiday company – was launched in 1994. This new brand identity was created from the original company Owners Abroad as a result of extensive research with customers. The aim of this rebranding exercise was to improve their image with existing customers and to give them a clear positioning strategy.

The value of established brand names such as Holiday Inn and McDonald's is closely related to the perceptions of consistency and quality which they represent internationally. The disadvantage of branding is that it requires large amounts of expensive advertising. This means that brands tend to be developed by large organizations because they have the necessary money.

Table 8.4 Brands as guarantors of quality in Europe

	Agree (%)	Disagree (%)
Spain	77	9
Italy	74	19
East Germany	66	23
France	58	20
West Germany	55	28
UK	47	41
Netherlands	43	37

Source: Henley Centre/Research International (1991/92).

Branding in Europe

Research has shown that consumers in Europe are expressing a growing desire for brands which are well-known. The Henley Centre/Research International (1991/92) survey in Europe *Frontiers* showed that consumers in European countries thought that 'buying branded articles is best as you can trust the quality'. There were differences, however, between consumers in different countries in Europe which are shown in Table 8.4. Consumers in the south of Europe were more brand loyal than those in the north of Europe.

Branding does therefore seem to offer an organization one way of developing a European or international marketing strategy. A multinational company can sell an identical product in the form of a global brand throughout the sales area. Alternatively, it can make modifications which will take account of local differences in taste. Local brands, although different in name, may also be endowed with corporate values (Wolfe, 1991).

The central question, therefore, is whether an organization marketing across national boundaries should **standardize** their product offering and branding or **customize** it to meet a local set of conditions. This will depend on the type of product which is marketed and the local conditions in the individual countries in which the product is sold.

The standardized approach is characterized by Holiday Inn. The company recognized early on that the Holiday Inn concept and brand could be standardized to offer customers high levels of service on an international basis. The customized approach is characterized by McDonald's. The company appears to have a standardized product on the surface. Despite this, it has had to alter the product to suit individual markets. The company offers beer, for example, in the French market, whereas no alcohol is sold in the UK. Salads are also on sale extensively in the French outlets, unlike the UK. The company has customized their approach within their brand identity.

The customized approach is also used by exclusive service organizations such as luxury hotels.

Table 8.5 Use of branding techniques in tourism, leisure and hospitality organizations – some recent examples

Sector	Examples	Comments
1. Destination	• Spain – 'España, Passion for Life' • The 'English Riviera', Torquay, Brixham and Paignton	Attempt to improve image of Spain Local authority created 'brand' intended to revitalize the market.
2. Accommodation	• Formule 1	Launch of budget sector – Accor
3. Attractions	• Nemesis ride – Alton Towers, Tussaud's Group • Port Aventura	The use of the Nemesis ride as a brand in its own right Launch of new attraction in Spain
4. Transport	• Le Shuttle • Eurostar	Development of the cross-Channel tunnel project
5. Tour operators	• First Choice	Rebranding and relaunch of Owners Abroad

New approaches in branding

There are indications that other sectors of the tourism, leisure and hospitality market are beginning to recognize the value of branding. Some recent examples of the use of branding are shown in Table 8.5. Branding is being used as a marketing technique by an increasing number of tourism, leisure and hospitality organizations.

Packaging

Packaging is very easy to understand in the case of manufactured goods, but what does it mean in the context of services? The answer will depend on what we mean by packaging. Packaging could be defined as the thing which makes it easier for customers to pick up, transport and use the goods.

Packaging in the context of services could therefore include:

• the use of brand names and logos;
• attractive entrances at premises;
• attractive merchandising materials;
• the use of other organizations such as tour operators to sell the product as part of a package.

PRODUCT POSITIONING

One of the key objectives of an organization's marketing strategy must be to create a favourable impression of the organization's products among their target customers. This is achieved by creating a favourable **product position**. It is also often referred to as **market positioning**. Kotler (1994) defines product position as:

> The way the product is defined by consumers on important attributes – the place the product occupies in the consumers' minds relative to competing products.

Market positioning is defined as:

> arranging for a product to occupy a clear, distinctive, and desirable place relative to competing products in the minds of target consumers. Formulating competitive positioning for a product and a detailed marketing mix.

The logic is that if a product is perceived to be exactly the same as that of a competitor then the customer will have no reason to buy or use it. The positioning of a product means that the organization must identify how it is going to offer greater value to chosen segments. This may be by charging lower prices than the competition or, alternatively, it may offer greater value associated with the product.

Effective positioning therefore, involves the organization **differentiating** its products and services in the eyes of the target customers. Dibb, Simkin, Pride and Ferrell (1994) suggest that there is a step-by-step approach which can be used to develop a positioning plan. This approach involves seven key stages as follows:

1. Define the segments in a particular market.
2. Decide which segment (or segments) to target.
3. Understand what the target consumers expect and believe to be the most important when deciding to purchase.
4. Develop a product (or products) which cater specifically for these needs and expectations.
5. Evaluate the positioning and images as perceived by target customers of competing products in the selected market segment (or segments).
6. Select an image which sets the product (or products) apart from the competing products, thus ensuring that the chosen image matches the aspirations of the target customers.
7. Tell target customers about the product (promotion) as well as making it readily available at the right price. This is the development of the marketing mix.

A good example of a positioning strategy in the hospitality industry has been the development of the **budget hotel chains**. In less than a decade, the budget market has become the fastest growing hotel sector in the UK and much of Europe. The UK now boasts nearly 300 units offering budget accommodation and it is estimated that about 460

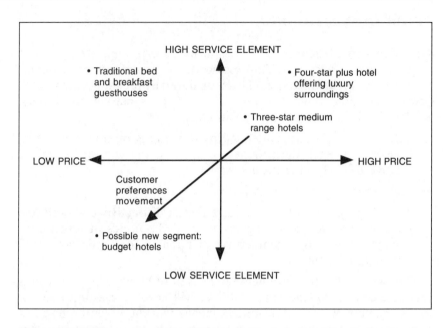

Figure 8.3 Position map of the UK hospitality industry prior to the development of the budget market.

branded budget hotels will be in operation by 1997. The opportunity for budget hotels was first recognized by companies such as Forte and Whitbread. The opportunity could be shown on a positioning map (Figure 8.3) which showed consumer preferences in the UK hospitality market and made predictions about the way these would move.

Research had shown that customer preferences in certain market segments were moving towards a hotel offering a lower service element, but offering accommodation of a reasonable standard and lower price. This was clearly a marketing opportunity. As a result of this, many hotel companies have now entered the budget sector as shown in Table 8.6.

The companies involved in the budget sector are now having to differentiate their products by developing their brands. This is particularly important because Holiday Inn Worldwide entered the UK market in the early 1990s with its own budget brand, Holiday Inn Express.

THE PRODUCT LIFE CYCLE CONCEPT

There is a view that products pass through stages during their lifetime, like people. This is the basic premise of the product lifecycle concept, which was originally developed by marketing academics for manufactured goods.

Figure 8.4 shows the traditional model for the product lifecycle. Table 8.7 illustrates the suggested characteristics and strategic responses at each stage of the lifecycle suggested by Kotler (1994).

There are a number of general points which can be made about the product lifecycle (PLC) concept:

- It is suggested that the product lifecycle curve will be 'S' shaped.
- The product lifecycle curve will comprise four stages which have been termed introduction, growth, maturity and decline.
- Product lifecycles are used to describe the sales behaviour of items, brands, types, lines or classes of products.
- The characteristics of each of the four stages are shown in Table 8.7. The cycle begins with **product innovation** and **development** when an organization finds an acceptable new product idea. The **introduction** stage is characterized by slow growth and low profits. If the new product is successful it then enters the **growth stage** which is characterized by rapid sales growth and increasing profits. The product then enters the **maturity stage** in which sales growth peaks and profits stabilize. The company seeks here to renew sales growth typically by relaunching the product. Finally the product enters a **decline stage** in which sales and profits decrease. The organization then has to decide whether to get rid of the product, maintain it, or harvest it.

Problems with the product life cycle concept

The PLC concept has been criticized by various individuals and groups. The most notable critics were Dhalla and Yuspeh (1976) who argued that:

> The PLC is a dependent variable, which is determined by marketing actions; it is not an independent variable to which companies should adapt their marketing programmes.

A further problem is the fact that a temporary plateau in sales can be interpreted as the onset of maturity, which may be an incorrect assumption. Some attractions, for example, have a bi-modal profile because they achieve an initial spectacular success which is temporary and are relaunched based on a change of core attraction or massive new product developments (Swarbrooke, 1995). The use of the product lifecycle curve as a predictive tool for this type of organization would be very dangerous indeed.

The shape of the PLC curve may not always follow the 'S' shaped model; it may be bi-modal with two peaks, or skewed, perhaps with the growth not occurring until the last quarter of the timescale. Researchers have found that there are at least 17 variants on the shape of the product lifecycle curve (Tellis and Crawford, 1981). For example, a fad product will show a shape which represents a period of rapid growth followed by an equally rapid collapse.

Table 8.6 Key players in UK budget market

Brand	Operator	No. of units	Total bedrooms	Price per room (spring 1995)	Restaurant	Expansion Plans
Travelodge	F	117	4500	£34.50	Sited adjacent to Little Chef, Happy Eater, Harvester or Welcome Break	Will continue to open 20–25 per year for foreseeable future
Travel Inn	W	68	2881	£34.50	Five Travel Inns incorporate Potters branded restaurant; the rest are sited alongside Beefeater, Brewers Fayre or TGI Friday's units	More than 90 Travel Inns due to be opened by end of Feb. 1996, with long-term growth plans of up to 175
Premier Lodge	P	4	900	Mon–Thur: £39.50. Fri–Sun: £29.50	10 Premier Lodges are attached to Miller's Kitchens	Two Premier Lodges opened in 1995. Seeking to acquire further sites in future
Granada	G	1	1000	£39.95	Restaurant is integral part of building or close by	Two Granada Lodges opened in Glasgow and Reading in 1995. Further expansion as market demands
Campanile	C	15	915	Mon–Thur: £35.75 Fri–Sun: £29.95	Integral hotel restaurant	Campanile's sixteenth unit in UK due to open in early 1996. A further six sites have also been purchased
Friendly Comfort Inn	FH	7*	477	£36.50	Integral bar and restaurant	Currently looking at possible development sites in UK and overseas

Pavilion Lodge	PA	7	376	£34.95 for 1 £38.95 for 2	Restaurants available in adjoining motorway service station	Looking to expand existing lodges. Expansion of additional lodges is undecided
Road Chef Lodge**	R	5	200	Mon–Thur: £35.50 Fri–Sun: 33.50	All meals available at adjoining service area restaurants	A further three units by 1996 and another three by 1997. Also looking at non-motorway suburban sites
Formule 1	A	3	220	£17–£19	Breakfast only available in the hotel	A fourth Formule 1 was due to open in 1995, by the M25, with a further 25 units by the year 2000
Holiday Inn Express	H	0	0	£39.95 including breakfast	Restaurant will be integral or in adjacent building	First four units due to be opened by end of 1995, 20 within five years, 80 in 'foreseeable future'

Key: F = Forte; W = Whitbread; P = Premier House, a division of Greenalls Group; A = Accor UK; C = Campanile UK; G = Granada; FH = Friendly Hotels; R = Road Chef Motorways Ltd; H = Holiday Inn; PA = Pavilion Services.

* Including one Comfort Inn operated by Friendly on behalf of Choice Hotels.
** Marketing link exists between Premier Lodge and Road Chef Lodge.

Source: *Caterer and Hotelkeeper*, April 1995.
Note: Forte has been bought by the Granada Group in 1996.

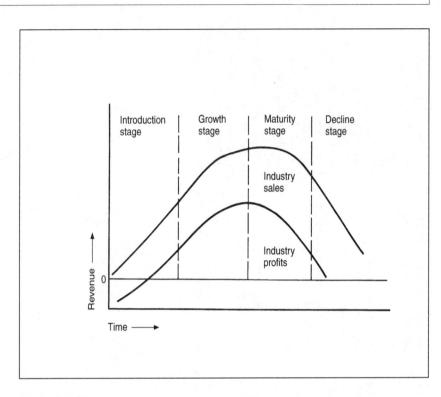

Figure 8.4 The four stages of the product lifecycle.
Source: Kotler (1994).

Product lifecycles can vary dramatically in their timespan. Products which are sold in a traditional market may have lifecycles measured in decades, whereas fashion-conscious products may last only a few weeks. Studies have also shown that products do not necessarily pass through all the four stages (Rink and Swan, 1979).

Many products sold by organizations seem to have been in the mature stage of their lifecycle for decades and show no signs of entering the decline stage. Old traditional hotels such as Claridges and The Savoy are examples of these types of organization.

Many products may also never enter the growth stage because they are refused in the marketplace and fail.

Decline of products is not inevitable. Most products in their mature stage are subject to intense marketing activity to delay any possible loss in sales. It is also possible to recycle the product lifecycle curve through further growth stages by increasing promotional spend, relaunching the product or introducing the product to new markets and users.

The relaunch of major attractions is an example of this type of activity. Most attractions introduce new rides, use new technology or improve support services to effectively relaunch the product. The introduction of a new 'white-knuckle' ride at a major attraction is often

Table 8.7 Summary of product lifecycle characteristics, objectives and strategies

	Introduction	Growth	Maturity	Decline
Characteristic				
Sales	Low sales	Rapidly rising sales	Peak sales	Declining sales
Costs	High cost per customer	Average cost per customer	Low cost per customer	Low cost per customer
Profits	Negative	Rising profits	High profits	Declining profits
Customers	Innovators	Early adopters	Middle majority	Laggards
Competitors	Few	Growing number	Stable number beginning to decline	Declining number
Marketing objectives	Create product awareness and trial	Maximize market share	Maximize profit while defending market share	Reduce expenditure and milk the brand
Strategies				
Product	Offer a basic product	Offer product extensions, service, warranty	Diversify brand and models	Phase out weak items
Price	Use cost-plus	Price to penetrate market	Price to match or better competitors	Cut price
Distribution	Build selective distribution	Build intensive distribution	Build more intensive distribution	Go selective: phase out unprofitable outlets
Advertising	Build product awareness among early adopters and dealers	Build awareness and interest in the mass market	Stress brand differences and benefits	Reduce to level needed to retain hard-core loyals
Sales promotion	Use heavy sales promotion to entice trail	Reduce to take advantage of heavy consumer demand	Increase to encourage brand switching	Reduce to minimal level

Source: Kotler (1994).

enough to revitalize the market. One such recent example of this is the introduction of the 'Nemesis' ride at the Alton Towers theme park in the UK.

Hotel chains have also shown evidence of relaunching their products. The introduction of leisure and health facilities within hotels has been a good example of this type of activity.

Organizations can therefore change the course of the lifecycle if they adopt a proactive approach to marketing activity.

There is also some dispute about the level to which the product lifecycle concept applies. It seems to have validity at the product level rather than the brand level (Dhalla and Yuspeh, 1976). This means that it could be applied to the beer market in general, for example, but it would be less appropriate to apply it to an individual brand such as Guinness.

The product lifecycle model cannot be used to predict when a product will move from stage to stage. This means that it only has limited value to product planners. Product lifecycle is therefore a generally

Table 8.8 The tour operator product portfolio and the product lifecycle

Product	PLC stage	Marketing strategy
Summer sun holidays or FITs	Maturity	Relaunch with new destinations Heavy promotion
Long-haul holidays or FITs	Introduction stage	Heavy promotion to build awareness Sales promotions with distributors
Fly-drive holidays to the USA	Growth stage	Use promotion to build brand preference Work on improving distribution

accepted, if rather simplified, model which can form the basis for discussion when formulating marketing strategies for individual products.

Product lifecycle in use

The product lifecycle concept cannot be applied to all products and its value to managers is highly questionable. However, it may allow an organization to focus attention on some of the key characteristics related to their products and markets. Let us consider an example of how a tour operator could use the product lifecycle concept in setting their marketing strategy, in relation to their product portfolio. This example is shown in Table 8.8.

PRODUCT DEVELOPMENT

Product innovation and product development are key activities in which any organization in the tourism, leisure and hospitality industry should be involved. The product lifecycle concept has shown that products at some time enter maturity and decline. It is very important that an organization replaces these outdated products with new innovative ideas.

Sources of new ideas

New product ideas may arise from sources both inside and outside the organization. Possible sources of new product ideas for a hotel which is part of a chain are shown in Figure 8.5.

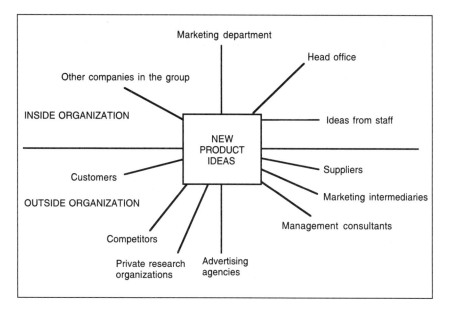

Figure 8.5 Sources of new product ideas for a hotel within a chain.

Inside the organization

New product ideas can come from a number of sources inside the organization. It will be one of the key functions of the **marketing department** to think about the future and the sort of products and services to be introduced. They should also be thinking about how to continually upgrade their current products and services to meet new customer demands.

The marketing department may look to ideas which originate from other sources in the company. If the hotel is part of a chain, new ideas may be generated at the **head office** level. They will supply new ideas and may even help the hotel staff with their introduction. If the hotel is strongly branded or franchised it is likely that new product development will be controlled by the head office of the company so that quality standards can be maintained throughout the group.

This is common in other organizations. The introduction of new products at the McDonald's chain, for example, is managed by the head office of the organization.

If the hotel is part of a large group, ideas may come from other parts of the organization. The ideas which are generated from other companies in the group can be particularly different and innovative if they originate from another country.

Other **staff members** can also have ideas for new products. These ideas should be encouraged at all levels in the organization and discussed openly and fairly. The senior managers of the company are also likely to be travelling abroad, both for work and in their leisure time. They should be encouraged to look around at other hospitality organizations and consider any new ideas which arise.

Outside the organization

Many new ideas originate from outside the organization. The marketers in the organization must make sure that they have systems in place to make themselves aware of these potential sources.

Customers can provide a vital source for new product ideas, particularly if the organization carries out regular quantitative and qualitative market research surveys with them. A customer, if questioned, can often talk about the area in the hotel where improvements could be made, and offer very good suggestions for possible additional products and services which would make the hotel more appealing.

Corporate customers can also give some vital clues to the ways in which the hotel could improve and offer new products and services. Corporate customers can represent a substantial part of the hotel's sales, and so it is particularly important that their ideas are considered.

Suppliers can offer new product ideas. This may be in the form of new equipment which will offer competitive advantages.

It is important to consider that the supplier may not necessarily be among the traditional sources of food, materials or equipment. The suppliers of compact business equipment, for example, have allowed hotels to develop sophisticated 'business' rooms where customers can use computers, faxes, etc. This has offered the leading hotels in this market significant competitive advantage.

Marketing intermediaries can offer new product ideas. The travel agent, for example, can suggest new product ideas to the tour operators as a result of customer feedback.

Competitors can also give the hotel ideas for the future. This may range from the marketers at the hotel noticing the new products that the competitor is developing and copying these, to working in a joint venture to produce new products. Joint ventures can be particularly attractive if the development costs are very large.

Management consultants can be used as a source of new ideas. Consultants are often used if the organization is planning major investment in new products. If the organization is planning to build a major extension to the hotel, or build a completely new hotel, it will often employ a management consultant to provide ideas and carry out feasibility studies.

Advertising agencies can also help with the development of new markets and products. They can be employed to look at one particular market area and make suggestions for future developments. Using an agency, like a management consultant, has the advantages of a 'fresh pair of eyes'. This may give the organization very innovative and novel ideas which they had not previously thought of.

Private research organizations are also a source of ideas for new products. They produce commercial reports which the hotel can buy and use. The hotel can also commission a specially designed piece of research on a particular market and use a private research organization to carry out the work.

Phases of new product development

Once the new product idea has been generated, the organization must then develop the idea so that it can be commercially sold. This involves a series of steps which the organization must carry out, as shown in Figure 8.6.

1. **Idea generation**. The organization must seek to generate new ideas. The possible sources of ideas have already been discussed. There will be more ideas generated than it is possible for the organization to develop, so there must be a screening process carried out to select those for further investigation.
2. **Screening**. All the new product ideas should be screened to see which are acceptable for the organization. This may involve talking to experts or market research with potential customers. This stage should prove that the ideas are suitable for the market.
3. **Business analysis**. Once the ideas have been selected, the organization should carry out a business analysis to see whether it is possible to develop the idea commercially. There should be estimates of predicted cost involved in the development. This should be balanced

1.   Idea generation
↓
2.   Screening
↓
3.   Business analysis
↓
4. Product development
↓
5.   Test marketing
↓
6.   Commercialization

Figure 8.6 The steps involved in new product development.
Source: Dibb, Simkin, Pride and Ferrell (1994).

against the likely payback period. It is only then that the organization can assess whether it can afford to carry on with the development process.

4. **Product development**. Work will now be carried out to produce a prototype product. For manufactured goods this involves the production of a mock-up product which can then be researched. In service organisations, the prototype ideas may be in the form of an illustration. Some of the elements of the new service may be produced. If the new service involves a new uniform for example, this can be made.

5. **Test marketing**. This is a very important step in the development process. The product or idea is test marketed before it is introduced commercially. In a hotel chain this could involve testing the new product or service idea in one hotel to see whether it is well accepted. This will prevent the organization spending the large amounts of money involved in the final commercialization process if the product or service idea is generally rejected.

6. **Commercialization**. This is the final stage when the new product idea is introduced to the market. This will usually involve a large marketing budget to promote the product or service and to build customer awareness and preference.

New product development in the tourism, leisure, and hospitality industries

New product development in the tourism, leisure and hospitality industries often involves investment in new facilities which involve a high capital investment. A 'feasibility study' is carried out to test the potential viability of the proposed project as accurately as possible before a decision is made to go ahead. This is particularly important if the project involves a large financial risk for the organization, in the case of attractions, for example. The stages of the feasibility study have been discussed by Swarbrooke (1995) and are summarized in Figure 8.7 in relation to a visitor attraction.

Key points of a visitor attraction feasibility study include:

- the 'penetration factor' – predictions of the proportion of people in each market segment who may visit the attraction;
- analysis of where the visitors will come from and when they will come;
- analysis of capital costs and estimated likely income – breakeven analysis may be used here.

However, where relatively little capital or financial risk is involved, the 'feasibility study' process may be shorter, quicker and far less structured. An example of this might be the decision to offer a new destination within a tour operator's 'summer sun' programme.

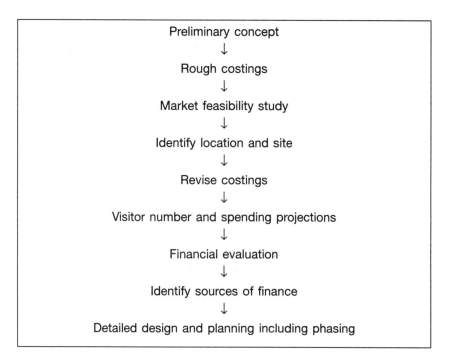

Preliminary concept
↓
Rough costings
↓
Market feasibility study
↓
Identify location and site
↓
Revise costings
↓
Visitor number and spending projections
↓
Financial evaluation
↓
Identify sources of finance
↓
Detailed design and planning including phasing

Figure 8.7 The feasibility study process for a visitor attraction.
Source: Swarbrooke (1995).

RECENT TRENDS

International trade in services is becoming more and more important because of several important market developments (Segal-Horn, 1989). There is an increasing importance in the use of information technology in services which leads to important economies of scale in service delivery. This is most notable in airline reservation systems.

A second development which Segal-Horn (1989) has identified which encourages the internationalization of services is the emergence of the 'global consumer'. This was looked at earlier in Chapter 4. A third factor is the internationalization of business itself which leads to the internationalization of services which are provided to the business traveller. The international hotel chains such as Hilton, Marriott and Intercontinental are examples of this development.

Segal-Horn (1989) also argues that the internationalization of services is just as important as the internationalization of manufacturing firms. It is, however, different: in services the internationalization process tends to involve the replication of the 'service delivery outlet' such as with a McDonald's hamburger outlet or a Hilton International hotel. This internationalization is often accompanied by a global marketing campaign. International services also offer a uniform quality of service delivery no matter where they are delivered.

If it is in fact possible to internationalize services on the supply side, then will the demand for these products be there? Chapter 4 has already looked at the convergence of customer behaviour in Europe. The new European segments have been identified by the Italian research company Eurisko (reported by Martin, 1988) as being:

- young people who have unified tastes across Europe in music, sports and cultural activities;
- the trendsetters and social climbers who are wealthier and more educated Europeans who tend to value independence, refuse consumer stereotypes and appreciate exclusive products;
- Europe's business people who are a rich target audience of approximately 6 million – they are about 40 years old, regularly travel abroad and have a taste for luxury goods

Targeting these market segments will involve a special approach to marketing strategy. It has been recognized that it is easier to standardize products and brand names, for example, than it is to standardize pricing and distribution (Porter, 1986). This is shown in Table 8.9.

For many organizations in the tourism, leisure and hospitality industries, they own the outlet anyway, which theoretically makes the introduction of European and global products an easier task.

Once the target market segment has been identified, the organization can develop its product strategy to meet their needs (Guido, 1991) These developments should focus on gaining production and marketing efficiencies. As more uniform standards are introduced, the organizations are more and more likely to target pan-European consumer segments. The ownership or acquisition of strong national brand names will allow the organization to develop these throughout Europe with common positioning strategies.

It is more important to carry out detailed market research to assess the potential response of customers to new products in all the countries in which the organization intends to market the product or service. Patenting and branding of products is also a significant step in the product development phase.

It is easy to be carried away with these new developments and assume that the market will be dominated by large companies targeting the new Euro-consumers with specifically designed products. It is important to remember, however, that although this is an important

Table 8.9 Marketing activities according to ease or difficulty of standardization

Easy to standardize	Difficult to standardize
Brand name	Distribution
Product positioning	Personal selling
Service standards	Training sales personnel
Warranties	Pricing
Advertising theme – packaging	Media selection

Source: Porter (1986).

recent trend, the industry is still fragmented and dominated by small operators. These two areas of business must continue to develop products hand in hand.

CONCLUSIONS

This chapter has explored a number of issues in relation to the product element of the marketing mix. It has looked at the augmentation of products and their positioning. The final part of the chapter has looked at the recent trends in products for tourism, leisure and hospitality organizations, particularly in terms of the implications of the internationalization of markets.

DISCUSSION POINTS AND ESSAY QUESTIONS

1. Discuss the main characteristics and components of **either** the tour operation product **or** a hotel product.
2. Examine the 'consumer benefit' concept in relation to **either** a visit to a theme park **or** the purchase of a fast-food meal.
3. Critically evaluate the current role of branding in the tourism, leisure and hospitality industries.
4. Discuss the value of the product lifecycle concept for marketers in tourism, leisure and hospitality.

Choose **one** of the following products: **EXERCISE**

- an airline flight;
- a theatre performance;
- a package holiday or FIT;
- a restaurant meal.

For your chosen product you should identify the core, actual and augmented elements of the product.

You should present your ideas in diagram form, together with a brief explanation of the content of your diagram.

CASE STUDIES

You may wish to look at some of the following cases which illustrate of the points made in the chapter:
 2. The Forte International Programme, UK;
 3. First Choice, UK;
 9. Bord Fáilte, Ireland;
 10. Club Méditerranée SA, France;
 11. The Hurtigruten, coastal voyage, Norway;
 12. Porta Carras complex, Halkidiki, Greece;
 13. Iceland: The marketing of a business tourism destination;
 18. Airtours plc, UK;
 19. British Airways, UK;
 20. The European Travel Commission;
 21. The Victoria and Albert Museum, UK;
 23. Futbol Club Barcelona, Spain;
 24. Abercrombie and Kent Ltd, UK;
 25. Accor, France;
 26. Thalassa International, France;
 27. Les Vins Georges Duboeuf SA, France;
 28. Center Parcs, UK;
 29. Port Aventura SA, Spain.

Price 9

Key concepts

The main concepts covered in this chapter are:

- traditional methods of calculating price;
- strategic and tactical pricing policies;
- state intervention in the setting of prices;
- differences in pricing issues within Europe.

INTRODUCTION

Pricing is clearly crucial to the successful marketing of any product or service. The prices that the organization charges for its products and services must strike a balance between gaining acceptance with the target customers and making a profit for the organization. Even for organizations that do not seek to make a profit, the pricing of products and services is the key to encouraging consumption.

The decision to offer a product free to encourage uptake should, however, also be a conscious decision which is made by the management of the organization in question.

Price is a key element in the marketing mix because, for a profit-motivated organization, the prices which are set relate directly to the total revenue and ultimately the profit made by the organization.

Many features of tourism, leisure and hospitality markets mean that the pricing of products and services is an extremely complex procedure. There is also the question as to whether an organization can adopt a European pricing policy.

This chapter will concentrate on the following issues:

- general pricing theory and the methods used for calculating prices;
- the use of pricing as a tactical and strategic weapon in the marketing process;
- the special nature of tourism, leisure and hospitality organizations and the effect that this has on pricing policies;
- the European dimension to pricing policy.

GENERAL PRICING THEORY

The setting of prices for products and services will be influenced by the objectives of the organization which is marketing them. The organization may have the objective of gaining maximum turnover and profits which will result in a satisfactory return on their investment for the shareholders. The organization may be trying to build market share which will have an effect on the pricing levels. Some organizations, particularly in the public sector, are simply trying to encourage usage of their products and services by customers. This may result in the product or service being offered free of charge or at reduced rates. Whatever the strategy of the organization is, clear pricing objectives should be established before price levels are set.

The key factors which determine pricing decisions have been summarized by Dibb, Simkin, Pride and Ferrell (1994). These are shown in Figure 9.1.

Organizational and marketing objectives

Organizations should relate the prices set to the organizational and marketing objectives. The Formule 1 chain which is the budget chain of the French company Accor, for example, is priced so that it is seen to be outstanding value for money. The prices are set at a reasonable level in relation to product quality. This will allow the company to develop this brand at the budget end of the market in line with their other brands.

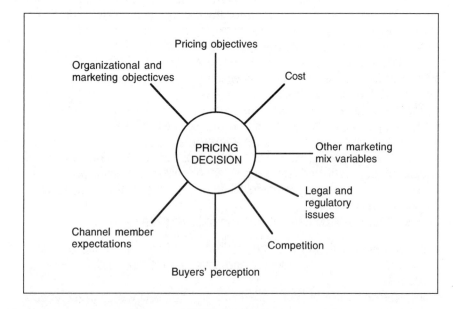

Figure 9.1 Factors affecting pricing decisions. Adapted from Dibb, Simkin, Pride and Ferrell (1994).

Other organizational goals may include the desire to be the brand leader in the marketplace. This will usually be reflected in higher prices in the long term. An organization may sustain a decrease in prices in the short term to try and gain market share in the long term. This strategy can be particularly relevant when an organization is launching a new product or entering a new geographical market area.

Pricing objectives

The organization should also have clear objectives in relation to their setting of prices. Organizations may have different objectives when prices are set. They may have a requirement for a certain target return on investment. There may also be a requirement to achieve a certain sales volume and a particular market share. The organization may also be looking for a period of rapid and sustained cash flow which can only be achieved by a temporary boost in sales.

For non-profit making organizations, the objectives may be to encourage new users. This is often achieved by **differential pricing strategies** where different prices are charged for different market segments. Museums, for example, often charge a lower admission for students, senior citizens and the unemployed to try and encourage people from these market segments to visit the museum.

Costs

The setting of prices should incorporate a calculation of how much it costs the organization to produce the product or service. If the company is profit oriented a margin will be added to the cost price to derive the selling price. An organization can decide, however, to sell below cost price for a period of time. This is often referred to as a **tactical price reduction**. Tactical price reductions can be made so that competitors' prices are temporarily matched or undercut with the aim of increasing sales, generating cash flow and gaining market share.

Other marketing mix variables

Pricing decisions always have an interaction with the other elements of the marketing mix, namely promotion, distribution and product design. Consider the example of the luxury hotel room for which the organization charges the customer a high price. This high price has to be reflected in other elements of the marketing mix. It is vital that the quality of the hotel service meets the expectations that the high price has generated in the minds of the customers. Price usually gives the customer the first indication of perceived product quality.

Distribution of the hotel room is likely to be via an exclusive channel to reflect the high-quality image and resulting high price. This may involve the use of a high-quality marketing consortium, for example, where luxury hotels are grouped together for distribution and selling purposes.

The promotion of the hotel will have to reflect the quality and prices. The messages which are given in the promotion will have to be of an appropriate standard. A high level of personal service will probably be included as part of the promotional package.

This example shows that pricing of the product or service is inextricably linked to all the other marketing mix variables.

Channel member expectations

A marketer must consider the intermediaries in the distribution channel when pricing a product or service. The sale of luxury hotel rooms by a particular organization, for example, may be carried out by an exclusive travel agency chain. This intermediary in the distribution channel will expect certain things from the hotel in relation to price.

The travel agency will have to make a profit in the form of a commission when the hotel rooms are sold. It will probably also require discount from the hotel, particularly if it sells a large number of rooms and obtains rapid payment from the customers. The agency will also require service support in the form of promotional materials and training. All of these items will cost the hotel money and they will have to be incorporated in the setting of the room rate and prices for other ancillary services.

Buyers' perceptions

The prices which are set for products and services must reflect the customers' perceptions in the target market.

It is important that the customer sees the link between the price charged and the product quality. In the tourism sector, for example, customers expect a high level of service and special features if a high price is being charged. This can be seen in the airline sector, where airlines charge high prices for first-class services. In return, the customer expects excellent check-in and waiting facilities, extra comfort and room on the plane, and extra personal service and benefits, such as free drinks. A speciality holiday company can also charge high prices if they are offering a higher level of service and individually tailored products.

The most important issue is whether the customer perceives that the price which they have paid represents good value for money and matches their quality perceptions.

Competition

Organizations which sell products and services in competitive markets will be trying to win customers from rival competitive organizations. This can be achieved in one of two ways.

Price competition is the first method that can be used. It involves offering the product or service at a lower price than the price charged by the competition. **Non-price competition** involves the organization in trying to increase market share or sales by leaving the price of the product or service unchanged but persuading the target customers that their offering is superior and has advantages compared to the competition.

Whether an organization uses price competition or non-price competition depends on the state of the market. In a very competitive marketplace, the organization is more likely to resort to intense price competition to sell their products and services.

In an oligopolistic market where there are few competitors, there is little to be gained from price competition and organizations tend to concentrate more on non-price competition.

The UK package tour operators are a good example of a sector which has competed largely on the basis of price to date. The focus in the past few years has been on price-cutting to gain market share and the customer for package holidays in the UK has come to expect substantial discounts. In an industry where operating margins can be as low as 2% spiralling discounts can be very damaging. The latest idea in this market is to try and compete more by non-price methods rather that by damaging discounting. First Choice, for example, is adopting a strategy of non-price competition. This has involved the company in differentiation of identifiable products and the development of a clearer branding strategy which is reflected in its advertising campaigns. It still discounts, however, because of competitive pressure.

Organizations can use a mix of price competition and non-price competition for different market areas. **Selective discounting** is a method used in service marketing to overcome the particular problems of perishability of services coupled with the burden of large fixed overheads. These ideas are explored in Figure 9.2.

A **seasonal discount** is often used by organizations marketing tourism, leisure and hospitality products to try and even out demand across the year. Hotels and airlines, for example, offer seasonal discounts in their slacker periods. Package holiday companies offer discounts in the form of free child places to encourage sales at quieter periods of the year.

Legal and regulatory issues

There may be legal and regulatory restrictions which control the ways in which an organization fixes prices. An organization such as a gallery or museum, for example, which is heavily subsidized by the government may be put under pressure to keep prices low to encourage visitors to come and visit. The state may also regulate prices which can be charged by commercial organizations. In Greece, for example, hotel prices are regulated by the state. There has also been traditional state intervention in Europe in relation to the prices charged for airline

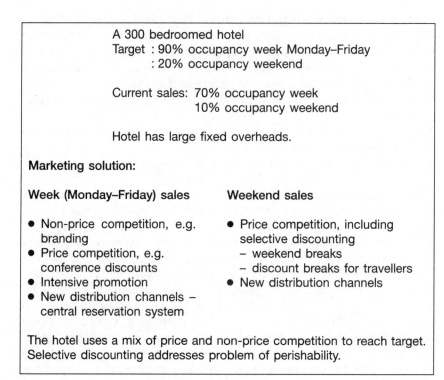

A 300 bedroomed hotel
Target : 90% occupancy week Monday–Friday
: 20% occupancy weekend

Current sales: 70% occupancy week
10% occupancy weekend

Hotel has large fixed overheads.

Marketing solution:

Week (Monday–Friday) sales	**Weekend sales**
• Non-price competition, e.g. branding • Price competition, e.g. conference discounts • Intensive promotion • New distribution channels – central reservation system	• Price competition, including selective discounting – weekend breaks – discount breaks for travellers • New distribution channels

The hotel uses a mix of price and non-price competition to reach target. Selective discounting addresses problem of perishability.

Figure 9.2 Examples of pricing.

seats, although this is declining within the European Union through the process of 'liberalization' in civil aviation.

On a more general level, legal restrictions are often placed on the practice of price fixing and collusion. The Monopolies and Mergers Commission in the UK, for example, looks at the likely effect on prices and the possibility of price collusion when a merger or takeover is proposed. If this results in a significant reduction in competitiveness in the marketplace, then they may take action to prevent the merger or takeover occurring.

DIFFERENT APPROACHES TO PRICING

Main types of pricing methods

Organizations involved in the marketing of tourism, leisure and hospitality products use different methods of calculation to set prices. Pricing methods fall into three main categories:

• cost oriented pricing;
• demand oriented pricing;
• competition oriented pricing.

Cost oriented pricing

This is where the price of a product or service is calculated and a margin applied to derive a selling price. This is the simplest method of pricing and is often used by companies for calculating prices. It has the disadvantage of not taking into account the economic aspects of supply and demand and often does not relate to pricing objectives. The concepts of mark-up and gross profit margin are used extensively in the tourism, leisure and hospitality industries.

In **cost-plus pricing** the seller's cost are calculated and the price is set by adding a specific amount which is often referred to as a **margin**.

Mark-up pricing is a commonly used method of pricing in retailing. The product's price is determined by adding a predetermined percentage of the cost of the item. Mark-ups obviously have to reflect the strategic vision regarding costs, risks and stock turnovers.

Demand oriented pricing

This method allows for high prices when the demand is high and lower prices when the demand is low, regardless of the cost of the product or services. One example of this is UK seaside resort accommodation which tends to be much more expensive in the summer than in winter due to demand. Demand oriented pricing allows an organization to charge higher prices and therefore make higher profits as long as the buyers value the products above the cost price.

Competition oriented pricing

The organization fixes the prices of the products and services in relation to competitors' prices. This has the advantage of giving the organization the opportunity to increase sales or market share. UK tour operators use this form of pricing due to intense competition.

In practice all three influences are often taken into account when setting prices. In the long term, organizations need to more than cover their costs if they are going to prosper. In doing this they can only go as far as competition and the prevailing strength of the market will allow.

Skimming and penetration pricing

Organizations use different methods of pricing when they are launching new products. If the organization is launching a product which is fairly unique and therefore offers the customer a new experience, it can afford to operate a **skimming pricing policy**. This is where a high initial price is charged in the hope of gaining maximum profit at the early stages of the product's life.

A specialist tour operator such as Abercrombie and Kent, for example (see Case study 24) can afford to charge higher prices for the unique service which it offers to the customer, particularly when new product development results in a holiday with unique features.

If the organization, on the other hand, is trying to get maximum distribution for the product or service in the initial stages, it will probably price at a lower level to get maximum sales and market share. This method is commonly used in the marketing of fast moving consumer goods where rapid distribution stocking is essential for the success of the product. This is referred to as **penetration pricing**. The fierce price competition which the UK tour operators are involved in is an example of this.

Discriminatory pricing

Organizations can often alter the prices charged to suit different customers, products, locations and times. Discriminatory pricing mean that the organization is selling a product or service at two or more prices, despite the fact that the product costs are the same. Discriminatory pricing is often used by organizations that are involved in the marketing of tourism, leisure and hospitality products for a variety of reasons. Consider the examples which are shown in Table 9.1. Each of the organizations shown are using discriminatory pricing for different reasons.

The leisure centre is trying to encourage groups in the community to take part in sports activities at the leisure centre. This may be profit motivated in that the centre can at least recoup some of the costs of opening the centre during quiet periods. The managers of the leisure centre may also have a social aim of trying to encourage particular groups of people who do not currently engage in recreational activities to use the centre with the aim of increasing general health in the population as a whole.

Table 9.1 Discriminatory pricing examples

Example	Approach	Reasons
Leisure centre	Customer segment based	• To encourage groups to take part in sporting activities • To increase revenue in quiet periods
Theatre	Location based	• To encourage different customer groups into the theatre • To get maximum revenue at each performance
Hotel	Time based	• To encourage 'off-peak' visitors • To cover high fixed overhead costs

The theatre will charge different prices for seats according to their particular location. This will enable the theatre to get maximum sales at any one performance and target different market segments.

Hotels also use discriminatory pricing, based on particular times. This will encourage off-peak visitors and help to contribute to the high fixed overhead costs.

The market must be capable of being segmented if discriminatory pricing is going to be an effective strategy. Care should also be taken that discriminatory pricing does not lead to customer resentment. It should also be legal. The deregulation of the airline industry in most European countries has meant that discriminatory pricing has been used much more in this market.

Strategic and tactical pricing

Organizations in the leisure, tourism and hospitality industries operate pricing policies at the strategic and tactical levels. This is very much because the nature of the business means that prices have to be set a long way in advance so that brochures and guides can be published. This means that prices are determined early on in the planning of the marketing strategy. These pricing decisions will be based on the long-term view of corporate strategy, product positioning and value for money in the marketplace.

The fact that organizations, however, cannot stock services means that if the planned supply exceeds demand in the marketplace for whatever reason, the organization must try to sell excess capacity. This often means that the organization has to resort to tactical pricing strategies, often in the form of discriminatory pricing or discounting.

One of the best examples of tactical pricing techniques is the moves which the UK-based package tour operator makes in response to a lack of demand. Last-minute highly discounted selling of package holidays in the UK to generate extra bookings has almost become the norm in the market. This has led analysts to worry that the long-term profitability of these package holiday companies will decline, because the customers have come to expect last-minute bargains and have therefore changed their purchasing habits. The only way out of the aggressive price discounting strategy it seems is to increasingly differentiate the product in the marketplace. The question is whether customers who are used to aggressive price discounting will accept this type of strategy.

The dumping of airline seats at heavily discounted prices is another good example of tactical pricing. The purchase of airline seats from newspapers, teletext services or 'bucket shops' means that the customer can often get a substantial last minute price reduction. This ensures that the airline fills the empty seats, which would otherwise represent lost revenue.

Hotels have also become skilled at operating last-minute tactical pricing methods to fill unoccupied rooms. The customer can often negotiate a substantial reduction on the rate if they ring the hotel during the evening that they want to stay.

This use of tactical pricing techniques means that pricing of tourism, leisure and hospitality products is an extremely complex and difficult task, which requires a great deal of knowledge of the market, ongoing customer demand and trading conditions.

THE SPECIAL NATURE OF TOURISM, LEISURE AND HOSPITALITY ORGANIZATIONS IN RELATION TO PRICING POLICY

We have already seen in this chapter that the fixing of prices for tourism, leisure and hospitality organizations is a difficult task which involves strategic and tactical measures. This section will now consider the special nature of the organizations involved in the sector and the effect that this has on their pricing policies.

It has been recognized by Cowell (1984) that the special characteristics of services have an influence on prices. He grouped the impacts of these service characteristics into five categories which are summarized in Table 9.2.

The characteristics of services outlined by Cowell indicate the importance of differentiating the service offered to gain competitive advantage and therefore give the organization more discretion in pricing. This is particularly important in service markets where perishability is common.

The special nature of travel and tourism products in particular has been considered by Middleton (1994). These characteristics are shown in Table 9.3.

Pricing for an attraction product as an example from the industry shows some of the difficulties in the fixing of prices for tourism, leisure and hospitality products in general. Swarbrooke (1995) illustrates the

Table 9.2 Characteristics of services and their influence upon service prices

1. Service perishability means that prices have to be adapted to meet fluctuating demands.
2. Customers can delay or postpone the use of services and may choose to perform them for themselves. This leads to keen competition between service providers.
3. Service intangibility has many price implications. The higher the material content of the service, the greater the tendency will be to standardize prices. Prices are often negotiated between buyer and seller.
4. Where services are homogeneous, price will be highly competitive. The more unique a service is, the greater will be the discretion in pricing. Price will be an indicator of quality and reputation of the organization.
5. The inseparability of the service from the person providing it places limits on the market that can be served. The degree of competition operating within these limits will influence the prices charged.

Adapted from Cowell (1984).

Table 9.3 The characteristics of travel and tourism services that influence pricing

- High price elasticity in the discretionary segments of leisure, recreation and vacation travel markets.
- Long lead times between price decisions and product sales. Twelve months or more are not uncommon lead times when prices must be printed in brochures to be distributed months before customer purchases are made, as is typically the case for tour operators.
- No possibility of stockholding for service products, so that retailers do not share with producers the burden and risk of unsold stocks and tactical pricing decisions.
- High probability of unpredictable but major short-run fluctuations in cost elements such as oil prices and currency exchange rates.
- Near certainty of tactical price-cutting by major competitors if supply exceeds demand.
- High possibility of provoking price wars in sectors such as transport, accommodation, tour operation and travel agencies, in which short-run profitability may disappear.
- Extensive official regulation in sectors such as transport, which often includes elements of price control.
- Necessity for seasonal pricing to cope with short-run fixed capacity.
- High level of customers' psychological involvement, especially with vacation products, in which price may be a symbol of status as well as value.
- The high fixed costs of operation, which encourage and justify massive short-run price cuts in service operations with unsold capacity of perishable products.
- High level of vulnerability to demand changes reflecting unforeseen economic and political events.

Source: Middleton (1994).

difficulty of setting prices for a visitor attraction product with reference to five main features. These are summarized in Table 9.4.

These features illustrate the complexities involved in the setting of prices for an attraction product which relate both to the supply side and the demand side of the market. On the demand side, the customer often expects entrance to an attraction to be free. If the customer expects to pay, their total price for their time spent at the attraction may include a sum of non-discretionary and discretionary spending. On the supply side, the attraction which is in the public sector may never have had to set market prices. This will often lead to a lack of awareness of competition by the manager of the attraction. It may also lead to general complacency in the management team and potential ignorance of customer needs.

The main complication in tourism, leisure and hospitality pricing is the role of **state ownership, regulation and subsidy**. Some examples will illustrate this point.

The public sector owns, and subsidizes, elements of the tourism and leisure product, for example museums, galleries, leisure centres and theatres. Due to these **subsidies** and the social objectives of many of these public sector bodies, a market price is not charged for the use of these products. The subsidies will usually hold down the price for all customers. In addition, concessions may also be made to allow people from disadvantaged sectors of society to pay an even lower price than other users for using these products, in the belief that they may otherwise not be able to use them. Such groups might include students, the elderly, disabled people and those who are unemployed. Concessions are offered either because it is thought morally wrong that such people should be deprived of the opportunity to use these products because they cannot afford the normal price, or because the product is thought to be so beneficial that everyone ought to be encouraged to use it. This is true of leisure centres because of the health benefits they can bring, or the cultural enrichment that is thought to be gained from visiting an art gallery, for example.

State subsidies are often seen as unfair by private sector providers offering similar products, who have to make a profit to survive and who do not receive any state subsidies.

The decision on what should be subsidized and what should not is a political choice which is often based on historical factors and tradition. In the UK for instance, opera is heavily subsidized while the cinema receives much less. Swimming pools often receive large subsidies but

Table 9.4 The features which explain the difficulty in fixing the price of an attraction product

1. Many of the organizations that operate attractions in the public sector are subsidized and do not look for an economic rate of return
2. The 'price' of buying the attraction product usually has three components, namely:
   - the direct cost of using the attraction, for example the entrance charge at museums;
   - the cost of extra discretionary purchases made by visitors such as meals and souvenirs;
   - the cost of travelling to and from the attraction, which can often be far greater than the direct cost of using the attraction.
   The many possible permutations of these three costs makes the pricing issue a very complex one.
3. Some attractions operate an all-inclusive price covering all on-site activities, facilities and services, while others charge on an item-by-item basis.
4. A number of attractions have no entrance or usage charge at all. For example, most natural attractions, some man-made attractions like churches and country parks and many events are to all intents and purposes free except for the cost of travelling to and from them.
5. The lack of perceived competition in some sectors of the attractions business and confusion over what exactly constitutes competition in other sectors makes it difficult to operate pricing based on what competitors are charging.
6. The prices charged for direct use of the product tend to vary depending on who the customer is with discounts being offered to groups and concessions being offered for families, the elderly, students and those who are unemployed.

Source: Swarbrooke (1995).

local bingo clubs do not. Subsidy is often used to maintain the viability of operations. If consumers were asked to pay the true cost of providing the product, it would not be a viable activity.

Subsidies take a number of forms in tourism, leisure and hospitality. This may be direct like those outlined above, or indirect where, for example, the infrastructure in a tourist resort is paid for by local taxpayers. Visitors who use this infrastructure such as roads and sewers pay nothing directly toward the cost of providing it, thus they receive an indirect subsidy from the local taxpayers.

THE EUROPEAN DIMENSION TO PRICING POLICY

Research by Porter (1986) has shown that pricing policy is one of the most difficult aspects of the marketing mix to standardize across national boundaries.

The different currencies and differences in the cost of living in different European countries means that it is very difficult to standardize the price for tourism, leisure and hospitality products across Europe. Customers in different countries of Europe also have different perceptions of the relationship between price levels and value for money. One example of this is the price which customers are prepared to pay for entrance to premier football matches. Prices in Spain and Italy for entrance to premier football grounds are relatively higher than the prices charged for top matches in the UK.

This can be explained only by the fact that customer perception of price for football entrance is very different in different European countries. The fanatical football supporter will pay any price to see their team. On the other hand, the idea that entrance charges to football grounds should be kept down as a social service is also a belief which has had an influence on the development of the market.

State regulation can affect the price consumers pay in a number of ways as follows:

- **Tourist taxes** may be levied by which tourists can be asked to make a contribution towards the cost of providing some of the services they require. An example of such a tax is the *taxe de séjour* in France, though this tends to be low at a few francs per person per night.
- There may be **state controls** on prices, for example in Greece where hotel prices are controlled by the State
- There may be **regulations in the transport sector**, as with air fares within Europe through cooperation between the relevant national governments. This often has the effect of making prices higher than they would be if free competition were allowed on the routes. Governments have often used this as a way of protecting national 'flag carrier' airlines which have usually been state-owned. However, this artificial price fixing is now being tackled, at least within the

European Union, through the 'liberalization' of air travel, which is part of the creation of a Single European Market.

As well as the factors that influence prices within tourism, leisure and hospitality specifically, there is an intra-European dimension to pricing in tourism, leisure and hospitality in Europe. These are briefly listed below:

- The widely differing levels of economic development found in the countries of Europe affect both the cost of producing tourism, leisure and hospitality products, and the ability of people in different countries to be able to afford to buy these products. For example, the lower level of economic development in Bulgaria, compared to Switzerland, is reflected in lower labour costs, and hence lower prices for skiing holidays. At the same time, these same low levels of economic developments in Bulgaria, compared to the UK and Germany, make Bulgaria a cheap holiday destination for British and German tourists. However, in time, tourism may help to reduce these differential levels of economic development between these countries. Ironically, this could lead to them becoming less attractive destinations for British and German tourists with a resultant loss of revenue.
- Policies on taxation and the differences in them between the various European governments can have a profound impact. An example of this are sales taxes (VAT in the UK, TVA in France, and so on). These vary dramatically within Europe, both in terms of the rate at which they are levied and the range of goods on which they are levied. Some governments have seen such taxes as a disincentive for tourism so have cut them on tourist-related services such as hotels, as happened in recent years in Ireland. Within the European Union, there are efforts towards harmonizing sales taxes across the states as part of the move towards a single European market.
- Given that tourism, leisure and hospitality are truly transnational industries, currency exchange rates also have an impact on prices. Fluctuations in exchange rates between generating countries and destination countries affect the price of hotel rooms, travel, meals and excursions. The devaluation of the pound sterling in 1992 and the fall in exchange from around 9.40 francs to the pound in summer 1992 to 7.40 in spring 1996 have severely affected the flow of UK tourists to France over the same period. Currency fluctuations make financial planning by tour operators difficult and can lead to supplements being charged to customers if the fluctuations are substantial and to the detriment of the tour operators. Within the European Union, therefore, the concept of a single European currency has significant implications for the tourism industry.

So far we have focused on the countries of the European Union. However, perhaps the most fascinating region of Europe currently in terms of the pricing of tourism, leisure and hospitality products is **Eastern Europe**. Political change in the region is generally leading to less state ownership and regulation at a fairly rapid rate. In many areas, almost overnight, a free-for-all is replacing decades of state price controls. This, coupled with often high inflation, is leading in some parts of Eastern Europe to enormous increases in prices for hotel rooms and domestic flights, for example. It is not always easy to see a reflection of these high prices in improved service and quality, so these prices may often not be seen to offer value for money.

One other interesting aspect of pricing seen in Eastern Europe, as well as in some Mediterranean regions, is differential pricing – in other words, situations where an identical product is sold at one price to local people and at another, usually higher price, to non-locals. This system reflects a belief that these 'foreigners' are more affluent than the locals and can therefore afford to pay the higher price. It may also, however, be a function of growing impatience with tourists on the part of local people, and a desire to make them pay higher prices almost as a form of punishment.

Finally, we must note that in some cases althought a direct price is charged for using a product in tourism, leisure and hospitality, indirect costs will also be incurred by the user, for example travel costs. Such costs include the entrance fee to a tourist destination such as a seaside resort and to some attractions such as public sector museums, traditional facilities which take place in the street and natural phenomena like beaches.

This discussion leads to the inevitable conclusion that standardization of pricing in Europe is a difficult strategic task. One of the best illustrations of these difficulties is a comparison of hotel prices in different European centres, as shown in Table 9.5.

The difference in price for comparable standards of hotel in different European cities is obvious when the figures are studied. The reasons for the differences are much harder to explain. They can be partly

Table 9.6 Pricing in tourism, leisure and hospitality in Europe

Type of product and organization	Market (M) or subsidized (S) or regulated (R) price	Method of pricing	Degree of tactical pricing to stimulate demand at less busy times (High, Medium, Low)	Pricing issue The emphasis is on discounting (D) for commercial reasons or the granting of concessions (C) for social reasons	Principal external bodies which are beneficiaries of a proportion of the income generated by the sale of the organization's products in addition to supplier	Opportunities for adding value	How similar are the pricing issues within the sector across Europe? Very similar (V) Quite similar (Q)
State owned scheduled airline seat	M/R/S	Competitive Cost plus	Medium	D	Taxes paid to government bodies. Commission paid to marketing intermediaries	Offering FITs	V
Hotel chain bedrooms	M (R in some countries)	Competitive Cost plus	High	D	Taxes paid to government bodies. Commission paid to marketing intermediaries. Shareholders' dividends where appropriate	Restaurant meals Mini-bars	V
Tour operators FITs	M	Competitive Cost plus	High	D	Taxes paid to government bodies. Commission paid to marketing intermediaries. Shareholders' dividends where appropriate. Financial bonds	Excursion programmes	V

Theme parks	M	Competitive Cost plus	Low	D	Taxes paid to government bodies. Shareholders' dividends where appropriate	Corporate hospitality catering	V
Private taxis	R (in most places in Europe)	Fixed price set by licensing authority – operator has no freedom to fix prices	Not applicable	Not applicable	Fees paid to licensing authority. Taxes paid to government bodies	Not applicable	V
Local municipal museum	S (or there may be no charge made)	Where there is a charge fixed, the price is to allow the organization to operate within its budget	Low	C	Contribution to the overall costs of the municipality	Guided visits	Q
Public sector theatre	S	The price is fixed to allow the organization to operate within its budget	Medium	C	Fees paid in return for the right to use copyrighted material such as plays and music	Pre- and post-performance suppers	Q
National park	No direct charge is made for using a national park	Not applicable	Not applicable	Not applicable	Not applicable	Charges may be levied for the use of car parks, the sale of publications and guided tours	V

explained by the fact that for each city in Europe, there is a different competitive position for each particular type of hotel – in other words, different market conditions. Customers must also have different expectations of hotel prices for different European cities. What is clear is the fact that hotel chains adjust the prices in their hotels according to their location in Europe.

CONCLUSIONS

Organizations involved in the marketing of tourism, leisure and hospitality products find that pricing is a difficult and complex strategic task. Pricing is used both as a strategic and tactical weapon in the marketing process. Standardization of prices across Europe is very difficult due to differences both in the supply and demand side of the market. Different European countries have different economic conditions and the level of competition in any particular market will vary from country to country.

The levels of state intervention in pricing policies varies in different European countries. All of these supply side factors will influence the prices which organizations can charge for products. On the demand side, the presence of the Euro-consumer has already been evaluated. Despite the growth of this target group, there is still marked differences in consumer perceptions in different European countries to prices and perceived value for money. This is particularly noticeable in certain markets, for example leisure products.

A summary of pricing for different categories of product in the tourism, leisure and hospitality industries is shown in Table 9.6. This shows the complexity of pricing for different kinds of organization and the impacts that the European dimension has on these processes.

DISCUSSION POINTS AND ESSAY QUESTIONS

1. Critically evaluate the different methods of calculating prices. Outline what you believe would be the most appropriate method or methods for calculating the price of **one** of the following products:
   (a) a restaurant meal;
   (b) an airline seat;
   (c) a theatre ticket.
2. Discuss the ways in which public sector agencies intervene in the pricing process in tourism, leisure and hospitality
3. Explain the differences between strategic pricing and tactical pricing.

> You should select both a public sector and a private sector organization   **EXERCISE**
> within tourism, leisure and hospitality.
>   For your chosen organizations you should discover the method, or
> methods, of pricing they use, and the factors they take into account when
> fixing their prices.
>   Finally, you should attempt to identify and explain differences in
> approaches adopted by your two chosen organizations.

CASE STUDIES

You may want to look at the following cases to illustrate some of the
points made in the chapter:

  2. The Forte International Programme, UK;
  7. Futuroscope, France;
 10. Club Méditerranée SA, France;
 11. The Hurtigruten, Norwegian coastal voyage, Norway;
 13. Iceland: The marketing of a business tourism destination;
 18. Airtours plc, UK;
 19. British Airways, UK;
 21. The Victoria and Albert Museum, UK;
 23. Futbol Club Barcelona, Spain;
 24. Abercrombie and Kent Ltd, UK;
 25. Accor, France;
 26. Thalassa International, France;
 27. Les Vins Georges Duboeuf SA, France;
 28. Center Parcs, UK;
 29. Port Aventura SA, Spain.

10 Place

Key concepts

The main concepts covered in this chapter are:

- the main distribution channels in tourism, leisure and hospitality;
- the impact of technology on distribution systems;
- the growth of direct marketing;
- factors which influence the type of distribution system in different sectors and different countries.

INTRODUCTION

Place is clearly a crucial aspect of marketing, for consumers may like a product and be willing to pay its price, but if they cannot gain access to it, no sale will result.

In this chapter, we will explore the nature of place, or distribution, in tourism, leisure and hospitality. In particular, consideration will be given to three aspects of distribution, namely:

- the distribution channels which operate in tourism, leisure and hospitality, and the role of marketing intermediaries such as travel agents;
- the growth of direct marketing, where producers communicate directly with potential consumers without the involvement of intermediaries;
- the development of European distribution channels in tourism, leisure and hospitality.

One clear theme that will be developed during the chapter is the increasing influence of technological developments on the distribution system in tourism, leisure and hospitality. These include computer reservation systems and multi-media systems, for example.

The distribution of tourism, leisure and hospitality products can take two forms as with other products, namely:

- directly from the producer to the consumer;
- indirectly from the producer to the consumer via one or more intermediaries.

DISTRIBUTION CHANNELS AND THE ROLE OF MARKETING INTERMEDIARIES

The distribution of tourism, leisure and hospitality products takes place using distribution channels. As stated above, distribution channels can take two forms, namely:

- directly from producer to consumer;
- indirectly from the producer to the consumer – when the product is distributed indirectly, there are one or more intermediaries that are involved in the distribution channel.

An organization may use one or a combination of direct and indirect distribution channels. The choice of these will depend on the costs involved, the predicted levels of success, the degree of control and the level of service required. The market characteristics will also determine the type of distribution channel which is used. In the tourism industry, for example, many domestic producers such as small hotels, bed and breakfasts, specialist tour operators, and holiday centres sell their products and services directly to the customer.

Direct sale has been helped with the growth of sophisticated targeting techniques for direct mail, and the use of advanced distribution technology. The products which constitute the outbound tourism market, however, are almost exclusively distributed directly via a series of travel agents. The travel agent acts as a retailer for the tour operator who negotiates the package from different suppliers and presents the finished result in a brochure.

A simple distribution channel consists of a producer who may sell directly to the final consumer or may use intermediaries. This is shown diagramatically in Figure 10.1.

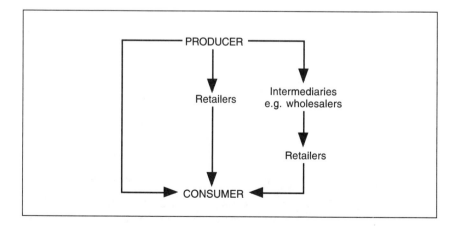

Figure 10.1 Examples of different distribution channels.

Table 10.1 The functions of the retail travel agent

- Stocks brochures
- Provides advice for customers
- Sorts the products ready for display
- Merchandises the products in attractive displays
- Handles promotions on behalf of the companies represented
- Negotiates terms of sale with the customer
- Uses computer reservation systems to expedite customer bookings
- Receives payment from the customer
- Transmits tickets to the customer
- Analyses sales data and provides companies with marketing information
- Offers ancillary products such as insurance and currency exchange
- Handles customer complaints

A **wholesaler** is a trader who buys a product or service in bulk from the producer and then sells it in smaller quantities, especially to retailers. A **retailer** is a person or company that sells products or services to the general public. The retail outlet may be in the form of a shop, a multiple, a supermarket, a restaurant, a public house, etc. The retailer is usually the last link in the distribution channel before the customer. The retailer will carry out a number of functions on behalf of the producer. Table 10.1 shows the functions which a retail travel agent carries out on behalf of the tour operators.

One of the key activities of the retail travel agent is to merchandise effectively so that consumers are attracted to the shop to purchase. The retail travel agency should also offer a reliable and efficient service which encourages sales.

A simplified model of distribution shows that the producer can use a number of intermediaries ranging from a wholesaler to a retailer. This general model can be applied to the tourism, leisure and hospitality industries. Airline seats, for example, are a good example of a product which is sold in a number of different ways using specific distribution channels. This is explored in Figure 10.2.

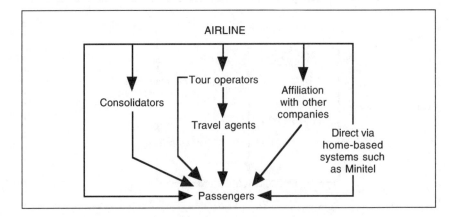

Figure 10.2 The distribution channel for airline seats.

This model shows that airline companies use a variety of distribution channels to sell airline seats to the final customer. They sell direct to the passengers using telephone or interactive systems like Minitel in France, for instance. They can also sell tickets in their own retail outlets. Most of the major national airlines have their own shops in major cities of the world. Airlines also sell seats by using the tour operators and travel agents as intermediaries in the distribution channel.

The airline can negotiate directly with the tour operator, which then presents a package which is either sold directly to the passenger or sold in a travel agent which serves as a retail outlet. Consolidators also act as intermediaries in the distribution channel, and may sell either direct to the passenger or may use other intermediaries. Airlines often form loose affiliations with other organizations in order to sell airline tickets to the final customer.

The distribution of airline tickets also relies heavily on the use of CRS (computer reservation systems). The use of technology in the distribution process is discussed in more detail later in this chapter.

Hotels also use many different forms of distribution channel. An example of a model for a hotel distribution system has already been discussed.

Organizations that are marketing tourism, leisure and hospitality products have developed special systems for distribution. This is probably partly explained by the intangible and perishable nature of services in general.

In some cases the organizations use marketing channels which are similar to those used by more traditional manufacturers. Examples of intermediaries in these types of distribution channel include company-owned, managed or franchised networks. In other cases, the organizations rely on unique distribution methods. Examples of intermediaries in these unique systems include consortia, central reservation systems, affiliations and specialist organizations such as tour operators and travel agents.

Organizations must also decide whether to own, manage or franchise the intermediaries in the distribution channel. A major hotel chain which is trying to expand internationally, for example, must decide on whether to **own** the new outlets itself. There are advantages and disadvantages to ownership which are summarized in Table 10.2.

Table 10.2 The advantages and disadvantages of expanding a hotel chain by ownership

Advantages	Disadvantages
Owning provides the best chance of controlling the product quality.	Capital monies are spread thin. The company may not have sufficient resources to fund rapid expansion plans.
Owning gives the company reassurance about consistent quality, internationally.	It may be a very slow process to own new hotels, particularly in areas where they have to be built from scratch.

Table 10.3 The advantages and disadvantages of expanding a hotel chain by management

Advantages	Disadvantages
The next best to owning for managing quality standards and consistency.	Can be difficult financially and can encourage over supply.
Much quicker than owning – managing usually involves existing properties.	Owners may refuse to refurbish when the managing company considers it is essential.
Little capital investment.	

Organizations can also **manage** properties owned by others. The advantages and disadvantages of this approach are summarized in Table 10.3.

The final method of expansion for the hotel chain is to enter into franchising agreements. **Franchising** is an agreement in which a retailer is granted the exclusive rights to retail certain products or services in a specified area in return for a payment. The franchiser grants the franchisee the use of its trade mark, promotional facilities and merchandising expertise.

Franchising has been used extensively by hospitality providers as a way of achieving an effective distribution channel in a short space of time. Hotel companies such as Holiday Inn and Accor, and fast food operators such as McDonald's and Burger King, have all used franchising as a way of developing distribution channels in extensive geographic areas. The development of a franchised network will allow the organization to spread the distribution of the product or service at a rapid rate. It also allows the organization to use the business experience of others which can be particularly important if the market is one in which the organization is not totally familiar. The control of quality and consistency may be difficult and will require very carefully designed management systems. Organizations often choose to use a mix of ownership, management and franchising agreements to develop an effective distribution system.

Other intermediaries in the distribution channels of tourism, leisure and hospitality organizations are discussed in the sections which follow.

Consortia

A **consortium** is a loosely linked group of independently owned and managed organizations which join up to operate a joint marketing distribution process. An example of a consortium of hotels is the French Logis de France which represents almost 5000 family-run hotels of varying sizes and quality. The properties are tied together by a logo and the consortium carries out marketing activities aimed at target markets. There is some measure of control placed on membership which differentiates them from reservation networks. Membership of a consortium offers an organization the advantages of access to improved marketing channels and exposure to more target customers. The organization can also use a brand identity which will often open up the possibility of distributing on an international basis. The fact that the organization needs to meet certain standards means that there may be some initial investment required.

There is also the danger that the members of the consortium are seen as a chain operation with little individual identity. The way that the Logis consortium in France has tried to overcome this potential problem is by the requirement that each Logis must have a local menu which reflects the local traditional cuisine. This ensures that each Logis has an individual and unique identity. Other examples of hotel consortia are:

- Best Western Hotels;
- Exec Hotels;
- Leading Hotels of the World;
- Quality International Hotels;
- Relais du Silence Hotels;
- Relais et Châteaux Hotels;
- Auberges de France.

Reservation networks

Central reservation systems have become a key factor in the marketing activities of hotels. Buttle (1986) has identified three forms of organization for these type of systems:

- a corporate group;
- a voluntary association or consortium;
- a franchise group.

The large hotel chains rely heavily on computerized reservation systems and the information which these systems generate can provide vital marketing information. Marriott hotels, for example, has a computer reservation system which provides the company with a massive database of marketing information which the company uses in a number of ways, including the accurate targeting of customers and potential customers.

Smaller groups and consortia of hotels have also joined together to establish reservation systems. Hotels of the World, for example, represent a group of luxury hotels which have joined together for reservation and marketing reasons.

Hotel reservation systems offer the hotel operator a number of advantages including:

- a convenient method of booking for the customer;
- automatic invoicing systems;
- marketing information opportunity;
- manipulation of room rates to improve profitability.

There are also a number of independent organizations which are using computer reservation systems as a central focus for their business. Companies have developed that offer to handle all the hotel reservations for corporate clients. The company then has direct links into hotel central reservation systems to arrange the booking. Because of bulk purchasing power, individual corporate clients can be offered more attractive rates than they can achieve for themselves. The reservation system intermediary also benefits through commission on its bookings. Hotels, however, have to decide whether the increased business which they can obtain compensates for the pressure on room rates.

Travel agents also use independent computer reservation systems to help with their complex booking operations. Most of the regions of the world are covered by global computerized reservation systems such as SABRE, GALILEO and AMADEUS. These offer the travel agent direct access into central systems for air seat booking. Most hospitality facilities could be members of global pre-booking systems, and this is certain to develop further in the next few years.

Travel agents

A travel agent is an intermediary in a channel of distribution who makes reservations on behalf of tour operators, airlines and hotels. The travel agent is compensated in the form of a commission. Travel agencies are nearly always equipped with computer systems to handle the complex set of variables involved in making bookings on behalf of individuals, business travellers and groups.

Tour operators

Tour operators are also intermediaries in the channels of distribution. Hospitality companies often rely heavily on tour operators to distribute their services. Tour operators may provide valuable custom and can generate substantial demand. This can be particularly valuable to hospitality companies at off-peak times although some businesses are permanently positioned towards the tour market. The disadvantages of being dependent upon this market are that the numbers arriving can fall short of that anticipated when room allocations were made. Also tour operators often demand extremely competitive rates. A further disadvantage is that tour customers may not 'fit' with other market segments being targeted by the company.

Future developments

The distribution and selling of tourism, leisure, and hospitality products is being revolutionized by the rapid development of new electronic databases which can be incorporated in telecommunication systems. The future of distribution in these markets will depend on the development of electronic channels via multimedia marketing.

Advances in indirect marketing channels in the last few years have included **computer reservation systems (CRS)** and **global distribution systems (GDS)**. These were developed initially by American airline companies in the 1970s with computers forming a link between the airline and travel agency.

The first CRS system was SABRE developed by American Airlines in the USA. This was followed by a similar system developed by British Airways in 1977 called TRAVICOM (now called GALILEO). The European market formed a number of consortia during the 1980s, Air France, Iberia, Lufthansa, Finnair, SAS, JAT, Braathens, Icelandair and Linjeflyge developing AMADEUS on the Unysis system, and Swissair, Alitalia, KLM, Sabena, Olympic, Austrian, Aer Lingus, Air Portugal and BA developing GALILEO on the IBM system.

The development of global distribution systems (GDS) arose from the initial development of CRS. GDS can now provide travel agents with access to the world's most comprehensive range of travel products and services. The top four distribution systems are SABRE, WORLD-SPAN, GALILEO and AMADEUS. These systems allow the buyers and sellers of travel products to be directly connected together. They also allow massive amounts of information to be ordered which can then ease the purchase of the product on a worldwide basis. The 'information superhighway' is therefore going to continue to have a significant effect on the distribution of tourism, leisure and hospitality products. It will also mean that the distribution of many products and services in the industry will be controlled by the owners of the global distribution systems rather than the owners of the outlets.

Viewdata is information which is transmitted by telephone line on VDU or TV. It excludes teletext (Ceefax and Oracle in the UK) which are communicated via TV transmitter. The first system to be introduced in the UK was PRESTEL which was developed by the Post Office. Thomson, the tour operator, developed its own system and installed direct access reservation systems in a wide network of travel agents in the 1980s. The trend is to link CRS and Viewdata systems together. ISTEL is connected to GALILEO and WORLDSPAN, for example. Such electronic distribution systems will play an increasingly important role in the future in the distribution of tourism, leisure and hospitality products.

Many organizations in the industry see the development of effective global sales and distribution as a key strategic objective. Forte, the UK-based hospitality company, for example, began the development of a global sales and reservation network within the hospitality industry in 1994. Fortress II was developed with a £20 m budget to link all Forte's sales offices and hotels throughout the world. The system interfaces with 400 000 travel agents and all the major airline systems. The company has developed a freephone system which can answer calls in

12 languages. Their newly acquired French chain Méridien was due to join the system in 1995.

THE GROWTH OF DIRECT MARKETING

The developments in multimedia systems mean that there are many opportunities to develop direct marketing channels. This will effectively remove the necessity for marketing intermediaries such as travel agents in the longer term.

The opportunities for increased use of direct marketing system means that it is easier for producers to distribute products and services on an international or European basis.

POI (point of information) systems are multimedia computers which stand alone and provide the customer with interactive services. POI systems have already appeared in travel agencies in Holland and are being investigated by other tour operators in other European countries.

POS (point of sale) systems are already operating in airports and stations. They allow the customer to buy their tickets directly and can be linked to electronic fund transfer at point of sale (EFTPOS) systems for direct payment. These systems can also be linked to POI systems so that the customer can buy direct in shops, departure points, or even in the home. This will allow multimedia systems of distribution to be located increasingly in the home on a personal computer or television screen. The customer will soon be able to make up their own holiday package to their own personal requirements in the home, which will make the systems of distribution more direct because the customer will have the ability to communicate directly with the supplier.

THE ISSUE OF PRE-BOOKING

Distribution networks tend to exist where pre-booking is the norm, which means airline seats, package holidays and hotel rooms, for example, in the context of tourism, leisure and hospitality. Where pre-booking is rare or there is no provision for pre-booking, it is difficult to identify anything that might be termed a distribution network. In this situation a distribution network is unnecessary or impractical. Examples of this in tourism, leisure and hospitality might include most visitor attractions and countryside recreation such as walking along footpaths.

LOCATION AND 'PASSING TRADE'

P for place in the marketing mix, as we know, means distribution channels. However, in some sectors of tourism, leisure, and hospitality, it can literally mean place or location. In sectors such as hotels and attractions, where so-called 'passing trade' is an important element of the market, this is the case. For example, someone walking around Bruges or Barcelona in the evening looking for a hotel room will select a hotel by walking up and down the street until they find a hotel they like the look of which has vacancies. Here it is the hotel's location which has given the customer access to the product.

THE DEVELOPMENT OF EUROPEAN DISTRIBUTION CHANNELS

It is well recognized that distribution is one of the most difficult parts of the marketing mix to standardize (Porter 1986). Distribution channels in different countries of Europe, for example, show very different patterns of development. Retailing has also been developed on an individual country by country basis.

The opportunity to standardize the distribution channels for tourism, leisure and hospitality products across Europe will depend on a series of factors, including those discussed below.

The market characteristics

The type of market will determine whether it is possible to standardize the distribution channels across Europe. The international airline business, for example, is showing increasing signs of standardization of distribution with the use of computer reservation systems (CRS) and global distribution systems (GDS). Standardization will become particularly well developed if the channels of distribution become shorter and direct selling becomes the norm. International airlines, however, still use a network of nationally based retailers in individual countries to distribute their product.

The hospitality industry is also beginning to show signs of a standardized approach to distribution. International hotel chains are beginning to develop distribution channels which use CRS and GDS systems, although nationally based retailers are also used to distribute their products and services. Fast-food chains such as Burger King and McDonald's have used a standardized approach to distribution in different countries. The fact that consumers in the market expect to go to a similar outlet in a major strategic location and buy a similar fast-food product has allowed the fast-food retailers to develop in a standardized way using a variety of techniques such as ownership and franchising.

The size of the supplier

The size of the supplier of the tourism, leisure or hospitality product will determine the approach to distribution. A small hospitality outlet such as a hotel or restaurant will have a small geographical market area. For this type of operation distribution or 'place' will literally mean the location of the operation rather than a channel of distribution. The question of whether to standardize or not will not be an issue for a small business such as this.

The leisure industry has also been characterized by small organizations which are often in the public sector. The small size of these operations such as leisure centres or theatres will also mean that distribution or 'place' will also mean the location of the operation.

It is the large organizations in the industry that have the ability to market in different countries which have the most opportunity to standardize their distribution channels. This includes international airlines, international hotel chains, and multinational fast-food chains. The use of computer reservation systems and global distribution systems will help in this standardization process.

The availability of standardized distribution channels

If an organization has the desire to develop a standardized approach to distribution it must have available standardized channels which the customer readily accepts.

Many large organizations in the tourism, leisure and hospitality industries have a mixed approach to distribution because of their portfolio of products and services. In some market areas they may be operating a locally developed distribution system to meet local trading conditions. In other market areas, they may be trying to standardise their distribution channels so that they can compete more effectively.

Bass, for example, the UK-based brewing and leisure group, operates different strategies in different areas of the business. This can be seen in a statement issued by the Chairman of the company in 1994:

> The competitive benefits of scale arising from size and brand leadership operate at different levels in different markets. Our strategy is, therefore, to focus our efforts sharply on the level that will yield most benefits locally for pubs and leisure retailing, nationally for brewing and soft drinks and internationally for hotel franchising.
>
> Ian Prosser, Chairman of Bass

Table 10.4 The strategy of Bass plc for different products and services

1. **Local focus:**
   Bass Taverns – public houses
   Bass Leisure – bingo, betting, bowling and electronic leisure

2. **National focus:**
   Bass Brewers
   Britvic soft drinks

3. **International focus:**
   Holiday Inn Worldwide
   International expansion by franchising

In other words, the company's focus is on a local, national and international basis according to the particular market. This is explored in more detail in Table 10.4.

DISTRIBUTION AND PROMOTION

It could be argued that some of the trends we have just been discussing are blurring the distinction between distribution and promotion. Consumers will increasingly be able to access promotional material directly, without the need for marketing intermediaries. They will then be able to book or buy the product at the same time, through interactive television for instance.

The choice of focus, whether it is local, national or international, has been determined by the market characteristics and consumer buying behaviour. In general there has been a growth in the number of indirect channels of sales in the tourism, leisure and hospitality industry. The closer that these intermediaries are to the consumer, the more local they have tended to become. Travel agents, for example, have developed at a local and national level in individual countries of Europe.

Distribution networks are likely to change in the next few years from the current structure of travel agencies, tour operators, corporate travel offices, hotel chains and government tourism promotion bodies. The role of these members in the distribution channel will change as the communications technology moves forward. Third parties with highly developed software and infrastructures will increasingly control the capacity. The revolution in the distribution of tourism, leisure and hospitality products across increasingly larger geographical areas has only just begun.

CONCLUSIONS

This chapter has explored the importance of place in the marketing of tourism, leisure and hospitality products. It has looked at the direct and indirect methods of distribution which exist in the industry. Important issues such as the growth of direct marketing are discussed. The chapter concludes by looking at the development of European distribution channels and the use of information technology to help with this process.

DISCUSSION POINTS AND ESSAY QUESTIONS

1. Discuss the different types of distribution channels which exist within tourism, leisure and hospitality.

2. Critically evaluate the ways in which technological developments are likely to affect the future distribution of tourism, leisure and hospitality products.
3. Examine the factors that will stimulate, and obstruct, the growth of direct marketing in tourism, leisure and hospitality.

EXERCISE Choose **either** of the following pairs of organizations:

- a mass market tour operator and a niche market specialist tour operator;
- a major international hotel chain and a small local private hotel.

Select a real organization from each of the two sectors. You should produce, for each organization, a model of their distribution network.

You should then identify the similarities and differences between the distribution networks of the two organizations and account for the differences.

CASE STUDIES

You may want to look at the following case studies to illustrate some of the points made in this chapter:

9. Bord Fáilte, Ireland;
11. The Hurtigruten, Norwegian coastal voyage, Norway;
13. Iceland: The marketing of a business tourism destination;
18. Airtours plc, UK;
19. British Airways, UK;
21. The Victoria and Albert Museum, UK;
23. Futbol Club Barcelona, Spain;
24. Abercrombie and Kent Ltd, UK;
25. Accor, France;
26. Thalassa International, France;
27. Les Vins Georges Duboeuf SA, France;
28. Center Parcs, UK;
29. Port Aventura SA, Spain.

Promotion 11

Key concepts

The main concepts covered in this chapter are:

- the role of promotion within marketing;
- the different forms of promotional technique or marketing communication;
- 'push and pull' strategies;
- the stages involved in the creation of a promotional campaign;
- the growth of pan-European media;
- the legal framework for promotional activities.

INTRODUCTION

The previous three chapters have looked at the development of well-designed products and services which are distributed effectively. The effective marketer must also communicate these product and service ideas to the target customers.

Effective communication with target customers is carried out by a variety of methods which in total are referred to as **marketing communication**. This chapter will look at the different promotional techniques which are used by tourism, leisure and hospitality providers.

For many people, marketing **is** promotion, for promotion is the highly visible, public face of marketing. However, this chapter is based on the view that promotion is only one of the four Ps, and is only part of marketing. It is the tip of the iceberg, the part which can be seen by passers-by, while only a few have an opportunity to see the whole iceberg.

We will look at the role of promotion in tourism, leisure and hospitality management. In doing so, consideration will be given to a number of promotional techniques, including:

- advertising;
- brochures;
- press and public relations;
- sales promotions;

- personal selling;
- direct mail;
- sponsorship;
- point-of-sale material.

The chapter will then go on to look at how organizations decide which promotional techniques to utilise and how to combine them in a promotional plan for a particular product.

Towards the end of the chapter, there will be a discussion of the ways in which technological developments are changing the nature of the promotional mix in tourism, leisure and hospitality. The chapter will finish by considering the role of pan-European promotion and whether this can be developed for tourism, leisure and hospitality markets.

THE ROLE OF PROMOTION

The role of promotion is to convince potential customers of the benefits of purchasing or using the products and services of a particular organization. This concept has been defined as:

> The role of promotion is to communicate with individuals, groups or organizations so as to directly and indirectly facilitate exchanges by informing and persuading one or more of the audience to accept an organization's products.
>
> Coulson-Thomas (1986)

The organization will use marketing communication methods to take potential customers through a series of steps before they adopt a product or service. These steps are considered below:

- **Awareness**. The potential customer becomes aware of the new product or service. This is often achieved by mass communication methods.
- **Interest**. The next stage is to get the potential customer interested in the new product or service. This is often achieved by linking the product or service to a well known brand name or company name. Mass communication methods are also used at this stage.
- **Evaluation**. The potential customer will then evaluate the product or service offered. This will often involve them referring to reports about the product or service and talking to friends and relatives about its potential benefits.
- **Trial**. The potential customer must then be encouraged to try the product or service. This is the stage that at which personal selling and sales promotions are often used to encourage trial.
- **Adoption**. The potential customer is finally convinced that adoption of the product or service is appropriate. This will be achieved by the perceived quality of the product or service. The customer will also talk to friends and relatives to reassure themselves that they have

made the right decision. Mass communication techniques will also reinforce their decision to adopt the product or service.

Organizations use marketing communications for many reasons other than simply launching new products. The main uses of advertising, for example, have been explored by Dibb, Simkin, Pride and Ferrell (1994) and are shown in Figure 11.1. Clearly the organization which is using marketing communication will be utilising a variety of techniques to achieve these particular objectives.

An organization may, for example, be trying to encourage potential customers to try their product or service at the same time as encouraging their existing customers to purchase or use the product and service again.

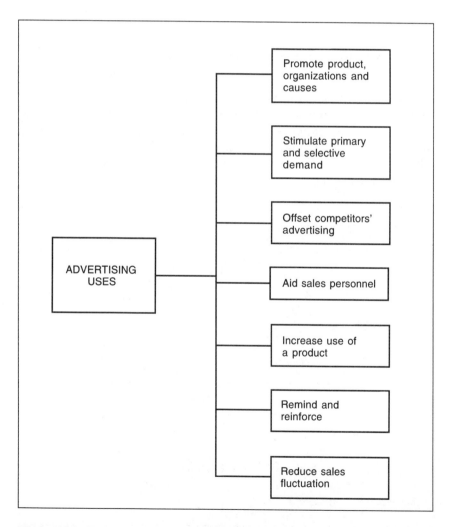

Figure 11.1 The main uses of advertising.
Source: Dibb, Simkin, Pride and Ferrell (1994).

METHODS OF MARKETING COMMUNICATION

Organizations use different methods of marketing communication to achieve their aims. It is important that they choose the correct mix of the different methods to achieve an effective **promotional campaign**. The different methods of marketing communication are shown in Figure 11.2.

Advertising

Advertising is a paid form of non-personal communication about an organization's product or services which is transmitted via the media of television, radio, newspapers, magazines, public transport, outside displays and catalogues. Advertising has been defined by Kotler (1994) as:

> Any paid form of non-personal communication and promotion of ideas, about goods, or services by an identified sponsor.

The choice of media to be used will depend on the objective of the campaign and the budget to be spent. Organizations often use a variety of methods and techniques at the same time to meet their marketing objectives. There are both advantages and disadvantages of using advertising as a method of marketing communication. These are summarized in Table 11.1.

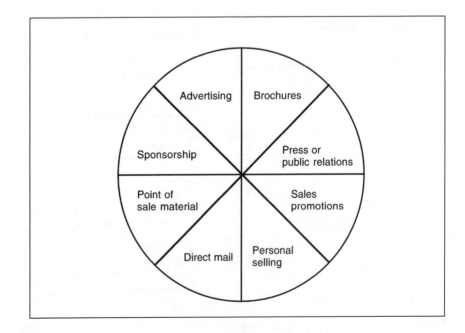

Figure 11.2 Methods of marketing communication.

Table 11.1 The advantages and disadvantages of advertising

Advantages	Disadvantages
It is very flexible and can target large audiences or more precise market niches.	Expensive to design and carry out, particularly on primetime television.
Can be cost efficient if the aim is to reach a large number of people at a low cost per person.	Relatively difficult to monitor its effectiveness. This is because the aims of advertising are often long-term in nature.
The message can be repeated regularly and via different media, e.g. TV, magazines, outdoor displays, etc.	

Advertising has the advantage of targeting large audiences via different methods, but it is expensive to design and implement and it is often difficult to monitor its effectiveness.

There are a wide range of advertising methods that an organization can use. Some large organizations such as airline companies, theme parks and important special events can afford television advertising which is expensive. Other smaller organizations may use advertising on a one-off basis to promote special events such as open days. The press is a major part of the main paid advertising medium which many organizations in this sector use. These may range from local, regional, and national newspapers to magazines and guides. Many organizations in the public sector have very low advertising budgets and therefore have to learn how to spend their budget wisely.

The cost of advertising media is related to a number of factors including the number of people who will see the advertisement and how influential the medium is thought to be in persuading people to buy or use the product.

Swarbrooke (1995) has pointed out that most visitor attractions are not mass market but rather niche market products. This means that they usually do not need to utilize the expensive mass media techniques. Highly targeted advertising strategies are usually more relevant. This targeting can take a number of forms including:

- targeting media which are aimed at appropriate niche markets;
- advertising at certain times of the year only;
- targeting potential customers in a particular geographical area.

The types of advertising that can be used by an organization are shown in Table 11.2.

Brochures

The brochure is one of the main forms of marketing communication in the tourism, leisure and hospitality industries. The services which are on offer by the organization are often depicted in a brochure to enable the potential customer to choose the right product. Boyer and Viallon

Table 11.2 The types of advertising that can be used by organizations

Type of advertising	Comments
Television	Visual and moving Reaches wide audience Expensive
Radio	Relatively low impact Inexpensive
Newspapers	Visual image Can be stored Modest production costs Often tied to particular times
Periodicals	Visual image Good for reaching target audience Often infrequent production
Annual guides and yearbooks	Often consulted by groups of people who are interested Often high cover price
Posters and visual displays	Visual image Colourful Stationary image May be expensive for prime sites

(1994) recognize that the brochure is of particular use in the communication of tourism products.

Brochures are increasingly being accompanied by video cassettes. These help the organization to show real images of the holiday, destination or hotel. In the future, the use of virtual reality images will allow the potential customer to view the actual location and even to 'try out' the potential purchase. In the meantime, the brochure production exercise forms a major part of the promotional activity budget of many major tourism, leisure and hospitality companies.

Marketers, clearly, also need to consider the importance of brochure distribution as a superb brochure is ineffective if it does not get into the hands of the right people at the right time.

Press and public relations

Publicity refers to non-personal communication in news story form about an organization and its products transmitted through the media for no charge. Kotler defines publicity as:

> Non-personal stimulation of demand for a product, service, or business unit by planting commercially significant news about it in a

published medium or obtaining favourable presentation of it on radio, television or stage, that is not paid for by the sponsor.

(Kotler, 1994)

The public relations mechanism should be well established by an organization and it should control and manage the use of effective publicity. Many large organizations are now employing **public relations agencies** to help them manage their publicity effectively. An organization should also develop an effective method of generating press releases and develop suitable relationships with the editors involved in the media with their coverage. Public relations is therefore an important part of the communications process. Buttle (1986) defines this role as follows:

> Improving awareness, projecting credibility, combating competition, evaluating new markets, creating direct sales leads, reinforcing the effectiveness of sales promotion and advertising, motivating the sales force, introducing new products, building brand loyalty, dealing with consumer issues and in many other ways.

Press and public relations activity is important in both the public and private sectors of tourism, leisure and hospitality. The opening of a new hotel, for example, would involve an extensive press and public relations campaign. Some of the activities which would be involved in the launch of the new hotel are shown in Table 11.3. It can be seen in this example that the activity involves both paid and non-paid communication methods.

For organizations that are operating in the public sector, the correct handling of press and public relations is very important. It is important for a museum, for example, which is funded by government or local authority sources of money to develop a very favourable impression with the local, regional and national media. This will encourage the media to cover the stories about the museum which show it in a good light. Unfortunately, the development of a high-profile image will equally encourage the media to cover any issues which show the organization in a bad light.

Table 11.3 The press and public relations activities involved in the launch of a new hotel

- Arranging press releases to regional, national and international media at the appropriate time.
- Arranging a 'pre-opening' campaign by inviting press, local dignitaries, etc. to look around the new hotel.
- Arranging an opening reception for the hotel with a major personality to carry out the official opening and having an impressive guest list for this event.
- Making sure that well known and liked dignitaries who make news are invited as the first guests to get maximum media attention.
- Making sure that the new hotel is well covered in all the major trade press in the country in which it is operating.

If an organization which has been developing a reputation for 'green' products and services, for example, is suddenly shown to have carried out an activity which is damaging to the environment, then it is almost guaranteed that the media will cover the story. The amount of coverage will depend on the interest of the story and the handling of the press and media by the press offices of the organization.

Organizations should also develop a well thought-out press and public relations strategy to cope with incidents which could damage the long term reputation of the business. Many large organizations have now established various forms of 'emergency committees' which are composed of a number of key individuals who assemble to deal with a major disaster. This could range from the death of a customer to a major pollution incident. The emergency committee will then deal with the incident and talk to the press and media in a well thought-out and planned approach to try and minimize the damage caused by the incident.

It is when these major incidents happen that it is vital that a good relationship with the media has been developed over a number of years. This will help the organization to deal honestly and effectively with the media with the objective of minimizing the long-term negative effects of bad publicity.

Press and public relations activity is therefore vital for any type of organization involved in the tourism, leisure and hospitality industries. It will help to show the organization in a good light and enable the organization to cope with major incidents which could damage the organization's long-term image.

Sales promotion

Sales promotion is an activity or material that acts as an inducement to sale for potential or existing customers. It includes the use of coupons, bonuses and contests which are all examples of techniques which an organization can use to boost sales. Sales promotion has been defined by Kotler as:

> Short-term incentives to encourage purchase or sales of a product or service.
>
> (Kotler, 1994)

The emphasis here is on the short term, rather than the longer-term objectives of advertising. Sales promotion is often used by companies at irregular intervals, particularly if the market is seasonal. The package holiday companies, for example, boost initial sales of their summer sum holidays by sales promotion techniques such as free holidays for children. Sales promotions can offer **discounts**. An example of this would be 'money off' promotions which are offered to stimulate demand. Sales promotions can also **add value** to the product or service offered. This means keeping the standard price but offering the customer more for their money.

Hotel companies have become very skilled at using added value sales promotion techniques. The bottle of champagne which is provided in the guests room on arrival is an example of the use of a sales promotion technique.

Personal selling

Personal selling techniques are of key importance to organizations which are marketing service products because of the inseparable nature of the offering. Personal selling involves persuading customers to purchase products and services in a personal face-to-face situation. The nature of tourism, leisure and hospitality products means that there should be a heavy emphasis on the personal selling effort as part of the marketing communications process.

Personal selling has been defined by Kotler, as

> Oral presentation in a conversation with one or more prospective purchasers for the purpose of making sales.
>
> (Kotler 1994)

The oral presentation may be made to the final customer and also to intermediaries in the distribution channel.

Personal selling has both advantages and disadvantages. It is directed at smaller groups of people or individuals compared to advertising but has the advantage of achieving greater impact and immediate feedback.

It is important to remember that all 'front of house' personnel in tourism, leisure and hospitality organizations are sales personnel. The person who serves you in a restaurant and the person who serves you in a travel agency, for example, are both carrying out selling activities. It is important that all sales personnel give the customer the right signals. Consider the example of the food server in a restaurant in Table 11.4. This example shows that the customer is looking to the food server as an important sales person and can have many expectations which will affect their overall experience in the restaurant.

The example in Table 11.4 shows that personal selling is very much an 'art' and is very complex in nature. There is a great difference between a 'soft' sell and a 'hard' sell approach. The 'soft' sell seeks to point out opportunities which the customer may wish to take advantage of. The 'hard' sell puts customers under pressure to purchase.

Restaurant companies often try to increase their spend per head by encouraging service staff to 'upsell'. This means that customers are encouraged to buy drinks or extra menu items which they had not otherwise considered purchasing. The sale of excursions by package holiday representatives at the resort is another example of upselling. It is important, however, that customers are not pushed into spending levels that they are uncomfortable with. This may increase their spend in the short term but significantly reduce their repeat customer level.

Table 11.4 The food server as a sales person

The customer of the restaurant will look for one or more of the following features:

- The way the food server dresses should befit the customers' expectations.
- The language which is used. This will be both spoken and unspoken. Body language such as how the food server moves his or her head, eyes, arms and hands is just as important as what they say. Hand gestures and head nodding are often important.
- The way in which the menu is presented to the customer, and what, if anything, is recommended.
- The way in which the food server gets the balance right between ignoring the customer and visibly hovering around them. The customer's requirements will depend on who they are with and their particular mood.
- The way in which the food server deals with children as customers.

It is important to remember that each customer will be looking for a different set of features.

Personal selling to the final customer or to intermediaries in the distribution channels is a key part of the marketing communications mix for tourism, leisure and hospitality organizations. It is vital that the methods are well developed and the front-line personnel are well chosen and trained to deal with their important selling function.

Direct mail

Direct mail and telephone selling are used to contact prospective customers to initiate sales. They are also used to contact existing and past customers to initiate repeat purchases. The use of these techniques has been developed over several decades and targeting of customers is becoming more sophisticated, particularly with the use of computers.

Many service organizations involved in the marketing of tourism, leisure and hospitality products have access to sophisticated customer databases. This makes the use of direct mail selling a particularly attractive proposition as a promotional technique, and a technique is not just confined to customers. It can also be used to target customers in the distribution channel when it is often referred to as **business-to-business marketing**.

It is essential that direct mail is correctly targeted, and that the material which is sent is designed so that it encourages the receiver to open it. To achieve effective targeting, organizations must develop **mailing lists**. These can be generated internally from previous sales data, which is very attractive for service organizations which deal directly with customers. Alternatively, the mailing list can be purchased from mailing houses or list brokers. Many of the geodemographic techniques of segmentation produce databases which are used for direct mail purposes.

Direct mail can also be customized to the individual which makes it an attractive method of marketing communication. The disadvantages include the fact that people often consider direct mail as junk and never open it. There are critics who are also opposed to the idea that organizations can 'buy' their name and address to send them targeted mail. These criticisms are likely to grow as organizations have more and more information concerning individuals and their associated lifestyles.

Point-of-sale materials

For many organizations marketing tourism, leisure and hospitality products, the point-of-sale (POS) material is often a very important promotional opportunity. Point-of-sale material is any material which is used to promote the products and services on offer, and is usually displayed close to retail units. Point-of-sale material has been defined as:

> A sales promotion method that uses items such as outside signs, window displays, and display rails to attract attention, to inform customers and to encourage retailers to carry particular products.
> (Dibb, Simkin, Pride and Ferrell, 1994)

Customers often enter into a hospitality, leisure or tourism business knowing that they are going to purchase something but not quite sure what. It is more likely that the customer has been attracted to the range and type of food on offer at a restaurant, for example, rather than a specific list. In a hotel setting, the customer knows they are staying there, but perhaps is unaware of the extra services which they will use. A customer entering a travel agents is often keen to buy a holiday, but is unsure of the various products on offer.

Here there is a promotional opportunity. The organization can use point-of-sale promotional material to influence the customer and steer them towards a particular choice. The restaurant, for example, may want to steer the customer to try a new dish on their menu, with the intention of broadening appeal and increasing the frequency of the visit. Alternatively, it may want to steer the customer towards selecting a dish which produces more profit. It may also wish to increase customer spend by encouraging the customer to purchase a starter, dessert, side dish or bottle of wine.

Care needs to be taken when designing point-of-sale material. It is not in the long-term interest of the organization to 'push' people into purchase decisions that they later regret. If a customer goes out for an everyday meal, but ends up spending more than anticipated, then they may not select the venue for another meal occasion.

Use of selective point-of-sale material which is sensitively designed has a very important role to play in communicating products and services to customers. In the restaurant setting, counter displays and posters are all forms of point-of-sale material. In hotels, for example, hotel service brochures play a vital role in promoting services of which the customer may otherwise be unaware. Reception staff can also use the check-in period as an important opportunity to promote other hotel services.

Point-of-sale material may also have a role to play in achieving objectives which are not financially related. A restaurant for employees, for example, may want to encourage their staff to eat more healthily. A public house or bar may want to encourage its customers to drive responsibly by not drinking and driving and to select low alcohol alternatives.

For these reasons, point-of-sale promotion is used extensively in tourism, leisure and hospitality organizations and is an important component in the overall promotional mix.

Sponsorship

Sponsorship has been defined as:

> The financial or material support of an event, activity, person, organization or product, by an unrelated organization or donor. Generally funds will be made available to the recipient of the sponsorship deal in return for the prominent exposure of the sponsor's name or brands.
>
> (Dibb, Simkin, Pride and Ferrell, 1994)

Sponsorship has become very popular in the arts. Some theatrical companies, museums and galleries rely more and more on sponsorship as government subsidy of the arts decreases. The Victoria and Albert Museum, for example, covered in Case Study 21, relies heavily on major sponsorship deals to finance many of the large-scale exhibitions.

Another area in tourism, leisure and hospitality which relies on sponsorship are organizations involved in sport. Football teams, for example, found that gate receipts were insufficient to cope with rising bills and operating costs. The way round this financial dilemma was to encourage sponsorship deals. Sponsors were encouraged to appear emblazoned on players' shirts and to finance new spectator stands, for example.

Sponsorship has also been a major part of promotional activity of major sporting events. The Olympics, for example, are always accompanied by an array of official sponsors, ranging from drinks to sportswear manufacturers.

If a company feels that its image or brand awareness will be helped by sponsoring an organization or event, then it will go ahead with this type of promotion. For the recipient organization, this is often an important part of their revenue.

PROMOTIONAL STRATEGIES

Organizations may use one of two different promotional strategies as part of their overall marketing communications mix. These have been referred to by Kotler (1994) as **push** and **pull strategies** and are shown in Figure 11.3.

A **push strategy** is a method by which the organization promotes directly to the intermediaries in the distribution chain, thereby hoping that these organizations promote the items to the final customer. For a package holiday company, this would involve the organization promoting their holidays to travel agents who will then sell them directly to the final customer.

A **pull strategy** relies on the idea that if an organization communicates to their final customer, then the customer will demand the item from the intermediaries. The package holiday companies, for example, would advertise directly to the customer via television, magazines and press advertising. It is hoped that the customer will then demand the

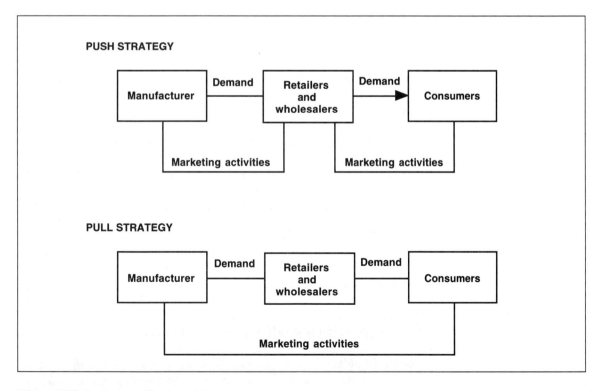

Figure 11.3 Push vs. pull strategies.
Source: adapted from Kotler (1994).

holidays from the travel agent. The package holiday company can also use data on their advertising programmes to convince the intermediaries – in this case the travel agent – to stock their brochures.

In reality, organizations use both types of strategy in their total marketing communications mix.

MARKETING COMMUNICATION IN SERVICES MARKETING

The **intangibility** of services means that they require special treatment when the marketer is planning the promotional campaign. It is difficult to know what to feature in advertising because of this intangibility. Service providers often use **symbols** to stress the nature of the service on offer. The package holiday company, Thomson, for example, uses the symbol of a bird in flight to demonstrate the idea that the customer will fly away on holiday. The symbol also gives an impression of freedom.

It has also become important in service organizations to differentiate effectively between competitors. Many service organizations have used **branding** as a very effective method of differentiation and a platform for their promotional activity. Accor, for example, the French hospitality group, has used a portfolio of brands including Novotel, Formule 1 and Thalassa International to differentiate their service offerings in a crowded market.

It is also important that the advertising for services emphasizes the special nature of what is on offer. This is often achieved by using a slogan or a phrase. British Airways, for example, use the slogan 'The World's Favourite Airline' to give the potential customer an idea about the sort of quality which they can expect when they purchase from them.

The **inseparability** of service means that the role of personal selling by front-line employees of the organization is paramount. Training of these staff in selling techniques should be an important part of the promotional activity. It is important that the customer can quickly recognize and associate with the front-line employees. This is often achieved by the use of a well designed and attractive uniform. One of the key activities in the relaunch of the British package holiday company Owners Abroad as First Choice was the creation of a series of uniforms for front-line staff, both in the UK and abroad in the resorts where the company was represented. This uniform was designed in the new company colours which also appeared in the brand name and all advertising literature.

The **perishability** of services means that organizations often have to try and smooth out demand by using sales promotions techniques. These are often combined with some form of discounting. Large leisure centres, for example, will try to target different groups in the population at quiet periods of operation with special packages. This will avoid closure of the facility during this quiet period as long as enough people in the target group are attracted to the facility.

The final special requirement for service providers is that word-of-mouth communication has been shown to be very important and for this reason should be encouraged. The restaurant which asks the customer to tell their friends about it if they enjoy their visit is an example of this. Hotels encourage word-of-mouth communication by offering customers free services or discounts for encouraging their friends or relatives to visit the hotel.

DESIGNING AN EFFECTIVE PROMOTIONAL CAMPAIGN

Marketing communication is a complicated concept and organizations often find it difficult to design effective promotional campaigns which persuade customers to buy. For this reason, organizations often rely on **advertising agencies** to help them design their promotional campaigns, to advise them where to place them in the media, and finally to help them buy the space in the appropriate media whether it be in print, or television or radio schedules. The organization should provide the advertising agency with an **advertising brief** which is a statement of the aims of the advertising campaign. This should be agreed between the client and the advertising agency before work begins on the promotional campaign. A creative brief to an advertising agency should contain the items shown in Table 11.5. Advertising agencies are very creative but will only produce effective campaigns if they are briefed correctly.

The organization should consider the objectives of the campaign and should decide on an appropriate budget. The types of messages which will be used in the overall campaign will be formulated and decisions made as to where the promotional campaign will be placed in the appropriate media. Finally, the organization will have to decide on how a campaign is to be evaluated. The whole process is shown diagramatically in Figure 11.4.

Table 11.5 The components of a creative brief for an advertising agency

- What is the advertising trying to achieve, e.g. address falling sales, increase sale levels in the next period?
- The size of budget
- What is expected exactly from the promotional mix?
- Who is being addressed? This should include a statement about the target customer
- What is the single most important point that the target customer should take from the promotion?
- Is there evidence of emotional support by the customer for the product/service, for example a well recognized brand name?
- Any other information which is relevant

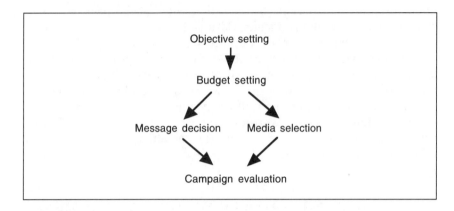

Figure 11.4 The main stages in creating a promotional campaign.

To examine the various stages in the creation and evaluation of a promotional campaign in more detail we will consider an organization opening a new hotel.

Objective setting

The organization should consider the overall objectives of the promotional campaign. There will be a mixed set of objectives for a campaign for the opening of a new hotel including:

● raising awareness amongst target customers;
● raising positive 'word-of-mouth' response from the general public, press and potential customers;
● encouraging trial of the hotel by target users;
● raising the profile of the hotel amongst important distribution intermediaries, e.g. travel agents, tourist offices;
● achieving a set sales level and occupancy level in a set period of time.

The organization will have to prioritize the objectives which have been identified.

Budget setting

The next stage in the design of the promotional campaign is to set a budget. This can sometimes be difficult for a new operation, since there is no established level of sales and profitability. The organization should, however, in the planning process, establish an estimate of expected levels of turnover for the new business.

The budget for the promotional campaign could be based on one or more of the following items:

● a percentage of predicted annual sales;
● the levels of promotional spend which competitive organizations are spending;

- past budgets which have been used by the organization;
- the amount that the organization can afford;
- the level of budget which the objectives of the campaign dictate. A huge capital investment in a new hotel, for example, will dictate the level of promotion necessary to recoup the money invested over a set period of time.

Message decision

Once the objectives of the campaign have been established, and the budget set, it is important that the type of messages which are to be portrayed in the campaign are established. The advertising agency often advises organizations about the style, tone and format of the proposed campaign. Creative copy is produced to portray the sorts of image proposed.

Media selection

The next stage in the design of a promotional campaign is to select the type of media in which the campaign will be featured, and the timing for the campaign.

The opening of the new hotel will probably use different types of promotion. These will probably include:

- media advertising;
- publicity launch;
- sales promotion.

The campaign will be featured in a number of media types including:

- local and/or national press;
- speciality magazines and trade press;
- direct mail to existing customers of the group.

There will be a series of timings which will be crucial for the successful launch of the new hotel. These will include:

- a press campaign leading up to the launch;
- major press activity at the time of the launch;
- direct mail prior to the launch and on an ongoing basis;
- a continuing campaign after the launch to sustain market growth.

The selection of the media used for a promotional campaign will vary for every organization, depending on the objectives of the campaign and the available budget.

Campaign evaluation

It is important that the results of the campaign are monitored by the organization on an ongoing basis to see if the original objectives are being met. There are a variety of ways in which the effectiveness of a campaign can be measured. Some of these methods include the following.

- **Sales**. The build up and continuing sales revenue from the hotel would be measured at regular intervals. This could be broken down into separate profit centres, e.g. restaurant, rooms, conference facilities, health clubs, etc.
- **Customer reaction**. The reaction of final customers and the distribution intermediaries to the promotional material for the hotel can be monitored.
- **Audience achievement**. The target audience for the promotional material would be monitored to see if they actually saw the promotion.

It is vital for the organization to establish whether the original objectives of the promotional campaign are being met on an ongoing basis. If this is not the case, then corrective action will have to be taken.

MARKETING COMMUNICATIONS IN EUROPE

We have seen that some of the organizations involved in the marketing of tourism, leisure and hospitality products have already established European markets. The question arises as to whether these organizations can adopt a European promotional strategy to market their products and services, or whether they will have to develop national campaigns for each country in which they have a presence.

Levitt (1983) stated that the whole world is becoming a single marketplace. If this is the case then it can be assumed that the standardized approach to marketing can be adopted. This will assume that all customers will want the same products which can be supported by identical promotional strategies.

The opposite view of this is that there will have to be a high degree of local adaptation to different market conditions. This is based on the idea that there will be cultural differences between countries and regions coupled with local differences in infrastructure and economic and technological differences.

Research has been carried out to look at the ease or difficulty of standardization of marketing activities. Porter (1986) found that it was easier to standardize some elements of the marketing mix than others. The results of this research are shown in Table 11.6. It is interesting to note that Porter (1986) considered many of the elements involved in promotion, including brand name, product positioning and advertising themes, as being easier to standardize than other elements of the marketing mix.

Research has also been carried out by Moriarty and Duncan (1990) to look at the ease of standardizing promotional campaigns. They found that it was easier to develop a standardized creative concept

Table 11.6 Marketing activities according to east or difficulty of standardization

Easier to standardize	Difficult to standardize
Brand name	Distribution
Product positioning	Personal selling
Service standards	Training sales personnel
Warranties	Pricing
Advertising theme	Media selection
Packaging	

Source: Porter (1986).

theme and that media planning was much easier to standardize than media buying.

The two important questions which an organization should ask itself, it seems, in tourism, leisure and hospitality are first, is there a common approach to advertising and promotion? If the answer to this question is yes then secondly, is it possible to develop a pan-European advertising strategy for these products?

Other requirements for adopting a standardized communication strategy are that pan-European advertising agencies are available to develop the ideas, and that the legal framework allows the organization to adopt a standardized approach.

The two questions posed above will now be considered.

Is there consumer demand for a common approach to advertising?

Research to date in this area seems to suggest that there is little evidence to suggest that there is a demand for a common European approach in advertising. Research by Munzinger (1988), for example, has shown that advertising styles are sensitive to different national cultures. Advertising in the UK, for example, reflects the British sense of humour and is often witty and entertaining. Germans, on the other hand, view their commercials as relatively less humourless, but entertaining in an emotional way. They also like their commercials to be informative. This study demonstrated the difficulty of finding a standardized European approach.

Research by Lannon (1992) has also shown that styles of advertising are very different in different European countries. The differences in styles were shown to be a reflection of the differences in cultural heritage and economic development of the individual countries studied.

One of the major problems with the adoption of a standardized approach is the choice of language for the advertisement. The area in which German is spoken is very large, but not everybody in Europe understands it. Countries like Sweden and the Netherlands, on the other hand, have a large audience for programmes in English. Table 11.7 shows how widely English, French, German and Italian are understood in Europe. In general, the better educated speak more languages and young people tend to speak English.

Table 11.7 Percentage of language comprehension in Europe

	Ger	Ita	UK	Fra	Spa	Neth	Bel	Por	Gre	Den	Swe	Aus	Swi	Fin	Nor
English	44	16	100	31	12	72	34	25	28	61	73	42	40	48	58
French	16	16	21	97	10	31	71	30	8	9	9	11	63	5	2
German	100	4	9	9	1	67	19	3	5	45	35	100	88	14	17
Italian	3	100	2	6	1	2	5	3	2	1	1	5	24	1	0

Source: *Reader's Digest* Eurodata, 1990.

The first Euro-consumers which are emerging – the well educated business traveller and the young – can be reached with advertising in English. The other possible approach is to translate some advertisements into different European languages.

According to Anholt, however, the approach of simple translation, particularly in press advertisements, is not sufficient. He states that:

> Advertising is so intimately linked with the popular culture, the social fabric, the laws, the conventions, the buying habits, the aspirations, the style, the humour, and the mentality of the people, that messages just cannot be communicated in precisely the same way in different countries.

(Anholt, 1993)

All of these reasons, he suggests, mean that the copy for advertising has to be written in a different way, rather than just written as a straight translation. The advertisement can have the same appearance and quote the same facts, but have equivalent but not identical 'noises'. He illustrates this point with reference to the Nike commercials developed in 1993, which had the same appearance but different copy in the English, French, Italian and Flemish regions.

Research by Toop (1992) has shown that it is feasible to run single sales promotions across national boundaries because of the emergence of a growing number of interests, tastes and activities which the peoples in Europe have in common. The lists of common interest which he mentions are shown in Table 11.8.

It is interesting to note here that many of the common interests which are quoted have strong links to tourism, leisure and hospitality products. The interest in Lego toys, Disney and the environment, for example, suggests ways of developing a European theme which will appeal to like-minded individuals in different countries. These common interests also suggest themes for advertising in general which will appeal to European consumers.

The conclusion to the first question is that, although there is evidence to suggest that there are substantial differences in the expectations of advertising by consumers in different European countries, there is the opportunity to build on common European interests to develop widely accepted advertising and promotion. This new advertising and promotion will have to be carefully designed to have appeal across Europe. The copy will also have to be subtly changed to suit the tastes and cultures of consumers in different European countries.

Table 11.8 Common European interests

Sporting events:
- The European Cup and World Cup soccer competitions
- The Olympic Games
- Wimbledon and other 'Grand Slam' tennis tournaments
- Grand Prix motor racing

Music:
- Leading pop groups
- The Eurovision Song Contest
- Festivals in Salzburg and Bayreuth

Travel and transport:
- Vacations in other European countries
- Concorde
- New York, San Francisco and Hollywood
- Luxury cars like Mercedes, BMWs and Jaguars
- Avis, Hertz and other car rentals

Television:
- *Dallas*
- *Dynasty*
- *Kojak*

Children's interests:
- Space travel
- Animals
- Dolls
- Pirates and buried treasure
- Lego toys
- Disney

Fashion
- Levis
- Benetton
- Gucci

Financial services:
- American Express, Visa, Mastercard
- Europ Assistance

Social concern:
- Red Cross
- World Wide Fund for Nature
- The environment
- Starvation relief
- Drug abuse

Source: Toop (1992).

Is it possible to develop a pan-European advertising strategy?

To answer this question regarding tourism, leisure and hospitality products we will focus on three main areas of discussion:

- the availability of pan-European media sources;

- the availability of pan-European advertising agencies;
- the legal framework.

The availability of pan-European media

The organization involved in the marketing of tourism, leisure and hospitality products in different European countries can develop the same advertising theme and then use national media to show the campaigns. Alternatively it can use the growing number of pan-European media sources which will allow the organization to show the same promotions simultaneously in different European countries.

The use of national media to show the campaigns is supported by the fact that the media scene in the countries of Europe is very different. The percentages of advertising spent on different forms of medium, for example, are very different in different European countries. This is shown in Table 11.9.

Southern European countries such as Greece, Italy and Portugal are heavy users of television. Northern European countries such as Denmark, Germany and the Netherlands rely heavily on print medium for advertising.

Consumer habits are also different in different European countries. Television viewing figures, for example, show that the United Kingdom is top in terms of average daily viewing figures. The Scandinavian countries watch television much less than many of their European neighbours. This is shown in Table 11.10.

Access to cable and satellite television is also growing across the whole of Europe. The growth in cable connections and satellite dish installations depends on the strengths and number of terrestrial channels in the country and the understanding of foreign languages. The percentage of television advertising which is directed to cable and satellite sources is currently small (apart from in West Germany where it is 39.7%), but this will grow as cable and satellite penetration

Table 11.9 Advertising expenditure by medium 1992 (% of total advertising expenditure)

EU	TV	Print	Radio	Cinema	Outdoor	Total
Belgium	28.7	51.6	5.5	1.2	13.0	100.0
Denmark	13.4	82.1	1.4	1.2	1.9	100.0
France	29.5	51.2	6.6	0.6	12.0	100.0
Germany	16.1	76.3	3.6	0.9	3.1	100.0
Greece	59.0	31.9	5.9	0.3	3.0	100.0
Ireland	28.6	52.4	12.3	0.4	6.2	100.0
Italy	49.5	40.9	3.5	0.2	5.9	100.0
Netherlands	15.6	72.2	2.4	0.4	9.4	100.0
Portugal	39.8	31.5	7.6	11.8	9.3	100.0
Spain	28.8	55.2	10.5	0.7	4.6	100.0
United Kingdom	31.7	62.2	2.0	0.6	3.6	100.0

Source: Euromonitor (1995).

Table 11.10 TV viewing

Country	Avg. daily viewing (minutes)
United Kingdom	232.8
Spain	220.0
Italy	219.0
Czech Republic	200.0
Ireland	199.8
France	193.0
Germany	186.0
Greece	184.3
Portugal	161.0
Belgium	156.0
Hungary	146.0
Netherlands	143.0
Austria	138.0
Switzerland	131.0
Finland	130.0
Denmark	128.0
Norway	128.0
Sweden	111.0

Source: *European Marketing Pocket Book* (1994).

increases. The current figures on cable and satellite television and the projections to the year 2003 are shown in Tables 11.11 and 11.12.

Many of the international cable and satellite channels can be seen in a growing number of European households. Eurosport and MTV (the global youth channel), for example, are viewed widely in Europe.

There has also been a growth in the number of printed newspapers and magazines which appear both internationally and across Europe. Women's magazines such as *Cosmopolitan*, *Marie-Claire* and *Elle*, and

Table 11.11 Cable and direct-to-home satellite television 1992

EU	Television households (000)	Cable households (000)	Cable households (% of TVHH)	Satellite households (000)	Satellite households (% of TVHH)	Cable/satellite TV ads (% of TV ads)
Belgium	4 025	3 497	86.9	27	0.7	0.8
Denmark	2 309	1 259	54.5	90	3.9	6.8
France	20 448	1 056	5.2	125	0.6	
Germany East				10		
Germany West	31 930	11 823	37.0	3 130	9.8	39.7
Greece	3 092			8	0.3	
Ireland	1 024	400	39.1	26	2.5	5.1
Italy	20 304			30	0.1	
Luxembourg	140	90	64.3			
Netherlands	6 100	5 350	87.7	240	3.9	2.1
Portugal	3 080			32	1.0	
Spain	11 350	600	5.3	100	0.9	
United Kingdom	22 088	652	3.0	2 294	10.4	0.7

Source: Euromonitor (1995).

Table 11.12 European cable and satellite dish penetration: projection to the year 2003 (Number of TV households: 143 400 000)

	Cable connections (%)	Satellite dish penetration (%)	Combined penetration (%)
1989	14	1	15
1990	17	1	18
1991	19	4	23
1992	22	5	27
1993	23	7	30
1994	25	9	34
1995	28	10	38
1996	31	12	43
1997	34	13	47
1998	36	14	50
1999	37	15	52
2000	39	15	54
2001	40	15	55
2002	41	15	56
2003	41	16	57

Source: de Mooij (1994).

men's magazines such as *Penthouse* and *Playboy* have a strong European presence. General publications such as those produced by American Express (*Expression*) Diners Club (*Signature*) and Readers' Digest also have wide European circulation.

The most noted growth in the circulation of European publications, however, has been in the business area. The European Business Man Readership Survey (EBRS) looks at this area every two years. Research is carried out with senior business individuals in seventeen European countries. The survey which was carried out in 1991 indicated that there were a number of publications which are read widely across national boundaries. These include dailies such as *The Financial Times* (English), weeklies such as *The Economist* (English), fortnightlies such as *Fortune* (English), monthlies such as *Euromoney* (English) and bi-monthlies such as *The Harvard Business Review* (English). Business people also read many of the in-flight magazines which are available on all the major European and international airlines.

The growth of the media barons such as Murdoch (television, newspapers and magazines) and Bertelsmann (television, newspapers, magazines, books, records) will also encourage multimedia synergy across national boundaries.

It is predicted that there will be a growing availability of pan-European media in the future. This means that for organizations which are marketing on a pan-European basis decisions about the design of advertising and media buying will become much more complex. The opportunities do exist, however, to develop pan-European promotional strategies.

The availability of pan-European advertising agencies

The organization which is wanting to develop a pan-European advertising strategy will have the best chance of success if it uses a pan-European advertising agency. This will allow a common theme to be developed. The agency will also be able to advise on European media planning and buying. There are a number of major advertising agencies which have a European profile. These are shown in Table 11.13.

The legal framework

Advertising in Europe is regulated by both international and European regulatory bodies. The International Chamber of Commerce is one of the most important international regulatory bodies. International professional advertising organizations also have an important role in the development of advertising regulation. The European Advertising Tripartite (EAT), for example, acts as the main lobbying body for the advertising industry in Europe.

There are also developments in the regulation of advertising in the EU. Extant legislation includes the Misleading Advertising Directive 1984 which provides procedures for the control of misleading advertising. There are also proposals to have a total ban on tobacco advertising and to introduce a nutrition labelling directive and food claims directive for foodstuffs.

According to Advertising Voices (1991) areas under threat of proposed regulation include:

Table 11.13 Top advertising agency networks in Europe

Rank	Network	Billings ($ million)		
		1993	**1992**	**1991**
1	Euro RSCG	4752.6	5358.3	5778.3
2	Publicis-FCB	3766.3	3772.2	3401.6
3	BBDO	2752.8	2767.1	2169.0
4	O&M	2744.8	2510.9	2418.5
5	Grey	2643.8	2585.0	2257.6
=6	McCann	2483.9	2790.8	2419.0
=6	JWT	2483.9	2452.3	2253.9
8	Y&R	2436.9	2845.6	3476.7
9	Saatchi	2355.3	2528.1	2780.6
10	Lintas	2137.1	2201.2	2115.8
11	BSB	2124.4	2263.6	2073.3
12	DDBN	2122.7	2184.4	1914.9
13	DMB&B	1957.9	1829.6	1685.7
14	Lowe	1288.6	1230.9	963.0
15	BDDP	1171.5	1306.0	1253.3
16	Leo Burnett	1087.4	1175.8	1076.2
17	TBWA	738.5	817.1	698.2
18	Armando Testa	690.0	677.7	
19	Ayer	662.0	1008.5	743.7
20	Alliance	385.3		

Source: *European Marketing Pocket Book* (1994).

- alcohol;
- sponsorship;
- direct marketing/data protection;
- taxation on advertising;
- comparative advertising;
- copyright;
- cross media ownership.

All of these proposed European regulations will affect the development of pan-European advertising strategies.

To conclude, therefore, it is possible for large organizations which have a European market to develop a pan-European promotional strategy. This can only follow, however, the development of a European product or service which is targeted at a Euro-consumer.

The development of the promotional campaign to support the opening of Disneyland Paris throughout the continent is a good example of a pan-European strategy. Promotion of the Barcelona Olympics was also developed to be shown throughout Europe. It is likely that European promotional strategies will be used in the first instance by large organizations for big budget products or events. It is predicted, however, that the convergence of customer tastes and the increase in the availability of pan-European media sources will also encourage an increased use of European promotional campaigns in the tourism, leisure and hospitality industries.

CONCLUSIONS

This chapter has looked at all the issues involved in the production of effective promotional campaigns for tourism, leisure and hospitality organizations. It has explored special features such as brochure production. The final part of the chapter looked at the possibilities for the development of pan-European advertising campaigns for the industry.

DISCUSSION POINTS AND ESSAY QUESTIONS

1. Outline the role of promotion within marketing, particularly in relation to the other elements of the marketing mix.
2. Compare and contrast the promotional techniques used by a major hotel chain with those adopted by a small local authority museum.
3. Discuss the obstacles that are restricting the growth of common pan-European approaches to advertising.

Choose **one** of the following hypothetical new products: **EXERCISE**

- a new long-haul holiday destination in a European tour operator's programme, which is aimed at an upmarket clientele which seeks exclusivity. You must base your project on a real destination;
- a newly-built theme park, aimed at a family market. You should specify where your hypothetical theme park is located;
- the launch of a new service between two cities within Europe by a European scheduled airline. You must specify which cities.

For your chosen product you should:

- design a brochure that will appeal to the target market;
- prepare an advertising campaign with a budget of £75 000 to promote this new product, including which media would be used and the design of proposed advertisements.

CASE STUDIES

You may wish to look at the following cases which illustrate some of the points made in this chapter:

2. The Forte International Programme, UK;
3. First Choice, UK;
4. The role of brochures in hotel marketing: The Hotel Vitosha, Sofia, Bulgaria;
5. The role of the media in tourism marketing in the UK;
9. Bord Fáilte, Ireland;
11. The Hurtigruten, Norwegian coastal voyage, Norway;
13. Iceland: The marketing of a business tourism destination;
18. Airtours plc, UK;
19. British Airways, UK;
20. The European Travel Commission;
21. The Victoria and Albert Museum, UK;
23. Futbol Club Barcelona, Spain;
24. Abercrombie and Kent Ltd, UK;
25. Accor, France;
26. Thalassa International, France;
27. Les Vins Georges Duboeuf SA, France;
28. Center Parcs, UK;
29. Port Aventura SA, Spain.

Conclusions to Part 3

In the preceding four chapters we have explored the key issues involved in the development of marketing mixes for different sectors of tourism, leisure and hospitality. It is important to remember that there are some general points which can be made about this process.

- The organization should consider each element of the marketing mix separately and have well defined plans.
- It is critical that the elements of the marketing mix interact effectively to give the organization products which are positioned and marketed effectively to their target groups of customers.
- The organization should consider their portfolio of products as a whole, rather than as individual products.

These points introduce us to the process of marketing planning which is covered in Part 4.

Marketing planning in tourism, leisure and hospitality

In this part of the book we examine the application of the principles and techniques of marketing planning to tourism, leisure and hospitality. Each of the four chapters in this part addresses one of the classic four questions which comprise the process of marketing planning, as follows:

- **Chapter 12: Where are we now? Current situation analysis.** This chapter looks at how organizations can analyse their current marketing situation as the context for a marketing planning exercise.
- **Chapter 13: Where do we want to go? The setting of goals and objectives.** In this chapter, we explore the setting of goals and objectives and the generation of mission statements.
- **Chapter 14: How will we get there? Developing the strategy.** This chapter looks at the evaluation of strategic options and the creation of marketing strategies. It then goes on to look at the role of marketing plans in implementing these strategies.
- **Chapter 15: How will we know when we get there? Monitoring, review and evaluation.** This chapter covers monitoring, review and evaluation, the techniques by which the implementation of the strategy is kept on the right track.

Where are we now? Current situation analysis | 12

Key concepts

The main concepts covered in this chapter are:

- current situation analysis at different levels, including whole organizations, complete product portfolios, strategic business units and individual products;
- SWOT analysis;
- Boston Consulting Group matrix;
- marketing audits.

INTRODUCTION

Strategic marketing planning always begins with an objective analysis of the organization's current marketing situation. This analysis needs to take place at a number of levels, including:

- the organization as a whole;
- its product portfolios;
- individual strategic business units (SBUs);
- individual products.

A number of techniques exist to help with the analysis of the current situation in terms of these respective levels, as follows:

- SWOT analysis is a good technique for considering the organization as a whole;
- the Boston Consulting Group matrix can be a useful framework for analysing the current performance of the organization's overall product portfolio, or even its strategic business units;
- product positioning and the product lifecycle are particularly relevant at the level of individual products.

Clearly, this is just a selection of relevant techniques and there are a number of others. Furthermore, many of these techniques not only relate to the current situation but can also can be used to see how a product, SBU or a whole portfolio are behaving over time.

In this chapter, we will look at how tourism, leisure and hospitality organizations can analyse their current marketing situation, and how the techniques outlined above contribute to this process. However, one has to bear in mind that a current situation analysis rarely begins with a clean sheet. It is undertaken in the context of existing strategies, the organization's history and culture, and involvement in physical planning, for example.

The book, up to now, has defined and explained the marketing concept and identified the ways in which it can be practically implemented. Marketing has become very fashionable in the tourism, leisure and hospitality industries. However, while this growing recognition of the importance of marketing is welcome, many organizations are becoming involved in marketing without a clear understanding of what it is and what the implications are of introducing a marketing approach.

Marketing should be planned in a systematic and rigorous way if it is to be implemented effectively. To help with this process the discipline of **marketing planning** has been developed. The marketing strategies will be developed for the organization in the marketing planning process.

A marketing plan has been defined as:

> A written statement of the marketing aims of a company, including a statement of the products, targets for sales, market shares and profits, promotional and advertising strategies, pricing policies, distribution channels etc. with precise specification of time scales, individual responsibilities etc.
>
> (Manser, 1988)

To achieve this marketing plan the organization will have to go through a number of stages which take the form of questions, as follows:

- **Where are we now?** – the analysis of the current marketing situation.
- **Where do we want to be in the future?** – setting the objectives.
- **How are we going to get there?** – creating the strategy.
- **How will we know when we get there?** – monitoring and evaluation.

This and the next three chapters give an overview of this four-stage process. If you require further in-depth analysis of the marketing planning process you should refer to the work of Ansoff (1988), Day (1990) Ohmae (1982), Porter (1980 and 1983) and Kotler (1994).

AN OVERVIEW OF THE MARKETING PLANNING PROCESS

The marketing planning process was developed as a systematic way of incorporating marketing into an organization. The marketing planning process is summarised in Figure 12.1, following McDonald, one of the leading academics and writers on the subject in the UK.

This model incorporates the stages which have to be completed in order to arrive at a finished marketing plan. The plan should contain:

- a summary of all the principal external factors which affected the organization's marketing performance during the previous year, together with a statement of the organization's strengths and weaknesses;
- the competition and how the organization is performing in the marketplace (SWOT analysis – Strengths, Weaknesses, Opportunities and Threats – can help with this);
- assumptions about the key determinants of marketing success and failure;
- setting of overall marketing objectives and strategies;
- programmes containing detailed timings, responsibilities, costs, budgets and sales forecasts;
- methods for measuring and reviewing progress made.

The feedback lines in the model indicate that in a real planning situation the steps will have to be completed more than once before the final plan can be written.

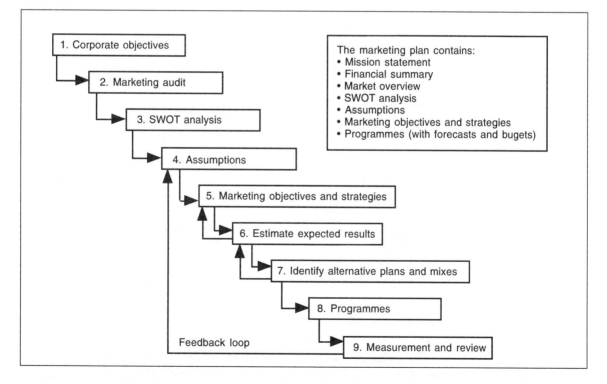

Figure 12.1 The marketing planning process.
Source: McDonald (1989).

Table 12.1 A suggested model marketing plan for an organization

- Management summary
- Current position of the product in the market
- Future prospects for the market
- Market research requirement
- Product strategy
- Promotion plan
- Sales plan
- Distribution plan
- Pricing policy
- Performance measures and controls

There are different models and concepts which can be used as the organization progresses to the finished marketing plan. These will be covered in more detail in this chapter, and in the following three chapters.

The style of the finished marketing plan will differ according to the type of organization. One suggestion for a marketing plan is shown in Table 12.1.

If the organization is planning to market the product in more than one country, then the plan will have to include important issues such as consumer views, the legal position and distribution plans. The process of marketing planning in international marketing is, however, in essence an identical process to that carried out in national markets.

THE MARKETING AUDIT

The analysis of the current marketing situation can be divided into three stages, as follows:

1. an evaluation of the organization itself in terms of its products, its markets, its customers, its structure and culture, and how it organizes its marketing;
2. an appraisal of the external business environment and how it affects the organization including political, economic, demographic, socio-cultural, natural and technological forces;
3. an examination of the organization's main competition.

The marketing audit will be composed of a number of sections, which will be produced as a result of a detailed review of internal and external factors. The parts of the audit are shown in Table 12.2.

To show the marketing audit in more detail, and to consider its application to the industry, the sections which look at the procedure which a UK tour operator would go through to complete a marketing audit.

Who should carry out the audit?

The tour operator could use one of its existing staff to carry out the audit. It is often better, however, if the company can afford it, for an impartial consultant to carry out the audit. This has the advantage of a person who is not involved in the day-to-day marketing activity giving a fresh view of the particular set of circumstances.

Table 12.2 An outline model for a marketing audit for an organization

External audit
- PEST analysis
  - Political factors
  - Economic factors
  - Socio-cultural factors
  - Technological factors

The market
- Total market size, growth and trends
- Market characteristics, development and trends
- Products, prices, distribution methods
- Customers
- Industry practice

The competition
- Major competitors
- Size
- Market share/reputation
- Production capabilities
- Marketing methods
- International links
- Profitability

Internal audit
- SWOT analysis
  - Strengths
  - Weaknesses
  - Opportunities
  - Threats
- Product range
- Customers
- The organization
- Sales
- Market share
- Profit margins
- Marketing organization
- Marketing mix variables:
  - product management
  - price
  - distribution
  - promotion

How should they start?

The audit should first look at the overall corporate mission of the organization. In the case of the tour operator this could be:

> We seek to maintain our number one position in the package tour business in the United Kingdom.

The corporate mission of the organization will give an overall view of where the organization sees itself going in the future.

EXTERNAL ENVIRONMENT

The next stage of the audit procedure will be for the tour operator to consider the external environment. This refers to the general forces which may affect the organization but which are outside its control, although it may of course influence some of them through lobbying. They include political, economic, socio-cultural and technological forces. This analysis is sometimes referred to as PEST or STEP analysis, and is covered in further detail in Chapter 8.

The most successful are those that accurately anticipate changes in these forces, and respond quickly and in the most effective manner. An example of an outline external audit for the tour operators is shown in Table 12.3. Factors have been identified in each category and then considered in relation to this particular organization so that they can be presented in rank order. By doing this, the organization will know which of the factors that have been identified they should concentrate on.

Table 12.3 External factors affecting the tour operator

Political factors	Technological factors
1. European Commission legislation, for example European Package Travel Directive	1. Developments in CRS systems
2. The Single Market in Europe	2. Virtual reality systems
3. Domestic legislation on consumer protection	3. Smart cards
4. Domestic legislation on timing of statutory holidays	4. Management information systems
Economic factors	**Socio-cultural factors**
1. Government economic policy affecting incomes	1. Growing interest in green issues
2. Recession and recovery from recession	2. Growing interest in independent travel
3. Availability of credit	3. Growing interest in health issues
4. Interest rates	4. Ageing population

Note: Factors have been presented in order of importance for the organization.

The consultant or individual who is carrying out the audit will find it very useful to use the **Delphi technique** to create this external audit. This involves speaking to industry and market experts concerned, in this case, with the package tour industry.
These experts may be found both inside and outside the company.

It is also important for the audit to have an international perspective. Too many companies have been caught out by restricting themselves to national issues, when a European or international issue has much more potential influence on the organization.

The next stage in the audit would be to look at the market.

THE MARKET

This section of the audit will look at the market for the tour operator. An example of the content of this audit for a UK operator is shown in Table 12.4. It is very useful for the individual or consultant carrying out the audit to seek expert advice to complete this section of the audit. The market characteristics are a very important part because it will provide general information about this particular market area. This will prove invaluable to the organization when it starts to set the marketing objectives later on in the marketing planning process.

COMPETITION

The next part of the audit would be an analysis of the competition in this market. For the tour operator, this will involve looking at other tour operators in the national market, and also considering potential new competition from European or international markets. The organization needs to recognize that it operates in a highly competitive environment and should analyse its main competitors in terms of their particular strengths and weaknesses. This will hopefully allow the organization to gain a competitive advantage over them.

In some parts of industry, particularly in the public sector, organizations and managers find it difficult to identify their main competitors. This is particularly so if there are many fundamentally different products and markets.

Competitors could be organizations offering similar products, targeting the same market segments, charging a similar price, or operating in the same geographical area. Competition might also include any activity that offers a similar benefit to the customer.

The identification of competitors in the leisure industry for example, is further complicated by the fact that in some instances such as local authority museum services, the main competitor in the geographical area may be a facility owned by the same organization.

Organizations in national markets also tend to view other national organizations in the same market sector as their competition. This may

Table 12.4 The market for tour operation

Total market
- Estimated at £X m in the UK
- The number of major players
- Growth in package holiday market
- Growth of large European players
- Seasonality of the market

Customers
- Are customers price sensitive and loyal to the company or not, for example?

Products
- Issues such as whether branding is important to customers
- A review of the image and reputation of the company products and how they are perceived by the customer

Price
- The features of the pricing strategies in the market. For example, are 'discounting' and 'inclusive' pricing common features?

Distribution
- The special features of distribution such as the use of dedicated travel agencies and direct sales

Communication
- The type of promotion which is currently used such as the importance of brochures, television advertising at specific periods and sales promotions

Industry practice
- Special industry practices such as ABTA bonding

---

be so in the short term, but long term there may be the unannounced arrival of a multinational competitor who views the national market as one window of opportunity.

An example of a model for a competitor audit for the tour operator is shown in Figure 12.2. It can be seen that this audit looks at both existing national competitors and potential international players.

INTERNAL BUSINESS ENVIRONMENT

By this stage, the organization will have a good knowledge of the external environment, its major competition and an overall view of the market. The next stage is to look internally at all the features which make up that particular organization. This will involve three stages:

- a SWOT analysis to look at overall features;
- a review of the current customers;
- a review of the organization's product ranges.

Competitor company	Market share	Turnover	Profitability	Geographical coverage	Major brands	International links	Marketing methods	Key strengths and weaknesses
Potential competitor company								

Figure 12.2 The competitor audit for the tour operator.

The SWOT analysis

The technique in the marketing audit often referred to as a SWOT analysis looks at the following:

S **Strengths**
   e.g. brand leader

                                  Internal to the organization

W **Weaknesses**
   e.g. poor staff training

O **Opportunities**
   e.g. growing market

                                  External to the organization

T **Threats**
   e.g. new legislation

Some of the factors which appeared in the PEST analysis will reappear in the SWOT analysis. The analysis should also help the organization to rank the individual items in the categories in order of importance. An example of a SWOT analysis for our hypothetical UK tour operator is shown in Table 12.5.

One of the important aspects of the SWOT analysis is that the links can be seen between the different categories. The best organization will be one which can turn threats into opportunities by the effective

Table 12.5 SWOT analysis for the tour operator

Strengths
1. Major market position with strong portfolio of brands
2. Ownership of own airline and travel agency chain
3. Good image with customers
4. Excellent marketing and operations staff

Weaknesses
1. Low profit margins
2. Poor labour relations
3. High cost operation
4. Bureaucratic management culture

Opportunities
1. Growth in market after recession
2. Potential development of specialist products to meet demand, e.g. holidays based on special interests and activities
3. Market entry in other European countries
4. Rebranding to reposition the product range

Threats
1. Entrance of major European tour operators into the UK market
2. Loss of consumer interest in traditional package holidays
3. The potential competition represented by virtual reality
4. New European Commission legislation

use of resources. For example, the tour operator may be threatened by the consumer who is worried about environmental issues and tourism. It may turn this threat into an opportunity by using its strength at branding to create a new 'green' holiday brand. This is an example of an organization linking the items in the audit together in a creative manner.

A review of the current customers

The next stage of the audit procedure is to establish who the customers are for the organization's products and services, and find out more about them and their attitudes to its products. This analysis should include:

- the place of residence of customers;
- demographic characteristics about the customers such as age, sex and stage in the family lifecycle;
- whether customers are using the product in their leisure time or when on business;
- if the customers use the products as individuals or as part of groups;
- socioeconomic data including education and income;
- lifestyles of the consumers;
- the benefits sought from the product including status, value for money and service;
- whether customers are frequent users, occasional users or first-time users;
- customers' opinions of the product and the organization in terms of strengths and weaknesses.

This exercise will demonstrate the different market segments which will have different motivations, different characteristics and display differences in behaviour. Each segment can then be targeted with a different set of messages about the product which can then be communicated through different marketing media. This concept of 'segmentation' is the key to successful marketing.

It is important to remember that the organization may also have intermediary 'customers'. For the tour operator, for example, this will be the retail travel agents. The customer analysis must reflect the importance of these 'customers' as well as the final 'customers'.

As well as finding out about existing customers, the organization will also need to look at people who are not using their product to identify what they need to do in the future to turn these potential customers into users of the product. When the organization is looking to market their product outside their own national boundaries, this will involve a detailed look at potential customers in the new markets. The concept of 'Euro-clusters' which can be applied here has already been discussed in Chapter 4.

Market research is an essential prerequisite for an organization to analyse its markets in the ways outlined above. Research data needs to be comprehensive, accurate and up-to-date, which means it is often expensive to gather. There are, however, relatively inexpensive but useful methods of collecting data that can be used including surveys of holidaymakers on their returning flights.

A review of the organization's product range

The next part of the audit will be to review the current product range. The organization should evaluate the products it offers, both individually and as a range or portfolio. Products in the tourism, leisure and hospitality markets are often an intangible experience rather than a tangible good and are therefore often difficult to analyse. Nevertheless, it is important for the organization to systematically examine what it offers to customers.

It is important to remember here that the customer is buying the **benefits** of the product, rather than just the product itself. The examination of the products offered by the organization should look at the type of factors shown in Figure 12.3.

The level of branding of the product will be a particularly important aspect of this analysis, since it is the branding which will give the product the 'added value' appeal to the customer. A leading brand will communicate an aura of quality and reliability which will provide a competitive advantage over lesser known brands.

The position in the product lifecycle is also of concern for all the organization's products. Products which have just been launched will be costing the organization money, with the hope of financial rewards later on. Products which are in maturity, on the other hand, will hopefully be bringing the company substantial cash turnover.

STRATEGIC BUSINESS UNITS

The concept of the strategic business unit (SBU) is important in the marketing planning process. The SBU is a division, product line or other profit centre within an organization that sells a distinct set of products and/or services to an identifiable group of customers. This set of products will compete against a well defined set of competitive products. Costs and revenue are directly attributable to the SBU, and should be monitored and evaluated by means of an effective control system. The SBU should also be regularly researched through marketing information systems.

The concept of the SBU can be applied to any type of organization, and has been applied to hospitality organizations by Calver (1994). The characteristics of the SBU are as follows:

- it is a division, product line or other project centre within an organization;

Product	Core attractions	Service component	Image and reputation	Branding	Guarantees and warranties	Main competing products	Pricing policy	Distribution	Promotion	Stage in the product lifecycle	Profitability	Other factors
Holidays for the elderly	Ready-made package holiday	Care and attention of all staff	Leading prestigious and reliable company	Strong brand name-X	After-sales help Money back offers	Other major tour operators	Value for money All inclusive	Via retail travel agents and direct sell	High quality brochure Company advertising	Recently launched Still in growth stage	Will break even this year	Recognized as premier product in this market First to be launched

Figure 12.3 Analysis of the product range of the tour operator.

Table 12.6 A hospitality organization in terms of SBU

SBU1 Food and Beverage Operations	SBU2 Accommodation Services	SBU3 Leisure Facilities	SBU4 Conference Facilities
Finance	Finance	Finance	Finance
Marketing	Marketing	Marketing	Marketing
Technology	Technology	Technology	Technology
Personnel	Personnel	Personnel	Personnel

- it has a distinct mission;
- it represents a market area and has identifiable competition;
- it can be independently financially planned.

The concept of the SBU can also be demonstrated with regard to a hospitality organization as shown in Table 12.6.

THE PRODUCT PORTFOLIO

One method of analysis which is used to help with the marketing planning process is the concept of product portfolios. This is based on the idea that products which are sold by organizations cannot be treated in isolation, but must be looked at as being parts of strategic business units or within product portfolios. An example of product portfolios, for a tour operator, is shown in Table 12.7. It can be seen that this tour operator has divided its business into four strategic business units. Within each SBU, there are a series of brands which make up the business unit.

The idea of a product portfolio is that the organization should meet its objectives by balancing sales growth, cash flow and risk. It is essential that the whole portfolio is assessed regularly and that the organization has an active policy of getting rid of old products and developing new ones.

Various models have been suggested which aim to help the marketing planner with the analysis of the product portfolio of an organization. One of the most famous of these is the **Boston Consulting Group (BCG) product portfolio analysis, or matrix**.

The Boston Consulting Group approach is based on the philosophy that **relative market share** and **market growth rate** are important considerations in determining marketing strategy. All the organizations products are integrated into a single overall matrix. The overall matrix can then be evaluated to determine the appropriate strategies for individual products or SBUs. The measure of market share used in the BCG matrix is the product's share **relative** to the organization's largest competitor. This is important because it reflects the dominance enjoyed by the product in the market. The BCG matrix is shown in Figure 12.4.

Table 12.7 An example of a product
portfolio for a tour operator

Strategic business unit 1
Summer sun:
- Brand A
- Brand B
- Brand C

Strategic business unit 2
Winter sun:
- Brand A
- Brand B

Strategic business unit 3
Winter sports
- Brand A
- Brand B

Strategic business unit 4
Long-haul holidays:
- Brand A
- Brand B

Strategic business unit 5
Specialist markets:
- Brand A
- Brand B

The BCG Matrix suggests that products can be categorized into four
main groups:

- The **star** is probably a new product which has achieved a high market share in a growing market.
- The **cash cow** is a leader in a market where there is little additional
  growth. These are excellent generators of cash.

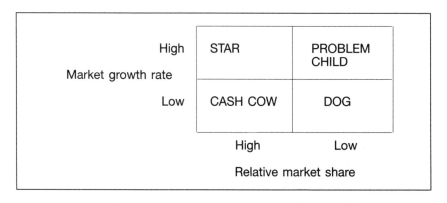

Figure 12.4 The Boston Consulting Group matrix.

- The **dog** has little future and can be a cash drain on the organization. The organization should be thinking of divesting this product unless there is good reason to keep it.
- The **problem child** (sometimes referred to as a question mark) is a product which has not yet achieved a dominant market position or perhaps it has slipped back from a better position. The organization will seek to move the question mark product into the star category

The Boston matrix can be used to illustrate market position of products. This is shown by the area of each circle which is plotted on the matrix. The bigger the area of the circle, the better the product's contribution to the total organization's sales volume. An example of the BCG growth-share matrix as applied to the tour operator's product portfolio is shown in Figure 12.5. It can be seen that the area of the circle for each product represents the contribution of the product to the overall organization's sales volume. The company can start to plan what to do with each of these products once armed with this information.

To summarise, therefore, the audit of the organization's product range should include a product lifecycle for each major product. It should also contain a product portfolio matrix showing the present position of the products.

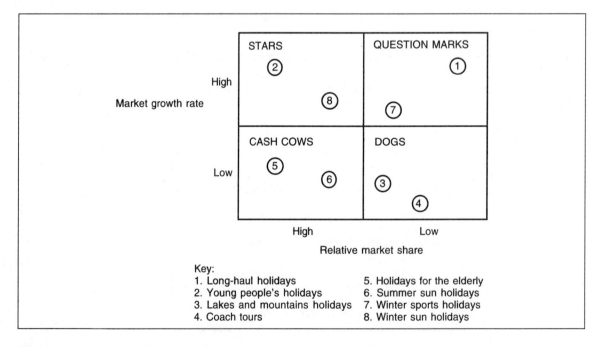

Figure 12.5 BCG growth-share matrix as applied to tour operator.

THE ORGANIZATION

A number of characteristics and features of the organization are relevant to the marketing of its products and should be included in the current marketing situation analysis, including the following:

- the influence of marketing within the corporate decision-making structure relative to other functions such as finance and operations, and the attitude of the organization as a whole towards marketing;
- the culture of the organization – is it innovative, adventurous, dynamic and risk-taking, or traditional, cautious, bureaucratic and stagnant?
- the financial performance and resources of the organization and the degree of control it exercises over its budgeting and financial management;
- what are the strengths and weaknesses of the staff and how willing is the organization to invest in training and staff development?
- to what extent do managers and staff have the power to make decisions and show initiative?
- the mission statement, objectives and corporate strategies of the organization;
- the organization's suppliers and its relationship with them;
- the organization's approach to quality and its quality control system.

This analysis should establish how the organization as a whole obstructs or facilitates the marketing function.

CONCLUSIONS

By the end of this stage of the marketing planning process, the organization should have a clear view of its current marketing situation and direction. The next stage of the process is for the organization to decide its future direction and where it wants to be at some future date. This involves the setting of objectives as the basis for the creation of a marketing strategy to guide the organization towards its desired future destination.

DISCUSSION POINTS AND ESSAY QUESTIONS

1. Outline a model for a marketing audit and explain the main reasons why it may be difficult for organizations to follow this model in reality.
2. Explain the ways in which an organization might seek to establish its current market position.
3. Critically evaluate the contribution which the Boston Consulting Group Matrix can make to an organization's analysis of its current situation.

EXERCISE Select **one** of the following organizations:

- KLM Royal Dutch Airlines;
- Madame Tussaud's, London,
- TUI;
- Accor;
- Legoland;
- Shannon Airport;
- Hermitage Museum, St Petersburg;
- Salzburg Music Festival;
- or a similar organization.

For your chosen organization, carry out a detailed SWOT analysis.

CASE STUDIES

You may want to use one of the following case studies to illustrate some of the points made in this chapter:

6. Scotland;
18. Airtours plc, UK;
19. British Airways, UK;
20. The European Travel Commission;
21. The Victoria and Albert Museum, UK.

Where do we want to go? The setting of goals and objectives

Key concepts

The main concepts covered in this chapter are:

- the setting of goals and objectives;
- the mission statement;
- generating and evaluating strategic options;
- Ansoff's matrix;
- the concept of the 'business mix';
- corporate and product positioning.

INTRODUCTION

This stage in the marketing planning process tends to consist of three main elements, as follows:

- setting goals and objectives that will guide the organization's marketing over a particular period of time, based on the outcome of the current situation analysis and a consideration of the organization's resources, history and culture;
- the development of an appropriate mission statement that reflects the goals and objectives;
- the establishment of a framework within which possible strategic options will be evaluated.

This stage is not about techniques; rather it is about judgement, and a clear sense of direction on the part of those making these judgements.

In this chapter we will consider the ways in which tourism, leisure and hospitality organizations may go about setting goals and objectives and developing mission statements. However, to begin with, we need to define what we mean by goals and objectives. The difference between the terms is a blurred one, but in this context, **goals** are defined as broad aims while **objectives** are the more specific aims which contribute towards the achievement of the goals, and **strategies** are how you plan to achieve those objectives. We may also say that marketing objectives are about products and markets.

In the previous chapter we looked at how an organization can assess where it is at one particular time. The organization will now know what its strengths and weaknesses are, and what the opportunities are for the future. It will have a clear view of its financial position and what it can afford to do next.

The next question in the marketing planning process is to set marketing strategies for the future. Where the organization will want to go depends on its corporate strategy on and where the various stakeholders would like to see the organization going in the future.

> 'Would you please tell me which way I ought to go from here?' said Alice to the Cheshire Cat.
> 'That depends a good deal on where you want to go,' said the Cat.
>   (Lewis Carroll, 1865)

One of the skills in marketing is deciding where you want the organization to go. In the McDonald's marketing planning model shown in Figure 12.1 in the previous chapter, this stage in the process involves both 'Step 5 – Marketing objectives and strategies' and 'Step 6 – Estimate expected results'.

STRATEGIC OPTIONS

Organizations can take a number of stances in relation to a particular market. The **market leader** is the organization which has the largest share of the market and will set the trends in the marketplace. **Market challengers** are not market leaders themselves but will attack the market leader at all times. These organizations are usually number two, three or four in the market. **Market followers** are low share competitors who copy the main innovators in the market.

Markets also usually have **market nichers**. These are companies which focus on a very small part of the market and offer speciality products. Speciality holiday companies and restaurants are examples of market nichers.

Michael Porter has described three generic strategies which he maintains can help organizations to achieve competitive advantage. These three generic routes to competitive advantage are shown in Figure 13.1.

- The **cost leadership** approach involves the organization in achieving a low-cost structure which allows high returns even when the competition is tough.
- **Differentiation** involves an organization in developing a product or service which is clearly superior in the customer's eyes to that of its rivals. Products and services which are developed by organizations which pursue a differentiation strategy are often superior in image

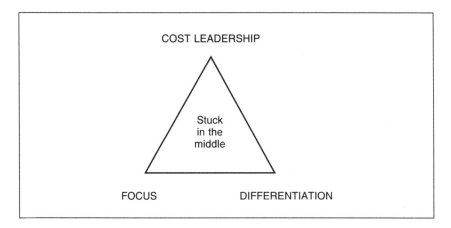

Figure 13.1 Generic routes to competitive advantage.
Source: Porter (1980).

or design which is usually reflected in their higher price. Branding of products and services is often a method which is pursued by an organization which operates a differentiation strategy.
- **Focus** is the third generic strategy outlined by Porter. This is where an organization concentrates on one particular segment of the market. Products and services are usually specialized and attract a specific customer group

Porter warns that organizations should not get 'stuck in the middle'; in other words, they should decide very firmly to pursue one of the three generic strategies.

MISSION STATEMENT

Once the organization has decided on the broad strategic direction in which to go, it is usual to write a **mission statement**.

The style and content of the mission statements of different organizations will vary – consider the examples of missions statements, or business visions, of the organizations from the tourism, leisure and hospitality industry shown in Figure 13.2. The mission statement or business vision should focus on the strategic direction in which the organization wishes to go. This vision should then be reflected in the marketing strategies and marketing objectives.

CORPORATE OBJECTIVES

The mission statement will have defined the organization and the boundaries of the business. Corporate objectives must now be set for the organization as a whole. These will concentrate on one or more of the following items:

1. **Whitbread**
   Whitbread's businesses are focused on large consumer markets where our skills have enabled us to build successful brands and concepts.
      Our future depends on our continuing ability to anticipate the changing lifestyles and tastes of our customers and to provide products and services which exceed their expectations.
      We will expand by further developing our existing businesses and by constantly seeking new ways of applying our operating skills in food, drinks and leisure.

2. **Forte**
   We have embarked on a strategy of building powerful hotel and restaurant brands through effective marketing, focused geographical expansion, innovative product development and a high customer service orientation amongst our people.

3. **Scottish Tourist Board**
   Vision – To enhance Scotland's reputation as a tourism destination, by building on its history, culture, environment and the hospitality of its people.

Figure 13.2 Mission statements or business visions of organizations in the tourism, leisure and hospitality industry. Sources: company annual reports.

- return on investment;
- profitability;
- image with the stock market, public, customers and employees;
- social responsibility;
- environmental policy.

The corporate objectives will set the framework within which the **marketing objectives** for each **strategic business unit (SBU)** will be set.

MARKETING OBJECTIVES

Once the corporate objectives have been set and the marketing audit completed, the organization can then move to setting the marketing objectives. This is one of the key activities in marketing because it seeks to match the organization's resources with the external environment.

The marketing model which has been used extensively in the marketing literature to describe the various options open to an organization when it is setting its marketing objectives is the product-market matrix developed by Ansoff, illustrated in Figure 13.3.

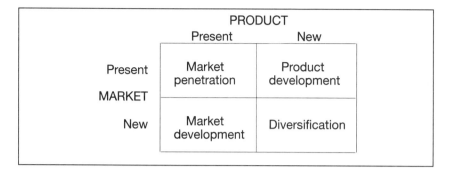

Figure 13.3 Ansoff's product-market matrix. Source: Ansoff (1988).

Market penetration

Market penetration involves an organization trying to sell more of its products and services in an existing market.

Burger King, the fast-food chain owned by Grand Metropolitan, tried to increase store traffic in their American and European outlets in 1994 by the introduction of a 'back to basics' strategy. The 'Get your burger's worth' campaign emphasized product quality and the convenience of 'hamburgers, fries and coke' coupled with value pricing. This activity in the US increased comparable store sales by over 6%.

Market development

Market development involves an organization in trying to sell its current products in new markets. Organizations often do this by selling their products and services in new geographic areas. The introduction by the French hotel chain Accor of its Novotel brand into the UK is an example of market development.

Before its takeover by Granada, Forte, the UK-based hotel chain, had been trying to develop products and services in new markets. The acquisition of the French hotel chain Méridien in 1994 added 53 hotels to the company's network of four- and five-star hotels. This allowed the company to combine the Méridien chain with the Forte Grand hotel brand giving it a major representation in the international hotel market. The acquisition of the Méridien chain also provided Forte with a significant representation in the important Asia Pacific market and the Middle East.

Product development

Product development is a strategy of developing new products for the existing market. The Victoria and Albert Museum's movement into the corporate hospitality market with a specially designed service is an example of imaginative product development.

It is very important for holiday centres and visitor attractions always to have significant product development plans, so that facilities are upgraded and new attractions are added. Center Parcs, the European-wide leisure company which is owned by Scottish & Newcastle plc, have carried out extensive product development and refurbishment pro-grammes in their holiday complexes. For example, the facilities at Het Vennenbos were improved with the introduction of a new Children's Pool and Lazy River, and at De Eemhof, a new Sports Hall was introduced. The bungalows at De Kempervennen, De Huttenheugte and De Eemhof have also been enhanced in an £8.2 m project during 1993/94.

Whitbread, the UK-based brewing and leisure group, have also car-ried out substantial product development programmes in a number of their businesses. They have attempted to make their public houses a welcoming place for every member of the family. To help with this, special children's menus have been developed and the company has put significant investment into the 'Charlie Chalk' fun factories which are branded children's play areas incorporated into the public house.

Whitbread have also developed new concepts for many of their pubs, including the use of 'virtual reality' technology. The introduction of the highly successful electronic game 'Bowlingo' is helping to increase turnover in 40 of their pubs, for example. In their restaurant sector, they control the franchised TGI Friday's chain. Recognizing that about 30% of their total business comes from children and famil-ies visiting at the weekend the chain has developed new children's menus and staff are specially trained to entertain young customers.

Diversification

Diversification is where an organization sells new products and ser-vices in new markets. Diversification is particularly important if the organization wants to spread its risk across a number of markets, and sees the opportunity of purchasing a brand or company. The Bass pur-chase of the American Holiday Inn chain is an example of a diversifi-cation strategy.

Setting the marketing objective

The marketing objectives which are set also have to be linked to the corporate objectives of the organization. Some examples of marketing objectives for an organization are:

- increasing market share;
- entering a new market;
- achieving number one market position;
- improving image.

The marketing objectives which are set in the end will of course result from the marketing audit which has already been completed.

The lifecycle and portfolio analyses will also allow the organization to come to some logical decisions. For example:

- It is important to maintain the position of a 'cash cow' product or a product in maturity.
- It is important to improve the sales position of a 'star' product or a product in the growth phase.
- It is important to decide what to do with a 'dog' product or a product in decline. The organization may decide to keep the product and 'harvest' the last remaining benefits or it may decide to exit from the market.
- It is important to decide when to enter a new business area with products and services. The development of new products and services will involve a market research programme so that expected results can be estimated.

The marketing objectives will also specify what the organization wants to achieve in terms of market share and volume.

THE BUSINESS MIX

Organizations in the tourism, leisure, and hospitality industries have a particular set of issues which must be considered when they are setting their objectives. Their demand is often highly seasonal and uneven in character which means that they must try and balance demand at different times by attracting different market segments and altering their marketing mix.

To illustrate this point, we will consider the case of a visitor attraction and a hotel. Both of these organizations have peaks and troughs in demand. It is important for each type of organization that the business mix maximizes profitably. This will mean that particular market segments are targeted in the quieter periods. It is also important that during periods of high demand the maximum revenue possible is collected. It is important too that the organization does not rely too heavily on one market segment. For example, if a visitor attraction tries to fill quiet periods by targeting educational groups only, problems may occur when educational budgets are cut. The development of the most appropriate and balanced business mix is an important part of the marketing planning process. Table 13.1 illustrates issues in relation to the business mix of attractions and hotels.

MARKETING STRATEGIES

Marketing objectives set the direction for the organization. Marketing strategies define how the organization is going to get there. Strategy is the overall route to follow to achieve the specific objectives. The strategy will describe the following things:

- the means to achieve the objectives;
- the time programme;
- the resources required to achieve the objectives.

Table 13.1 Getting the right business mix

Organization	Nature of demand	Marketing strategies to overcome the problem
Attraction	Very seasonal. Peak times at weekends and holidays	Offer different products at quiet periods to attract other market segments – educational trips/ corporate hospitality Alter marketing mix accordingly
Hotel	Seasonal peak times Business clientele on weekdays	Offer different products: – business – leisure – weekend breaks – health – special events Alter marketing mix accordingly

Table 13.2 Marketing objectives and marketing strategies

Marketing objectives	Marketing strategies
Increase market share	Range extension and/or price competition and/or high advertising spend
Enter new markets	Develop new products and/or acquire a product, brand or company
Achieve number one market position	Exclusive distribution and/or high quality promotion and/or high price
Improve image	High-profile public relations campaign and/or major relaunch of product range

The difference between the strategy and the detailed implementation plan is clear. Marketing strategy reflects the broad marketing aim of the organization. The plan which comes from the strategy will detail specifications and timing and will identify key responsibilities for people in the organization.

Marketing strategies are therefore designed to meet the requirements of the marketing objectives. They give a broad direction. Table 13.2 demonstrates the move from marketing objectives to marketing strategies.

CORPORATE AND PRODUCT POSITIONING

The concept of product positioning was introduced in Chapter 8. It is important that the organization also positions itself in a favourable light. This can be referred to as **corporate positioning**. When an organization is seeking to spread its marketing activity across national boundaries, it is particularly important to have an excellent corporate positioning strategy.

One of the best examples in the tourism, leisure and hospitality industry has been the conversion of British Airways into a serious global airline (see Case study 19). This included the 'Putting People First' campaign, which tried to change the staff's perception of the company, and the long-term ongoing public relations campaign.

There is also a link between corporate positioning and brand positioning. The French hotel chain Accor, for example, has tried to position its product range on an international basis using a number of well developed brands, Novotel, Sofitel, Thalassa, etc. The repositioning of the Hilton hotel chain by the Ladbroke Group in the early 1990s into a prestigious business-oriented hotel chain is another example of corporate positioning.

Beefeater, the Whitbread-owned dining chain in the UK, successfully repositioned itself in 1993/94. It achieved this by designing the interior to appeal to a broad range of ages and tastes, giving the pub restaurant a pleasant, informal and contemporary ambience. The repositioning strategy in combination with new menus helped Beefeater broaden its customer base and increase the number of visits from existing users.

SUMMARY

The organization has now set the overall marketing objectives and decided on an appropriate strategy to meet these objectives.

We considered a tour operator in Chapter 12 and looked at the process which such an organization would go through to gather together the information contained in the marketing audit. Table 13.3 summarizes the results discussed in detail below.

Table 13.3 The tour operator – results of marketing audit

Strengths
- Major national tour operator
- Major leading brands
- Number of cash generating products
- Cash rich
- Owns airline and retail outlet

Weaknesses
- No international strategy
- Some poorly performing products

Opportunities
- Wider European marketing opportunities
- New market 'niches'

Threats
- European Commission legislation
- International competitors

- **Competitive position**. Organization is in number one market position but the market is very competitive with some other strong players. There are signs that European companies are planning market entry.
- **Customers**. Customers in the UK are not brand loyal and they look for sales promotions and discounted products.
- **Market**. The market is strong and profitable while there is a trend by operators towards vertical integration through the ownership of airlines, retail travel agents and hotels. There are also signs that the market is fragmenting into smaller 'niches,' e.g. holidays on cruise ships, 'green' holidays and 'weddings in tropical places'.
- **Portfolio analysis**. This would give the organization some clues as to what to plan for each of the products within their range. The organization could carry out a portfolio analysis based on the Boston Consulting Group matrix discussed in Chapter 12. The results of this analysis could be as follows:

Cash cows	– Summer sun
	– Holidays for the elderly
Stars	– Young people's holidays
	– Winter sun
Question marks	– Winter sports
	– Long haul
Dogs	– Lakes and mountains
	– Coach tour holidays

An outline of the development of the marketing objectives and strategies resulting from the marketing audit is shown in Table 13.4. The overall objectives and the strategies for the organization are identified first of all. After this, the planning process can cascade down to each of the SBUs in turn. The example given here is for the Summer Sun product, which has a strong market position. The organization would carry out a similar activity for each SBU in the organization. The result of this planning exercise would be a logical marketing strategy for each area of operation.

CONCLUSIONS

At the end of this stage of the marketing planning process, the organization should have a clear view of what the objectives and strategies will be for the next period. The next stage will be to set detailed imple-

Table 13.4 The tour operator – setting market objectives and strategies

MISSION STATEMENT
 We seek to maintain our number one position in the package tour business in the United Kingdom.

THE ORGANIZATION
Marketing objectives
- To be the market leader in the UK in the package tour business
- To give excellent return on investment to satisfy shareholders
- To maintain our excellent image by strong differentiation
- To act in a socially responsible manner
- To look to develop in other European markets

Marketing strategies
- To intensify our marketing programmes
- To implement a high-profile public relations campaign
- To investigate the purchase of other European travel companies
- To implement an environmental policy

STRATEGIC BUSINESS UNIT 1: SUMMER SUN
Marketing objectives
- Keep our number one market position
- Take market share from our UK competitors
- Enter new market segments in the UK and overseas

Marketing strategies
- Relaunch the product
- Build brand awareness
- Introduce new destinations
- Aggressive pre-season advertising campaign and sales promotions
- Investigate opportunities which arise from planned company acquisition

mentation plans so that the objectives will be met within the broad strategies which have been set.

DISCUSSION POINTS AND ESSAY QUESTIONS

1. Briefly discuss the role of 'mission statements' and suggest a hypothetical mission statement for an organization of your choice, explaining the reasoning behind the statement you have devised.
2. Critically evaluate the concept of 'business mix' and outline how you would go about developing an appropriate business mix for a hotel **or** a visitor attraction **or** an airline.
3. Discuss the factors you might take into account when selecting a strategy from a range of options.

EXERCISE For a tourism, leisure and hospitality organization of your choice, you should:
(a) carry out a brief SWOT analysis;
(b) develop a set of marketing objectives and marketing strategies for both the organization as a whole and one of its strategic business units, based on the model found in Table 13.2.

You should present your ideas in the form of a written report, together with a verbal presentation.

CASE STUDIES

You may want to look at the following case studies which illustrate some of the points in this chapter:

6. Scotland
18. Airtours plc, UK;
19. British Airways, UK;
20. The European Travel Commission;
21. The Victoria and Albert Museum, UK.

How will we get there? Developing the strategy $\boxed{14}$

Key concepts

The main concepts covered in this chapter are:

- longer-term strategies and short-term tactical plans;
- sales forecasting;
- marketing plans.

INTRODUCTION

This stage in the marketing planning process is about turning goals, objectives and mission statements into clearly expressed policies and programmes of action.

The final strategy will usually have two elements, namely:

- a strategy covering the whole planning period, which will normally be measured in a number of years;
- tactical plans that detail the action which will be undertaken to ensure that the strategy is implemented. These are often produced annually so that there will be a number of them during the life of a single strategy. These plans are based on manipulating the four P's of the marketing mix to implement the strategy.

This difference is what distinguishes a marketing strategy from a marketing plan.

In this chapter we will look at the process of generating marketing strategies and plans within tourism, leisure and hospitality organizations. We will begin by looking at how strategy options are evaluated and the final one is selected. This will be followed by a detailed examination of the content of marketing plans and the issues which affect this content. Consideration will be given to the organization of marketing activities at this stage, too.

The organization has now progressed through the marketing planning to the stage where the broad marketing objectives and strategies have been set. The next stage of the process is to estimate the expected results for each strategic business in the organization and to plan the marketing mix which will achieve these objectives.

SETTING THE BUDGET

The marketing budget must be estimated. This will be determined once the marketing objectives have been set and will represent an estimate of the costs required for each planned activity in the different elements of the marketing mix, usually for the next year. The budget will be worked out by the relevant marketing manager and will determine the type of activity that can be planned. If the resource is inadequate then the plan will have to be amended. The setting of the budget and the agreement by the organization to the proposals will be dependent on the **sales forecast** which the marketing manager will also be required to produce.

The marketing budget is very often linked to the past sales and profitability of the individual product lines.

SALES FORECASTING

A sales forecast is the amount of a product that the company actually expects to sell during a specific period with a specified level of marketing activity. The sales forecast will be an essential piece of information which will be required so that the organization can set its marketing budget.

Sales forecasts also help the organization to measure marketing attractiveness, to monitor performances and to plan production levels.

There are various techniques which can be used by a marketer to produce a sales forecast. The methods which are used depend very much on the company history and culture, the levels of risk involved and the resources available. When the organization is taking a major financial risk, such as entering a new geographic market, the level of detail of the sales forecast should be great enough to minimize the risks involved.

Marketers tend to use a series of methods to develop sales forecasts. These methods include:

- **Executive judgement**. This is where the past experience and intuition of the key executives in the organization are used to develop the sales forecast.
- **Surveys**. This is where the organization carries out surveys with customers, sales personnel or experts to determine future trends. The **Delphi technique** is a very popular survey method which is often used by organizations when they are preparing sales forecasts. This

is where a series of experts are asked about their views of the market.

- **Time series analysis.** This technique is where a forecaster uses the historical sales data to discover patterns in the organization's sales over time. Computer programs can be used to help in this forecasting method. Time series analysis is very useful for organizations where the sales of the product or service is very stable. It is much less likely to be successful for organizations which sell products and services which have erratic patterns of demand.
- **Correlation methods**. This technique also involves the use of historical sales data. The forecaster tries to find a correlation between past sales and one or more variables such as per capita income.
- **Market tests**. This technique involves the organization in testing out the acceptability of a product or service with customers or distributors. This method is used extensively during new product development when there may be little or no historical sales data to help with the setting of the sales forecast.

The sales forecast should give a clear estimate of the expected results for a period of time, usually for a financial year. The sales forecast should include:

- predicted sales volume;
- predicted sales revenue;
- predicted profitability;
- predicted market share.

The organization will then be able to assess the suitability of the budget proposal and allocate resources effectively. This stage may require the organization to repeat this process on a number of occasions before the final decisions are made, as shown in Figure 14.1.

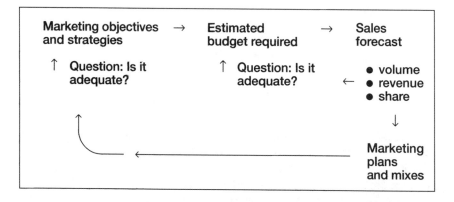

Figure 14.1 Coordination of marketing objectives, budgets and programmes.

IDENTIFYING ALTERNATIVE PLANS AND MIXES

Once the budgets and sales forecasts have been agreed, the organization can then set the action programmes for the individual products and segments. This is usually presented in the form of a **tactical one-year marketing plan**. The organization may of course produce alternative plans and mixes which are assessed before a final decision is made.

Once the final decision is made, the tactical marketing plan will be written and circulated to key personnel in the organization. It will include the major steps which are required in the implementation phase of the plan, who will be responsible for implementing the steps, and how resources and time will be allocated.

McDonald (1989) has suggested an outline model for a one-year marketing plan which is shown in Table 14.1. It is important to note that responsibilities have been clearly identified. There is also a contingency plan included which can be introduced if things start to go wrong during the implementation phase.

The marketing plan will have to include tactical activities which will help the organization to meet its marketing objectives. These could include items related to any part of the marketing mix, such as:

- Product:
  - product development;
  - relaunches;
  - introduction of a new product.
- Pricing:
  - discounting;
  - commission to retailers.
- Promotion:
  - sales promotions;
  - merchandising material;
  - advertising campaigns;
  - brochure production;
  - public relations.
- Place:
  - increase the number of marketing intermediaries
  - distribution and sales staff support.

The organization must check that all the planned activities fit in with the overall marketing strategies and can be funded within the planned marketing budget. It is also important that the organization checks whether the existing personnel are capable of achieving the plan. It is sometimes important that outside agencies, such as advertising agencies for example, are considered early in the planning stage and become actively involved if required.

Table 14.1 Suggested format for one-year marketing plan

1. (a) **Overall objectives.** These should cover the following:

   Volume or value: Last year   Current year estimate   Budget next year;
   Gross margins: Last year   Current year estimate   Budget next year.

   Against each there should be a few words of commentary/explanation

   (b) **Overall strategies** – e.g. new customers,. new products, advertising, sales promotion, selling, customer service, pricing.

2. (a) **Sub-objectives.** More detailed objectives should be provided for products or markets or segments or major customers, as appropriate.

   (b) **Strategies.** The means by which subobjectives will be achieved should be stated.

   (c) **Action/tactics.** The details, timing, responsibility and cost should also be stated.

3. **Summary of marketing activities and costs.**

4. **Contingency plan.** It is important to include a contingency plan, which should address the following questions:

   (a) What are the critical assumptions on which the one-year plan is based?

   (b) What would the financial consequences be (i.e. the effect on the operating income) if these assumptions did not come true? For example, if a forecast of revenue is based on the assumption that a decision will be made to buy new plant by a major customer, what would the effect be if that customer did not go ahead?

   (c) How will these assumptions be managed?

   (d) What action will you take to ensure that the adverse financial effects of an unfulfilled assumption are mitigated, so that you end up with the same forecast profit at the end of the year?

   To measure the risk, assess the negative or downside, asking what can go wrong with each assumption that would change the outcome.

   For example, if a market growth rate of 5% is a key assumption, what lower growth rate would have to occur before a substantially different management decision would be taken? For a capital project, this would be the point at which the project would cease to be economical.

5. **Operating result and financial ratios**
   - Net revenue
   - Gross margin
   - Adjustments
   - Marketing costs
   - Administration costs
   - Interest
   - Operating result
   - ROS (Return on Sales)
   - ROI (Return on Investment)

6. **Key activity planner.** Finally you should summarize the key activities and indicate the start and finish. This should help you considerably with monitoring the progress of your annual plan.

7. **Other.** There may be other information you wish to provide, such as sales call plans.

Source: McDonald (1989).

SUMMARY

When the programmes are set, the organization will know where it is going and how it will get there. It will also have a clear view of how this is going to affect the organization and its employees in the long and the short term.

We can now return to the tour operator which we looked at in Chapters 12 and 13. At that stage the organization had considered the overall marketing objectives and strategies. We will now consider the

Table 14.2 One-year marketing plan – Strategic Business Unit 1: Summer Sun

1. **Overall objectives**
   - Keep our number one market position
   - Take market share from our competitors
   - Enter new market segments in the UK and overseas

2. **Overall strategies**
   - Relaunch the product
   - Build brand awareness
   - Introduce new destinations
   - Investigate the purchase of European travel company to extend geographical market

3. **Financial objectives**

	Current year	Next year
Holidays sold	2 million	2.24 million
Turnover	£700 m	£874 m

4. **Marketing objectives**

	Current year	Next year
Market share	25%	28%

   NB: Assumes market remains static.
   The organization may also produce detailed weekly or monthly sales estimates to help with the monitoring and evaluation process.

5. **Detailed actions/tactics and estimated costs/responsibilities**
   A detailed review of the year plan is outlined in Table 14.3. It is important that the budget is available to fund this activity.

   Total marketing budget: £6.75 m

   NB: The organization should also prepare detailed planning documents for major activities such as a rebranding exercise.

6. **Contingency plan**
   - This one-year marketing plan is based on the assumption that the total market for package holidays in the UK remains static next year.
   - Problems will arise if overall market demand drops in the year. Monitoring will have to take place once a week to check weekly sales levels. Tactical measures will have to be taken if market demand drops.

writing and preparation of the detailed tactical marketing plan for the next year for Strategic Business Unit 1: Summer Sun.

The finished draft of the marketing plan is shown in Tables 14.2 and 14.3. The plan gives the overall objectives and strategies for the current year. A financial objective is also given to show the targets for this particular strategic business unit. This would, in practice, be expanded to a monthly or weekly sales estimate which would be used to evaluate performance on an ongoing basis. The plan also includes detailed plans, budgets and responsibilities for the various activities which will be required to meet the objectives of the plan.

This marketing plan would then have to be looked at in combination with all the other proposed marketing plans from other strategic busi-

Table 14.3 Detailed marketing activities

	Activity	Timing	Budget	Responsibility
1.	**Product range**			
	(a) Negotiate two new destinations for next season	Ongoing	£100 000	AB
	(b) Handle relaunch of Summer Sun brand	Ongoing – to be completed for next season	£500 000	TC
2.	**Promotion**			
	(a) Handle ongoing PR campaign	Ongoing	Central budget	Publicity manager
	(b) Prepare next year's Summer Sun brochure	Ongoing	£500 000	TC
	(c) Sales promotion with trade	January	£100 000	AC
	(d) Plan and execute TV/ press advertising campaign	Ongoing	£5 m	Liaise with advertising agency AB
	(e) Start work on rebranding exercise	Ongoing Initial ideas by May	£500 000	Liaise with advertising agency and design studio AC
3.	**Distribution**			
	(a) Work on direct sales ideas	Initial ideas by May	£50 000	BD
4.	**Prices**			
	(a) Set prices for next year	Initial ideas by May	–	Liaise with finance department
5.	**Other activities**			
	(a) Investigate possible purchase of European tour operator	Report on feasibility in June	–	'Purchase Team' AB – from marketing
	(b) Ongoing market research with customers	Final report available November	Central budget	Marketing research company controlled by AB

ness units in the organization to see if they were congruent. Once the marketing plan is agreed, it can be used as a means of communication to all staff within the company, and particularly to those in the marketing and sales departments.

CONCLUSIONS

The organization has now drawn up a detailed marketing plan for all of the strategic business units' brands and product lines. These can now be agreed and implemented for the next period. The organization must now move to the final part of the marketing planning process – the monitoring and evaluation stage or 'How will we know when we get there?'

DISCUSSION POINTS AND ESSAY QUESTIONS

1. Outline a hypothetical marketing plan for an organization of your choice, based on the model published by McDonald (1989).
2. Critically evaluate the one-year marketing plan for a tour operator's strategic business unit which is outlined in Table 14.2.
3. Discuss the main techniques involved in sales forecasting and examine the problems involved in sales forecasting.

EXERCISE Choose a tourism, leisure and hospitality organization which is based near where you live. For the organization selected you should:

(a) ascertain the organization's current marketing objectives;
(b) taking the organization's current marketing situation into account, develop a one-year marketing plan for the organization, based on the model set out in Table 14.1.

You should arrange to present your marketing plan to the organization and its managers, asking them to comment on its strengths and weaknesses.

CASE STUDIES

You may wish to look at the following case studies which illustrate some of the points made in the chapter:

  6. Scotland;
18. Airtours plc, UK;
19. British Airways, UK;
20. The European Travel Commission;
21. The Victoria and Albert Museum, UK.

How will we know when we get there? Monitoring, review and evaluation

Key concepts

The main concepts covered in this chapter are:

- performance evaluation techniques;
- marketing information systems;
- marketing control mechanisms.

INTRODUCTION

Last, but crucially important, in the marketing planning process is the issue of monitoring, evaluation and review. This is the control mechanism in the process which ensures that the outcomes are meeting expectations.

It follows a number of stages:

- monitoring the organization's performance against the targets set in the marketing strategy/plan;
- identifying variances and seeking to explain them;
- instituting action, wherever possible, to put the organization 'back on track' to ensure that the strategy/plan, as originally conceived, is implemented in full;
- where the pattern cannot be put right in this way because the original strategy was over-ambitious or circumstances have changed since it was adopted, then the strategy/plan has to be modified;
- the product of the monitoring review and evaluation phase of the process becomes the starting point for the current situation analysis stage of the next cycle of marketing planning.

In this chapter we will look at how monitoring, review and evaluation can be undertaken in tourism, leisure and hospitality. We will also consider the prerequisites for successful monitoring, review and evaluation.

CONTROLLING MARKETING ACTIVITIES

To achieve the marketing objectives the organization must control the marketing efforts. This control will consist of setting performance standards and establishing how the organization is achieving these standards on a regular basis. This is a fundamental activity in marketing, but evidence shows that organizations often fail at the final stage. The methods of control which are used will depend on the type of organization, the business in which it operates, and the culture and management style.

Performance standards must be set for all areas of the business. These will be a mix of financial goals and other standards which should also be met. Some examples of performance standards will appear in the detailed one-year marketing plan for an individual product.

Examples of performance standards might be planned weekly or monthly sales targets, or the successful completion of activities such as the production of brochures or a rebranding exercise, or increases in the total customer base. Performance standards can also relate to product quality.

The controlling process will involve looking at actual performance in relation to the performance standards and taking corrective action if necessary, as shown in Figure 15.1.

EVALUATING PERFORMANCE

There are various methods which can be used to evaluate the organization's performance in relation to set standards. The most commonly used method of evaluating performance is the use of sales data.

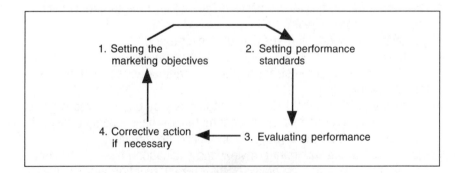

Figure 15.1 Summary of the marketing control process.

Sales analysis

Sales figures may be used to evaluate the organization's performance. Such data is usually available and it is the most direct method of analysing the customer reaction to changes in the marketing mix. The customer response to a new destination or a new brochure, for example, will be reflected in the level of sales which result from these developments.

The danger with sales data is that it is presented in a form which cannot be used by the marketing manager. Sales data should be summarized before presentation if at all possible. The data should be presented in a form which relates to the sales estimate. For example, if there is a target for £500 000 of sales in one month of trading, the manager can look at the resulting sales figure and judge exactly how close the sales of the product are to this estimate.

Sales data can also be presented in the form of sales volume, sales value or market share. Sales volume for a product will tell the marketer how the sales of a particular product are progressing. Market share data will tell the marketer how the product is performing in relation to the competition. It would be particularly serious, for example, if both the sales volume and the market share for a product were declining. The sooner the manager knows, the sooner corrective action can be taken to improve performance.

Total sales figures should be broken down by individual products. They can also be broken down by geographic area and customers. It would be particularly important for a tour operator, for example, to know the sales performance in different retail travel agents.

MARKETING INFORMATION SYSTEMS

Marketing information systems are the ways in which an organization measures whether it is meeting marketing objetives. The marketing information system for a large hospitality organization has been analysed by Calver (1994) and is illustrated in Figure 15.2. This model shows the

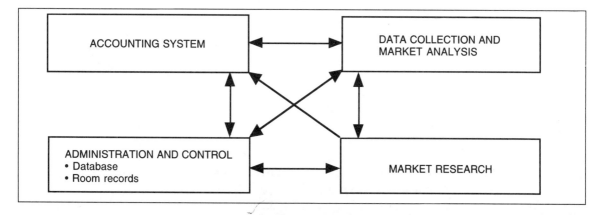

Figure 15.2 Marketing information system. Source: Calver (1994).

components of the system and the interrelationships between them, demonstrating the dynamic nature of such systems in a hospitality organization and which is typical of all business organizations.

One of the problems with this type of analysis is that it is often difficult to apportion central costs to specific product groups or individual products. The organization should have a way, however, of analysing the functional costs of specific product groups, geographic areas or customer groups.

PROBLEMS WITH MARKETING CONTROL

Organizations often have fundamental problems with their marketing control processes. These can be summarized under three main headings:

- **Environmental changes**. Organizations often introduce changes in marketing mix programmes at the same time as something happens in the business environment. Customer demand or economic conditions may change, for example. These will both have an effect on sales.
- **Time lags**. There is nearly always a time lag between carrying out marketing activities and their effects. The marketer must allow sufficient time before sales data is analysed. The definition of 'sufficient time' will largely be a matter of judgement by the marketer based on previous experience. In a completely new market, where experience is limited, the judgement will have to be developed.
- **Difficulties in determining costs**. It is often difficult for an organization to determine the full cost of a marketing activity for a particular product.

Despite these potential problems, the monitoring and evaluation of marketing activity detailed in a marketing plan is a very important activity. Marketing information systems should be developed which help the marketer to carry these out in a simple and effective manner.

WHAT TO DO IF THINGS GO WRONG

The advantages of a well developed monitoring and evaluation system is that the organization will know at an early stage when things are going wrong. For example, if sales and/or market share begin to fall, the organization can take corrective action immediately.

There may be a variety of tactical measures which an organization can use to help in these types of situation. For example, the organization may:

- introduce a sales promotion;
- temporararily reduce prices;

- increase advertising spend;
- reduce capacity.

The organization may also have to adjust the original marketing plan to reduce over-ambitious sales estimates.

It is just as critical to the organization if the indications are that the sales estimates were too low. This may mean that the company cannot meet demand and therefore will lose revenue. It may also mean that customers become unhappy and begin to look at competitors' products. This will be particularly damaging if customers are not 'brand loyal' because they will quickly change their allegiance to the competitors' products.

SUMMARY

The final stage of the marketing planning process is very important to ensure an organization's success. The marketer must review how the products are performing in relation to previously agreed performance standards.

We can now return to the tour operator which we looked at in the previous three chapters. At the end of Chapter 13 we saw how the organization had completed the one-year marketing plan for the Summer Sun Strategic Business Unit. It is important now that the marketing manager plans a method of review and evaluation for this area of the business so that ongoing progress can be evaluated.

The one-year marketing plan had proposed a series of performance standards. These are summarized in Table 15.1.

Table 15.1 Strategic Business Unit 1: Summer Sun – summary of performance standards

Source	Format
1. Financial performance data	(a) Yearly sales estimates
	(b) Sales estimates broken down into:
	(i) – weekly volume targets
	(ii) – destination volume targets
	(iii) – customer type targets
	(c) Marketing budget allocated to different activities, e.g. advertising budget
	(d) Market share data
2. Key activities for the year	(a) Overall plan with critical dates and budgets identified
	(b) Individual plan for specific projects, e.g. production of brochure
3. Market research of customer response	Overall targets

The marketing manager for the Summer Sun product should therefore make sure that the marketing information system outlined by Piercy (1992) is in place. Piercy describes the characteristics of a marketing information system as follows:

- it stores and integrates information on marketing issues from many sources;
- it provides for the dissemination of such information to users;
- it supports marketing management decision-making in both planning and control;
- it is likely to be computerized;
- it is not simply a new name for market research.

In the case of the tour operator the marketing information is coming from a number of sources.

The key activities which the manager should put in place are as follows:

- Make sure that there is a weekly summary produced of financial data, including weekly sales figures, market share and budget spend.
- Make sure that he or she has a regular review of marketing data, e.g. Mintel, press reports, etc. – ideally once a week or a minimum of once a month.
- Hold regular weekly/monthly meetings with key organization staff to monitor process on individual projects.
- Hold regular weekly/monthly meetings with key agency staff, e.g. market research agencies, advertising agencies, etc. to monitor progress.
- Hold monthly review of plans for individual high-profile projects, e.g. creation of the Summer Sun brochure.
- Ensure early feedback on key market research programmes. The research of customer attitudes is very important here.
- Hold regular review meetings with destination managers – how is business going? Are there any problems?

The marketer should then act on the information received and take corrective action if necessary. It is important that both quantitative and qualitative data is received, evaluated and responded to.

CONCLUSIONS

The marketing planning process is not finished until the plan is put into action and it is continually reviewed and evaluated. It is also important that any lessons which are learned from the previous year's planning process are incorporated into subsequent years.

DISCUSSION POINTS AND ESSAY QUESTIONS

1. Discuss the main methods of evaluating marketing performance, highlighting the difficulties involved in implementing these methods.
2. Evaluate the most important marketing control mechanisms and outline the problems associated with each of them.
3. Using examples, examine the role of performance standards in ensuring the effective implementation of marketing plans.

Choose **one** of the following Strategic Business Units (SBUs): **EXERCISE**

- the Business Class service offered by a privately owned scheduled airline;
- the short break product offered by a destination marketing agency;
- the ski holiday product of a tour operator;
- the food and beverage operation of a major hotel.

For the SBU you have selected, you should:
(a) suggest a range of performance indicators that would help an organization monitor the marketing performance of its SBU;
(b) outline the action that might be taken if an SBU failed to meet targets set for it in relation to these performance indicators.

CASE STUDIES

You may wish to look at one of the following case studies which illustrate some of the points made in this chapter:

6. Scotland, UK;
28. Airtours plc, UK;
19. British Airways, UK;
20. The European Travel Commission;
21. The Victoria and Albert Museum, UK.

Conclusions to Part 4

In the preceding four chapters we have explored the key issues involved in the process of marketing planning. Most people accept the logic of marketing planning even though they often find it very difficult to implement in practical organizational situations.

Many organizations in the tourism, leisure and hospitality sectors are operating in volatile business environments which may make marketing planning an impossible task. The process of marketing planning may also make the organization operate in a bureaucratic manner and prevent members of the organization thinking creatively and grasping opportunities. They may be too busy writing a marketing plan to think creatively and they may be frustrated by the apparently bureaucratic processes which are involved in the change process.

The marketing planning process may also be too time-consuming, particularly for small organizations. The process also requires detailed marketing research data which may not be available to the organization. Finally, it could be argued that the best ideas come from hunches and the judgements of individuals rather than the more psuedo-scientific approaches of marketing planning.

It can be argued that the most important aspect of the marketing planning process is that it forces marketers to think in a structured and systematic way about what they are doing. It also helps them to rationalize their marketing decisions.

Marketing in different sectors of tourism, leisure and hospitality

PART 5

In Part 5, we explore the role of marketing in 12 different sectors of tourism, leisure and hospitality, as follows:

- **Chapter 16: Visitor attractions;**
- **Chapter 17: Accommodation;**
- **Chapter 18: Tourist destinations;**
- **Chapter 19: Tour operation;**
- **Chapter 20: Transport;**
- **Chapter 21: Resorts;**
- **Chapter 22: Retail travel;**
- **Chapter 23: Arts and entertainment;**
- **Chapter 24: Recreation and sport;**
- **Chapter 25: Leisure shopping;**
- **Chapter 26: Catering;**
- **Chapter 27: Business tourism.**

The aim will be to identify the key factors which influence the practice of marketing in these sectors, and compare contrasting approaches to marketing between the sectors.

The main issues which will be covered to achieve these aims include:

- the marketing objectives of organizations within each sector;
- the marketing mix;
- the business environment;
- the nature of competition.

Any significant differences and similarities between countries across Europe will be identified where appropriate.

The 12 sectors we will be considering do not represent every aspect of tourism, leisure and hospitality. However, they are the major sectors and they do clearly illustrate the diversity of approaches to marketing that are found in tourism, leisure and hospitality.

Visitor attractions $\boxed{\textbf{16}}$

Key concepts

The main concepts covered in this chapter are:

- Types of attractions;
- differences between the marketing of attractions in the public, private and voluntary sectors;
- the marketing of attractions by other organizations;
- the role of marketing consortia.

INTRODUCTION

It is very difficult to generalize about the marketing of visitor attractions as it is such a heterogeneous field. This heterogeneity results from two main factors, namely that there are four different types of attraction and that attractions are owned and managed by three different sorts of organization.

TYPES OF ATTRACTION

The four main types of attraction are:

- natural features in the landscape, such as beaches, caves, woodlands and rivers;
- man-made phenomena which, while not designed to be visitor attractions, now function, at least in part, as attractions, including cathedrals and castles;
- man-made phenomena that have been designed specifically to attract visitors and for whom the attraction of visitors is their sole function. This category includes theme parks, for example;
- special events and festivals, which are neither physical or permanent, but which attract visitors to a particular location at a specific time. These may be traditional such as the Passion Plays of Oberammergau or more modern creations designed to encourage tourists to visit places they might not otherwise visit.

In the case of the first two types of attraction, the usual marketing objective is not to increase the number of visitors but rather to manage demand so that the attraction is not damaged by over-use. On the other hand, with attractions in the third category, the main aim of marketing is to increase visitor numbers and revenue. As far as the last category of attractions are concerned, the aim can be either managing demand to prevent the event being ruined by too many visitors, or increasing attendance to maximize the economic benefits of tourism for the local economy. In this chapter we will focus on these last two types of attraction which seek to attract more customers.

However, as we noted earlier in the book, there is an increasingly 'grey area' in terms of the distinction between attractions and destinations. Some man-made attractions, such as Disneyland Paris and Futuroscope in France, while technically attractions, appear to have more in common with destinations than with most other attractions. In terms of the area they cover and their visitor numbers, and the fact that they have on-site accommodation, for example, they appear to be more like destinations. However, the fact that they are usually in single ownership rather than multiple ownership confirms that they are not like other destinations, as does the fact that they usually have a single core product or theme, unlike most destinations.

OWNERSHIP AND MARKETING OBJECTIVES

The three types of organization which own and manage attractions have different motives and objectives, as discussed below.

Public sector

Public sector bodies tend to be particularly dominant in certain sectors of the attraction business, including museums, historic sites, galleries, theatres and leisure centres, for example. The marketing of public sector attractions is unusual in that the aim is rarely to make a profit but rather to break even or operate within a given deficit budget.

We can split public sector bodies into two types, namely national governments and agencies on the one hand, and regional and local governments on the other.

For national governments and agencies, ownership of attractions often has the following two major objectives:

- protecting the nation's heritage, in terms of historic buildings and archaeological sites, for example;
- to attract foreign tourists, with the result that the national balance of payments is improved.

In the case of regional and local governments, the objectives for operating attractions can often include:

- increasing the range of leisure facilities which are available to the local community;

- using museums to teach children about the history of their area;
- utilizing them as a way of improving the image of the area with external audiences;
- using attractions as a catalyst for the further development of the local tourism industry.

Perhaps the most significant development in Europe in recent years has been the growing trend towards the use of attractions to stimulate economic development and regeneration. A few examples will serve to illustrate this point, as follows:

- In urban areas in the UK central or local government has used attractions to try to regenerate industrial cities and towns which are suffering from unemployment, derelict land and social problems. Attractions have been used to try to improve the situation in such places. For example, the UK government has funded waterfront developments in cities such as Liverpool, and organized major Garden Festivals in Liverpool (1984), Stoke on Trent (1986), Glasgow (1988), Gateshead (1990) and Ebbw Vale (1992). At the same time we have seen attraction-led regeneration strategies in Bradford with its Museum of Photography, Film and Television, and Wigan with its famous Wigan Pier development.
- In the regions of France attractions have been used as a tool of regional development. For example, Futuroscope has been developed as a public sector-led project to help put the Poitou-Charentes region on the map. Further information on this successful development is contained in Case Study 7. Other examples include some of the major aquarium complexes which have been developed, including Nausicaa at Boulogne-Sur-Mer and Oceonopolis in Brest.
- In Spain, special event attractions have been utilized to help develop national economic development, most notably in 1992. In that year, the public sector in Spain spent billions of pesetas on three major event attractions, namely the Expo '92 in Seville, the Olympics in Barcelona and Madrid's role as European City of Culture.

However, in many cases, the role that public sector bodies can play in the attraction field is constrained by government policies on public spending.

Private sector

Private sector companies are particularly important players in certain sectors of the attraction business such as theme parks and industrial tourism. Usually, their main aim is to generate a certain level of profit or achieve a given rate of return on investment. Some of these companies, such as the Tussaud's Group in the UK, are transnational operators, owning and managing attractions in a number of countries. Tussaud's not only owns a number of leading attractions in the UK such as Warwick Castle and Alton Towers, but is also a partner in the company which owns the new Port Aventura theme park at Salou in the Murcia region of Spain. Likewise, the Lego Corporation of Denmark recently opened a new Legoland attraction at Windsor in the UK to add to its existing site in Denmark.

Many of these larger private attraction corporations have substantial financial resources for both product development and promotion. At the same time, the majority of private attraction operators are small and medium-sized enterprises with much more limited budgets.

Voluntary sector

Voluntary sector organizations play an important role in the attractions sector in some parts of Europe such as the UK and France. Tourism is often not their core business or their main interest; rather it is used as a means to an end where the end can be conservation and community development, for example. Income generated from tourism is used by voluntary bodies to further their main work. Two examples of such bodies will illustrate their role in the attractions field:

- The National Trust has more members than any other organization in the UK, and celebrated its 100th year in 1995. Its main concern is with the conservation of Britain's built and natural environment. It uses its income from tourism to further this, by buying and maintaining buildings and landscapes. Its tourism-related revenue comes from entrance charges to the properties it owns, income from self-catering cottages which it lets to tourists, together with money from its catering and retailing operations.
- The Ecomusées in France are usually run by voluntary sector bodies set up under the Association Law of 1901. One of the most impressive of these is that based at Puy-du-Fou in the Vendée region. However, Puy-du-Fou is not just an Ecomusée. It is also the site of, perhaps, Europe's largest theatrical spectacle. Each summer, over a thousand local people, all volunteers, dress up to help re-enact scenes from local history for visitors in a show called the Cinéscénie. These performances now attract hundreds of thousands of spectators. However, all the income from the event is used for the benefit of the local community. In the past this money has been used to provide grants for local students going to study elsewhere in France, and to fund a local radio station, for example. At the same time, the Cinéscénie has stimulated the local tourism industry and increased custom for local businesses. It has also funded the development of a heritage-based 'theme park' on the site.

THE ATTRACTION MARKET

The attraction market is interesting in a number of ways, notably:

- the distance people are prepared to travel to visit attractions. In some cases, attractions are the main motivation for people to travel thousands of kilometres away from their home, for example to Dis-

ney World in Florida or Disneyland Paris in Europe. At the same time some types of attractions such as local authority museums and most theatres appeal largely to a local audience;
- the frequency with which people visit attractions. Some people visit attractions regularly while others may rarely or never visit any attractions. Others may only visit one type of attraction;
- the motivation for visiting attractions. These can vary dramatically from the desire for excitement in the case of a 'white-knuckle' theme park ride to education in the case of museums and aesthetic pleasure at an opera performance, to give just three examples;
- the most relevant ways of segmenting the attraction market. These include education groups, coach parties, families and corporate users.

While little hard data exists, it also seems that there may be significant national differences in attraction visiting behaviour in Europe. This is certainly the implication of the differences in tourism and leisure markets detailed in Chapter 5.

PRICE

Pricing is a very complex issue in the attraction field because of the following issues:

- Some attractions which are publicly owned make no charge for using them, even though they may be world famous and of the highest quality. Others will be subsidized so that they do not need to charge a true market price.
- Discounts are used in a variety of ways for marketing purposes, either to attract market segments which are thought to be especially desirable, such as families which tend to be relatively high spenders and groups because of their size. Likewise, discounts can be used to attract visitors at quiet times of the year. Attraction discounts can take two forms, namely 'added value' such as 'two admissions for the price of one' offers or reduced price discounts such as 'fifty pence off'.
- Concessions may be offered, particularly by public or voluntary owned attractions for social reasons. The idea behind them is that they allow 'disadvantaged' people to visit an attraction who might not be able to afford to if they had to pay the full price. These concessions are often targeted at unemployed people, the elderly, the disabled and students.
- The concept of value-for-money can be more important than the price which is charged. Consumers are often happy to pay a relatively high price if they feel they are getting good value in return, rather than paying a low price for a less impressive product. Hence the fact that in Europe, the most expensive theme parks are also the ones which receive the most visitors such as Disneyland Paris.

Value for money in relation to attractions often seems to be based on the length of stay, the uniqueness of the attraction's product and the quality of on-site services and facilities. Some customers also believe that value for money means that the attraction charges an 'all-inclusive price' covering everything, rather than those attractions where one pays on an item-by-item basis.

DISTRIBUTION

Distribution, in the formal sense of the term, is little developed in the attractions sector as many purchases are made spontaneously when people pass an attraction they think looks interesting. Indeed, as there is relatively little advance booking of attractions – except for theatres and sports events, for instance – there is little need for distribution channels. However, there are a few specialist agencies which specialize in attraction bookings. Probably the largest in Europe is that operated by the Keith Prowse organization which offers tickets for a range of attractions in the USA as well as in the UK, France, Germany, the Netherlands and Scandinavia. Most of the attractions it deals with are theme parks with relatively high prices, so that the agency can generate a reasonable commission by selling their tickets.

PROMOTION

Most attractions in Europe have limited budgets for promotion, so that for most of them television advertising is not a viable option. Most of their advertising tends to be in the printed media such as newspapers and magazines. Perhaps the most important promotional device for most attractions is their general brochure which is designed to encourage people to want to visit the attraction and to provide practical information to help them when they do visit. Relatively little use is made by most attractions of other types of promotions such as direct face-to-face selling or sponsorship, for example. However, press and public relations are used by many attractions to gain free media coverage.

COMPETITION

The degree of competition varies between different sectors of the attractions field in Europe. The theme park business, for example, is highly competitive, while in the case of local council-owned museums and leisure centres, the council only operates these attractions in its own area. There is no overlap with other areas, so that one council does not operate such attractions in areas covered by other councils. In these cases, the only competition tends to be internal competition where the only museums in an area will belong to one council and the only real competition will therefore be between these museums which are owned by the one organization.

The competition for attractions is, however, not limited to other attractions. It can include any other use of leisure time or form of leisure spending, such as gardening or home entertainment systems.

Competition is also complicated in the attractions sector by the pricing issues discussed earlier; in other words, state subsidies mean that the prices paid do not always reflect the value of the product. This could be seen as a form of unfair competition by commercially managed attractions.

MARKETING BY EXTERNAL ORGANIZATIONS

Attractions are often marketed by other people as well as their own owners where they are used as part of other people's products. Examples of this phenomenon include the following.

- Tour operators, for whom attractions represent excursion opportunities for their clients and which may be a reason why some people choose to take a particular package holiday. For instance, some tourists may be encouraged to take a holiday in Crete because they can visit the temple site at Knossos. Likewise, tour operators selling Denmark promote Legoland in their brochures, and tour operators with programmes featuring Russia do the same for the Hermitage Museum in St Petersburg and the 'White Nights Festival' which takes place in June.
- Destination marketing agencies at national, regional and local levels. They use attractions to persuade visitors to make trips to their particular destination rather than to another place. Thus in its promotional campaigns in the UK market, Maison de la France, the French government national tourist office, uses Futuroscope and the many arts festivals in France, for instance. At the same time the promotional activity of many municipalities seems to be strongly based on major attractions which they have in their area, including the following, for example:
  - Thessaloniki in Northern Greece, with its famous archaeological museum and its many historic buildings and monuments;
  - the German city of Munich, with its annual Oktoberfest;
  - Sheffield in the UK, on the basis of its sports facilities;
  - Sofia, Bulgaria, and its proximity to the Rila Monastery and the Vitosha skiing areas.

Marketing consortia

Marketing consortia are also important in some regions of Europe, with attractions joining together to promote each other on a cooperative basis. These consortia tend to be of two types, namely:

- those made up of similar types of attractions such as stately homes or museums;
- those which bring together attractions in a certain geographical area.

These consortia can vary considerably in terms of their activities. In some attractions simply agree to display each others' brochures, while in other cases joint brochures are produced and joint advertising campaigns and sales promotions organized.

A good example from the UK of an attraction marketing consortia is the so-called 'Treasure Houses of England' group, which brings together eight of Britain's foremost stately homes. The group produces a joint brochure featuring a sales promotion offer, and in 1994 ran a joint photography competition in collaboration with Kodak.

Occasionally, these consortia can be transnational in nature. For example, after Disneyland Paris opened in 1992, a consortium of five leading European theme parks was formed. Its members were Alton Towers (UK), Parc Asterix (France), De Efteling (Netherlands), Europa Park (Germany) and Liseberg Park (Sweden).

CONCLUSIONS

As we have seen, attraction marketing is a complex, heterogeneous activity due to the nature of the attraction product and market, and the ownership structure of attractions.

Attraction marketing is particularly important for tourism and hospitality marketing in general because it could be argued that attractions are the reason why most people travel for pleasure with their resulting need for all the other tourism and hospitality services.

DISCUSSION POINTS AND ESSAY QUESTIONS

1. Discuss the different marketing objectives that are found between attractions in the public, private and voluntary sectors.
2. Examine some of the most important characteristics of pricing, distribution and promotion in the attractions sector.
3. Select one attraction which you believe has been particularly successful at marketing itself and explain the reasons why you believe it has been so successful.

From your local area choose an attraction from **two** of the following types of   **EXERCISE**
visitor attraction:

- museum;
- theatre;
- shopping centre;
- theme park;
- leisure complex;
- professional football club.

For your chosen attractions, produce a report of no more than 3000 words
which compares and contrasts them in terms of the following characteristics:

- ownership;
- size;
- marketing objectives;
- product;
- pricing policies;
- distribution channels;
- promotional techniques.

CASE STUDIES

You may wish to look at the following case studies which illustrate
some of the points made in this chapter:

7. Futuroscope, France;
21. The Victoria and Albert Museum, UK;
28. Les Vins Georges Duboeuf SA, France;
29. Port Aventura SA, Spain.

17 | Accommodation

Key concepts

The main concepts covered in this chapter are:

- types of accommodation;
- the influence of different forms of ownership on marketing objectives;
- the service element of the accommodation product;
- different forms of competition in the accommodation business.

INTRODUCTION

The idea of providing somewhere for tourists to sleep is simple, but the ways in which the industry provides for this need are myriad. There are many different types of accommodation which are usually categorized on the basis of whether they are fully serviced partly serviced or non-serviced. The following short, selective list of different types of accommodation in Europe will illustrates the diversity of accommodation types that exists:

- resort complexes;
- hotels;
- motels;
- 'bed and breakfast' establishments;
- state-owned historic hotels such as the Paradores of Spain and the Poussadas of Portugal;
- youth hostels;
- holiday centres and villages;
- clubs and institutions;
- inns, auberges and tavernas;
- farmhouses;
- cruise liners and ferries;
- narrow boats and canal boats;
- buses and coaches which can be converted for sleeping;

- sleeper trains;
- horse-drawn carriages;
- schools with residential facilities that are available during school vacations such as the Edda Hotels of Iceland;
- university and college halls of residence that are available during vacations;
- timeshare developments;
- campsites;
- caravans both touring and static;
- self-catering cottages, villas, apartments or gîtes;
- privately-owned second homes which are available for rent for part of the year;
- homes that used to be used for workers but are now available for use by tourists such as the former fishermen's shelters on Rorbus of the Lofoten Islands in Norway;
- mountain huts and refuges.

Even within some of these categories there are some major differences. In the private hotel sector, for example, there is a world of difference between a château hotel in the French countryside, a family-owned hotel in the suburbs of an industrial city and a high-rise chain-owned hotel next to a beach.

We will now move on to look at a number of the key issues that influence the nature and practice of accommodation marketing in Europe.

OWNERSHIP AND MARKETING OBJECTIVES

Let us begin by looking at the question of ownership which is a complex matter in the accommodation sector, yet it is important for it influences the marketing objectives which are set for the relevant accommodation unit. A few examples will illustrate this point as follows:

- The major privately-owned hotel chains set out to maximize the profits of their individual properties.
- The state-owned hotels such as the Poussadas and Paradores of Portugal and Spain respectively are designed to help conserve historic buildings while encouraging tourism to the regions in which they are located.
- Farm-based accommodation may be used as a way of supplementing the farmer's income so that the farm can remain financially viable.
- Voluntary sector-owned accommodation, such as many of Europe's youth hostels, have social objectives such as making it possible for people on limited incomes to visit the countryside and encouraging youth tourism.

LOCATION

A vital issue in accommodation marketing is the location of the accommodation establishment which determines the likely level of business a unit will receive and which target markets it will serve. Accommodation locations include:

- city and town centres;
- suburbs of towns and cities;
- major road junctions and roadside sites;
- villages;
- open countryside;
- mountains;
- coastal.

A unique, scenically attractive location can justify the charging of a premium price.

Location will also dictate the pattern of demand an accommodation unit will experience over a week and a year. For example, a city-centre hotel will probably be busier on weekdays than at the weekend due to its reliance on business travellers. Likewise, coastal hotels are likely to enjoy higher occupancy rates in the summer than in the winter. In the first case, the main aim of marketing activity may well be to create more weekend business, while the latter establishments may well wish to attract more business in the off-peak season.

Finally, some accommodation types are mobile, such as sleeper trains, while others are totally flexible, such as tents, so that their users can enjoy them virtually anywhere they choose.

SERVICE ELEMENT

The service element of the accommodation product is important in the accommodation sector in two contrasting ways, as follows:

- In those properties where a very high level of personal service is used to differentiate it from its competitors and to justify a higher price. This is particularly true of grand old hotels such as the Dorchester and Claridges in London and the George V and Crillon in Paris, for instance.
- In those units where little or no service is offered which is reflected in lower prices as their operation requires less labour. This is part of the thinking behind self-catering accommodation and the rise of budget motels like the French 'Formule 1' brand.

While service is usually provided by paid and trained staff, in some forms of accommodation much of the attraction to the tourist is that the service is not 'professional' as such. Hence the 'bed and breakfasts' of Britain are popular, partly because the 'hosts' deliver personalized attention rather than a professional standardized type of service.

PRICE

The pricing of accommodation is influenced by a number of factors, including:

- location;
- facilities in the unit and in the bedroom;
- level of service offered;
- time of the year and day of the week.

Discounting may be used to achieve many marketing objectives, with discounts being given for a number of different reasons such as:

- to attract volume business such as conferences and coach groups;
- to reward regular customers;
- to encourage people to use the hotel at quieter times.

Last-minute discounting is a common phenomenon because once the night comes the room no longer has any value. Therefore, hoteliers reduce prices dramatically once the evening arrives because they would rather receive some income for the room which they can set against their costs rather than nothing. They always hope that a guest may then spend elsewhere in the hotel, such as the bar and the restaurant.

Accommodation prices vary dramatically across Europe. Sometimes, a similar type of hotel might cost four, five or six times more in one European city than another. The factors that influence these price differentials include:

- the level of economic development in the country, which is usually reflected in land prices and labour costs, for example;
- the level of demand, both domestic and international, that is present in the area, region or country;
- state price controls in some countries such as Greece;
- differences between countries in terms of corporate taxation policies.

DISTRIBUTION CHANNELS

The main distribution channels for most accommodation establishments is still the travel agent. However, for large hotel chains, their own computer reservations systems are usually their main distribution mode. On the other hand, many small units often rely on local tourist offices in their home area. Accommodation is often also distributed via tour operators who function as wholesalers. Finally, in some cases, where accommodation units rely on 'passing trade' – people who see the unit, like it and make a spontaneous decision to purchase its product.

PROMOTION

Most accommodation establishments have limited budgets for promotion, with the majority of it being spent on simple promotional brochures. Their advertising is also usually limited to the brochures produced by local destination marketing agencies or national accommodation guides. It is the larger accommodation providers, such as the transnational hotel chains, that do spend considerable sums of money on advertising, such as happened when Forte rebranded its hotel portfolio in the early 1990s.

THE ACCOMMODATION MARKET

Because of the diversity of accommodation types, it is difficult to make generalizations about the accommodation market. However, we will endeavour to offer some comments which are relevant to the European situation, particularly in relation to hotels.

- The different target markets serviced by a unit have different needs which determine the types of facilities the unit must offer. For example, business travellers usually require single rooms, increasingly with features such as desks, fax machines and facilities for the use of portable computers. On the other hand, families look for rooms with two double beds and plenty of space, together with the availability of children's menus and baby-minding facilities.
- To be successful hotels need to develop a mix of customers that allows them to maintain their occupancy at all times of the week and year. Conferences and individual business people are the preferred weekday market while families and coach groups are looked to at the weekends.
- The nature of a unit's market can vary from the summer to the winter. An Austrian mountain resort hotel, for instance, will be used primarily by walkers on individually planned holidays and coach parties in the summer, and by skiers in the winter.
- As it is heavily dependent on business tourism as well as leisure tourism, the hotel market is greatly influenced by the economic state of particular countries. Thus, given the dramatic differences in national economies across Europe, it is not surprising that there are great variations in national hotel markets across Europe at any one time.

A report in *Hotels* magazine in June 1995, reporting a Horwath Consultancy survey, indicated that in 1994 European hotels overall had enjoyed an occupancy rate of 59%. In the same year, Horwath had estimated that guests in European hotels as a whole spent on average $57 per day, so that each available bedroom generated total income of $34 106 during 1994.

In January 1995, an article in the same magazine quoting a Pannell Kerr Forster report illustrated the state of national hotel markets

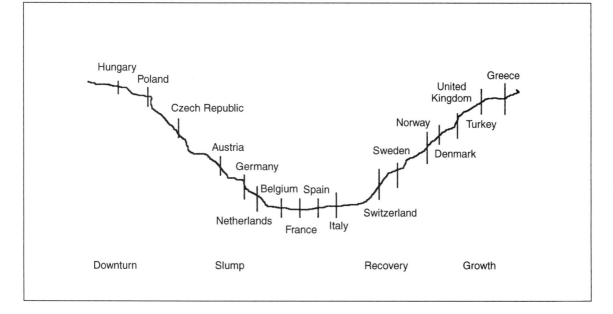

Figure 17.1 Hotel market business cycles in Europe.
Source: Pannell Kerr Forster/*Hotels* magazine (1995).

within Europe in terms of whether they were in downturn, slump, recovery or growth. This is illustrated in Figure 17.1.

Not surprisingly the countries in the downturn phase are in Eastern Europe, given the economic difficulties and political uncertainties which are currently being experienced in these countries. However, perhaps more surprising is the fact that the two countries where the hotel market was growing at the fastest rate at the time of the survey were Greece and Turkey.

COMPETITION

Competition is generally very strong in the accommodation sector. There are two main types of competition, namely:

- that between different types of accommodation such as hotel versus villas in Mediterranean resorts like Benidorm and Albufeira;
- that between different units which are all of a particular type of accommodation, such as major chain-owned hotels within a city centre.

Price has traditionally been the way in which accommodation operators have sought to achieve competitive advantage. Other methods can include the following:

- offering facilities for particular types of customer such as families and women business travellers;

- the development of in-house leisure facilities;
- in-bedroom services such as satellite television.

There are two particularly interesting forms of competition faced by some commercial accommodation establishments, as follows:

- those people who offer accommodation, wholly or partly as a 'hobby' rather than a commercial business. This is true of many people living in large houses who rent out one or two rooms. They often deliver an excellent service and provide large bedrooms at a low price, with which larger commercial hotels cannot easily compete.
- The phenomenon of 'visiting friends and relatives' (VFR), where people stay away from home as tourists at the homes of friends or relatives, free of charge. However, this is not really competition as most of these people would not travel in the first place to the location in question if they did not have friends or relatives there.

MARKETING BY EXTERNAL ORGANIZATIONS

Accommodation units are often marketed by other organizations apart from themselves because they are part of the product offered by other organizations. This usually relates to one of two different types of organization, namely:

- destination marketing agencies, for whom the stock of accommodation available in their area is a crucial part of their offering as a destination. Accommodation is usually promoted through the brochures produced by the destination marketing agency;
- tour operators who feature and promote accommodation units in their brochures to encourage their prospective clients to purchase the holiday based in the accommodation unit which is being offered by the tour operator.

MARKETING CONSORTIA

Consortia play a growing role in accommodation marketing. A number of authors, including Slattery (1988), have distinguished several types of consortia. Three of these types are particularly relevant to accommodation marketing, as follows:

- marketing consortia which provide marketing expertise for their members such as Relais et Châteaux;
- reservation systems which provide a central reservations service for their members, which was the origin of the UTELL organization;
- so-called 'referral consortia' which are often links between hotels and airlines where one would recommend the other to its customers – Golden Tulip Worldwide Hotels was an early example of such a consortium.

In some countries there are state-backed or state-controlled consortia designed to function as marketing consortia for particular types of accommodation. Gîtes de France in France is an example of such an organization.

GROWTH STRATEGIES

Accommodation corporations, particularly the major hotel chains, have in recent years started increasingly to use three modern types of growth strategy as a way of expanding at a relatively low capital cost.

- **Franchising** is where the organization or franchisor generally owns the brand name and sets a range of specifications which franchisees must follow. The franchisor usually also offers the franchisee a range of support services such as IT systems and marketing advice, together with training and purchasing.

  The franchisee can be an individual or a company, and they pay the franchisee fees based on room turnover, as well as providing all or part of the capital required to buy or build the unit. The main companies' own brands involved in franchising in the accommodation sector in Europe include Bass – Holiday Inn brand (UK), Accor – Mercure brand (France) and the Campanile brand (France).
- **Management contracts** involve accommodation corporations taking contracts to manage, rather than own, particular accommodation units. Their fee tends to have two components, a basic fee and a share of operating profits. Sometimes the contractor will take a minority equity stake in the unit in question. In Europe a number of hotel chains are involved in management contracting such as Bass plc in the UK.
- **Leasing** is where an accommodation corporation pays rent to the unit's owners and then keeps the rest of the hotel's profit for itself. This system has proved particularly popular with UK-based companies including Stakis and Ladbroke.

CONCLUSIONS

We can see from the above discussion that accommodation marketing is a diverse field due to the many very different types of accommodation that exist, and the different types of individuals and organizations that offer accommodation.

DISCUSSION POINTS AND ESSAY QUESTIONS

1. Discuss the main issues involved in pricing within the accommodation sector.
2. Evaluate the concept of competition within the accommodation sector and outline the different forms of competition that exist.

3. Explain the role of consortia within the field of accommodation marketing.

EXERCISE Choose an accommodation establishment which you are able to visit.

For your chosen establishment you should produce a report evaluating the quality of product it offers in relation to the following criteria:

- location;
- facilities;
- service;
- value for money.

CASE STUDIES

You may wish to look at some of the following case studies which illustrate the points made in this chapter:

2. The Forte International Programme, UK;
8. Timeshare accommodation in Europe;
12. Porto Carras complex, Halkidiki, Greece.

Tourist destinations

Key concepts

The main concepts covered in this chapter are:

- the geographical hierarchy of destinations from continents to individual resorts
- the complex objectives of destination marketing agencies and the fact that these agencies rarely own or control the product as a whole;
- the fact that no direct charge is made for the use of destinations;
- the role of marketing research in destination marketing.

INTRODUCTION

In this chapter we will consider the key issues involved in the marketing of tourist destinations in Europe. This is perhaps the most complex form of marketing in tourism, leisure and hospitality. There are a number of reasons for this complexity but there are, perhaps, four which are of most significance:

- destinations exist at a number of different geographical levels;
- the objectives of destination marketing tend to be more complex;
- the organizations marketing destinations have no direct control over the product;
- no direct charge is made for visiting the destination.

These issues and their consequences are explored in detail in the rest of this chapter.

GEOGRAPHICAL LEVELS

Destinations exist at a number of different geographical levels which are interrelated. Within the European context, some tourists can see the whole continent as a single destination, for example the 'Inter-

Railers' who tour Europe on a rail ticket that allows them to travel in most European countries. Other tourists talk about a country being their destination, for example 'this year we are going on a coach tour of Ireland'. Regions often function as destinations, such as the Lake District in the UK, the Loire Valley in France and Tuscany in Italy. Some of these regions can be natural regions that cross national boundaries like the Alps. Finally, there are individual resorts or urban areas such as Benidorm in Spain, or cities like Paris and St Petersburg. While even this breakdown appears complex, it is a simplification of the true situation!

Within Europe, there are organizations whose mission is to market destinations at all these geographical levels. One of the main challenges for these organizations is how their efforts can be co-ordinated with those other organizations which are responsible for the marketing of different geographical entities that encompass, but are not solely concerned with, their area.

This phenomenon is illustrated in the following list which gives all the bodies, at different geographical levels which have an interest in the marketing of the French resort of Nice:

Municipality (local authority)	: Office Municipale du Tourisme = Nice
Département (county)	: Comité Départementale du Tourisme = Alpes-Maritimes
Région (region)	: Comité Régional du Tourisme = Provence – Alpes – Côte d'Azur
National	: Central government = Maison de la France on behalf of the Ministère du Tourisme
Europe	: European Travel Commission

The situation is even more complex than this in a number of ways, for example:

- There are also transnational agencies are set up to market regions which cross national boundaries. For example, there has been significant cooperation between Kent County Council in the UK and the Nord-Pas-de-Calais Regional Council in North-East France.
- There are also sub-regional agencies based on cooperation between neighbouring local authorities. Indeed, in France, funding is available to encourage such cooperation. Such sub-regional groupings are terms 'Pôles Touristiques'. These consortia are potentially a good way of overcoming one of the major traditional problems of destination marketing in Europe, namely where local authority boundaries do not mirror the tourist's perceptions of destination boundaries.

In spite of these latter initiatives, coordination between the different geographical levels is still one of the major challenges of destination marketing across Europe.

OBJECTIVES OF DESTINATION MARKETING

The objectives of destination marketing tend to be more complicated than those for other types of marketing, reflecting the fact that most destination marketing is carried out by public sector bodies rather than private companies. These public bodies are often involved in destination marketing for a wide range of reasons, most of which involve tourism being used as a means to an end rather than an end in itself, including:

- improving the image of an area in the hope that this will encourage industrialists to relocate their factories and offices to the area;
- increasing the range of facilities and amenities that are available for the local community. Income from tourists can help keep local shops, theatres and restaurants viable, when they might go bankrupt if they had to rely solely on local residents. Tourist can also help justify and fund infrastructure development that might also benefit local people such as new roads and airports. The same argument applies to new attractions such as museums;
- giving local residents more pride in their local area, which can happen when people see that tourists want to visit their region;
- providing a rationale and funding for improvements to the local environment;
- trying to make the destination politically more acceptable to outsiders by giving them an opportunity to see for themselves either what the place is actually like or what the government wants tourists to think it is really like. In the former Soviet Union, for instance, tourism was used to try to give outsiders a positive view of the achievements of the political regime.

Where the objectives of the public sector destination marketing agencies are monetary rather than social, they are usually concerned with economic benefits for the community as a whole rather than profits for specific enterprises.

However, public bodies can have a vested financial interest in tourism for themselves, for they can earn income from tourism in a number of ways. Central government gains revenue from sales taxes and fares paid to some state-owned airlines, for example, while local authorities often gain from the charges paid by tourists to visit publicly-owned tourist attractions.

CONTROL OVER THE PRODUCT

The organizations which are charged with marketing destinations are largely promoting a product over which they have no direct control and which is not a single product. Destinations are a composite product which is made up of a number of components, including:

- accommodation establishments;
- restaurants;
- bars;
- theatres, cinemas and night clubs;
- transport systems such as taxis, metros and buses;
- natural features like beaches and cliffs;
- man-made attractions, including cathedrals, theme parks and museums;
- the availability of excursions to nearby attractions;
- sports centres and leisure facilities;
- special events, etc.

Generally the public sector organizations which market destinations neither own or control the vast majority of these elements of the destination product. Yet they have to endeavour to market them as a cohesive whole.

PRICE ISSUES

Finally, no direct price is charged for visiting the destination so that standard marketing approaches to pricing are not really applicable. This is why, for example, pricing has not as yet proved a very successful way of reducing peak demand in destinations which receive more tourists than they can cope with at peak times, like Venice.

Consumers pay to use the individual components of the destination product but not for the destination itself. Day trippers, therefore, can often use a beach for a whole day and use local infrastructure such as the road network without contributing any money to pay for the services they use.

This fact is at the root of one of the most controversial aspects of destination marketing. In other words, most destination marketing is funded by the whole community through taxes paid to public sector bodies. Yet most of the economic benefits go to private sector enterprises, while the consumer rarely pays the true cost of their visit. This is clearly a moral dilemma.

CONCENTRATION ON PROMOTION

The lack of control over the product which most destination marketing agencies experience, together with the absence of a pricing mechanism, has led many of these agencies to concentrate on the promotional element of the marketing mix.

Most destination marketing organizations are, therefore, involved in a range of promotional activities, including the following:

- **Brochures** are produced for both promotional and information purposes, although both functions may be served by a single piece of print. The promotional aspect, briefly, involves using colour photographs and prose laden with adjectives to sell attractive images of the destination to potential customers. The informative aspect of a brochure might involve hotel lists, a directory of services available within the destination, and information on travelling to the destination.

As well as a general brochure to cover the whole destination, a range of other brochures may also be offered. These may cover smaller geographical entities within the overall destination region. Alternatively, they could be targeted at specific market segments such as sports enthusiasts or business travellers. The potential economic value of this latter market leads many destination marketing agencies to create special packs of information specifically designed to meet their needs. These packs tend to focus on possible conference and exhibition venues within the destination. Coach operators and group visit organizers also tend to be given literature designed to meet their specific needs, for example they may include lists of hotels that can accommodate large groups.

- **Advertisements** are placed promoting the merits of visiting the destination. As the budgets of the relevant agencies are often limited, most advertisements are placed in the printed media rather than the more expensive, but more effective, medium of television. Most resort advertising is seasonal, and takes place when it is thought potential visitors will be making their holiday decisions. In the UK, for example, this leads to a plethora of resort advertising in late December and January. Most of the advertisements seek to encourage potential consumers to request a copy of the destination's brochure.
- **Press and public relations** play a significant role in the marketing activities of many destination marketing organizations. Journalists are offered free familiarisation trips to the destination, in the hope that this will result in them writing favourable articles. The same is true of television broadcasters. Likewise, many destinations undertake public relations activities to improve their image with the general public. They put out press releases on a range of 'good news stories' about the destination which they send to the media which they feel are used by their target markets. For agencies with limited budgets, this very low cost form of promotion is particularly attractive.
- Relatively little **direct selling** is carried out by destination marketing agencies. However, such selling is often used to attract high-spending, and thus economically valuable, conference business or coach groups.
- Due to the lack of control over the destination product and pricing, **sales promotions** are used relatively little in destination marketing. However, 'added value' promotional offers may be made available, featuring elements of the destination product over which the destination marketing agency does have control. Thus, a local authority

that owns a theatre and a museum could offer reduced price entry for people who visit the destination at certain times of the year.
- Attendance is made at **trade fairs and exhibitions**, aimed at both the public and the tourist trade.

TOURIST INFORMATION CENTRES

Most of the promotional efforts of destination marketing organizations are channelled through the **tourist information centres** which most of them operate. These centres are the public face of the agency, for visitors who are already in the destination as well as for those who are potential visitors.

In relation to the marketing mix, these centres also perform the 'place' function, in other words distribution, albeit usually for elements of the destination product such as hotels rather than for the destination product as a whole.

The role of tourist information centres varies across Europe but most of them distribute brochures and respond to requests for information. They may also perform a range of other services, including:

- hotel booking;
- currency exchange;
- selling local excursions;
- selling travel tickets.

However, the more commercial activities can bring them into conflict with local traders, who may see these public-sector subsidized centres as unfair competition. It is also vital for their credibility with the business community that these centres are seen to be impartial rather than promoting particular enterprises only. Thus they will often not recommend hotels but simply give customers a list.

Increasingly, many tourist information centres are seeking to increase their budget by engaging in more commercial activities. Some, such as the Syndicats d'Initiatives and Offices du Tourisme in France, have membership schemes. Private businesses pay to join in the knowledge that the centre will only actively promote the enterprises which are in membership.

DESTINATION PACKAGING

Some destination marketing agencies have sought to compensate for their lack of control of elements of the destination product by fulfilling the role of **packaging the destination product**. In part they have taken on the role of tour operators in putting together package holidays based in the destination. These packages usually include hotel accommodation as their core element, while extra elements may be incorporated including excursions, entrance to attractions, travel to/from the destination, transfers within the destination and special events.

These packages have particularly been utilized to try to attract visitors in the off-peak season, when accommodation providers are often desperate to increase their occupancy rates and will offer low prices. They can also be used in cities to stimulate demand at weekends when the business people have left and the hotels are quiet.

They can also be used to promote a certain image of a destination that the agency wishes to develop, such as arts and cultural breaks in industrial cities, for example. Such themed weekend breaks have become more popular in recent years. There are many types of such breaks, including:

- activity holidays such as those provided by the Loisirs Accueil agencies in France;
- breaks linked to special events such as arts festivals;
- breaks for people who want to spectate at sporting events, like the highly successful soccer weekends which are offered in Liverpool in the UK;
- themed holidays for people who want to visit areas where films or television programmes have been set.

However, the implications for small-scale public sector agencies of the European Package Travel Directive have discouraged some agencies from endeavouring to package their destination product.

PUBLIC–PRIVATE-SECTOR PARTNERSHIPS

In many European countries, in recent years, there has been a growth in **public–private sector partnerships** in destination marketing. This has occurred for a number of reasons, notably:

- the desire for a more coordinated approach to destination marketing;
- the need to use the financial resources of the private sector to supplement the limited budget available for public-sector destination marketing organizations;
- a wish to bring private-sector marketing expertise into the field of public-sector destination marketing.

Within the UK, for example, these partnerships have often followed the American model of visitor and convention bureaux. In Birmingham and Glasgow, to give but two examples, agencies exist which are funded by both local authority grants and contributions from private-sector enterprises such as hotels and attractions. However, many such partnership agencies find it difficult to consistently attract adequate private-sector funding and tend to rely heavily on the public sector for their financial stability.

MARKETING RESEARCH

A major potential role for destination marketing agencies that can increase their reputation with private-sector organizations is in **marketing research**. As we have noted elsewhere in the book, marketing research is a vital prerequisite for successful marketing, yet it is still at an early level of development in the tourism field.

Destination marketing agencies can play a vital role in this area because they can take an overview which an individual enterprise cannot, and because they have no commercial vested interest, they can be relatively impartial.

Good marketing research can be beneficial for destination marketing in three main ways, as follows:

- it can help the destination marketing agency to carry out its marketing function more effectively;
- it can assist private enterprises refine their marketing in terms of their product, price, place and promotion;
- it can be used to help attract entrepreneurs to invest in new projects in the destination. If reliable and detailed market research data exists, it gives these entrepreneurs the confidence to invest in a particular destination.

There are two types of marketing research, namely:

- **quantitative**: the number of visitors, when they come, where they come from, what they do in the destination, how much they spend, and so on;
- **qualitative**: why they come to the destination and their opinions on the various aspects of the destination.

Traditionally, marketing research in tourism focuses on existing customers who are easier to access. However, it is increasingly being recognized that we also need to focus on those who do not currently visit the destination and find out their reasons for not visiting. Future success may well depend on turning these non-users into users of the destination product.

To fulfil the potential benefits of marketing research, the data must be available at the appropriate geographical level. For example, data which is only available on a regional basis may be of little value to a single resort only in that region if its market is significantly different from the market of the region as a whole.

In France, marketing research data is particularly good, and is managed by a national, state-controlled body, the Observatoire Nationale du Tourisme. On the other hand, in the UK, public-sector marketing research is much less developed. Whereas in France, marketing research appears to enjoy a high status, in the UK it has until recently had something of a 'Cinderella' status. Marketing research has often been the first function to be cut if the tourist boards' or resort marketing departments' budgets were under pressure.

Good marketing research is expensive but the cost of not having good data in a competitive market will, increasingly, probably be even more expensive!

A more detailed discussion on marketing research is to be found in Chapter 32.

BEYOND EUROPE

So far, we have focused on destination marketing within Europe. However, there is also the issue of how Europe is marketed as a whole to attract non-European visitors. This has become a major issue in recent years with the realization that Europe is losing its share of the world tourism market. The European Commission, in particular, is striving to improve the way in which Europe, or at least the countries who belong to the European Union, promote themselves to the rest of the world as tourist destinations. The European Travel Commission is also trying hard to improve the marketing of Europe to defend the Continent's share of the world tourism market.

CONCLUSIONS

We have seen that destination marketing is perhaps the most complex form of marketing in the tourism, leisure and hospitality fields. It is largely carried out by public-sector bodies which have complex social, economic and political motives.

Destination marketing exists at a number of interrelated geographical levels and involves interrelationships between a myriad of public-sector organizations and private-sector enterprises.

At a time of growing international competition in the tourism market, it is vital that European destinations become even more effective at marketing themselves, to both European and non-European tourists.

DISCUSSION POINTS AND ESSAY QUESTIONS

1. Discuss what you consider to be the three main reasons why destination marketing is such a complex activity.
2. Using examples, evaluate the role of public–private-sector partnerships in destination marketing.
3. Discuss the contention that the public sector should play no role in destination marketing.

EXERCISE   Select a tourist destination with which you are familiar and which you are able to visit. You should investigate its current marketing situation and identify its strengths and weaknesses, together with its opportunities and threats.

You should then produce a five-year marketing strategy for the destination on behalf of the local municipality or relevant government body.

Finally, you should focus on how the strategy will be implemented, including the following issues:

- budgets and where the money will come from;
- who will be responsible for implementing the strategy;
- partnerships between private-sector and public-sector organizations;
- timescales.

CASE STUDIES

You may wish to look at some the following case studies which illustrate the points made in this chapter:

6. Scotland;
9. Bord Fáilte, Ireland;
13. Iceland: The marketing of a business tourism destination.

Tour operation  19

Key concepts

The main concepts covered in this chapter are:

- the role of tour operators in the tourism system;
- the highly interdependent nature of the tour operation product;
- the price elasticity of the European mass package holiday market;
- the highly competitive nature of the European tour operation market;
- vertical and horizontal integration as growth strategies.

INTRODUCTION

Tour operators are often described as the wholesaler in the tourism system, operating between the producer of the primary product and the retailer. However, the tour operator can also be seen as a producer who takes raw materials, like hotel beds and airline seats, and processes them into a 'manufactured' product which it then sells. The tour operator, it could be argued, represents the only genuine tourist industry that is not simply a sub-set of another industry. They perform a unique function in the tourism system.

However, as we will see, there is nothing homogenous about tour operation, either in its nature or its marketing function. In this chapter we will consider some of the factors that influence the approaches to marketing which are adopted by tour operators, together with some of the key issues in the practice of tour operation marketing.

SIZE OF OPERATION

The size of tour operators is an important factor. There are large differences in marketing between the major European mass market large-scale tour operators such as TUI and Thomsons who move literally millions of tourists around per annum, and the small, specialist operators who may only handle a few hundred customers a year.

This links to two other issues which relate to size and have implications for marketing, namely **ownership** and **marketing objectives**. The large tour operators are often part of big corporations with other business interests. On the other hand, the small operators are often owned by individuals or families and can often be run as a 'hobby' or part-time business. This is true, for example, of some special interest and activity holiday operators or some of the British tour operators who offer self-catering holidays in France. The two types of operator therefore tend to have different marketing objectives. Whereas for the big operators profit maximization is usually their main concern, these small operators are often willing to accept less than optimum profit levels provided that the business gives them an opportunity to indulge in their hobbies or interests, whether these be cycling in Wales or enjoying the food and wine of France, for example.

We must also recognise that while tour operation is the core business for tour operators, it is also an **ancillary activity** for some other tourism organizations such as airlines, for example British Airways Holidays. Destination marketing agencies with their short break programmes and even newspapers which offer 'reader's holidays' also function as tour operators.

TYPES OF PRODUCT

There are a number of differences in the nature of the product offered by tour operators, including the following:

- Some operators offer packages featuring destinations in their own country only while others offer products based on foreign destinations.
- On the one hand, operators can offer highly structured, all-inclusive packages where everything a holidaymaker will need is included in a single-priced package. This is the approach of Club Méditerranée. On the other hand, some companies are recognizing that other customers are looking for more flexibility and they are offering much looser packages, such as fly-drive and travel and accommodation-only holidays, with no meals and transfers.
- Many tour operators offer the services of in-resort representatives as part of the product they offer. The quality of the representative is usually considered to be a major element in the holiday experience of the customer.
- Because the tour operator is a wholesaler, they are totally reliant on their suppliers for the quality of their final product and their market-

ing intermediaries for the messages about their product which are relayed to customers.
- Some operators offer a broad portfolio of products, designed to service a range of markets, while others focus on either particular types of holidays (skiing or cycling for example) or specific countries.

Ultimately, perhaps, the most interesting aspect of the tour operation product is that it is a composite product, made up of a number of elements (destination, attractions, hotels, transport, and so on). In some ways, it could be argued that it is not a finished product but rather a set of opportunities for consumers to create their own self-service holiday product. A plane-load of tourists travelling to same hotel in Crete, for example, will all use the basic product in a different way. Some will stay around the hotel pool or the local beach while others will explore the island's archaeological sites, merely using the hotel as a base. Some will go to bed early while others will wake in the afternoon and dance through the night in the local clubs. The package tour offers customers an incredible variety of possible experiences from which the tourist chooses those which they prefer.

PRICE

Price has always been a key issue in the European tour operation sector. For the mass market operators in most countries their market is highly price elastic. These operators specialize mainly in inexpensive holidays with low profit margins, where profits come from volume rather than the margins on individual sales. Smaller and specialist operators on the other hand, tend to be able to offer prices that allow for more generous margins. This is important as they do not have the volume of sales to make a profit unless they can generate higher margins.

In some European countries, notably the UK, last-minute discounting is now an accepted part of the market. Consumers wait until near the departure time for a particular holiday and then look for bargains from operators who are keen to ensure that no capacity is left unsold when the holiday begins. The existence of these last-minute bargains has changed the market so that many clients do not now book their holidays until a few days before they wish to travel. This phenomenon affects profit margins and makes long-term capacity planning very difficult for tour operators.

The obsession with price, most notably in some Northern European markets, has implications for quality. Often the last-minute bargains are in unnamed accommodation so that clients do not know where they will be staying, which gives great scope for disappointment. Likewise, if people buy purely on price they can find themselves in places they do not like or would not have otherwise chosen. Likewise, for the operators and suppliers, low prices and discounts give little opportunity for the enhancement of quality standards.

DISTRIBUTION

Traditionally the distribution of the tour operation product has been via travel agents. However, increasingly some operators are looking to sell directly to their customers, thus saving the commission they pay to the travel agents. Technological innovations are making it easier for tour operators to communicate directly with their customers.

PROMOTION

As far as promotion is concerned, tour operators still rely very heavily on their brochure, which is often a thick, glossy, full-colour catalogue, designed to persuade people to purchase the product. One trend in recent years has been the replacement of the brochure which included every product offered by a company with several brochures featuring different products, such as activity holidays, city breaks or different countries.

Advertising is also heavily used, particularly at the start of the year when consumers are deciding on their holiday plans. Many operators may well make use of many advertising media such as television. For example, in 1994–95 in the UK, major television advertising campaigns were mounted by leading tour operators Thomson, Airtours and First Choice. Conversely, smaller, niche-market operators, tend to focus on printed media advertising in specialist publications that are popular with their target markets.

Substantial use is also made of other promotional techniques, including:

- press and public relations, with many operators trying to encourage travel journalists to take one of their holidays free of charge in the hope that they will then promote them via their television programmes and newspaper articles in a positive way to potential consumers. This relationship clearly raises some interesting ethical dilemmas;
- direct selling, largely in terms of tour operator sales staff encouraging travel agency counter staff to sell more of their company's holidays. This activity also involves giving travel agency staff gifts and financial rewards for selling particular products.

The promotional activities of some tour operators have drawn criticism because of their apparent lack of honesty. This ranges from the inducements to travel agency staff and the fake statements that have been found in some brochures, for example. The European Package Travel Directive was introduced, largely, to curb some of the more dubious practices in tour operation promotional activities.

THE TOUR OPERATION MARKET

There are also a number of aspects of the tour operation market that influence the way in which package holidays are marketed.

The first of these is whether the operator offers their products primarily within the domestic market or whether they also sell their holidays to people resident in other countries. In the latter case, operators have to take into account national differences in terms of consumer behaviour, business culture and statutory controls on tourism. This has been an issue for a range of European operators including:

- Club Méditerranée selling its holidays to people in the UK, Japan and the USA;
- Airtours which sells its Eurosites brand to people in the Benelux countries.

Secondly, consumers are not consistent in their behaviour patterns, for their decision-making has to take into account a range of factors that are always changing, such as their income, time availability, health, responsibility for caring for others, people they will be travelling with and so on. These behaviours can then change dramatically from one holiday to another. For example, this year a British consumer may goes on holiday with a friend to Spain's Costa Del Sol and have a 'hedonistic' holiday. Next year the same consumer may go on an educational field trip to the archaeological remains of Greece as part of their university course. The following year this person gets married and goes on honeymoon to Paris with their partner. By the following year they have a baby and stay in their own country as they are concerned that the food and sun in another country will make the baby ill.

Thirdly, there are a number of ways of segmenting the tour operation market, including:

- geographical methods in terms of where people live, which help determine which departure airports operators should offer their clients and the preferences of customers for different geographical areas. For example, some people like mountains while others prefer particular countries. Some from Northern Europe are drawn to Southern Europe because of the sun while others from Southern Europe travel north to escape from the heat in summer;
- much tour operation marketing is based on demographic segmentation. For example, holidays are labelled as family holidays and singles holidays, or they are aimed at young people or retired people, for example Club 18–30 and Saga in the UK. Likewise holiday advertisements can be linked to stereotypes relating to sex, such as men playing golf and women shopping. While European society has changed dramatically and made many of these stereotypes outdated, they still underpin much modern tour operation marketing;
- psychographic segmentation is becoming increasingly important, as we recognize that people often buy holidays that relate to their

everyday lifestyles. Thus we are beginning to recognize holidaymakers who are interested in healthy holidays or green holidays;

● the purpose of travel, which can include religious pilgrimage, health, education, business, making friends, enjoying new experiences and relaxing, for example.

Moreover, consumers often have unreasonable expectations of what they expect a holiday to do for them. For some people a holiday is used to recover from a bereavement or a broken relationship, or to put new life into a failing marriage.

It is also difficult for the operator to guarantee the quality of the consumer's experience as many of the factors that shape this experience are outside their control. These include strikes and civil disorder, bad weather or the behaviour of other people who are in the resort at the same time as the operator's clients. The consumer, therefore, may hold the operator at least partially responsible for weaknesses in the product which are outside their control.

Indeed, the behaviour of tourists can be contradictory because they may say they intend to do something which is socially or fashionably acceptable while in reality they will do something else. This can make it difficult for tour operation marketers to anticipate the needs and desires of their clients.

COMPETITION

In most European countries, competition is intense in the tour operation sector. This was not always the case, as we know in Eastern Europe, for example, state monopolies in the past prevented any real competition developing. However, now, competition is present in almost all aspects of tour operation in Europe.

Tour operators, therefore, are always looking to find ways of achieving competitive advantage, including:

● having lower prices than their competitors or offering their customers more services or benefits for the same price;

● opening up new destinations that are not offered by their competitors. For European operators this has in recent years largely meant offering new long-haul destinations in Asia, Africa, the Middle East and the Caribbean;

● pioneering new types of holidays such as particular special-interest activities that are not available from other companies;

● seeking to become a market leader in terms of the market for particular countries.

However, it is not always easy to identify who one's competitors are in the tour operation field. For a major European operator such as TUI, who are its competitors? Perhaps they are all the other German tour operators. However, it could be argued that a small operator in Bavaria offering short-break domestic holidays is no real competition for a major mass market tour operator which focuses on outbound holidays. Perhaps its competitors are the other mass market operators in Germany like LTU who are targeting smaller markets with similar products.

We could also ask if some of its competitors are perhaps foreign tour operators. At first the answer might seem to be no as relatively few foreign operators sell holidays to German clients. However, such an answer assumes that the only competition a tour operator faces is for customers. This is not the case, as competition also exists for the supply of the raw materials that make up the package holiday. In other words, TUI will find itself competing with foreign tour operators for hotel rooms in its destinations. If it fails to win this battle, it has no product, or a lesser quality product, with which to compete for clients in the German market.

In the most extreme cases, competition for TUI will not come from other people who offer package holidays. Instead it will come from 'substitution' – in other words, people choosing to buy a non-tourism product rather than a holiday. This phenomenon is very common in tour operation, with people in certain years substituting something else in place of a holiday, such as the following:

- the purchase of a new car;
- buying a new home;
- decorating or carrying out some repairs or renovation work on their home.

People may also substitute several short breaks or trips to friends and relatives for a main annual holiday because of a range of reasons, including lack of money, lack of time or their responsibilities and careers.

These forms of substitution are genuine competition for a tour operator, but they are forms of competition with which it is virtually impossible for tour operators to compete.

GROWTH STRATEGIES

When they wish to expand, European tour operators have used a number of growth strategies, of which the three most popular are as follows:

- vertical and horizontal integration, in other words taking over suppliers and marketing intermediaries on the one hand, and competitors on the other. The leading UK tour operator, Thomson, for example, developed its own airline, Britannia and owns its own travel agency chain, Lunn Poly. In addition it has taken over a number of competitors over the years. This form of expansion is clearly illustrated in the Airtours case study referred to at the end of this chapter;

- buying existing well-established brands in markets which are new ones for the operator which is seeking to grow. To take the Thomson example again, the company has purchased in the past two years several leading brands in the market for self-catering cottages in Britain;
- beginning to sell one's product to people who live in other countries. While this has happened relatively little to date in the European tour operation sector, there are signs that it is beginning to happen more and more. This is a logical consequence of a situation where some national markets are becoming saturated so that international market developments may be the only realistic prospect of large-scale future expansion. Possibilities of this form of expansion may exist, perhaps, in the growing outbound market in Southern European countries like Spain and Greece and the developing market of Eastern Europe.

TOUR OPERATOR CONSORTIA

Consortia of tour operators have also arisen, of which one of the best European examples is AITO, the Association of Independent Tour Operators in the UK. This organization represents many smaller specialist tour operators based in the UK; in 1995 its guide included 229 operators and their products. This consortium was set up to counter the marketing power of the major mass market operators. By pooling resources, its members can afford joint campaigns which they could not afford to undertake alone. AITO members claim to offer:

- a unique range of holidays;
- financial protection;
- personal service;
- value for money;
- high standards;
- tailor-made holidays.
- a dispute settlement service.

They also have a quality charter which emphasizes that companies have to meet strict membership criteria before they can join AITO. They also ensure that their brochures are accurate and that they listen to, and take action on, feedback from their customers. Briefly, the charter says that AITO is, 'committed to raising the level of environmental awareness within the industry'.

AITO also encourages its prospective customers to book their holiday through an independent travel agent rather than an agency owned by one of the large British tour operators. This way, AITO claims customers receive more choice, personal service and impartial advice. AITO has links with 400 independent agents and offers to provide a list of such agencies for consumers, on request.

This developing relationship between independent tour operators and travel agents represents an interesting response to the vertical integration of the major UK tour operators.

POLITICAL AND ECONOMIC CHANGES

Tour operators often have to respond, at short notice, to political and economic changes which can either affect their market dramatically almost overnight, or their ability to delivery their product as advertised. Several examples will illustrate this point, as follows:

- the Gulf War in 1991, which reduced the demand from Americans to visit Europe and of Europeans to visit places in the Eastern Mediterranean which were near to the conflict, such as Israel and Cyprus;
- the hostilities in the former Yugoslavia, which removed some popular destinations from Western Europe tour operator programmes;
- civil disorder like the *coup d'état* in Gambia in 1994, which resulted in European governments advising their citizens not to visit Gambia for a while until the situation improved
- dramatic changes in currency exchange rates, like the devaluation of the British pound sterling in September 1992. Interestingly, this made visits to Britain cheaper for many foreign tourists while it made traditionally popular destinations with British visitors, like France, much more expensive literally overnight.

CONCLUSIONS

In this chapter, we have briefly explored the key issues in the rapidly changing field of tour operation marketing, and outbound tour operations in particular. It is clear that there are major differences between large mass market tour operators and the smaller niche market operators.

DISCUSSION POINTS AND ESSAY QUESTIONS

1. Evaluate the suggestion that the only basis of competition in the European tour operation sector is price:
2. Discuss the value of the four classic methods of market segmentation to marketers within the tour operation sector.
3. Critically evaluate the range of growth strategies which have been adopted by European tour operators.

EXERCISE   Choose a mass market tour operator **and** a specialist tour operator. Obtain the main brochure of each operator.

For each brochure, answer the following questions, based purely on the contents of the brochure:

(a) Who is the brochure aimed at?

(b) What major selling points does the operator claim for their product or products?

(c) What pricing approaches is the operator using?

(d) What is the balance between subjective comments and factual information?

Compare the two operators in terms of the answers to these four questions. Finally, you should identify weaknesses in either brochure in relation to their role as a promotional tool.

The results of this project should be presented in a report and an oral presentation.

CASE STUDIES

You may wish to look at some the following case studies which illustrate the points made in this chapter:

  3. First Choice, UK;

10. Club Méditerranée SA, France;

15. TUI, Germany;

18. Airtours plc, UK;

24. Abercombrie and Kent Ltd, UK.

Transport

> **Key concepts**
>
> The main concepts covered in this chapter are:
>
> - the different modes of transport;
> - commercial versus subsidized transport operations;
> - state intervention in the transport market;
> - the complex distribution system in transport;
> - the nature of competition within transport.

INTRODUCTION

The transport sector is very broad in scope and approaches to marketing will vary greatly between different modes and countries. Some of the main factors that influence the nature of marketing within the sector are discussed in this chapter.

MODES OF TRANSPORT

There is diversity in the modes of transport which all have different strengths and weaknesses as far as consumers are concerned. These include:

- **air** – scheduled and charter services;
- **rail** – modern trains and historic steam railways;
- **water** – cruise liners, ferries, narrow boats and canal barges;
- **road** – private cars, car rentals, taxis, long-distance coaches, local buses, bicycles, motorbikes, horse-drawn carriages;
- **off-road** – horses, walking, cable cars, télépheriques.

The very different characteristics of these different modes make it difficult to generalize about transport marketing.

THE NATURE OF TRANSPORT OPERATIONS

Transport involves private, public and voluntary sector organizations with different marketing objectives. While private companies seek to maximize profit, state-owned operators often have broader aims including providing a service for the community. The limited number of voluntary-sector bodies in transport tend to use leisure and tourism as a means to an end rather than an end in itself. For example, most of Europe's steam railways are run by voluntary bodies who use the income from passengers to conserve the railways and maintain them.

Even within individual modes of transport, there can be distinct differences in ownership and marketing objectives. Perhaps the best current example of this is the airline business in the European context.

Many scheduled airlines in Europe are state-owned or controlled, so that they are allowed to make losses. British Airways, on the other hand, is a wholly private company which has to generate profits, and is thus very marketing and market orientated.

From a marketing 'point of view', an interesting point is that many charter airlines are owned by tour operators as part of their vertical integration strategies. Thus often they do not set their own marketing strategies, but rather play their part in the implementation of the strategies of the parent company.

This point is linked to the fact that while transport is sometimes sold as a self-contained product in its own right, it may also be sold as part of a larger composite product. For example, it may be combined with accommodation to form an inclusive tour. In this case the price the consumer pays is a single price for the complete package, so that they are unaware of the amount they have actually paid for the transport element.

Some transport markets are not free markets, but are state-controlled in some way, so that normal concepts of competition and pricing are of little relevance. Such markets include intra-European air travel and the private car sector due to state taxes on petrol and road use.

The transnational nature of many transport operations such as airlines, ferries, car hire and international rail services means that marketing policies have to take account of national differences in consumer behaviour, economic factors, legal regulations and operating practices.

Technological innovations can change the nature of existing transport products or create new ones. An excellent recent example of this is the Channel Tunnel which has given consumers a totally new mode of transport for crossing the English Channel/Manche, and given the ferries a new competitor.

THE NATURE OF THE TRANSPORT PRODUCT

The product offered by most modes of transport is the opportunity to be transported from one place to another at a time chosen by the consumer. But to achieve this the product represents a sophisticated bundle of elements and characteristics. These may be illustrated by taking the example of a scheduled airline, as shown in Figure 20.1.

Increasingly, transport operators are seeking to augment their basic product with **add-on services** that generate more income but also satisfy more of the consumer's needs. For example, the French state railway SNCF offers a range of extra services to its passengers, including car hire, bicycle hire and accommodation-inclusive packages. It also operates a range of coach excursions across France.

However, the transport product is also susceptible to changing factors outside its control which affect the quality of the product. For example, airport congestion across Europe is a problem at peak times and causes delays to flights. Strikes and civil disorder can also be a problem for transport operators, such as the situation in 1994 when Brittany Ferries had problems with its services from the UK to France because of protests and blockades by fishermen at French ports.

Finally, while most modes of transport are simply ways of travelling from place to place, some forms of transport can be attractions or even

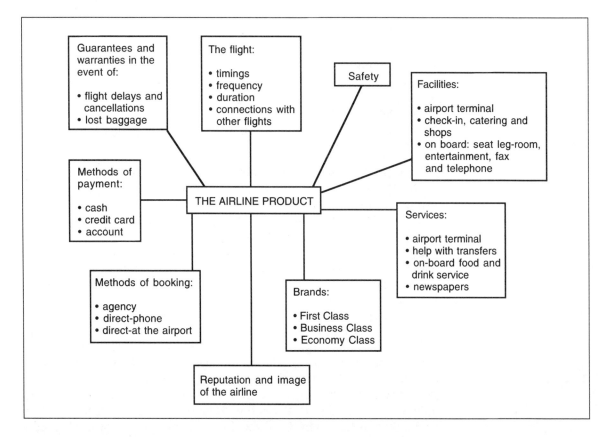

Figure 20.1 Elements of the scheduled airline product.

tourist destinations in their own right. These include Concorde, the Orient Express and major cruise liners.

PRICE

Pricing policies in the transport sector, are often influenced by state intervention in the market, either through statutory price fixing, subsidies or taxes on particular modes of transport. In sectors such as the European scheduled airlines there has been a tradition of price-fixing in relation to the state flag carriers in each country covered by a route. So, for example, until the current process of liberalization of European air travel initiated by the European Commission, the French and German governments might have met to fix the price that would be charged on the Paris–Frankfurt route by Air France and Lufthansa respectively.

However, both private and state transport operators also make use of commercial tactical approaches to pricing such as discounts. If we take the airline business as an example, discounts may be given to the following customers:

- franchisees;
- regular customers;
- group bookings including conference delegates and people on inclusive tours;
- people taking flights at less popular times such as midday flights on popular business travel routes;
- passengers who purchase promotion and offer tickets that have strict conditions such as no cancellation refunds.

Last-minute discounting is common, as airline seats are perishable products that have no value once the aircraft has taken off. Therefore, given this and the high fixed costs involved in operating a flight, airlines often heavily discount tickets at the last minute so that they can at least gain some revenue from the seats.

Many transport operators, particularly those in the public sector, also offer **concessions** for social reasons, to groups of customers who are thought to be disadvantaged in some way. These groups usually include the elderly and students, for example.

Most modes of transport appear to have complex pricing structures, particularly based on who the customer is and when they are travelling. This is particularly true of rail services and airlines. This can make it very difficult for customers to decide which ticket they should buy. It also often leads to a situation where people who are ostensibly receiving the same product or service can be paying very different prices. On a flight from London to Paris, for example, two people sitting next to each other in Economy Class, could have paid prices for their tickets that vary by a factor of up to several hundred per cent.

THE DISTRIBUTION NETWORK

Distribution networks in the transport sector can be very simple or very complex. The main distribution channels, however, are shown in Figure 20.2.

Some airlines, for example, are now seeking to sell directly to their customers to save the commission they have to pay to the intermediaries. This is being made more practical by technological developments which are taking place.

In general, technological innovations are changing the nature of distribution in transport in general – and airlines in particular – in a number of ways, including:

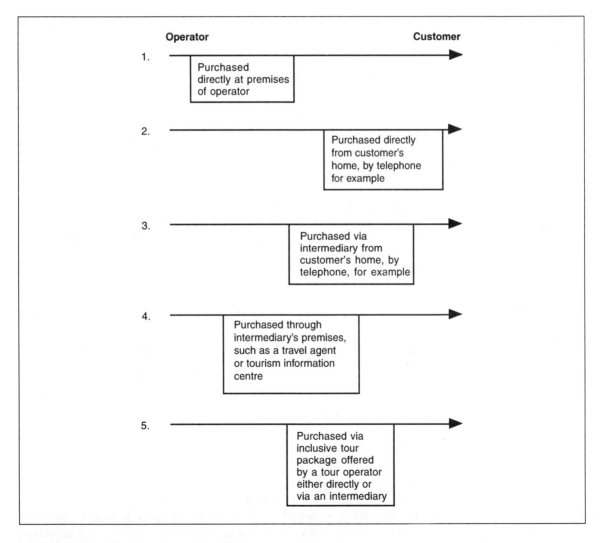

Figure 20.2 Distribution channels in the transport sector.

- the growing sophistication of the airline-based computer reservations systems such as GALILEO, AMADEUS, and SABRE, and the development of GDSs (global distribution systems);
- so-called 'smart cards' which facilitate late booking and ticketless travel, such as the experiment currently underway with Lufthansa on its domestic routes within Germany.

PROMOTION

The most important piece of promotional print used by transport operators is the timetable, which can be difficult for the ordinary traveller to read and is often only available to marketing intermediaries rather than customers in the case of airlines. The use of promotional brochures rather than informational publications is generally found most often in the transport sector in relation to ferry services.

In terms of advertising, television is used by major operators, particularly where new services are being launched. At the same time considerable use is made of the printed media.

Great use is also made of sales promotions, of which three examples will suffice to illustrate the point.

- Promotional fares which are used to introduce new routes or to fill seats at quiet times. These may simply be low fares or added-value fares where one adult pays a normal fare while their partner travels free of charge.
- Frequent flyer programmes offer a range of benefits for regular customers to encourage brand loyalty. Examples of these include KLM's 'Flying Dutchman' programme and the 'Frequence Plus' scheme operated by the Air France group.
- So-called 'piggy-back' promotions are where purchasing one type of product gives consumers an opportunity to enjoy a special deal in relation to another type of product. For instance, in the early 1990s, the UK food retailer Sainsbury's ran a promotion with British Airways where customers who spent a certain amount of money at Sainsbury's were eligible for reduced price tickets on British Airways. At the same time, in the UK market, a similar promotion was run between Martell Cognac and Air France. There are also examples from the UK in the ferry sector where special offers are available to people who read particular newspapers.

Some schemes allow certain groups of customers such as retired people and students to buy cards which entitle them to special prices. These are particularly common amongst state railways. In France, for example, SNCF has a range of cards with titles such as 'Carte Vermeil' and 'Carte Kiwi'.

Direct selling is largely restricted to relations between operators and marketing intermediaries such as travel agents and operators and major corporate clients.

THE TRANSPORT MARKET

The transport market can be segmented in a number of ways that also have an impact on the marketing function, as follows:

- geographical factors, in other words where people live and work, as this determines the potential demand for transport on particular routes;
- demographic factors such as age, sex, and even religion. The latter is particularly relevant in relation to the type of catering offered by airlines, for instance;
- the reasons why people travel, particularly the split between business and leisure. For rail operators, the former are more likely to use First Class services while for airlines they represent the main market for 'business class' brands;
- differences in purchasing behaviour such as how often in advance people purchase their tickets, where they buy them from and which payment method they use.

Some people are regular users of particular transport services while others use them rarely, maybe only once in their lives. While both sets of customers will demand safety and reliability, they will differ in terms of their main requirements of the product. Regular users will want an easy, hassle-free, low-key experience while the occasional user may want a more memorable experience.

Across Europe, one common fact in relation to transport is the preference of most people for the use of private cars rather than public transport wherever possible. Clearly this has implications for the quality of the environment. Therefore, many governments are taking measures to discourage private car use and encourage people to use alternative modes of transport.

COMPETITION

Competition within the transport sector tends to be of two types, namely:

- between different modes of transport;
- within the same mode of transport, between different operators.

Throughout the transport sector, operators tend to use the following tactics to achieve competitive advantage:

- speed, namely how quickly they can move the customer from where they are to where they want to be;
- convenience, so that the customer can travel when they want to with the least effort possible;
- price, including the use of tactical pricing such as discounts and concessions.

However, as we saw earlier, the transport market does not allow free and fair competition in a number of ways, particularly:

- where a state operator has a virtual monopoly within one mode of transport, for example rail services in almost all European companies;
- where the state subsidizes one or more operator within a market where non-subsidized operators are trying to compete. This is the situation in the domestic airline market in France, for example, where the private airline TAT seeks to compete with the state-subsidized Air France Group.

Perhaps the two most interesting examples of competition between modes of transport in Europe at the moment, are as follows:

- In the business travel market, there is competition between high-speed trains and aircraft in relation to short-haul routes in countries like France. Competition is intense, for example, on the Paris–Lyon route between SNCF with its high-speed TGV trains and domestic airlines. It appears that the train is beginning to win this battle with its ability to transport people at high speed from city centre to city centre, without the need to travel to and from out-of-town airports and check in for their flight. Competition for the airlines is set to grow with the introduction of trains in France, for example, which will be capable of travelling at some 500 kilometres per hour. The only way airlines may be able to compete with this is through the airports like London City, which are based within cities and use small aircraft that need little time or runway distance to take off. However, as yet, these do not appear to be very popular with business travellers.
- In the leisure travel field, there is competition between Le Shuttle and the ferry companies on the routes across the English Channel/ Manche. Le Shuttle offers speed, with a 35 minute crossing time. However, the ferries have fought back with new ships that offer shopping opportunities and sophisticated catering, and are selling the time spent on board as part of the holiday rather than merely as a mode of transport. The term 'mini-cruise' is being used to emphasize this point. A price war is taking place between the two modes, which was exacerbated in 1995 by the fact that the weakness of the pound sterling against the French franc has led to decline in the demand from Britons for holidays in France.

Good examples of competition between different operators within the same mode of transport include the following:

- car hire companies at European airports and in city centres;
- scheduled airlines on well-used intra-European routes such as London to Paris;
- ferry companies in the Baltic and the North Sea.

While competition is often beneficial for the consumer, the breaking up of state monopolies and the encouragement of private operators and competition can have a downside for the consumer. A good example of this is the case of Aeroflot in Russia, where the former state monopoly has been split into more than 400 private companies with a loss of coordination of services and a decline in safety standards as airlines have become more commercially motivated. However, this is clearly a unique situation.

GROWTH STRATEGIES

Transport operators who wish to expand and grow follow a variety of strategies, some of which we will now briefly discuss.

- **Marketing consortia** carry out cooperative marketing activities. A good European example of this is found in the rail sector through the consortium of rail operators who operate the 'Euro Domino' programme, a joint ticket which allows holders to travel on railways in a number of European countries.
- **Strategic alliances** are found particularly in the airline sector, where one such example links the British airline Air UK with the Dutch national flag carrier KLM. This alliance is based on Air UK services from regional airports in Britain to Amsterdam providing passengers for KLM international services. This brings more business for KLM and gives Air UK an extra benefit which it can offer to its passengers. It also gives Air UK passengers an opportunity to enjoy the benefits of KLM's frequent flier programme, the 'Flying Dutchman'. Likewise, KLM also has a strategic alliance with the US airline Northwest. They share routes across the Atlantic which gives KLM a chance to offer its customers direct access to Northwest's domestic network in the USA. This is important given that in the USA currently, foreign airlines may not fly on domestic routes.
- **Acquisition** or the purchase of equity in other operations, is how the Scandinavian-based Stena group has grown to become a major player in the ferry industry in Northern Europe.
- **Joint ventures** with other operators to create new carriers such as the project to create Air Russia by British Airways and Aeroflot.
- **Franchising** has been used by British Airways within Europe to increase its influence in the marketplace. Under the franchise agreement, the franchisees operate routes in British Airways livery and fly under British Airways flight codes. Such agreements exist between British Airways and Maersk Air UK, Manx Airlines (Europe) and Loganair.
- The development of **ancillary activities** either add value to or increase the amount of the organization's core business. This point is illustrated by the following examples:
  - Ferry companies, like Brittany Ferries (France) and the Color Line (Norway), for example, operate inclusive tour operations which combine ferry travel with accommodation, usually based on car travel. This clearly generates business for the ferry service.

- Likewise, airlines develop tour operation products based on their scheduled flights, such as Air France Holidays and British Airways Holidays.
- On-board facilities can mean that modes of transport become conference venues in their own right, rather than simply being the way in which people travel to a conference. Such facilities have been introduced on a number of ferries and are even available on some French trains.

One interesting development of transport marketing is the increasing tendency of different modes of transport to work together. In Germany, for example, there is cooperation between airports and state rail services, while there are well established, mutually beneficial relationships between car hire companies and airlines.

CONCLUSIONS

We have seen in this chapter that, while the various modes of transport differ greatly in their nature, there are also similarities in the ways in which they are marketed. This is particularly true of the modes which are most relevant to tourism, notably air, rail and ferry. However, we are aware that the most popular form of transport in Europe, namely the private car, has largely been excluded from this discussion. This is somewhat ironic given that the car has been at the heart of the history of leisure and tourism. In the early days it stimulated the development of both by making new places accessible and creating new types of activity such as caravanning. Now, however, the mass use of cars is making it more difficult to maintain the quality of leisure and tourism experiences because of pollution and congestion. It could be argued therefore that there is a need to concentrate on the **de**marketing of this particular mode of transport.

DISCUSSION POINTS AND ESSAY QUESTIONS

1. Compare and contrast the approaches to marketing taken by railway operators, ferry companies and airlines.
2. Identify and discuss the core, actual and augmented products within the airline sector.
3. Critically evaluate the range of promotional techniques which are used in the transport sector.
4. Discuss the nature of competition within the transport sector.

Prepare a list of all the transport operators – air, rail, sea – who are currently **EXERCISE** competing for business travellers and leisure travellers on the London–Paris route.

You should then undertake the following tasks:

(a) Describe the product each one offers and identify the key differences between them.

(b) Examine the prices they are charging, including the discounts that are on offer

(c) Evaluate their brochures and advertisements in terms of their likely effectiveness.

Finally, you should attempt to decide which of the organizations appears to have a competitive edge, and explain the reasons behind your choice.

CASE STUDIES

You may wish to look at the following case studies which illustrate the points made in this chapter:

11. The Hurtigruten, Norwegian coastal voyage, Norway;
19. British Airways, UK.

Resorts

Key concepts

The main concepts covered in this chapter are:
- the relationship between resorts and destinations or attractions;
- the integrated nature of the resort product;
- the distinctive benefits which are sought by resort customers;
- the marketing of resorts by other organizations.

INTRODUCTION

As we saw earlier in the book, the distinction between destinations and attractions is being blurred in Europe by the growth of resort complexes. These resorts offer both the attractions that motivate people to travel to visit them, together with the services and facilities they require. However, these resorts tend to be larger in size and area than most traditional attractions while they also differ from normal destinations in that they are in the ownership of just one organization and are managed as a single entity.

The idea of resorts is not particularly new, with Club Méditeranée or the UK's Butlins complexes both having been established for decades. Such resort complexes also have a relatively long history in the USA. Many American resorts are based on recreational activities such as golf, skiing or gambling. However, the Disney Organization also pioneered the idea of theme park based resorts through its complexes in Florida and California.

Resorts have also become increasingly common in other parts of the world, notably Sun City in Southern Africa, and in the Pacific Rim.

Nevertheless, Europe has in recent years witnessed the growth of resorts. Indeed they have been one of the fastest growing sectors of tourism, leisure and hospitality. They have been the basis of Club Méditeranée development as one of the world's largest accommodation chains, for example. At the same time the Center Parcs brand has expanded from its country of origin, the Netherlands, to France and the UK.

OWNERSHIP FACTORS

From a marketing point of view it is important to note that the vast majority of European resorts are privately owned and their main marketing objective is the optimization of profits.

We should also note that while some resorts are owned by independent companies that own just the one resort, the vast majority of those found in Europe are part of chains.

THE NATURE OF THE RESORT PRODUCT

The elements of the resort product can perhaps best be illustrated through the example of Disneyland Paris in France. This is particularly interesting as it is a resort conceived by an organization based in the USA but located in Europe.

The main components of the Disneyland Paris complex at the end of 1995 were as follows:

- the theme park which is split into five different areas or 'lands' each with a different theme. There are, in total, 39 major different rides and attractions;
- an entertainment programme featuring stage shows, outdoor parades and frequent displays;
- special events at certain times of the year such as Christmas;
- a selection of seven on-site accommodation establishments aimed at different market segments, all of which are themed. They range from the 'Davy Crockett Ranch' which offers log cabins and a caravan and camping site to the luxury Disneyland Hotel;
- there are some 34 themed catering outlets on the site, offering sit-down meals, fast-food and take-away meal services;
- on site, there are no fewer than 43 themed shops selling exclusive Disney merchandise;
- leisure facilities, although these are generally located within the individual accommodation units;
- organized activities such as the 'Character Breakfasts';
- the brand image and reputation of Disney;
- the high quality of service for which the Disney Organization is famed;
- easy accessibility via specially purpose-developed road and rail systems, and coach services from Paris and the local airport;
- opportunities for trips to the nearby city of Paris;
- guest services like wheelchair and pushchair hire, a pet care centre, and currency exchange facilities;
- the opening days and times – Disneyland Paris, for instance, is open every day of the year from between 9 am to 11 pm in the peak season to 10 am to 6 pm in the off-peak season.

The precise nature of the resort product depends on the type of resort it is; for example, the Center Parcs product lays a greater emphasis on leisure facilities and recreational activities than does Disneyland Paris.

Furthermore, we must also recognize that Disneyland Paris is Europe's largest resort. Most others are smaller, although they offer a similar range of product elements. While most resorts gear their product to the leisure user, some also offer facilities to attract the business user, namely conference rooms in particular.

Lastly, we should recognize that some European resorts are based on the timeshare principle. Here, guests buy the right to use the resort for one or two weeks every year for as long as they want. In these cases, the marketing challenge is the sale of the weeks in the first place rather than in needing to find new customers for them each year. However, it is important that the complex is self-contained as it must function as a 'home from home' for those customers who are committed to visiting the resort year after year.

PRICE

There are different approaches to resort pricing, as follows:

- what we might term the 'Club Med' approach of 'all-inclusive' prices where guests pay one price and that includes all or almost all of the elements of the product;
- the item-by-item approach, favoured by Disneyland Paris, for example, where each element of the product has a separate price and visitors buy only those elements they wish to, or can afford to, purchase.

Generally resorts are relatively highly priced to reflect both the costs incurred in their development and maintenance and their exclusivity value. However, discounts are used to attract business at the less busy times of the year.

Consumers do not always know what price they are paying for the use of the resort, as it may be part of a package holiday for which they have paid a single price.

DISTRIBUTION

The distribution of the resort product tends to be either by direct sale or via marketing intermediaries such as travel agents. Club Méditerranée, Center Parcs and Disneyland Paris all offer opportunities for clients to book direct but they are also available through travel agents. Some resort operators use specialist representatives in foreign countries from which they wish to attract tourists to help potential customers buy the product.

PROMOTION

As far as promotion is concerned, most of the major resort operators have large budgets and make use of television advertising as well as widespread printed media advertisements. Their brochures tend to be large and glossy and they make considerable use of sales promotions. Personal selling is used particularly to gain bookings from coach and tour operators and conference organizers, in other words those who control high-value business.

Many resorts also use direct mail based on their databases either to attract new customers or to persuade previous users to make a repeat purchase.

THE RESORT MARKET

The resort market can be segmented in a number of ways, such as:

- where customers live which determines whether their catchment areas are local, regional, national and international. This obviously influences where the resort operator will concentrate most of their advertising effort;
- where consumers are in terms of the family lifecycle, including young couples, families and so-called 'empty nesters', people aged around the early 50s whose children have left home;
- day visitors who are simply using the non-residential attractions on the site and those staying visitors who are also using the on-site accommodation units;
- those visitors who want to relax and those customers who want to spend most of their holiday indulging in active pursuits;
- people who use the resort in the peak season and those who visit in the off-peak season;
- gregarious people and those who prefer to be on their own, likewise extroverts and introverts, as some resorts suit one type while others appeal to the other;
- leisure visitors and business users.

The benefits sought by resort users vary depending on the nature of the resort in question and the personality of the particular guest. They can include the following:

- privacy or companionship;
- complete relaxation or the chance to practise a number of sports and recreational activities;
- the opportunity to enjoy a complete holiday without the need to leave the site, in other words convenience;
- value for money at those resorts where the price is all-inclusive.

Some resort operators specialize in offering certain benefits to their customers, and it is often the specialism on which they base their promotional activity. For example, Center Parcs are renowned for offering their customers the opportunity to take part in healthy activities in a rural-style environment. Club Méditerranée's reputation, on the other hand, is based on the quality of its food, the beachside locations of most of its centres and the activity programmes organized by its GOs or *gentils organizateurs*.

COMPETITION

There is competition in the resort sector, but as the product they offer is often very different and their target markets vary, much of the competition is between the resort and other types of holiday rather than between resorts themselves. For example, Club Robinson is aimed at German tourists and is for those who prefer a more individual type of holiday, whereas Club Méditerranée is aimed more at French- and English-speaking consumers, and is based on a more communal approach to holidaymaking.

As far as non-resort competition is concerned, it depends on the type of resort, but can include the following:

- destinations which offer a similar range of attractions and services, whether that be a seaside resort, a place with a local theme park or a skiing centre, for instance;
- attractions which offer on-site accommodation such as Futuroscope in France;
- package holidays that offer inclusive packages that comprise the elements that might otherwise be available at a resort such as accommodation, entertainment and activities.

In the case of theme park based attractions such as Disneyland Paris, the competition may be in terms of hotels outside the resort where customers use the theme park but not its accommodation. Clearly, this dramatically reduces the resort's income from that which it would receive if the visitor chose to stay in one of the resort's own accommodation establishments.

THE MARKETING OF RESORTS BY EXTERNAL ORGANIZATIONS

Many resorts are marketed by other organizations as well as by themselves, including:

- tour operators for whom they are the core product in particular packages that they offer. Thus UK tour operators promote Disneyland Paris through brochures purely on holidays to Disneyland Paris while the French state railways SNCF also offer combined rail–resort stay packages to the French market;
- destination marketing agencies who use the resort as a way of attracting particular market segments to their area. Hence the local

council in Nottinghamshire in the UK promotes the fact that there is a Center Parcs complex in their area;
* accommodation establishments which include an entrance ticket to the resort, where such tickets are available, as part of the package they offer to their clients, particularly in the weekend short break market.

However, some resort operators such as Disney, while happy to enjoy the benefits of joint marketing with other organizations, maintain strict control on the ways in which their product is packaged by these organizations. For example, they may insist on their logo and particular wording being used to describe aspects of the resort.

OTHER ISSUES

In addition to the resort chains like Club Méditerranée and Center Parcs, and the Disney Corporation, there are also many individual, independently-owned resorts in Europe. In the case of these resorts, it is difficult to draw a clear line between resorts and other sectors of tourism, leisure and hospitality. Two examples of where the boundary is blurred include:

* so called 'health farms' or health clubs, usually located in country houses or chateaux, which combine leisure facilities, recreational activities, accommodation and specialized healthy eating. There are many examples of such places in the UK including Champneys;
* hotels which offer a wide range of leisure facilities, are located in isolated localities and are largely self-contained. One example of such hotels in Europe is the Grecotel Hotel Meliton Beach at Porto Carras on Greece's Halkidiki peninsula.

It must also be recognized that not every complex that could justify the term resort is run by a private-sector organization. Some are owned by voluntary sector bodies and a few are in public ownership. Here the marketing objectives are largely social. These include the activity centres operated by the Youth Hostel Association in the UK, and the Villages Vacances Familiales (VVF) social tourism villages in France.

CONCLUSIONS

Overall, resort marketing tends to be a function of both the size of organization involved and the precise nature of the resort in question in terms of its core product and its target market. Given the growth of resorts in Europe, it is clearly a form of marketing with which we will become even more familiar in the future.

DISCUSSION POINTS AND ESSAY QUESTIONS

1. Choose **one** of the following resorts or resort companies and examine the nature of its product:
   - Disneyland Paris;
   - Center Parcs;
   - Club Med;
   - Butlins Holiday Worlds.
2. Discuss the main factors that may have contributed to the growth of resort complexes in Europe in recent years.
3. Evaluate the ways in which the resort market might be segmented.

EXERCISE You have been engaged as a consultant for a European based organization which wishes to develop a major new resort complex in Europe.

Your brief is as follows:

(a) to identify the optimum location in Europe for such a new resort complex and provide a rationale for your choice of location;

(b) to develop an overall concept for the complex;

(c) to create a two-dimensional plan of the proposed complex;

(d) to suggest who would be the main target market or markets for the new complex.

Your report should be presented to your client in the form of both a verbal presentation and a written report.

CASE STUDIES

You may wish to look at some of the following cases which illustrate the points made in this chapter:

10. Club Méditerranée SA, France;
12. Porto Carras complex, Halkidiki, Greece;
28. Center Parcs, UK.

Retail travel

Key concepts

The main concepts covered in this chapter are:

- the different types of retail travel outlet;
- the complex product offered by travel agents;
- the growing competition for retail travel outlets including direct marketing;
- the different markets served by travel agents.

INTRODUCTION

Retail travel, in other words the travel agency sector, is the distribution element in the tourism marketing system. It is, in general, the interface between the producers – tour operators, hoteliers, airlines and transport operators, for example – and their customers.

In some countries, including Germany and the UK, the main interests of travel agents are in outbound travel, helping their own nationals travel abroad on holiday or for business. However, in other countries, such as Greece and Turkey, travel agents are also often involved in inbound tourism, arranging excursions and car hire for inbound tourists, for example.

OWNERSHIP AND SIZE

In terms of ownership and size, travel agents tend to be of four types as follows:

- travel agencies which are part of chains with a number of branches in different locations in one country which are in turn part of larger corporations which have interests outside tourism. Such an organization is the French travel agency group, Havas Voyages, which also has substantial media interests for example;
- travel agencies which are part of chains with branches in different locations which are part of larger corporations with interests in other

sectors of tourism. Examples of this in the UK include the Lunn Poly and Going Places chains which are both owned by leading UK tour operators;

- privately owned, independent travel agencies that are not chains but do have several outlets;
- privately owned, independent single-outlet travel agencies which are owner-operated.

It is also possible in relation to the first two types of chain for them to have branches in more than one country, in other words to be truly international. Two examples of this are Thomas Cook which is owned by the German tour operator LTU, and American Express Travel which is part of the credit card group.

The final difference between types of travel agency is that distinction which can be made between those which specialize in leisure tourism and those which concentrate on business tourism.

THE RETAIL TRAVEL PRODUCT

Whatever the type of agency, the product it offers tends to be similar – a service or, more to the point, a range of services. These include:

- providing an opportunity for customers to purchase or book the product offered by tour operators, hoteliers, transport operators and theatres, for instance;
- offering advice and information both in relation to the products that are available and other matters such as currency rates, obligatory inoculations and visa requirements;
- being an outlet where consumers can obtain the brochures produced by tour operators and other producers in the tourism industry;
- collecting payment from the consumer and passing it on to the organization offering the product (less the agent's commission);
- operating as the first line of after-sales service to which problems and complaints can be referred;
- offering a range of other services such as currency exchange for the convenience of their clients.

It is clear from this selective list that the most important element of the travel agency product is the competence of the staff and their level of expertise in the various functions. Many complaints about travel agents relate to the lack of relevant expertise of some staff, in respect of unusual destinations for example.

PRICE

Agents do not charge the customer a price for their service usually. Their income comes in general from the commission they are paid by industry organizations on the sales of their products. These are expressed, usually, as a percentage of the purchase price of the product, and may range from 7 or 8% to 15%.

The fact that their income is dependent on commission leads to criticism that the agent may have a vested interest in not selling their client the cheapest appropriate product as this would give them a lower commission.

In the business travel sector, there are also sometimes arrangements where the client does pay for the agent's service, usually in the form of an annual fee.

DISTRIBUTION

As far as the third 'P' in the marketing mix, place, is concerned, it is not in general relevant to agents for they **are** the distribution element in the tourism system. However, the way in which their customers gain access to their service is, literally, place, in other words the location of their retail outlet.

Some are located in the high street of major urban areas, especially those involved in the mass market where casual passing trade is an important element. Perhaps this is particularly relevant to the budget end of the market where people may wish to compare special offers which are available at different agencies in an urban centre. Conversely, in the case of niche market agents or those which offer higher priced, more specialist products, they can really be located anywhere as people will travel to them because of their expertise. Some agents seek to become the major player in a particular neighbourhood.

It has to be said, however, that in general these comments are mainly applicable to Northern Europe. Given that we noted earlier that many Southern European agents also serve inbound tourists, agents in these countries are often located in the heart of the towns and cities which are most popular with tourists, to capture the passing trade.

PROMOTION

Methods of promotion in retail travel tend to vary depending on the size of the organization. Major chains of agencies tend to make use of television and press advertising, particularly at the main times of the year when people book holidays. Smaller agents on the other hand have to rely more on local newspaper advertisements.

However, there are other promotional activities which agents can undertake to raise their profile and increase awareness amongst potential customers. These include:

● running special evenings in a local hotel, for example, to inform customers about particular types of holidays that are available through the agency. These evenings often include some drink and food and are usually free of charge;

- services within the agency's premises when representatives of leading tour operators are on hand to advise clients;
- special offers, where people buying holidays receive a discount or do not have to pay a deposit. Most such offers carry conditions, however, which are often controversial, such as the requirement that people buy the agent's own insurance to be eligible for these offers.

Travel agencies also tend to make great use of visual displays in their windows to tempt customers to enter their premises to see what they have to offer.

Personal selling is important for travel agents, otherwise people will simply take away brochures and eventually buy a holiday elsewhere, or not buy a holiday at all.

RETAIL TRAVEL MARKETS

Travel agents service a range of markets, including:

- those who use them simply as sources of advice and information. This is particularly true of independent travellers thinking of travelling to lesser known destinations;
- people who wish to book travel services only such as air tickets or car hire, or who use the agency to make hotel bookings;
- individual customers who purchase an inclusive tour, who are, in general, the bulk of most leisure travel agents' business;
- associations and clubs who book group travel services via a travel agency;
- companies and organizations who use the agency to manage their business tourism needs;
- individuals who buy ancillary products from the agency such as foreign currency or travel insurance.

The aim of travel agency marketing has to be to ensure that the yield per consumer is maximized by effective personal selling and by offering a range of services that meet the needs of the majority of customers.

Most travel agencies in Europe rely for the bulk of their business on clients who wish to travel to other countries. In general, selling products based within their own country does not generate a substantial element of their income.

COMPETITION

At the present time, competition is intense in the retail travel sector in Europe. This competition comes in two forms, namely internal and external.

By **internal competition** we mean competition between different travel agencies. This takes several forms, as follows:

- that between the major chains based on the desire of each to increase their share of the relevant national market;
- that between the major multiple chains as a whole and the small independent agents;
- that between all the agencies, the multiples and the independents, in a particular geographical area.

The large chains tend to use their ability to offer big discounts as their way of achieving competitive advantage, which the small independents cannot afford to do. The latter therefore have to focus on service and building 'brand' loyalty, so that they attract repeat business.

External competition largely relates to the growth of direct selling in tourism in which products and consumers communicate directly with each other without the need for an intermediary or agent. This communications takes a number of forms, including:

- the computer reservations systems of some hotel chains which are available via toll-free telephone numbers;
- the newly developing GDS (global distribution systems) such as SABRE, which offer services that can increasingly be accessed by business tourists;
- flight consolidators in the air travel market, who sell discounted tickets directly on behalf of airlines but which are not travel agents in the usual sense of the word
- airlines and tour operators which sell their product via newspaper advertisements, and direct booking telephone lines to their offices;
- retailers in other industries who are seeking to offer travel agency services as part of their overall range of activities. In the past, in the UK for example, there have been rules preventing this happening, but these have now been relaxed and post offices, for example, have expressed an interest in providing a range of retail travel services;
- home-based information services such as Minitel in France and 'Teletext' in the UK;
- the media who are, in some European countries, increasingly offering advice that people would possibly have sought from travel agents.

Technological developments such as multimedia systems and smart cards are making it increasingly possible for those producers who wish to do so to market their products directly to their potential customers. It is not surprising, therefore, that more are seeking to do so, particularly in an industry where profit margins are low, as direct marketing can save the commission producers have to pay to agents. This is forcing agents to review their role and seek to improve the quality of their service in order to compete.

AGENCY–OPERATOR LINKAGES

A trend in many European countries has been the growth of travel agency links with tour operators often involving outright ownership of the former by the latter. Sometimes, as in the case of LTU and Thomas Cook, these developments have been transnational in nature. However, they have attracted criticism on the grounds that there are fears that agents may favour the products offered by their parent company whether or not it is the best product for a particular customer. This situation is particularly typical in the UK where the three largest agencies are owned or associated with the country's three largest tour operators. Concerns over these links in the UK even led to a government enquiry.

This enquiry is part of a growing phenomenon in Europe, namely the interest of national governments and supranational bodies such as the European Commission in the ethics of tour operation and travel agency marketing. This culminated in the EC Package Travel Directive. The result of this European legislation has been that some agents and operators have become much more careful about the accuracy of information they offer about products, and the claims they make on behalf of these products.

CONCLUSIONS

In some countries, such as France, travel agents have never become powerful players in tourism to the extent that they have in other countries like the UK. However, many commentators are now saying that technological innovations and changes in consumer behaviour are changing the very nature of the retail travel sector. These writers offer a vision of the future where customers prefer independent travel to package tours and have the home- or office-based technology to allow them to book the product they want.

If this prediction proves accurate, retail travel marketing in the future will not be about achieving competitive advantage – instead it will be about marketing for survival.

DISCUSSION POINTS AND ESSAY QUESTIONS

1. Identify the different markets which exist for the services of retail travel outlets and compare and contrast the needs of these different markets.
2. Discuss the various forms of external competition which retail travel organizations are increasingly facing and examine the approaches they might adopt in response to this competition.

3. Critically evaluate the relationship between tour operators and retail travel outlets in Europe and describe to what extent it benefits the consumer.

Select a local retail travel outlet which you are able to visit and where you can **EXERCISE** arrange an interview with the manager. For your chosen outlet you should visit, interview the manager and then undertake the following tasks:

(a) evaluate the strengths and weaknesses of the service which it offers;
(b) identify its competitors and see how it might seek to gain competitive advantage over them;
(c) examine the current role of technology within the business and see how technical developments might affect the way it operates in the future, both positively and negatively.

---

23 Arts and entertainment

Key concepts

The main concepts covered in this chapter are:

- the scope and nature of the arts;
- the different marketing objectives of arts organizations in the public, private and voluntary sectors;
- the arts product and the arts as a component of other tourism, leisure and hospitality products;
- competition within the arts, and between the arts and other leisure activities.

INTRODUCTION

The arts are a very important sub-set of the leisure market and arts marketing has developed dramatically across Europe in recent years.

THE SCOPE AND NATURE OF THE ARTS

However, before we begin to look at the practice of marketing in the arts, we must firstly define the scope of the arts. Figure 23.1 represents the view of the Arts Council in the UK as to the scope and nature of the arts.

Within these overall definitions, there are a number of other ways of classifying the arts. As these tend to affect either products or market segments, they clearly have a major influence on arts marketing and will therefore be briefly discussed.

- There is a distinction between the consumer as **spectator** and as **participant**. For example, a person may go to the theatre to see a professional drama performance, or they may be a member of an amateur theatre company which puts on its own performances as a hobby.
- There is a difference between **facilities** and **activities**, which can also be related to the difference between spectators and participants.

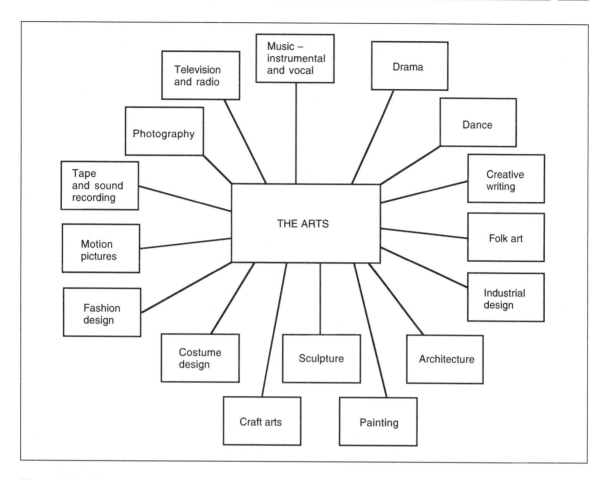

Figure 23.1 The scope and nature of the arts.

Arts facilities include art galleries, arts centres, theatres and cinemas, while arts activities include painting, making craft products, dancing and going to rock concerts or arts festivals.

- Some types of arts activity are usually **organized in advance**, such as a theatre visit, while others can be **spontaneous**, such as visiting a local art gallery. This difference is partly accounted for by the fact that pre-booking is normal for the former activity but not for the latter.
- Arts activities can be consumed either by **groups** or **individuals**; for instance, attending a concert is an example of the former while painting is often a solo activity.

OWNERSHIP AND MARKETING OBJECTIVES

There are also differences in terms of ownership and marketing objectives. The public sector tends to be a major provider of facilities such as art galleries and theatres, which are usually subsidized. The reason for the subsidy is that there is a belief that arts facilities like these are essential for the cultural life of an area and must therefore be provided, even if they lose money. The marketing of such public sector facilities is therefore largely about increasing usage as well as ensuring the budgeted targets are met. Voluntary sector involvement in the arts is largely in the field of activities, where the aim is to give opportunities for amateurs to develop their interest in particular hobbies. Their marketing objective is therefore often to generate enough income to allow them to carry on with their activities. Conversely, in the private sector, which is strongly represented in areas like the cinema, television and music, the aim is to maximize profits and boost market share where appropriate. These differences in marketing objectives can lead to these organizations adopting different approaches to marketing. In the first two cases there may be a tendency to concentrate on the product and hope a market can be found for it, while in the latter sector the focus is on looking at what the market wants and developing an appropriate product to satisfy this demand.

In the public sector, arts are a crucial element in the cultural and leisure policies of central and local government. They are often therefore called upon to help achieve broader social objectives such as education and providing activities for young people.

There have always been some blurred lines between the arts, entertainment and sport. The arts have traditionally been seen as rather highbrow activities that somehow uplift the soul and enrich people's lives. On the other hand, entertainment and sport are often somehow seen as activities that meet people's basic desires for amusement or exercise, but which do not merit the term arts.

However, in an era when we are talking about so-called 'postmodernism' it may well be that the demarcation lines are becoming less and less relevant. Indeed many would now argue that entertainment and sport can equally be considered as art, for example:

- developing and playing computer games;
- taking part in 'karaoke' evenings in clubs and pubs;
- circuses;
- playing sports such as football and tennis or taking part in sporting activities like skiing, for instance.

Finally, some would argue that the concept of the arts should be even broader and include other activities such as gastronomy, while Spanish people might argue that bullfighting is also an art form.

THE ARTS PRODUCT

The arts product can take a number of forms, including the following, for example:

- a permanent facility which offers opportunities for people to look at the tangible products of the arts, such as an art gallery or craft centre;
- a permanent facility which provides opportunities for people to participate in an arts activity, for instance a dance studio or recording studio;
- a club, association or society, membership of which allows someone to indulge in a particular activity and/or have access to equipment they require to take part in an activity. This might be an amateur dramatic club, for example;
- a special, temporary event such as a concert, a theatre performance, or an arts festival.

If we take one type of product, for example a theatre, the actual product consists of the following elements:

- its programme, in terms of what plays and other types of performances it offers;
- the building in terms of its location, seat comfort and facilities such as bars and restaurants;
- the days on which it is open and the times of its performances;
- its booking system, in terms of how customers can reserve tickets and which methods of payment are accepted;
- the theatre's image, reputation and brand name.

As well as being products in their own right, the arts can also be elements in the wider product of tourism and hospitality organizations. For example:

- Tourist destination marketing organizations may utilize arts festivals to attract tourists to their town, city or region. France has many examples of such festivals including the annual European Street Theatre Festival in Aurillac and a Festival of Bandes Dessinées, or illustrated comic books, at Angouleme, to give but two examples.
- Arts facilities and activities may be included in the excursion programmes offered by tour operators to holidaymakers in and around the resort where they are spending their holidays. For instance, tourists in London might be taken to the Museum of the Moving Image in the city, which illustrates the history of film and television. Likewise, tourists in countries such as Greece and Spain may be offered a national 'folklore evening'.
- Many hotels now offer weekend break products based on the arts. These can include painting, crafts, art appreciation and theatre weekends.

PRICE

Pricing is a complex issue in the arts, and it can also be controversial, particularly due to the role of public sector subsidies. These subsidies can mean that some arts facilities and activities of high quality may be offered at no charge, such as entrance to major art galleries. Subsidies may also mean that publicly owned facilities such as theatres may be able to offer their products at levels below the true market value. This is true of activities such as opera performances. As we will see later, this can be seen as unfair competition by commercial sector arts organizations.

A particularly controversial aspect of such subsidies is that they are often not linked to activities which are primarily enjoyed by people on limited incomes, where subsidies could be justified by the fact that they allow less affluent people to enjoy the art. In the case of opera, for example, where subsidies can be worth several pounds sterling per ticket sold, most customers are relatively affluent. There are, therefore, debates over the ethics of such subsidies and discussions about who should provide the subsidies and which arts should be subsidized.

Other pricing issues in the arts revolve around concessions which are given to economically and socially disadvantaged groups such as students and the elderly, and discounts which are offered for purely marketing reasons, such as the need to boost ticket sales at less busy times or the encouragement of group bookings.

DISTRIBUTION

Place or distribution is a relatively simple concept in the arts, with three major elements as follows:

- the use of marketing intermediaries from which consumers can purchase tickets for performances, such as travel agents and tourist information offices;
- direct booking with arts facilities or activity organizations by telephone or in writing;
- where pre-booking is not the norm, place can literally mean the location, where people are attracted to enter buildings or join in events simply because they happen to be passing by at the appropriate time.

PROMOTION

Most arts products are marketed using a limited range of promotional techniques because the budgets of arts organizations are also often limited. The most popular methods of promotion in the arts include:

- leaflets covering individual facilities or individual special events, or published programmes covering a season of plays at a theatre;
- advertising, largely in the printed media, either local or regional newspapers or specialist periodicals;
- sales promotion offers, both added value (two tickets for the price of one for a theatre performance, for example) and discounts (£1 off a ticket for students at a cinema);

- press and public relations, widely used to gain favourable media coverage that is largely free
- sponsorship of arts organizations to raise the sponsoring organization's profile and/or bring extra revenue.

The relatively few major transnational corporations in the arts also undertake more sophisticated advertising, such as television advertising when a new film is released.

Some arts organizations have combined the promotion of their core business with forays into the visitor attraction sector. In the UK, for example, the Granada Television company has set up the Granada Studios Tour in Manchester. This is in effect a media theme park, based on well-loved television programmes. It serves to promote the Granada brand and its programmes while also being an extra source of income for the company.

THE ARTS MARKET

There are a number of issues relating to the arts market which are relevant to marketing of the arts.

There are many different sizes of **catchment area** for arts facilities and events. Some have only a local catchment area while others can be largely international, and many others lie somewhere between these two extremes. For example, many cinemas may serve a local clientele while a major art gallery such as the Louvre in Paris has a truly international catchment area. The same is true of events where a small music festival may draw most of its visitors from the locality, and others such as the Salzburg Music Festival draw visitors from all over the world.

The market can be divided into a number of different **segments** on the basis of a range of criteria including age, sex, income, nationality, language, place of residence, lifestyle and personality. However, the market can also be broken down into those who like to watch and those who like to participate. There is also a difference between groups and individuals in terms of consumer behaviour.

The **benefits** sought by the users of arts products vary dramatically, and some of these differences are related to the existence of different market segments. Some of the most significant benefits sought include:

- status;
- aesthetic pleasure;
- learning a new skill;
- an individual experience or a collective experience;
- sensual pleasure;
- hedonism;
- ego enhancement;
- increased confidence;
- health and fitness.

This is but ten from a list that probably includes hundreds.

It is important to note how the benefits sought vary between different customers even in relation to purchasing what is ostensibly the same product. For example, the benefits sought by a young couple visiting a cinema to see a film might be one of the following:

- the cinema represents a place where they can enjoy a romantic experience in the dark!
- they may be keen to gain status by being able to say they have seen a particularly fashionable film;
- the film represents escape from the dullness of everyday life or fears, or the chance to learn something new, depending on the nature of the film;
- they may be able to enjoy the snacks and drinks on sale at the cinema;
- they may be taking advantage of a special discount offer, perhaps from a fast-food outlet which gives away cheap cinema tickets when people purchase particular meals.

Finally, in terms of the market, while most arts involve the use of leisure time, there is also a business-related market. For example, some companies use arts activities such as opera performances as part of corporate hospitality packages for their customers. This phenomenon may be developed to the point where it can form part of formal sponsorship arrangements between businesses and arts organizations.

COMPETITION

Competition is a complex issue in the arts field. As it is a leisure activity, the real competitors are all other forms of leisure activity or opportunities for spending disposable income. This can best be illustrated by taking an example such as a cinema which specializes in family films. Its competitors might typically include:

- other cinemas in the same geographical area with similar programmes;
- theatres in the same area offering family shows;
- special events targeted at families such as craft fairs;
- eating out at restaurants;
- visitor attractions which are aimed at families such as theme parks;
- recreational activities like taking a walk in the countryside, bicycle riding or swimming;
- visiting a leisure shopping complex;
- visiting friends and relatives;
- home-based leisure activities such as barbecues;
- home entertainment where the family stays at home and indulges in activities such as watching videos, playing computer games or simply playing games in the garden.

There are accusations that there is **unfair** competition in some areas of the arts. For example, our cinema above is privately owned, receives no subsidies and has to make a profit to survive. On the other hand, the local theatre with which it is competing is publicly owned and receives a subsidy so that it does not have to charge a market price for its tickets, unlike the cinema.

However, in the public sector in particular there is also **internal** competition where arts facilities owned by the same body may indeed be competing with each other. This may be true in relation to theatres or art galleries, for example. Marketing activity has to be carefully planned therefore to ensure that the organization is not spending money to allow it merely to compete against itself.

FURTHER ISSUES

Finally, there are several other miscellaneous issues relating to the marketing of arts products.

- **Consortia** play a significant role in arts marketing, with organizations particularly in the public sector which have limited budgets working together to increase their combined buying power in terms of advertising campaigns and brochure production and distribution. These consortia often relate either to a particular art such as dance or crafts or to art organizations within a specific geographical area. However, such consortia can also be found in the commercial sector, with perhaps the best example being the Society of West End Theatres in London.

- Many art organizations operate on a **transnational** basis so that they have to take into account national differences in terms of consumer behaviour, business practices, legal frameworks and so on. Examples of such transnational activities include:
  - foreign tours by dance companies and rock bands;
  - the sale of television programmes to networks in other countries;
  - international record sales;
  - art exhibitions mounted by galleries in one country that take place in a foreign country.

- The **size of marketing budgets** for arts organizations can vary dramatically from a few hundred pounds sterling for a small art gallery to major film companies which may spend millions of pounds sterling promoting just one film.

- In some of the arts there is a **tension** between the art and those who practise it, and the concept of marketing. Many people in the arts believe that marketing is harmful because it can mean having to compromise artistic principles and values to meet the wishes of consumers. This is particularly true in those art forms where professionals with a strong sense of vocation undertake performances, such as drama, dance and music.

CONCLUSIONS

Overall arts marketing is a complex but growing area of activity. Particularly in the public and voluntary sectors, there can be a very strong set of social marketing objectives. At the same time, in the private sector, one can see some of the most overtly controversial and aggressive types of marketing found in any industry.

DISCUSSION POINTS AND ESSAY QUESTIONS

1. Compare and contrast the approaches to marketing which are taken by public sector and private sector organizations in the arts.
2. Evaluate the nature of the product within the arts sector.
3. Identify all the main forms of competition which might be faced by an individual theatre **or** art gallery, both within the arts and outside the arts.

EXERCISE Choose **one** public sector body and **one** private sector company within the arts sector.

Compare and contrast these two organizations in terms of their:

- marketing objectives;
- the nature of the product offered;
- pricing policies;
- promotional techniques;
- policy in relation to competitors;
- performance indicators.

You should, finally, attempt to explain any differences which you may identify in relation to these six issues, between the two organizations.

Recreation and sport

Key concepts

The main concepts covered in this chapter are:

- types of recreational activity;
- the different objectives of organizations in the public, private and voluntary sectors;
- recreation and sport as an element in tourism and hospitality products;
- transnational marketing in recreation and sport.

INTRODUCTION

Recreation is defined by Torkildsen (1994) as 'activities and experiences usually carried on within leisure and usually chosen voluntarily for satisfaction, pleasure, or creative enrichment'. He goes on to say that, 'it may also be perceived as the process of participation. Physical recreation is closely allied to sport.'

In this chapter we are going to focus on the marketing of those aspects of recreation which are concerned with activities and sport, rather than the more passive forms of recreation. We will also concentrate on those forms of recreation which are most closely linked to tourism and hospitality. Figure 24.1 illustrates some of the major different types of recreational activity that people indulge in during their leisure time.

THE NATURE OF THE RECREATION AND SPORT SECTOR

Even the brief, selective picture shown in Figure 24.1 illustrates the diversity of forms of recreation which explains why it is such a complex sector as far as marketing is concerned. Some of the differences between forms of recreation which influence marketing practice in the sector include the following:

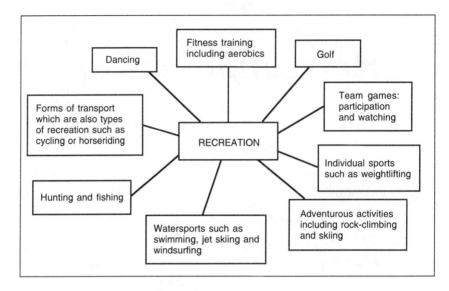

Figure 24.1 Types of recreational activity.

- some recreational activities can be practised in people's homes or in their local area, such as dancing and fitness training. Others require participants to travel considerable distances to the places where specialist facilities such as rock faces or water areas are located;
- partly for this reason, some forms of recreation can be indulged in on a daily basis, while others may only be undertaken once or twice a year, on an annual holiday, for example;
- some activities require special clothing and equipment such as skiing or golf, while others require little or none, as in the case of playing football in a public park, for instance;
- some forms of recreation are supported by a large physical infrastructure of facilities such as golf courses, while others are not;
- certain recreation activities can be controversial, politically sensitive, or even illegal in certain countries. The best example of this is, perhaps, hunting;
- some activities are conducted in groups such as playing team games while others are very much individual activities like horse-riding;
- while pre-booking is required for some recreational activities such as golf, it is not for others, including cycling and rock-climbing;
- recreation can be a matter of being a spectator watching others play football for instance, or it can be about participation, in other words playing in a football match.

Readers will have noted that in several of these aspects, there are links between recreation and sport, and arts and entertainment. The boundaries of the two are blurred – for example, dancing is a type of recreational activity but it is also an art form.

Another similarity between them is that the public, voluntary and private sectors play an important role in both. Their respective roles in recreation and sport are outlined below.

- The public sector owns many recreational facilities such as swimming pools and woodlands, for example, and makes them available, often at a subsidized price or even free of charge, to encourage people to take exercise for the sake of their health. Where participation rates in particular types of recreation are low amongst certain groups, such as countryside recreation amongst people from the ethnic minorities in the UK, the public sector may take positive action to encourage participation for purely social reasons.
- The voluntary sector tends to encompass the clubs, associations and societies which organize many recreational activities in those areas based on amateurism. Voluntary organizations sometimes also own and manage recreational facilities including golf courses.
- The private sector is involved in recreation on a commercial basis in three main areas, as follows:
  - the ownership and management of facilities such as dry ski slopes, and fitness and health clubs;
  - the ownership and management of teams in the areas of recreation where participation is based on professionalism such as professional football. Some football clubs such as Barcelona and AC Milan are businesses with large turnovers. In the UK, clubs like Manchester United are even quoted on the Stock Exchange;
  - the manufacture and supply of specialist equipment ranging from saddles to leotards, and climbing ropes to golf clubs.

Sometimes the boundaries between these three sectors can be blurred. For example, many public sector agencies are having to become more commercial in response to reductions in their state funding. Likewise some voluntary associations and clubs can have large turnovers on which they generate profits like private companies. Some may even be incorporated as private companies in respect of some of their activities.

Finally, it is important to note that all three sectors can be represented within one type of recreation. For example, some golf courses are owned by municipal authorities while others are in the ownership of voluntary bodies or private companies. Furthermore, most golfers are amateurs while a few are highly paid professionals.

Because of the diversity of the recreation sector, we will focus on just three different elements of recreation when we consider the application of the marketing mix to recreation and the recreation market. These are:

- countryside recreation in a national park;
- a golf course owned by a voluntary sector golf club;
- a major professional football club.

COUNTRYSIDE RECREATION IN A NATIONAL PARK

The countryside recreation **product** in a national park can be both 'natural' and artificially created. While much of the landscape will usually be natural its attractions may have been enhanced by the development of picnic sites and new footpaths. Further artificial product development may take place in the form of a programme of guided walks. The 'product' represents a series of opportunities from which users can build their own experience, whether it be a quiet picnic near their car or a long strenuous walk. A key element of the product is its accessibility from where people live, by private car or public transport.

As far as **price** is concerned, users rarely are asked to pay a direct charge for the use of the countryside for recreation purposes. Instead the cost of providing for their needs is usually met by taxation levied on the population in general.

As pre-booking is not the norm, **place** plays little real role in most countryside recreation in national parks. As most national parks are managed, if not owned, by the public sector, they have wider aims than simply encouraging countryside recreation. Their main responsibility is often conservation, so that frequently they have to indulge in demarketing to reduce demand and divert visitors to less popular areas to reduce pressure on the landscape.

Promotional techniques are often used to achieve this aim, through brochures, in particular, and press and public relations activities too. The limited budgets of most national park Authorities tends to result in relatively little advertising being undertaken.

As far as the **market** is concerned, several important points need to be made, as follows:

- Some national parks due to their remote location have relatively small visitor numbers while others which are nearer to urban areas have large visitor numbers (around 20 million in the case of the Peak District National Park in the UK).
- Many parks have a large local and regional market such as the Peak District, while others, particularly those in well established tourist destinations, have predominantly national and even international markets, like those in the French Alps.
- In some parks the majority of visitors are repeat visitors while in others most visitors will only visit once in their lives.

The **benefits** people seek from countryside recreation in a national park can vary dramatically, as we can see from the brief list below:

- passive relaxation or a chance to indulge in an energetic and even dangerous activity;
- the chance to escape from others and be alone or the opportunity to meet new people;
- the desire to try a new experience or the attractiveness of doing something with which you do often.

A GOLF COURSE OWNED BY A VOLUNTARY SECTOR CLUB

The **product** which the golf club offers has a number of elements as follows:

- the golf course itself with its golf-related features such as its bunkers and other hazards and the nature of its greens. The product also covers the environmental setting of the course and the views that are enjoyed by those playing the course;
- the days and times on which the course is available;
- the facilities available in the club-house such as bars and restaurants;
- the availability of advice and coaching from a resident golf professional;
- the image and reputation of the course locally, regionally, nationally and internationally;
- the social life involved in playing the course and/or belonging to the club.

The **pricing** structure tends to vary. Members may have to pay to belong to the club and then pay a modest sum for each round of golf they play, whereas casual players who are non-members may be asked to pay a higher price. Some municipally owned public-sector courses may also offer concessions to groups who are seen to be socially disadvantaged.

In terms of **place** and distribution, membership of the club is the way of gaining regular rights of access to the course, but often people have to be invited to join rather than simply apply. Thus they need to know people who are already members. The system of distribution for players seeking a casual one-off round of golf at such clubs and those wishing to play on municipal courses is a simple matter of pre-booking by telephone.

Promotion is often not relevant as in many cases demand outstrips supply, particularly at peak times. However, where newer courses have been established in countries like Spain and France to help attract tourists, substantial promotional activities may be undertaken by the golf course itself, the local destination marketing agency or a tour operator which is selling golf packages based on the course.

The **market** for golf courses can vary dramatically. With an old, well-established, famous course in the UK, most users are the members who live within the same region. Few non-members will be able to use the course in general, except when open tournaments are underway. On the other hand, at some of the new courses in Spain and Portugal, for instance, most users may well be foreign tourists, with relatively few local people making use of the course.

As far as the **benefits** sought by the consumers of golf courses and golf club services, status perhaps comes near the top of the list in relation to the more exclusive courses. However, in general, the benefits sought include:

- relaxation in the fresh air;
- gentle exercise;
- the social life and atmosphere that is part of the golf scene;
- the chance to gain satisfaction from improving one's ability to play the game;
- an opportunity to mix business and pleasure with business people using golf as a way of doing business in a relaxed, informal atmosphere.

A MAJOR PROFESSIONAL FOOTBALL CLUB

In many European countries, professional football is big business, with clubs having high turnovers and generating considerable profits. This is particularly true in Spain, Italy and the UK.

The **product** which is offered by a professional football club has two main elements as follows:

- the football team, which offers, in effect, a special event product, namely a 90-minute spectacle involving playing a competitive match against another team. However, a football match is about more than the 90 minutes of the game on the pitch. The team also offers opportunities for its fans to bask in their team's glory or lament its failures, and to look forward to the game throughout the preceding week. For a team, its image and reputation is all-important to its fans, to potential investors and to prospective players;
- the stadium, in terms of tangible features such as the quality of seating and catering facilities, together with intangible aspects such as the atmosphere. However, increasingly, football stadia are not just venues for football matches. They also act as a venue for concerts, for example.

In terms of the corporate market, football clubs often combine their two products, the team and the stadium, into a lucrative corporate hospitality product. Companies pay for facilities where important customers can be wined and dined and enjoy the match at the same time.

Prices tend to be relatively high for tickets at leading professional football matches, but there are different prices depending on where one sits within the ground. Season tickets are also offered to encourage brand loyalty and give the club cash flow at the beginning of the season. Corporate packages tend to be premium priced, particularly if the club is a famous one.

As far as **place** or distribution is concerned, pre-booking by post or telephone is the norm for football match tickets, and is obligatory for the purchase of corporate hospitality packages. For matches, a certain allocation of tickets may be given to the visiting club which it will then distribute to its supporters.

In relation to football matches, **promotion** is usually very low-key. Supporters are simply regular visitors and they buy their tickets almost automatically. All they need to be given is a fixture list for the season. The match brochure or programme can be used to promote particular matches. On the other hand, the corporate hospitality market, which is a very competitive and lucrative activity, merits glossy promotional brochures and a considerable amount of personal selling activity on the part of the clubs.

There are, as we have seen, a number of distinct **market segments** for a professional football club, namely:

- local people who support the team and go to watch all its matches;
- local people who go to some matches, particularly the most important ones;
- a small number of non-local supporters who will travel longer distances to watch some of its matches. This happens more in the case of the more fashionable clubs like Manchester United or Liverpool in the UK, for instance;
- business people who use the matches for corporate hospitality purposes;
- those people who use the stadium only when it is playing host to other kinds of events such as concerts.

The **benefits** sought from a football club depends on which segment one is talking about. Local supporters go to the match to see their friends, demonstrate their loyalty to the club and relax. For them the match is the focus of their trip to the ground. Conversely, for most business users, the game is a means to an end rather than an end in itself. In other words, the match is an opportunity to impress customers and discuss business in an informal setting.

While this and the previous two cannot represent the whole of recreation and sport, they at least demonstrate the great variety of marketing issues found in this sector.

COMPETITION

Competition in recreation and sport is also a complex matter and exists at a number of levels, including that between:

- different providers of the same product such as golf courses or gymnasia;
- different forms of recreation such as dancing, swimming and jogging for those interested in improving their health;

- free or subsidized publicly-owned recreation facilities and commercial promotion from private sector organizations;
- active recreation and sport and passive leisure activities such as watching television or eating out.

There can also be internal competition such as when a local council offers several types of recreation facility to its local population, and they can end up competing with each other for the local market.

OTHER ISSUES

Finally, we will consider a range of miscellaneous issues that influence the nature of marketing in recreation and sport.

The marketing of recreation and sports facilities by other bodies

Many facilities and activities are promoted by other bodies, as well as by the owners or operators themselves. For example, in the UK the Sports Council promotes a wide range of sporting activities and facilities.

Links with the marketing of tourism and hospitality

Recreation and sports products are increasingly being used as part of broader tourism and hospitality products as the following examples illustrate:

- tour operators developing holidays based on recreational activities as diverse as the following:
  - a golfing holiday in Portugal;
  - a hunting holiday in Bulgaria;
  - a walking holiday in the mountains of Spain;
  - a skiing holiday in the French Alps;
  - a scuba-diving trip to Malta;
  - a holiday based on going to see the European Football Championships in the UK in 1996;
- excursions available within tourist destinations which are based on recreational activities such as golf, horse-riding and wind-surfing;
- destination marketing agencies promoting an area on the basis of the natural and man-made resources it offers for recreational activities, including:
  - the golf courses of Ireland;
  - the surfing beaches of the Aquitaine coast in France or Cornwall in the UK;
  - the proximity of skiing facilities to Norwegian resorts such as Voss and Lillehammer;

- hotels developing leisure facilities within the hotel such as swimming pools and gymnasia to attract customers who wish to keep fit and take exercise while they are staying at the hotel

National differences in recreation and sport

These include:

- the popularity of different sports in different countries so that golf is very popular in Scotland and Ireland, but much less so in Greece, for instance;
- certain sports which are peculiar to individual countries or regions such as pelota in the Basque country of Spain and France and hurling in Ireland;
- differential levels of provision, from the massive football stadia in Spain and Italy to the small grounds of Iceland and Ireland;
- countries which have traditionally had a relatively small domestic market for recreation and sport and those where participation rates within the domestic market are much higher. While this distinction was often considered to exist between Northern and Southern European countries, respectively, it is a gross over-simplification. It is often simply that the people of the varying countries have different tastes for different types of activity, but that levels of participation in some form of leisure activity are relatively similar overall.

Transnational marketing

While most recreation and sport marketing is domestic, there is a significant amount of transnational marketing, particularly in the field of destination marketing. The organizations involved in such marketing clearly have to take into account national differences in consumer demand, legislation and business promotions. Examples of such transnational marketing include:

- destination marketing agencies in France attempting to attract UK golfers to the newly built courses of France;
- Irish destination marketers trying to attract anglers from the UK, Germany and the Netherlands;
- the marketing of sporting events which have an international appeal, such as the 1998 World Cup in France, the annual tennis championships at Wimbledon in the UK, and even the running of the bull festival in Pamplona, Spain.

Consortia

Consortia can play a significant role in recreation and sport marketing, particularly in the public and voluntary sectors. These consortia can either take the form of pressure groups and lobbying bodies on behalf of a particular activity, or a loose consortium of similar types of facilities such as golf courses.

CONCLUSIONS

As we have seen, marketing in the recreation and sport sector is complex due to a range of factors related to the nature of the product, ownership and marketing objectives, and different types of market demand. However, we have also noted that it shares some of these characteristics with the arts and entertainment sector.

DISCUSSION POINTS AND ESSAY QUESTIONS

1. Compare and contrast the marketing objectives of public, private and voluntary sector organizations in the recreation sector.
2. Evaluate the differences in terms of the application of the marketing mix between countryside recreation and a professional football club.
3. Discuss the links which exist between recreation and tourism and hospitality.

EXERCISE   You have been engaged as a consultant to undertake **either** of the following tasks:

- to encourage more people to take exercise by walking, riding, and bicycling in an area of your choice on behalf of a public sector body charged with promoting healthier lifestyles;
- to increase the income of a professional football club of your choice which owns its own stadium.

For your chosen project, you should:
(a) identify target markets;
(b) develop appropriate new products to meet the needs of these markets, and indicate how these products could be priced to make them attractive to these markets;
(c) outline the main distribution channels for these products;
(d) produce a promotional plan, indicating what promotional techniques would be utilized to persuade target markets to purchase these products;
(e) highlight key implementation issues, including funding.

CASE STUDY

You may want to look at the following case study which illustrates some of the points made in this chapter:

23. Futbol Club Barcelona, Spain.

Leisure shopping | 25

Key concepts

The main concepts covered in this chapter are:

- a typology of leisure shopping facilities;
- the nature of the leisure shopping product;
- the benefits sought by leisure shoppers;
- links between leisure shopping and other sectors of tourism, leisure and hospitality.

INTRODUCTION

While most shopping in Europe is utilitarian in nature, undertaken to purchase the goods which are the prerequisites for everyday life such as food and household goods, there has always been an element of pleasure shopping for non-essentials. However, it is only in recent years that we have seen the growth of a sector of tourism, leisure and hospitality which is solely concerned with retailing as a leisure activity. It is not the concept of leisure shopping which is new but its rapid expansion and the growing provision of purpose-built leisure shopping facilities.

LEISURE SHOPPING FACILITIES

Leisure shopping facilities come in a number of forms as follows:

- **Major leisure shopping complexes**. In such complexes all or most of the retail units sell products which are not essential to everyday life. They are purchased purely for pleasure as part of a leisure experience. An excellent example is the Albert Dock in Liverpool, UK, which has been used to spearhead the regeneration of the economy of the city through leisure and tourism on the model used in US cities like Baltimore and San Francisco. This is interesting because the idea of leisure shopping complexes or 'malls' originates in North America. In Europe, such complexes are found more in Northern Europe than in Southern or Eastern European countries.

- **Leisure shopping areas which are found within established tourist destinations**. These can range from the shops in UK seaside resorts selling 'rock' (candy confectionery) and novelty hats at cheap prices to the chic retail outlets of the French Riviera. This aspect of leisure shopping has a relatively long history compared to the complexes discussed above.
- **Industrial leisure-oriented shops in existing retail areas of towns and cities which are not major tourist attractions**. They are targeted both at locals and the relatively small number of tourists that visit the place, and are usually located in the districts which are most likely to be visited by such people.
- **Craft centres**. These sell craft goods, and may even provide opportunities for visitors to watch the product being made. These centres are particularly popular in the most popular tourist resorts in Europe as well as in rural regions in most European countries.
- **Leisure-oriented outlets which are part of visitor attractions**. For many attractions a significant element of their income is obtained from the sale of merchandise. This is equally true whether the attraction is a major theme park like Disneyland Paris or a museum such as the Victoria and Albert Museum in London.
- **Outlets linked to home-based leisure activities**, such as garden centres and 'do-it-yourself' centres.

At the same time, a leisure dimension is also being added to more utilitarian retailing activities, such as purchasing food and everyday clothes, as the following two examples illustrate.

- People are being encouraged to visit **food providers** as a leisure experience and buy some of their products directly. For example, in France one can buy cheese from a farmer who makes it and wine from the local cooperative. The pleasure is derived not just from the consumption of the product but also from the experience of seeing where it was made and meeting the producer.
- There is also the phenomenon of **factory shops** where producers, mostly of clothes, sell them directly from their premises. In the UK coach trips are often organized by groups and coach operators to such factory shops These are seen as a leisure experience as well as an opportunity to purchase clothes at below normal prices.

MARKETING OBJECTIVES

Most leisure shopping facilities are offered by the private sector whose marketing objectives are purely commercial. However, there is also a role for the voluntary and public sectors whose objectives are broader than the merely financial. For example, in the UK, one of the largest organizations involved in leisure retailing is the National Trust, a voluntary body. It uses the income generated from its retailing operations to fund its conservation work.

THE LEISURE SHOPPING PRODUCT

The leisure shopping product varies depending on which type of leisure retailing we are considering, but in general it contains the following elements:

- the products which are on offer in terms of their design, aesthetic appearance, features, reputation and exclusivity value;
- the retail outlet itself, including its location, decor and reputation;
- the service element, and the attitudes and product knowledge of the staff;
- the methods of payment which are acceptable;
- the outlet's opening times in terms of how convenient they are for prospective customers;
- the areas in which the outlet is located in terms of its environment, fashionability, accessibility, car parking facilities, ambience and the proximity of other services such as catering.

PRICE

The customer pays no price, usually, for entering a leisure shopping complex or an individual leisure retailing outlet. For some people, therefore, leisure shopping is a very economical leisure experience. They gain pleasure from looking rather than buying.

However, as many leisure retailing complexes and units are expensive to develop and their products often have a high degree of exclusivity, prices can be relatively high in order to recoup high costs and exploit the rarity value of products. Leisure shopping is often a seasonal activity, particularly where it takes place in an established tourist destination. Discounting, where it does exist, therefore, tends to take place at the end of the season when retailers need to sell stock which will lose its value once the season has ended.

DISTRIBUTION

Place or distribution is relatively simple in the leisure shopping sector in general. Pre-booking is not normal and therefore little use tends to be made of marketing intermediaries. In this case, 'place' really does mean location, for it is often where the complex or unit is situated that is one of its major attractions for visitors.

PROMOTION

The promotional techniques used tend to depend, as usual, on the size and budget of the organization. A small rural craft centre may rely on simple leaflets and word-of-mouth recommendations while a major leisure shopping complex may spend heavily on television and printed media advertising campaigns together with glossy brochures.

Many smaller leisure retailers rely heavily on repeat purchases so that they need relatively little promotional outlay designed to attract new customers.

THE LEISURE SHOPPING MARKET

The market for leisure retailing can be segmented in a variety of ways but is usually based on geographical and demographic factors, including:

- where people live, as most complexes or units have local, regional, national or international catchment areas;
- stage in the family lifecycle, in other words children, couples, families and older people, for example;
- sex, as women are seen to be far more enthusiastic leisure shoppers than men, for example.

The benefits sought from leisure shopping by consumers differ between the different types of leisure shopping. However, typically they might include:

- the chance to buy a unique and unusual product that is not available elsewhere;
- the pleasure of 'window-shopping' without buying anything;
- the opportunity to purchase a product directly from the producer at a lower cost than it would be available in a shop in the person's own area.

However, leisure shopping can also offer some more fundamental benefits. It is often the core attraction of trips made by people who are depressed; so called 'depression shopping' is becoming more widely recognized as an issue in some parts of Europe. For many people, leisure shopping trips are social activities which involve travelling with a group of friends. This can represent a break with routine, a form of 'escapism'.

In many cases the benefit sought is not an individual element but rather the overall experience, including:

- the journey to and from the retailing area;
- the company of friends;
- the pleasure gained from looking at goods or buying something special;
- a meal in the middle of the trip in an attractive restaurant.

COMPETITION

Competition takes a number of forms in leisure shopping including:

- between different types of outlets and complexes within a particular geographical area;
- between similar types of outlets and complexes in a wider geographical area;
- between leisure shopping and utility shopping;
- between shopping and other forms of leisure pursuits such as gardening, reading, eating out or sporting activities;
- between shopping and other forms of leisure spending on a day out, such as entrance fees to attractions and food and drink.

As we can see the form of competition will largely depend on the type of leisure shopping outlet or complex one is considering.

PROMOTION BY EXTERNAL ORGANIZATIONS

As well as marketing themselves, leisure shopping facilities are also often promoted by organizations in other sectors of tourism, leisure and hospitality. For example:

- The excursions organized by tour operators often feature a leisure shopping experience. This may be a rural craft centre in Ireland, gift shops on the Costa del Sol, a garden centre in the UK or a Christmas market in Bavaria.
- Hotels often promote leisure shopping facilities when they are trying to sell their weekend break packages. This is true of destinations from London to Lisbon, Paris to Prague, and Istanbul to Iceland.
- Transport operators such as the ferry operators offering services across the English Channel promote off-peak season shopping trips from the UK to France, for example.

LINKS WITH OTHER SECTORS

These examples lead us into a broader discussion of the links between leisure shopping and the other sectors of tourism, leisure and hospitality. These links take a number of forms, including the following:

- many accommodation establishments have installed retail outlets featuring largely upmarket leisure shopping products;
- leisure shopping complexes and units often enhance their attractiveness through the provision of catering facilities. Particular types of catering have become associated with leisure shopping such as 'tea rooms' or salons de thé, coffee shops, wine bars and unusual ethnic restaurants;
- social programmes and itineraries for conference delegates and their partners;

- airports, airlines and ferry companies are developing leisure shopping facilities of their own to increase income. This is particularly important as we approach the date when duty-free sales, which have hitherto provided much of their revenue, will disappear within the European Union;
- shops selling the equipment required for hobbies and recreational activities such as painting or skiing have grown considerably in recent years.

MARKETING CONSORTIA

Consortia play a limited but significant role in some areas of leisure shopping, notably:

- voluntary groupings of individual retailers within individual leisure shopping areas or complexes who combine to mount joint promotional campaigns;
- consortia of similar types of leisure shopping outlets, such as craft centres, which aim to promote their particular type of retailing and product.

CONCLUSIONS

Overall, leisure shopping is a growing area of activity within tourism, leisure and hospitality. It has strong links with other sectors in these three fields, but it also has some interesting characteristics of its own from a marketing point of view. It seems likely that in the future it will become increasingly recognized as a separate sector within tourism, leisure and hospitality.

DISCUSSION POINTS AND ESSAY QUESTIONS

1. Identify the main types of leisure shopping facilities which exist in Europe, and examine the differences between them.
2. Discuss the different markets that exist for leisure shopping products and outline the benefits each of these markets might seek from leisure shopping.
3. Examine the nature of competition within the leisure shopping sector.

Choose an example of a leisure shopping outlet, complex or facility which **EXERCISE** you are able to visit. You should visit your chosen outlet, complex or facility and spend some time there, looking at the product it offers and finding out the opinions of its customers. You should also endeavour to talk to the manager or owner about their marketing activities.

On the basis of evidence gained from this research you should:

(a) evaluate the strengths and weaknesses of the outlet, complex or facility from the point of view of both customers and the manager or owner;
(b) identify its main competitors in the opinion of both the customers and the manager or owner.

Finally, you should compare and contrast the views of customers with those of the manager or owner in relation to these two issues, identifying, where appropriate, those areas where their opinions differ markedly.

26 Catering

Key concepts

The main concepts covered in this chapter are:

- the wide variety of types of catering;
- catering as part of leisure and tourism products;
- the complex nature of the catering product;
- methods of segmenting the catering market and the benefits sought by these different segments.

INTRODUCTION

Catering is now a massive business across Europe and is a crucial element in the product offered by many European tourist destinations. It is primarily concerned with preparing meals which are consumed either on the caterer's own premises or at the consumer's home. The catering product is a combination of tangible elements such as the food and drink, together with an intangible service element.

Traditionally, catering has been seen to be distinctly different from food manufacturing and food retailing, but these distinctions have become blurred in recent years. Some aspects of catering, such as contract catering, have more in common with the production lines of food factories than with traditional restaurants. At the same time, more and more supermarkets are selling pre-prepared convenience dishes to compete with 'take-away' catering outlets.

However, even within mainstream catering, there are many sub-sectors with very different characteristics from a marketing point of view, some of which are illustrated in Figure 26.1. Clearly, this picture is simplified and relates largely to terms which are used in the UK. However, the types of catering it outlines are generally found across Europe, although the specific names may be different.

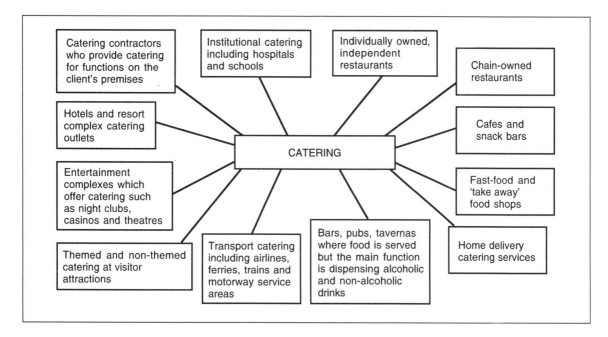

Figure 26.1 Different types of catering.

OWNERSHIP AND MARKETING OBJECTIVES

There are a number of general points that need to be made in terms of the marketing of catering in Europe that relate to ownership and marketing objectives. These include the following:

- Some of the major players in some areas of catering in Europe are non-European, for example McDonald's and Kentucky Fried Chicken. This had led to the introduction of American concepts of catering and service to the European market which have affected the approach of European players such as Burger King and the Quick chain in France.
- While most of the catering trade is in the private sector where profits and market share are the key marketing objectives, there is a welfare element which exists in the public sector, such as schools and hospitals, which have social objectives.
- The majority of catering outlets are small businesses operating single units, while the rest are generally parts of chains which offer a standardized product in a number of locations. In tourism, these chains may be part of larger corporations with interests extending beyond catering, such as the UK company Grand Metropolitan with its 'Burger King' brand.

LINKS WITH TOURISM AND LEISURE

There are some interesting links between catering and tourism and leisure which are becoming increasingly interrelated, as the two following examples illustrate:

- At many leisure facilities and visitor attractions, catering is a major element of the product on offer and contributes a significant proportion of overall income. In some cases, a particular catering outlet at an attraction can be almost as powerful a factor in a decision to visit as the attraction itself.
- Catering can be an attraction in its own right encouraging people to visit a particular location, usually a famous restaurant. Certainly the quality of catering outlets has been a major element of the marketing campaign of Kinsale in Ireland. Likewise, many people choose to travel to the Lyonnais region in France, amongst other reasons, because of the restaurant of Paul Bocuse which is located there. There is also a strong link between food production, catering and tourism which is clearly shown in the case of the Bourgogne (Burgundy) region of France. People travel to this region to visit wine producers and enjoy meals in local restaurants which feature traditional local dishes made using locally produced ingredients.

Therefore, as we can see, catering is not only marketed by caterers, but also by attraction and destination marketers, for example. However, it is also marketed by accommodation operators for whom catering is often a major source of revenue, through in-house catering operations such as hotel restaurants and banqueting facilities.

The general conclusion from this section of the chapter is that while catering is the core business of most catering businesses it is an important ancillary product for other tourism, leisure and hospitality organizations, which may encourage potential customers to purchase that core product.

CATERING AND THE MARKETING MIX

Now that we have looked at several issues that provide the context for catering marketing, it is now time for us to begin to look at the practice and techniques involved in such marketing, beginning with the marketing mix.

Clearly the precise nature of the catering **product** varies depending on the type of catering, but it usually includes the following elements:

- a meal, in a form in which it can be consumed immediately. The meal itself, a product, is a combination of the food itself and the way in which it is presented visually;
- the efficiency of the person serving the meal in terms of ensuring that the order is taken quickly and processed accurately to make

certain that the person receives the meal they ordered. However, as well as efficiency, the service element will also be judged by the consumer on other criteria such as the member of staff's knowledge of the product and their attitude to the customer;
- the decor, comfort and ambience of the catering outlet, whether it be a restaurant or a fast-food area where one collects a meal that will be consumed off the premises;
- the location of the outlet which will determine the type of customers that will be attracted;
- the days of the week the outlet is open and its opening times;
- the range of items which are offered and how clients are able to combine them through à la carte or fixed table d'hôte menus for example;
- the methods of payment which are accepted including cash, cheques and credit cards;
- the product's reputation which may be reflected in a brand name, whether it is an individual high-class restaurant such as Le Manoir aux Quat' Saisons of Raymond Blanc in the UK or a chain of restaurants such as Harvester in the UK or Flunch in France.

This list relates to mainstream catering but there are, as we saw in Figure 26.1, more specialist forms of catering where the core product is different. For instance, we also have:

- home delivery services where food is delivered to the consumer's home;
- contract catering where a catering service is provided for a client either on the client's premises, or at least on premises chosen by the client, which are not owned by the contract caterer.

Clearly in these cases, where the core product is not the standard catering product, different approaches to marketing have to be adopted.

In general, **prices** in catering are fixed and are based on the principle of cost-plus pricing. However, **discounts** are used and are usually given for one of two main reasons, namely:

- to stimulate business at quiet times such as the early evening and also particular days such as Mondays;
- for group bookings where the discount is given in recognition of the volume of business.

Customers, however, do not always pay a discrete, separate price for a catering product. Sometimes it can be included in a package for which an overall price is paid. An example of this are the in-resort excursions offered by tour operators. Thus, an excursion sold as a day trip to an archaeological site in Greece might include lunch in a taverna, with a total price for the excursion of 12 000 drachmas. However, the client will not know what proportion of this charge is specifically for the catering rather than the other elements of the package, such as transport and entrance charges.

Lastly, prices in catering are not always true market prices as in some European countries there are statutory regulations that control some food and drink prices.

The concept of **place** or distribution is generally very simple in the catering sector. Where pre-booking is the norm, reservations are usually made by telephone with the relevant outlet. However, in many cases there is no pre-booking and consumers simply look for an outlet when they are hungry and enter.

Likewise, in many cases the **promotional techniques** used by catering outlets are simple, reflecting the relatively low unit price of the product and the generally small capacity of outlets. Most restaurants, for example, rely on local press advertisements, 'point-of-sale' material such as advertising boards outside the restaurant and the occasional 'special offer' sales promotion, together with word-of-mouth recommendation to generate most of their business. However, the catering chains do indulge in more expensive and sophisticated promotional campaigns, involving national television and press advertising, together with sales promotions. Such promotions can be either added value (for example two main courses for the price of one), or discounts (such as £1 off a fast-food meal). Often these products are offered through partner businesses so that it is only the partner business customer that can benefit. Restaurants may, for example, use such joint promotions with cinemas or urban bus operators. Some of the more upmarket restaurants find they do not need to do any promotion as they are full because of their reputation and word-of-mouth recommendation, while most of the sophisticated marketing offers tend to be seen in the competitive fast-food sector.

THE CATERING MARKET

If we turn our attention to the catering market, it is difficult to make generalizations, both in terms of how the market is segmented and what benefits consumers seek from different catering products.

In terms of market segments, Table 26.1 illustrates how segments can differ depending on the type of catering outlet we are considering. There are similar differences in terms of the benefits which consumers seek from catering products, as we can see from Table 26.2.

Clearly, the real-world situation is never as simple as this for a variety of reasons. Firstly, different consumers in a restaurant will all have their own individual sets of benefits they are seeking, and they will all be different as with the case of the different users of a Greek taverna. Foreign tourists will see a taverna as a special place that offers them a chance to glimpse the 'real Greece' and try new dishes. For locals the visit will be an everyday activity which simply provides them with a chance to socialize with friends and eat the familiar foods. Likewise, in the case of the German conference venue, there is a difference

Table 26.1 Segments and different types of catering outlets

Type of outlet	Main segment or segmentation criteria
Famous Michelin three-star restaurant in France	• Affluent people from the region who can afford the price • Foreign tourists – business and leisure • Higher social classes • Occasional users, mainly couples
Fast-food 'fish and chip shop' in England	• People in lower social classes with limited income • People living within a kilometre of the outlet • Regular users • Couples, individuals and families
Greek taverna in a village	• Local people who live in the village • Greek tourists • Foreign tourists of different classes and incomes • Occasional and regular users • Families
Conference venue in Germany	• Business people – local, regional, national or international, or a mixture of all four

between the benefits sought by the customer (the company organizing and paying for the conference catering) and the consumer (the delegate who eats the food). The former sees the meal as a utilitarian activity where economy and efficiency of service are the key benefits sought. On the other hand the consumer will see the meal as a chance to enjoy the pleasures of eating and may want to try new dishes, and so on.

There are many other benefits which different groups of consumers look for in a catering product and, in marketing terms, these benefits can be used as a basis for segmentation. An excellent example of this are those people who are interested in healthy living and want to buy catering products which help them enhance their health. This may involve them seeking low calorie or low fat meals or dishes prepared using organically produced ingredients. These people represent a particularly lucrative, identifiable and targetable market segment.

At the same time, it appears that the European catering market is becoming ever more 'internationalized'. Chinese and Indian restaurants are very popular in many European countries, as are Italian and French restaurants. Japanese restaurants are becoming more common while much of the fast-food sector across Europe is dominated by major American competitors. However, at the same time, many European tourists who holiday in other European countries seek out the

Table 26.2 Benefits sought from different catering products

Catering product	Main benefits sought
Famous Michelin three-star restaurant in France	• Reputation • Once in a lifetime experience • Status • Special atmosphere • Aesthetic pleasure of a sophisticated meal
Fast-food 'fish and chip shop' in England	• Economy • Convenience • Reliability • Speed • Familiarity
Greek taverna in a Village	• Sociable atmosphere • Informality • Simple food • Relaxation
Conference venue in Germany	• Chance to talk about business to other people • Novelty of trying foods not tried before • The meal is served quickly enough that the conference timetable is not disrupted

type of food they eat at home while they are on holiday. Hence the British may look for fish and chips in Fuengirola and some Germans search for bratwurst in the Balearic Islands.

COMPETITION

Competition in catering is generally intense, but this competition can take a number of forms, as follows:

- competition between different types of catering outlets such as independent restaurants versus chain-owned outlets;
- competition between different types of cuisine including Italian, French, Asian and American fast-food, for example;
- competition within sectors of the catering trade such as the fast-food sector;
- competition between the major chains in the catering business;
- competition between catering outlets and food retailers who offer pre-prepared dishes such as Marks and Spencer plc in the UK and the traiteurs in France;
- competition between all types of catering outlets in a particular geographical location.

In some cases, however, there is no competition, namely in the case of hospitals and schools catering where there is in effect a captive market and a monopoly situation.

Finally, in relation to competition, catering can be used as a way of achieving competitive advantage by organizations in other sectors for whom catering is not their core business. Hence, many airlines promote the quality of in-flight catering when selling their business class brands. Likewise, hotels may promote their own restaurant's quality as a way of persuading clients to book into their hotel.

OTHER MARKETING ISSUES

We will conclude this chapter with a number of miscellaneous observations relating to the practice of marketing within the catering sector.

Where catering businesses wish to expand their main **growth strategy** has traditionally been through horizontal integration with the purchase of other existing catering outlets. At the same time catering companies may also, obviously, create new outlets or brands. However, franchising has also started to become common, particularly in relation to international chain-owned fast-food outlets and themed restaurants. For example, the UK brand Burger King now has franchises in a number of other European countries, most notably France, Germany and Spain.

Technological innovations in **management information systems** are providing more data for the catering marketer. Restaurant systems can provide information on indicators such as average spend per cover, customer profits, table turnover ratios, and the popularity of particular menus, dishes or drinks.

Because of the level of competition in urban areas in some countries in Europe, many urban hotels in these countries no longer offer a hotel restaurant. This is particularly true in France, for example. There is also a phenomenon in some European countries, most notably again France, where the restaurant within the hotel is franchised or leased to a separate operator.

In certain types of restaurant, particularly the chain-owned fast-food outlets and themed restaurants, a considerable amount of effort is expended in 'internal marketing'. This means encouraging staff to offer a better service and to conform to the organization's concept of quality.

CONCLUSIONS

Catering marketing is a complex matter, reflecting the diverse nature of the sector. There are clear distinctions in terms of marketing practice between independent and chain-owned outlets and take-away and eat-in outlets, for instance.

DISCUSSION POINTS AND ESSAY QUESTIONS

1. Compare and contrast the core, augmented and actual products of a fast-food outlet **and** a Michelin three-star restaurant.
2. Discuss the links which exist between catering and tourism and hospitality.
3. Evaluate the application of the four classic methods of segmenting a market to the catering sector.

EXERCISE You have been engaged as a consultant by an entrepreneur who wishes to develop a new restaurant in your local area. Your brief is as follows:

- to devise an overall concept or theme for the restaurant;
- to identify the target market or markets for the restaurant;
- to suggest an appropriate location for the restaurant;
- to advise the entrepreneur on how the proposed restaurant might differentiate itself from other restaurants in the area.

Your results should be submitted in report form supported by a verbal presentation.

CASE STUDIES

You may wish to look at some of the following cases which illustrate the points made in this chapter:

12. Porto Carras complex, Halkidiki, Greece;
25. Accor, France;
26. Thalassa International, France.

Business tourism

Key concepts

The main concepts covered in this chapter are:

- differences between business tourism and leisure tourism;
- the complexity and diversity of business tourism products;
- differences in marketing practice between destinations and hotels, for example;
- the nature of competition within business tourism.

INTRODUCTION

Business tourism is distinctly different from most of the sectors we have discussed in Part 5. It is primarily concerned with business activities rather than pleasure, and takes place in working time rather than leisure time.

It is also unusual in that most purchasing decisions are not taken by the end consumer, but rather by their employer, who is therefore the true customer. However, there is no doubt that the true picture is more complex than that for the business traveller's attitudes and experiences undoubtedly influence the employer's purchasing decisions.

Business tourism is a broad term but it covers a range of very different activities, namely:

- individual business trips;
- attendance at meetings, training courses and conferences;
- visiting and organizing trade fairs and exhibitions;
- undertaking product launches;
- incentive travel, where organizations use travel as an incentive or reward for the performance of their employees.

Business tourism, like leisure tourism, can be both domestic and international, and like the latter can be both outbound and inbound.

For the tourism industry, whether it be destinations, venues, transport operators or travel agents, business tourism is very attractive because it is generally the highest spending form of tourism. However, as we will see later there are areas where business and leisure tourism overlap.

In this chapter, we will look at the key issues in the marketing of business tourism, beginning with its structure.

THE STRUCTURE OF BUSINESS TOURISM

In many ways, the structure of business tourism mirrors that of leisure tourism, but it is handled by specialist departments or organizations, as can be seen in Figure 27.1. This is clearly a generalized and over-simplified picture as the structure varies somewhat between the different types of business tourism. Nevertheless it does illustrate the main points.

Business tourism is largely a private sector activity with the players seeking to maximize benefits if they are a buyer and optimize profits if

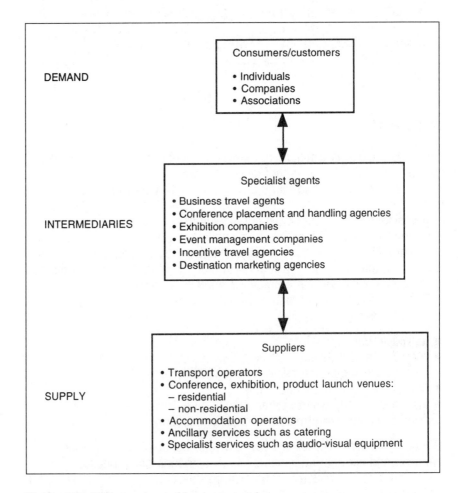

Figure 27.1 The structure of business tourism.

they are a supplier. However, there is also public-sector involvement through publicly owned venues and destination marketing organizations. In both cases, business tourism is often encouraged because of its spin-off economic and social benefits for the area.

The relationship between producer and consumer is not always as simple as Figure 27.1 might suggest. For example, a business tourism product can have several very different groups of consumers. A major exhibition has, for instance, to persuade the following audiences to 'purchase' its product to be successful:

- potential exhibitors have to be encouraged to buy space at the exhibition;
- efforts have to be made to ensure that enough visitors of the right kind visit the exhibition so that the exhibitors feel it has been worth their while attending the event;
- persuading the media to attend and give the event favourable coverage to ensure that enough exhibitors and visitors come to the exhibition, this year and in future years if it is a regular event.

Each of these audiences requires a different approach and set of messages.

THE BUSINESS TOURISM PRODUCT

The nature of the business tourism product varies depending on the type of business tourism. However, it does have something in common with the leisure tourism product, in that it can either be an integrated product made up of a number of components from different sectors, or it can be a single-sector product only. Thus, a conference delegate may buy an inclusive package that includes travel to and from the destination, attendance at the conference, accommodation, some meals and transfers within the destination. On the other hand, someone travelling to do a day's work from, say, Brussels to Amsterdam may simply need to buy a rail ticket between these cities. Normally, the former type of product is purchased by those attending conferences and exhibitions, for example, while the latter is usually restricted to relatively short-duration individual business trips.

The main types of business tourism products are outlined in Figure 27.2.

The different sectors of the tourism industry tend to develop specific sets of products for the business tourism market. These include:

- purpose-built conference and exhibition centres, which are often developed by the public sector. Major European examples include the National Exhibition Centre in Birmingham, UK, and the Acropolis in Nice, France;
- business-class cabins on airlines, with enhanced services, extra legroom, and perhaps access to fax machines, as well as business lounges at airports;

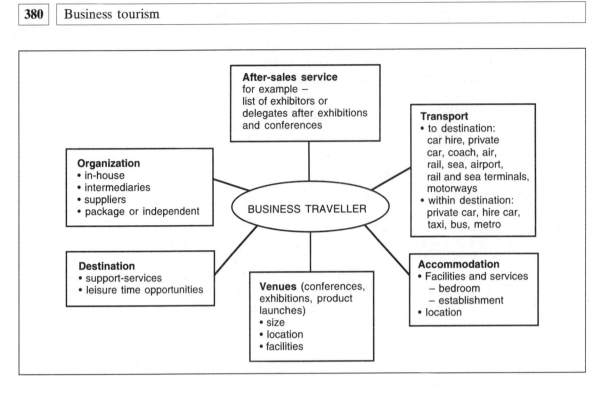

Figure 27.2 The business tourism product.

- conference and exhibition facilities within hotels and bedrooms designed to meet the needs of business travellers such as in-room computer facilities, for example.

In recent years, with the growth of competition in the sector, new types of products have been developed to try to meet the needs of the business traveller. These include:

- budget motel-style accommodation units for car-based business people working for companies which wish to minimize their expenditure. Such accommodation includes the Travelodge (Granada-Forte, UK) and Formule 1 (Accor, France) brands;
- programmes designed to encourage brand loyalty such as frequent flyer schemes with airlines and privilege card programmes with hotel chains;
- added value benefits for business and first-class travellers, such as free limousine services from the traveller's home to their departure airport.

PRICE

Pricing is clearly a key issue in business tourism. For many suppliers in tourism as a whole, their products which are aimed at business tourists are often the highest priced products in their portfolio. In some cases, such as incentive travel, a high price is almost a prerequisite to reflect the status and exclusivity which the product has to have to fulfil its purpose as a reward or incentive for employee performance. But even in relation to mainstream business tourism, the point about high prices is still true. The majority of business-class passengers on airlines, for example, are people on business.

On the other hand, one type of business tourism product, namely conference and exhibition venues, can be made available free of charge. This can happen if they are owned by local councils, for example, who are keen to attract conferences and exhibitions because of their positive economic benefits for the local community as a whole. This can lead to accusations of unfair competition from commercially owned venues which cannot afford to make such offers.

Discounting is used by some sectors of business tourism to attract business at times when demand is relatively low. However, rather than discounting, many organizations prefer to focus on providing packages which are seen as good value for money by adding in extras. A hotel, for example, may include free use of its leisure facilities in the package.

As we noted earlier, some customers buy a complete package when attending a conference or exhibition while others prefer to buy the elements separately. The latter is more common for customers who may not need the standard package, perhaps because they are not staying for the whole duration of the event.

Pricing in some sectors such as the conference field can be extremely complex for the conference organizer. Figure 27.3 illustrates the price-setting process for a conference. This diagram simply sets out some of the major steps; the process is far more complex.

THE BUSINESS TOURISM MARKET

The first thing to say about the business tourism market is that it is not a market. It is rather a number of markets, reflecting the different types of business tourism which we noted at the beginning of this chapter.

Nevertheless, speaking generally, we can identify a number of interesting characteristics of this market or these markets which have implications for business tourism marketing. Interestingly, these contrast with the case of leisure travellers. The main points are set out below:

- As we noted earlier, the consumer is usually not the customer, in other words the company which books the travel or arranges the event is the customer, but it is the individual business traveller who is the consumer. Both audiences, therefore, have to be satisfied even though the benefits they seek from a business tourism product can be different and potentially conflicting, such as economy and status, respectively.

- The business traveller does not usually choose the destination which will be determined by others, notably where the company has interests or where organizations have decided to site a specific conference or trade fair.
- The business traveller does not pay their own expenses so they may be a little more generous with their spending than a leisure traveller who pays their own bills.
- Most business trips are of short duration from one day to two or three nights, for example, but business tourists tend to travel more frequently than leisure tourists.
- Some trips can be undertaken at very short notice such as a 'trouble-shooting' visit to a branch factory, while lead-in times for a major conference can be measured in years.

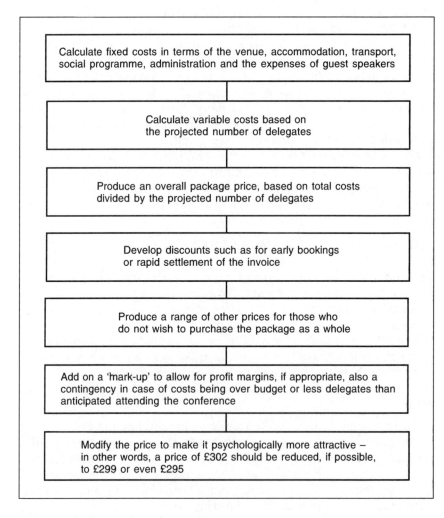

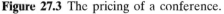

Figure 27.3 The pricing of a conference.

- Most business travellers are relatively experienced travellers with quite high expectations.
- Most demand is concentrated on weekdays rather than weekends and outside traditional holiday months such as July and August.
- The buyer can often be a large group rather than an individual, for example in the case of conferences organized by a professional association where the decision may be taken by a committee made up of very different people.

These differences in the demand side between business and leisure tourism are reflected on the supply side. Business tourism is like a parallel industry to hospitality, leisure and tourism, drawing on the services of these sectors to produce different types of product to their normal offering.

However, it would be wrong to say the markets for business and leisure tourism are completely mutually exclusive. There is a link between them both in two main ways, as follows:

- Business travellers become leisure tourists when the working day is over. They then indulge in standard leisure activities such as eating out, using hotel leisure facilities, drinking, going to shows and buying gifts for friends and families.
- Partners often accompany business travellers on their trips, so that while the business person is working, the partner is free to act as a leisure tourist.

Tourism marketers have to understand both of these phenomena and ensure that both sets of needs are satisfied if they are to be successful at business tourism marketing.

However, there can be an element to this link between business and leisure tourism which is sordid or even illegal. This can be seen in the 'red light districts' of major cities such as Hamburg and Amsterdam in Europe and Bangkok in Thailand.

In general, though, the desires of business tourists and the benefits they seek from business tourism products are more straightforward. As they are travelling for business their main needs are as follows:

- speed and reliability in their modes of travel and a minimum of time-wasting and bureaucracy at transport terminals;
- services in accommodation establishments that help them do their work such as faxes, computer points and efficient telephone systems;
- meeting and exhibition venues which are user-friendly;
- in-destination transport systems that are efficient.

However, there are more intangible things which the business traveller seeks, notably status. Suppliers realize this, hence products with names like 'Business Class' on airlines and 'Executive Bedrooms' in hotels. The way an executive travels and how they are accommodated give messages to the traveller about how they are viewed by their company, and give signals about this to their fellow travellers.

There are a number of segments of the business travel market which are increasingly being given greater attention by markets, of which women business travellers perhaps are the most important group. Suppliers are endeavouring to attract women travellers to buy their product. In doing so, though, they can face difficulties, for women are not an homogenous group. They, as individuals, want different things to each other, while some simply want to be treated like business travellers, regardless of their gender.

As far as the future of the market is concerned, there are also fears that it will be affected by technological innovations such as videoconferencing.

We will conclude this section with some facts and figures on the European business Travel market in the mid 1990s. Most of this data is taken from a paper presented by Rob Davidson at the 'Tourism: the State of the Art' conference which took place in Glasgow in 1994.

It has been estimated in a report published by American Express Europe Limited that companies spent a total of $141 billion in Europe on business tourism in 1993, a third of which was spent on international business travel. This spending is broken down as follows (note that these numbers do not add up to 100 because of rounding):

- Air fares   26 %
- Car travel   24 %
- Accommodation   20 %
- Meals   16 %
- Entertainment   11 %
- Rail travel   5 %

It has been found that some 27% of employees of European companies undertake at least one business trip per year, with 9% of employees taking international trips. Not surprisingly, employers of companies based in the smaller European countries such as Switzerland and the Netherlands, take a high proportion of the international trips.

Women make up 13% of business travellers in Europe, but the UK has the highest proportion with 23%.

One noticeable factor in the demand for business tourism is the state of national economies, for it is a sector which is very vulnerable to economic recession. The general recession in Europe in the early 1990s affected the market and resulted in some changes in buying behaviour as companies traded downmarket and looked for better value for money.

DISTRIBUTION

Figure 27.1 illustrated the important role of marketing intermediaries in the distribution of the business tourism product. However, these tend to be of two types, namely:

- those which are mainly concerned with individual business trips which include most business travel agencies;
- those which act as intermediaries by organizing conferences, exhibitions, product launches or incentive travel on behalf of client organizations.

While in the latter case more and more organizations are perhaps seeking to make use of specialist agencies, the opposite is possibly true for the former group, with many companies trying to organize more and more of their staff's business travel themselves. One reason for this is to try to get better deals from suppliers by buying hotel rooms and airline seats from them directly.

Conversely, sometimes a large organization will invite a travel agency to set up a branch or 'implant' within the organization's own premises. This trend may grow further in the future as new technologies such as multimedia systems and computer reservation systems are introduced into offices.

PROMOTION

As far as promotional techniques are concerned, these vary between the different sectors of business tourism.

Destinations, for example, tend to have limited budgets and can therefore only make limited use of advertising. Their most common methods of promotion include:

- glossy full-colour brochures featuring the attractions of the area as a whole together with information on individual venues. The venues may often pay for their section in the brochure, and paid advertising space may be offered to businesses within the brochure to help fund its production;
- exhibiting at trade fairs to distribute brochures, make contacts, generate enquiries and try to sell the destination to those attending the exhibition;
- running familiarization visits, where major buyers are invited to visit the destination to see what it has to offer at the expense of the destination marketing agency;
- press and public relations, in other words encouraging journalists to write favourable features on the destination in the trade press.

On the other hand, suppliers such as **hotels and airlines** make considerable use of advertising not only in specialist trade media, but also in newspapers and magazines which are read by business people. Considerable use is also made of direct, personal selling by telephone and in person. Sales promotions are also utilized extensively, usually in terms of added value packages where, rather than reduced prices, the customer receives more benefits when they purchase the product. This is interesting because the benefits are enjoyed by the consumer, namely the business traveller, whereas reduced prices would benefit the customer, namely the traveller's employer.

Some sales promotions, such as the frequent flyer programmes of airlines, are also aimed at the business traveller rather than their organization. For example, if a traveller uses a particular airline for business a certain number of times, then they receive reduced price tickets for flights for them and their partner for leisure purposes, such as a weekend break, for example. This is a controversial matter with many companies believing that they should receive the benefits of these promotions not their employees, at a time when they are trying to get better value for money out of their travel budgets.

Finally, we should note that as business tourism is a specialist activity, most relevant advertising and press and public relations activity is geared to specialist trade media publications such as *Conference and Incentive Travel* and *Business Traveller* in the UK.

COMPETITION

There is generally a high level of competition in the business tourism field. In the case of individual business trips, the main competition is between different modes of transport and accommodation establishments.

However, the situation is more complicated in the case of conferences and exhibitions, for example, particularly those for which there is an international market. In this case, competition exists at a number of levels, including:

- the destination, where the competition is between different countries, then regions, and finally towns and cities within an individual region;
- venues, both residential and non-residential, within the chosen destination;
- accommodation establishments within the destination;
- modes of transport that will be recommended to delegates or visitors.

Destinations tend to compete on the basis of a range of criteria, namely:

- accessibility, in terms of travelling times from the areas from which the majority of those attending will be travelling;
- the quality and variety of available venues found within the destination;
- the range of accommodation found within the area of the appropriate type and price level;
- the facilities within the destination for social programmes for the delegates during their leisure time, and for the programmes that are organized for partners. These facilities include museums, sporting events and themed restaurants, for example;

- the destination's infrastructure in terms of local transport, restaurants and the availability of services like photographers, florists and audio-visual suppliers;
- any packages of complementary services which are offered by local councils such as civic receptions and the services of local tourist guides.

Most of the other suppliers in the business tourism field such as hoteliers, transport operators and venues tend to compete on the basis of price and what is included in the package which the price covers. Airlines, for example, usually emphasize the following aspects of their product:

- pre-flight services such as complementary transport from home to airport and the convenience of check-in facilities;
- the airline's 'hub' airport and the range of connecting flights that are available from it, the convenience of flight-to-flight transfers and the availability of facilities such as duty-free shops;
- flight features such as timings and frequencies;
- in-flight services such as meals;
- aircraft facilities including seat leg-room;
- after-flight services such as help with connecting flights and airport to city centre transport.

Figure 27.4 illustrates the services which one European airline was offering to its business-class clientele in 1995.

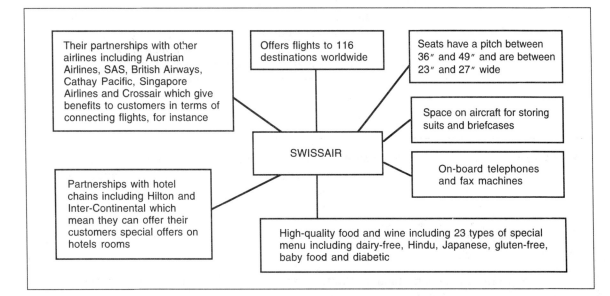

Figure 27.4 The business-class services of Swissair.

MARKETING CONSORTIA AND COOPERATIVE MARKETING

Marketing consortia and cooperative marketing play a significant role in one area of business tourism, namely the marketing of destinations. These consortia are usually led by the local government destination marketing agencies, usually in partnership with local venues, hotels, transport operators and ground handlers. These consortia are largely based on the visitor and convention bureaux of the USA. They engage in a range of activities including brochure production and distribution, exhibition and trade fair attendance, and familiarization visits for buyers, together with cooperative advertising features in the trade press.

CONCLUSIONS

We have seen that business tourism is a complex sector that is in fact made up of a number of different types of activities. These differences are reflected in the range of approaches to marketing, although there are also some similarities in marketing practice across business tourism as a whole.

DISCUSSION POINTS AND ESSAY QUESTIONS

1. Discuss the main differences between the business tourism market and the leisure tourism market.
2. Identify and examine the range of tourism, leisure and hospitality products which are used by the business traveller.
3. Compare and contrast the role of pricing policies, distribution channels and promotional techniques between a public-sector agency marketing a business tourism destination and a private-sector airline marketing its services for business travellers.

EXERCISE A group of students should undertake **one** of the following tasks:
(a) Planning every aspect of the organization of a residential conference for 150 people with the students selecting the subject of the conference.
(b) Planning every aspect of a major trade exhibition in relation to an industry of the students' own choosing.
(c) Planning every aspect of a product launch for a new product of their choice.

In each case particular attention should be paid to venue selection, budgeting and marketing.

CASE STUDY

You may wish to look at the following case study which illustrates some of the points made in this chapter:

13. Iceland: The marketing of a business tourism destination.

Conclusions to Part 5

In the preceding 12 chapters we have explored the key issues in marketing in the different sectors of tourism, leisure and hospitality. Many differences between these sectors can be identified but there are also some general points which can be made which appear to be relevant to a number of different sectors, including:

- Organizations in the public, private and voluntary sectors have different marketing objectives. These different objectives influence marketing activity in a number of ways including their pricing policies and their willingness to cooperate with other organizations in a similar business. The existence of different types of organization also has an impact on the nature of competition.
- The product which is offered is largely intangible, and the service element is highly important in determining the quality of the product which is enjoyed by customers.
- Tactical pricing is widely used to stimulate purchasing at times when demand is low.
- Place or distribution methods depend on whether or not pre-booking is the norm. Where it is, marketing intermediaries such as travel agents are widely used, while direct sales are the standard form of distribution where pre-booking is unusual or impossible.
- While large private organizations often make great use of advertising, particularly on television, smaller private companies and public and voluntary organizations often have to rely more on brochures, sales promotions and press and public relations, together with limited advertising. Face-to-face selling is only a key element in promotional strategies generally in relation to high spending customers or individual customers who purchase large amounts of the organization's products.
- Markets are often segmented on the basis of geographical and demographic factors, and they are frequently divided between leisure use purchasers and business people.

- Benefits sought by consumers vary between sectors but in all of them status is an important factor.
- Competition is intense in some sectors, particularly where the product is largely provided by private companies. On the other hand, there may be little real element of competition in a market which is largely the preserve of public sector organizations.
- In many cases the products of one organization in one sector are sold on its behalf by another organization in a different sector.

This last point raises the wider issues of links between tourism, leisure and hospitality. We have seen how closely these three fields can be in marketing terms. For example, tour operators sell hotel beds, hotels offer leisure facilities and leisure-based short break holidays, while resort complexes and business tourism, for instance, bring tourism, leisure and hospitality together. This conclusion is further justification of the fact that the three are brought together in the title of this book.

Unfortunately space precludes the possibility of looking at differences between marketing practice in different European countries. However, we have sought to use case studies from different European countries to illustrate some of the different approaches which are taken to marketing across Europe.

Nevertheless it is reasonable to assume that marketing will be different to some extent in different countries, even within a particular sector, in response to factors such as the following:

- government legislation and policies;
- economic situations;
- patterns of consumer demand;
- business culture and practices.

These differences are a particular challenge for those organizations, in all sectors, which are involved in operating in, or selling their product to people in, other countries.

Overall, however, it appears that the main characteristics of marketing in particular sectors are fairly standard across Europe. This may be because the nature of the product and its appeal to consumers in individual sectors is largely the same, regardless of which country we are discussing.

Having looked at marketing in individual sectors within tourism, leisure and hospitality, it is now time for us to look at five topical issues in tourism, leisure and hospitality marketing.

Topical issues in tourism, leisure and hospitality marketing in Europe

PART 6

In Part 6 we focus on five issues which are particularly important topics currently in the development of marketing in tourism, leisure and hospitality. These are as follows:

- **Chapter 28: Competition and competitive advantage**. This chapter covers the nature of competition and the ways in which tourism, leisure and hospitality organizations may seek to gain competitive advantage in their respective sectors.
- **Chapter 29: Quality**. This chapter covers the concept of quality, and the application of traditional and emerging approaches to quality management in tourism, leisure and hospitality.
- **Chapter 30: Green issues.** This chapter looks at the responses which tourism, leisure and hospitality organizations should make, and are making, to the challenges posed by green issues and the concept of sustainable development.
- **Chapter 31: Ethics and social responsibility**. This chapter covers the twin topics of ethics and social responsibility in relation to tourism, leisure and hospitality organizations.
- **Chapter 32: Marketing research**. This chapter covers a topic which is clearly crucial at a time when the conventional wisdom says that successful marketing means being consumer-led.

Competition and competitive advantage 28

Key concepts

The main concepts covered in this chapter are:

- differences in the degree of competition which exists in the markets in the various sectors within tourism, leisure and hospitality;
- the main types of competitive advantage strategies used within tourism, leisure and hospitality;
- the wide range of factors which influence the competitive advantage strategies an organization chooses to adopt.

INTRODUCTION

One of the clichés of marketing in the 1990s is that markets are becoming increasingly competitive and organizations must therefore strive constantly to find new ways of achieving competitive advantage.

In tourism, leisure and hospitality, these issues are particularly topical for two reasons. Firstly, the Europe-wide recession of the early 1990s made many markets more competitive and this competitiveness appears to be continuing after the economies have begun to recover. Secondly, increased competition is being seen in sectors where it has hitherto been limited such as the scheduled airline market in Europe, due to political factors such as deregulation.

In this chapter we examine both competition and competitive advantage strategies. In other words, we will look at the following:

- the nature of competition in tourism, leisure and hospitality, given that competition is intense in some sectors such as tour operation, but has traditionally been limited and even non-existent in some areas such as state-owned airlines or public sector leisure provision;
- the ways in which tourism, leisure and hospitality organizations may seek to achieve competitive advantage. We will look at what organizations in the three sectors are doing.

We should begin by noting that the ways in which an organization seeks to achieve competitive advantage often depend on the state of the economy and market at any one time. In a period of recession, competitive advantage is often based on cost reduction and price discounting, while in times of economic prosperity, mergers, acquisitions and new product development are commonly used methods.

Finally, we will try to identify any national differences and similarities that might exist within Europe in terms of the nature of competition and how organizations seek to achieve competitive advantage.

THE NATURE OF COMPETITION IN TOURISM, LEISURE AND HOSPITALITY

Competition is where two or more organizations are engaged in selling a similar product to a common target market. The customer thus has a choice of product and the competition between the organizations is to see which one can persuade the consumer to buy their particuclar product.

We have seen that in tourism, leisure and hospitality, there are great differences in terms of the degree of competitiveness which are found in the market in particular sectors. For example, competition is intense in the mass market tour operation sector but is very low, in general, in the non-commercial theatre sector. Likewise there is considerable competition in the market for fast food and budget hotels, but it is negligible in the area of local authority provision of leisure facilities.

Furthermore, competition can exist at a number of different geographical levels. This can range from local competition between organizations in the same town or city, for example in the restaurant sector, to truly global competition between organizations based on different continents, as is the case with major scheduled airlines.

However, there are also two other factors which complicate any discussion of competition in tourism, leisure and hospitality:

- internal competition where one part of an organization appears to be in direct competition with another part of the same organization. This can be true for local authority museums in the same city or for travel agents owned by one operator selling the product of a competitor operator, or for hotels in adjacent towns owned by the same chain chasing the same conference booking;
- competition from outside the sector altogether or what is sometimes termed 'substitution'. In other words, the competition for a tour operator trying to sell a holiday to a consumer may not be another tour operator but rather another form of consumer purchase. For example, the consumer may choose, in a particular year, to substitute the purchase of a new house or car for a holiday. Likewise, for many visitor attractions, their main form of competition is not

other visitor attractions, but other uses of leisure time and spending such as gardening or home entertaining.

The diversity of levels and types of competition within tourism, leisure and hospitality is a reflection of differences between individual sectors within these three fields in terms of a range of factors including the following:

- state intervention in the market through subsidies, regulation of entry into the market and the role of state-owned organizations as active players in the market;
- the number of major players who are in any one market, and the extent to which they may cooperate, formally or informally, together with the possible existence of implicit or explicit price-fixing;
- the lack of a profit motive for many public and voluntary sector organizations within the three fields which tends to modify the concept of competition;
- professional cultures in some sectors which are based on cooperation rather than competition such as in the case of museum curators.

Finally, it has to be noted that the lack of marketing research data in many areas of the three fields with which this book is concerned means that many organizations' attempts to identify their competitors are based more on perception than hard facts.

COMPETITIVE ADVANTAGE STRATEGIES IN TOURISM, LEISURE AND HOSPITALITY

We will now look at a number of approaches to achieving competitive advantage which have been used, or could be used, in tourism, leisure and hospitality. These include:

- rationalization and cost reduction measures;
- innovations in product development;
- product differentiation;
- pricing policies;
- improved distribution systems;
- more effective promotional techniques;
- relaunches and rebranding;
- developing brand loyalty;
- market focus;
- mergers and acquisitions including vertical and horizontal integration;
- strategic alliances;
- franchises;
- marketing consortia;

- diversification into other fields that reinforce the core business;
- selling corporate values to prospective customers as part of the organization's product.

We should, however, recognize that most successful organizations adopt a combination of these measures rather than relying on one approach alone.

We will now consider the approaches listed above, one by one, after which there will be a discussion of the factors that influence the approach an individual organization will choose to take.

Rationalization and cost reduction measures

In some sectors like hospitality, rationalization and cost reduction have always been a popular way of trying to achieve competitive advantage. The aim is to reduce the organization's cost base below that of its competitors, in line with the concept of cost leadership in Porter's model of generic competitive strategies. This usually involves reducing labour costs in particular, as these are a relatively high proportion of the costs of many service industry organizations. This strategy is particularly common in times of economic recession when the lack of consumer spending power is holding down prices or even forcing discounting to take place. With such limited prospects for increasing income, reducing costs may be the only real option for managers.

However, rationalization and cost reduction may also be used in anticipation of the arrival of a new competitor in the market. For example, the cross-Channel ferry companies operating between France, Belgium, Holland and the UK undertook such action in anticipation of the opening of the Channel Tunnel.

There is always a danger with such an approach, though, that cost reductions may lead to poorer standards of service which will cause competitive disadvantage in the longer term.

Innovations in product development

Many tourism, leisure and hospitality organizations have sought to 'leap-frog' over their competitors through innovative product development, by introducing new concepts and types of products. Examples of this in the last fifty years include the Club Med all-inclusive formula resorts, Center Parcs, the Disney theme parks and Concorde. However, such strategies are risky and expensive in terms of capital investment. Furthermore, if successful, this will spawn imitations so that the organization will need to be constantly seeking new ways of keeping ahead of its competitors. Thus, while Club Med now faces competition from a number of all-inclusive resorts, Concorde does not, largely because it has not been commercially successful.

Product differentiation

Rather than one-off innovations in product development, most product-related competitive advantage strategies in tourism, leisure and hospitality are concerned with differentiating the product of the organization from that of its competitors. The following examples serve to illustrate this point:

- the services offered to business class passengers on airlines including check-in facilities, exclusive lounges, in-flight catering and seat pitch;
- the range of destinations offered by tour operators and the departure airports which they can offer their clients;
- hotel chains competing in terms of hotel location and services such as leisure facilities, in-room computer link-ups for business clients and the number of people the room can accommodate for the family market;
- the desire of many theme parks to have the latest, most attractive 'white-knuckle' ride;
- tourist destinations that seek to develop reputations based on particular specialist aspects of their product such as Scheveningen in the Netherlands, with its casino, and those which have developed their sport facilities like Sheffield, in the UK;
- the different programmes of dramas and musical events offered by theatres.

Clearly, therefore, Porter's second generic competitive advantage strategy, product differentiation, is well represented in tourism, leisure and hospitality.

However, in some sectors differentiation is not a matter of strategy but is simply inevitable. For example, it is obvious that a museum telling the story of the history of Avignon will be a different product to those performing similar roles in Amsterdam, Athens, Augsburg or Assisi.

Pricing policies

Pricing is used as a competitive advantage tool in tourism, leisure and hospitality in a number of ways, as follows:

- low introductory prices for a new product entering a competitive market;
- low prices in general for organizations seeking to attract consumers for whom economy is a key benefit sought from any purchase;
- last-minute discounting to generate some income at least in the case of perishable products;
- discounting to attract particular market segments such as groups at visitor attractions and major corporate clients for airlines;
- premium pricing to differentiate the product on the grounds of exclusivity and status value.

Improved distribution systems

Tourism, leisure and hospitality organizations are constantly trying to improve the effectiveness of how they distribute their product to their potential consumers. This can include the following:

- looking to use new technology to allow the organization to communicate directly with customers rather than through marketing intermediaries. A well-established example of this is the Minitel system in France, but innovations such as multi-media and cable television are increasing the opportunities for such distribution;
- developing ever more sophisticated computer reservations systems (CRS) and global distribution systems (GDS), such as SABRE AMADEUS and GALILEO;
- offering more incentives for intermediaries to encourage them to sell more of the organization's product.

Even some intermediaries are attempting to improve the ways in which they distribute their service to their customers, for example the Thomas Cook Group's experiment in the UK with their multi-media kiosks.

More effective promotional techniques

Many tourism, leisure and hospitality organizations spend considerable sums of money on promotion and it is natural, therefore, that efforts should be made to achieve competitive advantage through making promotional activities more effective. Such efforts include:

- the use of video and multi-media to portray product images to prospective customers;
- more eye-catching, imaginative advertisements;
- joint 'piggyback' promotions with non-tourism, leisure and hospitality organizations which sell to similar target markets such as the promotions between British Airways and the UK food retailer Sainsbury's, and between Air France and Martells Cognac in the early 1990s.

Nevertheless, in spite of this it is noticeable that in areas like promotional literature there is often relatively little differentiation in style and format between most tour operator brochures across Europe, for instance.

Relaunches and rebranding

Relaunches are a well-established way of trying to gain or regain competitive advantage in tourism, leisure and hospitality. In the UK the old Butlins holiday camps have been relaunched as sophisticated modern 'Holiday World's'. On a grander scale, some seaside resorts have relaunched themselves, for example Scheveningen in the Netherlands, Majorca and Benidorm in Spain, and Torbay in the UK under the banner of the 'English Riviera'.

Rebranding has been also used by some organizations to respond to changes in consumer preferences. Hence, the Forte rebranding exercise of the early 1990s.

Relaunches and rebranding can help to reinvigorate an older organization or product range but they do not guarantee success.

Developing brand loyalty

At a time of great competition most organizations want to encourage brand loyalty for it is easier to keep customers than to try to win new ones. We have seen this particularly in the scheduled airline sector with its frequent flyer programmes such as the 'Frequence Plus' scheme of Air France and KLM's 'Flying Dutchman' programme. On a more modest scale, visitor attractions such as museums and theatres may also offer season tickets for the same reason.

Market focus

The third of Porter's generic strategies, market focus, has been used successfully by some tourism, leisure and hospitality organizations to achieve competitive advantage. In the UK, for example, the market has been segmented on demographic lines for this purpose with Saga focusing on older, retired customers, and Club 18–30, concentrating on younger customers in their late teens and twenties. Marketing in tourism, leisure and hospitality has often focused on demographic factors as we can see from destinations which advertise themselves as family resorts and those which concentrate on couples as their main market. Those organizations seeking to adopt a market focus in the future may perhaps target those who are particularly health-conscious, for instance, or may aim to attract those who are particularly interested in new technologies such as virtual reality.

However, many tourism, leisure and hospitality organizations will probably prefer to continue to hedge their bets by targeting several markets rather than focusing on one. Thus theme parks such as Alton Towers in the UK may seek to attract young adults, families, school groups and parties of older people by offering a varied product that appeals to all of these markets in different ways.

Mergers and acquisitions

Mergers and acquisitions have long been used, predominantly in the private sector, to develop competitive advantage within tourism, leisure and hospitality. This process often involves both vertical and horizontal integration. For example, the UK tour operator Thomson has grown by taking over other tour operators such as Horizon and Blakes Country Cottages, as well as buying up or creating suppliers and marketing intermediaries such as Britannia Airways and the Lunn Poly travel agency chain. The French Accor group has also grown through mergers and acquisition, even outside its core business of hospitality. Its purchase of the Wagon-Lits group also gave it a chain of travel agency outlets. However, mergers and acquisitions can be an expensive form of growth strategy.

Strategic alliances

In some areas of tourism, leisure and hospitality, such as the airline sector, strategic alliances have been more popular than outright mergers and acquisitions. This may be because the capital costs involved in civil aviation are so high so that acquisitions may be too costly at a time when most scheduled airlines in Europe are not making profits. However, it may also reflect state intervention in the market which can make some mergers and acquisitions particularly unacceptable to some governments when they involve foreign companies. Whatever the reason, strategic alliances have been widely used in the airline industry to achieve competitive advantage at relatively little cost. Two examples of such alliances will illustrate this point, as follows:

- Scandinavian Airlines System (SAS) and British Midland in the UK;
- Air UK and KLM Royal Dutch Airlines, and KLM with the American airline Northwest.

Strategic alliances may also exist between sectors such as hotels and airlines, car hire companies and airlines or theme parks and local hotels, to give just three examples.

Finally, it is interesting to note that strategic alliances in the form of joint ventures have been widely used by Western companies seeking to move into Eastern Europe markets, in the hotel field for instance.

Franchises

Another relatively inexpensive and low-risk way in which some tourism, leisure and hospitality organizations have sought to increase their power in the marketplace has been through franchising. The franchisor provides the franchisee with the right to use the franchisor's brand, together with a range of other support which might include assistance towards capital costs, marketing advice, purchasing services and so on.

However, the franchisor will also set a specification of minimum standards with which the franchisee must comply, together with standard operating procedures to ensure conformity with the overall brand. In this way, the franchise organization can grow the brand at minimal cost and risk to itself. Most of the risk and cost is shouldered by the franchisee.

Franchises have been used extensively in hospitality, for example in the case of Domino Pizza, Holiday Inn and the Campanile chain. They are also being used widely now by McDonald's. In addition, franchises can be found in the leisure sector in relation to sports facilities, for example. However, they have also now appeared in the transport sector too. For instance, there is British Airways Express in the UK, where British Airways has franchised certain independent carriers to operate in its livery and provide services under the British Airways Express brand. These carriers currently include Maersk Air (UK), GB Airways, Manx Airlines (Europe) Ltd and Loganair Ltd.

In an era of competition and economic uncertainty, franchises can be a very attractive way of attempting to gain competitive advantage. However, franchisors have to be careful to ensure that franchises maintain their own standards, otherwise the overall reputation of the brand may suffer.

Marketing consortia

Marketing consortia have been developed widely within tourism, leisure and hospitality, most commonly in the public and voluntary sectors. However, there are a number of well known consortia in the private sector too. In most consortia partners come together to undertake joint marketing activities which they could not afford to carry out on their own. Usually the partners will share a theme. In the UK, for example, there is a consortium of major stately homes which operate under the name the 'Treasure Houses of England'. France has a number of such consortia, many of which bring together different towns and cities as partners. For example, there is an association of Roman towns and cities which produce joint brochures on the Roman monuments of the respective partners.

Marketing consortia in the private sector are found most commonly in the hospitality sector. A good example in Europe is the Minotel group which brings together small privately owned hotels across Europe. Then there is Best Western which is also a consortium. The private sector consortia tend to be more sophisticated with central reservation systems, for example.

However, whichever sector they exist in, consortia have the same basic concept, namely to give individual organizations power in the marketplace they could not otherwise have though cooperation with other organizations in a similar field.

Diversification into other fields

Some tourism, leisure and hospitality organizations have sought competitive advantage, partly through diversification into other fields of activity which, nevertheless, reinforce their core business. An excellent example of this is the Georges Duboeuf organization in France. A renowned wine producer, the organization has opened a state-of-the-art visitor attraction devoted to telling the story of Beaujolais wine at its headquarters in Romaneche-Thorins.

The attraction also serves to remind visitors of the Georges Duboeuf brand and there is a shop where the customer may purchase the products of the organization. Such 'industrial tourism' is a major growth area in Europe in the 1990s.

Selling corporate values

In other industries, we have seen a trend towards some organizations attempting to sell their corporate ethical values as part of their product. Some of these have been very successful, such as the UK organization the Body Shop with its policy of not testing its products on animals and its involvement in aid projects in developing countries. Such organizations make customers feel good about buying their product because of the moral approach to business.

As yet, we have seen few such examples in tourism, leisure and hospitality. Perhaps such examples will develop in the future if consumer interest in ethical business and environmental issues grows in relation to tourism, leisure and hospitality. Perhaps we are already seeing the start of this trend with the rise of small tour operators which claim to offer environmentally friendly holidays, particularly in the Netherlands, and likewise with the action on environmental issues of major companies such as TUI in Germany and its partly-owned partner company Grecotel in Greece.

FACTORS INFLUENCING THE CHOICE OF COMPETITIVE ADVANTAGE STRATEGIES

Having now considered the main ways in which organizations in tourism, leisure and hospitality may seek to gain competitive advantage, it is an appropriate time to look at how organizations choose which strategy to adopt. As we noted earlier, most organizations utilize several approaches rather than just one.

The factors influencing the approach taken by an individual organization include those internal such as the organization's history, culture and financial resources, together with those external such as consumer behaviour and state intervention in markets. These factors will be different for each organization and represent a mixture of managers' perceptions and reality. Some of the most important are illustrated in Figure 28.1.

DIFFERENCES AND SIMILARITIES WITHIN EUROPE

In many respects there are perhaps greater differences between sectors than between countries in terms of the level of competitiveness in markets and competitive advantage strategies. National differences do, however, exist in relation to levels of competitiveness in particular sectors such as the hotel market. In the UK, there is virtually no regula-

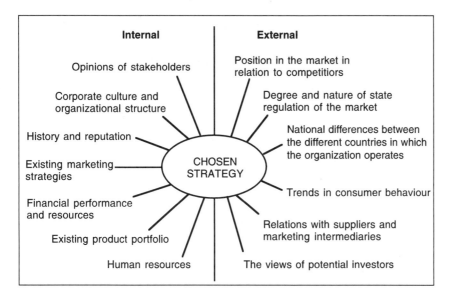

Figure 28.1 Major factors influencing the choice of competitive advantage strategies.

tion of hotel prices, whereas in Greece hotel prices are partly fixed by state intervention. In terms of competitive advantage strategies, some of the more modern approaches such as franchising, marketing consortia and strategic alliances are found more commonly in certain countries such as the UK and France.

Finally, organizations wishing to expand into certain countries within Europe may be forced to adopt particular approaches simply because national laws and government policy make other approaches impractical. For example, some European countries would not allow a foreign organization to wholly take over one of its major national companies, such as an airline or tour operator. Thus strategic alliance or franchising could be the only option for the organization which wished to expand.

CONCLUSIONS

We have seen that the level of competition varies between sectors within tourism, leisure and hospitality, and that there are a range of competitive advantage strategies that organizations may adopt. Presumably, within the European Union at least, EU competition policy will slowly create a 'level playing field' where companies from any member state can compete on equal terms with local companies. This should simplify the issue of choosing competitive advantage strategies for the growing number of European transnational companies in the field. However, that day still seems to be somewhere in the distant future.

DISCUSSION POINTS AND ESSAY QUESTIONS

1. Compare and contrast the nature of competition within tourism, leisure and hospitality.
2. Using examples, discuss the ways in which product differentiation has been used to gain competitive advantage in tourism, leisure and hospitality.
3. Evaluate the role of strategic alliances **or** franchising within tourism, leisure and hospitality in achieving competitive advantage.

EXERCISE Select an organization from **one** of the following sectors:

- scheduled airline;
- tour operation;
- accommodation;
- catering;
- arts;
- visitor attractions.

Evaluate the current marketing situation of your chosen organization.

You should then suggest what you consider to be the three most appropriate methods by which this particular organization might attempt to enhance its competitive market position. You must justify your decision to select these three approaches, rather than any of the others which are outlined in Chapter 28.

Quality 29

Key concepts

The main concepts covered in this chapter are:

- definitions of quality;
- the concept of the 'service gap';
- quality management systems;
- the links between quality and the marketing mix;
- quality and different audiences;
- official quality standards.

INTRODUCTION

Quality is perhaps the most fashionable word of marketing in the 1990s. However, while it is often used, it is rarely defined.

In this chapter we will take a broad view of the concept of quality in tourism, leisure and hospitality. To do this a number of issues will be examined, including:

- what the term quality means in the context of tourism, leisure and hospitality;
- the nature of quality in service industries;
- the different types of quality management systems that exist, including quality control, quality assurance, total quality control and total quality management;
- quality and the marketing mix;
- official measures of quality such as ISO 9000;
- quality and management functions;
- constraints on the operation of quality management systems in tourism, leisure and hospitality.

Furthermore, we will look at the different audiences that organizations must address if they wish to receive general recognition as quality organizations offering quality products. These include internal audiences such as staff and investors and external audiences such as customers, government regulators and the media, together with suppliers and marketing intermediaries.

Towards the end of the chapter, we will briefly attempt to conclude whether or not there are national differences in Europe in terms of the concept of quality.

WHAT DO WE MEAN BY QUALITY?

There is no universally accepted definition of quality, but certain principles do appear to be quite widely agreed upon. One is the idea that quality is about those features and characteristics of a product or service that affect its ability to satisfy the needs and desires of consumers.

Secondly, there is the concept of 'fitness for purpose' whereby quality is judged in terms of the extent to which a product measures up to its expressed purpose, usually defined in terms of a set of consumer needs. Both approaches put the customer at the centre, which fits neatly with the concept of customer-led marketing which is so popular at present.

QUALITY AND SERVICE INDUSTRIES

Most theory and practice in quality management grew out of the experience of manufacturing industries where the emphasis is on product standardization. The usual aim of manufacturing companies is to have every product coming off the production line identical, with no faults. Furthermore, this is an attainable goal, most of the time, providing that the right machinery is purchased, it is well maintained and its operators are correctly trained.

However, in service industries such as tourism, leisure and hospitality, this standardization is generally not attainable, and it may not even be desirable, for three main reasons. Firstly, the main element of the product is the individuals who perform the service and all staff are different. They have different abilities or attitudes and their moods are constantly changing. Secondly, in service industries the production process involves an interaction between consumers and staff, and the consumers are separate individuals with their own specific attitudes and expectations which they contribute to the process. Finally, most customers do not want to feel they are receiving a standardized product, with the possible exception of fast-food outlet customers and hotel chain clients. Most customers want to feel that the product will, at least in part, be tailor-made to meet their own particular needs and desires. This customization of the product is also important as a standardized product does not usually carry the status value that many customers seek from tourism, leisure and hospitality products.

It may also be that standardization is not an attainable aim in some parts of tourism, leisure and hospitality because in these specific parts of our industries, we do not give our customers a finished product. Instead, we give them a set of 'raw materials' and invite them to construct their own final product. For example, it could be argued that a tourist destination simply offers a range of attractions, accommodation, restaurants, bars and transport systems from which tourists can crate their own 'do it yourself' holiday experience which will be unique.

THE 'SERVICE GAP'

Quality management systems in service industries like tourism, leisure and hospitality tend to focus on the intangible service element of the product and the people who deliver it. Quality enhancement is often viewed in terms of reducing the gap between the perception of service quality held by an organization and that held by its customers.

In 1985, Parasuraman, Zeithmal and Berry identified the following five types of potential service gap, with which most tourism, leisure and recreation managers will probably empathize:

- gaps between consumer expectations and management perceptions of consumer expectations;
- gaps between management perceptions of consumer expectations and service quality specifications;
- gaps between service quality specifications and the service which is actually delivered;
- gaps between service delivery and what is communicated about this service to consumers which will shape their expectations;
- gaps between consumer expectations and their perceptions of the actual quality of service rendered.

QUALITY MANAGEMENT SYSTEMS

Most quality management systems originated in manufacturing industry, but they can be applied to some extent in service industries such as tourism, leisure and hospitality. This can be illustrated if we look at the case of a restaurant meal in relation to the four most common types of quality management system, as follows:

- **Quality control**. This is where the production process is monitored so that problems are eradicated before the product is delivered to the customer. This is well suited to manufacturing companies where problems are often easy to identify and there is a relatively long period between production and delivery to the customer. The equivalent in a restaurant meal situation would be an inspection of the dishes before they left the kitchen to be presented to the customer. However, while this does happen in some restaurants, the speed required to serve the dish while it is still at its best makes such careful inspection difficult. Furthermore, just because the dish looks and smells right, it does not follow automatically that it will satisfy the client. They may already have negative views about the restaurant because of its decor or how they were greeted. Or they may not like the chef's selection of vegetables, no matter how well they have been cooked. Even if quality control is possible in the case of our restaurant meal, it does not prevent waste arising in the first place, for if the dish is deemed not satisfactory, it may well be thrown away.

- **Quality assurance**. Here the emphasis is on prevention rather than cure. The aim is to prevent the problem arising in the first place, and rather than making quality the responsibility of one or two 'inspectors' the system places the onus on each member of staff involved to get it right first time. This prevents waste and removes the need for 'inspectors'.

- **Total quality control**. Under this system, a broader view is taken of the production or service delivery process. All possible factors that affect the final product or service are considered. In the case of our restaurant meal, this might include the quality of raw materials being provided by suppliers to the training of the kitchen staff. The aim is to ensure that by looking at these wider issues the quality of the product can be maintained and enhanced, on every occasion.

- **Total quality management (TQM)**. This is undoubtedly the most fashionable quality management system at present. It is predicated on the idea that quality must permeate the whole culture of an organization and involve every employee. It argues that organizations need to strive to make continuous improvements in quality.

    In other words, this approach acknowledges that quality is not an absolute standard which can ever be attained. Instead it is a continuous journey to an ever changing destination. In terms of our restaurant meal, therefore, a 'TQM' approach would involve looking constantly at how the meal might be improved in terms of its content, presentation, delivery and price, for example.

Benchmarking

Benchmarking is a quality management technique which is growing in popularity. It means 'measuring the performance of your business against the performance of other businesses in your own industry, or even in other industries' (Department of National Heritage, 1996). This helps organizations identify, and then seek to evaluate, best practice in a given sector of industry. This can lead to a greater efficiency, reduced costs, improvement in profitability and increased customer satisfaction.

The technique of benchmarking is already becoming widely used in the hotel industry. In March 1996, the Department of National Heritage published the results of a benchmarking exercise covering the performance of 70 independent hotels, guest houses and bed and breakfast establishments in England. The project involved the accommodation businesses being assessed by consultants relative to 30 different criteria, including among others:

- the answering of telephone enquiries;
- the handling of complaints;
- check-out procedures;
- breakfast service;
- the quality of public areas;
- frequency of checks on cleanliness and maintenance of bedrooms and bathrooms;
- training;
- business planning;
- marketing.

Composite scores were then established for each hotel to help owners see how their business compared to the industry norm, and also to identify areas where improvement were required.

Finally, a simple guide was published to help all accommodation operators to self assess their businesses.

THE MARKETING MIX AND QUALITY

We will now consider the implications of the concept of quality for the four elements of the 'marketing mix' which marketers in tourism, leisure and hospitality manipulate to achieve their objectives. We will begin with the product.

The **product** is crucial in that it is what the customer purchases in order to satisfy their needs and wants. A quality product is one which satisfactorily performs the task for which it was purchased and bestows the expected benefits on the purchaser. There are a number of ways in which quality and the product are linked in tourism, leisure and hospitality, as follows:

- There is what we might term the quality of the designed characteristics of the product, in other words those physical attributes of the product that have been deliberately designed. These might include the location and the leisure facilities of a hotel and the comfort and pitch of the seating in the business-class cabin of an airliner.
- There is the service element, including the service the customer receives and the attitudes and competence of the people who deliver this service.
- The reliability, or lack of it, of the product is also important. How often does the product promised to the consumer by the organization fail to materialize?. For example, it is not satisfactory to promise that a room rate includes a free morning newspaper each day if the person responsible forgets to deliver it to the room.

- The issue of what happens when things go wrong, and the systems which have been put in place to correct errors, also has an impact. For instance, if a guest complains that they have no clean towels in their room when they first arrive, how long will the guest have to wait before fresh towels are provided?
- Finally, there is the image and reputation of the product in the outside world at large. This is often an important factor in the decision-making process for first-time purchasers who have no previous personal experience of the product. It is also the basis on which some organizations are able to charge premium prices for their product. This image and reputation may derive from a variety of sources including popular culture and the media, together with the views of previous customers.

There is always a rapport between quality and **price**, for quality is not an absolute. We tend to buy the level of quality we can afford so that there is a trade-off between price and quality. However, contrary to some views which seem to equate quality with expensive, quality exists at all price levels although its precise nature will vary at these different price levels. Ultimately it is quality if it meets the desires and needs of the customer.

A good example of this argument occurs in the accommodation sector. Many overseas visitors are as thoroughly satisfied when they stay in private homes offering 'bed and breakfast' accommodation for, say, £20 per person per night as other people are when staying in a prestigious £200 a night hotel in central London. The different prices will lead the customer to expect different benefits from purchasing each product but they will probably both see each as a quality product if it meets their individual needs and expectations.

However, it is also important to note that the relationship between quality and price in tourism, leisure and hospitality can be complicated in the following ways:

- No charge is made, directly, to those who use some products such as some local authority museums and most tourist destinations.
- Some prices charged are not true market prices and reflect a level of public sector subsidy, for instance many opera performances.
- For many customers it is not the price that matters but rather whether they feel they have received 'value for money'. Thus, many of the most expensive visitor attractions in Europe also have the highest visitor numbers.

Quality is also an issue in the **place** or distribution element of the marketing mix, as follows:

- the ease with which potential consumers are able to purchase the product, through theatre ticket agencies and travel agencies;
- the quality of service offered by the operators who distribute the organization's product and their reliability;
- the accuracy of messages given by these agents to potential customers about the organization's product. Inaccurate messages may, in

the short term, increase sales but in the longer term they may well lead to customer dissatisfaction and a lack of repeat purchases.

Many tourism, leisure and hospitality organizations are seeking to develop tighter relationships with their distributors, partly because they are aware of these issues. However, these moves are also often a result of government legislation regarding product liability under which producers are held liable, increasingly, for the actions of their intermediaries.

There is, finally, clearly a quality dimension to the issue of **promotional** techniques, most notably brochures and advertisements but also face-to-face selling. Quality in promotional activities in our three industries has often been seen in terms of the glossiness of brochures and the ability of advertising campaigns and selling to persuade people to buy a product.

However, this is an industry view of quality in promotion. Consumers may see quality in a different way in relation to the promotional activities of organizations, namely the degree of honesty in brochures and advertisements such with regard to claims made about the quality of beaches in resort brochures, the noise levels in hotels and the walking times from accommodation to beaches in tour operators' brochures. To some extent the lack of self-regulation on the part of industry has led, at least in the tour operation field, to EU legislation to enforce such standards of honesty on the industry, hence the 1990 European Union Directive on Package Travel, Package Holidays and Package Tours.

Quality may also be seen in the advice provided to customers to help them enjoy the organization's product safely. This might include, for example:

- advice on areas of cities which should be avoided because of crime levels;
- information about potentially hazardous activities such as scuba-diving, and how those trying these activities for the first time can do so safely;
- advice about how to avoid skin cancer;
- suggesting people should not hire mopeds or ride horses if no safety helmets are provided.

However, such advice could obviously dissuade some customers from purchasing the organization's product, particularly in the tour operation sector. It is unlikely, therefore, that any organization would undertake such an approach alone. Instead it would probably only do so if competitors agreed to do likewise or there were government legislation.

On the other hand, it could also be argued that customers may well reward an organization that took the lead in being totally honest with its customers.

QUALITY AND MANAGEMENT FUNCTIONS

So far in this chapter we have focused on marketing and quality. How-ever, other management functions are crucial to quality within tourism, leisure and hospitality, namely financial management, human resource management and operations management. All three of these functions impinge directly on the quality of the consumer's experience and their ultimate satisfaction with the organization's product. We will therefore now consider each of these three other management functions in a little more detail.

In industries like tourism and hospitality where profit margins can be very low and the effects of recession severe, cost-cutting is a normal **financial management** response to an unfavourable financial climate or greater competition. Tour operators contract cheaper hotel rooms and airline seats and hotels reduce staffing levels, for example. However, in relation to quality, such cost-cutting may be necessary in the short term, but we must recognize that it directly affects the quality of the product and the consumer's satisfaction. For instance, cost-cutting in a hotel restaurant might mean fewer staff so customers wait longer for their meal or cheaper (poorer) ingredients.

Pruning spending may also lead to the postponing of routine main-tenance and decoration at hotels and leisure centres, for example. Again this leads to a deterioration in the physical appearance of the premises and further reduces the quality of the customer's experi-ence.

It is obvious that as people deliver the service which is the core of the product in our three sectors, **human resource management** has a crucial role to play in quality management within tourism, leisure and hospitality. Some organizations have built their whole reputation on the quality of their staff, notably the Disney organization in relation to its theme parks.

However, if human resource management is to make a full contribu-tion to quality in an organization, it has to be comprehensive in its approach. This includes:

- having recruitment procedures that ensure that the right people are recruited in the first place;
- providing adequate training;
- rewarding good performance in both financial and non-financial ways.

While few managers would argue with this approach, it is often diffi-cult to implement in industries which have a relatively high proportion of casual and seasonal staff.

Finally, **operations management** too has a vital role to play in achiev-ing and enhancing quality. It is concerned with how the customer experience is managed on a day-to-day basis. Its contribution to qual-ity covers a number of areas, including:

- ensuring that the organization's products are 'user friendly' for all groups of customers, whether they be disabled people, families with children or customers who speak a different language;
- keeping customers as safe and secure as possible from potential threats ranging from fire to food poisoning;
- operating an effective complaints procedure so that complaints are quickly resolved. On occasions, it could be argued that a well handled complaint might enhance an organization's reputation more than would have been the case if all had gone well in the first place, when the consumer might have taken the service for granted!

It is clear therefore that quality is a team game and the responsibility of all management functions within an organization.

QUALITY AND DIFFERENT AUDIENCES

Clearly the most important audience an organization needs to address in terms of the quality of what it sells is the customer. However, there are many other audiences which have an interest in the concept of quality in relation to any organization and its products. Each of these audiences will have their own particular interest in quality and will have different criteria for evaluating quality.

These criteria can be at odds with each other. If we look at a hypothetical example, a theme park, we can see how many different audiences there might be and what their likely definition will be of what constitutes quality at a theme park.

- Customers will see a quality theme park as one which is user friendly and offers the most enjoyment for the least cost. However, customers are not a homogeneous category for there are ex-customers, non-users, first-time users and regular customers.
- Theme park managers, on the other hand, view quality in terms of the smooth operation of the theme park together with its visitor numbers and financial performance.
- For the staff a quality theme park is one which provides good working conditions and where there are not too many customer complaints to handle.
- Investors and shareholders evaluate quality with how good a rate of return on investment the theme park earns for them.
- Suppliers might see quality in terms of a theme park that pays its bills promptly.
- For marketing intermediaries such as coach tour operators and tourist information centres, a quality theme park is likely to be seen as one which offers generous group discounts to the operator, and keeps the centre regularly supplied with brochures, respectively.
- Government regulators will judge quality in terms of the safety consciousness of the operator, for example.

In many sectors within tourism, leisure and hospitality, a major audience which needs to be convinced about the quality of an organization's products is the media. Guidebooks, television programmes and journals aimed at providing information and advice for tourism, leisure and hospitality customers have grown rapidly across Europe in recent years. Managers, therefore, have to be aware of the need to impress this audience.

One sector for whom the media is a particularly important audience is the hospitality business. There are a plethora of guidebooks which evaluate the quality of hotels and restaurants, most notably in Europe the '*Michelin Red Guide*'. Inclusion in, or exclusion from, one of these guides sends influential messages to potential customers.

OFFICIAL QUALITY STANDARDS

Public sector bodies play an important role in quality within tourism, leisure and hospitality in a number of ways. These bodies may be local authorities, national governments and the European Commission, or international bodies such as the International Air Transport Organization (IATO). The various official standards of quality in tourism, leisure, and hospitality, include the following:

- national government official classifications of hotel standards such as the 'star' system in France and the 'Crown' scheme in England;
- the licensing of premises such as restaurants to indicate that they meet certain health standards;
- the licensing of tour operators which often is in recognition of the fact that they have adequate financial resources;
- the licensing of tourist guides where knowledge is thought to qualify them to act as guides.

As one can see these different standards of quality all have different purposes and use different criteria. They can therefore be very confusing, particularly for the customer.

Furthermore, some are highly subjective, particularly hotel classification systems. Not only are the symbols different in the various European countries (stars, crowns, letters of the alphabet) but so too are the criteria on the basis of which they are awarded. These criteria might include:

- price;
- facilities in the hotel and/or individual rooms;
- location;
- services available and when they are available;
- size of the establishment.

This, again, is clearly very confusing for customers, hence the intention of the European Commission to harmonize these systems and produce a single European hotel classification system.

Public bodies may also try to improve quality through the use of voluntary codes of practice which they try to encourage organizations to follow. For example, in the UK, the government's domestic tourism agency, the English Tourist Board, has introduced a voluntary code of practice for quality management at visitor attractions.

In addition to these official standards which are specific to our three areas, there are also official measures of quality itself which are applicable across all industries, including tourism, leisure and hospitality. The most obvious example of this is ISO 9000 (BS 5750 in the UK), the internationally recognized standard of quality. It is a documentation driven system that has given rise to the criticism that it is more concerned with production processes than consumer satisfaction. There is also a worry that it might become a 'lowest common denominator' to which all organizations can aspire rather than a recognition of outstanding quality which only a few organizations will be able to attain at any one time.

Finally, if governments or supra-governmental bodies feel there are quality problems in particular industries they may seek to introduce legislation to raise standards by regulation. For example, the honesty of tour operators advertising in brochures has been increased by the European Commission's Package Travel Directive. At a national level, the UK government introduced the Food Safety Act 1991 to improve the standard of food production, handling and service in the UK.

CONSTRAINTS ON QUALITY MANAGEMENT

There are a number of constraints which affect the ability of tourism, leisure and hospitality managers to develop totally effective quality management systems, as follows:

- There are those factors which, while contributing to the quality of the consumer's experience, are largely outside the control of the organization. Such factors might include the following:
  - the weather which can delay flights and ruin holidays where it rains and sunbathing is the main aim of the customer, or where skiing is the purpose of the holiday and there is no snow;
  - the attitudes and expectations of the customers themselves. They may arrive with negative feelings because of dissatisfaction with their everyday life or their expectations may be unrealistic. A couple may, for example, take a weekend break holiday in Paris thinking it will bring romance back into their failing marriage;
  - industrial action which can ruin a holiday or business trip such as the Greek ferry strikes of 1995 or the almost annual industrial action of air traffic controllers somewhere in Europe!
- The limited financial resources which organizations have to fund product improvements is a particularly limiting factor where the capital cost of product improvements may be very high, such as in

the hotel and airline sectors, or where the organization is a local authority whose expenditure is controlled by central government.

- There is also the customer's willingness, or lack of willingness, to pay for quality. The level of quality an organization provides must be in equilibrium with the price its customers wish to pay for the product. A guest may dream of a centrally located plush hotel with porters to carry their luggage, 24-hour room service and expensive complementary items which guests may take away such as bath robes. However, the same individual may only be able to afford a budget, out-of-town motel-style hotel with neither porter or room service and no complementary gifts.

- Some organizations can be constrained when they seek to be seen as providers of a quality product if their history and existing culture has given them the opposite reputation.

- The lack of agreement on what quality achievement is and its purely subjective nature in tourism, leisure and hospitality makes it very difficult to develop effective, simple performance indicators for quality in our industries.

- The concept of quality is always changing and today's effective quality management system will become tomorrow's obsolete system.

DIFFERENCES AND SIMILARITIES WITHIN EUROPE

Quality as an explicit, defined subject within management is not an equally developed concept across Europe. However, it is rapidly becoming so. Yet, the idea of quality is well understood in the tourism, leisure and hospitality industries across Europe both by consumers and professionals. The quality of French and Italian restaurants, Greek beaches, and Irish hospitality are well known throughout Europe, while Eastern European professionals readily recognize the need to improve service quality in their countries.

The concept of quality probably does vary from country to country. For example, healthy food in the UK may be seen as diet and low fat processed foods, while in Mediterranean countries it may be equated with fresh produce rather than processed food. However, attitudes towards what constitutes quality in tourism, leisure and hospitality, are probably quite similar for certain segments which are pan-European such as international business travellers.

There can, however, be an element of patriotism involved, which can lead to large proportions of a population taking a similar view of quality in relation to the products of their own country, most notably food, but also cultural events for instance.

CONCLUSIONS

Quality is clearly an important issue for all tourism, leisure and hospitality organizations but it is a highly subjective concept. It could be said that quality is in the eye of the beholder and every beholder sees it differently. Furthermore, the concept of quality is constantly changing and evolving. The 'benchmark' of what constitutes quality has to be continuously moved in response to changes in consumer expectations and the ability of organizations to improve their product.

However, there is a danger that the current obsession with quality may debase the whole idea, particularly if quality becomes seen as a focus for marketing hype rather than reality.

DISCUSSION POINTS AND ESSAY QUESTIONS

1. Define what is meant by the term 'quality' and examine its application to service industries.
2. Identify the four main quality management systems and discuss their application to a tourism, leisure or hospitality product of your choice.
3. Evaluate the relationship between quality and price using examples.
4. Discuss the different 'audiences' that exist in relation to quality and consider how their ideas of quality may differ.

Choose a tourism, leisure and hospitality organization which you consider to be of particularly high quality and whose product you have never used. Identify the reasons why you hold this view of the organization. For example: **EXERCISE**

- Is it because of the experience of your friends and relatives, or have your views been influenced by the media or by the promotional activities of the organization itself?
- Is the quality reputation of the organization a result of the nature of its product, its pricing policies, its marketing methods, its culture and history or the quality of its suppliers?

The next stage is to find several people who have used the products of the organization and ask them if they view the organization as high quality or not, based on their experience of its products.

You should then contact people within the organization, namely its managers and staff. Ask them if they think the organization is high quality and, if they do, ask them on what basis they hold this view.

You should then endeavour to identify the differences and similarities in your view, that of customers and that of people within the organization.

30 Green issues

Key concepts

The main concepts covered in this chapter are:

- definitions of green issues;
- the concept of 'shades of green' in relation to consumer attitudes;
- different motivations for introducing greening activities;
- greening and sustainability;
- the idea of demarketing;
- greening as a competitive advantage tool.

INTRODUCTION

We are increasingly being told that organizations must modify their activities and products to reflect the growth of the 'green consumer' and governmental interest in green issues. However, much of what has been written on this subject appears vague and lacking in depth and detail.

In this chapter we will look at the current situation and future likely relevance of green issues in tourism, leisure and hospitality. To achieve this ambitious aim, we will consider the following issues:

- what is meant by the term 'green issues' and the link between green issues, environmental concerns and sustainability;
- the idea of the 'green consumer' and the notion that there is not a green consumer, but rather that consumers come in different 'shades of green';
- the motivations for organizations which seek to become greener;
- the greening of tourism, leisure and hospitality in terms of the product, the way in which the product is marketed, operations management, human resource management and financial management;
- greening as a source of competitive advantage;
- sustainability and the concepts of visitor management and demarketing in tourism;
- tourism as a positive force for conservation and rural development.

We will conclude by looking at national differences and similarities within Europe in relation to green issues.

WHAT DO WE MEAN BY GREEN ISSUES?

Green issues and 'greening' have become buzz words in the 1980s and 1990s, in Western Europe at least. Yet there is no generally accepted agreement on what constitutes a 'green issue'. It is merely an umbrella term which can be used to cover a myriad of different ideas and subjects. Each individual tends to see green issues from a different perspective depending on their attitudes and interests.

Green issues may, therefore, include the following:

- resource concerns such as the need to conserve water and energy and recycle what would otherwise be waste;
- an interest in the physical environment in terms of its aesthetic appearance and how it might be affected by pollution, for example;
- issues associated with healthy lifestyles including organically produced food and the question of additives in food;
- animal welfare including the testing of cosmetics on animals and the rise of vegetarianism.

Green is also a political philosophy, and the word is in the title of some political parties, most notably in Germany, but also in France and the UK.

In general, green tends to equate with the physical environment and with current, immediate issues. The hospitality industry has focused strongly on green issues and it still uses the term widely. This emphasis on the physical environment is also found in the tourism industries of many countries in Southern Europe.

However, in the tourism field, the concern is not so much with green issues, but with the wider challenge of **sustainability** in line with the Brundtland Report of 1987. Sustainability is about meeting the needs of the current generation without destroying the resources which will allow future generations to meet their needs. Sustainability is not just concerned with the physical environment, but rather with the relationship between the environment, society and economic systems.

Thus sustainable tourism means tourism which is economically viable, but which minimizes change to the physical environment and is as beneficial for both host community and tourist as possible.

THE 'GREEN CONSUMER' – MYTH OR REALITY?

Much of the stimulus for the growing interest of industries in 'greening' or sustainability has come from the idea that there is now a 'green consumer' who wants to buy products which are not environmentally harmful or socially irresponsible. For marketers, such customers, depending on the approach adopted by the organization, could be viewed as either a threat or an opportunity.

However, the idea of a homogeneous green consumer is a myth and is far too simplistic. The reality is there are **shades of green** in consumer attitudes. At one extreme, there are 'dark green' consumers for whom environmental issues or sustainability concerns are a major day-to-day element of their lifestyles, and are a great influence in their purchasing decisions. They are concerned with all or most such issues and are willing to make sacrifices, such as boycotting products or paying higher prices, in support of their beliefs.

Conversely, there are 'light green' consumers for whom such issues are only a minor concern. They will probably only be interested in a few issues and will not be willing to make more than the occasional minor sacrifice in pursuit of their beliefs.

Clearly, there are many shades of green between these two points, and there are also consumers who appear to have no interest whatsoever in such issues. These different shades of opinion tend to indicate that there is no single green consumer market segment, but rather a number of different segments based on different levels of concern and interest in different types of issues. Any tourism, leisure and hospitality organization seeking to achieve competitive advantage through 'greening' needs to be clear, therefore, about which segment or segments it is targeting.

Overall, it has to be said that in tourism, leisure and hospitality generally, there seems to have been relatively little consumer pressure on organizations to behave in a greener or more sustainable manner. Hotel chains appear to receive few complaints from their customers specifically about their impact on the environment. Likewise, few airlines passengers seem to worry about the effects of air transport. Perhaps the only area where consumer pressure has grown is in relation to tourist destinations where some tourists have been put off visiting places because of their poor environmental quality. However, here the tourist concern is not with green issues in general but rather with the quality of their own holiday experience. There is evidence that there is growing concern amongst consumers about these issues in Northern Europe.

MAKING TOURISM, LEISURE AND HOSPITALITY GREEN AND SUSTAINABLE

Motivations for taking action

There are a number of reasons why tourism, leisure and hospitality organizations might take action on the issues raised in this chapter, including the following:

- the need to comply with legislation such as that relating to aircraft noise and emissions which applies to airlines;

- the desire to undertake action voluntarily so that governments will not introduce legislation requiring even more drastic action;
- the selective introduction of those measures which will also bring benefits in terms of cost savings;
- responding to customer complaints;
- a belief that such action will improve the organization's image in the eyes of potential customers, peer groups, investors, government regulators and the media;
- the idea that being seen to be 'green' or 'environmentally friendly' or 'sustainable' might be a source of competitive advantage because it will attract new, perhaps higher spending customers;
- having to take action as a condition of contract imposed by companies to whom the organization sells its products. This could, for example, mean hotels having to introduce measures to make their operations more environmentally friendly as a condition of any contract entered into with a particular tour operator;
- occasionally the motivation can be linked to the personal beliefs of the owner or senior manager that such action is morally right and should be undertaken even if it may not bring immediate benefits for the business;
- responding to measures introduced by competitors;
- wishing to be seen to be part of initiatives undertaken by professional bodies and industry groups such as the International Hotels Environmental Initiative.

Actions being taken

We will now examine what action is being taken, and might be taken, to make tourism, leisure and hospitality greener and more sustainable. As this is such a broad subject, we will focus on two sectors only, namely hotels and tourist destinations. In the former we will see that most attention has, to date, focused on so-called green issues rather than sustainability. However, we will then look at the potential for taking a broader view and making hotels more sustainable.

As far as tourist destinations are concerned we will look at two issues:

- the potential role of demarketing on those historic cities and coastal resorts where there are problems in the relationship between tourists and the destination resource;
- the contribution which tourism marketing might make towards the development of sustainable rural areas in Europe.

While not a comprehensive approach the authors believe that this method will illustrate the main issues faced by organizations throughout tourism, leisure and hospitality. The method also neatly highlights the difference between those areas of the three industries where the emphasis is on greening and the physical environment, and those where the emphasis is on sustainability.

GREENING HOTELS AND MAKING THEM MORE SUSTAINABLE

In recent years a number of international hotel chains have developed a reputation for the action they have taken on environmental issues, most notably Inter-Continental and Canadian Pacific. This in turn has led to the International Hotels Environmental Initiative and a movement of good environmental practices for hotels. Most action has been in relation to the operations management side of existing units. However, we will begin by looking at the opportunities for greening the development of new units. Some of the ideas are drawn from the approach to the development of new complexes adopted by Center Parcs in the UK.

The development of new accommodation units can be made greener, if not totally green, in a number of ways, including:

- using local, traditional building materials and architectural styles;
- protecting wildlife habitats or developing new ones if the building of the unit damages the existing habitats;
- sensitive design that reflects the contours and relief of the land rather than ignoring it;
- ensuring that the size of the unit is appropriate for the location although economic considerations may make this impractical;
- being careful not to adversely affect water supplies by diverting natural sources to the hotel.

Once the unit is built an environmental audit can be carried out and a number of measures taken to 'green' the operation, including:

- developing recycling systems for materials such as packaging, paper, bottles and organic waste;
- using recycled supplies wherever possible like stationery and toilet paper;
- installing water-saving devices in showers and toilets;
- only using low energy light bulbs;
- energy conservation measures including insulation;
- using unbleached and undyed fabrics;
- developing solar powered water heating systems.

It is noticeable that for many of these measures there is a clear cost reduction benefit for organizations. This is perhaps the main motivating force behind the decision to undertake such actions.

However, in addition to these actions, which are in many ways reactive, defensive and operations-related, there are opportunities for hotels to undertake measures which are proactive, positive and marketing-driven. In other words, 'green' products can be developed to appeal to consumers with an interest in environmental issues. These might include:

- offering 'green rooms' in hotels where particular care has been taken to ensure that the room is environmentally friendly in every way;
- providing organically grown food in restaurants;
- developing weekend break packages based on green themes such as environmental awareness and holidays where guests might work on local conservation projects.

Marketing activities themselves may also contribute towards greening, through the reduced use of company cars by sales people and providing advice for guests on environmental issues in hotel brochures, for instance.

It is important to recognize that if hotels are going to be made more sustainable they must think wider than just green or environmental issues. They must also take into account people, whether they be the local community or the hotel's own staff. In the former case this could mean trying to reduce noise disturbance for the hotel's neighbours through measures such as using trees and fences as noise barriers, and siting car parks away from residential areas. This might be seen as good neighbourliness, bringing real commercial benefits, and if the hotel intends to expand at some stage, such an approach could minimize local opposition.

If a hotel is to become greener it needs the support of its staff who must be trained and empowered to take action. However, if we consider the broader issue of sustainability, there is another human resource dimension. A sustainable hotel is one which can recruit and retain good staff which means good working conditions and pay and following equal opportunities policies. It should also seek to support the local community through the recruitment of local staff. The emphasis upon community links also implies purchasing materials that are required from local suppliers.

Finally there is little evidence in the hotel sector of 'greening' being used to attempt to gain competitive advantage. Indeed, the pioneers like Inter-Continental and Canadian Pacific chose instead to share their approach with fellow hoteliers and through professional bodies. This raises interesting questions as to why such companies chose to take action on these issues in the first place.

DEMARKETING AND SUSTAINABLE TOURISM

Where tourist numbers are considered to be too great and/or tourist behaviour is perceived to be harmful, the traditional approach has been to introduce visitor management, in other words, rather than trying to reduce overall numbers, trying to manage the behaviour of tourists to minimize their negative impact. Such approaches have particularly been found in historic cities.

However, as marketing has become more sophisticated and highly developed, another approach has grown up – demarketing. This involves using marketing techniques to encourage consumers **not** to buy a particular product. There are, perhaps, three types of demarketing as follows:

- attempting to reduce the number of people using particular places, for instance the historic city of Cambridge in the UK;
- trying to reduce the number of people taking holidays in a place at a particular time of year, like August in the case of France;
- endeavouring to discourage certain types of people from visiting a place, such as young hedonistic so-called 'lager louts' in some Mediterranean resorts.

A number of ways can be used to implement demarketing including:

- not producing any promotional material;
- putting messages in advertisements and brochures that will discourage certain people from visiting the destination or to persuade people in general not to visit at certain times;
- promoting alternative places.

However, demarketing is fraught with potential problems. Changing established patterns of consumer behaviour is difficult and requires large sums of expenditure yet it is often attempted by destination marketing agencies with very limited budgets. Secondly, it assumes we have adequate data so that we can identify problems yet this is often not the case. Thirdly, if demarketing is too successful, tourist numbers may be reduced too much which could harm local businesses.

Finally, in a competitive market like international tourism, demarketing is a high-risk strategy as tourists whom you persuade to go elsewhere at times when you don't want them to visit your destination may discover other destinations which they prefer. They may not then come back when you want them!

TOURISM MARKETING AND SUSTAINABLE RURAL AREAS IN EUROPE

Commentators, such as Swarbrooke (1995), argue that tourism marketing can contribute not only to the development of sustainable tourism, but can also play a vital role in ensuring a sustainable future for rural areas in Europe. He argues that, by exploiting market trends and using marketing techniques, we can perhaps create a type of rural tourism which satisfies the tourist while, at the same time, maximizing the benefits of tourism for the host community and minimizing the negative impacts. Thus, such tourism might be used to help ensure the viability of Europe's rural areas, many of which are currently in a state of crisis.

The trends which might be exploited include the desire for new and exciting experiences, and the desire to feel temporarily part of a new community, to meet real local people and to enjoy the relaxing pleasures of the countryside.

However, for this to be sustainable tourism, it must be locally controlled, based on an authentic product and priced so as to maximize the economic benefits for the host community. Such a product might be termed, 'Discover the **Real** Countryside Holidays' and could include:

- staying with a local family in their home;
- visiting rural workplaces such as farms, craft workshops and forestry operations;
- taking part in everyday leisure activities;
- sampling local food and learning how to prepare traditional dishes;
- talking to older members of the community about life in the past.

Such a product should be on a small scale and would be highly priced to maximize the economic benefits while maintaining its exclusivity value and status. Distribution of the product might increasingly be undertaken directly with consumers in their own home through new technology, or it might be via intermediaries. Finally, promotional activities would be designed to give tourists realistic expectations of the product. This provides an excellent example of social marketing, in other words marketing carried out for public good rather than private profit.

We have seen from these examples that greening affects all areas of functional management. For example:

- it involves human resource management in terms of staff training;
- there is a financial management dimension in terms of the costs and financial benefits of greening;
- operations management has a contribution to make, through purchasing policies for instance;
- marketing too has a role to play through both the products that are developed and the ways in which they are marketed.

GREENING, SUSTAINABILITY AND COMPETITIVE ADVANTAGE

A number of tourism, hospitality and leisure organizations are taking the link with marketing further by seeking to use greening or sustainability to give themselves a competitive advantage. Examples include British Airways in the airline business and tour operators like LTU and TUI. Such a strategy involves not only taking action but telling key audiences what you are doing so that they may reward you in some way. There are three main such audiences, namely:

- consumers, where the hope is that they will begin to purchase the organization's product once they know about its activities in relation to green issues and sustainability;
- the media, so that they will give the organization's products and activities favourable editorial coverage, thus again influencing consumer choice;
- the government, who may then promote the organization as an example of good practice which other organizations in the industry should emulate.

However, as yet no major organization in tourism, leisure, and hospitality has decided to make its stance on these issues the main element in its competitive advantage strategy, like the Body Shop has in the retail sector. Perhaps there is a belief that there are not yet enough consumers who are 'dark green' in relation to tourism, leisure and hospitality products. Clearly, if such attitudes do develop the situation may well change.

In the meantime there is always a danger that some organizations will try to jump on the green or sustainable 'bandwagon' in the hope of gaining short-term competitive advantage. Should their actions be perceived by consumers to be tokenistic, opportunistic and more hype than substance, consumers may punish such organizations, who may then suffer competitive disadvantage. Staking a claim to being a 'green' or sustainable organization is therefore a potentially risky strategy.

Nevertheless, many tourism, leisure and hospitality organizations feel they must be seen to be making some concessions on these issues or their reputations will suffer. Each organization must decide how far it will go along the 'greening/sustainability continuum' and on what areas it will concentrate.

CONSTRAINTS ON GREENING AND SUSTAINABILITY

However, organizations and individual managers do not have total freedom in this field. Their actions are constrained by a number of factors, including:

- their knowledge about green issues and sustainability;
- the organization's resources both in terms of existing plant and equipment, staff and finance;
- the attitudes of staff;
- the organization's culture;
- the reputation the organization has in the marketplace.

Furthermore, it has to be recognized that tourism, leisure and hospitality organizations and their products can never be fully green, they can only be greener. A hotel will always produce some waste and an airline will always burn fuel, but both can be reduced.

DIFFERENCES AND SIMILARITIES WITHIN EUROPE

There is no doubt that green issues and sustainability are topical issues across the whole of Europe. However, the importance attributed to them varies greatly between European countries. In many countries the emphasis is still on the physical environment while in others it has developed to encompass the social and economic impacts of tourism, leisure and hospitality under the banner of sustainable development. The key issues also vary between countries from beach pollution in the UK to the impact of tourists on local cultural holidays in Greece.

However, the situation is complicated by the transnational nature of tourism in particular. For example, the attitudes adopted by Greek hoteliers are increasingly determined by the attitudes of German tourists. Likewise, the demands of German tour operators influence the actions taken by destination marketing agencies in the Balearic Islands. Finally, it could be argued, particularly within the European Union, that these differences in approach and attitudes will be reduced through the influence of European Commission training programmes and regulatory directives.

CONCLUSIONS

We have seen that the field with which this chapter is concerned is a complex one. It is still a relatively new area and we still do not have a clear idea of what type of tourism, for instance, is better than another. At first it was assumed that mass market resorts such as Benidorm were not green or sustainable because of their high-rise buildings and the great strain they placed on local infrastructure. However, good planning can overcome both problems, so that perhaps the concentration of such issues in certain areas will come to be seen as greener and more sustainable than independent travel which encourages tourism to spread everywhere.

Likewise, largely self-contained complexes such as those operated by Club Med or Center Parcs can be seen either as tourist ghettos or as ways of protecting an area's population from the 'pollution' of tourism.

Since there are as yet no answers to such conundrums it appears that it will be some time before organizations will be able to take action which will be guaranteed to be universally recognized as greener or more sustainable. In this situation, many organizations may decide that a minimalist approach may be the most acceptable.

DISCUSSION POINTS AND ESSAY QUESTIONS

1. Compare and contrast the meaning of the terms 'green' and 'sustainable'.

2. Discuss the factors which might motivate a tourism, leisure and hospitality organization to seek to become greener or more sustainable.
3. Evaluate the extent to which the concept of a green consumer in tourism, leisure and hospitality is a myth in Europe today.
4. Discuss the contention that most industry action to date in the environmental field has been largely cosmetic in tourism, leisure and hospitality.

EXERCISE   You have been engaged as a consultant by **one** of the following:

- a destination marketing agency;
- a hotel chain;
- a major airline;
- a fast-food catering company;
- a tour operator.

You should choose a real organization within your selected field.

Your client wishes you to advise them on how they may make their product and marketing activities greener or more sustainable, and how they may then use this to achieve competitive advantage.

Your advice to the organization should include:

(a) how the organization's products and operations should be modified to make them greener or more sustainable;
(b) how these actions should be communicated to internal and external audiences to help the organization achieve competitive advantage;
(c) the potential problems which might be involved in undertaking both these activities.

Your recommendations should be presented in a report, supported by a verbal presentation.

CASE STUDIES

You may wish to look at one of the following case studies which illustrate the points made in this chapter:

14. Grecotel: An example of greening and competitive advantage in the hospitality industry, Greece;
15. TUI, Germany.

Ethics and social responsibility 31

Key concepts

The main concepts covered in this chapter are:

- a typology of ethics and social responsibility;
- the variety of ethical dilemmas and social responsibility challenges which face organizations in the different sectors of tourism, leisure and hospitality.

INTRODUCTION

There appears to be a growing interest in the twin concepts of ethics in management and social responsibility in business. Perhaps, amongst other reasons, this is a result of the numerous scandals in political and economic life which characterized many European countries in the early 1990s.

Ethics and social responsibility are broad subjects with many elements, as can be seen from Figure 31.1. This same figure also illustrates the fact that some ethical dilemmas and issues of social responsibility are primarily internal to organizations while others relate to the organization's links with the outside world.

In this chapter, we will consider several types of ethical dilemma and issues of social responsibility which are found in the various sectors of tourism, leisure and hospitality. We will also consider the marketing implications of these for organizations within these sectors.

Later in the chapter we will consider how such ethical dilemmas can be seen as either threats or opportunities. Furthermore, the chapter will conclude with a brief discussion of national differences and similarities across Europe in attitudes towards ethics and social responsibility.

By definition the choice of issues in this chapter is selective but it does serve to illustrate the range of such issues which are encountered by managers in tourism, leisure and hospitality.

It is also important to note that, as ethical standards are highly personal, the choice of issues and the comments made about them are subjectiive and, at times perhaps, controversial.

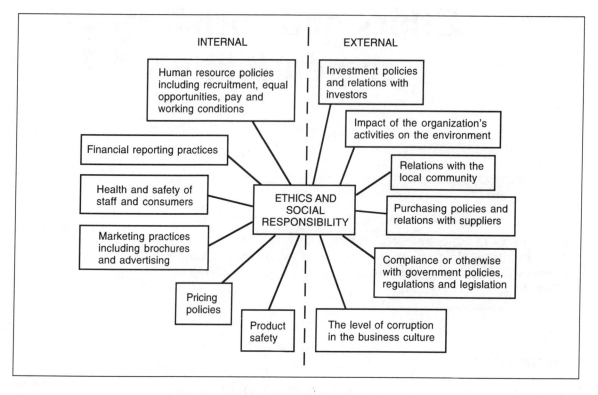

Figure 31.1 Aspects of ethics and social responsibility.

VISITOR ATTRACTIONS

The broad range of ethical dilemmas and questions of social responsibility in the attractions sector are illustrated by the following examples.

- In the museums sector there are the issues of how to handle **controversial and politically sensitive historical events and the ways in which the history of minority groups should be represented**. Such issues in Europe might include:
  - the role of British entrepreneurs in the slave trade;
  - The contribution of Turkish workers to the 'economic miracle' in Germany;
  - the treatment of the Jews by the Nazis;
  - the blurring of historical reality and nationalist aspirations in the Balkans;
  - telling the story of minority groups such as the Basques, the Corsicans, the Lapps and gypsies.

Tackling these issues can be a painful process that can lead to adverse publicity, reduced visitor numbers and the creation of a climate of conflict. On the other hand, ignoring these questions can lead to the story that is being told not offering a true picture of history. It may also discourage some potential customers from visiting the museum.

- The **safety of theme park and amusement park rides** is a more complex issue than it might at first appear. The attraction of many rides is the excitement which requires just a tinge of danger and, in any event, total safety is not possible. Furthermore, many theme and amusement parks live on narrow profit margins and employ casual staff, both of which can be constraints in terms of optimizing safety.

  However, an accident at a theme park or amusement park can result in very negative media coverage. Ironically, in the UK at least, such coverage rarely seems to adversely affect an attraction's visitor numbers. In some cases, it can even lead to an increase! Nevertheless there is a moral duty to optimize safety and, unlike the museums example, action is usually compelled by law rather than being a thoroughly voluntary matter.

- The **question of zoos and whether it is right to keep animals in captivity for the entertainment of visitors** is a long-standing debate. Many zoos, recognizing growing public distaste for traditional zoos, have responded by changing their promotional messages. They now sell the idea that their main purpose is education and conservation rather than entertainment. As many zoo owners are voluntary sector bodies acting on behalf of the 'public interest', it is vitally important to their credibility that they are seen to behave in a socially responsible manner. It is interesting to note that one of the first tourism-related applications of virtual reality that has been talked about is the idea of an animal-less 'virtual zoo'.

DESTINATIONS

Tourist destinations – countries, regions and resorts – also face a range of ethical challenges, as follows.

- **To what extent should those who do not gain financially from tourism subsidize the tourism industry?** Destinations keen to attract tourists spend vast sums of money on marketing and infrastructure, for example. This money usually comes from taxation which is levied on the community as a whole. Yet in many destinations, only a minority of the population will rely on tourism for their livelihood, directly or indirectly. Often relatively poor residents may find themselves subsidizing the promotion of private sector enterprises or the holiday costs of more affluent tourists. Such hidden subsidies distort the pricing system on which all private sector marketing concepts are predicated.

- **The degree to which public money is spent on tourism rather than other sectors of the economy and society** is a contentious issue.

Many developing countries, and even Eastern European countries, see tourism development as a good way of achieving short-term economic development. However, money spent on tourism is clearly not available for spending on other items such as health, education and housing. The marketing implication is that local resentment towards tourists may increase as people become frustrated by the priority accorded to tourism-related government expenditure. This resentment can reduce the quality of the holiday experience and lead to a decline in visitor numbers.

• Finally there is the **tension between short-term and long-term perspectives in the development of destinations**. This tension has been seen clearly in some Mediterranean countries and is currently evident in Eastern Europe. The need for the short-term benefits of tourism can lead to tourism development which is too rapid and uncoordinated. In the longer term this may lead to social and economic problems which will make the destination less attractive to tourists who may go elsewhere. The destination can then be left with huge capacity which is under-utilized.

ACCOMMODATION

The accommodation field offers many examples of ethical issues and social responsibility dilemmas, as follows.

• The existence of **many allegedly poor employment practices** in this sector is undoubtedly a contributory factor to the problems of recruitment and the high labour turnover that characterizes the accommodation sector. Long hours, low wages, poorly developed equal opportunities and racial and sexual harassment have all been identified within this sector. Yet employers would argue that some of this reflects consumers' unwillingness to pay a higher price for the product. This has underpinned the opposition of many hoteliers to the ideas of the European Commission on minimum wages and maximum working hours. However, the problems are clearly about attitudes as well as money, in relation to equal opportunities for instance. The result, from a marketing point of view, is that high turnover and low staff morale can lead to poor service and reduced levels of repeat custom.

• **Purchasing policies** can pose an ethical dilemma for accommodation operators. Buying from local suppliers aids the local community and increases local goodwill. However, if local suppliers are relatively expensive, operators may be forced to buy elsewhere for financial reasons. The most severe challenge may be when local products are best in terms of quality but are more expensive than those from elsewhere. Here there is a quality–cost dilemma which may be very difficult to resolve.

- The rapidly developing **timeshare sector** of the accommodation 'industry' has seen much controversy over the ethics of some of its selling methods. Images of aggressive sales people accosting people in Mediterranean resorts and using the prospect of 'free gifts' to invite people to view and buy timeshare properties is a common phenomenon across much of Western Europe. This reputation is hampering the growth of timeshare in parts of Europe and is forcing operators to introduce self-regulation and measures to reassure customers that they are ethical in the way they operate.

TOUR OPERATIONS

Tour operators live in a transnational and competitive business environment which contains many ethical dilemmas and social responsibility challenges, including the following.

- Firstly, there is the issue of **how honest they should be in their promotional activities**. Tour operators in many European countries have a poor reputation for honesty in their brochures, for example. Hotels have often been said to be 'just five minutes from the beach' when this would only be possible by helicopter! Some winter holiday brochures may feature photographs of the destinations taken in the summer when the temperatures are much higher and all the seasonal tourism businesses are open, and not a word may be said about the building work which may be taking place in a rapidly growing resort. Tour operators are reticent to take a lead in honesty in brochures in case they suffer competitive disadvantage if their competitors do not follow suit. However, in Europe, we have seen with the EU Package Travel Directive that such inaccuracy may result in compulsion through legislation.
- **Many tour operators do not provide adequate advice for their clients on potential hazards and inconveniences** in case such information might discourage them from purchasing the product. This might cover everything from diseases such as the severe infections which can come from drinking the water in St Petersburg to the annoying insects of Scotland and Scandinavia to street crime in major cities and the lack of plugs in many Eastern European hotels. In the short term, failing to give such guidance may not be a major problem, but in the longer term it may lead to customer dissatisfaction and a loss of business.
- The classic dilemma of **whether to add to the problems of already overcrowded destinations** by selling holidays to those destinations. On the one hand, a customer-led organization should continue because these are the places consumers want to visit. On the other hand, continued emphasis on such destinations may destroy them in the longer term. Where then will the operators take their clients?

TRANSPORT

The transport sector is a rich vein of ethical challenges and issues of social responsibility, of which the following are a brief selection.

- Firstly, there is the question of **'fair competition' in the airline sector** where state intervention has taken place in Europe, to protect state-owned national airlines. This is now changing as a result of 'liberalization' introduced in European Union countries as part of EU competition policies. However, the supporters of state intervention would argue that it is beneficial in that it protects the strategic interest of the nations concerned and safeguards non-profitable routes. Opponents, on the other hand, would argue that it artificially inflates prices and leads to inefficient operations. Liberalization is thus ushering in an era of massive change which also offers the prospects of lower fares for the consumer, and more competition.
- The **debate over the use of the private car** in leisure and tourism is highly topical. The car opened up leisure and tourism opportunities for many people in the 1950s, 1960s and 1970s and it created new forms of leisure such as caravan touring. However, increased car ownership is now harming the quality of experience as well as the environment. Yet we cannot bring ourselves to ban cars for they are a symbol of the basic right to freedom of movement. This dilemma is found from the clogged streets of historic cities to the narrow lanes of the countryside. Failure to tackle it effectively may result in certain congested destinations losing much of their appeal to tourists.
- **Safety on 'roll on-roll off' ferries** is a major issue in Europe now after the *Herald of Free Enterprise* and *Estonia* ferry disasters. However, greater safety means slower turnround times in ports and higher fares at a time when competition with other modes of travel such as the Eurotunnel and air transport is at a peak. Operators, therefore, have to balance their desire to achieve greater safety with the willingness of customers to put up with the effects of such action.

RESORT COMPLEXES

The main ethical issue which is specific to resort complexes is the question of their relationship with the area around them. Many appear like self-contained 'tourist ghettos' which have little to do with the local economy and communities that surround the complex. This can be said of the types of complexes managed under brands like Club Med and Center Parcs. One view suggests that this isolation is good in terms of protecting of the locals from the social, environmental and economic 'pollution' that tourism can cause.

Others are unimpressed saying such isolation is socially divisive. To some extent perhaps it is a matter of the extent to which tourists wish to mix with the host community and feel safe in the broader destination area. It is perhaps no coincidence that many modern resort complexes that are self-contained have developed in areas where tourists may feel a little uncomfortable or unsafe at certain times.

RETAIL TRAVEL

Retail travel includes a range of ethical dilemmas and moral challenges, as follows.

- The **incentives which a tour operator may give travel agency staff to sell its products** can be financial or non-financial (a free holiday, for example). This means that the client may not receive the impartial advice they expect to receive. This situation is exacerbated in the UK, for instance, by the fact that the leading travel agency chains are owned by the major tour operators. If this form of inducement continues, it may further convince customers that travel agents are not impartial, and in time technology will allow tourists to access products without the need for travel agents.
- **Many travel agents use sales promotions with restrictive conditions** to attract customers. For example, the client has to purchase the travel agent's own insurance policy, which may well be relatively expensive, to obtain the discount. This can be seen as a form of unfair, less than scrupulously honest promotion which again might reduce the reputation of travel agents as impartial intermediaries.

ARTS AND ENTERTAINMENT

There are numerous ethical dilemmas within the arts and entertainment field, including the following.

- Firstly, there is the issue of **subsidies**, in other words who should fund the subsidies and who should receive them. For example, there is the debate in the UK about the validity or otherwise of subsidizing a minority art form such as opera, where most opera goers are relatively affluent as a whole, while providing little or no subsidy to the cinema. Commercial operators who receive little or no subsidy believe such subsidies for their public sector 'competitors' amount to unfair competition. In any event, the existence of subsidies certainly distorts pricing mechanisms within the arts and entertainment sector.
- The question of subsidies is also linked to the debate about **the extent to which arts and entertainment organizations should seek to encourage participation from people who do not normally participate in, or even spectate at, arts and entertainment events**. Sometimes trying to attract such people can lead to what purists might see as a dilution or trivialization of the pure art form. This happens, for

instance, when directors attempt to increase the appeal of Shake-speare plays by staging them in the modern day and in modern dress. On the other hand, not seeking to attract new customers in this way can limit audience numbers and reduce income at a time when state subsidies are often being cut.

- **Some parts of the entertainment 'industry' are increasingly thought to be having a detrimental effect on society.** This is particularly true of television which is often accused of discouraging young people from playing outside their homes or taken part in healthy activities. It is also often blamed for violent behaviour amongst children. The influence of television is clearly spreading with the growth of satellite and cable television and computer games. This has serious implications for other sectors of tourism, leisure and hospitality such as visitor attractions, for whom they represent competition.

RECREATION AND SPORT

The broad field of recreation and sport offers a wide range of examples of ethical issues, including the following.

- In many European countries, **football is increasingly seen as a business where the owners of famous football clubs seek to use them to generate a profit**. At the same time these clubs are also an important part of the everyday life of the people who live in that area, they are part of the social fabric and heritage of the locality. Many clubs seek to charge prices that will be high enough to secure a good rate of return on investment while their supporters simply want to pay as little as possible to see their team play. Customers are seen as a captive market tied to a monopolistic product such that they will pay the price demanded in return for, what is to them, a unique experience. This polarity of interest is reinforced by the, some would say immoral, fact that clubs will pay huge salaries and transfer fees for top players, yet provide relatively poor facilities for their consumers, the spectators. How many other businesses could survive if they behaved in a similar manner?
- The ethical dilemma of **social engineering and paternalism** is evident in areas such as countryside recreation. In the UK, for instance, strenuous efforts have been made to encourage people from ethnic minorities to indulge in countryside recreation. This was based on two beliefs which may be or not be true, namely:
  - that countryside recreation is 'good for you' and is somehow an 'uplifting experience'. This view is probably not shared by everyone;
  - that people from ethnic minorities would visit the countryside if they only knew more about it. This appears a rather patronizing view that appears, in general, not to have been borne out by the results of the various marketing campaigns that have been undertaken by the relevant governmental agencies.

LEISURE SHOPPING

Leisure shopping, as we have seen, is a relatively recent arrival on the tourism, leisure and hospitality scene. Nevertheless it has already given rise to a range of issues relevant to this chapter, including the following.

- Firstly there is the criticism that **leisure shopping encourages people to spend money they do not have on goods they do not need**. Some commentators argue that it has fuelled the rise of materialism and the development of the all-embracing consumer society. On the other hand, it could be argued that it is simply offering consumers a choice which they are free to accept or reject. If many choose to take up the offer of the leisure shopping sector, who is to say it is a 'bad thing"?

- In many modern mixed-use developments it could argued that **leisure shopping complexes within such developments have helped ensure that the less affluent have been forced to move out**. In the UK, dockland development schemes in London and Liverpool, for example, have hardly any shops selling 'normal' products such as bread and vegetables. Instead they are packed with 'leisure' shops selling gifts, stationery, exotic foods and city souvenirs, usually at relatively high prices. Such shops can afford higher rents than everyday utility shops, and in any event developers prefer leisure shops because of their ability to attract visitors to the development. However, because they dominate retail provision, less well-off local people without access to a car cannot live in the area for there is nowhere for them to buy the things they need for everyday life. In the long run this means that such developments become 'leisure ghettos' with no indigenous resident population to give them a sense of continuity and purpose and a living heart. In the end this may reduce their attraction for visitors. Others would argue that this is simply an example of market forces in a postmodern world.

CATERING

Several major ethical dilemmas are found within the catering sector, namely the following.

- **Should priority in purchasing policies be given to products that are more animal friendly** such as truly free-range eggs and chickens that have lived in a natural environment? These products are usually more expensive than their industrially farmed counterparts and it is a matter of whether consumers care enough to pay the extra price.

- **There is also the issue of what is healthy and what customers like to eat**. Caterers have to decide if they will sell products which, while popular, are known to be harmful to people's health. They may contain sugar or be rich in fats, for instance, yet they are popular with customers. Surely the consumer-led approach to marketing dictates that such products should be sold, but to what extent does the caterer have a moral obligation to remind the consumer of the health implications of eating these products given that the customer may then not purchase the product?

- Many would, furthermore, argue that **caterers in any location should also have a responsibility to maintain local gastronomic traditions** by offering at least some traditional local dishes using local ingredients. However, often customers want more international dishes. Likewise it may well be cheaper to produce the dishes using non-local ingredients. Should this be done, and if so, should the customer be told?

BUSINESS TOURISM

As probably the most financially lucrative sector of tourism, leisure and hospitality, business tourism brings with it a host of socially responsible concerns and ethical challenges, as the following brief examples illustrate.

- There are **unfortunate social effects that can be caused by the demands of business tourists**, such as crime, prostitution and child sex. Yet destinations rarely want to intervene for controls on the activities of business travellers may reduce the volume of business tourism with a loss of the economic benefits that it brings. However, conversely, if these problems become very severe it may well ultimately make the place a less attractive venue for conferences and incentive travel packages, for example.
- There may also be **widespread corruption and fraud** in terms of 'bribes' of one kind or another, for example to locate a conference in a particular place or the falsification of expenses claims by business travellers. Again, attempts to clamp down on such practices might well result in a reduction in business travel.
- The **great gulf that can exist between very affluent foreign tourists and local residents** is a moral issue and can lead to the kinds of resentment outlined above. While this situation does not just relate to business tourism, it is within this sector that the extremes are most often seen.
- Sometimes **business travel to a destination may be based on business which is illegal** such as arms-dealing and trading in wild animals, for example.

MARKETING RESPONSES

Organizations can adopt a number of responses to such issues ranging from denial ('it is not a problem') to full ideological conversion leading to a total change of corporate policy. Most responses lie somewhere between these two extremes. Some may see such issues as a threat and seek to nullify them by making changes to policies and marketing practices so they are less vulnerable to criticism. On the other hand, certain issues may be viewed as opportunities by some organizations, to be exploited through the development of new products supported by a promotional campaign to inform potential customers about the stance the organization is taking.

Tourism, leisure and hospitality organizations have taken a range of proactive approaches on issues of social responsibility, including:

- the airline Virgin's legal battle with British Airways over what might be termed the issue of fair trade;
- German tour operators TUI and LTU's proactive action on sustainable tourism;
- Burger King setting out to employ more older people to counter criticisms that the hospitality sector is ageist in its recruitment policies.

However, as yet, no tourism, leisure or hospitality organization has gone as far as the 'Body Shop' in making its stance on ethical concerns, perhaps the main strand in its competitive strategy. This may change if De Bono's concept of 'sur-petition' or the selling of corporate values grows in popularity.

The decision as to which stance an organization should adopt on any particular ethical issue is determined by a range of factors including the views of major shareholders, the organization's culture and reputation, and the views of its customers – or more accurately, perhaps, the views which managers think are held by their consumers.

DIFFERENCES AND SIMILARITIES WITHIN EUROPE

There are apparently national differences and similarities in relation to this subject across Europe, at a number of levels as follows.

- There is a similar situation across most of Europe whereby interest in ethical issues in all industries in general has risen in recent years as a result of numerous scandals.
- Debates have developed in a number of European countries over a range of ethical issues and matters of social responsibility in tourism, leisure and hospitality, including employment policies, transnational organizations, promotional techniques and the whole field of sustainability.

At the same time there are also differences between individual countries and blocs of countries, as the following examples illustrate.

- In Eastern Europe the need to pursue short-term economic development has relegated many of the ethical issues we have explored in this chapter to matters of secondary importance.

● On most issues, concern seems greater in the Northern European countries that have traditionally been the tourist generating countries than in those Mediterranean countries that have generally been net receivers of tourists. This may simply reflect the way tourism has developed and may change as the economies of countries like Spain, Portugal, Italy and Greece develop further and they become ever greater generators of tourist trips.

Interestingly, the similarities may grow as the European Commission legislates on some of the issues covered in this chapter and enlargement means that more and more European countries join the European Union.

CONCLUSIONS

We have seen that there are many complex ethical issues in tourism, leisure and hospitality. Furthermore they appear to be growing in importance, particularly those which we might group under the heading of 'sustainability'.

It is also clear that there are similarities between the issues faced by organizations in different sectors within our three fields. For example, both destinations and tour operators face dilemmas in how they should present their product to potential consumers.

As yet, very few tourism, leisure and hospitality organizations appear to have been willing to take high-profile stances on ethical issues. Perhaps they see this as a risky strategy, particularly if consumer interest is not high enough that such an organization taking a proactive stance would be rewarded by increased custom. Some would also argue that either it is impossible to be highly ethical in any business or that ethics are really the responsibility of government and society, not individual organizations. Indeed if one were to argue from the point of view of customer-led marketing, it could be said that, ultimately, organizations have to respond to consumer pressure so that they should mirror the options of their customers in the ethical stance they adopt.

Whichever view one takes it seems likely that for tourism, leisure and hospitality marketers, ethical issues and questions of social responsibility will become increasingly important considerations in their working lives.

DISCUSSION POINTS AND ESSAY QUESTIONS

1. Discuss some of the major current ethical dilemmas in one of the following sectors:

    (a) visitor attractions;
    (b) tour operation;

(c) hotels;
(d) recreation and sport.
2. Evaluate the action which some tourism, leisure and hospitality organizations have taken on ethical issues.
3. Compare and contrast attitudes to ethics and social responsibility between different parts of Europe.

Select **one** sector within tourism, leisure and hospitality from those covered in   **EXERCISE**
Chapters 16–27 inclusive. Identify an ethical dilemma which currently exists
for organizations operating within your chosen sector.
   You should then·

(a) produce a short report introducing the dilemma and discussing its implications for organizations within your chosen sector;
(b) outline the range of possible stances which organizations in the sector might adopt in response to these implications;
(c) discuss the main factors which an organization should take into account when deciding which stance to adopt.

32 Marketing research

Key concepts

The main concepts covered in this chapter are:

- the difference between market research and marketing research;
- different types of marketing research;
- problems with the collection and interpretation of data;
- the lack of knowledge about why consumers behave in particular ways and how they make decisions;
- prerequisites for successful marketing research.

INTRODUCTION

In the era of so-called consumer-led marketing, marketing research must, by definition, be a key topical issue. Marketing research is a particularly crucial current issue in tourism, leisure and hospitality because in these three areas it is a relatively under-developed activity. We still know little about why consumers in tourism, leisure and hospitality behave in the way they do.

This chapter is not intended to provide a guide to how to undertake marketing research in tourism, leisure and hospitality. There are a number of texts which perform this task admirably, including those by Ryan (1995) and Veal (1992) for example. Instead, it is designed to simply highlight some of the problems and topical issues involved in marketing research in our three fields. To do this it will provide the following:

- an outline of the rationale for marketing research and the different types of research;
- a hypothetical case study that illustrates the problems involved in the collection and interpretation of data in tourism, leisure and hospitality;
- a short examination of five major current challenges in marketing research in tourism, leisure and hospitality;

- a brief discussion of the factors that assist the development of effective marketing research.

At the end of the chapter, an attempt will be made to identify similarities and differences between countries in Europe in relation to tourism, leisure and hospitality marketing.

Given the title and content of this book, it is appropriate that this chapter is about marketing research rather than market research. The difference between the two may seem pedantic but it is important. Marketing research is a precise, focused activity with the single aim of providing data which will be useful to help improve the effectiveness of an organization's marketing activities. On the other hand, market research is a broader, less focused activity where the main aim is to gather information about a market. The former is a more applied form of research than the latter. However, marketing people will also find market research valuable as background information. It can often help them to frame the objectives and content of their own marketing research projects.

THE RATIONALE FOR MARKETING RESEARCH

Marketing research is designed to allow organizations to evaluate their current performance, identify opportunities, and develop products and messages to allow them to exploit these opportunities. In other words, marketing research is about improving the efficiency of the organization's marketing activities.

What do organizations need to know?

Firstly organizations need to know about their markets, both existing and potential, and that is the main function of marketing research. Hence it is largely concerned with numerical data about its market together with the behaviour, opinions and perceptions of consumers. These issues will be explored in more detail shortly through a hypothetical example of a Mediterranean island and the organization responsible for marketing it. While this example is about a public sector agency, the points are equally relevant to private sector organizations.

However, a major distinction between marketing research and market research is that the former is not merely concerned with the consumer. It is interested in all research which might be of assistance to the marketing function. This might include information on the following:

- the activities and plans of competitors;
- changes in the macro environment such as new legislation, technological innovations and changes in the economic climate;
- the opinions of marketing intermediaries such as travel agents who deal directly with the organization's clients.

Having said this, most of the present chapter will focus on market-oriented research which, as we said earlier, is the primary concern of most organizations.

TYPES OF MARKETING RESEARCH

Marketing research tends to be of two types, namely:

- **quantitative** research, in other words facts and figures. This can include factual information on characteristics of the market together with statistics on the performance of the organization, including sales figures and market share;
- **qualitative** research, which is largely concerned with the perceptions, opinions and attitudes of consumers about organizations, their products and their competitors.

Traditionally, it has been easier and cheaper to collect quantitative statistics that to gather qualitative data: easier because it is simpler to count the number of times someone buys a product than it is to discover why they buy the product; cheaper because qualitative research requires long in-depth interviews with skilled interviewers, while quantitative data can usually be gathered through short, simple questionnaires that can be undertaken by less skilled staff.

Research data is generally compiled from two major sources as follows:

- original primary research to gather new information which is not available elsewhere. This may be used, for example, by an organization which wants to test consumer attitudes towards their own products, such as a hotel chain or an airline;
- the interpretation of existing secondary research data which has been produced previously and is available to an organization. Thus, the would-be developer of a potential new visitor attraction might use secondary data to establish whether a viable market existed for the potential attraction.

Middleton (1994) produced a useful model illustrating the range of primary and secondary research methods which are available to tourism, leisure and hospitality organizations. This is shown in Table 32.1.

The same author has also produced a classification of the ways in which research is applied to different functions within markets. This is illustrated in Table 32.2.

MARKETING RESEARCH APPLICATIONS

Several hypothetical examples will serve to demonstrate some of the main potential applications of the types of marketing research illustrated in Tables 31.1 and 32.2 in tourism, leisure and hospitality.

- A hotel owner might endeavour to discover how customers perceive his hotel in relation to its competitors, in terms of a range of criteria including its location, facilities and price. This would clarify on what aspect of the mix the hotel owner needed to concentrate his marketing, in other words on the product or the price for example.
- A tour operator might seek to see how satisfied its customers were with the product they purchase from the operator, to identify gaps which might affect the customers' satisfaction. Research could help the operator construct a gap analysis for a specific destination like that illustrated in Figure 32.1. This gap analysis would help the tour operator decide if it needed to remove the destination from its programme or use its brochure to modify customer expectations of the destination.
- Research by a scheduled airline might be undertaken to see how business travellers would respond to the introduction of a new business-class service. An airline would want to know if customers would use the service and, if so, how often. They would also like to

Table 32.1 The range of available marketing research methods

1 Desk research (secondary sources)
  - Sales/bookings/reservation records: daily, weekly, etc., by type of customer, type of product, etc.
  - Visitor information records by guest registration count, booking form data.
  - Government publications/trade organization data/national tourist office data/library.
  - Commercial analyses available on subscription or through purchased reports.
  - Previous research studies conducted; internal data bank.
  - Press cuttings of competition activities, market environmental changes.

2 Qualitative or exploratory research
  - Organized marketing intelligence, such as salesforce reports, attendance at exhibitions or trade shows.
  - Group discussions and individual interviews with targeted customers/non-users – to identify perceptions and attitudes.
  - Observational studies of visitor behaviour using cameras or trained observers.
  - Marketing experiments with monitored results.

3 Quantitative research (syndicated)
  - Omnibus questions of targeted respondents.
  - Syndicated surveys including audits.

4 Quantitative research (ad hoc and continuous)
  - Studies of travel and tourism behaviour and usage/activity patterns.
  - Attitude, image, perception and awareness studies.
  - Advertising and other media response studies.
  - Consumer satisfaction and product marketing studies.
  - Distribution studies amongst retail outlets.

Source: Middleton (1994).

Table 32.2 The application of different types of marketing research in marketing

Research category	Used in	Typical Marketing Use
1. Market analysis and forecasting	Marketing planning	Measurement and projection of market volumes, shares and revenue by relevant categories of market segment and product types
2. Consumer research	Segmentation and positioning	(a) Quantitative measurement of consumer profiles, awareness, attitudes and purchasing behaviour, including consumer audits (b) Qualitative assessment of consumer needs, perceptions and opinions
3. Products and price studies	Product formulation, presentation and pricing	Measurement and consumer testing of amended and new product formulations, and price sensitivity studies
4. Promotions and sales research	Efficiency of communications	Measurement of consumer reaction to alternative advertising concepts and media usage; response to various forms of sales promotion, and salesforce effectiveness
5. Distribution research	Efficiency of distribution network	Distributor awareness of products, stocking and brochures as effectiveness of merchandising, including retail audit and occupancy studies
6. Evaluation and performance monitoring studies	Overall concept of marketing results and product quality control	Measurement of customer satisfaction overall and by product elements, including measurement through marketing tests and experiments

Source: Middleton (1994).

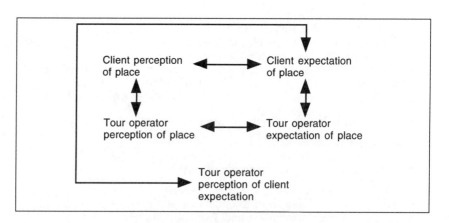

Figure 32.1 A gap analysis of a tourist destination. Source: Ryan (1995).
Note: Each line represents a potential gap that affects tourist satisfaction. The model can be extended by creating new partnerships and adding tourist intermediaries such as hoteliers.

know if the new service would persuade their competitors' customers to switch their allegiance to the organization.

- A major restaurant chain might wish to investigate the likely impact of potential prices on its existing customers. It will need to establish how many of its customers will stop using the restaurant after a price rise.

Clearly, the latter two types of research are more difficult to carry out than the former two as they involve hypothetical events rather than real ones which have taken or are taking place during the research period.

PROBLEMS WITH THE COLLECTION AND INTERPRETATION OF DATA

Most tourism, leisure and hospitality managers would probably agree with the statement that marketing research is inadequate in all three areas. We neither know enough facts and figures about our markets or sufficient about the attitudes and perceptions of our consumers. However, there are some good reasons why this is the case, particularly in the tourism area.

Perhaps these can be best illustrated if we imagine a small Mediterranean island which is becoming a popular tourist destination. The island government now wants to develop a marketing strategy and to this end it requires reliable, up-to-date marketing research. It has decided to undertake a survey of visitors to find out both quantitative and qualitative information. We will shortly look at the problems they might experience in carrying out such a survey, but first let us look at this island in a little more detail.

It is about 100 square kilometres in area and has an airport and a small port which is visited by both cruise liners and a ferry from the mainland. There are also several marinas which attract pleasure craft and some isolated inlets which provide safe anchorage for such craft. The accommodation stock ranges from luxury hotels in the two well developed resorts, to farmhouses which are available for rent, campsites and even the beach where some people sleep illegally. There are many restaurants and bars, particularly in the two main resorts. In addition the island has five beaches and several major tourist attractions including a museum, a water-based theme park and some nice old villages. There is also a small convention centre and spa and the north of the island has a reputation for its wildlife. Finally we should note that the island is within the European Union.

We will now look at what information the island government feels it might need to produce a marketing strategy and the difficulties it might experience in trying to collect and interpret such data.

Given the constraints of space, we will keep it simple by limiting questions to finding out the answers to just ten questions. These are as follows:

- how many tourists does the island receive?
- what is the purpose of their visit?
- when do they visit the island?
- where do they come from?
- how much do they spend?
- who are these visitors?
- what do they do when they are on the island?
- what do they think about the island as a destination?
- how do they believe the island compares to its competitors?
- will they make a return trip to the island?

Before we look at each question in detail, it is important to start by talking briefly about methodology and particularly sampling. To gain useful answers to these questions, what percentage of the island's visitors would have to be surveyed and how would they be chosen. The island receives 3 million visitors a year and the cost of interviewing all of them would exceed £30 million sterling, which is ten times the island's tourism marketing budget!

For financial and logistical reasons the survey would probably have to be small, perhaps 5%, but we must recognize that if we decide to interview less than 100% of all tourists we can never have the full picture.

The number of tourists

The first problem is to separate the island residents from tourists. After that it is a matter of how best to measure the tourist flows. The traditional way is through immigration controls, for example requiring all non-residents to complete an immigration form which is then collected on arrival in the country. However, as the island is in the European Union, it would not be normal practice any more to issue such cards to tourists who come from other European Union countries. As people from such countries represent the bulk of the island's tourist market, such a method would be ineffective.

Another method might be to use the passenger lists of the ferry and airline operators who serve the island. However, the ferries that visit such islands may only rarely have such lists and there is always the problem of separating residents from tourists. There is a further difficulty in that those people who arrive on private yachts will be excluded from such a count.

Finally, the numbers may be established by using the receipts of accommodation establishments. This is a totally flawed method for four main reasons, as follows:

- many people may not stay in officially recognized accommodation. This might include sleeping on the beach and rooms in private houses. These people would thus be excluded from such a count;
- those staying with friends and relatives which in some places might constitute a significant volume of tourists. This is particularly likely

to be the case on an island where there are a number of second homes owned by foreigners;

- day-trippers would be excluded from the count, and if the island is relatively close to the mainland, the ferries could bring significant numbers of such visitors to the island;
- some accommodation establishments may falsify and underestimate the number of tourists they accommodate to reduce their tax bills.

So far we have assumed that all the tourists are foreign, but it may well be that the island has a substantial number of domestic tourists. Measuring domestic tourism is particularly difficult because of the following characteristics:

- they cross no national boundaries;
- they are likely to travel by private car rather than ferry or bus;
- they will not use commercial accommodation but rather the home of a friend or relative, or their own second home.

The purpose of the visit

The reasons for people visiting could be interesting in terms of helping the island government to segment its market so that it can design appropriate products. Some reasons might include business, leisure travel, whether package holidays or independent, health, study or attending special events, for example. In general, such information can only be gathered through costly face-to-face interviews.

Furthermore, these purposes are not always mutually exclusive. For instance, business people may use package holidays as an inexpensive way of travelling to the island so that they can carry out their business. We have also noted earlier in the book that there is not always a clear dividing line between business and leisure travel. Business travellers become leisure travellers when the working day is over and many business travellers take partners with them who are leisure travellers for the whole of their stay.

When tourists come to the island

Tourism tends to have clearly defined patterns of seasonality which means that any survey designed to give an accurate overview of the island's existing market must cover the whole year. For example, most business travel will normally take place outside the summer months but most leisure travel will usually occur in these very same months. Different national markets may visit the island at different times during the summer, reflecting national differences in school holiday dates. There may also be particular times of the year when groups visit the island for specific reasons, which might include watching birds which migrate to the island in December, or attending an arts festival in February.

Where the tourists come from

This is clearly linked to the last question in some degree as it is in general a relatively straightforward issue. However, it can be a little more complex than it might at first appear. People may make a trip to the island from a location which is not of their normal place of residence. They may be staying with friends or relatives, for example. This is important from a marketing point of view because the island government needs to know in what geographical areas to concentrate its promotional activities so that its message reaches its target markets.

Tourist expenditure

What the island government may want to know is how much money tourists spend on the island, and where they spend it. However, it is often very difficult to differentiate money spent on the island from that spent off the island. If a tourist buys a 2000 Deutschmark trip to the island from a German tour operator, a significant portion of this money will never leave Germany. For example, it will be used to pay for the seat on a German charter airline on which the tourist will travel.

However, if we simply focus on the money tourists spend once they have arrived on the island, there are still some problems, as follows:

- some people will claim to spend more than they do in fact spend to appear more wealthy than they are in reality;
- other tourists say they have spent less than they have because they want to be seen as good bargainers;
- certain tourists may simply not know how much they have spent on holiday.

However, if the island government is keen to estimate tourism impact on their economy, there are two difficult to quantify sets of data they need to identify, namely:

- what proportion of tourist spending on the island leaves the island to pay for imports or as profits to foreign companies;
- the multiplier effect of tourist spending on the island.

A profile of the tourists

If one is trying to establish factual profiles of tourists there are difficulties that may be encountered. Some people may lie about their age or income, for instance. There may also be problems in applying the measures of social class used on the island to visitors from other countries where the concept of class may be different. Products based on family lifecycle can also be stereotypical and can lead to the idea that all families, for example, will require certain things which may well not be the case.

The activities of the tourists

It is usually not possible to discover tourists' activities through observation as it is very expensive. Normally, therefore, one relies on what tourists tell interviewers undertaking surveys or through self-completion questionnaires. However, tourists may not tell the truth, in other words:

- they may say they have not done certain things when they have in reality because they feel they are seen as not socially acceptable, such as indulging in casual sex or drinking heavily;
- alternatively, they may claim to have done things which are more acceptable such as visiting historic sites, when they have in fact done no such thing;
- some may give totally wrong information because they have been involved in illegal activities such as hunting or child sex.

Finally, some tourists may not even remember all or even most of the things they did on holiday!

Tourist opinions of the island as a destination

Some tourists will give an unrealistically positive opinion of the island because they feel it is what those conducting the survey want to hear. Others may give a negative view, not because they do not like the island, but rather because they are generally unhappy about their relationships or their life in general, for example. Generalized opinions can also mask views on specific aspects of the island which could be very useful to those responsible for marketing the island.

For example, someone who says they like the island overall may actually have been very unhappy about some aspect of the holiday such as their hotel or a particular beach. On the other hand, a tourist who in general appears to have a negative view of the island may have really enjoyed a particular leisure activity or a specific beach.

How does the island compare to its competitors

This is difficult to ascertain for several reasons, as follows:

- the tourist may not have visited any of the places the island has identified as its competitors;
- identifying the competitors can be a difficult task for they will be different for each different market segment, such as business travellers, hedonists and sightseers for instance;
- tourists' views of competitor destinations may be based on experiences which are a number of years old and are therefore out of date.

The likelihood of repeat visits

The response to this question may be distorted by the fact that people may at the end of their holiday say they are likely, or even certain, to return because they are filled with nostalgic feelings for the holiday they have just experienced. However, when they are home, and memories have faded and other destinations have targeted the same tourists with their promotional messages, the likelihood of a repeat visit in the near future is usually much reduced.

Summary

Even concentrating on just ten questions we have seen how difficult marketing research is in the field of tourist destinations. However, if would be wrong to say that it is as difficult in all sectors of tourism, leisure and hospitality. It is particularly difficult in relation to destinations because of their complexity and the fact that they are not in single ownership. In hospitality, for example, conducting research on the market is relatively easy for individual corporations such as hotel chains and fast-food outlet operators. Nevertheless, it can still be difficult to gain accurate information on these markets as a whole. Again consumers may give misleading answers; for instance diners may claim to eat healthier dishes than they do because such behaviour is more socially acceptable.

FIVE MAJOR MARKETING RESEARCH CHALLENGES

In spite of the advances made in marketing research in recent years, there are still five fundamental challenges in tourism, leisure and hospitality marketing research. These are discussed below.

The lack of reliable research on why consumers do what they do and how they make purchasing decisions

There is relatively little empirical research to show, for example:

- why people choose to visit particular attractions;
- how tourists select hotels;
- the reasons why people choose to use one travel agent rather than another.

The data that does exist on these issues tends to be based on small samples in one country or region so that it is difficult to draw any general conclusions.

In the absence of readily available and reliable such research, managers are left with only their experience and judgement on which to base their marketing decisions. Such judgements can often be inaccurate due to personal bias.

There have also been very few comparative studies designed to identify national differences and similarities in consumer behaviour in our three fields. This has made it difficult for organizations to evaluate whether or not their product may sell well in another country. At a time when many organizations in tourism, leisure and hospitality are seeking to expand internationally, this gap in marketing research is a particularly topical concern.

The difficult and high cost of finding out about non-users

Discovering why people are not purchasing the services provided by an organization is important as most tourism, leisure and hospitality organizations need to attract new customers if they are to thrive, or even to survive. There are several sectors where this is a major issue, namely:

- subsidized theatres where only a minority of the local population usually makes use of the theatre. Attracting more people from the local area to visit the theatre is crucial to management because it must be seen to be serving the whole community in order to justify the subsidy it receives;
- seaside resorts in the UK where many British people do not visit the resort and yet little is known about why they do not make use of the resort.

While research on non-users is difficult, it is vital for marketers. It can help them identify different types of non-users for whom different marketing messages need to be developed and transmitted, including:

- ex-users who need to be tempted back, either by being told about new features of the product or by being reassured that it has not changed;
- those who are aware of the product but have not yet been persuaded to buy it. They require a 'hard sell' message or perhaps a 'first-time user's special promotional offer';
- those who are not aware of the product's existence and who need to be informed about the product.

Problems with the identification of trends

This is due to the lack of longitudinal studies carried out over a lengthy period of time using a common methodology, and is unfortunate as trend extrapolation can be a valuable, if far from infallible, way of forecasting short-term future trends. If we cannot make such forecasts with any confidence, then our ability to undertake effective marketing planning is significantly reduced. While progress has been made on longitudinal studies in recent years, there are still too few of them, partly because of the high cost of mounting such studies.

Our lack of knowledge of the behaviour of individuals

We still tend to treat tourists and hotel users, for example, as homogeneous groups who will behave in a particular way. Yet we know, from our own experience as tourists or hotel consumers, that our individual behaviour changes over time and varies depending on circumstances. However, there is still little reliable research in tourism, leisure and hospitality on the behaviour of individual consumers. The lack of such data clearly limits our ability to realistically segment markets.

It also makes us develop stereotypes that may not reflect true behaviour. For example, we assume that some people prefer package holidays while others prefer independent travel and that some prefer the coast while others have a preference for the countryside. Yet we have not yet proved that these people are different people. It may be that they are the same people, doing different things at different times in response to changes in their circumstances or the 'determinants' which affect them.

We also know relatively little about how the behaviour of individual tourists or hotel customers, for example, changes over time. For instance, many commentators say one of the problems of the previously mentioned seaside resorts in the UK is that those who visited them in previous decades are now holidaying abroad. We all tend to accept this view as a truism, yet where is the empirical evidence?

We have to learn that markets are the result of the behaviour of individuals who are all different and who behave differently at different times. It is logical, therefore, that our research should start with the behaviour of individual consumers rather than with markets as a whole, for the overall picture includes major variations in individual behaviour which are very important from a marketing point of view.

Lack of funding

Inadequate budgets are still devoted to marketing research in most tourism, leisure and hospitality organizations. The many small operators and public sector bodies in these three fields often cannot afford research while many large organizations see it as a relatively low priority and one of the first areas that can be cut in times when resources are severely limited. This appears to be somewhat more of a problem in some countries such as the UK, where a lack of commitment to market research in the private sector is compounded by a lack of resources for marketing research in the public sector. Thus, potential developers and marketing people have difficulty in finding reliable, up-to-date, comparative data, collected and made available by the public sector, than would be the case in France, for instance. This undoubtedly is an obstacle to both the development of new products and the effective marketing of existing ones.

Marketing research is, increasingly, an expensive activity, but one which organizations need in order to optimize their marketing. Who pays for it – individual organizations or the public sector – is a major debate but it has to be paid for somehow, or the quality of tourism, leisure and hospitality marketing will suffer.

Attention needs to be directed to those five topical areas if we are to improve the effectiveness and professionalism of marketing in tourism, leisure and hospitality.

KEY ISSUES IN SUCCESSFUL MARKETING RESEARCH

For marketing research to be successful, in other words effective and useful for marketers, a number of prerequisites are required, as follows:

- having clear objectives as to what it is hoped will be gained from the research;
- selecting the appropriate methodology to achieve these objectives;
- only collecting data which has implications for marketing action;
- being able to carry out research on an ongoing basis rather than as a one-off 'snapshot' only;
- adequately briefing all staff involved in the research project;
- providing enough resources to allow the research to be conducted professionally;
- having the mechanisms to analyse all the results quickly before the research becomes outdated;
- having staff with the ability to accurately interpret the results;
- presenting the results in a user-friendly form for those who need to use them.

DIFFERENCES AND SIMILARITIES WITHIN EUROPE

While the principles of marketing research are largely the same in tourism, leisure and hospitality across Europe, there have been national differences in emphasis. In countries where inbound tourism is vitally important such as Spain and Greece, it is vital that data is gathered on the relevant foreign national markets. In countries like the UK where both inbound and outbound tourism are important, data on both types of markets is important.

There are certainly major differences in terms of the level of development and competitiveness of public sector marketing research. As one of the case studies illustrates, France, for example, has a highly developed system compared to other states such as the UK and Portugal.

One problem however, which all European states tend to experience is the difficulty of measuring domestic tourism flows. This is a serious problem in those countries where such tourism is on a particularly large scale such as the states of Eastern Europe.

CONCLUSIONS

Marketing research is in some ways relatively under-developed in tourism, leisure and hospitality in comparison with some industries. This might reflect the fact that all three are modern, at least they have only become major recognised industries in recent years. Or it may be a function of the tradition of entrepreneurship, based on hunches and judgements. However, it is more likely that it is because marketing research in our three fields is by nature very complex, as we have seen in this chapter. In such a situation it is tempting to rely on judgement when data is either non-existent or of dubious quality. However, at a time when markets are becoming ever more fragmented, consumers more sophisticated and business environments more complex, marketing research will become increasingly important. It may well be that the development of marketing research to a higher level may be the sign that tourism, leisure and hospitality have at last become mature industries.

DISCUSSION POINTS AND ESSAY QUESTIONS

1. Discuss the different types of marketing research and identify which ones are the most difficult to undertake.
2. Evaluate the main difficulties involved in collecting and interpreting qualitative data on tourists behaviour, perceptions and attitudes.
3. Examine what you consider to be the most important prerequisites for successful marketing research.

EXERCISE Your group has been retained as consultants by a destination marketing agency. The brief you have been given is twofold, namely:

- to discover the perceptions of their destination which are held by people who live in your local area;
- to identify which of these people have never been to their destination and to ascertain what the destination could do to persuade these people to visit.

You should choose a destination that is reasonably well known to people in your local area.

There are five stages to the project, as follows:

(a) deciding how you will go about handling this brief and deciding what survey or surveys you need to conduct;
(b) designing questionnaires for your survey or surveys;
(c) carrying out the survey with an appropriate sample of the population in your local area;
(d) analysing the results of the survey;
(e) delivering the results to your client through a presentation and a report.

CASE STUDIES

You may wish to look some of the following case studies which illustrate the points made in this chapter:

16. Marketing research in France;
17. The 'Ski Thomson' customer satisfaction survey, UK;
21. The Victoria and Albert Museum, UK.

Conclusions to Part 6

On the face of it, these five chapters have relatively little in common with each other. Yet if we look more closely we see that they are very closely linked in that they all focus on the consumer. In an era when the conventional wisdom is that marketing must be consumer-led, this is perhaps natural.

In Chapter 28 we noted that the key to achieving competitive success in tourism, leisure and hospitality marketing lies in anticipating and satisfying consumer demand more effectively than one's competitors.

Chapters 29, 30 and 31 looked at some of the emerging issues which our industries believe the consumer is becoming more interested in, namely quality, green issues and ethics or social responsibility.

Finally, in Chapter 32 we looked at marketing research, which has long been the 'Cinderella' of tourism, leisure and hospitality marketing. If we believe in consumer-led marketing then we clearly have to know more about the consumer.

However, before we become too enamoured of this concept of consumer-led marketing, perhaps we should sound a note of caution. Consumers may demand things which an individual organization with its heavy investment in buildings and equipment on a fixed site may be unable to accommodate in the short term. Therefore, if organizations are to be financially viable we must ask ourselves, can they ever be truly purely consumer-led?

Furthermore, in an era when our three industries are seeing the growth of major international players and concentration of ownership, just how much power does lie with the consumer? Will we really be consumer-led in the future, or will large corporations simply try to make the consumer believe that they are buying what they want when they are in fact simply buying what the corporation finds it profitable to produce?

The wider context

7

This brief part, which consists of just two chapters, is nevertheless of great importance, for it sets the content of most of this book in a wider context in two respects.

Firstly, Chapter 33 relates what we have been saying about tourism, leisure and hospitality to key trends and developments in other industries and sectors of consumer society within Europe. This is highly relevant, because in many ways what is happening in tourism, leisure and hospitality is mirroring, or even following on from, what has happened and is happening in these other industries.

Secondly, Chapter 34 relates what is happening in Europe to developments in the world as a whole. It therefore discusses the process of Europeanization in the context of the increasing globalization of supply and demand, both in tourism, leisure and hospitality, and other industries.

Where appropriate, the authors seek to identify differences between tourism, leisure and hospitality in respect of these two issues. Where any obvious national differences within Europe appear to exist, they are highlighted.

Tourism, leisure and hospitality, other industries and the wider consumer society

33

Key concepts

The main concepts covered in this chapter are:

- similarities with other countries as a result of political, economic, social and technological change;
- the continuing trend towards the concentration of ownership and transnational operation;
- similar trends in relation to the behaviour of consumers in tourism, leisure and hospitality with those in other industries.

INTRODUCTION

In this book the authors have made a number of comments about the ways in which marketing is developing in tourism, leisure and hospitality. These comments have covered the nature of the product, trends in market demand and the methods of marketing which are used.

However, it is, perhaps, a significant fact that many of these comments could have been applied, with modifications, to a number of other sectors of the consumer society. What is happening in tourism, leisure and hospitality is often mirroring similar developments in other industries. Indeed, in a number of cases, these developments are taking place at a slower pace than in some of these other industries.

This chapter will consider these links between trends in tourism, leisure and hospitality, and those in different industries. We will look at these issues under two main headings, as follows:

- the impact of political, economic, social and technological change;
- the structure of industries, including concentration of ownership and the growth of transnational corporations.

THE IMPACT OF CHANGE

While comparisons can be drawn between a wide range of industries and tourism, leisure and hospitality, the greatest similarities are with many other service industries, particularly perhaps the following:

- food retailing;
- financial services;
- media (press, radio and television);
- education.

However, similarities can also be identified with what is happening in a number of manufacturing industries, including food manufacturing and the car industry for example.

In terms of the impact of political, economic, social and technological change, the reader should compare the contents of Chapter 7 with the examples drawn from other industries which are discussed below.

Political change is creating new markets and new business environments for a range of industries in much the same way as it is for tourism, leisure and hospitality. In Eastern Europe, for example, food manufacturers are seeking to develop new markets for their products while wine and food products from Eastern Europe are increasingly finding their way into Western European retail outlets. Likewise the arrival of democracy in South Africa and relative peace in the Middle East is encouraging enterprises in a number of sectors to invest in these countries.

Finally, the Single Market and the enlargement of the European Union is also providing new opportunities for companies in a number of sectors. French insurance companies are developing links with British companies while British food retailers are opening branches in France. Rover and BMW have joined forces and Repsol – petrol stations owned by a Spanish corporation – are beginning to appear in the UK. Privatization and deregulation are also creating new opportunities in sectors such as the water industry where privatization in the UK has created investment opportunities for French utilities.

In many ways, **economic change** is clearly linked to political change, for many economic policies are clearly politically motivated. Differential levels of economic development between countries can stimulate the growth of branch factories in countries where costs are lower than in the company's home country. We have seen this phenomenon in the car and food industry, for example. At the same time, economic growth in particular countries can make them attractive places for inward investment as their domestic markets grow in purchasing power. Conversely economic instability and wildly fluctuating exchange rates can discourage such investment.

Social change is affecting both products and markets in a range of industries. Or perhaps it is more realistic to say that social change in markets is leading to the demand for new types of products. Examples of this include:

- growing interest in environmental issues leading to manufacturers modifying their products in response to criticisms. Hence the removal of chloro-fluoro-carbons (CFCs) from aerosol products in recent years;
- developments in the idea of healthy lifestyles which has created a demand for healthy food products such as diet foods and organic food, for example;
- the recognition of a growing youth culture in Europe which has led to new media and entertainment products being developed for this group of consumers;
- a desire by some people to retire at an earlier age than normal which has created a market for new types of personal pension products;
- the increasingly multi-cultural structure of many European national populations which has generated a need for education provision to be tailored to meet the needs of students from ethnic minority communities.

Technological change is also influencing other industries in the same ways that it is changing tourism, leisure and hospitality. Interactive television and multi-media systems are leading to the rise of 'tele-shopping'. Smart cards are being used increasingly in food retailing while virtual reality is beginning to play a significant role in education, in the training of surgeons for example.

THE STRUCTURE OF INDUSTRY

If we move on to the second heading, we can also see similarities between tourism, leisure and hospitality and other industries.

The trend towards **concentration of ownership** is being seen in most industries in Europe. Media 'empires' are growing like that of Signor Berlusconi in Italy, and mergers and takeovers are creating ever larger food manufacturers. In many sectors, small independent suppliers are being squeezed by the growth of these larger players with their considerable power in the marketplace.

At the same time, we are witnessing a general growth in **transnational corporations** across Europe in a range of industries through a variety of different mechanisms. For example:

- some education institutions are developing strategic alliances with other institutions to offer joint courses, or they are franchising their courses to certain foreign institutions;
- services such as financial consultants, estate agencies and civil engineering companies are establishing branches in the newly developing markets of Eastern Europe;
- joint ventures in the food industry are being created between partners based in two or more European countries;

- car manufacturers are working together in research and development;
- food retailers like Aldi and Netto are setting up units in the UK.

TRENDS IN MARKETING

The issues we have been briefly discussing in this chapter have led to a number of trends in terms of marketing in a range of industries including tourism, leisure and hospitality.

In terms of the **market**, they have led to a growth in segmentation, a recognition that most markets are made of sub-groups with shared characteristics as purchasers. Identifying these segments, developing products which are tailor-made for them alone and giving them the right messages about these products is increasingly seen as the key marketing challenge in a range of European industries.

Likewise, there is a growing belief that we are seeing the slow rise of some pan-European segments which behave similarly irrespective of their nationality. Such groups might include:

- young people and teenagers who share similar tastes in clothes, music and food;
- those interested in living a healthy lifestyle who take regular exercise and are careful about their choice of diet;
- people who are particularly concerned with environmental issues for whom this concern manifests itself in the household products they buy, the forms of transport they use and the food they choose to eat;
- business executives who are united by their use of particular modes of communication and the management theories by which they operate.

If this trend continues, then these groups will develop into the 'Euro-consumer'. What makes them fascinating from a marketing point of view is that their whole lifestyle is determined by the types of factors we have outlined above. Every purchasing decision is consciously or unconsciously designed to reinforce the lifestyle, both in the consumer's own eyes and in the eyes of other people.

Clearly this offers considerable opportunities for **new product development** by European companies. This is already being seen in a number of industries, including:

- the food industry where so-called health products such as 'bio-yoghurts' are being sold across Europe to health conscious consumers, whether they be Swedish or Spanish;
- European-wide clothing products, particularly in relation to the teenage market;
- pan-European management education courses, aimed at the 'Euro business executive' market.

The **way in which products are marketed** is also changing in a range of industries, largely in response to technological innovations. Direct marketing based on computerized databases is growing as the technology that underpins it becomes ever more efficient. This is clearly a threat to marketing intermediaries such as retailers. Technology is also leading to the growth of some forms of advertising media such as the Internet, multi-media systems like CD-Rom, and interactive television.

SUMMARY

This brief summary has hopefully shown that there are great similarities between trends in tourism, leisure and hospitality marketing and other industries, in Europe. However, we must be careful not to exaggerate these similarities, for there are differences, and the speed at which the trends are moving also varies between the different industries.

There are some intrinsic characteristics of tourism, leisure and hospitality that mean it may never be like other industries in some ways. For example, in general, the consumer still has to travel to enjoy the tourism product while in most industries the product can, in some form at least, be taken to the consumer. This point also leads to another relevant observation, namely that tourism, leisure and hospitality marketing is not in itself a homogeneous activity. While the tourism product requires the consumer to travel to it, many leisure and hospitality products can be taken to the consumer. We must therefore recognize the differences and similarities within tourism, leisure and hospitality marketing, as well as those with other industries.

However, ultimately, tourism, leisure and hospitality are merely a part of our overall consumer society. It is likely therefore that in many ways they will mirror and influence changes in marketing practice in other industries to some extent.

Finally, we should also recognize that in this chapter we have not disaggregated the discussion to the level of individual European countries. Yet this is important for a number of reasons, as follows:

- European countries differ greatly in terms of their business environments so that in some countries trends that we have discussed in this chapter will be almost unknown;
- in some countries the similarities between trends in tourism, leisure and hospitality marketing and marketing in other industries will be very close, while in others they will be much less obvious;
- trends such as industrial concentration and transnational operations are much more highly developed in some countries than others.

If the reader wants to test this view, he or she should simply look at the issues we have discussed and compare, almost at random, three different countries which all share the same first letter, namely Sweden, Spain and Slovakia.

CONCLUSIONS

We have seen that there are similarities between what is happening in tourism, leisure and hospitality, and developments in certain other industries.

We have now looked at the first aspect of the wider context of tourism, leisure and hospitality marketing, albeit briefly and selectively. It is now time for us to look at the second element, namely how Europe relates to the global situation.

DISCUSSION POINTS AND ESSAY QUESTIONS

1. Compare and contrast the impact of technological developments on tourism, leisure, and hospitality with their impact on other industries, now, and in the future.
2. Evaluate the differences and similarities in market trends between tourism, leisure and hospitality and other industries.
3. Discuss the extent to which tourism, leisure and hospitality organizations are using similar marketing techniques to organizations in other industries.

EXERCISE Choose **one** organization from **each** of the following industries:

- tourism, leisure or hospitality;
- financial services, media, education or food retailing;
- car manufacturing, food processing or textile production.

Identify the political, economic, social and technological factors which you believe will have the most important implications for your three chosen organizations over the next decade.

Compare and contrast these factors between the three organizations to see where there are similarities and differences.

Europe and globalization $\boxed{\textbf{34}}$

Key concepts

The main concepts covered in this chapter are:

- the process of globalization in terms of demand, supply and the business environment;
- globalization as an opportunity and a threat for European organizations.

INTRODUCTION

Naturally, given the title of this book, we have focused upon the marketing of tourism, leisure and hospitality in Europe. However, we must recognize that tourism, leisure and hospitality are global activities and transnational industries. Furthermore, there is a trend towards increased globalization in all three sectors.

By globalization we mean companies that increasingly operate across the world and sell their products to a worldwide market, which in itself is becoming more homogeneous. The position in Europe needs to be seen in the context of this process, and the concept of competition within Europe needs to be considered in relation to competition from outside Europe. Later in this chapter we will also look at the issue of competition between Europe and the rest of the world, and the ways in which they are influencing each other.

GLOBALIZATION

First of all, however, we will look at the three interrelated aspects of globalization, namely:

- consumer behaviour – the demand side;
- industry structure – the supply side;
- the business environment – the context for the relationship between the demand and supply sides.

In many ways it is the latter factor, which is the driving force behind changes in the other two areas. However, it is important to appreciate that the links between all three are blurred and they are all inseparably intertwined.

Nevertheless we can identify some forces in the business environment which are driving the move towards increased globalization. Some of these forces, in terms of both the macro- and the micro-environment are as follows.

- Technological developments such as global distribution systems are allowing companies to operate on a truly global basis. Likewise, increasingly sophisticated types of media technology such as the Internet are making it easier for consumers to gain access to products from all over the world.
- Political change has occurred in a number of regions of the world, such as Southern Africa, the Middle East, Eastern Europe and North America and Mexico (with the trade treaty between the USA, Canada and Mexico). In general these changes are making it less difficult for companies to set up operations in these regions and for investors to invest in new projects in such countries.
- Trade treaties such as the GATT Agreement are slowly creating a 'level playing field' on a global scale where companies from other parts of the world can compete with local companies on equal terms.
- Economic development in many countries outside the so-called 'developed world' is taking place often at great speed. These countries, such as those of South-East Asia for example, are thus becoming more attractive markets for foreign companies. They are also developing their own tourism, leisure and hospitality industries as their economies grow, and their companies are proving increasing competition for those from the older industrialized countries.
- The media is also becoming more globalized and that in turn is leading to some globalization of social and cultural factors in the business environment. For example, interest in environmental issues is growing in many countries and the media has played a major role in this. The same is true in relation to health, for example. Likewise the globalization of the media has also helped create some globalized social phenomena, such as the international teenage culture for instance.
- The growth of competition within individual countries and the impact of domestic economic recessions in the early 1990s has led to companies looking abroad for their future growth. Globalization through joint ventures, franchises, strategic alliances, takeovers and mergers has become the way in which many organizations have sought to achieve competitive advantage in the 1990s.
- Management theorists, particularly those from the USA and Japan, have had their ideas widely disseminated around the world and

many have been highly influential. Many companies are therefore now being managed in terms of standardized management theories, from Bradfield to Bogota, and Boston to Bangkok. In theory, at least, this should make it easier for companies to undertake transnational expansion.

This brief, selective list shows some of the factors which are driving the process of globalization in tourism, leisure and hospitality marketing. We can see therefore that globalization is a matter both of choice being exercised by the industries and changes in technology and the political environment which are making it possible for them to exercise this choice.

Some commentators tell us that we are moving towards the day when we will see the birth of the **global consumer** in tourism, leisure and hospitality, whose behaviour will differ little in relation to their nationality. If this is the case, it will probably be a result more of the actions of the three relevant industries than a desire for such a development on the part of the consumer.

Furthermore, globalization in tourism, leisure and hospitality marketing will also be promoted by some companies in other industries to help them achieve their broader aims. For example, the media companies and information technology industry will see tourism, leisure and hospitality as just three areas of application for their globe-shrinking new products such as smart cards and multi-media systems.

We should note that this process of globalisation is affecting many other industries apart from tourism, leisure and hospitality for example the food and drink industry, the entertainment business, financial services and retailing, for some of the same reasons that we noted earlier in respect of the three sectors with which we are primarily concerned. Indeed, it could be argued that globalization in these industries is much more highly developed than it is in tourism, leisure and hospitality. Hence the growth of truly global brands such as Disney and Coca-Cola.

Clearly, in some ways, tourism has always been a global industry by its very nature, moving people from continent to continent, and some hotel chains have been global operators for many years. However, the trend is now gathering pace, becoming more widespread, and is encompassing leisure increasingly too.

Nevertheless, there appear to be some obstacles to globalization, particularly in relation to national differences in consumer behaviour and government policies, for example. Patterns of demand and preferred holiday resorts can vary dramatically between different countries while some governments take a negative attitude towards the arrival of foreign companies into their national market. So the march of globalization will continue to vary in pace between different countries, and will falter from time to time in response to these obstacles.

OPPORTUNITY OR THREAT?

If we believe that the process of globalization will continue, then from a European perspective we have to see it as both an opportunity and a potential threat in terms of the tourism, leisure and hospitality markets.

Globalization is an **opportunity** for European organizations because it means opportunities for expansion and new markets to exploit. In recent years we have seen European companies growing through strategies based on becoming players on a truly global scale. Examples of these include:

- Club Méditerranée's expansion in terms of its recent new resorts in countries such as Mexico and Australia, together with its campaigns to attract customers in the US and Japanese markets;
- Accor's expansion into the USA hotel sector through its purchase of the Motel 6 chain;
- British Airways' purchase of shares in Qantas and US Air and its involvement in the creation of new airlines such as Carib Express.

This globalization has not just been seen in the commercial sector. Government-funded destination marketing agencies have also put some effort into marketing their product on a truly global scale. Two good examples of this include the sophisticated strategy of the Irish National Tourist Board, Bord Fáilte, and the French agency, Maison de la France's efforts in the Japanese market.

However, we already can see how globalisation could be a **threat** to Europe's tourism, leisure and hospitality industries in the following ways, for example:

- Europe is already losing its share of the worldwide international tourism market as new destinations outside Europe come.onto the scene;
- the rapid expansion of American fast-food chains such as McDonald's in Europe, which have changed the catering industry in Europe dramatically;
- the interest being shown in the liberalization of Europe's air transport industry by the lean and fit US airlines which have already survived the American deregulation process.

Clearly these opportunities and threats are similar to those which have already been faced by other industries, particularly in the manufacturing sector. In many older traditional industries, such as steel and textiles, and newer industries like computers and audio equipment, we have seen Europe lose out to non-European countries. These countries have tended to succeed for a variety of reasons including lower prices and being more in tune with changes in consumer demand.

We must, of course, appreciate that there are inherent differences between services like tourism, leisure and hospitality and manufacturing industries. However, we should recognize that some of the ways in which Europe is seeking to compete in manufacturing product markets may offer lessons for the situation with regard to tourism, leisure and hospitality. These include:

- concentrating on higher quality, premium priced products rather than competing purely on price;
- working on improving the service element of the product which is often compared unfavourably to those offered in other parts of the world, most notably South East Asia;
- becoming better at marketing in terms of research, new product development, promotion, distribution and selling;
- anticipating changes in consumer behaviour better, and adapting products quicker to meet changes in demand;
- utilizing technology to improve both efficiency of operation and the service which is offered to customers;
- the coming together of European businesses in particular sectors so that their combined strength allows them to compete with non-European companies.

CONCLUSIONS

If we look to the future, we will probably see a continued move towards globalization, which will be made increasingly possible by technological innovations. Each day we move a little closer to the so-called 'global village'.

It may well be that while we in Europe are concerning ourselves with the concept of Europeanization, Europe will find itself being 'leap-frogged' by the process of globalization. We must therefore always consider tourism, leisure and hospitality marketing in terms of a global context rather than behaving as if somehow Europe were a closed system.

DISCUSSION POINTS AND ESSAY QUESTIONS

1. Critically evaluate the extent to which the process of globalization is making the concept of Europe obsolete.
2. Discuss the opportunities and threats which the process of globalization represents for European tourism, leisure and hospitality organizations.

EXERCISE   You should choose **one** of the following sectors:

- tour operation;
- accommodation;
- air transport.

For your chosen sector you should produce a report covering the following issues:

(a) the role of European organizations in the relevant market or markets in non-European countries;
(b) the role of non-European organizations in the relevant market or markets within Europe;
(c) the extent to which the relevant market or markets may be considered to be global at present.

Conclusions to Part 7

In these two brief chapters we have attempted to remind readers that there is a broader context within which European tourism, leisure and hospitality marketing operates. There are other industries with which tourism, leisure and hospitality marketing has shared characteristics, and there is a global marketplace beyond Europe. The links between tourism, leisure and hospitality marketing and both of these wider contexts look likely to become closer in the future. The business environment in which we operate is changing in ways which are making distinctions between industries less clear-cut and are rendering geographical boundaries increasingly obsolete.

Looking to the future

In this section of the book, we will endeavour to draw together some conclusions, and then go on to look into the future, to see how the marketing of tourism, leisure and hospitality in Europe may develop in the years to come.

Our conclusions in Chapter 35 will be drawn from each of the seven parts of the book, together with some more general points.

When we attempt to predict future trends in Chapter 36 we will consider the likely impact of political, economic, social and technological factors on the future of marketing in the European tourism, leisure and hospitality industries. In general, we will concentrate on the foreseeable future – the next few years. However, we will also attempt to look further ahead, beyond the year 2005. In a rapidly changing world, this is a very difficult, some would say impossible task.

Conclusions  35

INTRODUCTION

At the end of such a long, complex, and wide-ranging text, attempting to draw conclusions is a necessary but awesome task. Perhaps the only real conclusion we can draw is that there are no generally applicable conclusions. However, this is too trite a statement, and we feel we must endeavour to pull together some broad conclusions for the benefit of readers.

SUMMARY OF THE TEXT

Before going on to outline these conclusions in some detail, we would like to begin by seeing how the book has, in our opinion, lived up to the objectives set out in the preface. However, it is for readers to decide how successful we have been in this respect, though we believe we have produced a text which is truly European in flavour, particularly through the case studies and examples that have been used. However, we are conscious of the fact that we have not been able to produce answers to questions such as whether there is any such person as the European tourist. This is not for want of trying, but simply because reliable data does not yet exist that would allow us to develop answers to this and other questions.

Part 1

Nevertheless, we believe that in relation to Part 1 of the book we can offer the following brief conclusions.

Firstly, the **marketing concept** appears to be viewed similarly across Europe, although perhaps in Eastern Europe it is still in its infancy.

Secondly, Europe is not homogeneous. There are **national differences** and there are **regional blocs** within Europe which appear to share similar characteristics, such as Southern Europe, Northern Europe and Eastern Europe. However, this situation appears to be changing in two ways, as follows:

- the policies of the European Commission and the enlargement of the European Union are slowly reducing some national differences between the relevant countries;
- economic growth in Southern Europe and political change in Eastern Europe seem to be gradually lessening some of the variations between these regions and the rest of Europe.

Thirdly, as we saw in Chapter 3, there are **significant differences between tourism, leisure and hospitality** in terms of marketing. These differences cover products, markets and marketing techniques.

Furthermore, even within each of these fields, we have seen that there can be significant variations in marketing practice. These are, perhaps, most noticeable in relation to the following criteria:

- the **marketing objectives** of organizations which tend to vary depending on whether the organization is in the private, public or voluntary sector. This characteristic can also reinforce the differences between our three fields for the private sector is much more powerful in tourism and hospitality than it is in many forms of leisure;
- The **size of organizations** ranging from small one-person enterprises to massive, transnational corporations. Marketing in the latter type of organization is usually well funded, heavily planned and carried out by specialist staff. In the case of small businesses, on the other hand, marketing often has limited budgets, is opportunistic rather than planned, and is usually carried out by the entrepreneur themselves, who may have little or no specialist marketing expertise.

Part 2

In Part 2 we looked at **consumers, markets, industry structure** and the **business environment** from a European perspective. While we were able to use copious examples from different European countries, it was not always easy to see a great deal of European homogeneity.

If we talk about markets and consumer behaviour, there is currently a generally heterogeneous situation. A French tourist, for example, still behaves differently to a British tourist. He or she is more likely to holiday in August, to stay in their own country for their main holiday, and to shun the package holiday in favour of more independent forms of holidaymaking.

However, we suggest that this heterogeneity is not the same as saying each country is very different. For example, regions of Europe do appear to share some characteristics and the French tourist is not dissimilar in many respects to tourists in Spain and Italy while the Dutch and German tourist shares many characteristics in common with his or her British counterpart.

Furthermore, we believe that trends are taking place which are making the picture more complex and perhaps leading to more homogeneity. For example:

- Certain **niche markets or market segments** are developing which appear to be more pan-European in nature than we have seen previously. Examples of these include the student traveller, who travels on study exchanges and then takes side trips from their study base.

  There also appear to be shared behavioural characteristics amongst many youth travellers in general, such as the 'hedonists' of Northern Europe. It is perhaps not surprising that the younger generation, with its greater language skills and lack of memories of wars past is taking the lead in this trend.

- There is growth in the **business tourism** market where consumer behaviour and demand patterns appear to show less variation than is the case with leisure travel. Perhaps this is because these travellers do not choose where, when and how they travel and are not motivated by a pleasure imperative. It is largely a utilitarian activity. Furthermore, much business travel is undertaken by employees of multinational companies who are by nature more international than national in outlook.

- The continuing **globalization** of the media is playing an increasing role in influencing consumer behaviour in tourism, leisure and hospitality.

- As more and more Europeans become **experienced tourists** they are alike in seeking ever more unusual new experiences and more flexibility from tour operators.

- **European Union regulations** are slowly standardizing a range of factors within members countries which affect tourism, leisure and hospitality marketing. These vary from controls on working hours to social benefits and consumer protection legislation.

- Many **new leisure activities** are sweeping across Europe, usually backed by huge promotional campaigns undertaken by major transnational corporations. These include everything from computer games to karaoke!

This is just a brief, selective list but it does indicate the range of such factors that are currently influencing the tourism, leisure and hospitality markets.

Clearly, there are links between trends in consumer behaviour and the **supply side**. Consumers can only buy what industries offer while organizations are always seeking to vary their offers in response to changing consumer preferences.

In Chapter 6 we identified several important issues in relation to the supply side, in other words the industrial structure of tourism, leisure and hospitality. These included:

- the polarization between small businesses and large corporations;
- the growth of transnational companies;
- the ongoing process of industrial concentration.

Chapter 7 went on to look at the European **business environment** and concluded that it is still largely heterogeneous in relation to tourism, leisure and hospitality. However, again we noted trends which will lead to greater standardization, including the following:

- technological developments which are truly global and for which geographical boundaries are of little relevance;
- political changes like the harmonization policies of the European Commission and the introduction of market or semi-market economies in Eastern Europe;
- the process of economic globalization;
- the growth of more and more standardized approaches to management education and training.

Part 3

In the next section of the book, Part 3, we examined the application of the concept of the marketing mix to tourism, leisure and hospitality. This resulted in the following points being identified.

- The **product** in all cases is intangible, a service, but it usually has tangible elements like the food in a restaurant or the seat on an aircraft.
- The **benefits** which the product bestows on the consumer vary between different sectors within tourism, leisure and hospitality.
- The same **pricing** mechanisms are available to most organizations but some show a preference for discounting for tactical marketing reasons while others offer concessions for social reasons.
- **Place** or distribution comes in both forms, namely direct from producer to consumer and via an intermediary such as a travel agent.
- While the range of potential **promotional techniques** is very similar for all organizations, they are used in different ways within different sectors. The main reason for this difference appears to be budgetary but there may well be others, notably the nature of the product, the size of the market and the price of the product.

Part 4

In Part 4 we looked at the **marketing planning process** in relation to tourism, leisure and hospitality. Using examples, we looked at how organizations seek to answer four questions, namely:

- where are we now?
- where are we going?
- how will we get there?
- when will we know when we have arrived?

However, as was indicated in Part 4, doubts have been expressed about the validity of traditional marketing planning in our three areas, mainly due to the volatility of the business environment.

Nevertheless, we did see that marketing planning is used by tourism, leisure and hospitality organizations, and we examined some of the issues involved in implementing such an approach.

Part 5

Part 5 was where we looked at a range of **individual sectors** within tourism, leisure and hospitality. This was very illuminating, for we believe that in terms of the practice of marketing there are greater differences between the sectors than there are between countries.

Three examples will illustrate this point, as follows.

- The **benefits sought** by those taking part in countryside recreation in Greece and Britain are probably similar but the benefits sought by Greek people from a restaurant meal or a shopping trip are likely to be very different.
- **Methods of distribution** are usually similar within the same sector in different countries, although to different degrees. For instance, most package holidays in France are sold through travel agents just as they are in the UK. However, in neither country, nor in any other European country, do travel agents play a significant role in the sale of tickets to visitor attractions, for example.
- The **promotional techniques** used are often similar between organizations in different countries within one sector. Airlines and hotel chains advertise widely while most museums rarely do. Tour operators across Europe tend to rely heavily on glossy brochures or catalogues while the main promotional literature of airlines tend to be their information-packed brochures.

This is not to say, however, that there are not significant differences between countries in terms of the marketing mix in some respect. All four elements of the mix are affected by a range of factors that can create major national differences in the framework within which the marketing mix is manipulated. Many of these factors are political and governmental and include laws on advertising, price controls and restrictions, or the lack of them, on the use of marketing intermediaries.

Part 6

In Part 6 we highlighted five topical issues within tourism, leisure and hospitality marketing, namely quality, green issues, competitive advantage, ethics and social responsibility, and marketing research. Even in a fashion-conscious area like marketing, these five areas stand out as being ones which are particularly exercising the attention of both academics and managers.

Two interesting points emerged from our examination of these topical issues, namely:

- that **they are interrelated**, in other words quality is a way of achieving competitive advantage and green issues are an ethical challenge for tourism, leisure and hospitality organizations;
- **all of them put the customer at the centre**. Organizations are interested in quality, green issues and ethics because they think these things are important to their customers. Competitive advantage is seen in terms of offering customers more benefits or different benefits to those offered by competitors. Lastly, marketing research is seen as crucial because we need to know who the customer is and what they are looking for in order to be effective and successful in marketing terms.

Part 7

In the last section, Part 7, we sought to place tourism, leisure and hospitality in a wider context. This led to some interesting conclusions, as follows:

- that **marketing in our three areas is very similar to that in many other industries**. There are few characteristics of marketing within tourism, leisure and hospitality that are not also found in at least one or two other industries;
- that **Europe is not a closed system**. It is involved in a two-way relationship with the rest of the world. Indeed some might argue that globalization is making the concept of Europe and Europeanization obsolete before they have even become a reality.

OVERALL CONCLUSIONS

Having drawn conclusions from each section of the book it is now time to look at more general points that have arisen from the book.

Firstly, **marketing in tourism, leisure and hospitality is a very complex and diverse field**. This diversity reflects a number of factors including:

- the differing objectives of organizations in the public, private and voluntary sectors;
- the variations in markets in terms of their size and the extent to which they are free or regulated;
- the size and resources of organizations;
- whether the organization operates on a purely domestic level or is transnational.

Secondly, Europe currently exhibits characteristics which illustrate that in many aspects of tourism, leisure and hospitality marketing, it is heterogeneous. However, **there are a forces at work which are making Europe ever more standardized, albeit at a slow pace**, for example:

- the enlargement of the European Union and the creation of a Single Market;

- the activities of transnational companies;
- management training and international education programmes which are spreading similar messages about tourism, leisure and hospitality marketing from Iceland to Italy and the Azores to Albania;
- technological developments which are making national boundaries less and less meaningful.

This last point has also to be put in the context of the steady march of globalization. In the emerging world order, Europe's traditionally strong position in the world of tourism, leisure and hospitality is clearly threatened by the rise of new geographical areas, most notably the countries of the Pacific Rim.

Whether or not the reader believes this book has achieved its original objectives it has, hopefully, highlighted two interesting points:

- Tourism, leisure and hospitality marketing is a fascinating and increasingly sophisticated field which merits more study by academics. We have not as yet even started to dig under the surface of this deep and ever-changing field. Such studies should also seek to place marketing in our three areas in the context of trends in marketing in other industries.
- The concept of Europe is slowly becoming more of a reality as a market, a political entity and an economic force, although this is taking place at a slow and uneven pace. This trend is not without its dangers, however. A 'transition' and 'Europeanization' of national and regional cultures, reinforced by the influence of American popular culture, could, potentially, make Europe a much less attractive cultural tourism destination for non-European tourists. It could also make international tourism within Europe less interesting for Europeans. Perhaps this has already gone too far to stop and instead a series of 'rearguard actions' may simply delay the inevitable outcome.

These conclusions are part of a continuum – they reflect trends that began some time ago and will carry on in some form into the future. It is therefore appropriate that we should conclude this book by taking a look at the future of tourism, leisure and hospitality marketing.

36 The future of tourism, leisure and hospitality marketing in Europe

INTRODUCTION

If drawing conclusions is a difficult task, then predicting the future is near impossible. Yet, we feel our task would be incomplete if we were not to attempt to suggest some likely possible future directions for tourism, leisure and hospitality marketing in Europe.

We will look at those factors which will influence this future direction and then briefly discuss the likely impact of these factors. These impacts will be considered in terms of their effect on products, marketing techniques and the market. As far as possible, we will group the factors into political, economic, social and technological.

Finally, there is the question of what do we mean by the future – what is our timescale? In such a fast-changing field, any attempt to look far into the future is of little value. Here, therefore, we will focus on changes which are likely to take place, or to be well underway, within the next ten years, say by the year 2005.

As we noted at the end of Chapter 35, the future is unlikely to see a revolution in tourism, leisure and hospitality marketing. Instead, there will be a continued evolution containing trends which are already established and which we discussed in the last section of the book.

POLITICAL FACTORS

A range of political changes will influence tourism, leisure and hospitality marketing over the next ten years, most of which are probably already underway. These may include the following.

- The further **enlargement of the European Union** is likely to encompass many Eastern European countries together with Malta and Cyprus. Norway may yet join as might Turkey and Switzerland. Any enlargement will bring yet more countries within the European Single Market. Furthermore they will become subject to European legislation on everything from working conditions to consumer protection.

- It appears likely that **political instability** may continue to hold back tourism development in parts of Eastern Europe, but in those countries where there is stability, tourism should grow at an impressive rate.
- National governments and/or the European Union may well pass **legislation** on a range of topics relevant to our three areas, for example:
  - imposing controls on some leisure applications of virtual reality technology;
  - outlawing 'ageism' so that job applicants cannot be discriminated against on the grounds of their age.
- The ongoing **process of liberalization, deregulation, and privatization** will probably continue with dramatic effects on the airline industry for example, where state support for national flag carriers will diminish and true competition will increase.

However, as we have seen in recent years, political factors can change overnight and upset the most carefully thought-out predictions. Events like the coming down of the Berlin Wall and the peace process in Northern Ireland have provided unexpected opportunities for the growth of tourism. At the same time, civil war has seriously damaged the tourism industry in the former Yugoslavia. Politics in Europe is currently a very volatile area and we must always recognize that we need to be ready to respond to unexpected events.

ECONOMIC FACTORS

As in Chapter 7, we can split these into those economic factors that are largely political in origin and those which are more purely economic in nature. We will begin with the former.

For at least 15 European countries, the European Union's economic policies will be crucial in relation to the following issues:

- the potential impact of a **single European currency** on the currency exchange business and on tourist flows which have traditionally been sensitive to changes in exchange rates;
- the **abolition of duty free allowances** which is a threat for many airlines, airports and ferry companies;
- the **harmonization of value added taxes** may lead to the prices of some tourism products rising in certain countries where they are currently taxed at relatively low rates, or indeed not taxed at all.

However, there are also more purely economic factors that will have a major influence on tourism, leisure and hospitality marketing between now and the year 2005, including:

- the **growing economies of many Southern and Eastern European countries** will lead to them generating more international tourist trips;

- **concentration of ownership** will continue, both through horizontal and vertical integration. In some markets, therefore, consumers may see less and less choice;
- in many sectors **competition** will remain intense, while in others it will become truly competitive for the first time through liberalization and deregulation. As domestic markets become saturated, organizations such as tour operators in particular may seek to grow by selling their holidays to residents of other countries.

SOCIAL FACTORS

Social and cultural change is also set to change marketing in our three areas over the next few years in a number of ways. The following few examples illustrate the range of such changes as we are likely to see.

- There will be **demographic change** such as more older people and an ever-increasing number of single-parent families, both of which represent expanding market segments for tourism, leisure and hospitality marketing to target.
- The trend towards **greater heterogeneity** in populations will continue to create more niche markets in place of the former mass markets. This has implications for product development and promotional strategies in particular.
- **The media will continue to raise awareness of issues amongst customers** which will then influence their purchasing decisions. These issues will probably continue to be environmental concerns, ethical standards in business, health and animal welfare, for instance.
- As education becomes more internationalized in different countries we will see new segments of, probably young, **consumers who see themselves as 'Europeans'** gradually emerge. These will be a good target market for those organizations which are seeking to expand into foreign markets.
- **Women** will become increasingly important in the tourism, leisure and hospitality marketplace, particularly as business travellers.
- **Groups who could be seen to be disadvantaged** in tourism, leisure and hospitality currently, such as the disabled and people from the ethnic minority communities, may step up their efforts to make the industry pay more attention to their needs as both potential consumers and prospective employees.
- The links between **marketing and lifestyle** which have resulted in much modern advertising and literature being designed to reinforce people's idea of their desired lifestyle will spread to tourism, leisure and hospitality from other industries, such as car manufacturers and the alcoholic drinks business. Thus, tour operator brochures, for example, will become more like designer lifestyle magazines.
- Finally, the debate over **postmodernism** will continue to rage but, whatever the merits of the argument, the 'postmodern' trend

towards the reducing of boundaries between different activities and markets will continue to be seen in tourism, leisure and hospitality.

TECHNOLOGICAL FACTORS

Technological innovations and their application to tourism, leisure and hospitality may in the years to come be the most significant set of factors in the shaping of the future. Their potential impact may well be felt in every aspect of marketing across all three areas with which we are concerned. This point is illustrated by the following examples.

- **New products** will be based on technological innovations such as virtual reality and the development of artificial environments.
- Certain technologies such as smart cards may **reduce the costs and therefore perhaps the prices** of certain products. For instance, a card that saves the need to print airline tickets will save the airline money. This will help the company to either reduce prices or increase its profit margins. Likewise, developments in catering technology will continue to be utilized to reduce labour input and costs in the hospitality sectors to allow organizations to remain competitive in the light of ever increasing competition.
- Innovations such as multi-media systems and CD-rom will facilitate the growth of **direct marketing** to the client who has such a system in their home or office. Again, marketing costs will be reduced for tour operators, for instance, as they will no longer need to pay commission to travel agents.
- **Promotional techniques** might also be changed by technological developments with the CD-rom replacing, or at least supplementing, brochures in the future.

However, while these developments may be good news for consumers, tour operators and airlines, they clearly pose a threat for intermediaries such as travel agents and other sectors of tourism, leisure and hospitality. Video- and computer-conferencing will, for example, lead to some reduction in the demand for business travel, although the authors believe that, for social reasons amongst others, this will not be a rapidly growing phenomenon.

There are also concerns that the technologies may be dominated by large corporations who may not make their competitors' products available on their systems. Ironically this could therefore mean less rather than more choice for the consumer.

Ultimately, the degree to which tourism, leisure, and hospitality marketing is affected by technological developments in the future will depend upon a number of factors including:

- the pace at which innovations are made and the speed with which they can be introduced within industry;

- the costs involved in introducing new technologies and the willingness of customers to pay the resulting price;
- the attitudes of consumers, as a whole and in individual market segments, towards technological developments, and their desire, or otherwise, to make use of them;
- the degree and nature of governmental and supra-governmental regulations which may be introduced in relation to the new technologies.

It is obviously difficult to gauge how far and how quickly technology will change tourism, leisure and hospitality marketing. 'Technophiles' predict massive, rapid and comprehensive change while 'technophobes' dismiss the idea that any significant change will occur. Certainly many organizations, particularly smaller ones, appear to be taking little concrete action in anticipation of rapid changes in their business as a result of technological innovations.

Perhaps history holds a lesson for us in this respect. Technology has stimulated great leaps forward in tourism in the past, particularly in the transport field. Yet the technological changes we are seeing are perhaps more fundamental and wide-ranging than we have ever seen before. It seems likely, therefore, that great change will take place as a result of current innovations.

Whatever happens, it is likely that the new technologies will bring tourism, leisure and hospitality organizations closer to other industries in two ways, as follows:

- the telecommunications, media and computer companies that are developing the technologies will become partners with companies in our three areas;
- other industries will seek to become sellers of tourism, leisure and hospitality products, for example high street retailers, due to the synergies of different new technologies.

IMPACT ON TOURISM, LEISURE AND HOSPITALITY MARKETING IN EUROPE

It might be helpful if we consider these matters in terms of the seven major parts into which this book has been divided. Let us therefore begin by looking at the future of the three questions which made up Part 1, namely:

- What is marketing?
- What is Europe?
- What are tourism, leisure and hospitality?

Marketing has been fashionable now for some years in Europe. It has perhaps been the most talked about and written about management function in recent years across the continent. However, there is no guarantee that this will continue, particularly in service industries where human resource management may become the next focus for attention by managers and theorists. Alternatively, the future may see a breaking down of the barriers between the different management functions and the emergence of a new form of integrated management. However, the principles and techniques of marketing will remain vital for any organization which aspires to be successful in a competitive market. We should therefore be interested in how the marketing concept itself may develop in the future. We have moved from the era of product and production-led marketing to the current idea of consumer-led marketing. Perhaps the future will see the emphasis switch to marketing that is concerned with society's attitudes and beliefs as well as the more traditional concerns of the marketer. Marketing may have to demonstrate it is socially responsible as well as being concerned with satisfying consumers.

The concept of **Europe** will clearly continue to change with the enlargement of the European Union and the harmonizing effects of EU policies. Europe will thus become an increasingly political and social rather than simply an economic phenomenon. However, this task will be far from complete at the end of our ten-year timescale.

Tourism, leisure and hospitality will continue to become increasingly interconnected in a complex web of relationships. New forms of leisure, hospitality and tourism will develop to meet the changing demand of the consumer. This may mean more emphasis on home-based entertainment systems, new forms of accommodation and innovative activity holidays.

Moving on to Part 2, as far as the **consumer and the markets are concerned**, certain trends are likely to occur, including:

- the growth of pan-European market segments such as student exchange travellers and 'empty-nester' travellers in search of new experiences, who will share similar characteristics regardless of their nationality;
- the further fragmentation of the mass markets into increasingly narrow niche markets;
- technology will allow consumers to gain direct access to some products without the need to use intermediaries.

At the same time our three **industries**, if they are industries, will also undergo change, most notably in terms of the continuation of the process of concentration of ownership and transnational expansion. Links with other industries will also grow, most notably with retailing, computers, telecommunications and the media as new technologies modify the pattern of distribution in tourism in particular.

The **business environment** will continue to be volatile and there appears no prospect of it becoming less changeable in the near future. The authors believe that most change will be seen in relation to the impact of political and technological factors.

In terms of Part 3, changes in the **marketing mix** will perhaps be focused on P for place or distribution, where technology will be both a threat and an opportunity. Technological developments will also facilitate the creation of new products, influence pricing policies and generate new types of promotional media.

Within the context of Part 4 the concept of **marketing planning** is not likely to change dramatically over the next few years. However, the work of researchers and management educators may result in the development of new techniques which make the process more effective in tourism, leisure and hospitality.

As far as Part 5 and the **individual sectors within tourism, leisure and hospitality** are concerned, the next ten years are likely to bring major changes in marketing for the following areas:

- airlines, where the European market will become freer and ticketless travel will become the norm while ever faster trains will increase competition on short-haul business routes within Europe;
- retail travel, where technology will allow consumers to bypass agents unless the travel agencies act quickly to reduce the threat;
- the attractions business, where technologies like virtual reality will underpin a range of new high-tech products;
- catering, where new ethnic cuisines will become fashionable and the distinction between food manufacturing and fast-food catering will become further blurred;
- in the arts and entertainment, and recreation and sport sectors, where technologies like multi-media systems and virtual reality will become potential competitors, encouraging consumers to substitute a passive at-home experience for an active, away-from-home activity;
- business tourism, where technology again in the form of video and computer conferencing will reduce some demand for business travel while those who do travel will demand better facilities from airlines and hotels.

Moving on to the subject of Part 6, it seems likely that the topical issues we discussed will remain topical between now and the year 2005. However, that is not to say that they will not change in terms of their focus and emphasis. For example:

- the rather simplistic concern with green issues may turn into a broader interest in sustainability;
- the idea of social responsibility may extend to the ways in which organizations recruit their staff and their employment practices;
- competitive advantage strategies could focus more on market forces and corporate values as well as on the traditional approaches of price and product differentiation;
- the emphasis on marketing research may shift from measuring tourism and collecting quantitative data to a concern with why consumers do what they do, in other words qualitative research.

EXTERNAL INFLUENCES

In line with Part 7 of the book, we must recognize that neither tourism, leisure and hospitality, nor Europe, are closed systems. The former influence and are influenced by other industries, while the latter enjoys a two-way relationship with the rest of the world.

It seems likely that the gaps between tourism, leisure and hospitality and other industries and activities will become increasingly blurred. Already highstreet retailers are interested in selling holidays and the media is playing an increasing role in tourism and leisure.

Tomorrow's 'travel agent' may well be a multi-media kiosk in a department store where the tourist can also buy their holiday clothes and may even obtain credit with which to purchase the holiday. Perhaps this development will come about because of shared technologies or it may be a result of postmodernism.

If it does happen it will not be a revolution, but rather a continuation of existing trends, whereby education institutions are offering tourist accommodation in their halls of residence, factories are becoming visitor attractions, and food shops are providing convenience foods that compete with fast-food catering outlets.

Europe's future in the wider world is a complex issue. The emergence of new tourist destinations seems likely to ensure that Europe's share of world tourism will continue to fall. However, the political changes in Eastern Europe might ultimately help to reverse this trend. It seems likely that European tourism, leisure and hospitality organizations will continue to expand in non-European countries, but that they in turn will face increased competition in their home markets from non-European organizations. Major competition may come from Pacific Rim countries in the airline and hotel sectors, for example, and the USA in terms of media and telecommunications companies in the distribution field across tourism, leisure and hospitality.

BEYOND THE YEAR 2005

Where are all these potential future trends going to take tourism, leisure and hospitality marketing in the years beyond 2005? Perhaps the following scenarios, which now appear like science fiction, will become reality sooner than we think. For example:

- the virtual reality 'holiday in the head' where there is no need to even leave home;
- Eastern European tourists filling the beaches of Western Europe's seaside resorts;
- people taking holidays in artificial environments including underwater resort complexes;
- the 'stay-at-home business traveller' who no longer needs to travel because of developments in communications technology;

- tourists buying their holidays from their local food store or post office, or from the armchair in front of their interactive television;
- limitations on where and when people can travel either because of the need to protect overcrowded destinations or due to the congestion of transport systems;
- the major tourism corporations of the future active in Europe may be from the newly industrialized countries of the Pacific Rim rather than from Europe or the USA;
- space-station holidays may even be on offer!

These are all possible scenarios – though some may never happen, others may become reality sooner than we imagine.

It should also be recognized, however, that some changes will occur in the longer term that cannot even be foreseen as yet. These may be triggered by a technological innovation, a change in the political situation, economic trends or changes in social attitudes.

CONCLUSIONS

The marketing of tourism, leisure and hospitality, has grown dramatically in recent years. In organizations which have been involved in it over a long time, the level of sophistication has become much greater while new organizations have come onto the scene such as public sector bodies and charitable trusts.

This growing interest in the subject is in many ways welcome, but it does pose potential problems for the future, for both the industries and society as a whole. These include:

- the danger that marketing can be hijacked by hype where exaggerated promises and bogus claims made on behalf of organizations are all too common;
- the potential damage that could result from the idea of taking consumer-led marketing too far. When do we tell the consumer their demand is unacceptable and cannot or will not be met?
- the difficulty in providing a good service product when the people who deliver the product, the staff, are often poorly paid or inadequately trained, sometimes resulting in high turnover rates but more often leading to demoralized and demotivated staff delivering the product grudgingly;
- the trend towards standardized products in hospitality, for example, may come into sharp conflict with the growth of niche markets and a possible rejection of mass produced products.

Tourism, leisure and hospitality marketing has undoubtedly helped to stimulate the consumer culture which seems to be growing in Europe and the rest of the world today. The implications of this for the environment and society are potentially enormous and largely destructive. Perhaps, therefore, the future will see tourism, leisure and hospitality marketing leading the way in the development of more sustainable and socially responsible approaches to marketing. The demarketing of tourist honey-pots, for example, may provide a lead for other industries in this respect. Many would argue that as marketing has helped create many of mankind's present problems, it is high time it started to contribute towards finding some solutions to those problems.

Perhaps tourism, leisure and hospitality marketing in Europe can spearhead this development, and in doing so secure competitive advantage for Europe in the future in the fields of tourism, leisure and hospitality.

Case studies

This book has used copious examples to illustrate points made in individual chapters. However, the authors also believe that readers might find a number of larger and broader case studies valuable.

The case studies which follow show how a number of European tourism, leisure and hospitality organizations currently carry out their marketing activities. These cases illustrate some interesting differences and similarities in marketing practice. Some are short and have been written to explore one particular issue. Others are much longer and give an overview of a whole business or organization.

At the end of relevant chapters in the book we have referred to the cases where appropriate. The following chart gives the reader a summary of the main areas of marketing which are covered in each case study. The cases which follow are arranged in the order in which they appear on this chart.

Wherever possible, the case studies have been developed using a standard questionnaire, with some minor modifications to reflect the differences between organizations. This, together with the fairly standard format in which the cases are presented, is designed to make it easier for readers to compare and contrast the approaches to marketing of the different organizations.

It should be noted that the material for these case studies was collected largely during summer 1995. They must therefore be seen, like all published case studies, as snapshots in time that will date quickly. Of course, this does not make the lessons that can be learned from them invalid.

Chart of main areas of marketing covered in each case study

Area of marketing

	Case study	The business environment	Product	Price	Place	Promotion	Marketing planning	Sector-specific Issues	Green issues	Marketing research and markets	Marketing in general
1.	Political change and hotel development in Eastern Europe	X						X			
2.	The Forte International Programme, UK		X	X		X		X			
3.	First Choice, UK		X			X		X			
4.	The role of brochures in hotel-marketing: The Hotel Vitosha, Sofia, Bulgaria					X		X			
5.	The role of the media in tourism marketing in the UK					X					
6.	Scotland						X	X			
7.	Futuroscope, France			X				X			
8.	Timeshare accommodation in Europe							X			
9.	Bord Fáilte, Ireland		X		X	X		X			
10.	Club Méditerranée SA, France		X	X				X			
11.	The Hurtigruten, Norwegian coastal voyage, Norway		X	X	X	X		X			
12.	Porto Carras complex, Halkidiki Greece		X					X			
13.	Iceland: The marketing of a business tourism destination		X	X	X	X		X			
14.	Grecotel: An example of greening and competitive advantage in the hospitality industry, Greece							X	X		
15.	TUI, Germany: Environmental policy of the tour operator							X	X		
16.	Marketing research in France									X	
17.	The 'Ski Thomson' customer satisfaction survey, UK						X			X	
18.	Airtours plc, UK	X	X	X	X	X	X	X			X
19.	British Airways, UK	X	X	X	X	X	X	X			X
20.	The European Travel Commission	X	X			X	X	X		X	X
21.	The Victoria and Albert Museum, UK	X	X	X	X	X	X	X		X	X
22.	The European youth travel market									X	
23.	Futbol Club Barcelona, Spain		X	X	X	X		X		X	
24.	Abercrombie and Kent Ltd, UK		X	X	X	X		X		X	
25.	Accor, France	X	X	X	X	X		X			
26.	Thalassa International, France		X	X	X	X		X			
27.	Les Vins Georges Duboeuf SA, France		X	X	X	X		X			
28.	Center Parcs, UK	X	X	X	X	X		X	X		
29.	Port Aventura SA, Spain		X	X	X	X		X			

Political change and hotel development in Eastern Europe

CASE 1

One outcome of the process of political change in Eastern Europe since the late 1980s has been the interest of Western hotel companies in developing new hotels in Eastern Europe.

A survey in *Business Traveller* magazine in July 1995 looked at some of the developments that had taken place in this field, including the following:

- Warsaw, Poland, where Marriott has built a 521-room unit as a joint venture with LOT, the Polish state airline. The city also has another hotel as a result of a joint venture, the 163-room Hotel Bristol, the result of cooperation between Forte and the Polish State travel agency, Orbis;
- Bucharest, Romania, in which the city's top hotel is the Sofitel hotel, part of the French Accor chain. At the same time a small upmarket hotel, the Helvetia, has been developed as a result of a joint venture with a Swiss company;
- Budapest, Hungary, has a new hotel, the Grand Hotel Corvinius, which has been developed by the German hotel company Kempinski. There is also a Marriott hotel which is the result of the refurbishment of an old Inter-Continental unit.

In addition, a number of hotels which have been developed and are owned by Eastern European companies, can be booked through Western European reservations networks. For example, in Prague in the Czech Republic, the Palace Hotel can be booked via Preferred Hotels, the Pariz via Concorde Hotels and the Diplomat through SRS.

A report published in March 1995 by Kleinwort-Benson indicated that Western companies owned some 40 hotels in Eastern Europe, with a total of 11 652 bedrooms. Poland is the most popular country with these companies, with 13 Western-owned hotels. Of all the cities within Eastern Europe, Budapest had the most 'Western-owned' hotels, with eight. The main companies involved in Eastern Europe in early 1995 were as follows:

Accor (France)	13 units
Seibu Saison (Japan)	10 units
Bass (UK)	4 units
Queens Moat (UK)	3 units
Marriott (USA)	3 units

The involvement of Western companies in Eastern Europe is dependent on a belief that demand justifies the development of new units, and on political stability. Any events that lead these companies to believe that either condition may no longer apply could lead to them withdrawing from the market. This is clearly illustrated in the case of the Serbian capital, Belgrade, where Inter-Continental has ended its involvement for the time being. This is not surprising given the current political situation in the former Yugoslavia and the impact of sanctions on the Serbian economy.

Clearly, the involvement of Western companies in Eastern Europe is a controversial area. On the one hand they bring expertise and much needed capital, but on the other hand they can be seen as exploiters who export their profits from the Eastern European countries where these profits are generated and needed. That is why some Eastern European governments have sought to develop hotels through joint ventures with foreign companies so that the benefits can be shared.

In many ways it could be argued, however, that the involvement of Western companies in Eastern Europe in the hotel sector has been more successful for all concerned than in some other sectors such as air transport. For example, Air Russia, a venture between British Airways and a Russian partner, has yet to take off, literally, while Air France's involvement in the Czech airline CSA was not satisfactory for either partner.

DISCUSSION POINTS AND ESSAY QUESTIONS

1. Account for the relatively small number of Western-owned hotels that are currently in operation within Eastern Europe.
2. Discuss the factors that will determine whether the number of Western-owned hotels will grow rapidly over the coming decade or not.

The Forte International programme, UK

The leading UK hotel company Forte* also owns a considerable number of hotels and resort complexes in other countries. Some of these properties are offered to English-speaking consumers through a programme entitled 'Forte International'. The main method of promoting this programme is a glossy colour brochure which comprised 68 pages in 1995.

The brochure contained photographs and descriptions of some 72 properties. It subdivided the hotels into a number of categories, as follows:

- the UK and Ireland (four hotels) featuring properties in Dublin and London. It may seem strange to include a London hotel in such a brochure. However, many British people take short-break holidays in London themselves and many overseas but English-speaking tourists may well be interested in taking a holiday, or part of a holiday, in London;
- European cities (27 hotels);
- European resorts (14 complexes);
- the Middle East and Africa (seven hotels);
- the Caribbean and Western Atlantic (six hotels);
- the USA and Canada (14 hotels).

The brochure notes the brand of each hotel featured such as Forte Grand, Exclusive Hotel or Forte Crest. The USA and Canada section also includes a number of hotels which carry the Travelodge brand. It also explains that some of the units carry other brand names such as Forte Agip in Italy and Hungary and several Forte Associate Hotels in Scandinavia.

In addition to the standard hotel product, the programme in 1995 also included a number of other products as follows:

- a combined package featuring the Forte hotels in Paris with a journey on the Orient Express, from £870 per person;
- a 'go-as-you-please' car-based tour in Italy where customers could buy vouchers for any one of 17 Forte Agip hotels, at £16 per adult per night;
- a five-day Nile cruise from £335 per person;
- a five night tour of Jordan from £795 per person;

* Since this case study was written, Forte has been acquired by the Granada Group.

- two-centre holidays in the USA and Canada, including Washington, New York, and Toronto.

Some of the packages include only the accommodation with breakfast, and sometimes, dinner, while others include flights and airport taxes.

A number of sales promotions are offered by individual hotels of which the following examples serve as an illustration:

- Hotel Pennine Golf and Resort Hotel, Portimao, Portugal – one free round of golf per night of stay was offered;
- Hotel Bristol, Warsaw, Poland – a client who booked a six-night stay in January, February and August received a seventh night free of charge;
- Grand Hotel, Nuremberg, Germany – here, in 1995, customers received an automatic upgrading to a deluxe room, subject to availability;
- Hotel Phoenicia, Malta, in 1995, up to two children under 12 years old were accommodated free of charge if they were sharing the room with two adults.

Exhibit 2.1 Forte International programme prices (£ sterling 1995)

Property	Accommodation price – bed and breakfast, per night, per adult sharing a twin/double room	Flight inclusive (two nights, bed and breakfast and flights from London), per person
Shelbourne Hotel, Dublin, Ireland	69	295
Hotel Plaza Athénée, Paris, France	186	565
Forte Crest, Milan, Italy	36	310
Royal Christiania Hotel, Oslo, Norway (Forte Associate hotel)	64	360
Forte Agip Hotel, Budapest, Hungary	35	310
Hotel Cala Viños, Majorca, Spain	45	299
Hotel Dona Filipa, Vale du Lobo, Portugal	65	445
Villa del Parco, Sardinia, Italy	275	(See note)

Note: Not available, but a seven-night, flight-inclusive package cost from £1435 to £2245 per adult.

The brochure also stated that Forte could create tailor-made holidays for customers and that they also offered a special package for honeymooners. **Exhibit 2.1** gives some high season prices, from the brochure.

The brochure also offers its customers the chance to reserve airport hotels at special prices, for those who are buying a Forte International product. These prices also include a period of free car parking at the home airport.

At the end of the brochure, there is a small feature about Forte's 'Leisure Breaks' programme, their short break brochure featuring their UK and Ireland hotels. The main slogan used to sell these domestic market breaks highlights the fact that prices begin at £26 per adult per night, including breakfast.

DISCUSSION POINTS AND ESSAY QUESTIONS

1. Taking into account the product offered, discuss the segments at which you believe this programme is targeted.
2. Explain the substantial differences in prices charged for accommodation at the different hotels featured within the programme.

First Choice, UK

On 16 August 1994 First Choice was born with the relaunch of the UK tour operator Owners Abroad. This relaunch was the culmination of a review and restructuring of the company's activities.

THE REASONS FOR RELAUNCH

Owners Abroad was relaunched to meet the aims of the company strategy which was to improve brand positioning and marketing. The company had grown by acquisition which had resulted in a range of disparate brands. Research with customers had also shown that the name 'Owners Abroad' did not reflect the business that the company was in and led to confusion. It was therefore decided to change the company name and to create a new brand identity.

HOW DID THEY ACHIEVE IT?

The relaunch programme took the company seven months to achieve. The main stages involved in this process are shown in Exhibit 3.3. The project was very complex and hard work for all the people who were involved.

WHAT WAS ACHIEVED?

The name of the company became First Choice and three new brands were created from the original brands:

- First Choice: Enterprise, Falcon, Martyn, others.
- Sovereign: 'old' Sovereign and Martyn.
- Freespirit: Sun Med, Enterprise, Twenty's, Falcon, Martyn and Sovereign.

The old brands that were absorbed into the new structure were Enterprise, Falcon, Martyn, Olympic, Sun Med and Twenty's. The company retained the Sovereign brand because this was seen to have a good quality image with customers. The company also retained the Eclipse direct sale brand and the airline brand Air 2000.

Exhibit 3.1 First Choice – Key Facts

- In the last 10 years the group has provided holidays or flights for over 20 million people.
- During the last 12 months the group has provided holidays for over 2.5 million holidaymakers.
- The group's 1992–93 turnover, on a pro-forma basis including ITH, was £910 million.
- The group employs over 3600 staff.
- The group provides holidays in 400 different resorts centred on 80 airport destinations in over 50 countries.
- The group makes use of over 6200 hotels and apartments.
- Group Company Air 2000 is the 11th most profitable airline in the world, and the 76th largest in turnover.
- Group subsidiary ITH is Canada's largest tour operator, with sales in 1992–93 of over £200 million.
- The group's direct brand, Eclipse, is the UK's largest.
- For summer 1995 alone First Choice produced a range of 19 different brochures.
- The group's IT capacity is in excess of 250 gigabytes. Its reservations information technology is one of the largest single-application digital computer platforms in Europe, with a capacity sufficient easily to meet peak seasonal demand from travel agents.
- Air 2000:
  - flies over 10000 flights per year, totalling over 72000 hours of flying time;
  - carries over 4 million sector passengers;
  - serves over 4.5 million meals per year;
  - has won the UK Charter Airline of the Year Award for three out of the last four years;
  - has the best punctuality record of any UK charter airline: 67% of flights leave on time, and 85% within half-an-hour of scheduled departure.

Source: First Choice 1995

Exhibit 3.2 First Choice Destinations

Andorra	Columbia	Finland	Honduras	Luxembourg	Romania	Sweden
Antigua	Costa Rica	France	Hong Kong	Malaysia	Sardinia	Switzerland
Aruba	Cuba	Gambia	Hungary	Malta	Seychelles	Thailand
Austria	Curacao	Germany	Iceland	Mauritius	Singapore	Tunisia
Barbados	Cyprus	Greece	Indonesia	Mexico	Slovenia	Turkey
Belgium	Czech Republic	Greenland	Ireland	Morocco	Spain	UK
Belize	Denmark	Grenada	Israel	Norway	St Kitts	USA
Bulgaria	Dominican Republic	Hawaii	Italy	Panama	St Lucia	Venezuela
Canada	Egypt	Holland	Jamaica	Portugal	St Maarten	

Source: First Choice 1995.

Exhibit 3.3 Stages in the relaunch programme for Owners Abroad

January 1994
  A strategy group was established to review all marketing, corporate and branding strategies.

January – March 1994
  The team reviewed the marketplace to identify key market segments. This process used internal customer satisfaction questionnaires and external market research data. This resulted in three market segments which were to become the three new major brands.

April 1994
  The team submitted preliminary proposals to the main board.

May 1994
  Decision made to go ahead. The brand team were reorganized to reflect the new direction.

June onwards
  Work continued on implementing the rebranding strategy. Working parties were established to work on key issues:
  - corporate identity;
  - brochure design and production;
  - signs and clothing;
  - overseas requirements;
  - Air 2000;
  - information technology;
  - public relations;
  - launch events;
  - sales promotion;
  - advertising;
  - direct marketing.

  A steering committee had overall responsibility for planning the project. All the external agencies such as the advertising agency were represented on this committee.

16 August 1994
  Day of relaunch. Announcements made to press and all staff.

Source: First Choice 1995.

First Choice

First Choice was chosen as a name because it was seen to emphasize a fresh, colourful approach to holidays. The brand was designed to be aimed at the family market which is very important to the company.

Sovereign

Sovereign was maintained and is being used to target the higher-value sector of the market. It is targeted at the growing number of holiday-makers who are looking for high levels of quality and service. These customers tend to be more mature.

Free Spirit

Free Spirit was developed as a new brand to target adults that want to go on holiday on their own. Market research had shown that a growing number of people wanted to relax and unwind on holiday without the presence of children. The company planned to promote this programme of holidays targeting 25–45 year olds, lively and 'child-free'. They estimated that this market represented 4 million holidays a year in the UK.

Each of the new brands has a clear distinctive positioning. They have also been tested and validated by extensive customer research. First Choice, as well as being the leading brand, has become the new 'umbrella brand' name and appears on all promotional and advertising material.

Relaunch of the Kids Club

The company has a well developed market for family holidays. To support these sales, the company has developed Kids Clubs in the major resorts, which has meant that it is well recognized as a high quality provider for children's initiatives. The Kids Clubs allow parents on holiday to take time out from the constant demands of their children.

The Kids Club programme was relaunched at the same time as the major brands were relaunched. The total number of clubs has been reduced to three : 'Nippies' for 3–6 year olds, 'Surf Seekers' for 7–11 year olds, and 'Beach Hounds' for 12–16 year olds. The logo design for each age group makes use of the corporate colour palette which links them to the First Choice brand. The designs have been incorporated on to a Kids Club kit which includes T-shirts, Club Membership cards, dairies and the in-flight funpacks on Air 2000 flights.

THE ADVANTAGES OF THE NEW BRAND IMAGE

The advantages which the new brand image has given to First Choice can be summarized as:

- increased economies of scale in marketing costs have been achieved because of the reduced portfolio;
- clear positioning strategy – each brand reflects a well defined market segment;
- new company name 'First Choice' avoids the confusion which the 'Owners Abroad' name gave to customers;
- the new name 'First Choice' reflects the company activities much more closely than 'Owners Abroad';
- the simplification of the brands has made it much easier for travel agents to advise their customers on holiday selection.

KEY ACTIVITIES IN THE RELAUNCH OF THE COMPANY AND THE BRANDS

A number of key activities had to be achieved before the relaunch was completed and could be announced to the press. Two example activities are shown below.

The development of the new brand names

A market research company worked on the development of the new brand names. They worked with customer focus groups to look at the strength of the Owners Abroad brand portfolio. Only the Sovereign brand name was viewed by the groups as being positive so it was decided that the Sovereign brand logo would be given a facelift only, which was completed by a design agency.

The new brand names – First Choice and Free Spirit – were generated after company personnel worked with an agency. The company was lucky that the proposed brand names could be registered in the company name and there were no legal problems.

Designing the new range of clothing for employees

Once the main palette of colours for the company and its branches had been decided on, a new range of clothing for employers had to be developed. An outside clothing design specialist was employed for this. The design company had to produce a sample of the main items of the new range which included, men's and ladies' suits for the UK and overseas, casual wear for the overseas teams and special items such as ladies' dresses and blouses, and men's shirts and ties. The finished designs ensured that the uniform colours were very distinctive and that all the accessories matched the overall effect. Uniforms for all employees in the company colour palette formed a major part of the rebranding exercise. It means that the customer recognizes the employees very easily either in the UK or when they are abroad. The uniform, therefore, helps to develop a strong corporate identity.

LOOKING TO THE FUTURE

First Choice has ambitious plans for the future to support the rebranding exercise and to build First Choice into a strong and stable holiday company. These activities include the following.

- The company plans to actively market the award winning airline Air 2000.
- The company plans to invest further in ITH – their Canadian tour operations business. This investment has allowed the company to smooth out the cyclability of the UK holiday business because the demand pattern is the reverse of the UK.

- The company has invested heavily in information technology which has improved their response time to travel agents. This cost the company over £8 million in 1994 and makes the company's cumulative investment in excess of £20 million.
- The company has invested in a sophisticated new process for the design and publishing of all the company brochures. The company produces over 14 million brochures every year and it is important that this process is as streamlined as possible. The new process interlinks databases, photo libraries, layout and design grids and electronic scanning and imaging in order to be able to produce high quality, accurate and better structured brochures more responsively and more cheaply. The company intends updating and improving this system every year.

CONCLUSION

The rebranding exercise was the third important element in the marketing strategy for the company. The first element was the restructuring of the company's management systems and cost structure. The second element was the introduction of new information systems and the improvement of internal controls. Finally, the rebranding exercise itself provided the company with a fresh look and a new positioning strategy.

DISCUSSION POINTS AND ESSAY QUESTIONS

1. Discuss the reasons which, you believe, led to the relaunching of Owners Abroad as First Choice in 1994.
2. Examine the potential costs and benefits that may arise from a rebranding exercise.
3. Critically evaluate the outcome of the First Choice relaunching and rebranding exercise.

CASE 4

The role of brochures in hotel marketing – The Hotel Vitosha, Sofia, Bulgaria

The Hotel Vitosha is located on the edge of the city of Sofia in the foothills of the Vitosha Mountains. It is a 21-storey hotel built on a site of some 30 000 square metres. It was designed by a Japanese architect and was opened in 1979. Since the onset of political and economic change in Bulgaria, the hotel has been refurbished and relaunched, as a five-star unit. It is promoted as a 'Summit International hotel'.

As part of its promotional activities, the hotel produces a glossy folder into which are inserted the business cards of the hotel's marketing manager and general manager. A number of other brochures are also produced and included in this folder, depending on what the potential client's interests are.

The four main brochures are as follows.

GENERAL HOTEL BROCHURE

The general brochure is a 30–page glossy, full colour brochure portraying images of the hotel that suggest it is luxurious and combines modern facilities with traditional decor. The 'strap line' at the beginning of the brochure reads: 'There is no place like home ... and Hotel Vitosha.' The brochure begins with two views of the outside of the hotel before it goes on to talk about the hotel's public areas. There is then a section on the hotel's suites, after which there is a photograph and text relating to the hotel's standard bedrooms. The emphasis then changes to the subject of eating, with eight pages being devoted to the hotel's different themed restaurants. Other brief sections cover the following aspects of the hotel:

- the Viennese themed café;
- the night club;
- the casino;
- the in-house art gallery;
- the business centre;
- the sports and leisure facilities.

The brochure ends with a page of facts and figures about the hotel and an atmospheric photograph of the hotel grounds.

Like all the other brochures, no prices are given in the literature so that the brochures do not become dated if prices change, and potential clients are not put off by the prices before a sales person has had an opportunity to 'sell' the hotel to them.

The other three brochures are not specifically about the Hotel Vitosha. However, all three carry the hotel's imprint and feature sections on the hotel.

'BULGARIAN BEAUTY – DISCOVER IT WITH US'

This brochure features a range of tourist attractions in Bulgaria as well as some general information on Bulgaria itself. Two pages at the beginning of the brochure and several inserts then tell readers that the tour operations desk at the hotel can book day and weekend package trips to these attractions on behalf of clients. For example, it offers a seven-day tour of Bulgaria called the 'Luxury Circle' at a cost, in 1994, of US$475 per adult sharing a double room. The same brochure also offers weekend breaks, including excursions based on staying at the Hotel Vitosha. The brochure also includes an advertisement for Balkan Bulgarian Airlines. This brochure represents a very interesting phenomenon, namely a hotel acting as a tour operator.

'SKI BULGARIA'

This is a six-page brochure with inserts which is about ski resorts in Bulgaria. It also carries the Hotel Vitosha imprint and contains a map of Europe that shows the location of Bulgaria. The brochure includes 'flyers' or loose inserts, which set out two skiing programmes which are offered by the Hotel Vitosha. One package is based on seven nights accommodation and five days skiing while the other offers five nights accommodation and three days skiing. Both packages contain similar elements, namely:

- half board accommodation in the hotel with meals taken in the hotel's Bulgarian, Italian and Japanese themed restaurants, together with a tavern in Sofia;
- airport transfers;
- the ski package including tuition, equipment hire and lift pass;
- transfers from the hotel to the ski slopes;
- an evening in a traditional local tavern with folk dancing and music;
- a guided visit to the Rila Monastery;
- a gift.

In 1994–95 the cost of these packages for adults sharing a double room was US$595 for the five-night package and US$825 for the seven-night package.

'SOFIA – YOUR CONVENTION CROSS POINT'

This is a well produced high-quality brochure promoting Sofia as a convention destination. It is a mixture of editorial about Bulgaria and Sofia specifically, together with features on the main convention venues in Sofia. Of the five hotels featured, the Hotel Vitosha has the largest section, four pages out of a brochure that contains 32 pages in all.

The Hotel Vitosha section contains photographs and text about the hotel, together with plans of its conference rooms and details of their size and capacity. The slogan used is: 'Our experience will guarantee your successful conference'.

The rest of the brochure is divided up as follows:

- general editorial and photographs of Bulgaria and Sofia which cover nine pages;
- six pages on the Congress Centre in Sofia;
- five pages of advertising features on four other Sofia hotels;
- a three-page advertising feature about Balkan Bulgarian Airlines;
- advertisements for the Hertz and Avis car hire companies;
- a one-page feature on an art gallery in Sofia;
- a one page feature about a local, traditional folk song and dance ensemble.

The outside back cover is an advertisement for the Hotel Vitosha, while the inside back cover is an advertisement for the *Bulgarian Beauty – Discover It With Us* brochure discussed above. Most interesting of all is an imprint at the end of the brochure which indicates that the brochure has been produced by the 'Hotel Vitosha Advertising Studio'.

CONCLUSIONS

This case study is fascinating because it does not just show the ways in which hotels can use different types of brochures to promote themselves. It also illustrates how some hotels in Eastern Europe are responding to the new political and economic climate by becoming involved in a number of new entrepreneurial activities.

DISCUSSION POINTS AND ESSAY QUESTIONS

1. Critically evaluate the range of brochures which are used to promote the Hotel Vitosha.
2. Discuss the factors that influence the success of a brochure as a means of promoting a hotel **or** a tour operator's programme **or** a visitor attraction.

The role of the media in tourism marketing in the UK

CASE 5

The media is increasingly influencing the holiday and day trip decisions of UK tourists in terms of where they go, the types of trips they take and when they choose to travel. In this case study we will focus on non-advertising media as advertising media are covered in Chapter 11.

The tourist market in the UK is influenced by two distinctly different types of media, as follows:

- **travel media**, including guidebooks, editorial features in newspapers and periodicals, and specialized radio and television programmes which are concerned with tourism solely;
- **non-travel media**, which covers literature, films, and radio and television news programmes, wildlife shows and drama series, for example.

In the first case, the media are part of the tourism industry and are designed to inform and influence their users in terms of their behaviour as tourists. In relation to the latter group they are not explicitly tourism-related so that their influence on tourists is indirect and largely unintentional. Nevertheless, their influence on tourists can be as great as if not greater than the travel media.

From the point of view of the UK tourism industry, the travel media are easy to identify and can be influenced. Marketers can use promotional techniques to attempt to gain favourable coverage for their product. On the other hand, the non-travel media are much broader in scope and can rarely be influenced by tourism marketers. As a result, in general, marketers can take a proactive approach towards the travel media, while they usually have to adopt a reactive approach to the non-travel media.

Having made these general points, we will now briefly examine the current nature and scope of media influence in the UK tourism market, beginning with the travel media.

THE TRAVEL MEDIA

Guidebooks

The supply of guidebooks that await the prospective tourist in most UK bookshops is now enormous and has grown dramatically in recent years, particularly in relation to foreign destinations. These guidebooks fall into a number of categories, including:

- guides to countries and regions, including the *Rough Guide, Let's Go, Lonely Planet, Cadogan* and *Fodors* series, for example;
- hotel and restaurant guides such as the *Michelin Red Guide* series;
- guides for people who want to take special interest holidays, such as walking, climbing and cycling;
- books for consumers advising them about modes of transport, such as travelling around Europe by rail or finding inexpensive air tickets;
- guides aimed at particular market segments such as families, gay people and disabled travellers.

Some types of guide books are followed, almost religiously, by tourists, for example the *Michelin Red Guide* and the *Rough Guide* series. A favourable entry in such a guide therefore usually guarantees extra business for a destination or individual business.

Conversely, unfavourable coverage can threaten an area or establishment's reputation and this often ensures a strong response from the people who stand to lose.

Newspapers

Most national, regional and local newspapers in the UK have regular tourism features designed to inform their readers about holiday opportunities. These are often linked to advertising features. Some of the tourism features can be lengthy, running to a number of pages.

Periodicals

In the UK, a number of periodicals have been created which are solely devoted to tourism, both for leisure and business. These periodicals are of several types, namely:

- those linked to travel programmes on the television;
- those concerned with an individual country which is popular with UK tourists, including France and the USA;
- those relating to a particular type of holiday such as caravanning or skiing;
- periodicals for people who own second homes abroad or would like to own such a property;
- specialist magazines for the business, rather than the leisure, traveller.

These publications have audiences who are very interested in their content. They are thus highly influential in their relevant readership's behaviour.

Television

Every one of the four terrestrial television stations in the UK has its own regular programme about holidays. In addition, the satellite channel Sky TV has a separate travel channel while there is also a travel programme on one of the BBC's radio stations.

Because of the fact that it can show visual images, television is a particularly powerful medium in the tourism field. Most television travel programmes tend to offer fairly uncritical features on particular destinations. The fact that often these programmes are made with the actual cooperation of the tourist industry, which offers services free of charge to the programme makers, means the objectivity of such programmes may be criticized.

THE NON-TRAVEL MEDIA

Literature

Literature has always inspired tourists to visit places where books were set. However, in recent years there have been a number of books which have had a particularly profound impact on the behaviour of UK tourists. Perhaps the best example of this are the books of Peter Mayle, such as *A Year in Provence*. This autobiographical tale of a couple who moved to France to live encouraged literally thousands of Britons to visit the village where they had settled. In time, this became a real problem with locals feeling that their lives were being harmed by this influx of 'literary tourist pilgrims'.

Films

Seeing films featuring particular locations can encourage people to want to visit these locations for themselves. This has happened to a limited extent in the UK market, in relation to films such as *Manon des Sources* (Provence, France), and a number of films based in Ireland, from *Ryan's Daughter* to *The Commitments*.

Radio and television

News coverage

Radio and television news can often give negative images of a place that discourages tourists from visiting them. For UK tourists this was certainly the case in relation to Northern Ireland before the peace process began in 1994. Likewise, the publicity surrounding criminal attacks on tourists in Florida had an effect in the early 1990s.

Wildlife programmes

Wildlife programmes have become very popular in the UK in recent years. They give positive images of many destinations and make some people want to visit them to see the wildlife at first hand. This phenomenon has, perhaps, been most noticeable in relation to the wildlife reserves and national parks of Africa.

Drama series

Drama series set in the regions of the UK have stimulated a number of new domestic tourist flows in the UK in recent years. Some notable examples include:

- *Last of the Summer Wine*, a programme based in West Yorkshire in the North of England;
- two programmes based in North Yorkshire, *Heartbeat* and *All Creatures Great and Small*;
- *Howard's Way*, a programme based on the world of boating around the Solent Estuary in Southern England;
- *Peak Practice*, a series about doctors set in the southern Peak District region of Northern England.

All of these programmes have created demand from people who wish to visit the places associated with these programmes. In one case, the appeal of 'soap operas' has been such that a themed visitor attraction has been created to exploit this audience interest. The attraction is the Granada Studios Tour in Manchester based on the *Coronation Street* soap opera which was first transmitted in 1960.

Meanwhile, in London and Bradford there are museums devoted to film, television and photography that themselves attract hundreds of thousands of visitors.

CONCLUSIONS

This brief summary illustrates that the media, both travel and non-travel, is an influential factor in the decision-making of UK tourists. It can represent opportunities for free promotion for destinations and individual businesses, but occasionally it can also represent a threat to both areas and individual enterprises.

DISCUSSION POINTS AND ESSAY QUESTIONS

1. Identify the main types of travel media and evaluate their role in shaping tourist behaviour.
2. Discuss some of the ways in which non-travel media can have an impact on consumer behaviour in tourism.

VISION: 'To enhance Scotland's established reputation as a tourism destination, by building on its history, culture, environment and the hospitality of the people.'

INTRODUCTION

Following a major review of the government tourism policies for Scotland in 1992/93, the Secretary of State for Scotland asked the Scottish Tourist Board (STB) to prepare a National Strategic Plan for Scottish Tourism. This involved working closely with Scottish Enterprise (SE) and the Highlands and Island Enterprise (HIE) and under the supervision of the Scottish Tourism Coordinating Group (STCG).

This resulted in a draft plan being produced in 1994 which was sent out for comments. The production of the strategic plan involved the Scottish Tourist Board in a number of stages as follows:

- analysis of the tourism industry in Scotland;
- analysis of the international market situation;
- analysis of Scotland's tourism markets;
- analysis of the strengths, weaknesses, opportunities and threats of Scotland as a tourist destination;
- formulation of key issues and priorities.

This work led to the STB proposing overall aims and objectives and targets for the industry to achieve by the year 2000.

ANALYSIS OF THE TOURISM INDUSTRY IN SCOTLAND

The main factors highlighted in 1994 were:

- the accommodation sector is central to the industry – Scotland has over 20 000 hotels, guest houses, B & B's, caravan parks, catering establishments and youth hostels;
- the majority of tourism businesses in Scotland are small and family-run – there are very few major players;

- tourism is an industry where commitment to training and staff development is generally weak;
- Scottish tourism is a strong performer in economic terms – it made a major contribution to the scottish economy accounting for almost £2.1 billion of expenditure in 1993;
- Scottish tourism employs 8% of the workforce.

AN ANALYSIS OF THE INTERNATIONAL MARKET SITUATION

General market trends of the international tourism market for the next decade were highlighted in the report, as follows.

- Markets will become segmented as they increasingly reflect the particular lifestyles and interests of different demographic groups. The tourism industry will have to focus more on new destinations, closely tailored holidays, special interest holidays and short breaks – all against the background of generally higher standards of product and service.
- The traditional package holiday will gradually go out of fashion as package tours, like other holidays, become increasingly customized.
- Tourists today are more discerning and more affluent. They expect higher standards and, as they travel more widely, they become more experienced at comparing destinations and products.
- Tourists are also becoming more sophisticated. They are more interested in the culture and heritage of their destinations, and perhaps more likely to want their holidays to include an educational element.
- Concern for the environment has reached an all-time high and will continue to intensify throughout the rest of the decade. This will put pressure on the industry to demonstrate that new and existing tourism developments are environmentally friendly and sustainable.
- More effort will have to be devoted to creating visitor attractions out of the natural and built surroundings. These attractions will have to satisfy – in a carefully controlled manner – the international tourist's growing interest in the environment and culture of different parts of the world.
- The industry will need to be increasingly professional to meet the demand for higher standards. Shortages of skilled labour may restrict development in some areas.
- The development of the European Union will be important in encouraging tourism between member countries as trade barriers fall and there is more freedom of movement for visitors, workers and investment. This in turn will enhance Europe's competitiveness in the world markets.

Exhibit 6.1 Volume and value of all tourism in Scotland in 1993

	Trips (million)	Nights (million)	Expenditure (£m)
Scots	4.9	17.4	535
Rest of UK	4.1	24.2	885
Overseas*	1.8	19.0	670
Total	10.8	60.6	2090

* Estimated.

- Eastern Europe and Russia will gradually offer new destinations, alternative investment opportunities and at a later date, as economic recovery takes hold, a new source of visitors.

ANALYSIS OF SCOTLAND'S TOURISM MARKETS

Other important factors which the report highlighted were:

- 60% of trips were made to Scotland by overseas visitors and about 40% by UK visitors;
- overseas visitors came from the US (over a quarter of the total), Germany (11%), Italy (6%), Ireland, France, Canada, Australia (5%), the Netherlands (4%), Spain and Switzerland (3%).
- European countries would provide the greatest growth in overseas visitors to Scotland throughout the 1990s;
- visiting friends and relatives was an important part of the business;
- business trips represented a much lower percentage of overseas trips in Scotland compared to the UK as a whole;
- there was a need to develop a strong positive and consistent brand image of Scotland;
- Scotland must develop an increasing business in the second-holiday market.

SWOT ANALYSIS OF SCOTLAND AS A TOURIST DESTINATION

A summary of this analysis is shown below.
Strengths:

- environmental appeal, heritage, ethnic and historic links with other countries;
- excellent image amongst visitors;
- good choice of accommodation;
- wide range of attractions;

- relatively crime-free.

Weaknesses:

- on the periphery of Europe in geographic terms;
- some concerns about the price and standard of accommodation;
- lack of entertainment for bad weather;
- unpredictable weather;
- expensive to access;
- environmental problems such as dirty beaches and mountain erosion.

Opportunities:

- extending the season;
- building on unique advantages;
- linking holidays to culture and the natural environment;
- development of all-weather holidays;
- development of package holidays.

Threats:

- complacency;
- lack of investment in facilities;
- competitors such as Ireland, France and Norway.

FORMULATION OF KEY ISSUES AND PRIORITIES

The report recognized that Scotland should have a number of key issues and priorities which would allow the country to capitalize on its strengths. These were summarized as follows:

- The facilities do not meet the needs of all the target markets. There are shortcomings in accommodation, visitor attractions, sports and recreation, entertainment, facilities for children.
- The standard of facilities and services varies widely and individual businesses often do not make the best of resources available to them. For example, Scotland has a poor reputation for catering despite the very high quality of much Scottish produce.
- The promotion of Scotland itself and of individual products and places has been fragmented and often not as effective as it could be.
- Many of the weaknesses have been compounded by poor levels of skill throughout the industry.

SETTING THE PRIORITIES FOR THE MAIN AREAS OF SCOTTISH TOURISM

The report recommended detailed targets for each of the sectors of the industry including:

- accommodation;
- visitor attractions;
- the natural environment;
- things to do;
- service and transport.

The report also looked particularly at programmes which could tackle the seasonality issue. Marketing was considered to be an important aspect of this section.

Marketing

The main objectives of the marketing programme were set out as follows.

UK market

- To increase overall levels of tourism expenditure, in particular holiday expenditure.
- To increase tourist expenditure outside the main summer period, particularly in the second and fourth quarters.
- To increase the percentage of touring holidays, particularly outwith Edinburgh and Glasgow.
- To increase the percentage of activity and special interest holidays.

A well coordinated, industry-wide campaign with the twin aims of consolidating existing market sectors and opening up new ones will be critical to the success of these objectives. As the leading marketing organization for Scottish tourism, STB will aim to:

- develop a coordinated long-term marketing campaign to establish and maintain Scotland as a serious competitor in the top 25% of holiday destinations;
- continue to evaluate, develop and promote geographical and product-based niche markets;
- continue to bring together the consumer, the travel trade and the tourism product operators and suppliers through a programme of exhibitions and publications;
- continue to operate Scotland's Travel Fair and examine the feasibility of collaborating with other Scottish industries at the Travel Fair;
- develop awareness of Scotland around a common theme or image in co-operation with other public and private sector organizations which market Scottish products.

Within the UK, the main markets will be Scotland, the North of England and the South East of England. Here there are varying levels of potential for activity and special-interest holidays, city break holidays, family holidays, holidays for the 55-plus group, coach tours, short breaks and independent car touring holidays.

Overseas market

- Increase overseas visitors' intentions to choose Scotland as a destination.
- Increase levels of visitor expenditure.
- Increase the spread of visitor expenditure throughout Scotland.
- Increase the seasonal spread of visitor expenditure in Scotland.

The USA, Germany and France currently offer the greatest potential and this is where the major part of our resources will be devoted. The rest of Western Europe, Japan, Australia, New Zealand and Canada represent secondary markets where there will be moderate investment to develop incremental business. Ireland deserves particular consideration as a single market combining the domestic market of Northern Ireland and the overseas market of the Republic.

Tackling the seasonality issue

It is proposed that a number of ideas will be looked at to see whether they can be used to encourage a greater uptake of holidays. These include:

- special events;
- spring and autumn activities (sporting and non-sporting);
- Easter activities for children (sporting and non-sporting);
- entertainment for adults;
- entertainment for children;
- extending opening periods for visitor attractions;
- food events and holidays;
- holiday shopping;
- child minding;
- wet weather facilities;
- joint ticketing;
- transport offers;
- accommodation discount offers and quality assurance.

Overall aims and objectives

The STB identified a number of aims, objectives and targets as a result of the report. These are set out below.

Scotland's tourism product – the landscape, the culture and the people – has outstanding potential. The main aim of this plan is to establish the means to maximize that potential and so realise the greatest benefits to Scotland. To achieve this the industry must have as its broad aims:

- to ensure that a variety of tourism businesses offer a range of products targeted at a mix of domestic and overseas market sectors;
- to build on Scotland's real advantages in terms of scenery, environment, history, culture and opportunities for activities and special interests;
- to increase tourism in the off-peak period;

- to increase the spread of tourism throughout Scotland;
- to offer a well balanced and integrated tourism product within the main regions of Scotland;
- to provide secure and worthwhile employment and good returns on investment;
- to be environmentally sensitive and sustainable;
- to build up solid repeat and referral business based on customer satisfaction and a reputation for quality and value for money.

These broad aims are supported by the following principal objectives:

- to create new facilities, and improve existing ones, which cater for particular target markets;
- to promote tourism in a more effective and co-ordinated way at all levels in the industry;
- to enhance skills, especially management skills, throughout our industry.

Targets

To give a clear focus to objectives, STCG has identified a number of realistic targets for tourism in Scotland which the industry should achieve by the year 2000:

- to increase total visitor expenditure from £2,090 m in 1993 to £2,500 m in 1993 prices;
- to increase the number of bednights from 60.6 m in 1993 to 72.5 m;
- to increase the number of jobs in tourism from 171 000 in 1991 (latest employment census figure) to 210 000;
- to increase the percentage of tourism expenditure from October through June from 55% in 1993 to 60%;
- to increase the value of tourism expenditure outwith Edinburgh and Glasgow from 51 per cent of the total in 1993 to 55%;
- to increase Scotland's market share of UK domestic tourism expenditure from 11.4% in 1993 to 13%;
- to improve visitor perceptions of Scotland, as quantified in market research surveys, using 1994 as a base.

It was recognized that, to be successful, Scottish tourism must be of the highest quality which requires greater capital investment as well as more money for marketing.

DISCUSSION POINTS AND ESSAY QUESTIONS

1. Examine the SWOT analysis of Scotland contained in this case study and discuss its implications for the future international marketing of Scotland as a tourist destination.
2. Evaluate the measures outlined in the case study which were designed to tackle the problem of seasonality.

Futuroscope, France

Futuroscope is unusual amongst theme parks, in that it was conceived by a public sector body, namely the Conseil Général of Vienne, a *département* in the West of France centred on Poitiers. This Conseil is still the leading player in the mixed economy organization that continues to manage the park.

The attraction is a high technology 'hands-on' theme park based on state-of-the-art technology. It calls itself 'Le Parc Européen de l'Image' in view of its theme of the moving image. It is also unique in that it is part of a development that also includes a high technology industrial complex and a set of separate education institutions which all specialize in different aspects of modern technology.

The site looks like a set from a science fiction film with striking ultra-modern buildings in a parkland setting. Its location is excellent, being just a few kilometres off the A10 Paris–South West France motorway. It also benefits from being near Poitiers which is linked to Paris and Bordeaux by the high-speed TGV train.

Futuroscope opened in 1987 and in its first year attracted some 225 000 visitors. By 1993, it was attracting around 1 900 000 visitors, an increase of more than 800% over the 1987 figure. The operators are confident that visitor numbers per annum could reach four million before the end of the 1990s.

Rob Davidson, writing in 1994, estimated that 6% of the visitors were from other countries. However, given the marketing effort in foreign countries that Futuroscope has recently undertaken, it is likely that this figure is now higher. The same author writing in *Insights* reported that 84% of all visitors to Futuroscope came from outside the region.

Apparently, some 88% of all visitors expressed a desire to return to Futuroscope at some time in the future. It is a very educational attraction, and while it is popular with all age groups, it appears that some 60% of all visitors are adults.

Futuroscope is very professionally marketed both within France and in other European countries. A range of brochures are produced in a number of languages, some of which are designed to persuade people to want to visit the place, while others are mainly informational, giving opening times, prices and details of on-site services. These brochures are readily available, free of charge. Furthermore, there are staff available on site who can answer telephone queries in a range of languages. This is important for an attraction which is receiving more and more international visitors.

The pricing policy is quite complicated, and in 1995 the charges were as follows, in French francs:

	Individual		Groups (minimum of 20 persons)	
	One day	Two days	One day	Two days
Adults	145	260	135	240
Children	110	195	95	160

However, the entrance charge gives access to every part of the park together with the laser show, while children under five years of age are admitted free of charge.

Furthermore, there are a range of accommodation-inclusive packages which are designed to encourage use of the on-site hotels. In 1995, packages ranged in price from 1155 French francs to 1955 French francs. The first price includes a one-day entrance ticket plus dinner, bed and breakfast at a one-star hotel for two adults and one child, while the latter price is based on staying in a superior hotel. If the child shared the room with two adults a discount applied to both prices. Group prices were somewhat lower than these prices for families and individuals and included the services of a guide.

Futuroscope is widely advertised in France and in other countries. In 1995, for instance, double-page Futuroscope advertisements appeared in British newspapers as part of a Maison de la France joint promotion of the French regions in the UK market. Point-of-sale displays about Futurscope may also be seen in some French travel agents' windows.

Futuroscope is also represented at major tourism exhibitions such as the World Travel Market. It also engages in press and public relations and tries to encourage travel journalists to write about it, and television programmes to use it as a set from which to broadcast.

As well as offering their own packages, Futuroscope also distribute their product through the packages offered by tour operators in France and other countries. Operators will often include entrance to Futuroscope free of charge to their prospective customers, as an 'added value' sales promotion designed to encourage them to buy the main product.

Futuroscope also relies on representatives to help market it in other countries. For example, it has a representative in the UK based in London. Furthermore, it is twinned with the Museum of the Moving Image in London.

Cooperative joint marketing also takes place between Futuroscope and the Conseil Général de la Vienne. Futuroscope promotes the Vienne area in its brochures while the Conseil Général and the

Regional Council of Poitou-Charentes features Futuroscope in its marketing activities. This approach to marketing is beneficial for both parties.

Finally, the marketing effort does not end when the customer arrives on site. The aim of the marketers is then to ensure that the customer has such an enjoyable experience that they will want to visit again. To this end there are free children's push chair and wheelchair hire, free kennels for pet dogs, guides, a left luggage office and free walkman headsets so that visitors can enjoy a self-guided tour of the site.

DISCUSSION POINTS AND ESSAY QUESTIONS

1. Suggest reasons why visitor numbers to Futuroscope have grown rapidly since it was opened in 1987.
2. Discuss the reasons why a similar attraction may, or may not, prove as successful if it were to be developed somewhere in the UK or Greece.

Timeshare accommodation in Europe*

CASE 8

The concept of 'timeshare' accommodation originated in Switzerland in the 1960s and is thus a European creation. However, it did not really begin to grow until the 1970s, since when it has grown at a steady pace. In spite of the controversy which has often surrounded this type of accommodation, Haylock (1994) estimated that there are 2.5 million households all over the world who own timeshare. After the USA, Europe is the second biggest world market for timeshare sales.

It was in Britain that the European timeshare market developed first, with British holidaymakers purchasing property in popular Mediterranean holiday destinations such as the Canary Islands. There are also well established markets for timeshare in Germany, France and Italy, while new markets are emerging in Spain, where the number of owners grew from 3000 families in 1990 to 23 000 in 1992. There are also growing numbers of timeshare owners in Eastern Europe who are particularly purchasing timeshare rights in Spanish developments.

On the supply side, there are relatively large numbers of timeshare complexes in Britain, France, Italy and Scandinavia. Many European companies have been involved in the development and management of timeshare complexes including:

- the builders, Barratt (UK);
- the Metro Group (Germany) who are largely retailers in their home country;
- Club Méditerranée (France);
- Banco Bilbão Vizcaya (Spain);
- the Berlusconi Group (Italy).

In spite of its continued growth, there are a number of challenges facing this sector if it is to continue to grow and prosper. These include the following.

- The sector has a generally poor reputation in terms of the sales methods used by some timeshare developers, involving hard-sell

* The authors are pleased to acknowledge that much of the data in this case study is based on a conference paper presented by Haylock at the 'Tourism: The State of the Art' Conference which took place in Glasgow in July 1994.

techniques and pressurized face-to-face selling, together with alleg-edly false offers and misleading advertisements. However, this repu-tation is not true for all types of timeshare but, is perhaps, mainly true of some of the developments in the Mediterranean which are aimed at those who are there on holiday. Nevertheless, this reputa-tion may serve to put off some potential purchasers.

- While most timeshare developments are of high quality in terms of both their design and management, some well publicized cases of poor quality and badly managed complexes have somewhat tarn-ished the reputation of timeshare overall.

- There is a problem with exchanges, given that many people will want, from time to time, to swap a week at their resort for another somewhere else in the world. This overcomes the problem of peo-ple's fears that they will get bored of visiting the same destination year after year. However, many owners find that, although in theory they can exchange with other owners, in reality it is difficult or impossible to achieve.

With this latter point in mind, some companies have grown up to handle this process of exchanging weeks between owners. The world's largest such company, RCI, was founded in 1974, and is still privately owned by Christel De Haan. In 1994, the company had 57 offices in 29 countries, employed 3600 people, and in 1993 acted as an agent for some 4.5 million timeshare tourists worldwide, including 2.5 million in Europe. Over 2600 timeshare projects are now affiliated to the RCI exchange system out of a world total of some 4000. RCI tries to ensure that there is a match in terms of quality between those who exchange weeks to ensure that one party is not disappointed by the quality of what they receive. They also elicit considerable post-holiday feedback from consumers on their experience and those resorts that regularly receive good feedback are given awards, such as the 'Gold Crown Resort' appellation or the 'Resort of International Distinction' award.

Timeshare developments can be very popular with local authorities and destination marketing agencies in tourist regions for two main reasons, namely:

- the economic benefits that can flow from the construction and operation of timeshare complexes. A 1993 study carried out by the European Timeshare Federation estimated that European owners generated revenue of some £387 million. An Ernst & Young survey of 1990 found that timeshare developments in the Canary Islands involved nearly £1 billion worth of investment and visitor expend-iture;

- the fact that as most timeshare resorts sell 50 weeks a year, the 'season' lasts virtually all year, in contrast to the much shorter sea-son for most traditional resort hotels.

Timeshare development can also increase a destination's overall visi-tor numbers. For example, a study of Malta carried out by Dean in

1993, and quoted by Haylock, showed that occupancy levels and visitor arrivals grew dramatically after several of the island's hotels were converted to timeshare complexes. Clearly, however, there may have been other contributing reasons for this growth in visitor numbers and occupancy levels.

It seems likely that timeshare will continue to grow in Europe in the future, although some feel that a spate of legislation across Europe in recent years may slow down this growth.

DISCUSSION POINTS AND ESSAY QUESTIONS

1. Discuss the reasons why the timeshare concept has not grown as rapidly in Europe as it might have done under different circumstances.
2. Evaluate the factors that may influence the growth of timeshare accommodation in Europe in the future.

Bord Fáilte, Ireland

Bord Fáilte, created in 1955, is the government agency responsible for tourism development and marketing in Ireland. Its main functions are outlined in the organization's mission statement, including the following:

> Bord Fáilte's core mission is through promotion to maximize foreign tourism revenue in Ireland, thereby contributing to job creation throughout the economy.
>
> To support and further this objective the Bord also encourages and assists product development in tourism.
>
> The Bord carries out its functions in partnership and cooperation with the tourism industry in Ireland and in the market and is committed to enabling entrepreneurs in tourism to develop sustainable businesses that are profitable and enduring.

In 1993, the total budget of Bord Fáilte was some 52 million Irish Punts (IR£) which represented a reduction of approximately 6% on the 1992 figure. A little over two-fifths of this budget came from grants from the Irish government, while a further IR£7 623 221 came from income generated by commercial activities, such as the sale of publications, the sale of advertising space and registration fees.

The budget figure involves a sum of IR£20 415 983 for the European Commission Operational Programme for Tourism which involved financial assistance from the European Regional Development Fund. This money was all spent on projects eligible for funding under the scheme which is designed to assist the development and marketing of resort amenities in Ireland to meet demand from international tourists. Seventy per cent of the money was used to aid capital funds while the other 30% was used to fund marketing activities.

If we exclude this particular funding and several other categories of money which were earmarked for one purpose only, we are left with a figure of approximately IR£22.4 million, which was spent as follows (expressed as percentages):

	%
Marketing	72.31
Development	7.12
Administration	8.37
Regional	7.57
Tourism organizations	
Superannuation	4.63

We will now discuss the activities of Bord Fáilte in 1993 in more detail.

MARKETING

The marketing budget was spent on a range of activities, as follows:

- advertising campaigns in the main target markets, and on which IR£6.78 million was spent in 1993;
- the production of brochures in no fewer than 16 languages which took up IR£1.83 million of the 1993 budget;
- undertaking trade and consumer promotions and trade fairs, at home and overseas, in partnership with the industry. Some of the events attended in 1993 included the World Travel Market in London, ITB in Berlin and BIT in Milan, together with events in North America;
- events were also held for foreign tour operators in Cork and Galway;
- linking all the principal tourist information offices in Ireland to 'Gulliver', Ireland's computerized tourist information and reservation system. They were also connected to a new nationwide free fax reservation system;
- the publication of guides to help small and medium-sized businesses to improve the effectiveness of their marketing activities;
- hosting visits by some 942 overseas media representatives to encourage them to portray positive images of Ireland in the media in their home countries;
- the annual Marketing Forum which acts as a mechanism for the exchange of views on marketing between the Bord and the industry;
- a continuation of the Conference Ambassador Programme, which had helped boost conference revenue to IR£76 million by 1993;
- the production of a video promoting the Irish countryside, entitled 'Rural Ireland – the Living Tradition';
- cooperating with the state television company RTE to present positive images of Ireland to the international audiences watching the Eurovision Song Contest which took place that year in Ireland.

INVESTMENT AND PRODUCT DEVELOPMENT

Between 1988 and 1993, during the lifetime of the Operational Programme for Tourism, the Bord took a proactive role in the encouragement of new product development. During this period the investment levered by grant aid from Bord Fáilte totalled IR£261.5 million. Grants made under this project in 1993 alone varied from sums as small as IR£191 to Leitrim County Council in respect of a walking, cycling and riding product project to IR£2 million for the Temple Bar urban regeneration scheme in Dublin.

The categories of project under the Operational Programme for Tourism involved: inland waterways, cycling, walking, culture, heritage, activities and special interest, language and craft centres, health and leisure facilities, and conference facilities.

There was also the Interreg Project and the European Union initiative which covered the border regions (adjacent to Northern Ireland) and County Sligo. Grants totalling IR£1.34 million were granted to 14 projects in 1993, of which the largest single project to which a grant was made was IR£367 093 to the Garton Outdoor Pursuit Centre in County Donegal.

Between 1991 and 1993, Bord Fáilte received IR£4.2 million from the Irish government to aid agritourism projects. Some 192 schemes were supported under the Agri-Tourist Grant Scheme. Most of the money was spent in the West of Ireland.

In 1993, under the Business Expansion Scheme (BES), some 20 tourism-related projects were approved for funding with a total investment value of IR£9.6 million, with IR£6.3 million of BES funding being allocated for this purpose. In the event only IR£3.1 million was required for the 14 projects that went ahead in 1993.

Finally, in 1993, grants totalling IR£1.98 million were made to 33 projects which were split into three categories, namely:

- the Accommodation Amenity Scheme;
- the Tourism Amenity Development Scheme;
- the Hotel and Guest House Improvement Scheme.

The size of the grants made under these schemes ranged from IR£300 for improvements to the Woodhill Home guest house in County Donegal to IR£270 000 for the Tay Island Hotel, also in County Donegal.

The strategic guidelines for Bord Fáilte grant aid were set out in relation to the Operational Programme for Tourism. They listed five priorities for new product development, including the following:

(i)   introduce new high-quality facilities, particularly weather independent attractions

(ii) encourage development of ancillary facilities – such as golf, leisure and conference facilities – to complement investment in accommodation and give it long-season capability

(iii) improve the quality and scale of existing products

(iv) improve and develop identified centres and touring routes.

More specifically, Bord Fáilte is trying to use grant aid to persuade the private sector to:

- develop a national convention centre;
- establish a holiday park for foreign visitors;
- create a centre based on health tourism;
- build a large-scale integrated holiday complex featuring high quality accommodation, conference facilities and a mix of activity holiday opportunities.

REGIONAL TOURISM ORGANIZATIONS

These were established by Bord Fáilte in 1964 to provide a wide range of services at the local level including tourist information services and accommodation reservation services.

In 1993 the regional tourism organizations serviced 2.7 million visitors and booked 486 814 hotel and guest house bednights on behalf of clients. In addition, 190 000 bednights were booked through the self-catering reservations system.

IRELAND'S INTERNATIONAL MARKETS

In 1994, Ireland received 3 679 000 overseas visitors, compared to 3 274 000 in 1993 and 2 884 000 in 1989. The 1994 figure for visitor numbers was made up as follows:

Mainland Britain	2 038 000
Mainland Europe	988,000
North America	494,000
The rest of the world	159,000

In addition, there were around half a million visits made to the Republic of Ireland by visitors from Northern Ireland.

The main national markets for Ireland in 1993 were, in order of importance, Britain, the USA, Germany, France and Italy. Some 40% of all international tourists using Ireland in 1993 were classified as being in social classes A and B, in other words professional and management. In the same year, nearly half of all overseas visitors were in the 25 to 44 age group and, interestingly, just under a half of all international visitors in any one year are repeat visitors.

In 1993 total earnings from foreign tourism were worth IR£1367 million to the Irish economy compared to IR£641.7 million from domestic tourism. The spending of foreign tourists in 1993 was 11% higher than the figure for 1992 and had grown by more than a third between 1989 and 1993.

Between 1992 and 1993 the fastest growing national markets in terms of spending were Italy (52%) and Germany (29%). Over the same year spending on domestic tourism fell by 1.6%.

THE 1995 MARKETING PROGRAMME

Bord Fáilte believes the strengths of its products are as follows:

- superb scenic landscapes
- a quiet island with a relaxed pace of life
- a distinctive heritage and culture
- the absence of mass tourism
- a friendly welcoming people
- an excellent location for outdoor activities and sports
- a green unspoilt environment.

To exploit these strengths, the Bord's Annual Marketing Programme set out a detailed plan to increase visitor numbers from international markets. The Programme was set in the context of a new Operational Programme for Tourism which is set to run from 1994 to 1999.

The plan envisaged a growth of 7% in the British visitors over the 1994 figure, which would largely be achieved through attracting more upmarket high-spending visitors through city breaks and golf and angling holidays. Priority was given to attracting visits from British tourists in the off-peak season.

The Bord envisaged in addition that the number of visitors from mainland Europe would also increase, with potentially strong growth in the Swiss, Austrian, Benelux and Scandinavian markets. In mainland Europe the bulk of resources were to be devoted to 'above the line' activities such as advertising, publicity and consumer sales promotions. This campaign emphasized the friendly welcome, history and culture, leisure pursuit opportunities and accommodation as major selling points.

In addition, the Bord highlighted a number of small but important niche markets such as shopping trips from Iceland and language teaching holidays for the Greek markets.

The US and Canadian market grew by 16% in 1994 and the Bord were looking for continued growth in 1995. This dramatic growth was put down to four factors, namely:

- an improving economic situation in North America;
- lower prices in 1994 due to the devolution of the Irish punt;
- extra marketing expenditure;
- reorganized and improved Aer Lingus air services to the USA.

The main markets in North America from Ireland included major cities like New York, Boston, Chicago and Toronto, and states like Texas and Florida. California generated more trips to Ireland than any other region of North America.

Bord Fáilte was also putting significant effort into attracting visitors from Australia and New Zealand through roadshows for the tourist trade in both countries, backed by representation at trade fairs attended by consumers. In 1995, the Bord was also introducing a new horse-racing product for the Australasian market.

At the same time, Bord Fáilte was encouraging the domestic Irish market to take holidays at home in the low season months.

The Bord's marketing activities are a partnership with the Irish tourism industry, which provides funding for the Bord's promotional activities. The industry also makes an input to the strategic and tactical planning process of the Bord, through the Marketing Information Group and the Promotions Review Group.

CROSS-BORDER MARKETING INITIATIVES WITH NORTHERN IRELAND

The peace process in Northern Ireland has led to growing cooperation between Bord Fáilte and the Northern Ireland Tourist Board. In 1995, a joint campaign was planned in terms of cross-border marketing activities using IR£6.8 million from the European Union, the International Fund for Ireland and the public and private sectors. The campaign was designed to have three main elements, as follows:

- a joint television campaign in the USA, Britain, France and Germany;
- pilot programmes on themes such as angling, golf, literature and heritage;
- links between Northern and Southern Ireland heritage and cultural attractions.

A NEW DIRECTION FOR BORD FÁILTE

At the present time, the Bord is undergoing a period of change in its role, following a report produced by Arthur D. Little. In future it will concentrate on the following three core activities:

(i)   selling and promoting Ireland overseas
(ii) helping the Irish industry develop its marketing and product development capabilities
(iii) providing information for enhanced decision-making by marketers, investors and managers in the industry as well as government.

At the same time, a number of non-core functions will be transferred or diverted to other organizations. These include:

- hotel and guest house registration and grading;
- domestic marketing;
- the operation of the Gulliver Information and Reservation System.

The main focus of the Bord's work in the future will be international marketing. The Bord is recruiting 20 marketing graduates with tourism industry experience. It is envisaged that of a full-time staff of 230 in the future, up to 90 will be working overseas.

However, Bord Fáilte will increasingly be less of a doer and more of a facilitator. Hopefully, it will be as successful in this new role as it has been throughout its 40-year history.

DISCUSSION POINTS AND ESSAY QUESTIONS

1. Critically evaluate the current activities of Bord Failté.
2. Discuss the impact which you believe the re-organization of Bord Failté may have on its effectiveness in the future.

Club Méditerranée SA, France

Founded in 1951, Club Méditerranée is now a worldwide organization. It is a major player in the global hospitality industry, being ranked the third largest hotel chain in Europe and thirteenth in the world in 1993 (*Hotelier*, July 1994). In addition, it is also a major tour operator. During the early 1990s, it was the sixth largest tour operator in Europe (EIU, 1992).

Over the years since its creation, the company has developed in a number of ways. However, it has also maintained many of its original unique selling points such as the 'all-inclusive' nature of the package offered and the role of the on-site staff or GOs ('Gentils Organisateurs').

Although it has diversified into new activities, its core business remains the operation of its resort complexes. In summer 1995, Club Méditerranée was offering 80 resorts in 30 countries under its brand name of Club Med, from Australia to Ireland, Florida to Bulgaria. The countries with the most Club Med resorts included France (10), Italy (7), Morocco (6), Greece (5), Switzerland (4) and Mexico (4).

The types of resort vary, and include the following:

- straw hut villages, which are a reminder of the origins of the company when its villages were simple affairs, consisting literally of straw huts on or very near to a good beach. In the summer of 1995, there were nine such resorts, all located around the Mediterranean with three being found in Greece;
- resorts in mountain areas, mostly in France and Switzerland, which function as ski resorts in the winter season;
- modern purpose-built complexes, usually in coastal locations;
- existing hotels which have been converted to the Club Med formula.

Club Med emphasizes that while its prices are above average, the package is fully inclusive, in that it includes:

- transport to and from the resort from the client's home;
- full board, in other words usually three meals a day, while in the resort;
- wine with all meals;
- sports activities and tuition;
- the children's club and activities;
- entertainment;
- insurance.

Clients can also buy the inclusive stay without the flights and transfers. Interestingly, however, Club Med has also developed two resorts, in Turkey and Sicily, which are based on an 'à la carte' formula, rather than the 'all-inclusive' approach. In other words, the basic package includes bed and breakfast accommodation, collective sports and evening entertainment. Clients are then free to choose and pay for extras such as other meals, the children's club and excursions. This has been done, according to the company, because they have 'recognized the need for flexibility in order to suit everyone's holiday needs'.

Club Med also emphasize the atmosphere of their resorts, which they describe as the 'village ethos', and they also talk in their promotional literature about the fact that their complexes are self-sufficient. This fact has at times been criticized by those who believe that interaction between visitors and the host community is beneficial. Conversely, for those who believe that tourism can be a form of cultural pollution, this aspect of Club Med is attractive.

It also stresses the informal relationship between staff and guests, or as they are called 'GOs' ('Gentils Organisateurs') and 'GMs' ('Gentils Membres').

Prices for a one-week all-inclusive stay in the high season, including flights for British clients in summer 1995, were as follows (in pounds sterling):

		[£]
Corfou Ipsos	(Greece)	568
Waterville	(Ireland)	761
Opio	(France)	1117
Cancun	(Mexico)	1259
Phuket	(Thailand)	1372
Bali	(Indonesia)	1576
Moorea	(Polynesia)	1684
Lindeman Island	(Australia)	2074

All-inclusive prices for the accommodation only, excluding flights, in 1995 ranged from £27 per adult per day at the 'straw hut village' resort at Al Hoceima in Morocco, to £105 per adult per day at the luxurious Opio complex in the hills of Provence in France.

In its early days, Club Med sold simple resort complexes to people looking for a relaxed, relatively unsophisticated holiday. However, over the years as it has grown and its customer-base has widened, it has had to change its product to attract and retain new customers. This has been particularly true as the company has sought to attract customers from non-French speaking markets such as the USA and Japan. This, and its recognition that consumers are becoming more selective and concerned with quality, has led it to develop a number of new products in recent years. These include the following:

- *Club Med 1* and *2*, which are cruise ships, designed with sails to look like olden day sailing ships. They offer the traditional 'all-inclusive'

Club Med resort product in a cruise setting. In 1995, one of the ships was cruising in the Mediterranean while the other was operating in Polynesia;

- City Club, Vienna, which is very unusual for Club Med in that it is located in the suburbs of a major city. It contains a luxury hotel with a conference complex and leisure and sports facilities;
- Club Med Business, which offers all-inclusive packages for corporate clients in relation to conferences and incentive travel;
- winter sun and winter ski holidays, using their resorts to attract customers on one of these types of holidays which are growing in popularity;
- Club Med Découverte, the brochure for which unlike all the others as produced by the company, is currently only available in French. This is a programme of guided tours and organized visits to historic and cultural tourism destinations around the world;
- the Villas in Mexico, which are smaller hotel-style complexes located near the archaeological sites of Mexico. They are designed for those who wish to use Club Med resorts simply as a base for exploring the archaeological sites;
- joint ventures with a Japanese company to help Club Med gain access to this important market.

The brochures produced by Club Med also reflect their growth in new markets and their perception of their customers' concern with quality. For example, their brochures include the following:

- a Club Med quality rating system for their own resorts, the 'Trident' system, with each resort being given from 1 to 4 'Tridents';
- a section emphasizing the environmentally friendly nature of Club Med resort complexes, particularly in terms of recycling and the efforts which are made to build in traditional regional styles and use local contractors.

Furthermore most brochures are available in English-language versions and the company stresses the fact that many of its reservations staff can speak English. In addition, Club Med has agents in a number of countries in which it sells its holidays, including the UK.

While in recent years the company has suffered some disappointing financial results, it is still clearly established in the resort complex market as a unique phenomenon and a by-word for quality.

DISCUSSION POINTS AND ESSAY QUESTIONS

1. Discuss the reasons why Club Méditerranée has been so successful since it was founded in 1951.
2. Examine the ways in which Club Méditerranée is seeking to keep up to date with developments in consumer behaviour.

The Hurtigruten, Norwegian coastal voyage, Norway

The Hurtigruten, or 'Fast Route', is a coastal steamer service which links some 34 ports along the West Coast of Norway between Bergen and Kirkenes, and back again. Fundamentally these are working boats providing a lifeline for coastal communities.

However, the service has also been developed and marketed as a tourism product by a number of tour operators, including NSR Travel, a Norwegian company which is part of the Norwegian State Railways.

The ships are working vessels which are capable of carrying between 142 and 490 passengers. There were 11 different ships plying the route in 1995 owned by three different companies and were built between 1986 and 1994. The older ships have a kind of 'old world charm' while the modern vessels are larger and more like modern ferries.

Stops are made at the ports but in general these stops are short. Nevertheless they do offer an opportunity for shore excursions. If we take the NSR Travel product on sale in the UK in 1995, for example, the basic packages offered by tour operators typically include the following elements:

- a berth in a cabin for the duration of the voyage which is 11 days. The cabins vary in standard from inside cabins with wash basin only to luxurious suites with bedroom, sitting room, shower, WC, radio and telephone. The higher grades of cabin tend not to be available on the older ships;
- travel between the tourist's home country, for example the UK, and Bergen, either by air or sea. Rail tickets may also be included in the package for rail travel between the tourist' home town and their departure airport;
- hotel accommodation on the night before/after the voyage in Bergen if this is required due to the timing of flights and sailings;
- three meals per day during the 11-day voyage;
- an on-board courier, usually in the summer only.

Items not included in the package are:

- drinks on board the ships;

- shore excursions – pre-booked packages of excursions are available ranging in price from £54 to £130;
- insurance, which in 1995 cost £28 per adult passenger.

In addition to the inclusive package tours, it is possible for independent travellers to book places on either the whole voyage or part of it without needing to buy a package holiday.

The service operates all year round and prices vary dramatically depending on the time of year and the type of cabin. Some typical prices for 1995 are outlined below, per person (in pounds sterling) from the UK, in twin cabins:

		Air inclusive packages £	Sea inclusive packages £
March 1995	Suite	1711	1677
	Inside twin with wash basin only	951	917
July 1995	Suite	2813	2829
	Inside twin with wash basin only	1493	1509
October 1995	Suite	1819	1769
	Inside twin with wash basin only	1019	969

Reduced prices are offered for senior citizens and children under 12 years of age.

The Hurtigruten is promoted either in specialist tour operator brochures which just feature the service, or as just one package in a tour operator's brochure that features other products.

The 1995 NSR Travel brochure for the Hurtigruten for the UK market took the following form:

- a full-colour 32-page glossy brochure illustrated by many spectacular photographs designed to persuade people to want to take the coastal voyage;
- a simpler, less glossy insert containing information and no photographs.

The glossy brochure highlighted a number of reasons why people might enjoy taking the voyage, including:

- the chance to be part of a Norwegian tradition, given that the voyage has been part of Norwegian life for decades;
- the opportunity to observe everyday Norwegian life at close quarters;
- the spectacular coastal scenery;
- the various types of shore excursions which are available
- the opportunities for talking to local people;
- the fact that the ships all have different characters;

- the novelty of crossing the Arctic Circle and seeing the 'Midnight Sun' and the 'Northern Lights' at certain times of the year.

The non-glossy information brochure contained a variety of information, including:

- the dates of each sailing and which ship will be operating the particular sailing;
- data on each of the 11 ships;
- prices;
- details of the different types of cabins;
- information on the different shore excursion packages;
- general information about life on board the ships, health, visas and the currency which is used on board ship;
- insurance;
- the climate in the West of Norway;
- the type of meals served on board;
- the clothes that people should wear during the voyage;
- details of the ferry services and flights between the UK and Norway;
- information on AITO, the Association of Independent Tour Operators given that NSR Travel is a member of AITO;
- detailed booking conditions;
- a booking form.

The Hurtigruten is not just sold in the UK, as the NSR Travel brochure acknowledges when it says 'From Moss (Norway), Manchester (UK) and Michigan (USA) come the landlubbers, with the sea in mind and a longing in their hearts.'

The distribution channels for the Hurtigruten are as follows:

- shipping company → customer;
- shipping company → tour operator → customer;
- shipping company → sales agent → customer;
- shipping company → tour operator → travel agent → customer.

Finally, it is worth noting that the coastal voyage is so popular that it is often necessary to book many months in advance to secure a berth in the peak season.

DISCUSSION POINTS AND ESSAY QUESTIONS

1. Examine the reasons why the Hurtigruten has become a popular tourism product with foreign visitors.
2. Evaluate the ways in which the Hurtigruten is distributed and promoted in the UK market.

Porto Carras complex, Halkidiki, Greece

Porto Carras is a self-contained resort complex located on the Sithonia peninsula of the Halkidiki region of Northern Greece. Developed by a Greek shipowner, the late John Carras, the complex covers some 1800 hectares and stretches along more than 10 kilometres of privately owned coastline. It is built on land purchased from a monastery in the 1960s and most of the buildings date from the 1970s and early 1980s.

The complex contains a number of different elements, including the following.

- **Hotel accommodation**. There are three separate hotel units. First there is the Hotel Grecotel Meliton, a deluxe hotel which is part of the Grecotel Group, Greece's largest hotel chain. The hotel has 428 double rooms and 18 suites. There is also the Sithonia Beach Hotel, a Category A hotel with 46 single rooms, 402 doubles and 20 suites. Finally, there is the Village Inn, a more informal, smaller Category B hotel with nine single bedrooms, 79 doubles and one suite.
- **Restaurants**. There are 10 different restaurants in the complex, some of which are within hotels while several are independently situated in the grounds. The list of restaurants is as follows:
  - an upmarket traditional Greek cuisine restaurant by the marina – 'Taverna Ambelos';
  - 'The Oasis' – spit roast meats and 'mezes';
  - 'Marina Restaurant' – an à la carte seafront restaurant;
  - 'Restaurant des Ports' – international and Greek cuisine within one of the hotels;
  - 'L'Orangerie' – attractively decorated à la carte restaurant;
  - 'Sangria' – specialising in traditional Greek 'mezes' in one of the hotels;
  - 'Pergola' – an informal beachside restaurant specializing in grilled and roast meats;
  - 'La Brasserie' – à la carte 'brasserie' restaurant in one of the hotels;
  - 'Epicurus Table' – the main restaurant of the Sithonia Beach Hotel;
  - 'Pefko' – informal self-service restaurant offering Greek and international cuisine.

- **Bars**. There are six bars on the site ranging from the Oriental themed 'Samovar' bar to poolside bars to a sophisticated cocktail bar.
- **Entertainment facilities**. There is a hall for functions which seats 450 people and an open-air cinema with 705 seats. There is also a disco and a night club. The hall also functions as a conference venue with sophisticated audio-visual and simultaneous translation facilities.
- **Leisure facilities**. These include the following:
  - a 166 berth marina, the only privately owned marina in Northern Greece. It has a customs office and repair yard;
  - an 18-hole, par 72 golf course, which again is unique in Northern Greece and has a resident professional;
  - a driving centre called 'Proteus';
  - watersport facilities including water-skiing, boat hire and windsurfing;
  - a tennis court with a resident professional instructor;
  - a riding school;
  - a gym club with a weight room and supervised training programmes.
- **The casino**. Opened in 1995, it is located within the Sithonia Beach Hotel.
- **The winery**. Visitors to the complex have the opportunity to taste and buy wines produced on the Porto Carras domaine, Château Carras. The winery claims to be the producer of Greece's 'finest luxury wines'.
- **The pottery**. Where visitors can watch traditional style Greek pottery being produced. There are also opportunities for adults and children to learn how to make these pots themselves.
- **A shopping centre**. A range of shops sells jewellery, clothes and leather, for example. There is also a bookshop and a supermarket which sells drinks, gifts and even bread baked in the complex's own bakery.
- **Private beaches**. These have been awarded the European 'Blue Flag'.
- **Visitor services**. These include a beauty salon for men and women and a full guest laundering service.
- **Children's facilities**. These include a crèche, playgrounds and donkey rides. There are also organized daytime activities for children and special children's menus in many of the restaurants.
- **Transport services**. A shuttle bus service travels around the main attractions on the site, and a boat that ferries visitors to the nearby village of Neo Marmaris.

It can be seen that the complex provides both hospitality services for its guests and opportunities for them to make full use of their leisure time.

The Porto Carras complex is also tied into the tourism field in a number of ways, including:

- the fact that most customers are tourists in the true sense of the word, in that they are staying away from home for at least one night. Most of the hospitality services and leisure facilities are designed to be used primarily by those who are staying in the on-site hotels. The tourists who use the complex are both domestic Greek tourists and foreign tourists, mainly German and British;
- the complex is a popular business tourism venue because of its conference facilities and attractive environment;
- part of the complex, namely the Grecotel Meliton Hotel, is owned by Grecotel which is partly owned by the leading German tour operator TUI;
- much of the bedroom capacity of the complex is contracted by foreign tour operators such as Thomson in the UK and TUI in Germany;
- national and regional destination marketing agencies use Porto Carras as part of their campaigns to attract foreign tourists to visit Greece because of its uniqueness and the quality and variety of its leisure facilities.

Thus, this complex provides an excellent example of the integrated nature of modern resort complexes, and illustrates the difficulty, and perhaps the irrelevance, of trying to distinguish between tourism, leisure and hospitality in such modern resort developments.

DISCUSSION POINTS AND ESSAY QUESTIONS

1. Critically evaluate the core, augmented and actual products offered by the Porto Carras complex.
2. Discuss the strengths and weaknesses of largely self-contained resort complexes such as Porto Carras in terms of the concept of sustainable tourism.

CASE 13 | Iceland: The marketing of a business tourism destination

BACKGROUND

The marketing of Iceland as a business tourism destination is the responsibility of a government agency, the Iceland Convention and Incentive Bureau, which is an arm of the Iceland Tourist Board.

Because of its geographical location and expensive cost of living, Iceland has decided not to try to become a mass tourist destination. After all, it is an affluent, highly developed country, and there is therefore no strong economic imperative to develop high-volume tourism.

Instead, the island seeks to promote more specialist forms of tourism, including:

- business tourism;
- off-peak season weekend breaks which increase occupancy at weekends when the business travellers have gone home;
- activity holidays such as riding, walking and nature watching;
- stopovers for people using the services of the state airline, Icelandair, between Europe and North America.

The emphasis is on types of tourism which involve low volumes but high per head spending. It is clearly a successful strategy as some 11% of Iceland's national earnings in 1993 came from tourism. In recent years, considerable effort has been put into marketing Iceland as a business tourism destination. However, even within the field of business tourism there has been specialization in certain elements of business tourism, namely:

- conferences;
- incentive travel;
- product launches.

The choice of these three reflects the range of facilities available together with the attraction of Iceland for the latter two types of business tourism because of the uniqueness of its landscape and lifestyles.

To develop business tourism in Iceland, people have had to be made aware of the island's existence, as few people know about it. There are also many misconceptions about Iceland which have to be tackled by those who market the island as a business tourism destination. These include:

- 'it is cold and snowy all year round';
- 'it is inaccessible';
- 'there are no good restaurants';
- 'there are no fax machines'.

And so on.

The Iceland Convention and Incentive Bureau has undertaken considerable press and public relations to improve the image of Iceland. This is illustrated by the fact that in the spring of 1995 in the UK two major business tourism journals, *Conference and Incentive Travel* and *Business Traveller* carried features on Iceland. Indeed much of the data contained in this case study comes from these two articles. This emphasis on the international market is understandable given that with a population of only 260 000, Iceland's domestic business tourism market is very limited.

PRODUCT

The product which Iceland offers its business visitors involves the following:

Transport

Direct flights are available to Iceland from Amsterdam, Baltimore, Barcelona, Copenhagen, the Faeroe Islands, Frankfurt, Glasgow, Gothenburg, Greenland, London, Luxembourg, Milan, Munich, New York, Orlando, Oslo, Paris, Stockholm, Vienna, Washington and Zurich with the state airline, Icelandair. A number of other destinations are available around the world through connections with the services of other countries, namely SAS via Copenhagen. Very few foreign airlines fly to Iceland.

In terms of domestic transport, there are air services, long-distance buses and car hire, but no rail services. Road conditions can be bad, particularly in the winter.

Destinations and attractions for conferences

The capital Reykjavik is the only real destination as it is the only place with suitable facilities. However, incentive travel programmes and product launches utilize a range of unique Icelandic attractions outside Reykjavik. These include:

- the Myvatn area in Northern Iceland which is volcanic terrain where the earth literally moves and bubbles under visitors' feet;
- Hveragerdi, a village where greenhouses fed by natural steam produce tropical fruit in the middle of Iceland!

- Thingvellir, the site of the world's first Parliament;
- mountains where people can cross a glacier on foot and engage in off-road 'jeep' driving;
- trips to the Westmann Islands where in 1973 a volcanic eruption created a new island;
- an inland desert where no one lives and few people venture;
- sea cruises daily during which one can see whales, dolphins and seals.

Conference venues

Most venues are small to medium size and consist of facilities within the large hotels. However, there are also some purpose-built conference centres such as the Haskolabio Centre in Reykjavik which has five different auditoria seating a total of some 1600 delegates. It also offers simultaneous translation and exhibition facilities.

Accommodation

Most conference delegates stay in one of Reykjavik's modern hotels, wherever their conference is taking place. Reykjavik has no five-star hotel but it has a range of three- and four-star properties including the Saga, Esja and Loftleidir. Two of these are owned by Icelandair but there is now some which are owned by a foreign chain, after the Holiday Inn chain changed ownership in the mid 1990s. Growing demand has led to a number of new hotels being opened in recent years.

In addition, Reykjavik has a number of small 'boutique-type' hotels which are relatively small (around 30–40 rooms) and of high quality. Perhaps the best known of these are the Borg and the Holt hotels.

As well as new hotels, there has also been considerable recent renovation work on the older properties such as the £250 000 spent on refurbishing one floor of the Hotel Saga in 1995.

As many of the incentive travel packages involve attractions outside Reykjavik, they make use of the accommodation stock found in the rest of Iceland. This varies between small and medium-sized privately owned hotels, schools which are used as hotels during vacations (Edda Hotels), guest houses, farms and mountain refuges.

Catering

There has been a growth in restaurants in Iceland in recent years, both within hotels and independents. Icelandic food is very distinctive, but international cuisine is also widely available.

Ground handlers and destination management companies

There are a number of specialist organizations in Iceland that specialize in arranging and managing conferences, incentive travel packages and product launches in the country. These include Urval Utsyn, Sam-vinn-Travel and Iceland Incentives.

PRICE

Prices in Iceland are undoubtedly high so the emphasis has to be on value for money rather than low cost. To give the reader an idea of prices, here are some as they stood in 1995:

- London–Reykjavik, Business Class return airfare with Icelandair – approximately 90 000 Icelandic kroner (£855);
- a one-night stay in a single room of a four-star hotel in Reykjavik, including breakfast – 9900 Icelandic kroner (approximately £95);
- a restaurant meal for one person without wine – 2000 Icelandic Kroner (approximately £19);
- a bottle of wine – 2600 Icelandic kroner (approximately £25).

It is not surprising, therefore, that given these prices Iceland has specialized particularly in perhaps the least price-elastic aspect of business tourism, namely incentive travel. Iceland can offer unique incentive products to justify these high prices, including opportunities to:

- sleep next to a glacier in a mountain hut, that has its own 38°C naturally fed hot water pool;
- go on whale watching cruises;
- bake bread in the lava of the volcano on the island of Heimaey which was created by a volcanic eruption in 1973;
- soak in mineral rich hot pools while sipping cocktails;
- be 'hijacked' by 'Vikings' and enjoy a 'Viking Feast' which features the exotic traditional foods of Iceland;
- experience buffets on tables which have been carved out of ice on the edge of glaciers.

However, in spite of all the efforts that have been made to spread the image about Iceland, at least 60% of Icelandic conferences still have their origin in the other Nordic countries, both through companies or professional associations.

However, in addition to conferences, incentive travel packages and product launches, there is also a market in terms of individual business trips to Iceland. These trips are particularly linked to the main economic activities of Iceland including fishing and fish-processing and the generation of energy from natural sources.

PROMOTIONAL TECHNIQUES

The Iceland Conference and Incentive Bureau uses a number of types of promotional techniques to attract business tourists. These include:

- specialist literature for those planning to organize events in Iceland;
- familiarization visits for potential buyers;
- press and public relations activities to ensure that Iceland receives favourable coverage in the business tourism trade press, such as the two articles referred to earlier in this case study;
- advertisements in these trade press journals, such as the one-page colour advertisement that was placed in *Conference and Incentive Travel* in June 1995. This talked about incentive programmes and post-conference activities. This advertisement also carried a reader enquiry number so that readers could request further information on Iceland, via the journal.

CONCLUSIONS

Iceland is a good illustration of the links that can exist between business tourism and leisure tourism. It offers excellent opportunities for social programmes for business people after the working day is over and for partners' programmes for those travelling with business people who are not involved in the business side of the trip.

Overall, Iceland is a good example of a destination which is taking a niche marketing approach to business tourism.

DISCUSSION POINTS AND ESSAY QUESTIONS

1. Discuss the reasons why Iceland seeks to market itself as a business tourism destination.
2. Examine the problems which Iceland faces as a business tourism destination.

Grecotel: An example of greening and competitive advantage in the hospitality industry, Greece

Grecotel is the largest hotel management company in Greece. In 1994, the Crete based company, which is partly owned by leading German tour operators TUI, managed nearly 10 000 bedspaces in 18 units. Four of these units were designated as either luxury or five-star hotels.

In 1993, the group's turnover was just under 14 billion drachmas (approximately £40 million at 1995 exchange rates). In the same year, over 3000 people were employed while some 124 000 guests stayed at one of its hotels. Some 30% of these guests were repeat customers, and occupancy levels reached 92% in 1993.

The company reported that in questionnaire surveys conducted between 1990 and 1993, 89% of guests declared that they were satisfied with the Grecotel product.

Grecotel claims to be the first Mediterranean resort hotel company to have set up an Environment and Culture Department. Their interest in environmental issues is said to have developed out of their concern for the strain which tourism growth was placing on the natural resources of Crete.

In 1991, the Grecotel group outlined its first environmental policy, and in 1992 they successfully applied to the European Commission for a grant of 100 000 ECUs to conduct research on the links between tourism and the environment in Crete.

Following on from this, in July 1993 the company signed up to the 'Charter for Environmental Action' as part of the International Hotel and Catering Industry Initiative on the Environment.

Grecotel has achieved peer recognition of its work in the environmental field through the receipt of several international environmental awards.

The company's activities in relation to the environment take a number of forms, including the following.

- It has developed an **Environment and Culture Department** and **employs a professional environmentalist** to advise the company on the action it should take in relation to the environment and to supervise the implementation of the policy.
- The company undertakes **environmental audits** at its hotels and implements their findings wherever possible. These audits cover subjects such as water conservation and quality, sewage, waste management, energy conservation, purchasing policies, architectural styles and building materials, and pollution (air, noise, water and soil).
- The company operates **purchasing policies** which are more friendly towards the environment, by reducing waste and pollution. Examples of such policies include:
  - reducing the use of disposable materials such as individual plastic portion packs;
  - replacing disposable plastic laundry and refuse bags with recyclable paper ones;
  - using bio-friendly products wherever possible;
  - addressing wider ethical issues through the purchasing policies. For instance, wherever possible, fruit and vegetables are purchased locally to benefit the local economy and dolphin-friendly tuna is used.
- The hotel operations are managed in ways which **reduce the wasteful use of water and energy**. Water is reused for irrigating gardens, for example, while final rinse water in laundry machines is recycled as pre-wash water in the laundries. Solar energy is used to heat water while double-glazing is used to reduce energy conservation and noise pollution.
- **Management and staff are encouraged to 'think green'** to ensure that the company's policies are implemented at the level of individual hotel units.
- Initiatives are undertaken in relation to the **architectural design and decoration** of Grecotel hotels. This includes using local materials in the construction and renovation of hotels and the use of local plant species in hotel gardens. More questionable in terms of the principles of sustainability is the policy of developing features in hotels which resemble traditional Greek village squares.
- **Environmental causes outside the hotel are sponsored**, including:
  - involvement in the conservation and promotion of the archaeological site at Eleftherna;
  - the Sea Turtle Protection Society of Greece;
  - the establishment of the Doron Society, a charitable cultural trust, in Crete;
  - the protection of wetland environments which are important habitats for migrating birds.

- Participation in **European Commission environmental programmes** such as the Blue Flag beaches, EPET II and EC Life.
- Attempts are made **to educate guests** about green issues through guest bulletin boards and information packs in bedrooms.
- Attempts are made **to influence tour operators'** attitudes to green issues through mailshots to operators and persuading them to include the relevant sectors in their brochures.
- **The awareness of local communities** is raised in relation to environmental issues through talks at schools and colleges, for example.
- **The media are made aware** of what the company is doing in relation to the environment.
- Attempts are made to **persuade local and central government to adopt more positive environmental policies**.
- **Advice and help are offered to fellow hoteliers**, nationally and internationally, on the greening of hospitality organizations.

The Grecotel approach to greening is interesting in two main ways:

- it is not only concerned with the internal operations of the company, but also with the wider environment and community in which the hotels exist;
- as well as the physical environment, the company has become involved with cultural issues such as the conservation of heritage attractions.

The company promotes what it does in the area of greening to help it achieve competitive advantage in the international tourism market. To fulfil this aim it targets its message at a number of audiences including:

- existing guests;
- fellow hoteliers;
- tour operators;
- the media;
- public sector decision-makers in local and central government, together with the European Commission.

The motivation behind Grecotel's growing interest in green issues probably includes the following:

- improving the company's reputation with a range of audiences and showing it cares about the environment in which it operates;
- reducing costs through recycling and energy conservation, for example;
- genuine concern at the damage being done to part of Greece by the effect of many tourists;
- the views of major stakeholders such as the German tour operator TUI;
- a belief that some consumers will be more likely to visit a hotel if it is seen to take a more responsible attitude towards the environment.

Some people might accuse companies like Grecotel of tokenism and opportunism. However, in a commercial world, it is perhaps naive to expect any company to take action on environmental issues unless there is some commercial gain as a result. Providing that there are real benefits for the environment as a result, perhaps the motivation does not really matter.

The actions of Grecotel have clearly brought benefits in relation to the environment. Hopefully, other hotel groups around the Mediterranean will follow suit to reduce the problems caused by tourism in what is perhaps the world's most popular holiday region.

DISCUSSION POINTS AND ESSAY QUESTIONS

1. Critically evaluate the environmental measures which have been undertaken by Grecotel.
2. Discuss the range of possible motivations for the stance which Grecotel has taken on environmental issues.

TUI, Germany: Environmental policy of the tour operator

TUI (Touristik Union International), Europe's largest tour operator, has been heavily involved in environmental initiatives since it appointed an Executive Director in 1990 to head up its conservation and environmental activities. The postholder reports directly to the executive board of the company.

TUI claims that the reason it spends millions of Deutschmarks each year on environmental activities is because 'holiday regions and resort hotels cannot remain successful in the long term without clean beaches, clean water and unspoiled landscape.' For a tour operator, therefore, it could be argued that environmental action is an issue of enlightened self-interest.

The company has outlined its stance on environmental issues in a 1994 publication, with the apt title, *Better Environment, Better Business – Tourism and Environmental Compatibility as Practised by a Tour Operator.*

The organization splits its objectives in the environmental field into two parts, namely ecological and economic. Both sets of objectives are then divided into those which are short, medium, and longer term.

The short-term ecological objective is to reduce pollution, while in the medium-term the company wants to see pollution prevented at source and to promote conservation. In the longer term, its aim is to see positive proactive improvements to the environment in addition to a continuation of both medium-term objectives.

The company's short-term objectives are, according to the previously mentioned report, linked to 'quality assurance, product optimization and securing commercial returns'. In the medium term, TUI says it hopes to be more adventurous in its environmental activities. Finally, it states that in the longer term its aim must be to 'secure the group's own future, to safeguard and improve profits'.

This illustrates the need to reconcile environmental objectives with business objectives in a competitive market like tourism. It also demonstrates that TUI, like other tour operators involved in environmental initiatives, believes there is a close link between environmental management and quality management. The environment in which a client takes their holiday is seen as a crucial element in the quality of holiday experience they enjoy.

And this mention of the client is at the heart of TUI's involvement in environmental issues, for they believe that consumers will reward companies that are seen to share their concern with the environment in holiday destinations. This is borne out of a survey conducted by BAT-Leisure Research Institute in 1993 which is quoted in the TUI report. The survey claimed that of ten criteria for a quality holiday listed by consumers, seven related to the environment.

However, TUI does not simply seek to respond to consumer concerns about the environment. It also sees its role as trying to persuade 'these hedonistic citizens of the leisure era to save water and energy and to avoid discarding litter, even during the most relaxed weeks of their year'. In other words, it also tries to persuade its customers to behave in a more environmentally friendly manner.

TUI has realized that it cannot take effective action on the environment alone. It has therefore established the TUI Environmental Network, or TEN for short. This means trying to 'export' its environmental ethos to other organizations with which it works such as tourist boards, local authorities, subsidiaries and contracted hotels. An interesting example of this exporting of the environmental ethos of TUI relates to Case study 18 in this part namely Grecotel which is 50 percent owned by TUI. TUI also cooperates with a number of external organizations such as the UNEP, UNESCO, the FOEI Med Net, and the International Hotels Environmental Initiative.

The company has already introduced a range of simple measures to help reduce the negative environmental impact of its operations. For example, their clients are given carrier bags which are reusable rather than disposable plastic ones, and the company produces its brochures on paper which is made using environmentally friendly techniques.

However, TUI's major innovations are in terms of their environmental checklists for both destinations and accommodation establishments, and transport operators. These environmental reports on destinations are written by the company's locally based representatives. Exhibit 15.1 illustrates the scope and content of the destination environment report in 1996. Issues raised in these reports can then be taken up with the relevant authorities by the company.

As far as accommodation establishments are concerned, TUI buyers insist on hotels meeting basic minimum fixed standards on environmental good practice as a precondition before they will contract bedrooms. The company asks every hotelier it works with to complete and sign an environmental checklist. Hotels that are identified as being particularly good in terms of their environmental practices are highlighted in TUI brochures.

Exhibit 15.2 reproduces the checklist for hotels, clubs and holiday apartments which TUI used in 1996, while Exhibit 15.3 shows the checklist for airlines.

Exhibit 15.1 TUI destination environment report 1996

TUI
Schöne Ferien!

1996 TUI Environmental Criteria for Destinations

Suggested points of interest for environmental reporting:
(where available, please submit in addition, photos, press clippings, documentation, reports by environmental groups, or videos)

1) Bathing Water Quality and Beach Quality

Optical and odour assessment of the quality of bathing waters [= sea, lakes, rivers] and of the beaches/banks? Are water analyses conducted regularly? At how many sampling points? Analysis results available [perhaps upon request] and/or made known by public postings? Beaches clean and well-kept? Method of beach cleaning? Regular waste collection? "European Blue Flags"? Toilets, showers? Bans on cars and dogs? Any other special points?

2) Water Supply and Water-saving Measures

Source of drinking water [groundwater, springs, dam, seawater desalination, etc.] and capacity? Quality/treatment of drinking water? Regular quality monitoring? Are water-saving measures implemented? Are there state/regional/local water-saving awareness campaigns for the public and/or tourists? Measures to reduce groundwater consumption by re-use of treated wastewater? Any other special points?

3) Sewage Disposal and Utilization

Public sewer system? Sewage plants [technologies used, capacities]? Cesspools? Other forms of sewage treatment? Where exactly are the wastewaters discharged to? Is treated wastewater re-used [e.g. in agriculture, on golf courses, etc.]? How and where are the sewage sludges and residues arising from treatment disposed of? Any other special points?

4) Waste Management and Prevention

Regular waste collection services [by whom, how often]? Uncontrolled flytipping [where]? Locations, numbers and types of controlled landfills and/or waste incineration plants? Separation of different types of wastes? Recycling possibilities or composting in the destination area? Treatment of hazardous wastes? Are there state/regional/local waste prevention awareness campaigns for the public? Any other special points?

5) Energy Supply and Energy-saving Measures

Type of energy generation [which sources of energy]? Utilization of renewable sources of energy [wind, solar]? Are there energy-saving measures? State/regional/local awareness campaigns for the public and/or programmes promoting energy conservation? Any other special points?

6) Traffic, Air, Noise and Climate

Impairment of air quality by industry, traffic, or incineration of wastes? Are air quality analyses conducted regularly? With what results [if available]? Measures to reduce traffic (traffic control, contingents, park&ride, public transport]? Traffic calming or car-free zones? Measures to reduce noise [traffic, machinery, building sites, public localities]? Noise protection facilities? Noticeable impacts of climatic changes? Any other special points?

7) Landscape, Built Environment and Building Density

Scenic features? Landscape care? Agriculture? Golf course construction? Are there green areas, parks, public amenities? Regional or land-use planning? Environmental impact assessment procedures? Local development plans and ordinances? To what extent are these implemented and observed? Concentration of building on the coast/building density? Urban planning? Regionally typical architecture? Much concrete buildings? Any other special points?

8) Nature Conservation, Species Preservation, Animal Welfare

Nature reserves? National parks? Biosphere reserves? Soil erosion? Flood hazards? Forest fires [and their control]? (Re-)Afforestation measures? Crop protection? Particular animal welfare problems? Are there animals and/or plants in the destination area that fall under the provisions of the Washington species preservation convention? Are there state/regional/local awareness campaigns for the public and/or tourists on protected species [if such species exist in the destination area]? Any other special points?

9) Environmental Information and Offers

Information materials of state/regional/local information bodies [e.g. municipalities, environmental agencies, health authorities, etc.]? Notices, placards, leaflets etc.? Guided tours, excursions, courses? Educational walks or rambling tours? Bicycle tracks, rental? Regulations governing jeep safaris? Car rental with catalytic converters? Unleaded petrol available? Any other special points? Are there for instance problematic holiday offers [heli-skiing etc.]?

10) Environmental Policy and Activities

State/regional/local environmental policy? Environmental legislation? Are environmental requirements integrated into tourism development? Willingness of authorities to provide information and to make efforts? Environmental officers? Environmental protection established in media, schools? Environmental awareness and behaviour of public/authorities/TUI partners/other service providers? Environmental competitions/prizes? Environmental organizations? Environmental seminars? Environmental projects? Environmental conferences? Any other special points?

Exhibit 15.2 TUI Environmental Checklist 1996 – Hotels, Clubs and Holiday Apartments

Schöne Ferien!

Environmental Checklist 1996

Hotels, Clubs, Holiday Apartments

Object: _____

Destination: _____ Area:_____

Built in: _____ TUI-Cat: _____ -star

No. of floors: _____ Beds (total):_____

_____
Date, stamp of the hotel

_____
Name, function, signature of the hotel representative

TUI Environmental Checklist 1996 HOTELS, CLUBS,

Destination: _ _ _ *Area:* _ _ _ _ _ _ _ _ _ _ *Object:* _ _ _ _ _ _ _ .

1) Hotel management

a) **Waste water treatment**
Cesspool? Connection with public waste water treatment plant? Own waste water treatment plant (which technique: mechanical, biological etc)? Re-use of grey sewage? etc.

b) **Waste disposal**
Waste aviodance (no small packages, returnable bottles, no-can policy etc.)? Separation of waste for recycling? Composting? Gathering of special waste (how)? etc.

c) **Water economy measures/Water supply**
Water-saving measures, e. g. flow limitation devices, adjustable WC water consumption, etc? Variable laundry exchange? Desalination? Re-use of water? Quality of drinking water? Own well? etc.

d) **Energy-saving measures/Energy supply**
Energy saving (how)? Low-energy light bulls? Automatic cut-out air-conditioning equipment? Alternative energy production (solar or wind energy)? etc.

e) **Management**
Detergents? Insect pest control? Local produce/wholefoods? etc.

2) Noise protection in/at hotel

Traffic abatement; traffic-free zones? Other noise protection measures e.g. insulation? etc.

3) Gardens of hotel

Layout and upkeep of gardens? Water economy measures/use of purified waste water? Pesticides (which)? etc.

4) Architecture and building materials of hotel

Building style and materials typical of particular region; problematic building material? etc.

5) Environmental information and environmental offers of hotel

Information leaflets? Bicycle rental? Courses und guided tours? Non-smoking areas? etc.

6) Location and immediate surroundings of hotel grounds

Surrounding landscape? Buildings around hotel? Traffic? Industry? etc.

7) Sea- and poolwater and beach quality in hotel area

Hygien/action to clean up beach and pool? Natural state? Blue Flag? Analyses? etc.

8) Other aspects of hotel either causing concern or being particularly environment-friendly

HOLIDAY APARTMENTS

TUI
Schöne Ferien!

_ _   *TUI-Cat.:* _ -star   *Built in:* _ _   *Beds (tot.):* _ _ _   *Date:* _ _ _ _

**Please provide the fullest possible explanations,
if necessary using an additional sheet**

| ++ | + | o | - | -- |

_____   ☐ ☐ ☐ ☐ ☐

_____   ☐ ☐ ☐ ☐ ☐

_____   ☐ ☐ ☐ ☐ ☐

_____   ☐ ☐ ☐ ☐ ☐

_____   ☐ ☐ ☐ ☐ ☐

_____   ☐ ☐ ☐ ☐ ☐

_____   ☐ ☐ ☐ ☐ ☐

_____   ☐ ☐ ☐ ☐ ☐

_____   ☐ ☐ ☐ ☐ ☐

_____   ☐ ☐ ☐ ☐ ☐

_____   ☐ ☐ ☐ ☐ ☐

_____   ☐ ☐ ☐ ☐ ☐

TUI-Umwelt:
8. Fassung (1996)

Do you measure consumption? If you do, then which consumables (e. g. water, electricity, diesel, heating oil, gas)?

....

How much is consumed per season?

Water (m³): ....

Electricity (kWh): ....

Diesel (l): ....

Heating oil (m³):..

Gas (m³): ....

What is the volume of waste produced (in t) per season?

....

How many days are your premises open per year?

....

How many overnight stays per year?

....

FURTHER DETAILS OF ENVIRONMENTAL ASPECTS
- Please attach photographs and information material if necessary -

Exhibit 15.3 TUI Checklist – Airlines.

TUI Checklist: Carriers and Environmental Acceptability

Schöne Ferien!

A *The minimization of environmental impacts is part of the practical work of the carrier.*

The carrier names to TUI a responsible contact person who is always available for queries on all aspects of the environmental acceptability of the carrier, and who reports regularly to TUI on all relevant actual and prlanned aspects and on-going developments.

	Yes	No	Notes

Contact person: _____ (name, position)

	Yes	No	
Environmental and resource profile analysis?	☐	☐	
Environmental audit (pursuant to EC Regulation)?	☐	☐	

B *Reduction of emissions (air/noise) and energy consumption*

	Yes	No	Notes
1. Use of aircraft satisfying Chapter III? (ICAO noise values at take-off and landing)	☐	☐	
2. Implementation in the power units of the state of the art in emission abatement (noise, air) and fuel consumption?	☐	☐	
3. Are pilots instructed to observe environmentally more acceptable take-off and landing procedures? (short take-off and landing (STOL), low drag / low power approach)	☐	☐	

C *Maintenance*

	Yes	No	Notes
1. Reuse of parts, environmentally sound repair techniques?	☐	☐	
2. Reduction of static tests of power units conducted outdoors? (Use of noise control installations)			
3. Application of biodegradable cleaning agents?	☐	☐	
4. Controlled disposal/recycling of			
- paints and varnishes?	☐	☐	
- solvents?	☐	☐	
- fats?	☐	☐	
- oils?	☐	☐	

D Catering / Waste prevention

	Yes	No	Notes
1. Is tableware reusable, or recyclable?	☐	☐	
2. Metal cutlery?	☐	☐	
3. Avoidance of multiple wrappings?	☐	☐	
4. Restricted use of plastic cups for beverages?	☐	☐	
5. Avoidance of plastic bags for in-flight sales?	☐	☐	

Catering / Waste separation, recycling and disposal

	Yes	No	Notes
1. Is waste collected separately?	☐	☐	
If so, what is separated:			
- Glas?	☐	☐	
- Aluminium?	☐	☐	
- Paper?	☐	☐	
- Plastics?	☐	☐	
- Hazardous/special waste (e.g. medicines, batteries)?	☐	☐	
Consignment to recyclers or other specialized firms?	☐	☐	
2. Recycling of organic wastes / food remnants?	☐	☐	
3. Must particular hygiene regulations (e.g. foot-and-mouth disease etc.) be observed?	☐	☐	

E Environmental commitment/information

	Yes	No	Notes
1. Environmental information contained in the			
- on-bord journal?	☐	☐	
- audio/video system?	☐	☐	
2. Technical information given from the cockpit addressing aspects relating to the flight and environmental acceptability?	☐	☐	
3. Non-smoker flights offered?	☐	☐	

Carrier, stamp, date

Name, position

TUI also tries, in general, to encourage good practice in destination regions regarding the following:

- biological water treatment plants;
- alternative regenerative energy sources;
- intelligent beach cleaning technology.
- sustainable land-use, and tourism development

TUI staff are also involved in applied research projects within destinations on matters such as environmental impact assessment.

The fact that many environmental initiatives in the tour operation sector in Europe feature German tour operators such as TUI may reflect the high level of concern with environmental issues amongst German consumers. Such concerns are far less visible in many other European countries.

However, within the European Union at least, there are developments taking place which mean that all European tour operators may have to take environmental issues more seriously in future. These include the concepts of 'eco-labelling' and 'eco-auditing'.

DISCUSSION POINTS AND ESSAY QUESTIONS

1. Critically evaluate the contents of the TUI destination environment report of 1996.
2. Discuss the potential contribution of the TUI environmental checklist for accommodation establishments 1996 to the development of more sustainable and environmentally friendly forms of tourism.

Marketing research in France

Marketing research in tourism and hospitality is a highly developed and sophisticated activity, largely carried out by the public sector at the national, regional and local levels. Two recent examples will illustrate the type of data which is collected and how it is used to help improve the effectiveness of the marketing undertaken by professionals within the tourism and hospitality industries.

THE 'BONJOUR' INITIATIVE, 1994–95

This was a government initiative organized by the Ministère de l'Equipement, de Transport, et du Tourisme. It was designed to improve the efficiency of both the marketing of France to foreign tourists by private tourism interests and to improve the quality of welcome extended to these foreign visitors. Using research data gathered by the Observatoire Nationale du Tourisme, a guide was produced to help French tourism businesses tailor their product to the tastes of individual foreign markets and to help them give the right messages about their product to different foreign markets. To this end the booklet provided information on some 30 national markets that are important to France, from Britain to Australia and Japan to the USA. This information included:

- dates of school holidays in each of these countries;
- market trends;
- the personality types that are typical of particular nationalities;
- their preferences for particular tourist destinations apart from France;
- their perceptions of France;
- their behaviour and likes in terms of things as diverse as the consumption of alcohol, the types of bed and bedding they prefer, when they like to eat, and the types of holiday they favour.

Based on research undertaken the booklet also identified ten examples of activities that tourism professionals could take to improve their quality of welcome for foreign tourists. These included:

- endeavouring to speak at least a few words of the tourist's own language;
- providing more services for families with children;
- putting extra effort into improving hygiene and sanitation;

- improving security measures, particularly for tourists' cars;
- offering inexpensive leisure activities.

This initiative is a good example of the applied use of marketing research, but it can only be attempted if comprehensive, reliable data has been collected in the first place.

LES CHIFFRES DU TOURISME EN MIDI PYRENÉES

At the regional level, most French regional councils tend to publish an annual set of statistics covering tourism in their region. These can be purchased by tourism professionals or any one else with an interest in tourism in the region.

The annual report of the Midi Pyrenées region published in February 1995 was some 200 pages long. It was produced by the regional equivalent of the Observatoire Nationale du Tourisme in cooperation with other central and local government agencies. It covered both the domestic and international markets as well as providing data on the supply of tourism and hospitality products in the region. The report contained figures for the 1993 season in the following sections:

- employment figures for tourism and hospitality;
- income from local accommodation taxes;
- public spending on tourism;
- tourist expenditure;
- types of accommodation available and the number of bedspaces in each of them;
- how the accommodation stock had developed over time;
- occupancy rates for different types of accommodation;
- tourist numbers, broken down by the month in which they visited;
- lengths of stay;
- tourist profiles;
- participation in activity holidays;
- information on short stay holidays;
- specific types of tourism including cultural tourism, industrial tourism, ski-resorts, and spas, together with business tourism;
- air transport statistics.

In addition the report provided definitions and information on how the figures were collected, together with a list of sources of further information. Such data is valuable not only to private tourism enterprises, but also to public sector agencies in the fields of destination marketing and tourism planning.

CONCLUSIONS

These two examples show how data can be produced in a format that makes it useful for practitioners in tourism and hospitality. However, it would be wrong to assume that the situation in France was true of Europe as a whole. The situation is different in each country. For example, it appears that less data is collected and disseminated in the UK than is the case in France.

DISCUSSION POINTS AND ESSAY QUESTIONS

1. Critically evaluate the weaknesses in the type of guide produced under the 'Bonjour' initiative which seeks to describe the behaviour of tourists of different nationalities in a small number of words and a few statistics.
2. In relation to the Midi-Pyrennées example, discuss the problems which can arise when there is a delay of some eighteen months between the events taking place and the publication of the data.

CASE 17

The 'Ski Thomson' customer satisfaction survey, UK

The UK tour operator Thomson is renowned for its comprehensive questionnaire surveys of its clients. These are undertaken on its behalf by an independent market research company. The results are analysed and presented to Thomson in the form of regular reports on customer satisfaction. The questionnaires are distributed on all charter flights that operate on Thomson's behalf. This makes it easier to administer the questionnaire and ensure a high response rate. The 1994–95 questionnaire for customers who had purchased skiing holidays with Thomson is reproduced in Exhibit 17.1.

It can be seen that this survey not only helps Thomson modify its product to meet the expectations of its clients, it also provides information on its customers and helps the organization develop a comprehensive consumer database which can be used later for direct mail marketing purposes. It is thus a very effective form of marketing research activity.

DISCUSSION POINTS AND ESSAY QUESTIONS

1. Examine the ways in which the results of this survey might help Thomson in its marketing activities.
2. Suggest any ways in which you feel the survey could be improved to make it even more valuable, from a marketing point of view.

Exhibit 17.1 Ski Thomson customer satisfaction survey 1994–95.

Please ✓ appropriate box or write in answer as requested

YOUR HOLIDAY DETAILS...

▶ **Was this holiday:**

Full board [1]	Self catering [4]
Half board [2]	Chalet [5]
Bed/breakfast [3]	Flights only [6]	(27)

▶ **Was this a Ski Drive/Self Drive holiday?**

Yes [1] No [2] (24)

▶ **The name of your resort(s)**

....
....

▶ **The name of your Hotel(s)/Chalet/Apartments (name all accommodation stayed in)**

....
....

▶ **How long before departure was the holiday booked?**

Less than 1 week [1]	3-4 months [4]
1-4 weeks [2]	5-6 months [5]
1-2 months [3]	Longer ago [6]	(22)

▶ **Was the name of your accommodation specified:**

In advance [1] On arrival at resort [2] (25)

If in resort, was this a: ↓

Ski Deal [1]
Price Breaker [2] (26)

▶ **Number of nights abroad:**

6 or less [1]	14 [4]
7 [2]	15-20 [5]
8-13 [3]	more [6]	(23)

▶ **How many children are travelling in your personal holiday party?**

	None	One	Two	Three or more	
Children age 0-1	[0]	[1]	[2]	[3]	(29)
2-11	[0]	[1]	[2]	[3]	(30)
12-15	[0]	[1]	[2]	[3]	(31)

▶ **Not counting this holiday, in the past five years how many times have you been on a ski holiday to:**

	None	One	Two	Three or more	
This country	[0]	[1]	[2]	[3]	(34)
This resort	[0]	[1]	[2]	[3]	(33)
This accommodation	[0]	[1]	[2]	[3]	(32)

▶ **How did you book this holiday?**

Direct with holiday company [1]
With a travel agent [2] (102)

↓

▶ **With which travel agent did you book this holiday?**

A.T. Mays [1]	Co-op Travelcare [5]
Thomas Cook [2]	Callers Pegasus [6]
Lunn Poly [3]	Dawson & Sanderson [7]
Going Places [4]	Other [8]
(incl. Hogg Robinson/Pickfords)	Write in.......................... (35)

FLIGHTS...

Please rate:

	Excellent	Good	Fair	Poor	
▷ UK airport check-in arrangements	1	2	3	4	(36)
▷ Resort airport check-in arrangements	1	2	3	4	(37)
▷ In-flight comfort	1	2	3	4	(38)
▷ In-flight food	1	2	3	4	(39)
▷ Cabin crew helpfulness and manner	1	2	3	4	(40)
▷ In-flight audio/visual entertainment	1	2	3	4	(41)

IN-RESORT SERVICE...

	Excellent	Good	Fair	Poor	
▷ On arrival: assistance at resort airport/transfer journey	1	2	3	4	(42)
▷ On departure: assistance at resort airport/transfer journey	1	2	3	4	(43)
▷ Representatives/Chalet girls: availability and punctuality	1	2	3	4	(44)
▷ Representatives/Chalet girls: attitude and manner	1	2	3	4	(45)
▷ Representatives/Chalet girls: knowledge	1	2	3	4	(46)
▷ Welcome meeting	1	2	3	4	(47)
▷ Excursions: choice	1	2	3	4	(48)
▷ Excursions: value for money	1	2	3	4	(49)

YOUR ACCOMMODATION...

Please give an average rating of all accommodation stayed in.

	Excellent	Good	Fair	Poor	
▷ Location	1	2	3	4	(50)
▷ Reception service	1	2	3	4	(51)
▷ Bar service	1	2	3	4	(52)
▷ Cleanliness and maintenance	1	2	3	4	(53)
▷ Comfort of public areas	1	2	3	4	(54)
▷ Bedroom comfort	1	2	3	4	(55)
▷ Breakfast	1	2	3	4	(57)
▷ Midday/evening meals	1	2	3	4	(58)
▷ Waiter service/buffet efficiency	1	2	3	4	(58)
▷ Leisure facilities (eg. sauna, pool, gym etc.)	1	2	3	4	(171)
▷ Facilities and services for children	1	2	3	4	(172)
▷ Apartment equipment	1	2	3	4	(59)

OVERALL...

Taking everything into account:

	Excellent	Good	Fair	Poor	
▷ Flights	1	2	3	4	(62)
▷ Holiday weather	1	2	3	4	(63)
▷ Resort	1	2	3	4	(64)
▷ Accommodation	1	2	3	4	(65)
▷ Representatives/Chalet girls	1	2	3	4	(66)
▷ Holiday overall	1	2	3	4	(69)
▷ Thomson company overall	1	2	3	4	(67)
▷ Value for money	1	2	3	4	(68)

OUT & ABOUT...

▶ **Did you yourself:**

	Yes	No	
▷ Go to the welcome meeting	1	2	(74)
▷ Go on any Thomson company excursions	1	2	(75)
▷ Go on any other organised excursions	1	2	(76)

▶ **Please rate:**

	Excellent	Good	Fair	Poor	
▷ Après-ski entertainment	1	2	3	4	(173)
▷ Children's day kindergarten/creche	1	2	3	4	(174)
⌐ Children's ski classes/ski kindergarten	1	2	3	4	(175)

THIS HOLIDAY...

▶ **Did you:**

	Yes	No	
▷ Ski on holiday	1	2	(176)
▷ Book a Learn to Ski Week	1	2	(177)
▷ Ski with the Thomson Ski Ranger	1	2	(178)

▶ **What standard of skier were you at the start of this holiday:**

First time skier [1]   Beginner [2] (snow plough turns)   Early Intermediate [3] (basic swing/Stem Christie)

Intermediate [4] (basic parallel)   Advanced [5] (carved parallel)   Expert [6]   (179)

▶ **Please rate:**

	Excellent	Good	Fair	Poor	
▷ Fluency of ski instructor's English	1	2	3	4	(180)
▷ Snow conditions	1	2	3	4	(181)
▷ Range of skiing for your standard	1	2	3	4	(182)
▷ Efficiency of lift system	1	2	3	4	(183)
▷ Ski hire equipment	1	2	3	4	(184)
▷ Ski school tuition	1	2	3	4	(185)
▷ Ski Ranger: overall service	1	2	3	4	(186)
▷ Learn to Ski Week: overall service and organisation	1	2	3	4	(187)
▷ Learn to Ski Week: value for money	1	2	3	4	(188)

HOLIDAY EXPERIENCE...

▶ **How did this holiday compare with the impression you gained from the brochure?**

Better [1]   The same [2]   Worse [3]   Did not use brochure [4]   (82)

▶ **How likely are you to choose Ski Thomson for your next skiing package holiday?**

Definitely [1]   Probably [2]   Possibly [3]   Not likely [4]   (83)

▶ **With which company did you take your last skiing package holiday?**

a Thomson company [1]   Crystal [2]   Inghams [3]   Enterprise [4]   Neilson [5]   (84-85)

Ski Bound [6]   Airtours [7]   Other [8]   Write in . . . .

	None	One	Two	Three	Four	Five or more	
▶ Not counting this one, how many skiing holidays have you taken abroad in the past 5 years? . . .	0	1	2	3	4	5	(189)
▶ How many of these were skiing package holidays?	0	1	2	3	4	5	(190)
▶ How many of these were with a Thomson company?	0	1	2	3	4	5	(191)

ABOUT YOU...

▶ I am: Male [1]   Female [2]   (97)

Married [1]   Single [2]   (98)
(incl. living with partner)   (incl. widowed, separated, divorced)

▶ Age: 16-24 [1]   35-44 [3]   55-64 [5]

25-34 [2]   45-54 [4]   65 + [6]   (99)

▶ How many adults are travelling in your personal holiday party including yourself?

	One	Two	Three or more
Adults age 16 & over	[1]	[2]	[3]

(28)

▶ I am:

In full/part time employment or self employed [1]   (100)

A student [2]   A full time housewife [3]

Retired [4]   Otherwise not employed [5]

▶ If you are in employment, which best describes the type of job you do, or if retired, the last job you did?

Skilled trade/craft [1]   (101)

Plant and machine operator/driver etc. [2]

Foreman/supervisor [3]

Manual worker/factory worker [4]

Service worker [5]
(eg. shop assistant/cleaner/catering/caretaker/goods delivery etc.)

Clerical/secretarial/other office work [6]

Technical [7]
(eg. programmer/technician/nurse/representative)

Junior management/junior professions/executive [8]

Senior & middle management/professions [9]

Other (write in) .... [0]

▶ **Name:**   Mr / Mrs / Miss / Ms   Initials [ ]

Surname
[ ]

Address (Street – Town/City)
[ ]

[ ]

[ ]

County
[ ]

Postcode [ ] [ ]   Date [ ] 199 [ ]

Please can we assure you that your name and address will not be passed to any third party. However, from time to time we may wish to send you brochures or other details of our holidays. If you would prefer not to receive this information, please tick this box. [1]   (109)

▶ Which daily newspaper do you read regularly/often?

The Sun [1]	The Express [7]
The Mirror [2]	Daily Star [8]
The Times [3]	The Independent [9]
The Guardian [4]	Today [10]
Financial Times [5]	Daily Mail [11]
The Telegraph [6]	Daily Record [12]

(110-111)

▶ Do you have:

Cable television	Satellite dish	Ceefax/ Teletext	None of these
[1]	[2]	[3]	[0]

(112-114)

▶ In which of the following categories is your personal annual income from all sources before tax and deductions?

£13,001 – £17,000 [4]

£5,000 or under [1]   £17,001 – £24,000 [5]

£5,001 – £9,000 [2]   £24,001 – £32,000 [6]

£9,001 – £13,000 [3]   £32,001 or over [7]   (116)

▶ Have you been ill at any time during your holiday?

Yes [1]   No [2]   (117)

If yes, please write in illness:...................................

THANK YOU VERY MUCH! ANY OTHER COMMENTS?

We find your comments interesting and helpful, but cannot reply individually. If you have specific points to which you need a reply, please write to: Thomson, Customer Service, Greater London House, Hampstead Road, London NW1 7SD.

_____

_____

_____

_____

_____

_____

_____

_____

_____

_____

_____

_____

_____

_____

Source: Thomson (1996).

Airtours plc, UK

Exhibit 18.1

Airtours is perhaps the United Kingdom's fastest growing holiday company, operating in the world's largest and still expanding industry. The company is a large multinational employing over 8000 people in 12 countries. The company has grown by vertical integration into one of the major players in the leisure travel industry.

> We consider that vertical integration is essential to profitable growth in the leisure travel industry and that the growth is driven by distribution capability.

David Crossland, Chairman, 1994.

The company now offers customers the opportunity to visit over 300 worldwide resorts from 19 UK departure points. In 1994, the company also started marketing holidays in Scandinavia following the acquisition of the Scandinavian Leisure Group.

HISTORICAL DEVELOPMENT

The development of the Airtours business has been spectacular. The company came to the stock market in 1987 and since this time has

---

Exhibit 18.2 Airtours plc: key dates

1987	:	Airtours comes to the stock market.
December 1989	:	Commencement of the Euro Sites business.
September 1990	:	The creation of an in-house airline.
Winter 1990/1	:	Commencement of one-day city trips to major European cities.
September 1992	:	Acquisition of Pickfords Travel Service Limited.
January 1993	:	Company seeks capitalization issues.
June 1993	:	Purchase of Hogg Robinson Leisure Travel Limited's 210 retail outlets.
June 1993	:	Purchase of Aspro Travel Group.
September 1993	:	Opening of Airtours departure hall Manchester Airport.
December 1993	:	Launch of the 'Going Places' brand for combined retail shops.
December 1993	:	Acquisition of the Tradewinds brand.
1993/1994	:	Introduction of the Ski programme.
April 1994	:	Acquisition of the Scandinavian Leisure Group (SLG) for £80 m.
June 1994	:	Announcement of the purchase of the MS *Seawing* cruising ship to develop fly/cruise programme.
October 1994	:	Announcement of the purchase of the MS *Carousel* cruising ship to develop fly/cruise programme further.
October 1994	:	Acquisition of Late Escapes telephone sales business.
December 1994	:	Acquisition of Winston Rees (World) Travel.

Source: Airtours Annual Accounts 1990/1991/1992/1993/1994.

---

pursued a strategy of vertical integration. The company has acquired many businesses to enable this strategy to be pursued. The key activities which the company has been involved in since 1987 are shown in Exhibit 18.2. It can be seen that in a short space of time, Airtours has developed its own airline, has developed a fully branded nationwide retail outlet system and has started to develop markets in other countries.

MARKET SHARE

Airtours has grown rapidly in the years since flotation on the stock exchange. It is now estimated that it controls over 20% of the market share of self-catering holidays abroad in the United Kingdom (Exhibit 18.3).

PRODUCT RANGE

The company offers a comprehensive range of summer and winter sun holidays. It has developed holidays to the Caribbean and tropical destinations. The latest addition to the product portfolio has been the addi-

Exhibit 18.3 Market shares for inclusive self catering holidays abroad, 1994

	millions of customers	%
Thomson Travel Group	1.6	26
Airtours	1.1	17
First Choice (formerly Owners Abroad)	0.7	11
Cosmos/Avro	0.6	9
Iberotravel	0.2	3
Other inclusive operators	2.1	34
Total	6.3	100

Source: Mintel.

tion of a fly/cruise business which offers customers the opportunity to cruise in the Mediterranean for reasonable prices.

FINANCIAL PERFORMANCE

The company has benefited from the advantages of marketing holidays in a period of rapid growth. Exhibit 18.4 shows that the UK air-inclusive 'package' holiday market has grown gradually since suffering a slight decline in 1990. Airtours' performance in this market has been

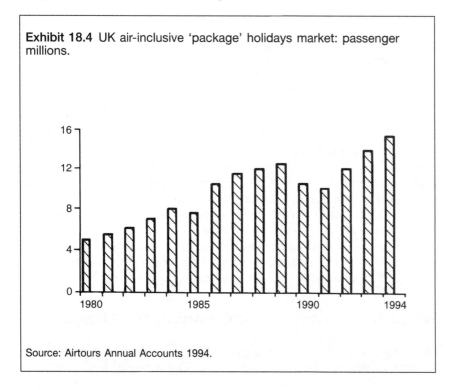

Exhibit 18.4 UK air-inclusive 'package' holidays market: passenger millions.

Source: Airtours Annual Accounts 1994.

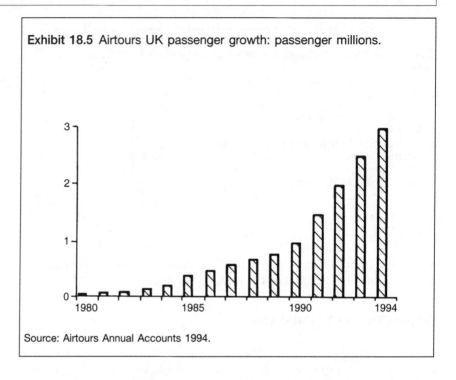

Exhibit 18.5 Airtours UK passenger growth: passenger millions.

Source: Airtours Annual Accounts 1994.

Exhibit 18.6 Airtours: customer volume, 1993–1994

Retail	3.6 million
Tour operations	3.5 million
Airline	2.6 million
Hotels	0.2 million

---

spectacular. Exhibit 18.5 shows the growth in millions of Airtours UK passenger numbers in this period.

The size of the Airtours business which has developed over a relatively short period of time can be seen by looking at the volume which the company handles in specific parts of the business. Exhibit 18.6 shows the volumes of people which were handled by the business during the year ending 30 September 1994.

The financial performance which has resulted from this level of business has been very satisfactory. Exhibit 18.7 shows the turnover and profit performance over the last few years.

ACQUISITION STRATEGY AND MARKET DEVELOPMENT

The company has pursued an aggressive acquisition and development strategy to develop its market position. This strategy has given the

Exhibit 18.7 Airtours: turnover and profit, 1990–94.

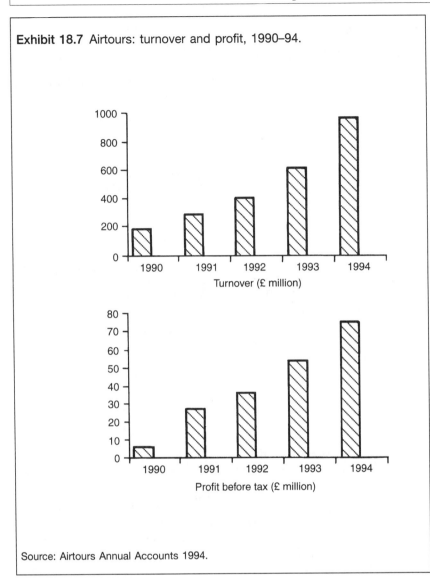

Turnover (£ million)

Profit before tax (£ million)

Source: Airtours Annual Accounts 1994.

company considerable market strength in the travel retail and tour operations business supported by its ownership of airlines and hotels. Exhibit 18.8 shows the areas in which the company has developed.

The acquisition of the Scandinavian Leisure Group (SLG) has opened up a new Scandinavian business for the company using the major brand names of Ving, Saga and Always. The acquisition also means that Airtours now own 50% of Premiair which is a Scandinavian joint venture formed out of the merger of SLG's charter airline (Scanair) with the Danish airline Conair. Exhibit 18.9 summarizes the most recent developments in the Airtours business.

Exhibit 18.8 The product portfolio

Retail	Going Places is the UK's second largest travel agency with a network of 685 shops across the UK. This provides invaluable support for the distribution of Airtours' own products together those of other major tour operators.
Tour operations	Building upon support provided by Going Places, Airtours Holidays has further increased its market share and consolidated its position as the second largest tour operator, resulting in a significant increase in total customers carried and in cost-saving opportunities.
Fly-cruise	This latest venture derives substantial added value from the Group's existing cost structure. The fly-cruise product is marketed by Airtours Holidays in the UK and by SLG in Scandinavia. Passengers fly to their embarkation points on existing Airtours International and Premiair flights.
Airline	With profitable utilization of aircraft guaranteed by Airtours Holidays, Airtours International has maintained its position as the UK's most effective leisure airline with the highest utilization of its fleet and the highest load factors on its aircraft.
Hotels	The Group now controls 16 hotels and holiday complexes located in the principal resorts served by the Group's tour operators. This keeps within the Group a higher percentage of the money spent in resort by its customers as they utilize on-site facilities and services.

Source: Airtours Annual Accounts 1992, 1993, 1994.

The company has developed a portfolio of 16 accommodation complexes in the principal holiday destinations served by the Airtours Group. Fourteen of these properties, shown in Exhibit 18.10, were acquired as part of the Scandinavian Leisure Group and operate under the brand name Sunwing.

KEY PERSONNEL

Development of the Airtours company has been carried out by David Crossland who is chairman and principal shareholder. David Crossland started in the travel industry over 30 years ago, and it has been his skill, expertise and imagination which has led the company to its current strong position.

The company also appointed George Marcall in 1986 after his 13-year career with Marks & Spencer plc. He was appointed to the board in 1991 and has responsibility for sales and marketing for the group.

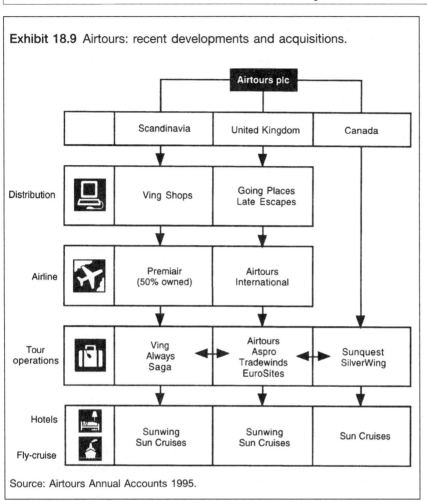

Exhibit 18.9 Airtours: recent developments and acquisitions.

Source: Airtours Annual Accounts 1995.

THE COLLAPSE OF THE INTERNATIONAL LEISURE GROUP

The collapse of the International Leisure Group in 1991 provided Airtours with a substantial opportunity to put on additional capacity for summer 1992. The demise of a major competitor meant that Airtours was able to capitalize on the capacity. Airtours had a successful early booking season and were able to make the necessary adjustments to the portfolio to sell remaining capacity at satisfactory margins.

Airtours has considerable skill in managing its capacity and its cost base in line with rapid changes in demand.

David Crossland, Chairman, 1992.

Exhibit 18.10 The Airtours hotel portfolio

Hotel	Freehold/ leasehold	Rooms
Sunwing Alcudia, Majorca	L	429
Sunwing Cala Bona, Majorca	F	394
Bouganvilla Park, Majorca	L	609
Mimosa, Majorca	F	287
Binimar, Menorca	F	404
Sunwing Arguineguin, Gran Canaria	F	266
Sunwing Playa Ingles, Gran Canaria	L	250
Sunwing Sandy Bay, Cyprus	L	342
Sun Garden, Cyprus	L	259
Sunwing, Rhodes	F	359
Beach Hotel, Rhodes	F	168
Helios, Rhodes	L	31
Sunwing, Crete	F	355
Sunwing Åre (Ski), Sweden	L	206
Sunwing Ekerum (Golf) Sweden	Management contract	65
Sunwing, Gambia	L	200

Source: Airtours Annual Accounts 1994

NEW PRODUCT DEVELOPMENT

The latest Airtours venture has been the development of the fly-cruise business. This venture derives substantial added value from the Group's existing cost structure.

The fly-cruise product is marketed by Airtours Holidays in the UK and by SLG in Scandinavia. This has opened up further opportunities for European marketing for the company.

Passengers fly to their embarkation points on Airtours International or Premiair flights. The company has invested £16 m in the 800 berth MS *Seawing*. Customer demand for this new product has been very strong and as a consequence the company has a £35 m investment in a second cruise ship, the MS *Carousel* (Exhibit 18.11).

PROMOTION AND CUSTOMER CARE

Airtours rely on a collection of well produced brochures to sell their holidays. The company uses the term slogan 'Airtours – We go a long way to make you happy' to promote their holidays.

The company has also developed a customer promise (reproduced in Exhibit 18.12) which is included in all of the brochures.

Airtours was also a pioneer of offering sales promotions of free children's holidays and reduced children's prices as an early incentive for holiday purchase. The development of special offers for children has meant that the company has targeted the family holiday market in their marketing strategy.

Exhibit 18.11 The Airtours cruise liner MS *Carousel*. Reproduced courtesy Airtours plc.

THE FUTURE

It is predicted that Airtours is set to embark on further buying sprees. There have been suggestions in the trade press that the company will look to purchase a tour operator in Germany and a third cruise ship. Airtours Chairman, David Crossland, is believed to be looking to enter Germany because it ranks as the most mature market with the UK.

In late 1995 a Danish acquisition looked imminent, according to the Copenhagen newspaper *Borsen*, which reported that Airtours will take over the operator Spies in the near future. Airtours plc, as a public limited company, cannot comment on this speculation. Whether these

---

Exhibit 18.12 The Airtours customer promise

We are wholly committed to your holiday enjoyment. Only by meeting the expectations of our customers and listening carefully to what they have to say are we able to count on their custom in the future:

- We promise to give you the best possible choice of destinations.
- We promise to give you the best possible choice of hotels and apartments.
- We promise to give you the best possible value for money.
- We promise to do our utmost to make your holiday happy and trouble free.
- We promise to respond promptly and efficiently if you are dissatisfied with any aspect of your holiday or our service.

Source: Airtours promotional brochure 1995.

latest developments happen or not, it is likely that the dynamic Airtours company will continue to develop a European tourism market by strategic acquisition.

DISCUSSION POINTS AND ESSAY QUESTIONS

1. Evaluate the strengths and weaknesses of the way in which Airtours has grown since 1987.
2. Discuss the challenges that Airtours will face in the future in the macro-environment as it seeks to enhance its position in the tour operation market.
3. Examine the branding strategy which has been adopted by Airtours and outline the rationale for the approach which has been taken.

British Airways, UK

Exhibit 19.1 BA: The Mission

'To be the best and most successful company in the airline business.'

INTRODUCTION

British Airways has developed into one of the world's leading passenger airline. It is also one of the most profitable passenger airlines in the world. It has been built by a dedicated workforce into a company with excellent marketing, financial management and operational expertise. This has created a company which regularly receives accolades for its quality of service in all categories of business.

British Airways serves 169 destinations in 80 countries. BA flight numbers, including all the above, all franchise services and specific Deutsche BA, TAT European Airlines, Qantas and USAir, cover 278 destinations in 84 countries. British Airways has the biggest market share of the scheduled market into and out of the UK. The airline competes with more than 90 other airlines at the UK hub, Heathrow. Exhibit 19.2 shows the UK scheduled market.

BRIEF HISTORICAL REVIEW

The company has developed rapidly into a major world player in the airline industry over the last 15 years. A brief historical review of the company is shown in Exhibit 19.3. The move of British Airways from the public into the private sector was a long and highly involved process. In 1982, Gordon Dunlop, the airline's Financial Director, said that the company was technically bankrupt to the tune of £300 million and if the company had been in the private sector it would have found itself in the bankruptcy courts.

Exhibit 19.2 The top five UK scheduled airlines for calendar year 1994

	** Total number of passengers (m)	Overall load factor (%)	Passenger load factor (%)
British Airways (incl. Brymon)	27.9	68.0	49.6
British Midland	4.5	47.8	46.2
BA Euro Ops LGW*	2.3	53.8	51.3
Air UK	2.6	45.4	44.7
Virgin Atlantic	1.7	56.9	40.9
Others	4.9		
Total	43.9	65.4	48.4

* Formerly Dan Air.
** To/from and within the UK. Data is airline reported and therefore excludes non-commercial passengers
Source: Annual CAA UK Airlines booklet.

Restructuring of the airline commenced with reducing the number of routes served, divesting property interests, closing the College of Air Training and transferring catering operations to outside contractors.

The airline was shown by Campbell-Smith (1986) to offer a 'peasant class' of travel and to show general subservience to trade union pressure. Internal studies showed that the managers' jobs were highly specialized, interdepartmental communications were poor and British Airways was technically bankrupt.

This was the basis for the appointment of Lord King of Wartnaby as Chairman and Colin Marshall as Chief Executive in 1980 who were seen by the British government as the saviours of the business. Colin Marshall joined from the successful service company Avis Rent-a-Car, a significant move for the airline, since the post was not filled by a person from the airline industry.

In 1983, a steering group was established to investigate ways of improving customer service in the British Airways market. Customer service was identified as being the cornerstone to British Airways' offering in the market place.

The steering group recommended two courses of action which shaped the subsequent decisions made by the company. A Marketing Policy Group was established which worked on the reorganization of the company. Secondly, a programme of courses was implemented – 'Putting People First' – throughout the whole company.

These moves resulted in a complete revue of the management structure with 60 of the top 100 managers leaving the company. The overall age profile of the management team was reduced and these managers were chosen for their entrepreneurial abilities. The cultural revolution of the company was underway with the aim ultimately, of putting the customer first.

This changing philosophy of the company was underpinned by an extensive programme of marketing research which started the process

---

Exhibit 19.3 Brief historical review of British Airways

1979 Announcement that BA was to be privatized.
1980 Appointment of Lord King as Chairman and Colin Marshall as Chief Executive to lead company to privatization.
1983 Steering group established to lead the company. This established the Marketing Policy Group and the 'Putting People First' courses throughout the company.
1987 Privatization of British Airways.
1987 British Airways acquires British Caledonian.
1988 Announcement of branding policy for individual classes of customer service.
1989 Launch of First Class Service.
1989 Launch of the British Airways Travel Clinic.
1989 Company presses for deregulation of the airline industry.
1989 Development of the links with the Galileo Company Limited (computer reservations).
1990 Launch of the 'World's Biggest Offer' travel promotion in an attempt to boost trade after the Gulf War.
1991 'Winners for Customer' development initiative.
1991 Continued commitment by BA to globalization.
1991 BA obtains 49% stake in the German airline Deutsche BA.
1991 Development of Air Russia with partners in Russia.
1991 Allegation by Richard Branson that British Airways had conducted a hostile and concerted campaign against Virgin Atlantic Airways Limited (Virgin), and himself. This developed into 'The Dirty Tricks Affair'.
1992 Investment in the USAir Group Inc., in Qantas of Australia, in TAT European Airlines of France and in Deutsche BA in Germany.
1992 Acquisition of the principal scheduled European and domestic routes of Dan Air.
1993 Improvements made to major international departure areas.
1993 Investment in Australian airline Qantas. Gained control of Brymon Aviation, the UK regional courier.
1993 Acquisition of the Air Miles Travel Promotions Limited company.
1994 Franchise agreements made with Loganair, Manx Airlines (Europe) and GB Airways.
1994 £70 million investment in the Club Europe brand. Improvements made to check-in facilities, seating, improved catering and on-board service.
1995 Litigation brought by Virgin Atlantic in the English courts was settled.

Source: British Airways Annual Accounts 1988–1989; 1990–1991; 1991–1992; 1992–1993; 1993–1994; 1994–1995.

towards a campaign aimed at improving standards of service. This programme of marketing research looked at customer attitudes and experiences. The research focused on the following elements:

- customer service standards monitor;
- regular business traveller survey;
- advertising and image monitor;
- requirements for service, change and enhancement by a well defined product development programme.

The results of the research were communicated to all staff, even though much of the data demanded a strategic rather than a tactical response.

The post-privatization policy of British Airways has been well documented by Laws (1991). The policy involved the creation of a clear mission statement, clear corporate objectives and clear corporate goals. These are shown in Exhibit 19.4.

The mission, objectives and goals quoted Exhibit 19.4 all demonstrate the change from a product orientation to a market orientation, including concentration on customers, markets and competitors. The success of the company can be attributed to a series of factors which are shown in Exhibit 19.5.

By the early 1990s the company had effectively been turned around and was receiving a number of major accolades. These are shown in Exhibit 19.6.

The recession and the Gulf War halted the growth of the global airline business in the first half of 1991. Despite this, British Airways managed to become one of the most profitable airline companies. The company used the 'World's Biggest Offer' travel promotion in which it gave away every seat on every flight on one day to boost trade after the Gulf War.

The 1990s has been a period of rapid development for British Airways. It has been strengthening its brands and growing strong partly-owned, partly-franchised global alliances, opening up many new market opportunities for the company. The development of the company and its brands has been fostered by a long running advertising and promotional campaign which has been engineered by the Saatchi & Saatchi advertising agency, and more recently M & C Saatchi. This will be looked at in more detail later in the case study. There has also been an emphasis placed on the development of an environmental policy.

THE EVOLUTION OF THE AIRLINE MARKET IN THE UNITED KINGDOM

The world airline industry is of immense size and has been in a period of growth during the 1970s and 1980s, although stagnation and decline

Exhibit 19.4 BA: Post-privatization policy

1. The BA Mission – To 1990 and Beyond

- BA will have a corporate charisma such that everyone working for it will take pride in the company and see themselves as representing a highly successful worldwide organization.
- BA will be a creative enterprise, caring about its people and its customers.
- BA will develop the kind of business capability which will made BA the envy of its competitors, to the enhancement of its stakeholders.
- BA will be a formidable contender in all the fields it enters, as well as demonstrating a resourceful and flexible ability to earn high profits wherever it chooses to focus.
- Whether in transport or in any of the travel or tourism activity areas, the term 'BA' will be the ultimate symbol of creativity, value, service and quality.

2. BA's corporate objectives

The paramount objective is profitability, underpinned by subsidiary objectives:

- To match at least the annual average growth of the total world airline market.
- To achieve standards of performance at least as high as the best of our competitors.
- To serve existing routes and markets, to identify new opportunities for branded services and products and to ensure BA's freedom to compete in world markets; all being undertaken in such a manner as to meet the paramount and subsidiary objectives.
- To attract, develop and retain sufficient well-trained staff with the skills to meet customer expectations.
- To be more efficient than relevant competitors in the marketplaces we choose to operate.
- To provide a continuity of service from the initial point of customer contact through to the completion of the service.

3. BA's corporate goals

- The corporate goal in British Airways is to be the best airline in the world.
  To achieve this goal, the corporate objectives are:
- To provide the highest levels of service to all customers, passengers, shippers, travel agents and freight agents.
- To preserve high professional and technical standards in order to achieve the highest levels of safety
- To provide a uniform image worldwide and to maintain a specific set of standards for each clearly defined market segment.
- To respond quickly and sensitively to the changing needs of present and potential customers.
- To maintain and, where opportunity occurs, expand the present route structure.
- To manage, operate and market the airline in the most efficient manner.
- To create a service and people-oriented work environment, assuring all employees of fair pay and working conditions, and continuing concern for their careers.

Source: British Airways.

were experienced during the mid-1980s. The industry had been greatly affected by the cyclical patterns of the world economy, and the average passenger journey was getting longer.

The industry has historically had an immense amount of government involvement in all areas of business. Governments have been committed to owning state airlines, although this picture is now changing with a market trend towards the privatization of airlines. Despite the privatization process, the industry still experiences government regulation which has limited the freedom of action of airlines to devise their own marketing policies. The trend which is now occurring towards deregulation and liberalization is allowing the industry greater freedom in business operations.

Regulation of the airline industry was carried out for a series of reasons. Governments have viewed regulation as being crucial to maintaining safety standards in the industry, even though safety is also of prime importance to a privately owned airline.

Regulation is also seen to guarantee a reliable 'scheduled service' which operates on a year round basis to a published timetable, and

---

Exhibit 19.5 Factors which led to the success of the company

- Change in management personnel and recruitment of strong leaders into the business.
- Emphasis on marketing philosophy, customer service and performance related pay.
- Creation of a clearly defined marketing department.
- Reductions in costs in the business achieved by savage labour cuts, slimming down of the business and concentration on key strategic business areas.
- Clearly defined segmentation policies and the targeting of these in well developed branding programmes.

Exhibit 19.6 BA: awards and reports

- UK travel agents picked British Airways as best airline in Europe in *Travel Trade Gazette's* annual awards 1991.
- Readers of the *Observer* voted British Airways their favourite airline for the fourth year running in 1991.
- The media reported on the performance of the company in the early 1990s, for example:

'BA remains the most robust of the world's leading airlines.'
The Independent
'The turnaround story of the decade in the airline industry is unquestionably British Airways.'
Financial World

Source: Press Articles

therefore provides a valuable business and social service to the community. Regulation has also been explained by the governments concerned as being important in preventing fierce competition which in the end will not favour the consumer, and being important in protecting national interest since airlines are often viewed as part of the national defence capability and have an impact on national balance of payments statistics.

Deregulation has occurred in a number of key domestic airline markets over the last 20 years which has had a profound effect on the total industry. In October 1978, the US domestic industry was deregulated to allow free competition with the passing of the Airline Deregulation Act which eliminated regulation and pricing control. Deregulation has spread to other markets including Canada in 1986 to 1988 and Australia in 1990. The UK domestic market has only been partly deregulated with an example of a deregulated market being that from Heathrow which was a monopoly for British Airways before 1982.

The European market is also undergoing a gradual liberalization process which began amid much controversy in December 1987.

Pricing regulation still exists in practice in airline marketing although increasingly airlines are beginning to compete on price by offering cheaper fares to consolidators and back-street 'bucket shops', control of which has proved ineffectual. The liberalization process has meant that the world's airlines have faced growing competition. Some airlines have been unsuccessful in this new environment and have gone out of business.

Shaw (1990) has stated that an airline facing deregulation must control its operations in the following way:

- optimize their route network;
- develop new market segments with different fare structures such as the leisure market;
- control marketing opportunities via effective computer reservation systems;
- develop market loyalty;
- control costs particularly in the area of labour.

Privatization is the second area which is having a considerable influence on airline marketing. Complete privatization of a number of state-owned airlines has already been achieved including Japan Airlines, British Airways, Air Canada and Air New Zealand. The privatization process is transforming the marketing environment of the airline industry. British Airways, for example, has been transformed from being technically bankrupt in 1981 to a financially strong formidable competitor in the airline industry in the 1990s.

The final change which is occurring in the environment is the emergence of mega carriers, the globalization of markets and the development of strategic alliances between companies. Airlines which seek to increase the scale of their operations do so for a variety of reasons. Shaw (1990) has identified these as being:

- to act as an insurance policy against competition;
- to allow greater flexibility in pricing due to cross subsidy opportunities;
- to allow the development of expensive branding programmes;
- to create economies of scale in aircraft purchase.

Certain airlines are also investigating and implementing marketing alliances where airlines agree to cooperate, although ownership is retained along with independent market identity. The problems associated with marketing alliances has been the difficulty of compromise and agreements between organizations with different strategic visions.

Shaw (1990) suggests that a successful airline should pursue the following strategy:

- appreciate the importance of a sound understanding of the environment within which their marketing activity takes place;
- acknowledge that the trend towards deregulation and liberalization is well established and will continue;
- accept that if an airline can make a series of well understood adaptations, deregulation can prove to be far more of an opportunity than a threat;
- accept that deep-seated, structural changes are taking place in the airline industry at the moment. Knowledge and understanding of these changes are essential prerequisites of successful marketing;
- accept that a thorough analysis of the competitive scene is necessary with the analysis updated regularly to take account of the evolution of competitive relationships.

A summary of the changes facing the airline business are shown in Exhibit 19.7.

THE BRITISH AIRWAYS MISSION 1995

British Airways has developed a mission and a series of goals to achieve this mission. The company is aiming to be the best and most successful company in the airline industry. Exhibit 19.8 shows the detail of the mission and the goals of the company.

FINANCIAL PERFORMANCE

Despite the problems which occurred with airline sales following the Gulf War, British Airways is still continuing to make healthy profits. Group results for 1994–95 are shown in Exhibit 19.9.

BOARD MEMBERS, PRESIDENT AND EXECUTIVE MANAGEMENT

Lord King was Chairman from 1981–93. He retired from the post of Chairman in 1993 and became President. Sir Colin Marshall then took over as Chairman.

The Board of British Airways plc comprises four executive directors and seven non-executive directors. The Executive Management Group which has overall management responsibility for the company is shown in Exhibit 19.10. It is interesting to note that the company has created the posts of Head of Communications, Head of Public Relations and Director of Customer Service to strengthen the marketing operations.

MARKETING AT BRITISH AIRWAYS

The transformation of British Airways into a profitable private sector business has been the result of restructuring, financial management and expert marketing ability. The emphasis of marketing was made by senior management in the early 1990s.

Exhibit 19.7 Changes occurring in the airline business

Change or proposed change	Effect of change
1. Trend towards deregulation and liberalization	• Increased competition • More freedom in marketing programmes • Shorter time horizons in strategic planning • Removal of 'barriers to entry'
2. Trend towards privatization of state-owned airlines	• Business becomes similar to other private sector business • Culture change required • Marketing opportunity • Freedom in recruitment
3. Trend towards large-scale operations and strategic alliances	• Development of global brands • Economies of scale • Combined marketing programmes • Possible name change and image building

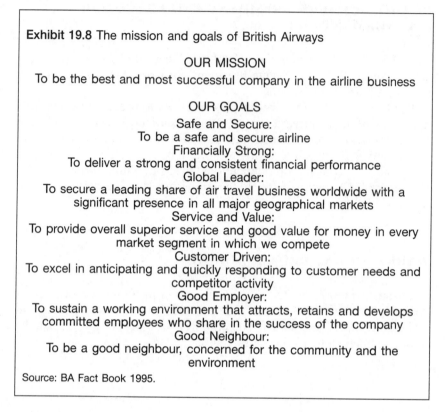

Exhibit 19.8 The mission and goals of British Airways

OUR MISSION
To be the best and most successful company in the airline business

OUR GOALS
Safe and Secure:
To be a safe and secure airline
Financially Strong:
To deliver a strong and consistent financial performance
Global Leader:
To secure a leading share of air travel business worldwide with a
significant presence in all major geographical markets
Service and Value:
To provide overall superior service and good value for money in every
market segment in which we compete
Customer Driven:
To excel in anticipating and quickly responding to customer needs and
competitor activity
Good Employer:
To sustain a working environment that attracts, retains and develops
committed employees who share in the success of the company
Good Neighbour:
To be a good neighbour, concerned for the community and the
environment

Source: BA Fact Book 1995.

> We know all 50 000 of us in BA around the world – that the only
> way we can operate is by providing customer service that is at least
> as good as the best of the rest at value for money prices.
> Sir Colin Marshall, BA, 1991.

The company in the early 1990s also recognized that marketing
would have to be central to every role within the organization. Customer service backed by excellent market research was the central
theme for the company.

> British Airways' marketing policy is driven by the objective of pro-
> viding overall superior service and value for money in every market
> segment in which we compete. We seek to excel in anticipating and
> quickly responding to customer needs and competitor activity.
> Liam Strong. Director of Marketing and Operations, 1991

This statement summarizes the overall marketing philosophy which the
company has incorporated into the business over the last ten years.

In 1995, emphasis has been placed on improving the strength of the
British Airways brands particularly by improving customer services.

> We have continued to invest in improving our customer service
> facilities through the opening of nine new Executive Lounges. This

was to support the introduction of the new Club Europe cabin and service on almost all of our shorthaul routes.

Sir Colin Marshall, 1995

MARKET SEGMENTATION AND BRAND DEVELOPMENT

British Airways announced in 1988 that it was introducing a policy of branding their individual classes of customer service. This was to ensure that each individual sector of the market would have its own distinctive style of customer service which would make it unique.

The first application of this policy, which has been widely used in the consumer goods industry, was very new to service industries in Britain.

Exhibit 19.9 British Airways Group results

Group Result			1994–5	1993–4*
Turnover	£m	up 9%	7 177	6 602
Operating profit	£m	up 32%	618	468
Profit before taxation and exceptional provision	£m	up 61%	452	280
Provision against investment in USAir Group Inc.	£m		(125)	
Profit before taxation	£m	up 17%	327	280
Profit after taxation	£m	down 9%	250	274
Capital and reserves	£m	up 21%	2 090	1 730
Earnings per share:				
Basic	p	down 13%	26.2	30.0
Basic adjusted **	p	up 31%	39.3	30.0
Dividends per share	p	up 12%	12.40	11.10
Employees and productivity				
Average number of employees		up 3%	53 060	51 530
Revenue tonne kilometres per employee	000	up 5%	233.3	222.5
Available tonne kilometres per employee	000	up 3%	345.1	334.4
Operating statistics				
Revenue tonne kilometres	m	up 8%	12 380	11 467
Available tonne kilometres	m	up 6%	18 311	17 233
Passengers carried	000	up 9%	35 643	32 749
Cargo carried (tonnes)	000	up 10%	666	607
Overall load factor (scheduled services)	%	up 1.3%	67.8	66.5

* Restated in accordance with Financial Reporting Standard 5
** Adjusted to exclude exceptional provision against investment in USAir Group Inc.
Source: BA Annual Accounts 1994–5.

The first brands to be introduced were the **Club World** and **Club Europe** classes of business travel. These brands proved to be very successful in a highly competitive marketplace. Volume of traffic during the year increased by 31% in Club World and by 12% in Club Europe.

In 1989, the company extended the range of branded services with the launch of the new **First Class** service. Young passengers, particularly those who are flying alone, have also been recognized as an important market in their own right. The company have launched a new range of facilities for the under-18s called **Skyflyers**. Other brands which have been developed include **Euro Traveller** and **World Traveller** for the economy service, and **Super Shuttle** for the domestic service.

British Airways have therefore branded their various distinct segments. This has created specific brands of service which are designed to meet the needs of specific sectors of the market. This branding exercise was only carried out after substantial customer market research to discover what each segment of the market required.

Exhibit 19.10 The executive management structure of British Airways plc 1995

Terry Butfield (54) Head of Network Management
Anthony Cocklin (52) Head of Communications
Alistair Cumming (60) Managing Director, BA Engineering
Dr Michael Davies (57) Director of Health Services
Robert Falkner (47) Group Chief Accountant
Tony Galbraith (56) Treasurer
Valerie Gooding (45) Director of Business Units
Kevin Hatton (50) Managing Director World Cargo
Brian Haydon (49) Director of Information
David Holmes (60) Director of Government and Industry Affairs
David Hyde (58) Director of Safety, Security and Environment
Peter Jones (46) Head of Public Relations
Captain Jock Lowe (51) Director of Flight Operations

Clive Mason (51) Deputy Managing Director, BA Engineering
Roger Maynard (52) Director of Corporate Strategy
John Patterson (47) Director of Operational Performance
Valerie Scoular (39) Director of Human Resources
Mike Street (47) Director of Customer Service
Walter van West (52) Group Financial Controller
Ken Walder (52) Secretary and Legal Director
Mervyn Walker (36) Director of Purchasing and Supply
John Watson (51) Director of Regions and Environment Sales
Ford Ennals (39) Director of Marketing

Membership as at July 1995.
Source: BA Fact Book 1995.

PROMOTIONAL STRATEGY OF BRITISH AIRWAYS

The growth of the British Airways brands and the globalization of the business have both been fostered by the long-term development of advertising and promotion which has been engineered by Saatchi & Saatchi Advertising agency. A brief review of the development of this long term promotional campaign by the agency is shown in Exhibit 19.11.

Maurice Saatchi gained the British Airways account from Foote, Cone Belding in 1982. The agency then tried to take the globalization theory of Professor Theodore Levitt and put it into practical use.

The advertisements which followed this featured celebrities such as Joan Collins, Peter O'Toole and Omar Sharif, and were part of the 'disappointment' campaign. The theme of the campaign was to get the audience to imagine the disappointment that they would feel if they couldn't get a BA ticket.

Exhibit 19.11 A brief review of promotional strategy – the Saatchi years

1982 Advertising agency Foote, Cone Belding sacked after 36 years' work for British Airways. They produced the 'Fly the Flag' and 'We take more care of you' promotion.

1982 Maurice and Charles Saatchi gained the British Airways account under the leadership of Lord King.

1983 The 'Manhattan' advertisement introduced the idea of the 'World's favourite airline'.

1983 The 'Joan Collins' advertisement generated much media coverage.

1985 The superwoman BA stewardess advertisement brought the concept of BA staff as superheroes. This introduced the idea of BA being a customer service oriented airline.

1988 'Red eye' advertisement introduced which recognized improvements for business people in the BA service.

1990 'Global' breaks all the rules of airline advertisements and introduces the Delibes music soundtrack. Reflected BA's confidence.

1991 'The World's Biggest Offer' attempts to kick-start the airline travel out of the Gulf War slump.

1991 Interactive cinema advertisement where actress planted in the audience recognizes her boyfriend Malcolm on the screen.

1991 Campaign's 'Advertiser of the Year'.

1993 'Where is everybody' campaign.

1994 'Island' advertisement – cost £1.4 million to make.

1994 IPA Advertising Effectiveness Award. Best long-running campaign.

1995 BA nominated for ITV award for Marketing for Brand of the Year in the category of service.

Source: Adapted from *Campaign* 5 May 1993, pp. 32–3.

The 'Red Eye' advertisement in 1988 showed that British Airways could offer a good service for business travellers. This was developed, hand in hand, with the brand development plan.

The most famous Saatchi advertisement, however, must be the 'Global' which changed the face of airline advertising. Using a soundtrack from Delibes the advertisement was fresh and exciting and is still shown today.

On 22 March 1991, the 'World's Biggest Offer' was launched simultaneously in 69 countries in 29 languages. The campaign was aimed at stimulating sluggish airline trade following the aftermath of the Gulf War and generated an estimated £60 million of free publicity in Britain alone.

Other extravagant developments have included the 'Surprise, Surprise' interactive cinema advertisement and the more recent hugely expensive 'Island' advertisement which cost £1.4 million to make.

The development of the global business of British Airways can be partly attributed to the advertising expertise of the Saatchi and Saatchi agency, and M & C Saatchi since May 1995.

DEVELOPMENT OF A GLOBAL ALLIANCE

One of the key features involved in the strategic marketing development of the British Airways business has been the development of global alliances to develop an extensive scheduled route network. The results of this development can be seen in Exhibit 19.12.

The historical development of the global network can also be seen in Exhibit 19.13. The benefits of scale in the airline industry can be summarized as follows:

- expanding operations allows carriers to compete in more markets;
- expanding allows carriers to dominate their home markets;
- big carriers can market more effectively and squeeze their rivals as a result;
- big carriers can dominate distribution.

Globalization of an airline tends to follow a trend. Firstly the airline will try to dominate their domestic market. Then they will try to establish links in neighbouring countries which in Europe will involve setting up European alliances. The airline will then try to establish links with carriers in other countries leading to the final globalization of the airline. Exhibit 19.13 shows the development towards globalization in the airline industry.

The importance of the development of significant alliances to help British Airways develop into a global player, cannot be underestimated.

Exhibit 19.12 British Airways Global Alliance scheduled route network, June 1995

- The British Airways Global Alliance network has 492 scheduled destinations in 99 countries across the world's major markets, offering an average of 7000 departures every day.
- The British Airways route network, including Brymon Airways, covers some 169 destinations in 80 countries. A further 33 points in Europe and North Africa are served by the airline's franchise partners CityFlyer Express, GB Airways, Loganair, Maersk Air UK and Manx Airlines (Europe).
- In Europe, partners Deutsche BA and TAT European Airlines operate to 53 European destinations. Together the British Airways Alliance serves a total of 142 scheduled destinations across Europe.
- In the United States, the largest market in the world, USAir and USAir Express together serve some 195 destinations. In addition USAir operates an international route network of 19 destinations in 11 countries.
- Based in the Pacific, the fastest growing major market in the world, Qantas flies to over 50 destinations in Australia, and a total of some 86 scheduled destinations across 25 countries.

Source: BA Annual Accounts 1994–5.

'The investments in USAir and Qantas have provided significant alliances in the major markets of North America and within the Pacific region. In Europe, British Airways' presence has been strengthened by establishing a number of franchises, which operate

---

Exhibit 19.13 The trend towards the globalization of an airline

Dominate domestic market
For example:
US industry
Air France + UTA + Air Inter
BA + Loganair + Manx Airlines
+ GB Airlines + Brymon + Maersk Air UK

↓

Establish links with neighbouring countries
Air France + Sabena
BA + TAT + Deutsche BA

↓

Establish links with other continents
KLM + Northwest
Delta + Singapore + Swissair
BA + USAir + Qantas

↓

Globalization

---

feeder services under the British airways name, along with investments in Deutsche BA and TAT European Airlines'.

BA Annual Accounts 1994–5.

THE FUTURE

British Airways is committed to maintaining its position in the forefront of the globalization of the airline industry. The company is expected to gain more franchises and to take stakes in a limited number of other airlines in key geographic areas. The company also expects to put a continuing emphasis on a consistent quality of customer service and the delivery to the marketplace of value for money.

DISCUSSION POINTS AND ESSAY QUESTIONS

1. Critically evaluate the strengths and weaknesses of the way in which British Airways has grown since it was privatized.
2. Discuss the reasons why British Airways has become one of the world's most successful airlines in the past decade.
3. Critically examine the British Airways 1995 Mission Statement.
4. Discuss the promotional activities which have been undertaken by British Airways since 1982.

European Travel Commission

INTRODUCTION

The European Travel Commission (ETC) is an organization which was established in 1948. It has responsibility for promoting Europe as a tourist destination for non-European tourists.

HISTORY

The ETC was established first as part of the OEEC (Organization for European Economic Cooperation, now OECD), then as a voluntary autonomous organization.

Europe had become more conscious of the importance of tourism as an economic factor between the years 1918 and 1938. It was at this time that the first cooperative activity took place between European countries on the development of tourism. Exhibit 20.1 shows a brief historical development of the ETC to date.

EUROPEAN COUNTRIES CURRENTLY INVOLVED

The countries which are involved in the ETC are shown in Exhibit 20.2. It can be seen that all the European Union countries (except the Netherlands) are members, as well as other European countries.

OBJECTIVE/MISSION

The objective of the ETC is to promote Europe as a tourist destination. A long-term policy and strategic aims were set out in 1983. The corporate identity, objectives and strategy which were formulated from this in 1983 are shown in Exhibit 20.3.

A Resolution was passed by the Assembly of the European Travel Commission in Lisbon on 6 May 1994. This recognized that tourism

---

Exhibit 20.1 The development of the ETC

1925	–	Creation of the International Union of Official Tourist Publicity Organization.
1927/8	–	Circulation of 100 000 copies of *Europe Calling* in the United States.
1947	–	'International Union of Official Travel Organizations' established in Paris
1948	–	Principle of Regional Commissions adopted in Oslo. The foundation of the European Travel Commission (ETC) in Stalheim, Norway.
1958	–	Formal incorporation of the ETC in accordance with Belgian law. Commission transferred to Dublin.
1962	–	European Travel Conference.
1971	–	A permanent Executive Unit established headed by Executive Director.
1976	–	A Conservation Committee (subsequently the Environment Committee) established.
1978	–	A member of ETC designated to ensure positive links with industry.
1983	–	Statement of 'Long-Term Policy and Strategic Aims'.
1987	–	Robert Hollier appointed Executive Director.
1987	–	ETC/ETAG International Conference on Europe's Tourism (ETAG – European Tourism Action Group). Transfer of ETC Executive Unit to Paris.
1994	–	Resolution passed by ETC, Lisbon.

Source: European Travel Commission, *40 Years of Joint Action 1948–1988.*

---

has not been recognized in either the Treaty of Rome or in that of Maastricht. Details of the Resolution can be see in Exhibit 20.4.

CURRENT STRUCTURE AND MEMBERS

The members of the ETC are the directors of each European National Tourist Organization (NTO) which handles national tourism promotion. They elect a Chairman, two Vice-Chairmen, a Steering Committee, and a Planning Committee for revolving two-year terms. A Research Working Group exchanges information and identifies market segments for investigation. There is also a small permanently staffed Executive Unit. A summary of the ETC structure is shown in Exhibit 20.5.

FUNDING AND BUDGET

The ETC is financed by members' contributions which are individually calculated according to a set of agreed criteria. Additional financial support for specific campaigns is raised overseas. The ETC also gets support from local industry. In 1994, the ETC's said money of about ECU 1 million was multiplied to around ECU 4 million.

Exhibit 20.2 ETC member organizations in 1994

Austria (Autriche)
Osterreich Werbung
Margaretenstrasse, 1
1040 Wien IV

Belgium (Belgique)
Vlaams
Commissariaat-
General voor Toerisme
Grasmarkt, 61
B-1000 Bruxelles

Office de Promotion
du Rue du Marché
aux Herbes, 61
B-1000 Bruxelles

Bulgaria (Bulgarie)
Committee of Tourism
1, Sveta Nedelya
Square
1040 Sofia

Croatia (Croatie*)
Ministry of Tourism
Avenija Vukovar, 78
Zagreb

Czech Republic
(Republique Tcheque*)
Czech Tourist
Authority
Staromestske Nam, 6
110 15 Praha 1

Cyprus (Chypre)
Cyprus Tourism
Organization
19 Limassol Avenue
PO Box 1390 Nicosia

Denmark (Danemark)
Danmarks Turistrad
Vesterbrogade 6D
1620 Copenhaven V

Finland (Finlande)
Finnish Tourist Board
PO Box 625,
Töölönkatu, 11
SF-00101 Helsinki

France (France)
Maison de la France
8, Avenue de l'Opéra
75001 Paris

Germany (Allemagne)
Deutsche Zentrale für
Tourismus
Beethovenstrasse, 69
D-6000 Frankfurt
(Main) 1

Greece (Grèce)
National Tourist
Organization of Greece
2 Amerikis Street
Athens 10564

Hungary (Hongrie)
Hungarian Tourist
Board
Kargit Krt., 85
1024 Budapest

Iceland (Islande)
Iceland Tourist Board
Tourisme
Laekjargata, 3
101 Reykjavik

Ireland (Irlande)
Bord Failte Eireann
Baggot Street Bridge
Dublin 2

Italy (Italie)
ENIT
Via Marghera, 2
00185 Roma

Luxembourg
(Luxembourg)
Office National du
Tourisme
Boîte Postale 1001
77 rue d'Anvers
L-1010 Luxembourg

Malta (Malte)
National Tourism
Organization-Malta
280 Republic Street
Valletta

Monaco (Monaco)
Tourisme et Congrès
Principauté de
Monaco
Boulevard des
Moulins, 2a
98030 Monte-Carlo

Norway (Norvège)
NORTRA
Norwegian Tourist Board
PO Box 2893, Solli
Drammensveien, 40
N-0230 Oslo

Poland (Pologne)
State Sports and Tourism
Administration
12 Swietokrzyska Str.
00-916 Warsaw

Portugal (Portugal)
ICEP (Investment Trade &
Tourism of Portugal)
Av. 5 de Outubro 101
1000 Lisboa

Slovenia (Slovenie)
Ministry of Economic Affairs
Tourism & Catering
Cantarjeva, 5
61000 Ljubljana

Spain (Espagne)
TURESPANA
Secretaria General de Turismo
Castello 115
28006 Madrid

Sweden (Suède)
Swedish Travel and
Tourism Council
PO Box 10134
Arenvägen, 41
12128 Stockholm

Switzerland (Suisse)
Swiss National Tourist Office
Bellariastrasse, 38
CH-8028 Zurich

Turkey (Turquie)
T.C. Turizm Bakanligi
Tanitma Genel Müdürlügü
Ismet Inönu Bulvari, 5
Bahcçelievler, Ankara

United Kingdom (Royaume-Uni)
British Tourist Authority
Thames Tower, Black's Road
London W6 9EL

Source: ETC 1994 Report.
* Since 1995.

Exhibit 20.3 Policies and methods of the ETC

Corporate identity
ETC is a voluntary umbrella organization for European national tourist organizations with the following aims:

- to increase the level of tourism from other parts of the world to Europe as a result of its marketing as a result of its marketing activities;
- to provide a forum for individual members to exchange ideas and experiences for the benefit of each member and the group.

Objectives

- ETC is a cooperative marketing and servicing organization for:
  (a) all members;
  (b) part of its membership – normally in respect of specific projects;
  (c) the tourism industry.
- Activities undertaken concentrate on marketing or subjects supporting the marketing activities.
- ETC undertakes only that which can be more effectively carried out collectively than separately.
- The range of activities should be optimum in relation to resources.
- Every effort is made to ensure that common activities are in the interest of all members.
- Activities are not undertaken:
  (a) which are among the objectives of other organizations;
  (b) which can be carried out more effectively by another organization;
  (c) in which a substantial number of ETC members are not interested in the long term.
- ETC provides specific services to its members or to part of its membership based on the exchange of ideas and set on a year-to-year project basis to match members' requirements.

Strategy
Following this, a Strategic Market Plan was approved in 1985. This Plan included an independent consultant's re-statement of ETC's role and relationships, namely:

> The European Travel Commission's marketing role is a unique one. Only the ETC can provide marketing support for Europe. It can undertake market research or launch 'generic' promotional pro-grammes on behalf of Europe. These programmes can be of invaluable support to National Tourist Offices (NTOs) in their task of marketing individual countries.
>
> The ETC has also proved that as a catalyst it can influence the marketing efforts of the industry and harness considerable funds for the promotion of Europe.
>
> The existence, in source markets for long-haul traffic to Europe, of operational groups comprised of European NTO representatives can be a very considerable contribution to the marketing of Europe – through the exchange of intelligence, ideas and joint public relations operations.

Source: European Travel Commission, *40 Years of Joint Action 1948–1988*.

Exhibit 20.4 The ETC Resolution – 6 May 1994

RESOLUTION
At the General Assembly of the **European Travel Commission** in Lisbon on 6 May 1994, the heads of the National Tourist Organizations of 26 European states noted that:

- although tourism is a major industry in terms of jobs and revenues for many national economies in the last decade of the twentieth century, it has not been recognised as such in the **treaty of Rome** or in that of **Maastricht**, to be revised in 1996;
- in this context, it is essential that all European Tourism Ministers and their colleagues in related fields of government take every possible step to emphasize the **importance of the tourism industry** to their respective national and European economies;
- with the extension of its borders, Europe must ensure that its attractions receive **greater exposure** in the face of growing international competition from emerging foreign destinations, at the very time when the transformation of the European Communities into the European Union marks the opening of new possibilities for Europe as a partner and marketplace in the world;
- there was a need to create a **synergy** between the European Union and EFTA countries on the one hand and the ETC which has consistently demonstrated an unrivalled level of expertise in researching and marketing Europe as a travel destination;
- consequently, **a broadly based promotional campaign** designed to portray Europe as a reliable, attractive and financially competitive destination should be carried out jointly with the European Union and the EFTA and participating countries.

In conclusion, they confirm that the ETC, which is the expression of the national tourist organizations in 26 countries in Europe, is available at all times to **cooperate actively** in such a policy.
Source: ETC Report (1994).

The European Union has also participated actively in joint campaigns and has supported ETC market research projects. Joint ETC/EU action to promote Europe overseas is considered to be a very cost-effective method of promotion.

The ETC operates in all the major markets where at least six NTO's are represented. These markets are USA, Canada, Latin America, Japan, Australia and occasionally elsewhere. It also funds research and the preparation of statistics. Global budgets for the ETC are shown in Exhibit 20.6.

FUNCTIONING OF THE ETC OVERSEAS

The representation of the European national tourist organizations (NTOs) join together to form an ETC chapter and then they elect a

Exhibit 20.5 The structure of the ETC.

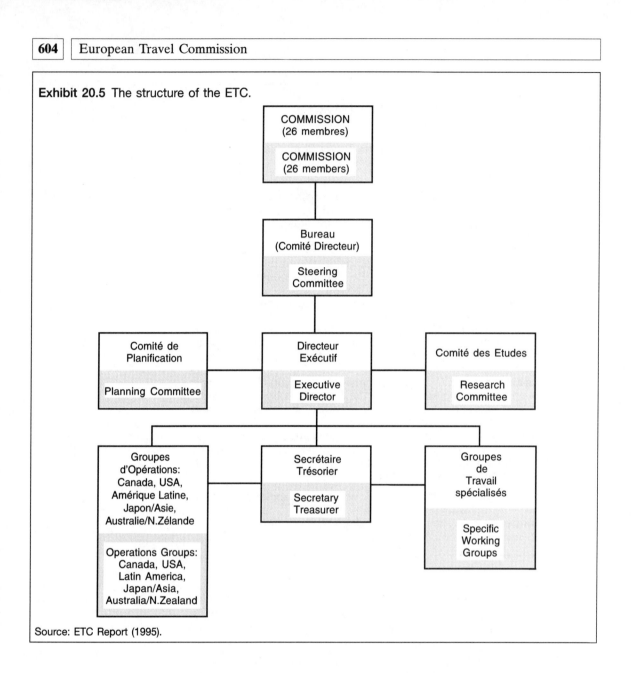

Source: ETC Report (1995).

chairman. They propose joint activities for the year, propose a budget and seek local industry support.

In Europe

The programme is then submitted to the ETC's members in Europe who meet in the spring and autumn every year. After voting, they allocate a budget for each of the five overseas markets. Each Operations Group then may hire a public relations agency which can be responsible for raising local industry support. The ETC itself has very

Exhibit 20.6 Global budgets ETC joint promotion overseas – for total year 1994 (revised) and Operations Groups estimates for 1995 (ECUs)

	USA 1994	USA 1995	Canada 1994	Canada 1995	Latin America 1994	Latin America 1995	Japan 1994	Japan 1995	Australia 1994	Australia 1995	Europe/Others 1994	Europe/Others 1995	TOTAL 1994	TOTAL 1995
1. Promotion														
ETC funds	364 217	500 000	59 000	100 000	22 000	45 000	129 000	10 000	52 000	70 000	—	—	626 217	725 000
Local industry	2 064 000	2 700 000	—	75 000	22 000	30 000	18 700		>200 000	>300 000	—	—	2 304 700	3 105 000
Local NTO reps	481 400	539 500	107 200	125 000	21 000	16 000	3 110		50 000	100 000	—	—	662 710	780 500
TOTAL	2 909 617	3 739 500	166 200	300 000	65 000	91 000	150 810	10 000	302 000	470 000	—	—	3 593 627	4 610 500
2. Research														
ETC funds	—	(1)	—	(1)	3 500	3 500	—	(1)	—	(1)	24 100	1 500	27 600	42 000
Other sources	—	(1)	—	(1)	3 500	3 000	—	(1)	—	(1)	71 000	(1)	74 500	60 000
TOTAL	—	(1)	—	(1)	7 000	6 500	—	(1)	—	(1)	95 100	(1)	102 100	102 000
3. Statistics (ETM)*														
Joint NTO funding											—	136 500	—	136 500

Source: ETC; *Marketing Opportunities 1995*.
(1) Was to be decided by Working Group on 3 February 1995
* ETM – European Travel Monitor

low running costs which means it can allocate the major proportion of the funds to overseas activities.

ETC MARKETS

Statistical data suggests that there is considerable market potential available from the overseas markets which the ETC targets. Exhibit 20.7 shows the visitors which came to Europe from these markets in 1993 and the resulting budget in billions of ECUs.

It can be seen that the United States still represents the largest market, but that other markets also contribute substantial amounts of revenue.

There is also a growing proportion of 'repeat' visitors to Europe and business travellers from the USA, Canada and Japan. Some of the business travellers only visit one country or even one city. The first-time visitors generally opt for around Europe packages. The ETC has recognized that it must concentrate its activities on these two very different types of visitor.

The European Travel Commission also considers that there is a need for further market research to help with the development of Europe as a tourist destination. Research is important to track trends in established markets and identify potential new segments. The ETC has identified gaps in the information, including an overall gap in information regarding the rapidly expanding Latin American markets. Research data is also required on the Japanese and USA markets. Research is also regularly commissioned on the European market. For example, the European Youth Travel Market report was completed in

---

Exhibit 20.7 Overseas visitors to Europe 1995.

Visitors from:	1995 visitors	1995 expenditure[1] (billion Ecus)
USA	8 700 000	14,1
Canada	1 600 000	2.1
Latin America	1 260 000	2,4
Mexico (150 000)		
Argentina (290 000		
Brazil (500 000)		
Australia	543 500	1,96
Japan	1 880 000	1,6
Total for overseas markets covered by ETC	13 983 500	22.16

Source: ETC (1996)
[1] Excluding airfares

1994. In 1995, 21 ETC members will collectively purchase data produced by the Munich based European Travel Monitor (ETM) which surveys overall and holiday travel flows inside and out of Europe.

OTHER ORGANIZATIONS

The European Travel Commission works actively with other organizations to promote Europe as a tourism destination. These organizations include the following.

- **ETAG**. The European Tourism Action Group was formed in 1981 at the ETC's initiative by the leading international trade associations. It brings together representatives of hoteliers, restaurateurs, carriers, tour operators, travel agents, major city tourism authorities, travel journalists, youth hostels, conference organizers and theme park managers. ETAG works closely with the European Union, OECD (Organization for Economic Co-operation and Development) and WTO (World Tourism Organization).
- **The European Union (EU)**. Tourism comes under the Directorate-General XXIII within the European Union. The Director-General of the ETC regularly represents the ETC on the Advisory Committee to DG XXIII's Tourism Unit.
- **The European Parliament**. The ETC regularly liaises with MEPs and other contacts within the European Parliament.
- **The World Tourism Organization (WTO)**. The ETC is Vice Chairman of Affiliate Members.
- **The Federation of European City Tourist Offices (FECTO)**. Cooperation between the ETC and FECTO is well developed.

THE FUTURE

It is important that the ETC continues its good work of promoting Europe as a tourist destination. The organization will try to continue attracting money from the industry which will be used to ensure that all the major European markets hold their own against the growing competition from America and the Asia/Pacific areas.

The increased emphasis on market research will ensure that the information will be available to be used as a valuable marketing tool to help with these initiatives.

DISCUSSION POINTS AND ESSAY QUESTIONS

1. Critically evaluate the role and operation of the European Travel Commission (ETC).

2. Discuss the potential significance of the ETC Resolution of 6 May 1994.
3. Examine the link between the ETC and other bodies such as the European Union, the World Tourism Organization and the European Tourism Action Group.

The Victoria and Albert Museum, UK

INTRODUCTION

The Victoria and Albert Museum (the V&A) is the National Museum of Art and Design in the UK devoted to increasing the understanding and enjoyment of art, craft and design through its collections. Originally opened in 1852 as a Museum of Manufacturing situated in the centre of London in Marlborough House, the museum moved in 1857 to the fields of Brompton, where it became known as the 'South Kensington Museum'. In 1899 it was renamed 'The Victoria and Albert Museum' in honour of Queen Victoria and Prince Albert. Queen Victoria laid the new foundation stone of the new building in that year. It

Exhibit 21.1 Location of the Victoria and Albert Museum, London

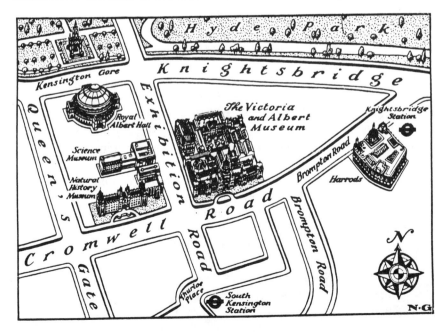

is not, however, a museum of Victoriana. The strength of the collections lie in the combination of great works of art with a broad range of objects of many different types and styles. It contains the national collections of furniture, silver, fashion, ceramics, glass, sculpture, watercolours, jewellery, and photographs drawn from Britain and over the world and spanning 4000 years.

The museum is now one of the major attractions in the city of London and in the UK. In 1994, the V&A welcomed over 1.4 million visitors.

FACILITIES

The V&A is situated in South Kensington. It is near to other major museums of London – the Science Museum and the Natural History Museum.

The main museum is situated on four floors and houses the core collections of: sculpture, ceramics, furniture, glass etc. The guide book suggests that the visitor should walk around these galleries following colour marked routes in the book.

The remainder of the exhibits are housed in the Henry Cole Wing which is accessed from the ground floor. This wing of the museum houses Fine Art including an impressive collection of paintings by Constable, water colours and English miniatures. The museum also has the following facilities.

- **V&A shops**. The shops sell products associated with the museum. The shops stocks an excellent range of quality gifts, stationery, books, ceramics and textiles. There is also a Crafts Council shop.
- **The new restaurant**. Open:
  Mon   12.00–17.00
  Tues–Sun 10.00–17.00
  The restaurant is well furnished and provides an excellent range of food and drink. There is a jazz brunch on Sunday mornings.
- **V&A picture library**. Offers pictures for loan including commercial loan.
- **Research services**. The V&A offers an extensive range of research services and opinion services. These include:
  – the National Art Library housing 1 million books – the national collection of books on art;
  – the Archive of Art and Design;
  – The Print Room;
  – The Textile Study Room;
  – India and South East Asia Study Room;
  – Theatre Museum Archive and Study Room.

Exhibit 21.2 The branch museums of the V&A

- **Bethnal Green Museum of Childhood, Bethnal Green, London.** The national museum of childhood displays. Facilities include a shop and café. Free entrance
- **Theatre Museum, Russell Street, Covent Garden.** The national museum of the performing arts. Admission charges.
- **Apsley House, 'Number 1 London' Hyde Park Corner, London.** The home of the Duke of Wellington. Fine collection of art, sculptures, furniture and personal relics of the Duke. Admission charges.

BRANCH MUSEUMS

The museum has just finished an extensive programme of structural repair to and redecoration of Apsley House which is situated at Hyde Park Corner. This was given to the nation in 1947 by the Seventh Duke of Wellington. It is a palatial London townhouse which houses a spectacular collection of paintings with works by Velázquez, Murillo, Correggio, Rubens and Van Dyck.

The V&A also has branch museums at Bethnal Green and Russell Street, Covent Garden. Details of the branch museums are shown in Exhibit 21.2.

MARKET POSITION

The V&A is one of the major museums which are open to the public in London. It is also an example of a leading national museum.

Museums and galleries are one of the few segments of the UK tourist attraction market which did not suffer a decline in visitors during the recession. This can be partly explained by the fact that many of the museums have no charge for admission (Key Note 1994).

Visits to tourist attractions numbers show the importance of the V&A as a major national museum. This can be seen in Exhibits 21.3 and 21.4.

The V&A has recorded the highest number of visitors in almost 10 years. In 1994, the V&A welcomed over 1.4 million visitors which was a large increase on figures for 1993. Director of the V&A in 1995, Elizabeth Esteve-Coll reported this success in the following statement:

> There is no doubt that members of the public are enjoying our exhibition programme, and, more importantly, are taking time to explore and get to know the permanent collections during their visits.

Visitor numbers have grown steadily over the last 10-year period. These are shown in Exhibit 21.5.

Exhibit 21.3 Visits to the major museums and galleries 1993

1.	British Museum, London	5 823 427	F
2.	National Gallery, London	3 882 371	F
3.	Tate Gallery, London	1 760 091	
4.	Natural History Museum, London	1 700 000	F
5.	Science Museum, London	1 277 417	F
6.	Victoria and Albert Museum, London	1 072 092	D
7.	Royal Academy, London	922 135	F
8.	National Museum of Photography, Bradford	853 784	F
9.	Glasgow Art Gallery and Museum	796 380	F
10.	Jorvik Viking Centre, York	752 586	

F = Free   D = voluntary donation on entry

Source: British Tourist Authority, *Visits to Tourist Attractions* (1994).

Exhibit 21.4 Visits to the major museums and galleries 1994

1.	British Museum, London	5 896 692	F
2.	National Gallery, London	4 301 656	F
3.	Tate Gallery, London	2 226 339	F
4.	Natural History Museum, London	1 625 000	
5.	Victoria and Albert Museum, London	1 440 334	D
6.	Science Museum, London	1 268 839	
7.	National Portrait Gallery, London	1 044 149	F
8.	Royal Academy, London	952 472	
9.	Glasgow Art Gallery and Museum	903 680	F
10.	National Museum of Photography, Bradford	737 096	F

F = Free   D = voluntary donation on entry

Source: British Tourist Authority, *Visits to Tourist Attractions* (1995).

PROFILE OF VISITORS

The origin of visitors to the V&A is shown in Exhibit 21.6. It can be seen that in the spring and summer months, a higher proportion of the visitors to the V&A come from overseas. London residents and UK daytrippers also represent a significant proportion of total visitors to the museum.

The gender and age of respondents of a V&A visitor survey is shown in Exhibit 21.7. Schoolchildren were not sampled in this survey. These figures show that a higher proportion of females compared to males visit the museum. There is a reasonable spread of visitors across the various age groups.

Exhibit **21.5** Visitor figures 1984–94

1984	–	1 690 122
1985	–	1 733 314 (voluntary donations introduced in November)
1986	–	1 022 328
1987	–	916 476
1988	–	996 501
1989	–	952 992
1990	–	903 688
1991	–	1 066 428
1992	–	1 182 402
1993	–	1 072 092
1994	–	1 440 334

Source: V&A.

Exhibit **21.6** Profile of visitors to the V&A

Total sample	1993 Spring 376 %	Summmer 354 %	Autumn 373 %	1994 Spring 341 %	Summer 349 %	Autumn 360 %
Origin of respondents						
Total overseas	54	52	35	34	49	38
Europe	16	21	12	12	15	15
North America	30	21	17	17	24	18
Rest of the World	8	10	6	3	10	4
Total UK	46	48	65	65	51	62
Greater London	17	25	26	24	17	27
Resident of V&A area	3	6	6	6	3	3
Rest of South East	12	12	17	24	15	16
Rest of UK	16	11	21	17	19	20
Type of UK Visitor						
London resident	17	25	26	24	17	27
UK daytripper	22	15	24	33	21	25
UK resident staying in London	6	8	14	7	13	10

NB: Figures are rounded.
Base: All respondents.
Source: V&A visitor survey.

Exhibit 21.8 shows the social class profile of UK visitors taken from the same visitor survey. It can be seen that a large proportion of the UK visitors questioned in the survey came from the ABC1 social groups.

Exhibit 21.7 Gender and age of visitors

		1993			1994		GB (average across country)
	Spring	Summmer	Autumn	Spring	Summer	Autumn	
Total sample	376	354	373	341	349	360	
	%	%	%	%	%	%	%
Gender							
Male	40	36	38	41	39	38	48
Female	60	64	62	59	61	62	52
Age							
14–15	2	1	2	0	2	3	} 20
16–17	3	3	2	2	3	3	
18–24	17	19	11	7	7	24	
25–34	21	24	20	21	18	20	18
35–44	19	22	20	20	19	13	15
45–54	17	14	18	26	20	19	14
55–64	11	11	16	13	13	9	14
65+	10	7	11	10	16	8	19

NB: Schoolchildren not researched. Figures are rounded.
Base: All respondents.
Source: V&A visitor survey.

Exhibit 21.8 Social class of UK visitors

		1993			1994		GB (average across country)
	Spring	Summmer	Autumn	Spring	Summer	Autumn	
Total sample	171	169	242	218	173	231	
	%	%	%	%	%	%	%
AB	31	42	49	39	51	36	18
C1	45	35	38	42	33	48	23
C2	11	14	6	9	10	6	28
DE	10	9	7	6	3	6	31

NB: Figures are rounded.
Base: UK visitors.
Source: V&A visitor survey.

FINANCING THE V&A MUSEUM

The Museum is funded through a number of sources:

- **Government grant**: approximately £32 m broken down between building maintenance and acquisitions grants.

- **Donations from visitors**: amounting to over £1 m annually.
- **Development Office**: dealing with corporate Patrons and Benefactors of the V&A; raising sponsorship for the refurbishment of existing galleries and the creation of new galleries (e.g. the Tsui Gallery of Chinese Art, the Toshiba Gallery of Japan, the Samsung Korean Gallery, the Nehru Gallery of Indian Art) and for temporary exhibitions (e.g. Elida Gibbs sponsorship for Fabergé and Pearson plc sponsorship of Pugin, both in 1994).
- **V&A Enterprises**: the trading arm of the V&A. V&AE's areas of activity include running the two museum shops and a mail-order catalogue service; licensing and development of new product lines based on objects in the collections; corporate entertaining through the Special Events Department using the V&A as a different and unusual place for corporate events such as dinners, receptions, recitals, private views of exhibitions and galleries, etc.
- **Friends of the V&A**: the Friends – numbering 7000 – are very productive in raising funds for the museum. The annual adult membership currently costs £30. All revenue generated is used to finance various projects such as gallery improvements; in 1994 the Friends helped to fund the development of a multi-media system in the newly refurbished Glass Gallery. Benefits of being a Friend include private viewings of exhibitions, a newsletter three times a year, access to late view, exclusive use of a Friends Room, free access to all exhibitions.
- **International & American Friends of the V&A**: a new charity set up in 1993 to complement work done by the UK Friends.

Admission charges

The V&A introduced a voluntary donation scheme in November 1985. This means that as customers enter the museum, they are asked to make a voluntary contribution to the museum funds. It is suggested that a reasonable donation is £4.50 for adults (children under 12, Patrons and Friends of the V&A free).

THE MARKETING DEPARTMENT AT THE V&A

The Marketing Department at the museum, in early 1996, was managed by the Head of Marketing and PR, Robyn Griffith-Jones. She had a team of 12 people plus over 100 part-time staff reporting to her. The work within the department is divided into specific projects which are reviewed each year when the annual marketing and public relations strategy is produced.

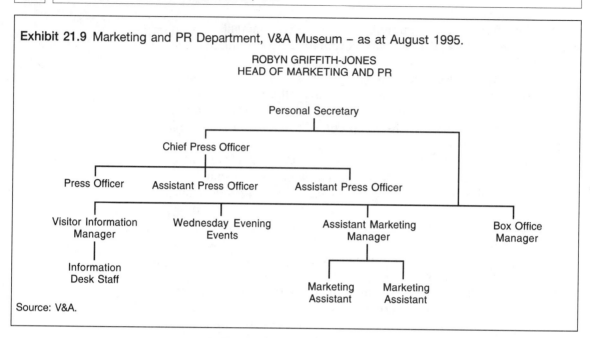

Exhibit 21.9 Marketing and PR Department, V&A Museum – as at August 1995.

Source: V&A.

Organization structure

The organization structure of the V&A marketing and PR department is shown in Exhibit 21.9.

The Victoria and Albert Museum has been transformed into a marketing orientated organization over the last few years. This move was consolidated with the establishment of a new position, the Head of Marketing and PR. The post-holder has changed the image of the museum and introduced an organization-wide marketing programme.

Current marketing issues

> Museums will stand or fall not only by their competence to care for collections, but by their ability to care for people. In other words, they need to be market-oriented if they are to survive.
>
> Cossons (1985).

The aim of the marketing and public relations department of the Victoria and Albert Museum is to position the V&A as the natural museum of choice for leisure, education, and association in support of its mission.

The museum is faced with competition from all leisure activities but must maintain an increasing annual visitor number. It is also being faced with more financial constraints and is seeking to increase revenue wherever possible. The main issues which are facing the museum are therefore common to other visitor attractions.

The V&A is a Grade 1 listed building. One of the main strategic issues facing the museum is how to make the building attractive to

---

Exhibit 21.10 Main objectives of the marketing and PR plan

● Build awareness, understanding and influence.
● Increase visitor numbers.
● Increase revenue.
● Improve visitor experience through information.

---

visitors and incorporate services which will not alter the fabric of the building.

High-profile public relations campaigns are an essential part of the marketing effort.

The main objectives of the current marketing and PR plan are shown in Exhibit 21.10. and were derived after considering the strategic vision of the museum.

Build awareness, understanding and influence

The marketing department of the V&A ensures that the museum has a high profile so that people know about the museum and want to do something about preserving it. This means that visitors continue to come and also helps to support relationships with business contacts who provide an important source of sponsorship.

The museum also has strong links with the tourism and attractions industry. It has a close relationship with bodies such as the LTB (London Tourist Board), London First, and the BTA (British Tourist Authority).

The V&A considers itself to be a **leisure attraction** and uses the marketing techniques which have been developed in the private sector service industries.

It is important that media coverage of the museum is always achieved, particularly when the excellence of research, education, sponsorship, conservation and scientific development can be covered.

An example of an educational development which the V&A used to gain media coverage was the work that the museum staff have completed with teachers to develop the National Curriculum. Scientific breakthroughs can also offer the V&A the opportunity for press coverage. The V&A science staff, for example, have worked with scientists from the neighbouring Imperial College in the area of glass conservation and have made major scientific advancements.

Special events give the V&A a particular opportunity for raising the profile of the museum. The hosting of prestigious conferences or exhibitions are examples of special events which can be used to give the museum media coverage. The reopening of Apsley House to the public also gave the V&A the opportunity to target media coverage while exhibitions and gallery openings provide the largest opportunity for media coverage.

The V&A plans a balanced programme of large and small, scholarly and popular exhibitions to attract a broad range of audiences and to enhance the visitors' understanding of the museum's collections. Exhibitions planned for the next five years include:

- William Morris;
- American Photography 1890–1960;
- British Fashion since the War;
- Designing Modernity: The Arts of Reform and Persuasion 1885–1945;
- The Swedish Style: Carl Larsson (1853–1919);
- The Excellence of Every Art: The Life of London's Victoria and Albert Museum;
- Sikhs and the Art of the Punjab;
- Grinling Gibbons.

The V&A has an ongoing programme of redisplaying the permanent collections. Recently, the V&A has opened the Nehru Gallery of Indian Art, the T.T. Tsui Gallery of Chinese Art, the European Ornament Gallery, the Twentieth Century Gallery, the Samsung Gallery of Korean Art, the Frank Lloyd Wright Gallery and the Glass Gallery. Over the next three years, the V&A will complete the following galleries:

- Raphael Gallery;
- English Silver Gallery;
- British Art and Design Galleries;
- The Photography Gallery;
- The Ironwork Gallery;

Increasing visitor numbers

It is very important that the museum continues to increase the visitor numbers each year, particularly as the numbers are published annually. There are various methods which the museum can use to help the continued increase in visitor numbers, including effective market segmentation and targeting. The museum carries out quantitative market research at the main museum and during special exhibitions to identify a profile of visitors.

The four press officers who work within the Marketing Department have the job of maintaining a strong, open and positive relationship with the press. The majority of this work is carried out in the UK but the press officers are also responsible for communicating with the overseas press.

Special exhibitions are often promoted overseas. The 'Wedgwood' exhibition, for example, which took place in 1995 was launched in France. The V&A sent a Japanese speaking press officer to support a touring exhibition of Japan and promote the V&A in London as a tourist attraction.

Work on publicity leaflets and visitor services must continue on an ongoing basis to encourage increased numbers of visitors. This material should enable the museum to develop a strong image. The use of the V&A logo, for example, in all publicity material is a very important aspect of this work. The visitor's first impression of the museum should be favourable, so the design of information desks and the training of front-line staff in this area are ongoing marketing activities.

The museum Marketing Department also identifies key activities which are developed each year. This can be in the form of a joint marketing activity with other museums. The development of overseas markets for a major museum is a key area of marketing activity and the V&A is busy developing the Japanese and American markets.

The main ways that the V&A is increasing visitor numbers may be summarised as:

- effective targeting and planning;
- effective advertising and promotional campaigns;
- the development of new propositions.

Specific campaigns are devised for particular exhibitions. These campaigns include leaflets, promotions and ticket offers. Each exhibition will have a different market segment. An exhibition or fashion, such as the 'Streetstyle' exhibition which took place in 1994/95, had a younger audience, for example, than the more traditional exhibition such as the 'Wedgwood' exhibition of the same year.

The Marketing Department also liaises with the **Development Department** and the **Education Department**. The Development Department has the job of financing the exhibitions and obtaining major sources of sponsorship. The Education Department is responsible for developing school and academic links. It is heavily involved in developing community education programmes.

The Marketing Department has also used sales promotion techniques to increase visitor numbers. The **jazz brunch**, for example, was so successful as an initial sales promotion when the V&A was opened on a Sunday morning that it has remained as a permanent fixture! Exhibit 21.11 shows the key market segments that the V&A is attracting.

Exhibit 21.11 Key market segments for the V&A

- Local and regional residents living near to the museum.
- National visitors who are visiting London on a day trip, a short or longer break.
- Overseas visitors travelling on their own.
- Overseas visitors travelling in a group, usually in association with a package company.

Increase revenue

The V&A marketing aim is to increase revenue from donations and exhibition revenue. This work has been concentrated in a number of areas including:

- focusing on special exhibitions and thereby encouraging secondary spend in café/restaurant and shop;
- working to increase donation levels;
- working in partnership with marketing and travel operations.

In addition the PR function helps support the wider museum aim of increasing sponsorship.

Improve visitor experience through information

The V&A aims to continually improve the levels of information and service which are available in the museum. This includes improvements to desks, signposting and ancillary services such as the restaurants.

The V&A has developed a prominent presence in London with the use of leaflets and posters. This is very important because the location of the museum, which is out of the main tourist area, means that it has to attract visitors from the centre of London.

The V&A carries out extensive market research with visitors to the museum and to the special exhibitions so that improvements can be made. The front-of-house service staff at the museum have all been trained in customer care techniques. Every two months all the areas dealing with visitors meet in the 'Visitor Services Group', including the security staff, the restaurant staff, education department, the desk staff, the buildings maintenance and cleaning staff, and the Marketing Department.

The V&A was awarded a Charter Mark in October 1994. Specially cited by the government in awarding this honour were: the quality of information and multilingual free leaflets, customer training programmes for warding and front-of-house staff, access for the disabled, visitor surveys, and the courtesy and knowledgability of the staff.

OTHER ACTIVITIES

Friends of the V&A

Friends of the V&A is an organization which has been set up to support the work of the museum. Friends give their time in voluntary work and financially support a wide range of projects including the purchase of objects, refurbishment of galleries and grants for research.

Friends and Patrons of the V&A and their guests can attend special events including late viewing in the museum and late lectures. Drinks and buffet suppers are also served in the restaurant to accompany these events.

Special events

The V&A is housed in a magnificent Victorian building with remarkable rooms of the period. This has allowed the museum to offer clients the opportunity of entertaining in the heart of London.

The V&A can cater for receptions, dinners, lunches, conferences and presentations of up to 700 guests. Events can be booked in a number of key locations in the museum including The Dome which is the museum's resplendent main entrance, the Gamble Room and the Morris Room which is smaller and elegant. The Pirelli Garden can also be used for entertaining and can be floodlit at night.

One of the most spectacular corporate venues in the country was opened in June 1995 as a result of Apsley House reopening. Apsley House can be booked as a corporate venue and cost £10 000 per night in 1996. Alicia Robinson, the V&A's Head of Special Events, has added this to her list of venues on offer to companies. These efforts have contributed to the £3.5 million turnover which V&A Enterprises in total raised for the museum.

> The V&A was ripe for development when I took over five years ago. I'm always aware that we are working in a sensitive environment, but it has been successful and profitable, and our bookings have increased.
>
> Alicia Robinson, V&A Head of Special Events.

CONCLUSION

The Victoria and Albert Museum is one of the national monuments in the UK. The marketing activity carried out by the museum is critical for the success and development of the museum in the future.

DISCUSSION POINTS AND ESSAY QUESTIONS

1. Evaluate the implications of the 1994 visitor profile data for future promotional strategies that might be undertaken by the Victoria and Albert Museum.
2. Identify the main competitors for the Victoria and Albert Museum and discuss how it might seek to gain competitive advantage over these competitors.
3. Discuss the challenges which the Victoria and Albert Museum will face from likely future changes in its macro-environment.

CASE 22

The European youth travel market

In 1995, the European Travel Commission (ETC) published a report which highlighted some interesting national differences between European countries in respect of the important youth travel market. For the purposes of this report, the youth market was defined as being tourists aged between 15 and 26.

This case study, based closely on this report, examines the European youth travel market in terms of the following issues:

- the intra-European market;
- travel by Europeans to other continents;
- domestic youth travel;
- non-European visitors to Europe;
- suppliers and intermediaries.

THE INTRA-EUROPEAN MARKET

The intra-European market means trips taken by residents of one European country to another European country. If we divide the number of trips taken by people aged 15–26 resident in any country by the population of that country aged 15–26, we have an index which may be termed, the 'travel propensity'. This is an index of the average number of trips taken per year by the youth population of the country. This 'travel propensity' varies dramatically between European countries as we can see from Exhibit 22.1.

Young people in Europe clearly have strong preferences for particular countries when they travel around Europe. For example, in 1993, 7 707 000 youth visits were made to France by Europeans while a further 5 505 000 trips had Spain as their destination. At the other extreme, Sweden attracted 1 116 000 such trips and Hungary 1 032 000.

In 1993, the three largest volume flows of youth tourists between individual European countries were as follows:

1. Germany to Austria   1 934 000
2. Germany to France   1 636 000
3. UK to Spain   1 384 000

Exhibit 22.1 Youth travel propensity 1993

Country	Youth trips (millions)	Youth population (millions)	Travel propensity
Switzerland	2.0	1.2	1.67
Denmark	1.3	0.9	1.43
UK	5.7	10.2	0.56
France	2.4	8.1	0.30
Poland	0.9	5.4	0.17

Source: Adapted from Wheatcroft and Seekings (1995).

Sun, sand and sea holidays were the type of trip most often taken by European youth travellers, but other types of holiday were also popular, including visiting friends and relatives (VFR). While this latter type of trip represented 5.5% of intra-European trips overall, some countries showed a particular preference for this type. In France, visiting friends and relatives represented 17% of all trips, while in Poland the corresponding figure was 13%, still well above the European average.

TRAVEL BY EUROPEANS TO OTHER CONTINENTS

In 1993, European youth travellers took 3.5 million trips to other continents, compared to 42 million trips they took within Europe. The USA attracted 40% of these trips while a further quarter had the Pacific, Asia and Australasia as their destination.

Of the overall volume of 3.5 million trips, nearly a million were taken by Germans and a further 23% by Britons. At the other extreme, Finland contributed 51 000 trips and other Eastern European countries generated 50 000 trips, between them.

There are clearly different preferences for particular non-European destinations, between the youth populations of different European countries, reflecting shared languages, traditions of emigration and historical links. For instance, visits to Latin America represented 11% of non-European trips by German youth tourists in 1993 while they amounted to a third of all trips made by Spanish youth travellers. Likewise, 10% of Britons visited the Caribbean in 1993, a region with which the UK has had links for centuries, while only 3% of trips made by Swedish youth travellers had the Caribbean as their destination. For almost all European countries, the USA was the single most popular destination region, but not for Greek tourists who showed a preference for the Pacific, Asia and Australasia region, perhaps reflecting the recent migration of many Greek people to Australia.

Exhibit 22.2 The percentage of long holidays (four nights or more) which are domestic in different European countries in 1993

Country	Percentage of holidays which are domestic
Italy	87
Portugal	85
Greece	83
Ireland	67
Norway	63
UK	63
Netherlands	45
Germany	30
Belgium	27

Source: Adapted from Wheatcroft and Seekings (1995).

DOMESTIC YOUTH TRAVEL

Exhibit 22.2 illustrates the national differences within Europe in terms of the percentage of holidays taken by youth travellers which are domestic trips.

There are also variations between individual European countries in terms of the domestic youth travel markets in relation to the types of holidays which are taken, as can be seen from the following examples based on data for 1993:

- 35% of domestic trips by Britons involve visiting friends and relatives while VFR represents only 23% of domestic holidays taken by Italians;
- cities were the main destination for 18% of Spanish youth travellers but only 10% of young Italian tourists;
- Between 8 and 9% of French youth tourists used hotels compared to 22% of Spanish youth travellers.

NON-EUROPEAN VISITORS TO EUROPE

Non-European youth travellers have clear preferences for particular European countries, as can be seen from the following examples:

- France in 1993 attracted some 37 000 Canadian visitors compared with Portugal which attracted just 3 500 such tourists;
- the UK in the same year attracted a third of all Israeli youth travellers who visited Europe, while just 9% visited Germany;
- the UK was the destination for 79 000 Japanese tourists aged 15–24 in 1993 compared to Greece which attracted a mere 6 000 such travellers.

What is clear from the data is that for all non-European tourists, Eastern Europe was far less popular than Western Europe, attracting less than a tenth of Western Europe's share of such tourists' trips.

SUPPLIERS AND INTERMEDIARIES

Differences in the youth travel market between European countries are mirrored in differences within the supply side, the organizations which serve the youth travellers of Europe. There are also differences in how trips are purchased. These points are illustrated by the following examples:

- ISIC (International Student Identity Cards) in 1994 were sold to 301 000 British young people and 140 000 Irish students, but only 25 000 were bought by Swedish young people and less than 25 000 were purchased by Greek and Portuguese youth travellers;
- there are nearly 80 000 beds in official youth hostels in Germany compared to only 12 000 in France;
- some 45% of youth trips taken by Britons are packaged holidays, while only 16% of trips taken by young Italians are packaged.

CONCLUSION

We have seen that there are significant national differences within Europe in the youth travel market. Yet, it is amongst young people, who have grown up in the era of European cooperation and widely available foreign language instruction, that many believed we would see the first truly pan-European markets.

DISCUSSION POINTS AND ESSAY QUESTIONS

1. Discuss the factors that might account for the differences between European countries in the 'travel propensity' of their youth markets.
2. Evaluate the reasons that might explain the figures on domestic youth tourism in Exhibit 22.2.

CASE 23

Futbol Club Barcelona, Spain

Exhibit 23.1 F.C. Barcelona.

FUNDAT EL 1899

FUNDADO EN 1899

FOUNDED IN 1899

FONDÉ EN 1899

INTRODUCTION

Futbol Club Barcelona is one of the major European football clubs. The club was founded in 1899 and since this time has continued to grow and develop in the city of Barcelona, Spain. The club has won many prestigious cups over a long period of time. It has a strong financial position with many corporate backers who help the club buy the best players in the world. The club has set up a foundation which receives donations and prevents the club becoming a limited company.

Barcelona has also developed a multi-sport base. It has 11 sports sections including basketball, hockey, athletics and ice skating, all of which take part in leading competitions. These clubs are followed with the same passion as the football club.

F.C. BARCELONA – A BRIEF HISTORY

F.C. Barcelona was founded on 29 November 1899. Hans Gamper, a Swiss businessman, along with 11 other men, founded the city's first football club. Since this time, the club has had 31 chairmen. After an initial period of consolidation, a great step forward was made when the Les Corts football ground was built in 1924 signalling a period of unstoppable expansion. The Barça Club, as it had become affectionately known, grew because Barcelona was also growing, the club soon becoming Catalonia's representative all over the world. The Catalan people found that football helped them through long years of political repression and gave them a way of expressing their identity.

The Les Corts ground soon became too small. In 1957, the Camp Nou Stadium was opened to take 90 000 Barcelona supporters. Twenty years later in 1977, the Club needed a further boost in capacity. The arrival of Josep Lluís Núñez and his management team marked the beginning of the Club's modern era.

The stadium was enlarged to lift its capacity to 120 000 spectators. Barça then became the football club with the largest number of season-ticket holders in the world.

BARÇA'S SPORTING RECORD

Barça's sporting record is no doubt amongst the finest anywhere in the continent. The list of great victories and mythical football stars who have played with the team is an important part of Barcelona's collective memory. The club has become part of the story of an entire people over the last hundred years and throughout its long history, F.C. Barcelona has attracted major football stars. The club has triumphed, as a result, both at home and in European competitions.

Barça started a long history of winning European competition when it won the first Fairs Cup in 1957–58. Since then it has played more internationals than any other club. Taking part in European competitions has led to many victories: – the European Cup, the European Super Cup, the European Cup Winner's Cup, and the Fairs Cup (now known as the UEFA Cup). This record of achievement is shown in Exhibit 23.2.

This record of achievement has meant that the supporters will always travel en masse wherever Barça goes to play. These achievements have also placed Barça at the very top of the European league of football clubs as is shown in Exhibit 23.3.

Exhibit 23.2 European titles since 1978: F.C. Barcelona

1978–79	European Cup Winner's Cup
1981–82	European Cup Winner's Cup
1988–89	European Cup Winner's Cup
1991–92	European Cup
1992–93	European Super Cup

Source: F.C. Barcelona.

Exhibit 23.3 Major European Clubs and their title records since 1978

Club	No.	Title
F.C. Barcelona	1	European Cup
	3	European Cup Winner's Cups
A.C. Milan	3	European Cups
Juventus	1	European Cup
	1	European Cup Winner's Cup
	2	UEFA Cups
Liverpool	2	European Cups
Nottingham Forest	2	European Cups
Ajax	1	European Cup
	1	European Cup Winner's Cup
	1	UEFA Cup
I.F.K. Göteburg	2	UEFA Cups
Real Madrid	2	UEFA Cups
Inter Milan	2	UEFA Cups

The club was also recognized in 1994 when their player Christo Stoitchkov (Barcelona and Bulgaria) was awarded the prestigious title of European Footballer of the Year.

The city of Barcelona is transformed when Barça wins any important competition. Catalonia also becomes one great fiesta. When the club won the European Cup, over one million people came onto the streets to welcome their idols. This phenomenon has become a real tradition in Barcelona.

THE FACILITIES AT F.C. BARCELONA

The F.C. Barcelona sports complex is located in a privileged position right in the city centre of Barcelona. The sports complex consists of a number of key facilities as follows:

- F.C. Barcelona Stadium: capacity – 120 000 spectators;
- Ice Palace: capacity – 2 000 spectators;
- Mini-Stadium: capacity – 16 000 spectators;
- Blaugrana Building: capacity – 6 000 spectators;
- training field;
- training ground;
- 'La Masia' residence – school for footballers;
- club ticket windows.

The F.C. Barcelona stadium has become known as the Camp Nou ground. It is well recognized as being one of the city's architectural marvels and is currently the largest in Europe in terms of capacity.

The Ice Palace is open to the public every day. The Mini-Stadium, which has a capacity of 16 000 places, is used by the lower teams such as the Barça B team and the amateur team. The Blaugrana Building houses the indoor sports arena and has a capacity of 6 000 spectators. The club also has a dedicated training field and training ground in the city.

'La Masia' is the F.C. Barcelona football nursery where young men who aspire to play in the great stadium come to learn their skills. The club also has a museum and visitor centre, where visitors can learn about the history and current operation of Barça.

The inside of the club incorporates a full array of ancillary services. Everybody is catered for – sportsmen and women, members, visitors and managers, all have access to a wide range of facilities.

The club has a kindergarten, a day centre for the most senior members and a museum for visitors. There are also impressive dressing rooms, gymnasiums and full medical services. The hospitality suites include a boardroom and a public authorities reception room.

Special facilities are provided for the media because of the extraordinary amount of information which is demanded by the public about the club. There are 200 seats for sports journalists, 24 radio booths, an interview room holding 250 people, two work rooms, two telephone rooms, a television studio and other ancillary services.

THE CATERING FACILITIES AT F.C. BARCELONA

F.C. Barcelona has a full range of catering facilities within the complex, for the general public, for corporate visitors and for visitors from the media. There is a main restaurant next to the ice rink and a full range of bars and tapas bars throughout the complex. Media representatives and corporate visitors are entertained in impressive facilities.

THE SUPPORTERS OF BARCELONA FOOTBALL CLUB

Barcelona Football Club has supporters and members in five continents. The club has the largest number of season ticket-holders in the world. These supporters live and breathe football passionately, and have a major effect on spreading a positive image of the club. The board of directors have been actively trying to encourage the supporters and increase their numbers in Catalonia, Spain and worldwide. This is seen as an important part of the marketing and public relations activities of the club.

Barcelona Football Club have worked closely with the Barça bank – Banca Catalana. This excellent relationship has allowed the club to develop The F.C. Barcelona Bank. The collaboration has given club members new and better services, such as the sale of tickets through the 400 branches of the Banca Catalana. Season tickets and members cards are therefore sold more efficiently and effectively. The club has also developed the Visa Barça which enables all club members to become a 'player' in the Barça team.

THE FINANCIAL POSITION OF F.C. BARCELONA

The 'patrimoni' or net worth of the club was 4 633 million pesetas in 1995. The current board of management of the club does not have to credit the budget for 1996 because the network of the club, which was formed in 1978/79, now has assets exceeding 3 303 million pesetas which is the required legal minimum. This means that the members of the board are trusted to manage the club financially. The club has also gained the status of an anonymous sport association. The club has restructured the whole of the first tier of the stadium which has been financed from the income produced from 1744 new members joining the club and help from some of the old members.

The most important change in the assets of the club has been in the investment of sport and social facilities. The club has always had the improvements of the facilities as its main aim.

The amount of money coming from members, ticket holders and takings has been decreasing over the last 20 years to represent 54% of total earnings in 1994/95. Money from other sources has been increasing during the same period to represent 46% in 1994/95. This increase in 'atypical earnings' has meant that the club has extra resources to provide the following:

- keeping the membership fees and subscriptions to a minimum;
- no increase in the annual fees during 1991 and 1992, and an increase proportional to the retail price index in 1993, 1994 and 1995;
- free entrance to the European Cups with the payment for the member card and the subscription fee;
- free entrance in the Super Cup.

The budget summary of the club for the 1995/96 season is shown in Exhibit 23.4.

Exhibit 23.4 F.C. Barcelona: budget summary 1995/96 season

	(Pta million)
Sports competitions	1032
Members and ticket holders	3749
Accessories	3479
Other additional earnings	560
Expenses	
Purchases	189
Work, supplies and external services	2450
Tributes	159
Staff and players	4620
Other expenses	76
Redemptions/repayments	1319
Extra costs (restructuring plan)	102

SPONSORSHIP AND PROMOTIONAL ACTIVITY OF F.C. BARCELONA

The F.C. Barcelona foundation keeps successfully growing thanks to the support of all the promoters and sympathizers of the club. The club has encouraged sponsorship with major corporations such as AGFA, Ballantine's, Banca Catalana, Iberia, Sony, Coca Cola, etc.

F.C. Barcelona has hosted many historic events in the sporting world which have allowed the club to gain promotional coverage. The Camp Nou ground has been particularly important in this respect. In 1982, the ground hosted the 1982 World Cup inauguration which was watched by 500 million television viewers worldwide. The Pope also visited the ground in 1982 and celebrated mass for 120 000 people. The ground also provided the venue for the Amnesty International event in 1988. The Olympic football final was also held at the Camp Nou ground in 1992 during the Barcelona '92 games. All of these major events are remembered by the Barça supporters with great feelings of nostalgia. This helps to promote a very positive image with the supporters of the club.

A joint agreement was reached between the club and Warner Brothers on 11 May 1995. This agreement means that the club can use the characters of the Warner Brother company on merchandising products. The characters will be used in combination with the 'El Barça' symbols and colours. Bugs Bunny will be the main motif used for the making of T-shirts, caps, shorts, and other cotton products.

'Bideko' is the branding which will be used to put these products onto the market with the licence held by the two organizations. In the presentation ceremony, the President of the Barcelona Football Club and the Vice President of the Warner Brothers Corporation signed the agreement surrounded by their new animal characters.

THE FUTURE

F.C. Barcelona will be 100 years old in 1999. In response to this, the club is planning for the future and facing new challenges. The club has created an F.C. Barcelona foundation – The Asociació promotora de la Fundació F.C. Barcelona – which has produced its own logo. All the members of the club have played a part in the founding of this body so that the characteristics which make F.C. Barcelona more than just a club can be preserved forever.

DISCUSSION POINTS AND ESSAY QUESTIONS

1. Evaluate the importance of corporate backers to the success of F.C. Barcelona.
2. 'Success on the field is the most important attribute a football club can have' (Horner and Swarbrooke, 1996). Discuss this statement.

Abercrombie and Kent Ltd, UK

INTRODUCTION

For many years, Abercrombie and Kent has led the field in offering exclusive holidays of distinction, sometimes sophisticated, sometimes escapist, sometimes adventurous, but always rather special. The range of products which the company offers demonstrates the quality, flexibility and variety of holidays which the company sells. The company prides itself on the professional and personalized service which it offers to customers. Many of the holidays which the company arranges are 'tailor-made' in the UK and by operating offices in many locations around the world. Abercrombie and Kent has become a respected name worldwide.

THE MARKET

Abercrombie and Kent offers inclusive tours, a market in the UK dominated by major operators such as Thomson, Airtours and First Choice. There are, however, over 600 operators in the UK market (Mintel). Many of these companies are small in size and often they compete in a specialist niche market. The largest of these specialist operators include Kuoni Travel, Hayes and Jarvis, Cox and Kings, and Abercrombie and Kent.

Abercrombie and Kent is recognized as a specialist operator which offers products at the very top of the market. The company specializes in tailor-made holidays to exotic locations such as East Africa, South Africa and Uganda. It is estimated that the average Abercrombie and Kent price per person in 1994 was £2 600 (Mintel).

COMPANY DETAILS

Abercrombie and Kent was originally established in 1962 in Nairobi. The company has grown and developed over a 30-year period and established offices in many worldwide locations. A brief historical development of the company is shown in Exhibit 24.1.

Exhibit 24.1 Brief historical development of Abercrombie and Kent

1962	Established in Nairobi as a safari operator.
1973	Abercrombie and Kent Ltd opened in London. Abercrombie and Kent International Inc. opened in Chicago.
1988	Hotel management company Windsor Hotels Ltd was formed in Nairobi.
1994	Acquired share in Conservation Corporation, South Africa.
1995	Abercrombie and Kent, London employs 94 staff. Worldwide operating offices network.

Source: Abercrombie and Kent.

The company has its own operating offices in the following locations:

Australia	: Auckland, Melbourne
Egypt	: Aswan, Cairo, Luxor
Far East	: Bangkok, Hong Kong
India	: Delhi
Kenya	: Malindi, Mombasa, Nairobi
South Africa	: Cape Town, Johannesburg
Tanzania	: Arusha, Zanzibar
Uganda	: Kampala
Zimbabwe	: Harare, Victoria Falls, Kariba

The local representatives in countries where there are no Abercrombie and Kent operating offices have been carefully selected for the quality of their local expertise and their identification with the high standards which Abercrombie and Kent require for their clients.

The company has become well known for its ability to tailor holidays to the requirements of customers. The company can design virtually any 'tailor-made' itinerary which is devised especially to suit the customer's inclination, budget and schedule. In this way, Abercrombie and Kent is very different from the traditional package tour operator. Abercrombie and Kent has become recognized worldwide for their active involvement in wildlife conservation and environmental issues. The company is committed to helping to save the environment and ecosystems to ensure the future of the natural habitat of the animal and plant world, its wildlife and the cultural heritage of all nations.

The company operates in three main areas of business:

- tour operating;
- ground handling;
- IATA agents:

- general travel;
- corporate business.

FINANCIAL PERFORMANCE

The sales turnover of Abercrombie and Kent Ltd is shown in Exhibit 24.2.

MANAGEMENT STRUCTURE

The managing director of Abercrombie and Kent has overall responsibility for the company controlling five main divisions:

- Tours Division – Long and Short haul;
- General Travel and Corporate Travel;
- Sales and Marketing – Direct and Agency Sales;
- Accounts;
- Reception.

Exhibit 24.2 The sales turnover of Abercrombie and Kent Ltd

Sales turnover		£000s
Year ended 31 August	1973	1
	1974	90
	1975	174
	1976	176
	1977	317
	1978	451
	1979	629
	1980	708
	1981	732
	1982	965
	1983	1 872
	1984	2 503
16 months ended 31 December	1985	6 916
Year ended 31 December	1986	7 546
	1987	10 752
	1988	13 258
	1989	16 931
	1990	17 984
	1991	16 582
	1992	17 565
	1993	18 789
	1994	24 428

Source: Abercrombie and Kent Ltd.

COMPANY OBJECTIVES

Abercrombie and Kent is quite unique. A family business founded in 1962 has grown into an international concern with 14 companies worldwide and many associated companies. The Abercrombie and Kent philosophy of service, quality and style, is expressed in the company marketing statement:

'Simply The Best Way To Travel'

Abercrombie and Kent is a member of the Association of British Travel Agents (ABTA), and is a fully bonded ATOL-holder licensed by the Civil Aviation Authority. ABTA has been at the forefront of the travel industry since its formation in 1950, offering the holidaymaker a financial protection scheme, professional service and peace of mind. ABTA's principal role is to ensure decent standards of service and business throughout its membership.

THE ABERCROMBIE AND KENT PORTFOLIO

The Abercrombie and Kent Portfolio of holiday products is shown in Exhibit 24.3.

Abercrombie and Kent has its own vehicles in countries where they have operating offices. This allows the company to monitor standards of transport and driver care in Kenya, Tanzania, Uganda, Zimbabwe and Egypt. The company also has direct association with a number of hotels and boats in Africa and Egypt. In Egypt, the company owns three luxurious boats on the Nile – *Sun Boats I, II* and *III*. In East Africa, the company is involved with a number of hotels which are managed by the Abercrombie and Kent associated company, Conservation Corporation, East Africa. In South Africa, the company also has an association with the Conservation Corporation of South Africa. This means that the company is involved with a number of game reserves and lodges.

Abercrombie and Kent also offers the customer the possibility of upgrading to first and club class flights at special rates.

THE CUSTOMERS OF ABERCROMBIE AND KENT

Research has shown that customers choose to purchase an Abercrombie and Kent holiday because of the reputation of the company as a worldwide specialist tour operator which offers a personalized service. Customers also like the freedom that Abercrombie and Kent offers to allow them to create their own 'tailor-made' holidays. The staff at Abercrombie and Kent are knowledgeable and have a great deal of expertise. This feature, coupled with the more unusual and off-the-beaten-track holiday products which the company offers, means that

---

Exhibit 24.3 The Abercrombie and Kent portfolio

- **The World of A & K**
  Exotic world-wide destinations, tailor-made for the discerning traveller.
- **ExplorAsia**
  Specialist holidays to India, Tibet and Nepal including trekking in the Himalayas.
- **A & K's Africa**
  Highlights of A & K's exclusive safaris throughout this intriguing continent.
- **Honeymoons**
  Hand-picked selection of romantic hideaways around the world.
- **World of wildlife**
  Escorted wildlife and bird-watching tours to a range of destinations.
- **Italian and French Journeys**
  Tailor-made fly-drive itineraries, select hotels, canal and river cruises, and cookery courses.
- **Andalucia Safaris**
  Walking holidays in the spectacular countryside of hidden Spain.
- **The Ski Company**
  Stylish skiing holidays in France, Switzerland and the USA, in luxury villas and chalets.
- **Private Label: Tours by Invitation**
  A series of personally escorted tours in Europe and beyond.

Source: Abercrombie and Kent.

Exhibit 24.4 The Abercrombie and Kent customer

Country of origin	–	Great Britain (predominantly South East).
	–	Some Europe – France, Switzerland, Belgium, Italy.
Demographic profile	–	ABC1.
Repeat purchase	–	Repeat purchase is approximately 40%. Customer loyalty is a key feature of the Abercrombie and Kent market.

Source: Abercrombie and Kent Ltd.

---

customers choose Abercrombie and Kent products. A profile of the Abercrombie and Kent customer is shown in Exhibit 24.4.

Repeat purchase by customers represent a large proportion of the Abercrombie and Kent business. Repeat purchase is encouraged by a number of marketing activities which may be summarized as follows:

- the development and upkeep of a good customer database;
- follow-up mailing of activities;
- customer evenings;
- company representative at the game fair, bird fair, destinations travel show, etc;
- publishing and distribution of 'Sundowner' a biannual customer magazine. This allows the company to keep existing customers up to date with the products on offer.

NEW PRODUCTS

Abercrombie and Kent prides itself on the introduction of new and off-the-beaten track destinations. The ideas for new destinations come from a variety of sources:

- the personnel working in the Abercrombie and Kent ground offices in 14 countries introduce the company to new areas;
- Abercrombie and Kent staff travel globally and look around for new destinations;
- the company is often approached by hotels and tourist boards;
- Abercrombie and Kent staff have extensive expertise and contacts on a world-wide basis.

The development of a new destination involves the use of in-house expertise and contacts. The company will liaise with the appropriate ground agent, property owner and airlines during the development of a new destination.

THE PRICE OF ABERCROMBIE AND KENT HOLIDAYS

The price of Abercrombie and Kent holidays is sometimes higher than the competition. The holidays are priced on an all-inclusive basis with no extras and no supplements. Customers are prepared to pay more for the holidays because of the expertise of the staff and the added value of the company owning its own ground offices, shops and hotels. The company operates an 'all-inclusive' pricing strategy wherever possible. They do not offer discounts but sometime arrange special offers such as seven nights for the price of six nights stay one week and get the second week accommodation free, etc.

DISTRIBUTION OF ABERCROMBIE AND KENT HOLIDAYS

Distribution of the Abercrombie and Kent holidays is carried out in two mains ways:

- direct sale brochures are requested and sent out daily. A mailing house also sends out brochures which may also be personalized;
- brochures are distributed to agents by a mailing house and by direct visits made by sales staff.

PROMOTION

Abercrombie and Kent produces a full range of brochures for their portfolio of products on a yearly basis. These are then either sent out directly to customers or distributed to retail travel agencies. The company currently deals directly with 800 travel agents in the UK who regularly book Abercrombie and Kent holidays. The company also use other methods of promotion including:

- direct marketing;
- public relations/media features;
- limited press advertising;
- customer evenings;
- personalized mailing by customer database containing approximately 38 000 names;
- encouragement of word of mouth and personal recommendation;
- occasional joint promotions with other organizations.

CONCLUSION

Abercrombie and Kent is a specialist holiday company which has developed a market for specialist, flexible, tailor-made holidays to exotic and different locations. This approach has enabled a small family-owned company to grow into a large group offering a wide range of products to customers from a range of European countries.

DISCUSSION POINTS AND ESSAY QUESTIONS

1. Discuss the advantages of a high level of repeat purchase for a specialist tour operator such as Abercrombie and Kent. Explain the methods which can be used to establish and maintain high levels of repeat purchase.
2. 'The marketing of a specialist holiday product will allow a tour operator to develop a truly European market more effectively and efficiently than the marketing of a mass market product' (Horner and Swarbrooke, 1996). Discuss this statement.

Accor, France

Exhibit 25.1 The Accor Group: A World of Travel, Tourism and Services.

HOTELS

TRADITIONAL HOTELS

 Hotel Sofitel

 NOVOTEL

  mercure HOTELS

 ibis

CORALIA
THALASSA
ATRIA
HOTELIA
PARTHENON

RESINTER

BUDGET HOTELS

 HOTEL FORMULE 1

 MOTEL 6

 ETAP HOTEL

BUSINESS SERVICES

SERVICE VOUCHERS

 ticket restaurant TR

TICKET ALIMENTAÇÃO
TICKET TRANSPORTE
RIKSKUPONGER
LUNCHEON VOUCHER
TICKET SERVICE
CHILDCARE VOUCHER

INSTITUTIONAL CATERING

 EUREST

GEMEAZ CUSIN
GR RESTAURANTES
DE COLETIVIDADE

TRAVEL AGENCIES

Carlson
Wagonlit
Travel

OTHER ACTIVITIES

RESTAURANTS

 L'ARCHE RESTAURANT

CAFE ROUTE
LE BŒUF JARDINIER
MEDA'S
ACTAIR
L'ECLUSE

 CourtePaille

 LENÔTRE

RAILWAY SERVICES

 WAGONS-LITS

CAR RENTAL

 Europcar Inter rent

TOURISM AND LEISURE

GROUP SET :
AKIOU
AFRICATOURS
ASIETOURS
AMERICATOURS
EL CONDOR
JET EVASION

EPISODES
ISLANDS IN THE SUN
PARC ASTERIX
CROISIERES
COSTA / PAQUET

 ACADEMIE ACCOR
l'université de service

CREORD
DEVIMCO
INCENTIVE HOUSE
PRESS CLUB

Source: Accor, 1996.

INTRODUCTION

Accor is a French-based multinational travel, tourism and services company. The Group's activities fall into two strategic areas: Travel and Tourism, and Business Services. The company has recognized that synergy has developed among the operating sectors and considerable economies of scale have been gained. Geographical diversification is playing an increasingly crucial role in the Group's strategy. In 1993, for example, it allowed Accor to absorb the volatile economic and political environment and the wide currency fluctuations.

Accor has developed a multinational travel tourism and services business by the development and acquisition of businesses over a long period. A brief history of Accor is shown in Exhibit 25.2.

Exhibit 25.2 A brief history of the Accor Group

1970	Novotel International founded.
1973	Ibis hotel chain founded.
1974	Courte-Paille restaurant chain founded.
1975	Acquisition of the Mercure hotel chain.
1980	Acquisition of the Sofitel hotel chain.
1983	Merger of Novotel SIEH (hotels) and Jacques Borel International (restaurant and service vouchers) into Accor.
1985	Creation of the Accor Academy – the Group's training centre. Formule 1 budget hotel chain founded. Acquisition of the Lenôtre gourmet boutiques and catering services.
1989	Tourism division founded.
1990	Acquisition of the Motel 6 chain in the USA.
1991	Acquisition of Compagnie Internationale des Wagons-Lits et du Tourisme which added a wide portfolio of hospitality and transport services.
1992	The introduction of a new motto 'Accor, A World of Travel, Tourism and Services'.
1993	Accor becomes the largest shareholder in Pannonia, a Hungarian hospitality group. Introduction of the Coralia brand name to differentiate resort hotels from business hotels.
1994	Agreement between the North American Travel network and Wagonlit Travel to form Carlson Wagonlit Travel. The opening of two new senior citizen hotels in Paris and Bordeaux under the Hotelia brand name.
1995	Development of the Resaccor hotel reservation system with IBM. The system will be operational in 1996. Carlson Wagonlit Travel enters Hong Kong and Japanese markets.

Source: Accor' 1995.

FINANCIAL DATA

A summary of the financial position of Accor in 1994 is shown in Exhibit 25.3. It can be seen that the hotels division and the business services division make up a similar and major part of the Group turnover. Revenues from Europe excluding France have grown to a stage where they are greater than the revenue from France.

Exhibit 25.3 The Accor Group: financial details.

	1994 **(FRF millions)**
Total revenues	33472
Operating income	2938
Consolidated net income, Group share	711
Cash flow from operations	3522

	(FRF)
Earnings per share	28.60
Cash flow from operations, per share	141.80

Breakdown of total revenues by activity (FRF millions)

Hotels	13829

Business Services	13063	Service vouchers	1578
		Institutional catering	7475
		Travel agencies	4010

Other Activities	6580	Public restaurants	3612
		Railway services	1932
		Miscellaneous	1036

Breakdown of total revenues by geographical area (FRF millions)

France	11350
Rest of Europe	15770
North America	3681
Latin America	2120
Other	551

Source: Accor 1995.

BUSINESS ACTIVITIES OF ACCOR

The business activities of Accor are divided into three main groups:

- hotels;
- business services;
- other activities.

Each of the three groups has a well developed branding strategy which differentiates each product offering. A summary of the portfolio of brands for hotels is shown in Exhibit 25.4, for business services in Exhibit 25.5, and for other activities in Exhibit 25.6.

Exhibit 25.4 The hotel portfolio

Hotel Sofitel	4-star
Novotel	3-star
Mercure	3-star
Atria	Hotel with full business and conference centres – 3-star
Ibis	2-star
Hotel Formule 1	Budget hotel
Etap Hotel	Budget hotel
Motel 6	Budget hotel
Parthenon	First-class hotel with suites
Hotelia	Senior citizen hotels
Coralia	Resort hotels
Thalassa International	Thalassotherapy centres

Source: Accor 1995

Exhibit 25.5 The Business Services portfolio

- **Service vouchers**
    Ticket Restaurant
    Ticket Service
    Ticket Transport
    Childcare Voucher

- **Institutional catering**
    Compass
    Eurest
    Gemeaz Cusin
    Restaurantes de Coletividade

- **Travel agencies**
    Carlson Wagonlit Travel

Source: Accor 1995.

Exhibit 25.6 The Other Activities portfolio

- **Public restaurants**
  - L'Arche
  - Café Route   }   motorway restaurants
  - Le Boeuf Jardinier
  - Actair   –   airport catering
  - Terminal   –   railway station catering
  - Restaurants et Sites   –   exhibition and attraction catering
  - Quick   –   fast-food restaurants
  - Meda's   –   Spanish motorway restaurants
  - CourtePaille   –   popular traiteur French restaurant chain
  - Lenôtre   –   prestigious restaurants and cooking school, France

- **Railway services**
  - Wagons-Lits   –   railway catering and sleeper car service

- **Car rentals**
  - Europcar

- **Travel and leisure**
  - Episodes   –   hotel booking service for the Accor Group
  - Groupe Set   –   tour operators:
  - Islands in the Sun   –   American tour operator
  - ATS tours
  - Croisières Costa   –   cruise line operator
  - Paquet
  - Parc Asterix   –   theme park

Source: Accor 1995.

HOTELS

Accor enjoys a strong position in the hotel business as both owner and operator of over half of its hotel portfolio, comprising 265 000 rooms in 2 400 properties around the world at the end of 1994. The balance of the portfolio consists of hotels managed under rental management or franchising contracts. Accor's unique owner-operator status has given the group a number of advantages, including a high degree of control over its properties and the development of a unique expertise in hotel engineering and all aspects of hotel operations ranging from purchasing and quality control to personnel training and motivation.

The future of the Accor Group in the hotel business will involve growth by franchising and management contracts. The group sees the Asia-Pacific region as having particular growth potential.

By 1997 Accor expect that their hotel portfolio will have grown by an additional 50 000 rooms to encompass 100 000 company-owned rooms, 100 000 rooms under management contracts and 100 000 franchised rooms.

Accor has carried out an extensive programme of hotel brand portfolio streamlining which was completed in 1993. Sofitel and Pullman, Mercure, and Altea, Ibis and Arcade were combined to allow the group to position their product range clearly in various niches of the international hotel market. Alongside the major international hotel brands, the group has developed the Hotelia chain for senior citizens and the Thalassa International chain for thalassotherapy and health treatment. The Mercure name covers a broad range of hotel categories, and the chain has traditionally seen itself as essentially a franchising service organization.

Hotels now represent the leading activity of the Accor Group, operated under the brand names Sofitel, Novotel, Mercure and Ibis in the traditional upscale and midrange segment, and Formule 1, Etap Hotel and Motel 6 in the no food, no frills, budget segment.

BUSINESS SERVICES

Service vouchers, institutional catering and travel agencies make up the Group's Business Services sector. Ticket Restaurant is the Group's best known product in service vouchers, but the product line is much broader and growing. Institutional catering through Eurest International is rapidly growing around the world. Eurest International is the number one institutional catering company in several European countries, including Germany and Spain.

In travel agencies, Accor and Carlson Companies of the US brought their activities together in March 1994. This merger created the Carlson Wagonlit Travel network, which is one of the world leaders in the business travel market. Carlson Wagonlit Travel have developed a motto:

'Global Presence, Local Power'

This reflects the business's investment in global networks and the service which is offered at a local level.

> For Accor, the 1995 outlook is bright. Our overall activity levels are improving, we are clearly focused on our core Hotels and Business Services activities, our indebtedness is falling, synergies across businesses are bearing increasing fruit, quality is up; we are responding to challenges with increasing innovation and resourcefulness.
>
> Paul Dubrule and Gérard Pélisson, Co-Chairmen, Accor.

CONCLUSIONS

The Accor Group has grown rapidly from being a national chain to a multinational organization and a leader in the travel and tourism industry, which is the first in the world in terms of GDP (12% of the worldwide GDP) and employment (200 million jobs) (Source UTCC data 1996.) The Group has relied on a well developed branding strategy to develop hospitality business.

DISCUSSION POINTS AND ESSAY QUESTIONS

1. Discuss the strengths and weaknesses of the portfolio of products and brands which Accor has currently.
2. Evaluate the likely future changes in the European business environment which are likely to be most significant to Accor.

Thalassa International, France

INTRODUCTION

The Accor Group has recognized that there is a substantial opportunity for it in the rapidly growing leisure hotel segment. The Group has developed two brands to help with this marketing activity – Coralia which is the resort hotel and Thalassa International which is the brand name for the thalassotherapy seawater spas. Accor has undisputed leadership in the thalassotherapy market.

THE HISTORY OF THALASSOTHERAPY

The use of seawater treatments as a prevention or cure for illnesses is based on an ancient tradition. Six centuries before Christ, the Greeks discovered the value of thalossotherapy treatment (the Greek word *thalasso* means the sea). The Romans also used thalassotherapy treatments in combination with thermal bath techniques. Thalassotherapy was developed in France in the nineteenth century. The first establishment was opened in Dieppe in 1882 and many more establishments developed at seaside locations on the Channel coast, the Atlantic coast and the Mediterranean coast. The term 'thalassotherapie' was first used by a French Dr Labornardière in 1869. In 1898 the therapeutic effects of the sea were studied at an experimental centre in Roscoff, and in 1902 a congress was held in Biarritz on the subject of thalassotherapy. In 1904, René Quinton, a famous biologist, published the book *L'eau de mer, milieu organique*, which has become the contemporary reference book for thalassotherapy experts.

Exhibit 26.1 Thalassa International logo.

THALASSOTHERAPY TODAY

Thalassotherapy involves the use of all the elements of the sea (including climate, water, and seawater plants and animals) to prevent or cure medical conditions. Seawater is rich in plankton and micro-elements, which in turn are rich in vitamins, minerals and amino acids. Application of these elements in a variety of treatments is claimed to be extremely beneficial. Sea air is also rich in ozone and has a beneficial effect. Thalassotherapy centres have developed to offer thalassotherapy treatments often coupled with diet and exercise programmes.

The thalassotherapy centres have become very popular in France and offer customers the possibility to gain both a physical and mental tonic. Customers use the centres for a variety of reasons including :

- to improve overall physical well-being and limit the effects of age;
- to improve mental well-being and to experience rejuvenation;
- to reduce stress and eliminate psychosomatic conditions such as anxiety and fatigue;
- to help in the treatment of rheumatism and arthritis;
- to change eating habits and reduce the consumption of alcohol and smoking;
- to improve relationships between partners and families.

The growth of thalassotherapy centres reflects the growing interest in the importance of health, well-being and physical and mental health. There has been a widespread reaction to the effects of stress on overall well-being. The popularity of this type of holiday has also been boosted by the growing number of people over 50 in Europe. The French package holiday company Havas Voyages, for example, offer 'Tonique' holidays in the 32 thalassotherapy and balnéothérapie centres in France, Morocco and Portugal.

THE ACCOR BUSINESS IN THALASSOTHERAPY

In 1989 the six thalassotherapy centres in France were unified under the brand name Thalassa International. The Group launched an advertising campaign in 1990 to promote the centres. The Accor Group has launched their Thalassa International brand to allow development of the thalassotherapy market and currently markets thalassotherapy holidays via the seven centres in France given in Exhibit 26.2.

Details of the various cures on offer at the thalassotherapy centres are shown in Exhibit 26.3. It is interesting to note that these cures combine features of hospitality, leisure and recreation.

Two-thirds of the customers for the Accor thalassotherapy centres are women, the majority are 45 to 65, and they are overwhelmingly from urban areas. Forty per cent of customers are repeat customers which shows the high level of customer loyalty which is present in this market.

The Accor Group has made a series of innovations in the thalassotherapy market in 1994. These innovations include:

Exhibit 26.2 The Accor Group thalassotherapy centres in France

---

Le Touquet – The Resort for all Seasons
  Cures – 'Health', 'Fitness', 'Post-Natale', 'Male Tonic', 'Heavy Legs'

Dinard – The Pearl of the Côte d'Emeraude
  Cures – 'Health', 'Fitness', 'Active Woman', 'Male Special', 'Sea Rest', 'Thalasso and Golf'

Quiberon – The Birthplace of Modern Thalassotherapy
  Cures – 'Health', 'Fitness', 'Special Legs', 'Biological Cure', 'Special Cellulite', 'Health Check-Up', 'Smoker's Cure'

Les Sables-d'Olonne – A Cure of Vendéen Mildness
  Cures – 'Health', 'Fitness', 'Special Legs', 'Post-Natal', 'Energizing Cure'

Oléron – Between Sea and Forest
  Cures – 'Health', 'Fitness', 'Future Mother', 'New Wave'

Hyères – The Sunshine of Provence
  Cures – 'Health' or 'Fitness', 'Relaxation-Energy', 'Fitness and Beauty'

Porticcio – All the Charm of the Isle of Beauty
  Cures – 'Fitness Health' or 'Fitness Slimness' (health diet), 'Fitness Beauty', 'Male Tonic', 'Young Mother'

Source: Accor Thalasso International.

- the development of a well targeted programme including an anti-stress cure, and an anti-cellulite cure;
- the introduction of new underwater jet technology;
- the launch of a beauty product and body-care line 'Thalocéan'.

Accor has been seeking to expand the Thalassa International chain. The company signed two new contracts in 1994 for the development of hotels and adjoining thalassotherapy centres in Arachon, France, and near Athens in Greece. International development commenced in 1992 when the company developed an institute comprising a five-star hotel, private beach and thalassotherapy centre under franchise in Shima, Japan. The company is currently negotiating on a number of projects outside France. In 1995, Thalassa International is focusing on:

- developing and implementing a dietetic chart in each centre;
- expanding the Thalocéan range;
- further adapting the Thalassa concept to international markets.

The leader in the French thalassotherapy market, Thalassa International is expanding outside France and looking to diversify into related water therapies to become the world leader in this area within the next five years.

Exhibit 26.3 Cures on offer at the Accor Thalassa International centres

'Health' or 'Fitness' Cure
Fatigue, stress, prevention and re-education: this is the standard cure for toning or relaxing, depending on individual needs. Accompanied by a diet full-board to boost the benefits, the ideal length is 6 days with 4 treatments a day.
Featured in all Thalassa centres

'Fitness and Beauty' Cure
To cope with the pace of everyday life. Because your body, your face and your hair deserve all the combined attention of thalassotherapy and beauty care. Facials, peeling, back treatment and body modelling come on top of marine treatment. Gently recover your natural radiance.
Featured in Hyères and Porticcio

'Male Tonic' Cure
Take good care of yourselves, gentlemen.
This is the 'Fitness & Beauty' cure in its male version: thalassotherapy and skincare treatment together with a programme of physical activity. Day after day men recover the tone and physique they need to feel good about themselves.
Featured in Le Touquet, Dinard and Porticcio

'Active Woman' or 'New Wave' Cure
Women's hectic everyday life can lead to a number of ills such as anxiety, depression, smoking, poor blood circulation and risks of cardio-vascular problems. Certain important periods in life, before menstruation or menopause, can sometimes be a trying experience. Four treatments a day, sessions of aquagymnastics in a heated sea-water pool and beauty care (depending on the centre) help you to recover fitness and vitality.
Featured in Dinard and Oléron

'Thalasso and Golf' and 'Fitness and Golf' Cure
Combine the well-being of marine therapy with relaxation in the open air on the fairways. For tip-top physical fitness, take advantage of either unrestricted access to the Espace Forme (fitness unit comprising body-building room, gym, sauna and Turkish bath) or 3 thalasso-theraphy treatments a day for a 6 day cure.
Featured in Dinard (3 golf courses)

'Special Legs' Cure
Every day, your legs suffer from exterior aggression, and without a fluid blood flow quickly becomes heavy and painful. Five special thalassotherapy treatments such as pressotherapy and pediluve improve the blood flow, slim down legs and reduce the risk of ede-mas.
Featured in Le Touquet, Quiberon and Les Sables-d'Olonne

'Sea Sleep' or 'Relaxation and Energy' Cure
Depending on the prescription, marine treatments tone or relax. Make the most of waking or sleeping states: thalassotherapy treatment is combined with techniques of relaxation, sophrology, oxygenation and special exercises.
Featured in Dinard and Hyères

'Future Mother' Cure
Between the first and eighth months of pregnancy, live in gentle harmony with relaxation, breathing, oxygenation, back statics and well-balanced eating. Lie back and quietly enjoy this 10 day cure (minimum 6 days).
Featured in Oléron

'Post Natal' Cure
Young mums, let yourself be mothered for a change! Every day, 3 thalassotherapy treatments, a session of aquagymnastics and perineal or abdominal re-education therapy to tone up the stomach and lower abdomen. Build new body balance by combining the benefits of health eating and beauty care.
Featured in Le Touquet, les Sables-d'Olonne and Porticcio

Biological Cure
To fight stress, overwork and poorly balanced diets.
On arrival you are given a blood check-up to determine your 'trace element/vitamin' profile and establish the number of thalassotherapy treatments given each day. Ideally, this cure lasts 6 days.
Featured in Quiberon

Health Diet Cure
Rebalance your diet and lose weight effortlessly, if that's what you want. This is your invitation to taste new and delicious living hygiene by combining your cure with full-board and a health diet.
Featured in all Thalassa centres

Beauty Care
At all Thalassa institutions a Beauty Centre offers a full range of facials and body care treatment, high-pressure UVAs and a hair salon.

Source: Accor Thalassa International.

AN EXAMPLE OF AN ACCOR THALASSA INTERNATIONAL CENTRE

Thalassa Les Sables D'Olonne is one of the French thalassotherapy centres. The centre faces the sea and is sheltered by pine forests. Seawater is used for many of the treatments at the centre. Les Sables D'Olonne is also recognized for good sunshine records and invigorating sea air. The health spa has been developed next to the Mercure Hotel and guests can walk between the two wearing the bathrobe which is provided by the hotel. The hotel has a restaurant and bar, both of which have been designed to be casual and comfortable. The restaurant offers dietetic food as well as French cuisine. The hotel also has a fitness centre where guests can use the swimming pool, sauna, whirlpool, bubble bath and water bed.

Health care at Les Sables-d'Olonne

Treatment is given at the centre by staff under medical supervision using the most advanced techniques and equipment. Seawater treatments are used because of their therapeutic benefits. When a guest arrives, they have a thorough medical examination and are then prescribed a treatment programme tailored to the individual's personal needs. The main seawater treatments which the centre offers include the following.

- **Seawater Therapy**. The bubble bath, hydromassage, jet shower, underwater jet massage, effusion shower, massage under effusion, foot bath and jet pool have been conceived to give perfect massages, to relax, to alleviate all sorts of physical pain which result not only from modern ways of life such as overweight, effects of traumatism, tiredness and stress, but also from rheumatism.
- **Seaweed Therapy**. A natural hot seaweed paste used as an algo-pack alleviates painful symptoms, and both trace elements and mineral salts are absorbed into the body.
- **Dry Treatment**. Manual massage, lymphatic drainage, pressure therapy and physical rehabilitation may also be included in the programme to foster the synergy between the treatments.
- **Aerosol**. Sea air with a high proportion of negative ions is sprayed in a special room. This is particularly recommended for heavy smokers and all people with breathing problems.
- **Relaxation**. Sophrology, Do-In Shiatsu and other methods of relaxation are taught by specialist staff. These help relaxation and combat stress.

The centre also offers packages as follows.

- **Classic Seawater Therapy**. To those who suffer from lower-back pain or the effects of traumatism, or stress and fatigue, this treatment provides the solution to your problem. It is the ideal way to return to fitness and to improve physical condition.

- **Fitness for Women**. Women have to face not only difficult time due to their age, but also all the consequences of a modern active way of life. A special treatment which combines seawater treatment and aesthetic care has been developed.
- **Special Leg Treatment**. A special treatment developed to improve legs.
- **Dietetics**. A treatment which concentrates on diet, with the help of a dietician who gives personal consultations with nutritional test and advice. Relaxing and invigorating seawater treatment together with gourmet dietetic cuisine are combined together.
- **Post-Natal Course**. The weeks following the birth subject the mother to a particularly trying physiological and psychological upheaval. This course includes the latest techniques among which is perineal physiotherapy. Abdominal rehabilitation and seawater treatments form part of this programme to help the mother to be reconciled with her body. The baby may have his own special course of seawater treatment, – '**the baby swimmer**' – providing he has got 2nd DTP and Polio injections.

The centre also concentrates on aesthetics and hairstyling and offers the following services.

- **For The Face**. Full treatment, lifting, and other treatments to make you look good.
- **For The Breast**. Strengthening treatment.
- **For The Body**. Energetic drainage, algo-pack, abdominal massage, Californian massage, 'fisiotron' treatment, cold treatment for legs, make up, manicure, etc. UVA sessions. Special cosmetic range of products 'Thalocean' based on seaweed and seawater are used by professional aestheticians. These products are available from the aesthetic shop for those of you who wish to continue treatment at home. Hairdressers carry out special scalp treatment and also cut style, perm and colour, as a final touch.

CONCLUSION

Thalassa International has become an important part of the leisure business of the Accor Group. It has managed to segment the market very effectively and target the group of customers who are interested in the use of thalassotherapy methods for tonic effect. Accor has recognized that this fairly unique combination of leisure, hospitality and tourism features has the potential to be developed for European and international markets.

DISCUSSION POINTS AND ESSAY QUESTIONS

1. Discuss the advantages of a brand for the development of a speciality service such as thalassotherapy.
2. Evaluate the significance of health and fitness as market trends which European tourism, leisure and hospitality organizations may exploit.

Les Vins Georges Dubœuf SA, France

27

INTRODUCTION

Les Vins Georges Dubœuf SA is situated at Gare de Romanèche-Thorins, France, which is in the heart of the Beaujolais vine growing area. The complex consists of a wine producing and bottling plant and a visitor attraction, 'Le Hameau du Vin', which was opened in 1993 to illustrate the wine production process.

Les Vins Georges Dubœuf SA is a good example of a food and drink business which has diversified into the tourism business. This is becoming increasingly important for food and drink manufacturers because it offers an organization excellent publicity and public relations advantages.

THE HISTORY OF LES VINS GEORGES DUBŒUF

The company was founded in 1964 by Georges Dubœuf. The original buildings were situated in the south-east of Romanèche-Thorins. The company expanded in 1989 when 20 million francs were invested in an ultra-modern wine production plant at Romanèche-Thorins. This expansion included the installation of an automatic bottling plant.

In 1993, Georges Dubœuf opened the attraction 'Le Hameau du Vin' at Romanèche-Thorins. The museum was designed as a way of communicating the 'glory' of Beaujolais and Mâconnais wines to visitors. It explores the production of wine from start to finish.

Les Vins Georges Dubœuf SA has more than 100 workers and accounts for 15% of total Beaujolais wine production. The company exports to 110 countries and has an annual turnover of around 450 million French francs.

Georges Dubœuf is the founder of the fête of Romanèche-Thorins which takes place on the third Wednesday of November when the new season's Beaujolais reaches the market. Everybody then proclaims 'The New Beaujolais has arrived – Le Beaujolais Nouveau est arrivé'.

Beaujolais primeur represents about 20% of the production of the company and forms a major part of its marketing activity. The company does, however, produce many classic Beaujolais wines and other wines including Rhône Valley wines, Vins de Cépage and Vins de Table.

Georges Dubœuf has helped to take the Beaujolais name from relative obscurity to great respectability. The wines have been developed to have good flavours and recognized brand names. They are now world renowned.

GEORGES DUBŒUF – THE MAN

Georges Dubœuf has become known as 'The King of Beaujolais'. He is now 62 and is probably the most famous wine merchant in history. Twenty million bottles of wine are sold each year with his signature on. This remarkable development was carried out by a man who has a passion for quality, outstanding taste and a great capacity for work. He always visits the 400 supplying vignerons every year to check the quality of the wines, and he refuses to buy any which does not meet the company's high standard of requirements. He has personally contributed to the recognition of Beaujolais as a prestigious wine growing region. Georges Dubœuf has become world renowned for his good quality wines.

LES VINS GEORGES DUBŒUF SA – THE COMPANY TODAY

The company was formed with a capital investment of 4 959 000 French francs and was originally created in 1964 by Georges Dubœuf. The turnover of the company in 1993/4 was 496 million French francs. The company has a 310 million French francs export business to 110 countries, principally Belgium, Canada, the UK, Switzerland, Holland, Germany, Japan and the USA.

Details of the company are shown in Exhibit 27.1.

LE HAMEAU DU VIN

Georges Dubœuf opened the attraction 'Le Hameau du Vin' in 1993. The attraction was developed to demonstrate the ancient and skilled craft of wine production in the Beaujolais and the Mâconnais regions of France.

'Le Hameau du Vins' is situated close to the wine production and bottling factory of the company in the village of Romanèche-Thorins.

Exhibit 27.1 Les Vins Georges Dubœuf – company information

General information

Company name: Les Vins Georges Dubœuf SA

Address: 71570 Romanèche-Thorins

- Type: SA with capital of 4 959 000 French Francs
- Created in: 1964 by Georges Dubœuf
- President/Director General: Georges Dubœuf
- Administrator: Franck Dubœuf

Wine merchant and bottler

Turnover at 31.07.94: 496 million French francs – 310 million French francs obtained from export to 100 countries

Principal trading countries: United States, Canada, United Kingdom, Switzerland, Holland, Germany, Japan

Commercial volume: 300 000 hectolitres
30 million bottles

Clientele

- France: wholesalers
restaurants
specialists

- Export: agents or importers

Wine merchants

- 400 wine growers – 20 wine cooperatives

Equipment

- 5 bottling lines, capacity of 3000 to 10 000 bottles/hour
- 1 mobile bottling plant
- wine stores (4 oenological)
- 85 000 hectolitres, capacity storage (in vats)
- analytical laboratory

Organization

- 100 personnel in 8 divisions

Source: Les Vins Georges Duboeuf SA.

The attraction is housed in a number of old buildings which are characteristic of the Beaujolais and Mâconnais architectural style. Within the buildings, the visitor is led through a series of exhibition halls which demonstrate the wine production process and the origins of wine. A plan of the attraction is shown in Exhibit 27.2.

The visitor enters the attraction by the side of the old railway station. There is a cafe, toilets and ticket hall in the preliminary hall which

Exhibit 27.2 Map of Le Hameau du Vin – The Village of Wine.

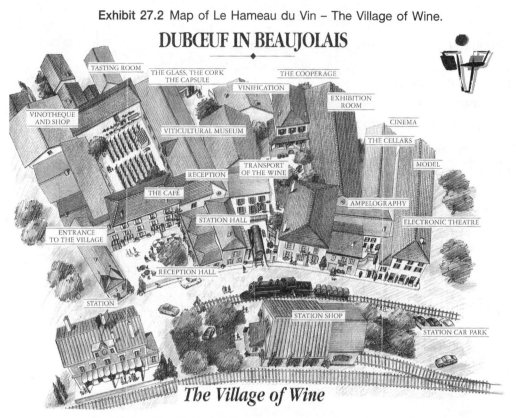

Source: Les Vins Georges Dubœuf SA.

has been made to look like a station waiting room. The remainder of the exhibition halls are listed in Exhibit 27.3.

CUSTOMERS OF 'LE HAMEAU DU VIN'

The customers of 'Le Hameau du Vin' can be divided into distinct groups as follows.

- **Corporate clients of Les Vins Georges Dubœuf SA**. European and international clients of the wine producer are taken around the attraction as a public relations exercise.
- **Corporate visitors**. French companies take their customers around the attraction.
- **Coach groups**. Coach tours visit the Beaujolais wine production area. These are encouraged to stop for a visit at 'Le Hameau du Vin'.
- **Individual visitors**. These visitors usually arrive by car and visit the attraction as part of a day-trip from France or as part of a holiday in France. This group of customers comes from France, Europe and even further afield.

Exhibit 27.3 Le Hameau du Vin – visitor attractions

Visit time – 1 h 30 min

1.   **Station Waiting Room**. Ticket booths and cafe.

2.   **Exhibition of the transport of wine**.

3.   **The museum of viticulture**.

4.   **Poully-Fuissé production**.

5.   **Moulin-à-Vent production**.

6.   **Crûs production**.

7.   **The geology of wine producing regions**.

8.   **Electronic Theatre**. The wine seasons are demonstrated using animatronics.

9.   **Interactive diarama**. The Beaujolais–Mâconnais region is shown in the diarama and the types of wines which originate from different soil types are discussed.

10.   **Cinema**. A film is shown to demonstrate the wine production process.

11.   **The Art Gallery**. Temporary exhibitions are held in this room on different aspects of wine production. The gallery is designed to look like a 'grenier'.

12. ⎫
13. ⎬   **Rooms which demonstrate different stages of the wine production process** including vinification, bottle production and cork production
14. ⎭

15.   **Tasting Hall**. The visitor enters the final hall where there is an electronic organ which plays while visitors can sample different varieties of wines.

16.   **Shop**. Sale of wines and a full range of merchandising objects.

Source: Les Vins Georges Dubœuf SA.

'LE HAMEAU DU VIN' AS A PUBLIC RELATIONS TOOL

'Le Hameau du Vin' introduces the corporate and individual visitor to the wines of the Beaujolais region. The tasting session which takes place in the final room of the visit is used to show the quality of the Georges Dubœuf wines. Customers are then encouraged to purchase wines and other merchandising materials in the extensive shop at the end of the visit. The shop also offers a mail-order service. In this way, customers on a world-wide basis are encouraged to purchase a full range of Georges Dubœuf wines. The attraction therefore has an important public relations role in the overall marketing strategy of the company.

CONCLUSION

'Le Hameau du Vin' is an important new venture for the Georges Dubœuf company. It helps with the raising of the company profile and with the development of wine sales on a world-wide basis.

DISCUSSION POINTS AND ESSAY QUESTIONS

1. Evaluate the importance of the visitor attraction at Georges Dubœuf to the development of their wine business.
2. The use of national, regional and local food and drink traditions as a theme for visitor attractions can be very successful. Using examples, discuss the reasons which may explain this phenomenon.

Center Parcs, UK

Exhibit 28.1 Center Parcs – 'a truly unique short break experience'.

INTRODUCTION

Center Parcs has been developed as a European leisure business. The company currently has 13 villages spread across Europe. All of the villages are based on the original ideas of a Dutch entrepreneur, Piet Derksen, who developed the first village in 1967. The holiday villages which have been developed all have high occupancy levels, and the concept of Center Parcs has been well received in all the European countries in which it has been developed. Center Parcs is now a world leader in short-break holidays.

HISTORY OF CENTER PARCS

The first village was established in the south of Holland in 1967. Since this time, villages have been developed in five countries of Europe. A brief history of the development of Center Parcs is shown in Exhibit 28.2. The location of current Center Parcs villages is shown in Exhibit

---

Exhibit 28.2 History of Center Parcs

1967	Piet Derksen, a Dutchman, establishes the business under the original name Sporthuis Centrum Recreatie. The first village opened in the south of Holland and was designed by Professor Jaap Bakema, an eminent Dutch architect.
1967–1993	Development of the Center Parcs idea into Belgium, France and the United Kingdom.
1987	Opening of first UK village in Sherwood Forest.
1989	Scottish and Newcastle Breweries plc, the UK-based brewing, leisure and retail group, obtains the major shareholding in Center Parcs.
1989	Opening of second UK village in Elveden Forest.
1991	Scottish and Newcastle Breweries plc acquire the outstanding equity interests in Center Parcs.
1992	Center Parcs called in by the Belgian government as an environmental expert to oversee the greening of a vast area as a nature reserve at Maasmechelen.
1993	Opening of the second French village at Chaumont-Les Hauts de Bruyères in the Loire Valley.
1994	Opening of the third UK location – Longleat Forest.
1995	Opening of first German village. Company now operates 13 villages across Europe. Plans for third Belgian village.

Source: Center Parcs Annual Accounts 1990, 1991, 1992, 1993, 1994.

Exhibit 28.3 Locations of Center Parcs in Europe

In Holland

- Het Meerdal
- De Huttenheugte
- De Kempervennen
- De Eemhof
- Het Heijderbos

In Belgium

- Erperheide
- De Vossemeren

In France

- Les Hauts de Bruyères
- Les Bois-Francs

In England

- Sherwood Forest
- Elveden Forest
- Longleat Forest

In Germany

- Bispinger Heide

Source: Center Parcs.

28.3. The Mission and Goals of the company are shown in Exhibit 28.4.

Scottish and Newcastle plc, the UK-based brewing, leisure and retail group, obtained a major shareholding in the Center Parcs business in 1989. At this stage the company was a market leader in all-year-round residential leisure recreation operating at 13 locations – eight in Holland, two in Belgium, one in France, and two in England. Center Parcs remained a publicly quoted Dutch company at this stage. The management board of the company introduced a new decentralized management style which on the one hand coordinated management by geographical market, and on the other gave general managers greater control and responsibility. During 1992, Scottish and Newcastle plc offered to acquire the outstanding equity interests in Center Parcs. This was completed during 1991 which meant that 1% of the equity interests remained outstanding.

Exhibit 28.4 The Mission and Goals of Center Parcs

MISSION STATEMENT
To give our guests a truly unique short break holiday experience
which far exceeds their expectations

OUR SIX GOALS
In order to carry out our mission successfully, we have formulated six
basic goals which we call the Center Parcs' Goals

Goal 1
A visionary approach to creative
management

Goal 2
Striving for the highest standards of product possible

Goal 3
An approach to guest service that is second to none

Goal 4
A positive approach to the genuine recognition of our own
employees

Goal 5
A commitment to invest in the business and in the personal
development of each and every individual in the organization

Goal 6
This will result in our guests returning, in satisfying our employees' needs
and ultimately in optimizing the profitability of our Company

Thus maintaining our position as market leader

And securing our own future

If we can achieve these goals, we will have accomplished our mission,
which is to give our guests a truly Unique Short Break

Source: Center Parcs.

Scottish and Newcastle plc have continued to develop the Center Parcs concept since 1991.

THE MARKET FOR CENTER PARCS

The concept was developed to appeal to families from ABC1 socio-economic groups, usually with young children. The growth in the interest of these groups in the environment has fuelled the Center Parcs growth. The idea of staying in a village which demonstrated environmental sustainability appeals to the A, B, C1 family group.

THE CENTER PARCS PHENOMENON

The appeal of Center Parcs involves a combination of features which together give the organization a uniquely positioned product. The features of this unique product are shown in Exhibit 28.5. Each village has developed a series of facilities to reflect these features. These include:

- a full range of villas located discreetly in a forest setting with all 'mod-cons';
- the all-weather dome which is a tropical paradise and is at the centre of the development;
- a full range of ancillary services, including sporting facilities, health farms, restaurants, etc.

The Center Parcs concept reflects concern for the environment and quality of life. The customer can have the pace and excitement of a country club and sports complex. Alternatively if they want the peace and pampering of a health farm, they can have it. If they want the flexibility of a village in a forest setting, it is waiting for them. The villages have an exciting Continental feel, yet they are in the heart of the countryside. The beautiful natural settings afford both space and privacy but also absorb an unrivalled range of sports and leisure facilities. Center Parcs offers unrivalled services for families and encourages children to gain their independence in a safe environment because there are no busy roads within the village.

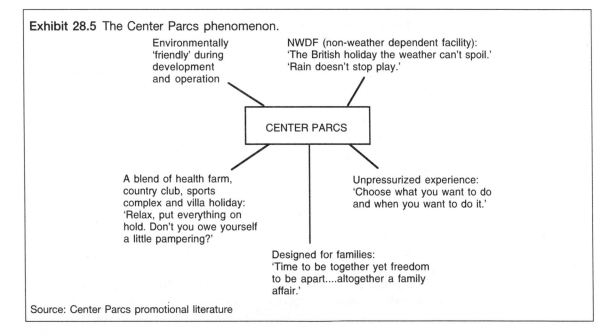

Exhibit 28.5 The Center Parcs phenomenon.

Environmentally 'friendly' during development and operation

NWDF (non-weather dependent facility): 'The British holiday the weather can't spoil.' 'Rain doesn't stop play.'

CENTER PARCS

A blend of health farm, country club, sports complex and villa holiday: 'Relax, put everything on hold. Don't you owe yourself a little pampering?'

Unpressurized experience: 'Choose what you want to do and when you want to do it.'

Designed for families: 'Time to be together yet freedom to be apart....altogether a family affair.'

Source: Center Parcs promotional literature

The two weeks we spent at Center Parcs were most notable for the sense of harmony we felt as a family – and you can't say that about most holidays where growing children are involved.

Nursery World (1994).

CENTER PARCS AND THE ENVIRONMENT

Concern for the environment is fundamental to Center Parcs' whole philosophy and plays a major role even before a site is selected for a Center Parcs village.

Site selection

To ensure that Center Parcs selects the least environmentally sensitive sites for any proposed new village, a team of ecologists and landscape consultants, together with Center Parcs' own specialists, first makes a detailed inventory and appraisal of a potential site and, in consultation with both statutory and non-statutory bodies, identifies environmental constraints and opportunities for each potential location.

Landscape consultants carry out a visual appraisal and ecologists survey both the potential site and surrounding areas to ensure its relatively low existing ecological value and identify any habitats of value which will require protection. Engineers appraise traffic and highway arrangements to ensure minimal disruption to the site and its environs.

The criteria for a new site include that it should be medium-aged conifer woodland for several reasons. The mature trees provide screening during both construction and operation, and provide a green backdrop all year round. The age of the trees allows them to be selectively thinned and interplanted with younger trees and other diverse species. Conifer plantations also have a comparatively poor diversity of indigenous plant and animal life but considerable potential for enhancement.

A detailed environmental statement is prepared bringing together the various studies carried out and is used in consultations with not only the local authorities but the local community, the Countryside Commission, English Nature and any other interested bodies.

Design and construction

Environmental constraints are vitally important influences on the planning process and ensure that area of conservation and wildlife interest are protected.

The siting and detailing of villa clusters, central buildings and the car park is meticulously carried out to ensure as many trees as possible are retained. Any areas identified by the ecologists as having particular interest, e.g. remnants of broad-leaved woodland and particularly fine individual specimens, are retained and protected during the construction phase and plans are incorporated to protect resident wildlife.

During construction, the contractor is required to work within strict limitations to prevent damage to the environment. Routes for new waterways are used for access, avoiding unnecessary tree felling, pre-fabricated elements minimize on-site construction and any areas not affected by the construction are fenced off. There is strict supervision by Center Parcs' own technical staff, consultants and also the contractor's construction project manager to ensure plans are adhered to.

Landscaping is carried out throughout the construction of the village, commencing with thinning of the forest and underplanting with native broad-leaved species. Seeding takes place with selected grass and wildflower species (e.g. cornflowers, poppies and wood sorrel) and over 500 000 trees and shrubs are planted at each new village. The network of lakes and waterways form key elements of a village and the plants introduced to these areas arrive from local sources with all their indigenous insect life ensuring new habitats are quickly established. Bird boxes are introduced to attract a wide variety of birdlife – green and greater spotted woodpeckers, nuthatches, tawny owls and woodcock can be seen, along with the scarce nightjar. Bats are also encouraged with the introduction of nesting boxes.

Operation

Concern for the environment doesn't stop at the end of the construction of a village. A team of trained forest rangers supported by ecologists manage the ecological systems. Their role covers not only the day-to-day maintenance of the village, but encompasses the establishment and implementation of the Landscape Management Plan which includes habitat management and forest thinning and management. Center Parcs also works closely with outside bodies such as the Forestry Commission and local wildlife trusts.

The villages are traffic-free with guests' cars allowed further than the car park only to unload at the villa on arrival and load again on departure on Mondays and Fridays. During the rest of the week bicycles are the only form of transport.

Ecological monitoring takes place regularly.

Recognition

For many years Center Parcs has been deeply committed to not only conserving the environment, but enhancing it. In particular the company strives to create habitats that encourage the indigenous flora and fauna.

It is generally accepted by ecologists and conservationists alike that Center Parcs' villages form a richer, more attractive and better balanced ecological environment than existed before the company took over a site. As Dr David Sheppard of English Nature commented:

Center Parcs' overall record of environmental care is impressive. What is more impressive is the company's positive response to any suggestions to improve the environmental quality of their village.

Center Parcs has received the recognition of such bodies and individuals as the government, the Secretary of State for the Environment and the Director of the Countryside Commission. It has received many awards – amongst others in 1988 Sherwood Forest Holiday Village was awarded the Business and Industry Environment Award and in 1990 the company received the English Tourist Board's inaugural Green Tourism Award. Center Parcs was also awarded the 1993/94 Business Commitment to the Environment Premier Award in recognition of its 'human and social responsibility and environmental quality in respect of its development of its villages at Sherwood, Elveden and Longleat Forests'.

Tropical landscapes

Center Parcs' environmental expertise also extends to the creation and care of its internal tropical landscapes in the Subtropical Swimming Paradise, Plaza and Jardin des Sports. The plants are brought from all over the world by Center Parcs' own landscape architect who has developed a technique for putting the plants into hibernation during transportation. On arrival at the company's nurseries in Holland they are revived and gently acclimatized for anything from a month to a year, depending on the individual plant.

More than 5000 tropical plants from 800 species are selected for each village, and themed to recreate, for instance at Longleat Forest, a Burmese wood, at Elveden Forest a South American tropical forest and a replica of the Florida Everglades at Sherwood Forest.

As trade in endangered plants is monitored through the Convention on International Trade in Endangered Species, Center Parcs take special care over which plants are selected and they will never take a plant if there are fewer than 100 specimens within the vicinity.

Only environmentally safe sprays and organic feeds are used, with natural predators being used to eradicate pests – but it is essential that the right species are used as, for example, ladybirds from Europe will turn away from Brazilian bugs!

The soil is checked regularly and gradually replaced to maintain its richness and all pruning and replanting is carried out at night whilst guests are sleeping.

Statement of environmental objectives and policy

Center Parcs strongly believes the tourism industry needs a code of practice which involves continued 'environmental stewardship'. The approach evolved by Center Parcs demonstrates an industry standard which ensures that every aspect of the environment is included in the provision of tourism and recreation facilities.

The company environmental objectives and policy are:

- to make a positive contribution to the global environment by our efforts at a local level;
- to accept responsibility for the environmental consequences of our activities and therefore to aim to minimize any adverse environmental impacts we may have;
- to conduct all our activities in the spirit of being custodians of the environment within and around our villages;
- to enable our guests and employees to experience the process of environmental care at first hand, so that they too will be encouraged to make a contribution in their daily lives;
- to be acknowledged as setting the standard for our industry by demonstrating that sustainable tourism is achievable and by offering to share our experience with others.

MARKETING

The marketing strategy for the launch and early development of Center Parcs in the UK – including both the consumer promise, creative strategy and media strategy – was of course tailored for the British target audience and has evolved over the course of the last 10 years.

In Holland, where the experience is much more mature and targeted at a slightly different audience, and yet again in France and Germany, where it is an even more recent experience, both require appropriate strategies. Notwithstanding that, the appeal of the concept and the care elements of the experience are essentially the same.

Center Parcs is very much a marketing-driven organisation. Its positioning statement on launch was as follows:

Center Parcs offers a new upmarket holiday experience where, for 52 weeks of the year, guests can get away from the hassle of everyday life to enjoy a special environment with people who share the same values and want the same things out of a holiday break in terms of facilities, service etc.

The target audience profile for the UK to which sales and marketing activities are directed is:

- upmarket – A,B,C1, aspiring C2;
- young – 25–50;
- family unit – parents with children still holidaying as a unit.

Almost 100% of sales come from direct sales, with less than 2% coming through selected travel agents.

Sales and marketing strategy

There is a programme of advertising (mainly television), public relations and selected promotions drives sales activity.

The media plan

As noted above, the primary medium is television, with some radio and selected national press and specialist consumer magazines for specific audiences as a secondary media. The objective of the television strategy is to book brochure response, rather than sell directly from the screen.

PR is considered important to give third party endorsement.

Research is carried out into different aspects of the organization, with the main programme being the Guest Satisfaction Monitor which is carried out continuously in all the villages. This provides the company with valuable information not only on how accurately they are targeting their audience and where they can make changes, but also on development and operational aspects of the villages, which either provide excellence or require particular attention.

FINANCIAL PERFORMANCE

The Leisure Division of Scottish and Newcastle plc, of which Center Parcs is the major part, has shown a consistent pattern of profit growth over the last few years. Operating profits have also been growing. Since its inception in 1989/90, when Center Parcs was first acquired, the division has nearly doubled its contribution to group operating profits and in 1994 it contributed 32% of the total group profits. The financial performance of the leisure division (which also includes the Pontin's business) is shown in Exhibit 28.6.

Exhibit 28.6 Turnover and operating profit of the Leisure Division, Scottish and Newcastle plc

	1994 £m	1993 £m	1992 £m	1991 £m
Turnover	367.5	335.4	310.9	295.1
Operating profit	83.1	77.0	74.6	65.5

Source: Center Parcs 1995.

THE FUTURE

There is potential for the Center Parcs idea to spread further across Europe, in East Germany and beyond. The forests in Eastern Europe and Russia, for example, offer tremendous potential. The problem with this, however, will be the development of the organizational infrastructure to support the project. The company is also looking to continue developments at their existing villages. The range of services on offer are constantly growing and the company will continue to develop and upgrade their facilities. Health and relaxation facilities, country clubs and golf courses are all recent additions to the range of facilities at existing villages.

CONCLUSIONS

Center Parcs is the market leader in the short-break holiday market in Europe. It has created a unique product which appeals to families from ABC1 socioeconomic groups across Europe.

The Center Parcs business has had to cope with varying economic conditions from country to country. These economic conditions have been reflected in very diverse consumer attitudes to spending.

It remains simplistic to consider mainland Europe entirely as one trading entity and there is a need to anticipate and react to local market needs. Indeed this is reflected in our own Center Parcs organization, which continues to reflect national boundaries.

Scottish and Newcastle plc, Accounts 1994.

Center Parcs will continue to develop across Europe reflecting local national trading conditions.

DISCUSSION POINTS AND ESSAY QUESTIONS

1. Discuss the importance of the environmental objectives and policy of Center Parcs UK in their marketing activities.
2. Evaluate the reasons for the nationally developed marketing strategy as opposed to a European marketing strategy for the Center Parcs business in the UK.

Port Aventura SA, Spain

Exhibit 29.1 The Port Aventura Theme Park

Source: Port Aventura SA. Reproduced with kind permission.

INTRODUCTION

Port Aventura is a new European theme park which opened to the public on 2 May 1995. It is located 100 km south of Barcelona in a 295-acre ark and is being managed by the Tussauds Group which has a 40% shareholding in the project. The theme park is split into five 'lands', each of which has its own themed rides, food and merchandising. It is estimated that 2.5 million people will visit the theme park in the first year of operation to produce a predicted turnover of $64 million for 1995. it is hoped that the theme park will bring tourists into the Costa Dorada area within the Murcia region of Spain which already has a well developed tourist infrastructure.

THE INITIAL IDEA FOR THE PROJECT

The initial idea for the project came about when the US brewing to theme park giant, Anheuser-Busch, worked with the Spanish development company Grand Tibidabo. Anheuser-Busch already had experience of running attractions such as Sea World and Busch Gardens, and owned the Budweiser beer brand. The project stalled a number of times due to commercial, political and legal reasons, and Anheuser-Busch finally decided to take on more partners which would reduce their shareholding in the park. The Tussauds Group entered the business in 1994. The original planning of the park, which was based loosely on the Busch Garden parks theme, was, however, kept, and the layout remained much the same as it had originally been designed.

CURRENT ECONOMIC DATA

Port Aventura is a multinational company which consists of four major shareholders. The whole company was founded with a capital investment of 15800 million pesetas by the four major shareholders. Details of these shareholders and their percentage investment are shown in Exhibit 29.2.

Port Aventura is a 48 000 million peseta project which is broken down into three main areas:

• Real estate:	6 000 million pesetas
• Construction, theming and rides:	25 000 million pesetas
• Previous studies, architectural and engineering projects, start-off and financial expenses:	17 000 million pesetas

Of note are the 5000 million pesetas in the construction, theming and rides area which has been dedicated to the design, construction and installation of rides. Of this 1000 million pesetas has been spent on the

---

Exhibit 29.2 Major shareholders in the Port Aventura Company

Company	Country of origin	Type of company	% investment*
The Tussauds Group	UK	Leisure and entertainment business	40.01
La Caixa	Spain	Spanish savings bank	33.19
Anheuser-Busch	US	Brewing and theme park business	19.99
FECSA	Spain	Spanish utility company	6.79

*Because of rounding this column does not add up to 100.0%.
Source: Port Aventura 1995.

---

construction of the major attraction, the 'Dragon Khan' roller coaster, which is the first in the world with 8 loops.

Port Aventura expects a turnover of 12 000 million pesetas in its first year of operation which will be broken down as follows:

- Sale of entrance tickets: 60%
- Consumption in the Park: 40%

The Park will have 170 permanent workers and 2500 seasonal workers.

THE PARK DESIGN

The Park is divided into five 'lands', each of which has its own theme, rides, food and merchandising. Details of the five 'lands' are shown in Exhibits 29.3 and 29.4.

The five 'lands' invite the visitor to become an adventurer and enjoy a day in typical villages from the Mediterranean, Polynesia, China, Mexico and the Far West. There is an array of rides, attractions, shows, restaurants and shops that together are said to create a unique sensation of travelling the world in one day. The Mediterranean village is the welcoming area and contains typical building and boats in a harbour. Polynesia, with an assortment of huts and cabins, brings the visitor back to the times of Captain Cook. Marco Polo's China is the home of the Dragon Khan, the Park's major ride. Mexico is recreated by two historical periods – Mayan and Spanish colonial. The Far West recreates the experience and atmosphere of a Western town in the middle of a 4th of July independence day celebration.

Exhibit 29.3 Map of the Port Aventura Theme Park.

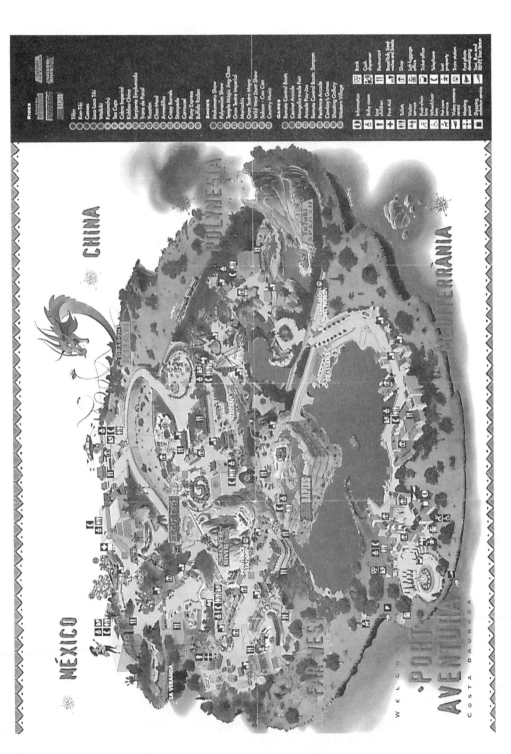

Source: Port Aventura SA. Reproduced with kind permission.

Exhibit 29.4 The five 'lands' of the Port Aventura complex

- **Mediterranean** – This is styled on a Mediterranean village and is at the entrance to the park. It has a boating lake and services. The streets feature local handicrafts, dancing and other entertainment.
- **Polynesia** – This 'land' is a series of islands which are linked by bridges and covered in dense vegetation. This 'land' has the Tutuki Splash water ride which features a boat being hurled out of an erupting volcano.
- **China** – This 'land' is composed of a fishing town and an imperial city. The central theme of the park, the Dragon Khan roller coaster, is in this area. There is also a 1200-seat theatre which offers acrobatics and magic shows.
- **Mexico** – Mexico features a Mayan temple and a colonial hacienda. Attractions include a runaway mine train and a large screen film show.
- **The Wild West** – The Wild West recreates 4 July 1876 and features country and western music, cowboys and can-can dancers. Rides include rafting through the Grand Canyon and shooting the Colorado rapids.

ACTION IN THE STREETS

One of the main features of the theme park is the street entertainment which is carried out by the Performance Department of Port Aventura. There are 46 actors involved in bringing life to the different 'lands'. These make the open areas of the park into a continuous spectacle for the visitors. The themes of the different zones in the park are reinforced by the live performance. The different shows include Polynesian Island folklore dances, Chinese acrobats, Mariachis, Wild West action, and a Wild West saloon show.

> The finest setting in Port Aventura is the street itself.
>
> Teresa Escudé, Director of Port Aventura show

Details of the shows and the performance table are shown in Exhibit 29.5.

THE UNIFORMS AT PORT AVENTURA

The wardrobe is one of the identifying characteristics of Port Aventura. The colour, vivacity and a feeling of light-heartedness in the designs, all express the fun and entertainment that Port Aventura offers in its 'fantastic journey' through the different national cultures presented in the Park.

The official presentation of the costumes took place on 22 March 1995. These are worn by the personnel teams of Port Aventura in the

Exhibit 29.5 The shows and performance table

Polynesia	– Bird Shows, (Makamanu Show), Dances, (Polynesian Show)
China	– Magic Shadows, (Jing-Cou Temple), Chinese Acrobats, (Imperial Theatre)
Mexico	– Mariachi Band, Cantina, Films, Maya Theatre
Far West	– Western Stunt Show, Country Music, Saloon Show

Performance table

Performance	Duration	Capacity	No. per day
Polynesian Island			
Dances	20 minutes	800	8
Bird Shows	20 minutes	860	6
Magic Theatre	20 minutes	448	10
Chinese Acrobats	25 minutes	1190	6
Mariachis	20 minutes	1000	9
Western Stunt Show	20 minutes	1160	5
Saloon	15 minutes	275	10
Country Music	20 minutes	364	8

various sections and areas which comprise the first Spanish Theme Park. According to Teresa Escudé, Director of Productions at Park Aventura:

> The object we concentrated on when designing the clothes and choosing the cloth was to achieve the necessary balance in manufacturing a working uniform which at the same time would transmit the ethnic image of the area where it was to be located, would be practical, and above all would be easy to maintain.

The first decision, therefore, was to choose the fabrics which fulfilled these requirements, and to this end more than 20 textile companies were contacted. This was followed by a period of trial and selection when the durability and ease of maintenance of the fabrics was tried out.

Barcelona designer Gemma Sénder was commissioned with this important task of creating over 100 different types of uniform. Sénder has shown her designs in some of the most representative collections in the Salon Gaudi and has a broad experience in the design of costumes for shows, ballets and even films.

The vivid colours, which attempt to portray the image of the Park Aventura Logo in the costumes and a certain feeling of light-heartedness and fun, are consonant with the youthfulness of most of the Park's employees, with an average age of less than 25 years.

Another of the aspects treated with great care in the design of the costumes has been the accessories to the uniforms – the hats, necklaces and head-dresses – which have generally been imported from their countries of origin in order to produce the kind of realism and detail so important at Port Aventura.

SHOPS

The various theme areas in the Park have a series of shops which, just like the attractions and the refreshment areas, are carefully decorated with excellent detail. The articles for sale in these shops have been very carefully selected, a process which has taken the Port Aventura representatives to a good number of trade fairs and brought them into contact with suppliers from all the zones represented in the theme park.

Around 130 suppliers have been contacted to obtain the articles, most of them produced by craftsmen, for the 22 shops situated in the different areas of the Park. There are also many products which have been specially designed for Port Aventura.

Mexico

There are two shops in the Mexico Theme Area: **Taxco**, where one can buy articles specially made by craftsmen, and **Tianguis**, with typical articles from a Mexican market (coloured paste made into necklaces, seeds, paper flowers, craft-made wooden toys, etc).

Polynesia

Most of the articles for sale in the shops in this area come from Fiji, Samoa, Tonga and New Zealand. These articles were found in the same way as those from the Mexican villages. At certain times the inhabitants of the islands of the different Polynesian archipelagos send their products to local markets where they are sold for export.

Far West

Some 40 companies supply the principle goods for this theme area: gifts and decoration, clothing, art and literature, all arising from country and western inspiration.

The goods can be characterized as Western (cowboy and indians) and Country (colonizers). Among the stock can be seen Red Indian pottery, porcelain, silver and alpaca, games of Far West inspiration, decorative Red Indian objects, dolls, leather, music, videos and country textiles.

China

The China of tradition and craftmanship visits us through the articles that you can buy in the shop in this area. Visitors can admire the china, pottery, woodwork, enamel, silks, works of art, glass and bronzes. One of the most unusual articles among the Chinese crafts is the jewellery made from bone.

THE CRAFTSMEN OF PORT AVENTURA

In addition to the various shops throughout the Park, the visitor can follow the process of production of some of the craft products, representative of the different theme areas. There are nine craftsmen working in the Park using the original techniques of these areas.

- In the **Mediterranean** area there are three craftsmen. One of these engraves glass with a diamond needle, another paints ceramic floor tiles and the third is occupied in the *dégorgement* of cava, using techniques from the early years of the century, adding the *liqueur d'expedition*, inserting the cork, and finally fixing the wire and the foil capping.
- In **Polynesia** three native craftsmen give demonstrations in the huts which surround the shopping area. They work with different techniques and with materials originating from their country. The demonstrations consist of the production of canoes from treetrunks, the carving of figures in wood and coconut, and the preparation of bark paintings.
- In the **Chinese** zone, there is a demonstration of Chinese calligraphy on ricepaper, personalizing the names of the visitor. There are also painters who, as in the Mediterranean, make caricatures of the visitors.
- In the **Mexican** area there is a craftsman working on special products from the Mexican culture, such as painting on amate paper, preparing celebration jars and making *papier maché* figures.
- The **Far West** craftsman displays leatherwork to the visitors, using techniques from the end of the ninetenth century. The workshop makes several products (belts, bags, etc.) which are subsequently sold in the shops.

RESTAURANTS AND SNACK BARS

The catering outlets at the Park have been designed to fit in with the theme areas. Each one of the theme areas of the Park has a variety of offers. In the first place, the visitor can choose between three types of establishment. There are 15 **restaurants** of which three are self-service cafeterias, and there are four fast-food establishments.

Take-away meals are also on offer. There are 15 **trolleys** decorated in the style of the theme area where they are located, from which drinks, ices and other similar products can be purchased.

The visitor can choose from a variety of restaurants, Ximpang, La Hacienda, The Iron Horse, Emma's and the Racó del Mar. Located in the Mediterranean area, El Racó del Mar may be considered as one of the finest restaurants in the province. Its menu is based on representative dishes of Catalan cuisine.

Another notable place is La Cantina – a restaurant with seating for 1000, it is the biggest of all those in the Park. It offers exclusively typical dishes from Mexican cuisine, and with its special decor achieves an atmosphere which transports the visitor to a traditional fiesta in the main square of a little Mexican town.

The Polynesian area is as exotic in its gastronomy as in other aspects. Bora Bora is a restaurant of 3-star status, specializing in typical dishes from Polynesia, dishes such as fish with sweet 'n' sour sauce or moa sausages grilled Polynesian style, and traditional tropical fruits.

The catering services which are on offer at Port Aventura are shown in Exhibit 29.6. It can be seen that the hospitality outlets have been developed to make gastronomy an important aspect of the visitor experience.

THE MARKET FOR PORT AVENTURA

Port Aventura has been developed as a theme park which will appeal to the holidaymaker who is taking a longer break holiday. The park has therefore been located in a traditional holiday destination. The park is targeting the Costa Dorada's traditional holiday market as well as visitors to nearby Barcelona. It also hopes to attract visitors from Majorca following the announcement of a new trans-Mediterranean ferry route linking Palma with Tarragona. It is hoped that the Park will bring substantial revenue into the area. Tarragona tourist authority, for example, estimate that Port Aventura could bring in an additional £38.2 million in tourist revenue in its first year of operation.

The nature of the market has meant that Port Aventura has not developed accommodation at the Park. Port Aventura is relying on the tourist beds which are within an hours drive. A good tourist infrastructure is already in place with 285 hotels and 175 000 apartments along the 200 km coastline.

OPENING TIMES AND PRICES (1995)

Port Aventura was open from 2 May to 29 October 1995, and the park was open as follows:

May to 22 June	10–20 h
29 June to 16 September	10–24 h
17 September to 29 October	10–20 h

Exhibit 29.6 Catering outlets at Port Aventura

Mediterranean
- Racó del Mar   Restaurant 4-star
- La Fleca   Restaurant 2-star
- Cururutxo   Ices
- El Posit   Tapas
- El Glop   Snacks, drinks

Polynesia
- Bora Bora   Restaurant 3-star, cafeteria
- Capitan Cook   Ices and tapas
- Tropical   Juices
- King Kamehameha   Snacks, cold drinks
- Bamboo   Snacks

China
- Ximpang   Restaurant 4-star
- Canton   Restaurant 3-star
- Sichuan   Restaurant 2-star
- Mandarin   Juices and ices
- Altai   Snacks, cold drinks

Mexico
- Economato   Juices and Ices
- Palma Real   Ices and tapas
- La Cantina   Restaurant 2-star
- La Veranda   Picnic
- La Papaya   Snacks, cold drinks
- La Hacienda 'El Charro'   Restaurant 4-star

The Far West
- The Iron Horse   Restaurant 4-star
- Barbecue   Restaurant 3-star
- Big Bill's   Restaurant 2-star
- Cold Drinks   Snacks, cold drinks
- Logger Drinks   Snacks, cold drinks
- Grand Canyon Drinks   Snacks, cold drinks
- Long branch saloon   Drinks, tapas
- Emma's   Restaurant

The price list (in pesetas) for 1995 was as follows:

Bonus	1 day	2nd day*	2 days	Season pass	Holiday
Adults	3 800	1 400	5 200	9 500	8 500
Senior	3 000	1 200	4 200	7 500	6 500
Children	3 000	1 200	4 200	7 500	6 500

*To be used on two consecutive days only.

Senior: 65 or more.
Children: 4 to 12 years.
Children under 4 enter free.
Consult special prices for schools, special groups and special events.

Visitors on wheelchairs pay Senior/Children rates.

CONCLUSION

Port Aventura is destined to become a major player in the European theme park market. The reliance on existing tourism infrastructure and distribution channels will allow the Park to develop a substantial European market. The Park has combined tourism, hospitality and leisure features to produce a major new European attraction.

DISCUSSION POINTS AND ESSAY QUESTIONS

1. Discuss the advantages and disadvantages of locating Port Aventura in a traditional holiday destination.
2. Evaluate the importance of themed catering outlets in the theme park experience, at Port Aventura and elsewhere.

Glossary of terms

The following glossary of terms is important for the following reasons:

- As marketing has become a more popular topic, marketing terms have been used more widely, and perhaps increasingly with less clarity. It is vital, therefore, for the authors to define key words and phrases in terms of what they have been taken to mean when they have been used in this book.
- The meaning of some relevant terms varies between different countries in Europe, and some terms may not been known to readers in some European countries.
- At a time when marketing in tourism, leisure and hospitality has an increasingly European dimension, there is no widely available published glossary of relevant terms.

It is clear that most of the terms used in marketing are English, or perhaps more accurately American. However, many relevant words also exist in other national languages. While it is beyond the scope of this book, if we seek to better understand European tourism, leisure and hospitality marketing, we should perhaps be demanding the publication of a dictionary of tourism, leisure and hospitality, which brings together and translates relevant terms in all the major European languages.

ACORN. A method of clarifying residential neighbourhoods on the basis of who live there for use in direct mail or marketing research.

Advertising. Paid-for types of communication, designed to influence the attitudes and behaviour of the public as a whole, or particular sections of people.

Allocentrics. A term coined by Plog (1977) for customers who are adventurous, outward-looking and like to take risks.

Ansoff's matrix. A model developed by Igor Ansoff that suggests four different marketing strategies which organizations can adopt. Further details of the matrix are to be found in Chapter 13.

Arts. Creative activities carried out for commercial gain or personal pleasure.

Boston Consulting Group Matrix. A technique designed to show the performance of an individual product in relation to its major competitors and the rate of growth in its market. This technique is discussed in more detail in Chapter 13.

Brand. Kotler (1994) defines a brand as 'a name, term, symbol, or design, or combination of them, intended to identify goods or services of one seller or group of sellers, and to differentiate them from those of competitors'. Well known brands in tourism, leisure and hospitality include Disney World, Center Parcs, Club 18–30 and Big Mac.

Brand loyalty. The propensity or otherwise of consumers to continue to purchase a particular brand.

Business environment. The business world in which an organization lives and the factors within it that influence the organization's products and marketing activities. This subject is covered fully in Chapter 7.

Business mix. The overall balance of the different types of markets and products of an organization.

Business tourism. Tourist trips that take place as part of people's business occupational commitments largely in work time, rather than for pleasure in people's leisure time. This aspect of tourism is discussed in more detail in Chapter 27.

Cash cow. A product that generates a high volume of income in relation to the cost of maintaining its market share.

Catchment area. The geographical area from which the overwhelming majority of a product, or organization's, customers are drawn.

Chain. A term used to describe an organization which owns a number of hotels, restaurants or travel agencies, for example, that offer a generally standardized product.

Commission. Money paid to an external agent who assists the organization in selling a product, usually expressed as a percentage of the price paid by the customer.

Competition. The process by which organizations attempt to gain new customers from other organizations whilst retaining their existing customers.

Computer Reservations Systems (CRS). Computer-based systems used widely in tourism and hospitality for making and recording bookings and payments made by customers.

Consumer. The person who uses a product or service. *See also* Customer.

Consumer behaviour. The study of why people buy the products they do and how they make decisions.

Cost leadership. A competitive advantage technique identified by Porter (1980), in which organizations attempt to produce a product at a lower price than their competitors.

Customer. The person who purchases a product or service. This term is often used inter-changeably with the word consumer, but they can be different. For example, in business tourism, a company pays for the travel services but it is its employee who uses (or 'consumes') the services. *See also* Consumer.

Demand. The quantity of a product or service that customers are willing and able to buy at a particular time at a specific price.

Demarketing. Action designed to discourage consumers from buying particular goods or services. This is discussed further in Chapter 30.

Demography. The study of population structure including age, sex, race and family status.

Destination. The country, region or locality where a tourist spends their holiday.

Determinants. Factors which determine whether or not a tourist is able to take a holiday, and if so, then the type of holiday they are able to take. These are covered in detail in Chapter 4.

Direct marketing. Selling directly from producer to customer without the aid of marketing intermediaries such as retailers or agents.

Discounts. A reduction in the list price of a product designed to encourage sales.

Disposable income. Money remaining after essential expenditure has been subtracted from a person's income.

Distribution. The process by which products are transferred from producers to consumers. *See also* Place.

Diversification. An extension of an organization's activities into new markets.

Domestic tourism. Tourism where the residents of a country take holidays wholly within their country of residence.

Ethics. The moral values and standards that guide the behaviour of individuals and organizations.

Europe. In this book, Europe is defined broadly to encompass the mainland from Portugal and Iceland in the West, to the Ural Mountains in the East. It stretches from Lapland in the North to the islands of Malta and Cyprus in the South and, of course, the offshore Spanish and Portuguese islands, namely the Canaries and Madeira respectively. The definition has also been stretched to include Turkey, the Western part of which at least is generally considered to be part of Europe. The concept of Europe provides the focus for Chapter 2.

Family lifecycle. The stages through which people pass between birth and death that influence their behaviour as consumers.

Fast food. A form of hot food that can be prepared and served in a very short time.

Feasibility study. A study which is carried out to test the potential viability of any proposed development project or new product. A feasibility study will usually examine both the financial viability of the project or product as well as try to establish the size of its potential market.

FIT. Fully inclusive tours.

Four Ps. The elements of the marketing mix, namely produce, price, place and promotion.

Franchising. The process by which an organization agrees to permit another organization to sell its product and use its brand name in return for a payment.

Green issues. A commonly used but rather ill-defined term used as an umbrella for a range of issues relating to the physical environment. These may range from pollution to recycling, wildlife conservation to 'global warming'. The impact of green issues in tourism, leisure and hospitality is discussed fully in Chapter 30.

Gross Domestic Product (GDP). The total value of a nation's output of goods and services produced in one year.

Growth market. A market where demand is growing significantly.

Heterogeneous. A market, product type or industry sector that contains non-identical elements that differ significantly from each other.

Homogeneous. A market, product type or industrial sector that contains elements which are wholly or largely identical.

Horizontal integration. The process by which organizations take over organizations who are, or could be, competitors.

Hospitality. In this context, hospitality is used in the way it is in the USA, namely as an umbrella term for the whole hotel and catering field. This term is defined in more detail in Chapter 3.

Intangibility. The characteristic of service products by which they lack physical form and cannot be seen or touched.

International tourism. Tourism where the residents of one country take business or leisure trips which have their destination in another country.

JICNARS. Joint Industry Committee for National Readership Surveys.

Launch. The introduction of a new product or service into a market.

Leisure. According to Collin (1994), leisure is 'free time' but it is also seen by some as an industry, or set of industries, providing products for consumers to use in their leisure time. The term leisure is fully discussed in Chapter 3.

Leisure shopping. Leisure shopping is different to ordinary shopping in that it involves consumers choosing to shop as a leisure activity rather than treating it as a necessary task. It also implies that the products they buy will be chosen purely for the pleasure involved in their consumption rather than because of their utilitarian value. This largely modern phenomenon is covered in more detail in Chapter 25.

Lifestyles. The way of life adopted by an individual or community.

Market. A market is those consumers who currently are, or might potentially be, purchasers and or users of a particular good or service.

Market focus. This is a term coined by Porter (1980) whereby an organization seeks competitive advantage by focusing on one specific market segment and trying to become the market leader with this particular segment.

Market leader. The product which has the largest share of an individual market.

Market positioning. The position in the market of a product as perceived by customers in terms of variables such as price, quality and service.

Market share. The proportion of sales in a market achieved by a product or organization.

Marketing. There is no single definition of marketing but a range of different definitions are offered in Chapter 1.

Marketing audit. An analysis of the current performance of an organization's marketing activities.

Marketing consortia. These are formal or informal groupings of organizations who cooperate in mutually beneficial marketing activities.

Marketing intermediaries. Intermediaries are organizations who provide the interface between producers and consumers. They are the retailers in the distribution system, for example travel agents in the field of tourism.

Marketing Mix. This term refers to the four marketing variables or techniques which organizations manipulate in order to achieve their objectives, namely product, price, place and promotion. Part 3 of the book contains separate chapters on each of these four variables.

Marketing plan. A written statement of an organization's marketing aims and the ways in which those aims will be implemented.

Marketing planning. This is the process through which organizations plan and implement their marketing strategies. Part 4 of the book focuses on the stages in the marketing planning process.

Marketing research. Research which is designed specifically to help an organization increase the effectiveness of its marketing activities. This topic is discussed in more detail in Chapter 32, including the difference between market research and marketing research.

Media. This term has two meanings in the context of this book. First, it relates to the news communications media in society, including newspapers, magazines and television for example. But one can also talk specifically about advertising media, in other words the media where advertising can be placed. These include the four previously mentioned plus cinema and poster sites for instance.

Mission statement. A brief simple phrase or sentence which summarizes the organization's direction and communicates its ethos to internal and external audiences.

Model. A representation that seeks to illustrate and/or explain a phenomenon.

Motivators. The factors which motivate consumers to buy a particular type of holiday. These motivators are discussed in Chapter 4.

Niche marketing. This is where an organization to target its product specifically at a particular market segment which is numerically much smaller than the size of the total market.

Off-peak. A period when demand for a product is habitually lower than at other times which are termed peak times.

Outlet. A place where products or services are sold or distributed to customers.

Pan-European Phenomena which share similar characteristics across Europe as a whole.

Perception. The way in which people interpret the data which is available to them about a product or organization.

Perishability. A characteristic of tourism, leisure and hospitality products whereby they have limited lives, after which they no longer exist and have no value. An example is a seat on a particular flight which ceases to exist as a product that can be sold when the aircraft departs.

Personal selling. This is defined by Kotler (1994) as an 'oral presentation in a conversation with one or more prospective purchasers for the purpose of making sales'. Such selling is found in tourism, leisure and hospitality where hotel staff try to persuade conference buyers to use their hotels as conference facilities for example.

Place. An element of the marketing mix which is concerned with distribution and the ways in which consumers may gain access to products. This is the subject of Chapter 10. *See also* Distribution.

Point of sale. Dibb *et al.* (1994) define this as 'sales promotion methods that attract attention, to inform customers and to encourage retailers to carry particular products'. While this definition relates primarily to manufactured goods, it is also found in tourism, leisure and hospitality, for example in window displays in travel agents' premises.

Postmodern. A sociological theory that has major implications for the study of consumer behaviour based on the idea that in the industrialized nations, the basis on which people act as consumers has been transformed in recent years. The impact of postmodernism in tourism is discussed in the *The Tourist Gaze* by John Urry, for example.

Press and public relations. A range of activities usually involving the free use of the media designed to raise awareness and or enhance the image of an organization or product amongst the population in general.

Price. An element of the marketing mix concerned with the money which the customer pays in exchange for a product. Chapter 9 focuses on price.

Primary data. The data collected by direct original surveys and observations.

Private sector. Those organizations in a market or industry which are owned by individuals or groups of individuals and are motivated by commercial objectives.

Product. What an organization offers to satisfy customers' wants and needs. Chapter 8 discusses the product in detail.

Product differentiation. A term coined by Porter (1980) which describes a technique whereby organizations can seek to gain competitive advantage by offering a product which has features not available in the offerings of competitor organizations.

Product lifecycle. The concept by which a product has a 'life', in that it is born, grows and eventually dies. More detail on the product lifecycle is to be found in Chapter 8.

Product portfolio. This term refers to the range of products offered by a single organization at any one time.

Product positioning. The process by which an organization seeks to give a particular impression of its products to potential consumers in order to encourage them to purchase these products.

Product-service mix. Renaghan (1981) defined this term as 'the combination of products and service aimed at satisfying the needs of the target markets'.

Promotion. This is an element of the marketing mix and refers to all the different techniques which are used to communicate the attributes of a product to potential customers to persuade them to buy it. This includes advertising, brochures, sales, public relations and personal selling. Chapter 11 discusses promotion in some detail.

Psychocentrics. A term coined by Plog (1977) for inward-looking, less adventurous consumers.

Psychographic. The analysis of people's lifestyles, perceptions and attitudes as a method of segmentation.

Public sector. Those organizations which are owned and managed by either central or local government. They are generally not commercially motivated and act on behalf of the community as a whole.

Qualitative research. Research concerned with customers' attitudes and perceptions which cannot be quantified.

Quality. The features and standards of a service. Quality is the subject of Chapter 29.

Quantitative research. Research which is concerned with data which is measurable and can be expressed numerically.

Recreation. Defined by Torkildsen (1994) as 'activities and experiences usually carried on within leisure and usually chosen voluntarily for satisfaction, pleasure, or creative enrichment'.

Relaunch. The reintroduction of a previously available product or service into a market, usually following modification.

Repositioning. The process by which organizations attempt to change the image of a product in the minds of consumers with a view to improving the product's reputation with consumers.

Resort complex. A self-contained site, usually in single ownership, which provides all or most of the products and services required by a tourist. They tend to combine attractions with support services such as accommodation and catering. Examples include brands such as Club Med and Center Parcs. For more details, see Chapter 21.

Sales promotions. In general, these are short-term tactical offers designed to stimulate demand. This often takes the form of either price discounts or added value (giving consumer more for the same price).

Secondary data. Data which comes from existing sources such as reports and databases rather than being collected by original research.

Segmentation. The practice of dividing total markets up into subgroups which have similar characteristics. Segmentation methods are discussed in Chapter 4.

Service gap. A term used by Parasuraman *et al.* (1985) to describe the potential gaps which can exist between expectations of a service and the reality of the way in which the service is actively delivered.

Services. Products which are intangible processes designed to meet consumer needs.

Social marketing. Marketing in non-commercial organizations where the objectives are social rather than commercial.

Sponsorship. A phenomenon whereby an unrelated organization provides material or financial support for another organization's activities or products in return for some benefit, which might include raising the awareness of the organization's products amongst the latter organization's market.

Strategic. Thinking or action which is longer term, broad in scope and generally at the macro level.

Strategic alliances. A competitive advantage tool which involves working with other organizations in a close relationship for mutual benefit. Such alliances are a common feature of the modern airline industry, for example.

Strategic business unit (SBU). A self-contained subdivision of an organization concerned with a particular product or set of products.

Subsidy. Financial support provided by an organization to improve the financial performance of the organization which receives the subsidy, or to allow customers to afford to buy a product they could not otherwise afford to buy.

Suppliers. The organizations which provide the supplies or 'raw materials' from which suppliers can produce products. For example, hotels are suppliers for tour operators by providing the accommodation element of their package holiday product.

Sustainability. The concept of using resources to meet our needs in a way that will not threaten the ability of future generations to do the same.

SWOT analysis. A technique used by organizations to assess their current marketing situation. It involves analysing the organization's current internal strengths and weaknesses, and identifying specific external opportunities and threats in its business environment. This technique is covered further in Chapter 12.

Tactical. Thinking and action which is shortterm, narrow in scope and at the micro level.

Target marketing. Marketing activity aimed at a particular subgroup within the population.

Theme park. A type of attraction, usually in single ownership, which is largely based on a central theme, for example Disneyland Paris and Legoland.

Timeshare. A type of accommodation where customers pay a lump sum and in return receive the right to use a unit of accommodation for specific times in the year.

Total Quality Management. A fashionable management approach to quality which emphasizes that quality is the responsibility of all staff and that quality is about constantly seeking to improve performance. See Chapter 29 for more details.

Tour operator. Organizations which assemble 'package holidays' from components provided by other sectors such as accommodation operators and transport organizations. They then sell those packages to consumers, often through travel agents. Chapter 19 deals more fully with tour operators.

Tourism. The activity in which people spend a short period of time away from home for business or pleasure. It is defined in detail in Chapter 3.

Tourist. A consumer of tourism products.

Transnational corporations. Organizations which operate across national boundaries.

Travel agents. The retailer in the tourism system, selling the products of organizations within tourism to consumers. Travel agents are considered in more depth in Chapter 22.

Unique selling proposition (USP). A feature that is so unique that it distinguishes one product from other products.

Upmarket. Products aimed at the more expensive, high status, higher quality end of the market.

Vertical integration. The process by which an organization takes over other organizations involved in a different stage of production or distribution from itself, for example where a tour operator takes over a travel agency and/or an airline.

Visitor. A widely used term in the visitor attraction field for someone who makes a visit to an attraction. It recognizes that not all visitors are tourists in the technical sense of the term, in that they are not all spending at least one night away from home. Indeed, most customers at attractions are not tourists but excursionists or day trippers.

Visitor attraction. A single site, unit or entity which motivates people to travel to its location to see, experience and participate in what it has to offer. Attractions can be natural or man-made, physical entities or special events. More information on attractions is contained in Chapter 16.

Voluntary sector. Organizations which are composed of volunteers who join together to achieve a shared objective or work on a common interest. Examples include the National Trust and many steam railway operators in the UK.

Word-of-mouth. This is where consumers who have experienced a product or service pass on their views about this product or service to other people.

Bibliography and further reading

Advertising Voices (1991) 'Legislation passed by the European Community', *International Journal of Advertising*, Vol. 10.

Anholt, S. (1993) 'Adapting advertising copy across national frontiers', *Admap*, October, pp. 16–17.

Ansoff, H.I. (1988) *The New Corporate Strategy*, John Wiley & Sons, New York.

Archdale, G. (1994) 'Destination databases: issues and practices', in Seaton, A.V. *et al.* (eds), *Tourism: The State of the Art*, John Wiley & Sons, Chichester.

Ashworth, G.J. and Goodall, B. (1990) *Marketing Tourism Places*, Routledge, London.

Ashworth, G.J. and Voogd, H. (1990) *Selling the City: Marketing Approaches in Public Sector Urban Planning*, Belhaven Press, London.

Ayton, P. (1994) 'Spending Time', *Leisure Management*, February, pp. 24–6.

Babbie, E.R. (1979) *The Practice of Social Research*, 2nd edn, Wadsworth, Belmont, CA.

Bateson, J. (1977) *Do we need service marketing*? New Insights Report, Marketing Science Institute, Boston, November, pp. 77–115.

Bateson, J.E.G. (1995) *Managing Services Marketing. Text and Readings*, 3rd edn, Dryden Press.

Beoiley, S. and Denman, R. (1988) *Industrial Heritage Attractions in North West England*, North West Tourist Board, Bolton.

Boniface, P. (1995) *Managing Quality in Cultural Tourism*, Routledge, London.

Booms, B.H. and Bitner, M.J. (1981) 'Marketing strategies and organization structures for services firms', in Donnelly, J. and George, W.R. (eds) *Marketing of Services*, American Marketing Association, Chicago, pp. 47–51.

Boston Consulting Group, The (1970) *The Product Portfolio*, The Boston Consulting Group Inc., Boston, MA.

Bould A., Breeze, G. and Teare, R. (1992) 'Culture, customisation and innovation: a Hilton International service brand for the Japanese market', in Teare, R. and Olsen, M.D. (eds), *International Hospitality Management*, Pitman, London.

Boyer, M. and Viallon, P. (1994) *La Communication Touristique*, Presses Universitaires de France, Paris.

Bramham, P., Henry, I., Mamm, H. and Van der Pool, H. (eds) (1993) *Leisure Policies in Europe*, CAB International, Wallingford.

Brent-Ritchie, J.R. and Goeldner, C.R. (1994) *Travel, Tourism, and Hospitality Research: A Handbook for Managers and Researchers*, John Wiley & Sons, New York.

British Tourist Authority (1995) *Visits to Tourist Attractions*, BTA, London.

Bull, A. (1991) *The Economics of Travel and Tourism*. Longman, Melbourne.

Burns, P.M. and Holden, A. (1995) *Tourism: A New Perspective*, Prentice-Hall, Hemel Hempstead.

Burton, R. (1995) *Travel Georgraphy*, 2nd edn, Pitman, London.

Buttle, F. (1986) *Hotel and Food Service Marketing: A Managerial Approach*, Cassell, London.

Cadotte, E.R. and Turgeon, N. (1988) 'Key factors in guest satisfaction', *The Cornell Hotel and Restaurant Administration Quarterly*, Vol. 28, No. 4, February, pp. 44–51.

Calantone, R.J. and Mazanec, J.A. (1991) 'Marketing management and tourism', *Annals of Tourism Research*. Vol. 18, No. 1, pp. 101–99.

Campbell-Smith, D. (1986) *Struggle for Take-off – the British Airways Story*. Hodder & Stoughton, London.

Carroll, Lewis (1865) *Alice's Adventures in Wonderland*, First Edition, First Presentation Copy, MacMillan, London.

'Chain Reaction' (1995) *Business Traveller*, July, pp. 22–26.

Chartered Institute of Marketing (1984) *Definition of Marketing*, Chartered Institute of Marketing, Cookham.

Chisnall, P.M. (1985) *Marketing: a behavioural analysis*, 2nd edn, McGraw-Hill, Maidenhead.

Collin, P.H. (1994) *Dictionary of Hotels, Tourism and Catering Management*, P.H. Collin, Teddington.

Cohen, E. (1979) 'A phenomenology of tourist experiences', *Sociology*, 13, pp. 179–201.

Connell, J. (1994) 'Guide to hospitality marketing literature and intelligence', *Insights*, September, pp. 129–42.

Cooper, C., Fletcher, J., Gilbert, D. and Wanhill, S. (1993) *Tourism: Principles and Practice*, Pitman, London.

'Corporate hospitality' (1995) Leisureweek, 30 June.

Cossons, N. (1985) 'Making museums market oriented', in Scottish Museums journal, *Museums are for People*, HMSO, Edinburgh.

Coulson-Thomas, C. (1986) *Marketing Communications*, Heinemann, London.

Cowell, D. (1984) *The Marketing of Services*, Heinemann, London.

Crompton, J.L. (1979) 'Motivations for pleasure vacations', *Annals of Tourism Research*, Vol. 6, No. 1, pp. 408–24.

Crossley, J.C. and Jamieson, L.M. (1988) *Introduction to Commercial and Entrepreneurial Recreation*, Sagamore, Champaign, IL.

D'Arcy, Masius, Benton and Bowles (1989) *Marketing: Communicating with the Consumer*, Mercury Books/CBI, London.

Davidson, R. (1992) *Tourism in Europe*, Pitman, London.

Davidson, R. (1994a) European business travel and tourism, in Seaton, A.V. *et al.* (eds), *Tourism: The State of the Art*, John Wiley & Sons, Chichester.

Davidson, R. (1994b) 'Themed Attractions in Europe', *Insights*, May, pp. A159–A166.

Davidson, R. (1994c) *Business Travel*, Pitman, London.

Day, G.S. (1990) *Market Drawn Strategy: Processes for Creating Values*, Free Press, London.

De Bono, E. (1993) *Sur petition – Going Beyond Competition*, Harper Collins, London.

Department of National Heritage (1996) *Tourism: Competing with the Best. Number 2: Benchmarking for Smaller Hotels*. Department of National Heritage, London.

Dewailly, J.M. and Flament, E. (1993) *Géographie du Tourisme et des Loisirs*, SEDES. Paris.

Dhalla, N.K. and Yuspeh, S. (1976) 'Forget the product life cycle concept', *Harvard Business Review*, January–February, pp. 102–12.

Dibb, S., Simkin, L., Pride, W. M. and Ferrell, O.C. (1994) *Marketing: Concepts and Strategies*, 2nd European edn, Houghton-Mifflin, London.

Douglas, S. and Wind, Y. (1987) The myth of globalization. *Columbia Journal of World Business*, Winter, pp. 19–29.

Driscoll, E. (1995) 'Fire and ice', *Business Traveller*, May, pp. 51–4.

Drucker P.F. (1969) *The Practice of Management*, Heinemann, London.

Drucker P.F. (1985) *Innovation and Entrepreneurship*, Heinemann, London.

Economist Intelligence Unit (1992) *The European Tour Operator Industry*, EIU Special Report No. 2141.

Economist Intelligence Unit (1993) *Tourism in the European Community*, EIU Special Report No. R451.

Economist Intelligence Unit (1994) EIU International Tourism Report No. 3.

Economist Intelligence Unit (1995) EIU International Tourism Reports Nos 1, 2 and 3.

Eiglier, P. and Langeard, E. (1981) *A Conceptual Approach to the Service Offer*, Working Paper No. 217. April, Centre des Hautes Etudes Touristiques (CHET), Aix-en-Provence.

Euromonitor (annual) *European Marketing Data and Statistics*, Euromonitor, London.

Euromonitor (annual) *European Travel and Tourism Marketing Directory*, Euromonitor, London.

Euromonitor (1994) *European Domestic Tourism and Leisure Trends*, Euromonitor, London.

European Marketing Pocket Book (1995, 1996) NTC Publications, Henley-on-Thames.

Eurostat (1995) *Statistics in Focus – Regions*.

Feiffer, M. (1985) *Going Places*, Macmillan, London.

Getz, D. (1991) *Festivals, Special Events, and Tourism*, Van Nostrand Reinhold, New York.

Gianluigi, G. (1991) 'Implementing a pan-European marketing strategy', *Long-Range Planning*, Vol. 24, No. 5, pp. 22–33.

Gilbert, D.C. (1991) 'An examination of the consumer decision process related to tourism in Cooper, C. (ed.), *Progress in Tourism, Recreation and Hospitality Management*, Vol. 3, Belhaven Press, London.

Gold, J.R. and Ward, S.V. (eds). (1994) *Place Promotion: The Use of Publicity and Marketing to sell Towns and Regions*, John Wiley & Sons, Chichester.

Goodall, B. and Ashworth, G. (1988) *Marketing Tourism Places – The Promotion of Destination Regions*, Croom-Helm, London.

Gotti, G. and van der Borg, J. (1995) *Tourism in Heritage Cities*, Centro Internazionale di Studi sull' Economia Turista, Na11.

Gratton, C. (1993) 'A perspective on European leisure markets', *ILAM Guide to Good Practice in Leisure Management*, 2nd edn, Longman, Harlow.

Gratton, C. (1994) *The Single Internal Market, European Integration and the Development of International Leisure Markets and Transnational Leisure Corporations*, Conference Paper.

Gratton, C. and Richards, G. (1995) 'Structural Change in the European Package Tour Industry'. Conference paper presented at the International Conference on the Economics of Tourism, University of Crete and Fondazione ENI Enrico Mattei, Rethymnon, Crete, October 1995.

Greaves, S. (1995) 'Fired up but freezing Iceland', *Conference and Incentive Travel*, June, pp. 33–8.

Grönroos, C.L. (1980) *An Applied Service Marketing Theory*, Working Paper No. 57, Swedish School of Economics and Business Administration, Helsinki .

Grönroos, C.L. (1990) 'Marketing redefined', *Management Decision*, Vol. 28, No. 8.

Guido, G. (1991) 'Implementing a pan-European marketing strategy', *Long-Range Planning*, 24, No. 5, pp. 23–33.

Hall, C.M. (1992) *Hallmark Tourist Events: Impacts, Management, and Planning*, Belhaven Press, London.

Hall, D.R. (ed.) (1991) *Tourism and Economic Development in Eastern Europe and the Soviet Union*, Belhaven Press, London.

Halliburton, C. and Hünerberg, R. (1993) *European Marketing – Readings and Cases*, Addison-Wesley, Wokingham.

Hamill, J. (1993) 'Competitive strategies in the world airline industry', *European Management Journal*, Vol. 11, No. 3, September, pp. 332–41.

Haylock, R. (1994) 'Timeshare: the new force in tourism' in Seaton, A.V. *et al.* (eds) *Tourism: The State of the Art*, John Wiley & Sons, Chichester.

Headland Business Information (1995) 'Cross-Channel tourism', *New Travel and Tourism Markets*, No. 2.

Henley Centre/Research International (1991/92) *Frontiers*, Henley Centre/Research International.

Herbert, D.T., Prentice, R.C. and Thomas, C.J. (eds) (1989) *Heritage Sites: Strategies for Marketing and Development*, Avebury, Aldershot.

Holloway, J.C. and Robinson, C. (1995) *Marketing for Tourism*, 3rd edn, Longman, Harlow.

Homma, N. (1991) 'The continued relevance of cultural diversity', *Marketing and Research Today*, November, pp. 251–8.

ILAM (1992) *Guide to a Good Practice in Leisure Management*, 2nd, edn, Longman, Harlow.

James, W.P.T. (1989) *Healthy Nutrition*, WHO Regional Office for Europe, Copenhagen.

Jefferson, A. and Lickorish, L. (1988) *Marketing Tourism*, Longman, Harlow.

Johnson, G. and Scholes, K. (1993) *Exploring Corporate Strategy*, 3rd edn, Prentice-Hall, Hemel Hempstead.

Johnson, P. and Thomas, B. (eds) (1990) *Proceedings of the Tourism Research in the 1990s Conference*, December. Durham University.

Johnson, P. and Thomas, B. (eds) (1993) *Choice and Demand in Tourism*, Mansell, London.

Judd, R.C. (1968) 'Similarities and differences in product and service retailing', *Journal of Retailing*, Vol. 43, Winter, pp. 1–9.

Kanter, R.M. (1984) *The Changemasters – Corporate Entrepreneurs at Work*, Allen & Unwin, London.

Kanter R.M. (1989) *When Giants Learn to Dance*, Simon & Schuster, New York.

Kashani, K. (1989) Beware the pitfalls of global marketing, *Harvard Business Review*, September–October, pp. 89–98.

Key Note Report (1994) *A Market Sector Overview – Tourist Attractions*, Key Note Report, Key Note Ltd, London.

Key Note (1995) *Travel Agents and Overseas Tour Operators – A Market Sector Overview*, Key Note Report, Key Note Ltd, London.

Kossoff, J. (1988) 'Europe: up for sale', *New Statesman and Society*, Vol. 1, No. 8, pp. 43–4.

Kotler, P. (1975) *Marketing for Non-Profit Organizations*, Prentice-Hall, Englewood Cliffs, NJ.

Kotler, P. (1984) in Fisher, A.B. 'The ad biz gloms on to global', *Fortune*, 12 November, pp. 77–80.

Kotler, P. (1994) *Marketing Management: Analysis, Planning, Implementation, and Control*, 8th edn, Prentice-Hall, Englewood Cliffs, NJ.

Kotler, P. and Andraeson, A.R. (1987) *Strategic Marketing for nonprofit Organizations*, Prentice-Hall, Englewood Cliffs, NJ.

Kotler, P., Haider, D.H. and Rein, I. (1993) *Marketing Places*. Free Press, New York.

Krippendorf, J. (1987) *The Holiday Makers: Underestimating the Impact of Leisure and Travel*, Butterworth-Heinemann, Oxford.

Lannon, J. (1992) 'Asking the right questions – what do people do with advertising' *Admap*, March, pp. 11–6.

Lanquar, R. and Hollier, R. (1989) *Le Marketing Touristique*, 3rd edn, Presses Universitaires de France, Paris.

Law, C. (1993) *Urban Tourism: Attracting Visitors to Large Cities*, Mansell, London.

Laws, E. (1991) *Tourism Marketing: Service and Quality Management Perspectives*, Stanley Thornes, Cheltenham.

Laws, E.C. (1995) *Tourist Destination Management – Issues, Analysis and Policies*, Routledge, London.

Leadley, P. (1992) *Leisure Marketing*, Longman/ILAM, Harlow.

Lendrevic, J. and Lindon, D. (1990) *Mercator*, 4th edn, Dallas, TX.

Levitt, T. (1960) Marketing Myopia, *Harvard Business Review*, July–August, pp. 45–6.

Levitt T (1972) 'Production line approach to services', *Harvard Business Review*, September–October, pp. 41–5.

Levitt, T. (1983) 'The globalization of marketing', *Harvard Business Review*. May–June, pp. 92–102.

Levitt, T. (1986) *The Marketing Imagination*, Free Press, New York.

Lewis, R.C. and Chambers, R.G. (1989) *Market Leadership in Hospitality*, Van Nostrand Reinhold, New York.

Littlejohn, D. and Beattie, R. (1992) The European hotel industry – Corporate structures and expansion strategies. Butterworth Heinemann Ltd in Tourism Management, March, 1992.

Lundberg, D.E. (1990) *The Tourist Business*, 6th edn, Van Nostrand Rheinold, New York.

MacCannell, D. (1976) *The Tourist: A New Theory of the Leisure Class*, Macmillan, London.

MacCannell, D. (1992) *Empty Meeting Grounds*, Routledge, London.

McCarthy, E.J. (1960) *Basic Marketing: A Managerial Approach*, Irwin, Homewood, IL.

McDaniel Jr, C.D. and Gates, C.R. (1993) *Contemporary Marketing Research*, 2nd edn, West Publishing, Minneapolis St Paul, MA.

McDonald, M.H.B. (1989) *Marketing Plans – How to Prepare Them: How to Use Them*, Heinemann, London.

Manser, M.H. (1988) *Marketing Terms. Chambers Commercial Reference*, W.R. Chambers Ltd, Edinburgh.

Mantanari, A. and Williams, A.M. (eds) (1995) *European Tourism: Regions, Spaces and Re-structuring*, John Wiley & Sons, Chichester.

Market Research Europe. (1995) *European Markets*. June.

Marketing Services Institute (1977) *New Insights*, Report 75–115, Marketing Services Institute, Boston.

Martin, B. and Mason, S. (1993) 'The future for attractions – meeting the needs of new consumers', *Tourism Management*, February, pp. 34–40.

Martin, J. (1988) 'Beyond 1992: lifestyle is key', *Advertising Age*, 11 July, p. 57.

Mathieson, A. and Wall, G. (1982) *Tourism: Economic, Physical and Social Impacts*, Longman, Harlow.

Mazanec, J.A. and Zins, A.H. (1994) 'Tourist behaviour and the new European lifestyle typology', in Theobold, W. (ed.), *Global Tourism: The Next Decade*, Butterworth-Heinemann, Oxford.

Middleton, V.T.C. (1990) *New Visions for Independent Museums in the UK*, Association of Independent Museums, Chichester.

Middleton, V.T.C. (1994) *Marketing in Travel and Tourism*, 2nd edn, Butterworth-Heinemann, Oxford.

Mills, P. (ed.) (1992) *Quality in the Leisure Industry*, Longman, Harlow.

Mintel (1995) *Product Inclusive Tours*, London.

Mintel (1994) *Inclusive Tour Report*, London.

Mooij, M. de (1994) *Advertising Worldwide*, Prentice-Hall, London.

Moorcroft, S. (1987) 'Lifestyle and values: the european dimension', *Admap*, May, pp. 27031.

Moriarty, S.E. and Duncan, T.R. (1990) 'Global Advertising: Issue and Practices', *Current Issues and Research in Advertising*, Vol 13. Nos 1 and 2 J.H. Leigh and C.R. Martine (eds) Division of Research, School of Business Administration. The University of Michigan.

Morrison, A.M. (1989) *Hospitality and Travel Marketing*, Delmar, Albany, NY.

Moutinho (1987) 'Consumer behaviour in tourism', *European Journal of Marketing*, Vol. 21, No. 10, pp. 1–44.

Mullin, B.J., Hardy, S. and Sutton, M.A. (1993) *Sport Marketing*, Human Kinetics, Champaign, IL.

Munzinger, U. (1988) *Ad Vantage/AC-T*, International Advertising Research Case Studies, ESOMAR, Seminar on International Marketing Research, 16–18 November.

Myerscough, J. (1988) *The Economic Importance of the Arts in Britain*, Policy Studies Institute, London.

Nykiel, R.A. (1989) *Marketing in the Hospitality Industry*, 2nd edn, Van Nostrand Reinhold, New York.

Ohmae, K. (1982) *The Mind of the Strategist: Business Planning for Competitive Advantage*, Penguin Books, London.

Ohmae, K. (1989) 'Planting for a global harvest', *Harvard Business Review*, July–August, pp. 136–45.

Olsen, M.D., Teare, R. and Gunnerson, E. (1995) *Service Quality in Hospitality Organizations*, Cassell, London.

Packard, V. (1957) *The Hidden Persuaders*, Longmans, Green and Co, London.

Page, S. (1994) *Transport for Tourism*, Routledge, London.

Page, S. (1995) *Urban Tourism*, Routledge, London.

Paitra, J. (1993) quoted in Halliburton, C. and Hünerberg, R. (eds), *European Marketing: Readings and Cases*, Addison-Wesley, Wokingham, p. 67.

Parasuraman, A., Zeithmal, W.A. and Berry, L. (1985) 'A conceptual model of service quality and its implications for future research', *Journal of Marketing*, Vol. 49, No. 4, pp. 41–50.

Pearce, W. and Butler, R.G. (1992) *Tourism Research – Critiques and Challenges*, Routledge, London.

Peters, T. and Austin, N. (1985) *A Passion for Excellence*, Collins, Glasgow.

Peters, T. and Watermann, R.H. Jnr (1982) *In Search of Excellence*, Harper & Row, Scrantan, PA.

Piercy, N. (1991) 'Developing marketing information systems', in Baker, M. (ed.), *The Marketing Book*, 2nd edn, Butterworth-Heinemann, Oxford.

Piercy, N. (1992) *Market-Led Strategic Change*, Butterworth-Heinemann, Oxford.

Plog, S. (1977) 'Why Destination Areas Rise and Fall in Popularity', in Kelly, E. (ed.) *Domestic and International Tourism*, Institute of Certified Travel Agents, Wellesley, Ma.

Plog, S. (1991) *Leisure Travel: Making It a Growth Market Again*, John Wiley & Sons, New York.

Pompl, W. and Lavery, P. (eds) (1993) *Tourism in Europe: Structures and Developments*, CAB International, Wallingford.

Poon, A. (1993) *Tourism, Technology and Competitive Strategies*, CAB International, Wallingford.

Porter, M.E. (1983) *Competitive Advantage – Creating and Sustaining Superior Performance*, Free Press, New York.

Porter, M.E. (1986) *Competition in Global Industries*, Harvard Business Press, Boston, MA.

Py, P. (1992) *Le Tourisme: Un Phénomène Economique*, La Documentation Française, Paris.

Reed, A. (1990) *Airline. The Inside Story of British Airways*. BBC Books, London.

Reid, R.D. (1989) *Hospitality Marketing Management*, 2nd edn, Van Nostrand Reinhold, New York.

Renaghan, L.M. (1981) 'A new marketing mix for the hospitality industry', *Cassell Hotel and Restaurant Administration Quarterly*, April, pp. 31–35.

Rink, D.R. and Swan, J. (1979) 'Product lifecycle research: a literature review', *Journal of Business Research*, September, pp. 219–42.

Ross, G.F. (1994) *The Psychology of Tourism*, Hospitality Press, Melbourne.

Rushton, A.M. and Carson, M.J. (1985) 'The Marketing of Services', *European Journal of Marketing*, March. Hospitality Press, Melbourne. p. 23.

Ryan, C. (1991) *Recreational Tourism: A Social Science Perspective*, Routledge, London.

Ryan, C. (1995) *Researching Tourist Satisfaction: Issues, Concepts and Problems*, Routledge, London.

Sasser, W.E., Olsen, R.P. and Wycoff, D.D. (1978) *Management of Service Operations – Text and Cases*, Allyn & Bacon, Boston, MA.

Schmoll, G.A. (1977) *Tourism Promotion*, Tourism International Press, London.

Scholes, K. (1991) *Development in Local Government*, Occasional and Conference Paper, Sheffield Hallam University, Sheffield.

Seaton, A.V. (ed.) (1994) *Tourism: The State of the Art*, John Wiley & Sons, Chichester.

Segal-Horn, S. (1989) 'The globalisation of service firms', in Jones, P. (ed.), *Management in the Service Industries*, Pitman, London.

Sharpley, R. (1994) *Tourism, Tourists and Society*, Elm, Huntingdon.

Shaw, S. (1990) *Airline Marketing and Management*, 3rd edn, Pitman, London.

Shaw, G. and Williams, A.M. (1994) *Critical Issues in Tourism: A Geographical Perspective*, Blackwell, Oxford.

Shostack, G.L. (1977) 'Breaking free from product marketing', *Journal of Marketing*, Vol. 41, No. 2, pp. 73–80.

Sinclair, M.T. and Stabler, M.J. (1991) *The Tourism Industry: An International Analysis*, CAB International, Wallingford.

Slattery, P., Feehely, G. and Savage, M. (1995) *Quoted Hotel Companies: The World Markets 1995*, March, Kleinwort Benson Research.

Smith, S.J. (1995) *Tourism Analysis*, 2nd edn, Longman, Harlow.

Stone, M. (1990) *Leisure Services Marketing*, Croner, Kingston-upon-Thames.

Swarbrooke, J.S. (1994a) 'Greening and competitive advantage in the hospitality industry', in *Proceedings of the Hospitality Marketing Conference*, Gloucester and Cheltenham College of Higher Education, Pavic, Sheffield.

Swarbrooke, J.S. (1994b) 'Greening and competitive advantage', *Insights*, May, pp. D43–D50.

Swarbrooke, J.S. (1994c) 'The future of heritage attractions', *Insights*, January, pp. D15–D20.

Swarbrooke, J.S. (1995a) *The Development and Management of Visitor Attractions*, Butterworth-Heinemann, Oxford.

Swarbrooke, J.S. (1995b) 'Towards Sustainable Rural Tourism in Europe, A Marketing Approach'. Conference paper presented at the 2nd Ecological Conference of the Halkidiki Hoteliers Association. Halkidiki, Greece. July 1995.

Teare, R., Mazanec, J.A., Crawford-Welch, S. and Calver, S. (1994) *Marketing in Hospitality and Tourism*, Cassell, London.

Tellis, G.H. and Crawford, C.M. (1981) 'An evolutionary approach to product growth theory', *Journal of Marketing*, No. 4, pp. 125–132.

Theobold, W. (ed.) (1994) *Global Tourism: The Next Decade*, Butterworth-Heinemann, Oxford.

Toop, A. (1992) *European Sales Promotion*, Kogan Page, London.

Torkildsen, G. (1993) *Torkildsen's Guide to Leisure Management*, Longman, Harlow.

Torkildsen, G. (1994) *Leisure Management A–Z: A Dictionary of Terms*, Longman, Harlow.

Tourism Planning and Research Associates (1993) *The European Tourist: A Market Profile*, Tourism Planning and Research Associates, London.

Tourism Research and Marketing (1994) 'Theme parks – UK and international markets', October.

Urry, J. (1990) *The Tourist Gaze: Leisure and Travel in Contemporary Societies*, Sage, London.

Urry, J. (1995) *Consuming Places*, Routledge, London.

Uysal, M. (ed.) (1994) *Global Tourist Behaviour*, International Business Press, New York.

Van Kraay, F. (1993) *Tourism and the Hotel and Catering Industries in the EC*, European Community Law Series No. 6, Athlone Press, Canada.

Vandermerwe, S. and L'Huillier, M.A. (1989) 'Euro-consumers in 1992', *Business Horizons*, Vol. 32, No. 1, pp. 34–40.

Vandermerwe, S. (1989) 'Strategies for pan-European Marketing', *Long-Range Planning*, Vol. 23, No. 3, pp. 45–53.

Veal, A.J. (1992) *Research Methods for Leisure and Tourism: A Practical Guide*, Longman, Harlow.

Voase, R. (1995) *Tourism: The Human Perspective*, Hodder & Stoughton, London.

Wackerman, G. (1993) *Tourisme et Transport*, SEDES, Paris.

Wahab, S., Crompton, L.J. and Rothfield, L.M. (1976) *Tourism Marketing*, Tourism International Press, London.

Wheatcroft, S. and Geekings, J. (1995) *Europe's Youth Travel Market*, European Travel Commission, Brussels.

Williams, A.M. and Shaw, G. (1991) *Tourism and Economic Development: Western European Experiences*, 2nd edn, Belhaven Press, London.

Witt, S.F. and Moutinho, L. (1995) *Tourism Marketing and Management Handbook*, Student Edition, Prentice-Hall, London.

Witt, S.F. and Witt, C. (1991) *Marketing and Forecasting Demand in Tourism*, Academic Press, London.

Wolfe, A. (1991) 'The Single European Market: national or Euro-brands?', *International Journal of Advertising*, Vol. 10, No. 1, pp. 49–58.

Wood, K. and Hase, S. (1991) *The Good Tourist: A Worldwide Guide for the Green Traveller*, Mandarin, London.

Worcester, R.M. and Downham, R. (1986) *Consumer Market Research handbook*, 3rd edn. Elsevier for ESOMAR: McGraw-Hill, Maidenhead.

World Travel and Tourism Council (1994) *Travel and Tourism: Progress and Priorities*, World Travel and Tourism Council, Oxford.

Yale, P. (1995) *The Business of Tour Operations*, Longman, Harlow.

Index